WHITE OVER BLACK

The Omohundro Institute
of Early American History
and Culture is sponsored
jointly by the College of
William and Mary and the
Colonial Williamsburg
Foundation.

Published for the
Omohundro Institute
of Early American
History and Culture
at Williamsburg, Virginia,
by the University of
North Carolina Press,
Chapel Hill

WHITE

OVER

BLACK

American Attitudes
Toward the Negro, 1550–1812

WINTHROP D. JORDAN

© 1968 by The University of North Carolina Press
All rights reserved
Manufactured in the United States of America
ISBN 0-8078-1055-X (cloth: alk. paper)
ISBN 0-8078-4550-7 (pbk.: alk. paper)
Library of Congress Catalog Card Number 68-13295

07 06 05 04 03   14 13 12 11 10

TO PHYLLIS

PREFACE

THIS STUDY ATTEMPTS TO ANSWER A SIMPLE QUESTION:
What were the attitudes of white men toward Negroes during the
first two centuries of European and African settlement in what became the United States of America? It has taken a rather long
time to find out, chiefly because I have had to educate myself about
many matters concerning which at the outset I was very ignorant.
This book does something to answer the question, but I am aware
that it affords only partial illumination. Like most practicing historians today, I have assumed the task of explaining how things
actually were while at the same time thinking that no one will ever
really know. Which is to say that this book is one man's answer and
that other men have and will advance others. I hope that mine is a
reasonably satisfactory one, but I shall be enormously surprised—and greatly disappointed—if I am not shown to be wrong
on some matters.

Some, but not *too* many. I have tried to read a good deal in the
extant remains of a literate culture which, however greatly it
influenced its current heirs, is no longer in existence. Some of the
inherent biases in these remains are discussed in the Essay on
Sources. I have tried to read these sources with mind and eyes open
and to listen with as much receptivity as possible to what men now
dead were *saying*. Some readers will think that this book reads too
much *into* what men wrote in the past. To this objection I can only
say that an historian's relationship with the raw materials of history
is a profoundly reciprocal one and that I read in these materials for
several years before I became partially aware, I think, of what
meaning they contained, of what thoughts and feelings in their
authors they reflected. This is in part to say that I became aware of
the power of irrationality in men because and not before I read the
source materials for this study.

Some, but by no means all readers schooled in the behavioral sciences will discover a disgraceful lack of system in the approach taken here toward the way societies are held together and toward the way men think, act, and feel. There is, however, a certain sloppiness in the available evidence. If it were possible to poll the inhabitants of Jamestown, Virginia, concerning their reaction to those famous first "twenty Negars" who arrived in 1619 I would be among the first at the foot of the gangplank, questionnaire in hand. Lacking this opportunity, I have operated with certain working assumptions which some readers will detect as drawing upon some "psychologies"—the assumptions about how people operate—of the twentieth century and upon some of the psychological imagery of the eighteenth. I have taken "attitudes" to be discrete entities susceptible of historical analysis. This term seems to me to possess a desirable combination of precision and embraciveness. It suggests thoughts and feelings (as opposed to actions) directed toward some specific object (as opposed to generalized faiths and beliefs). At the same time it suggests a wide range in consciousness, intensity, and saliency in the response to the object. We are all aware that our "attitude toward" sex is not of precisely the same order as our "attitude toward" Medicare, and the same may be said of our attitudes toward the neighbor's cat or Red China or rock-and-roll or the Ku Klux Klan—not, of course, that it is right to suppose that our various attitudes toward these objects are altogether unconnected with one another. This book treats attitudes as existing not only at various levels of intensity but at various levels of consciousness and unconsciousness; it is written on the assumption that there is no clear dividing line between "thought" and "feeling," between conscious and unconscious mental processes. The book therefore deals with "attitudes" toward Negroes which range from highly articulated ideas about the church or natural rights or the structure of the *cutis vera,* through off-hand notions and traditional beliefs about climate or savages or the duties of Christian ministers, through myths about Africa or Noah or the properties of chimpanzees, down to expressions of the most profound human urges—to the coded languages of our strivings for death and life and self-identification.

Which is the way things are and—this book suggests—have been for a long time with white men. This is not a book about Negroes except as they were objects of white men's attitudes. Nor is it about the current, continuing crisis in race relations in America. As a point of personal privilege I wish to state that work on this study was begun several years before Mrs. Rosa Parks got "uppity" on that bus. I might also say that at a later date when I first read some remarks by James Baldwin my first reaction was that *he* had plagiarized *my* unfinished and unavailable manuscript. I have attempted, indeed, to avoid reading widely in the literature of the present crisis because it is frequently so tempting to read the past backwards—and very dangerous. The relevance, if any, of this study to the present is left principally to the reader to determine, though I confess to having written two sentences on the subject. My assumptions about the value of historical study are the same as those of most historians. A comprehension of the past seems to have two opposite advantages in the present: it makes us aware of how different people have been in other ages and accordingly enlarges our awareness of the possibilities of human experience, and at the same time it impresses upon us those tendencies in human beings which have *not* changed and which accordingly are unlikely to at least in the immediate future. Viewed from a slightly different vantage point, an understanding of the history of our own culture gives some inkling of the categories of possibilities within which for the time being we are born to live.

To say this is, I suppose, to make something of a claim for the value of studying current attitudes toward Negroes by taking, as they say, "the historical approach." What the historian contributes, inevitably, is a sense and appreciation of the important effect— perhaps even the great weight—of prior upon ensuing experience.

I embarked on this project without suspicion of how very strong this effect could be. I assumed that when Englishmen met Negroes overseas there would be "attitudes" generated, and I first looked for evidence in the writings of English voyagers to West Africa and of their readers at home. It only gradually dawned that I was oafishly cutting into the seamless web of time at just the wrong moment, that it was necessary to probe the characteristics of Englishmen before rather than when they first confronted Africans. But from the first the sources made evident that there existed certain traditions about these Africans which were already in existence elsewhere in Europe in the days when Englishmen painted themselves blue and were otherwise notorious savages. Some of these traditions are discussed in chapter I, and in both chapters I and II there are the results of my attempt to learn what Englishmen were like during the years immediately prior to first-hand contact with Africans and during the seventy-five years following while their contact remained infrequent and casual.

The second chapter focuses especially upon the problem of the origins of American Negro slavery. Understanding the way racial slavery began is both extremely difficult and absolutely essential to comprehension of the white man's attitudes toward Negroes. For once the cycle of debasement in slavery and prejudice in the mind was underway, it was automatically self-reinforcing. It is so easy to see the dynamics of this cycle that most students of race relations in the United States have looked no further; they have assumed that the degraded position of the slave degraded the Negro in the white man's eyes—without pausing to wonder why Negroes came to be slaves in the first place, a question which cannot be answered by thinking entirely in terms of the Negro's condition since he was not fully a slave for Englishmen until they enslaved him.

Once the cycle was fully established, it is possible to obtain satisfactory answers as to the way it operated. From about 1700 until shortly after the middle of the eighteenth century, slaves were imported and worked by white men without effective challenge or even effective questioning of the rationale underlying what had rapidly become an important New World institution. It is therefore possible to treat this period as a unit, which in Part Two is discussed in four major aspects. It has seemed essential to deal first with the geographic and social patterns of the institution and with the problems generated by the necessity, as white men thought, of maintaining control over Negroes who no one thought would be lovable and happy and civilized and contented if left to themselves. The problem of maintaining control was in part a matter of white men controlling themselves, and a special aspect of this necessity is dealt with in the next chapter on interracial sex. It came to me as a surprise that many of the patterns of behavior, beliefs, and emotional tensions which are well known in the twentieth century were in existence more than two hundred years ago. The evidence suggests the great importance of demographic patterns in shaping white attitudes toward sexual intermixture, and it also shows that white men projected their own conflicts onto Negroes in ways which are well known though not well acknowledged today.

In the eighteenth century the role of explicitly religious ideas and impulses was of the utmost importance in shaping men's attitudes. The injunctions of Christian belief placed the keepers of Negroes under the task of doing what they could or would not do, of converting Negroes and treating them as brothers at least in Christ. This made (and sometimes still makes) things difficult, and the results of this difficulty are treated in chapter V. But Negroes were for white men not merely souls, which by definition were the same before God, but also corporeal creatures whom the merest glance revealed to be different from "white" men. In conceptualizing this difference provincial Americans drew upon certain prevailing cosmological and scientific concepts, and they showed themselves pulled by opposing tendencies—the need to explain why Negroes looked both the same as and different from white men and the twin senses that man both is and is not an animal.

While there were of course changes during the first sixty years of the eighteenth century, there was a remarkably sudden onset of self-examination among white Americans beginning with the Quakers about 1755 and among others during the gathering crisis which climaxed in the War for Independence. During the Revolutionary era Americans suddenly came to question not only the rightness of slavery but also to realize for the first time that they had a racial problem on their hands, that the institution which their ideology condemned was founded on perceptions of physiological differences which they thought they could do little or nothing about. The Revolution entailed upon Americans a dilemma of tragic proportions. It irreversibly altered the context in which "all men"—and hence Negroes—had to be viewed.

From the Revolutionary era on, there are greatly more abundant sources upon which investigation can be rested. It has seemed essential to concentrate first of all upon certain economic and ideological changes; new agricultural developments and the process of nation-building both created constant pressures upon white men. It is then possible to trace three interrelated strands of development during the twenty-five years following the Revolution. Since opposition to slavery was widespread and in some quarters intense, tracing its decline and virtual collapse after official abolition of the slave trade in 1808 affords one basic periodization of fundamental changes in American thought after the Revolution. In one important fashion, the Revolution perpetuated itself and thereby drove home to Americans the dangers of their own thinking. They watched in fascinated alarm as their own magnificent principles spread, as they thought, to France, then to the black island of Santo Domingo, and then to their own slaves. Gabriel's slave rebellion in Virginia in 1800 was real, half-expected, self-justifying, and utterly dangerous. As much as any single event it caused the sons eventually to repudiate their founding fathers' principles. Given this over-all pattern of retreat it is possible finally to sketch briefly the hardening of slavery and the separation of free and religious Negroes from the white community, processes whose timing was in virtual lockstep with economic changes, with the integration of the unified nation, with the course of antislavery, and with the pattern of response to slave rebelliousness.

Once these social and ideological developments become clear, there comes the chance to see how articulate white Americans dealt conceptually with the people who had become a standing problem. With one man only, though, is there opportunity to glimpse the interactions among deep emotions, intellectual constructs, long-accumulated traditions concerning the Negro, and the social problem of slavery in a free society. Thomas Jefferson combined, publicly and painfully, a heartfelt hostility to slavery and a deep conviction, inconsistently expressed, that Negroes were inferior to white men. He therefore has a dual role to play in this book. His remarks on the Negro were the most influential utterances on the subject, and they need to be considered as causally important. It was his comments concerning the Negro's lesser intellect which brought the sharpest challenge from defenders of the Negro's fundamental equality, and the resultant discussion, which coincided with the crisis concerning the existence of the new nation from 1787 to 1790, did a great deal to sharpen the distinctions which reign today in a still common if somewhat subterranean debate. At first sight the question of the Negro's mental ability would seem to have rather little to do with Thomas Jefferson's personal affective life, but it is precisely the connection between the two which requires emphasis. Here, in a different and more difficult arena of historical analysis, lies his other role. In seeking to understand the way his emotions interplayed with his ideas and his society I have not attempted to model feet of clay but rather to shed whatever light possible upon this interplay as a generic phenomenon. A great and good and admirable man, Jefferson like others of that description requires our comprehension and our sympathy, the second of which in this case flows from the first.

He discussed the Negro's nature within the confines of a specific intellectual milieu, as who does not. Two important traditions, the Chain of Being and Linnaean biological classification, did a great deal to shape the terms of his thinking and that of his fellow natural philosophers. It seems to me that such "ideas" have been too infrequently related by historians to the social milieu in which they found sustenance, and I have attempted to suggest that the prevalence of ordered arrangement and hierarchical imagery was connected with a feeling, which had been strengthening for more than a century, that the arrangement of society was becoming disorderly and rather the opposite of hierarchical. What seems particularly to make the debate on the Negro's nature different after the Revolution than before was the rapid growth in Europe and America after 1775 of interest in anatomical investigation of human differences. From the first voyages of discovery Europeans had seen these differences with their eyes, but it is from the final quarter of the eighteenth century that we may date widespread interest in elucidating and characterizing these differences with scalpels and calipers. At the same time, men devoted to the ancient Christian ideal of human unity began to scent danger, partly because there was good reason to fear the effects of probing into physiological differences among men and partly because they rightly felt that the cause of revealed religion was otherwise undergoing challenge. In this age it was still possible for them to defend religion with the principles of science, a procedure which was to become in the nineteenth century rather more difficult.

Heightened interest in man as a physical creature meant that the long-standing puzzle of the Negro's color underwent intensified investigation or, rather, speculation. That the Negro's complexion had also become a social problem made for some extraordinary suggestions which were animated by the hope that his blackness would eventually go away. What American intellectuals did in the post-Revolutionary decades was, in effect, to claim America as a white man's country. The impulses behind this claim were as deep and powerful as any in American culture. They became evident in proposals for removing Negroes from the United States, and these proposals, which became common at the end of the eighteenth century, tell, as much as any body of historical material can "tell," how profound were Americans' feelings about Negroes. They reveal, especially in Virginia where the great turning point came in 1806 in the form of forcing emancipated Negroes to leave the state, that white men were scarred by fear of racial intermixture which they equated with Negro insurrection, with free Negroes, with their own freedom, and with their own lack of mastery and self-control.

All of which means that this book ends where it begins, with the uncertainties inherent in a venture of a people into a new land. It focuses narrowly upon the attitudes of only one of the European peoples who settled in the New World because the story seems worth telling in its own right and because comparison with the experience of other nations, while potentially fruitful, is frequently misleading, as is always the case with comparisons between two unknowns. It deals with the overseas English, including those in the Caribbean islands until the War of Independence when white men there began to slip protesting from their seats of mastery. It deals also with the American Indians, for it is impossible to see clearly what Americans thought of Negroes without ascertaining their almost invariably contrary thoughts concerning Indians: in the settlement of this country the red and black peoples served white men as aids to navigation by which they would find their own safe positions as they ventured into America.

There are other "themes" in this book, ones which derive from basic, long-term trends in Western culture, most notably the gradual secularization of thought and leveling of society. As much as these changes were important, they did not alter such fundamental constants as the opportunities offered by America, human avarice and exploitation, and the need of transplanted Englishmen to know who it was they were. This last constitutes the thread which I hope binds this study together. For white men had to know who *they* were if they were to survive. They had to retain control of themselves and of their liberties if they were to succeed in America. Whether they "succeeded" is a question of standards. This study seems to suggest that the success of white Americans was also their failure, that how it was with Negroes was how it was with themselves.

ACKNOWLEDGMENTS

A FRIEND (AN HISTORIAN WHOSE NAME APPEARS BELOW) once warned me that "if the present tendency is not curbed we will all find ourselves reeling off fulsome acknowledgments for every paper clip we borrow during the course of preparing a manuscript." I have been careful about paper clips ever since. Yet a great many people have lent information or advice which has helped strengthen and clarify this book, and since I am very grateful to them I shall quietly succumb to the present tendency.

Thanks are owing to the Editor of the *William and Mary Quarterly* for permission to incorporate portions of two articles (cited in the footnotes) which I wrote several years ago. Parts of another, copyright 1962 by the Southern Historical Association, are reprinted by permission of the Managing Editor of the *Journal of Southern History*. The Note on the Concept of Race and several paragraphs in the text are reprinted by permission of the publishers from Samuel Stanhope Smith, *An Essay on the Causes of the Variety of Complexion and Figure in the Human Species*, ed. Winthrop D. Jordan, Cambridge, Mass.: The Belknap Press of the Harvard University Press, Copyright, 1965, by the President and Fellows of Harvard College.

Librarians in various parts of the country have generously proffered assistance; Jeannette D. Black and Thomas R. Adams of the John Carter Brown Library, Brown University, and Sarah De Luca and Dorothy Day of the Brown University Library were especially helpful. I am also grateful to the various past and present members of the staff of the Institute of Early American History and Culture who did so much to forward completion of this long book: Patricia Blatt, Susan L. Foard, Jack P. Greene, Stephen G. Kurtz, Marise L. Rogge, Beverly Schell, James Morton Smith, Thad Tate, Robert J. Taylor, and the Institute's director, Lester J. Cappon.

Many persons in the historical and medical professions have

furnished me with information and good counsel. I should like to thank these friends especially (while being acutely conscious that I cannot name everyone to whom thanks are due): Richard M. Brown, Robert Coles, David B. Davis, Emory G. Evans, Leon Golden, James B. Hedges, Sydney V. James, Benjamin E. Potter, Eugene M. Sirmans, Lawrence W. Towner, and Alfred Young. I want also to thank several students and non-students who helped me with research and with the mechanics of this book: Mary Rae Donaldson, Mimi Drain, Barbara Falcon, Judy Ryerson, Julia Selfman, Katherine E. Top, Ronald Walters, Virginia Warfield, Beverly Wellings, and especially Sharon Cabaniss and Stephen Thewlis (who helped do the index) and David Hollinger. And I am indebted to colleagues at several institutions who at various times read part or all of this study and gave me valuable suggestions: William W. Freehling, John Higham, William G. McLoughlin, Robert Middlekauff, George W. Stocking, Jr., and William B. Willcox. I am especially grateful to Donald Fleming, who at a crucial juncture during this undertaking did me the great favor of helping to readjust the level of my intellectual sights.

The person to whom I am most indebted intellectually—as in many other very important, private ways—is my wife, who knows why and how fully this book is dedicated to her.

TABLE OF CONTENTS

Preface   vii
Acknowledgments   xv

Part One. GENESIS 1550–1700

I. FIRST IMPRESSIONS: INITIAL ENGLISH CONFRONTATION WITH
    AFRICANS   3
    1) The Blackness Without   4
    2) The Causes of Complexion   11
    3) Defective Religion   20
    4) Savage Behavior   24
    5) The Apes of Africa   28
    6) Libidinous Men   32
    7) The Blackness Within   40

II. UNTHINKING DECISION: ENSLAVEMENT OF NEGROES IN
     AMERICA TO 1700   44
     1) The Necessities of a New World   45
     2) Freedom and Bondage in the English Tradition   48
     3) The Concept of Slavery   52
     4) The Practices of Portingals and Spanyards   56
     5) Enslavement: The West Indies   63
     6) Enslavement: New England   66
     7) Enslavement: Virginia and Maryland   71
     8) Enslavement: New York and the Carolinas   83
     9) The Un-English: Scots, Irish, and Indians   85
     10) Racial Slavery: From Reasons to Rationale   91

Part Two. PROVINCIAL DECADES 1700–1755

III. ANXIOUS OPPRESSORS: FREEDOM AND CONTROL IN A SLAVE
      SOCIETY   101
      1) Demographic Configurations in the Colonies   102

2) *Slavery and the Senses of the Laws*   103
3) *Slave Rebelliousness and White Mastery*   110
4) *Free Negroes and Fears of Freedom*   122
5) *Racial Slavery in a Free Society*   128

IV. FRUITS OF PASSION: THE DYNAMICS OF INTERRACIAL SEX   136
1) *Regional Styles in Racial Intermixture*   137
2) *Masculine and Feminine Modes in Carolina and America*   144
3) *Negro Sexuality and Slave Insurrection*   150
4) *Dismemberment, Physiology, and Sexual Perceptions*   154
5) *The Secularization of Reproduction*   164
6) *Mulatto Offspring in a Biracial Society*   167

V. THE SOULS OF MEN: THE NEGRO'S SPIRITUAL NATURE   179
1) *Christian Principles and the Failure of Conversion*   180
2) *The Question of Negro Capacity*   187
3) *Spiritual Equality and Temporal Subordination*   190
4) *The Thin Edge of Antislavery*   193
5) *Inclusion and Exclusion in the Protestant Churches*   198
6) *Religious Revival and the Impact of Conversion*   212

VI. THE BODIES OF MEN: THE NEGRO'S PHYSICAL NATURE   216
1) *Confusion, Order, and Hierarchy*   217
2) *Negroes, Apes, and Beasts*   228
3) *Rational Science and Irrational Logic*   234
4) *Indians, Africans, and the Complexion of Man*   239
5) *The Valuation of Color*   252
6) *Negroes Under the Skin*   259

Part Three. THE REVOLUTIONARY ERA
1755–1783

VII. SELF-SCRUTINY IN THE REVOLUTIONARY ERA   269
1) *Quaker Conscience and Consciousness*   271
2) *The Discovery of Prejudice*   276
3) *Assertions of Sameness*   281

4) *Environmentalism and Revolutionary Ideology* 287
5) *The Secularization of Equality* 294
6) *The Proslavery Case for Negro Inferiority* 304
7) *The Revolution as Turning Point* 308

Part Four. SOCIETY AND THOUGHT
1783–1812

VIII. THE IMPERATIVES OF ECONOMIC INTEREST AND NATIONAL
IDENTITY 315
1) *The Economics of Slavery* 316
2) *Union and Sectionalism* 321
3) *A National Forum for Debate* 325
4) *Nationhood and Identity* 331
5) *Non-English Englishmen* 335

IX. THE LIMITATIONS OF ANTISLAVERY 342
1) *The Pattern of Antislavery* 343
2) *The Failings of Revolutionary Ideology* 349
3) *The Quaker View Beyond Emancipation* 356
4) *Religious Equalitarianism* 361
5) *Humanitarianism and Sentimentality* 365
6) *The Success and Failure of Antislavery* 372

X. THE CANCER OF REVOLUTION 375
1) *St. Domingo* 375
2) *Non-Importation of Rebellion* 380
3) *The Contagion of Liberty* 386
4) *Slave Disobedience in America* 391
5) *The Impact of Negro Revolt* 399

XI. THE RESULTING PATTERN OF SEPARATION 403
1) *The Hardening of Slavery* 403
2) *Restraint of Free Negroes* 406
3) *New Walls of Separation* 414
4) *Negro Churches* 422

Part Five. THOUGHT AND SOCIETY
1783–1812

XII. THOMAS JEFFERSON: SELF AND SOCIETY 429
1) *Jefferson: The Tyranny of Slavery* 430

2) *Jefferson: The Assertion of Negro Inferiority*　435
3) *The Issue of Intellect*　440
4) *The Acclaim of Talented Negroes*　445
5) *Jefferson: Passionate Realities*　457
6) *Jefferson: White Women and Black*　461
7) *Interracial Sex: The Individual and His Society*　469
8) *Jefferson: A Dichotomous View of Triracial America*　475

XIII.　THE NEGRO BOUND BY THE CHAIN OF BEING　482
1) *Linnaean Categories and the Chain of Being*　483
2) *Two Modes of Equality*　486
3) *The Hierarchies of Men*　491
4) *Anatomical Investigations*　497
5) *Unlinking and Linking the Chain*　502
6) *Faithful Philosophy in Defense of Human Unity*　506
7) *The Study of Man in the Republic*　509

XIV.　ERASING NATURE'S STAMP OF COLOR　512
1) *Nature's Blackball*　512
2) *The Effects of Climate and Civilization*　513
3) *The Disease of Color*　517
4) *White Negroes*　521
5) *The Logic of Blackness and Inner Similarity*　525
6) *The Winds of Change*　530
7) *An End to Environmentalism*　533
8) *Persistent Themes*　538

XV.　TOWARD A WHITE MAN'S COUNTRY　542
1) *Emancipation and Intermixture*　542
2) *The Beginning of Colonization*　546
3) *The Virginia Program*　551
4) *Insurrection and Expatriation in Virginia*　560
5) *The Meaning of Negro Removal*　565

EPILOGUE

XVI.　EXODUS　573

Note on the Concept of Race　583
Essay on Sources　586
Select List of Full Titles　610
Map: Percentage of Negroes in Total Non-Aboriginal Population, 1790　615
Index　617

Part One

GENESIS 1550–1700

I FIRST IMPRESSIONS

Initial English Confrontation with Africans

WHEN THE ATLANTIC NATIONS OF EUROPE BEGAN EXPANDING overseas in the sixteenth century, Portugal led the way in Africa and to the east while Spain founded a great empire in America. It was not until the reign of Elizabeth that Englishmen came to realize that overseas exploration and plantations could bring home wealth, power, glory, and fascinating information. By the early years of the seventeenth century Englishmen had developed a taste for empire and for tales of adventure and discovery. More than is usual in human affairs, one man, the great chronicler Richard Hakluyt, had roused enthusiasm for western planting and had stirred the nation with his monumental compilation, *The Principal Navigations, Voyages, Traffiques and Discoveries of the English Nation*. Here was a work to widen a people's horizons. Its exhilarating accounts of voyages to all quarters of the globe (some by foreigners, in translation) constituted a national hymn, a sermon, an adventure story, and a scientific treatise. It was these accounts, together with ones added during the first quarter of the seventeenth century by Hakluyt's successor Samuel Purchas, which first acquainted Englishmen at home with the newly discovered lands of Africa.

English voyagers did not touch upon the shores of West Africa until after 1550, nearly a century after Prince Henry the Navigator had mounted the sustained Portuguese thrust southward for a water passage to the Orient. Usually Englishmen came to Africa to trade goods *with* the natives; the principal hazards of these ventures proved to be climate, disease, and the jealous opposition of the "Portingals" who had long since entrenched themselves in forts along the coast. The earliest English descriptions of West Africa were written by adventurous traders, men who had no special interest in converting the natives or, except for the famous Hawkins voyages, in otherwise laying hands on them. Extensive English participation in the slave trade did not develop until well into the seventeenth century. The first permanent English settlement on the African coast was at Kormantin in 1631, and the Royal African Company was not chartered for another forty years.[1] Initially, therefore, English contact with Africans did not take place primarily in a context which prejudged the Negro as a slave, at least not as a slave of Englishmen. Rather, Englishmen met Negroes merely as another sort of men.

Englishmen found the natives of Africa very different from themselves. Negroes looked different; their religion was un-Christian; their manner of living was anything but English; they seemed to be a particularly libidinous sort of people. All these clusters of perceptions were related to each other, though they may be spread apart for inspection, and they were related also to circumstances of contact in Africa, to previously accumulated traditions concerning that strange and distant continent, and to certain special qualities of English society on the eve of its expansion into the New World.

1. THE BLACKNESS WITHOUT

The most arresting characteristic of the newly discovered African was his color. Travelers rarely failed to comment upon it; indeed when describing Negroes they frequently began with complexion and then moved on to dress (or rather lack of it) and manners. At Cape Verde, "These people are all blacke, and are called Negros, without any apparell, saving before their privities." [2] Robert Baker's narrative poem recounting his two voyages to the West African coast in 1562 and 1563 first introduced the natives with these engaging lines:

> And entering in [a river], we see
> a number of blacke soules,

1. Kenneth G. Davies, *The Royal African Company* (London, 1957), 38–46; John W. Blake, trans. and ed., *Europeans in West Africa, 1450–1560; Documents to Illustrate the Nature and Scope of Portuguese Enterprise in West Africa, the Abortive Attempt of Castilians to Create an Empire There, and the Early English Voyages to Barbary and Guinea (Works Issued by the Hakluyt Society, 2d Ser., 87 [1942]), II, 254–60.*

2. "The voyage made by M. John Hawkins . . . to the coast of Guinea and the Indies of Nova Hispania . . . 1564," in Richard Hakluyt, *The Principal Navigations, Voyages, Traffiques and Discoveries of the English Nation . . . ,* 12 vols., 1598 ed. (Glasgow, 1903–05), X, 15. See Katherine Beverly Oakes, *Social Theory in the Early Literature of Voyage and Exploration in Africa* (unpubl. Ph.D. diss., University of California, Berkeley, 1944), 120–23.

> Whose likelinesse seem'd men to be,
> but all as blacke as coles.
> Their Captaine comes to me
> as naked as my naile,
> Not having witte or honestie
> to cover once his taile.[3]

Even more sympathetic observers seemed to find blackness a most salient quality in Negroes: "although the people were blacke and naked, yet they were civill."[4]

Englishmen actually described Negroes as *black*—an exaggerated term which in itself suggests that the Negro's complexion had powerful impact upon their perceptions. Even the peoples of northern Africa seemed so dark that Englishmen tended to call them "black" and let further refinements go by the board. Blackness became so generally associated with Africa that every African seemed a black man. In Shakespeare's day, the Moors, including Othello, were commonly portrayed as pitchy black and the terms *Moor* and *Negro* used almost interchangeably.[5] With curious inconsistency, however, Englishmen recognized that Africans south of the Sahara were not at all the same people as the much more familiar Moors.[6] Sometimes they referred to Negroes as "black Moors" to distinguish them from the peoples of North Africa. During the seventeenth century the distinction became more firmly established and indeed writers came to stress the difference in color, partly because they delighted in correcting their predecessors and partly because Negroes were being taken up as slaves and Moors, increasingly,

3. "The First Voyage of Robert Baker to Guinie . . . 1562," in Richard Hakluyt, *The Principall Navigations, Voiages and Discoveries of the English Nation* . . . (London, 1589), 132. The entire poem was omitted in the 1598 edition.

4. "The Voyage of M. George Fenner . . . Written by Walter Wren" (1566), Hakluyt, *Principal Navigations*, VI, 270. All ensuing references are to this reprinted 1598 edition unless otherwise indicated.

5. Warner Grenelle Rice, Turk, Moor and Persian in English Literature from 1550–1660, with Particular Reference to the Drama (unpubl. Ph.D. diss., Harvard University, 1926), 401–2n; Robert R. Cawley, *The Voyagers and Elizabethan Drama* (Boston, 1938), 31; Samuel C. Chew, *The Crescent and the Rose: Islam and England during the Renaissance* (N. Y., 1937), 521–24; Wylie Sypher, *Guinea's Captive Kings: British Anti-Slavery Literature of the XVIIIth Century* (Chapel Hill, 1942), 26.

6. An early instance is in "The Second Voyage to Guinea . . ." (1554), in Hakluyt, *Principal Navigations*, VI, 167–68. See the associations made by Leo Africanus, *The History and Description of Africa and of the Notable Things Therein Contained* . . . , trans. John Pory [ca. 1600], ed. Robert Brown, 3 vols. (London, 1896), I, 130.

were not. In the more detailed and accurate reports about West
Africa of the seventeenth century, moreover, Negroes in different
regions were described as varying considerably in complexion. In
England, however, the initial impression of Negroes was not appreciably modified: the firmest fact about the Negro was that he
was "black."

The powerful impact which the Negro's color made upon Englishmen must have been partly owing to suddenness of contact.
Though the Bible as well as the arts and literature of antiquity and
the Middle Ages offered some slight introduction to the "Ethiope,"
England's immediate acquaintance with black-skinned peoples came
with relative rapidity. While the virtual monopoly held by Venetian
ships in England's foreign trade prior to the sixteenth century
meant that people much darker than Englishmen were not entirely
unfamiliar, really black men were virtually unknown except as
vaguely referred to in the hazy literature about the sub-Sahara
which had filtered down from antiquity. Native West Africans
probably first appeared in London in 1554; in that year five
"Negroes," as the legitimate trader William Towrson reported, were
taken to England, "kept till they could speake the language," and
then brought back again "to be a helpe to Englishmen" who were
engaged in trade with Negroes on the coast. Hakluyt's later discussion of these Negroes, who he said "could wel agree with our meates
and drinkes" though "the colde and moyst aire doth somewhat
offend them," suggests that these "blacke Moores" were a novelty to
Englishmen.[7] In this respect the English experience was markedly
different from that of the Spanish and Portuguese who for centuries
had been in close contact with North Africa and had actually been
invaded and subjected by people both darker and more highly
civilized than themselves. The impact of the Negro's color was the
more powerful upon Englishmen, moreover, because England's principal contact with Africans came in West Africa and the Congo
where men were not merely dark but almost literally black: one of
the fairest-skinned nations suddenly came face to face with one of
the darkest peoples on earth.

Viewed from one standpoint, Englishmen were merely participating in Europe's discovery that the strange men who stood revealed
by European expansion overseas came in an astounding variety of

7. Hakluyt, *Principal Navigations*, VI, 176, 200, 217–18. Just how little Euro-
peans knew about Africa prior to the Portuguese explorations is evident in T.
Simar, "La géographie de l'Afrique central dans l'antiquité et au moyen âge,"
La Revue Congolaise, 3 (1912), 1–23, 81–102, 145–69, 225–52, 288–310, 440–41.

colors. A Spanish chronicle translated into English in 1555 was filled with wonder at this diversity: "One of the marveylous thynges that god useth in the composition of man, is coloure: whiche doubtlesse can not bee consydered withowte great admiration in beholding one to be white and an other blacke, beinge coloures utterlye contrary. Sum lykewyse to be yelowe whiche is betwene blacke and white: and other of other colours as it were of dyvers liveres." [8] As this passage suggests, the juxtaposition of black and white was the most striking marvel of all. And for Englishmen this juxtaposition was more than a curiosity.

In England perhaps more than in southern Europe, the concept of blackness was loaded with intense meaning. Long before they found that some men were black, Englishmen found in the idea of blackness a way of expressing some of their most ingrained values. No other color except white conveyed so much emotional impact. As described by the *Oxford English Dictionary,* the meaning of *black* before the sixteenth century included, "Deeply stained with dirt; soiled, dirty, foul. . . . Having dark or deadly purposes, malignant; pertaining to or involving death, deadly; baneful, disastrous, sinister. . . . Foul, iniquitous, atrocious, horrible, wicked. . . . Indicating disgrace, censure, liability to punishment, etc." Black was an emotionally partisan color, the handmaid and symbol of baseness and evil, a sign of danger and repulsion.

Embedded in the concept of blackness was its direct opposite—whiteness. No other colors so clearly implied opposition, "beinge coloures utterlye contrary"; no others were so frequently used to denote polarization:

> Everye white will have its blacke,
> And everye sweete its sowre.[9]

White and black connoted purity and filthiness, virginity and sin, virtue and baseness, beauty and ugliness, beneficence and evil, God and the devil.[10]

8. Francisco López de Gómara, in Peter Martyr (D'Anghera), *The Decades of the Newe Worlde . . .* , trans. Richard Eden (London, 1555), in Edward Arber, ed., *The First Three English Books on America . . .* (Birmingham, Eng., 1885), 338.

9. Thomas Percy, *Reliques of Ancient English Poetry . . .* , ed. Robert A. Willmott (London, 1857), 27 (Sir Cauline, pt. 2, stanza 1).

10. Numerous examples in Middle English, Shakespeare, the Bible, and Milton are given by P. J. Heather, "Colour Symbolism," *Folk Lore,* 59 (1948), 169–70, 175–78, 182–83; 60 (1949), 208–16, 266–76. See also Harold R. Isaacs, "Blackness and Whiteness," *Encounter,* 21 (1963), 8–21; Caroline F. E. Spurgeon, *Shake-*

Whiteness, moreover, carried a special significance for Elizabethan Englishmen: it was, particularly when complemented by red, the color of perfect human beauty, especially *female* beauty. This ideal was already centuries old in Elizabeth's time,[11] and their fair Queen was its very embodiment: her cheeks were "roses in a bed of lillies." (Elizabeth was naturally pale but like many ladies then and since she freshened her "lillies" at the cosmetic table.) [12] An adoring nation knew precisely what a beautiful Queen looked like.

> Her cheeke, her chinne, her neck, her nose,
> This was a lillye, that was a rose;
> Her hande so white as whales bone,
> Her finger tipt with Cassidone;
> Her bosome, sleeke as Paris plaster,
> Held upp twoo bowles of Alabaster.[13]

Shakespeare himself found the lily and the rose a compelling natural coalition.

> 'Tis beauty truly blent, whose red and white
> Nature's own sweet and cunning hand laid on.[14]

By contrast, the Negro was ugly, by reason of his color and also his "horrid Curles" and "disfigured" lips and nose.[15] As Shakespeare wrote apologetically of his black mistress,

---

speare's Imagery and What It Tells Us (Boston, 1958), 64, 66–69, 158; Arrah B. Evarts, "Color Symbolism," *Psychoanalytic Review*, 6 (1919), 129–34; Don Cameron Allen, "Symbolic Color in the Literature of the English Renaissance," *Philological Quarterly*, 15 (1936), 81–92; and for a different perspective, Francis B. Gummere, "On the Symbolic Use of the Colors Black and White in Germanic Tradition," *Haverford College Studies*, 1 (1889), 112–62.

11. Walter Clyde Curry, *The Middle English Ideal of Personal Beauty; As Found in the Metrical Romances, Chronicles, and Legends of the XIII, XIV, and XV Centuries* (Baltimore, 1916), 3, 80–98.

12. Elkin Calhoun Wilson, *England's Eliza* (Cambridge, Mass., 1939), 337; Charles Carroll Camden, *The Elizabethan Woman* (Houston, N. Y., and London, 1952), chap. 7; Cawley, *Voyagers and Elizabethan Drama*, 85; Elizabeth Jenkins, *Elizabeth the Great* (London, 1958), 62, 100, 159, 296; Gamaliel Bradford, *Elizabethan Women*, ed. Harold O. White (Boston, 1936), 82, 212; Violet A. Wilson, *Queen Elizabeth's Maids of Honour and Ladies of the Privy Chamber* (N. Y., n.d.), 4–5. Hugh Plat, *Delightes for Ladies, Written Originally by Sir Hugh Plat, First Printed in 1602, London, England*, ed. Violet and Hal W. Trovillion (Herrin, Ill., 1939), 87–94, 99, 102–3, contains advice on cosmetics.

13. [George Puttenham?], *Partheniades* (1579), quoted in Wilson, *England's Eliza*, 242.

14. *Twelfth Night*, I, v, 259–60, W. J. Craig, ed., *The Complete Works of Shakespeare* (London, N. Y., Toronto, 1943). For other expressions of this ideal, *A Midsummer-Night's Dream*, I, i, 128–29; III, i, 98–99; III, ii, 137–44.

15. *Love in Its Ecstacy*, quoted in Cawley, *Voyagers and Elizabethan Drama*, 86n; "A Letter written from Goa . . . by one Thomas Stevens . . . 1579,"

> My mistress' eyes are nothing like the sun;
> Coral is far more red than her lips' red:
> If snow be white, why then her breasts are dun;
> If hairs be wires, black wires grow on her head.
> I have seen roses damask'd, red and white,
> But no such roses see I in her cheeks.[16]

Some Elizabethans found blackness an ugly mask, superficial but always demanding attention.

> Is *Byrrha* browne? Who doth the question aske?
> Her face is pure as Ebonie jeat blacke,
> It's hard to know her face from her faire maske,
> Beautie in her seemes beautie still to lacke.
> Nay, she's snow-white, but for that russet skin,
> Which like a vaile doth keep her whitenes in.[17]

A century later blackness still required apology and mitigation: one of the earliest attempts to delineate the West African Negro as a heroic character, Aphra Behn's popular story *Oroonoko* (1688), presented Negroes as capable of blushing and turning pale.[18] It was important, if incalculably so, that English discovery of black Africans came at a time when the accepted standard of ideal beauty was a fair complexion of rose and white. Negroes not only failed to fit this ideal but seemed the very picture of perverse negation.[19]

From the first, however, many English observers displayed a certain sophistication about the Negro's color. Despite an ethnocentric tendency to find blackness repulsive, many writers were fully aware that Negroes themselves might have different tastes. As early as 1621 one writer told of the "Jetty coloured" Negroes, "Who in their

---

Hakluyt, *Principal Navigations*, VI, 384. Curry, *Middle English Ideal of Personal Beauty*, 64–66, 113–14, indirectly makes abundantly clear how very far Negro women were from matching prevalent English ideals for beautiful noses, lips, and breasts.

16. Sonnet CXXX; see also nos. CXXVII, CXXXI, CXXXII. Shakespeare's "Dark Lady" is discussed by George B. Harrison, *Shakespeare under Elizabeth* (N. Y., 1933), 64–67, 310.

17. Harrison, *Shakespeare*, 310–11, quoting Weever, *Epigrams* (1599), Third Week, Epig. 12, *In Byrrham*.

18. Aphra Behn, *Oroonoko; Or, the Royal Slave*, Montague Summers, ed., *The Works of Aphra Behn*, V (London, 1915), 145.

19. In the Middle Ages a man's "complexion" was conceived as revealing his temperament because it showed his particular blend of humors, each of which was associated with certain colors: Lynn Thorndike, "De Complexionibus," *Isis*, 49 (1958), 398–408. Yet Englishmen seem not to have made efforts to link the Negro's skin color specifically to his bile or dominant humor and hence to his temperament.

native beauty most delight,/And in contempt doe paint the Divell white"; this assertion became almost a commonplace and even turned up a hundred and fifty years later in Newport, Rhode Island.[20] Many accounts of Africa reported explicitly that the Negro's preference in colors was inverse to the European's.[21] Even the Negro's features were conceded to be appealing to Negroes. By the late seventeenth century, in a changing social atmosphere, some observers decided that the Negro's jet blackness was more handsome than the lighter tawny hues; this budding appreciativeness was usually coupled, though, with expressions of distaste for "Large Breasts, thick Lips, and broad Nostrils" which many Negroes "reckon'd the Beauties of the Country." [22] As one traveler admiringly described an African queen, "She was indifferently tall and well shap'd, of a perfect black; had not big Lips nor was she flat Nos'd as most of the Natives are, but well featur'd and very comely." [23] By

20. P[eter] H[eylyn], Microcosmus, or a Little Description of the Great World. A Treatise Historicall, Geographicall, Politicall, Theologicall (Oxford, 1621), 379; Peter Heylyn, ΜΙΚΡΌΚΟΣΜΟΣ. A Little Description of the Great World, 3d ed. (Oxford, 1627), 735; The Golden Coast, or a Description of Guinney . . . Together with a Relation of Such Persons, As Got Wonderful Estates by Their Trade Thither (London, 1665), 3; Thomas Phillips, A Journal of a Voyage Made in the Hannibal of London, Ann. 1693, 1694, from England to Cape Monseradoe, in Africa; and Thence Along the Coast of Guiney to Whidaw, the Island of St. Thomas, and So Forward to Barbadoes. With a Cursory Account of the Country, the People, Their Manners, Forts, Trade, etc., in John and Awsham Churchill, comps., A Collection of Voyages and Travels, Some Now First Printed from Original Manuscripts. Others Translated Out of Foreign Languages, and Now First Published in English . . . , 6 vols. (London, 1704–32), VI, 219; Thomas Browne, "Of the Blackness of Negroes," Charles Sayle, ed., The Works of Sir Thomas Browne, 3 vols. (London, 1904–07), II, 383–84; Newport [R. I.] Mercury, Jan. 11, 1768. See Karl Pearson, E. Nettleship, and C. H. Usher, A Monograph on Albinism in Man (Department of Applied Mathematics [or Statistics], University College, University of London, Drapers' Company Research Memoirs, Biometric Ser., 6, 8, 9 [6 vols.] [London, 1911–13]), I, 48.
21. Peter Martyr (D'Anghera), De Orbe Novo: The Eight Decades of Peter Martyr D'Anghera, trans. Francis A. MacNutt, 2 vols. (N .Y. and London, 1912), II, 39; Morgan Godwyn, The Negro's and Indians Advocate . . . (London, 1680), 21; The Works of Michael Drayton, Esq., 4 vols. (London, 1753), III, 1177; W. Gifford, ed., The Works of Ben Jonson, 9 vols. (London, 1816), VII, 11; Cawley, Voyagers and Elizabethan Drama, 32n. Cf. Katherine George, "The Civilized West Looks at Primitive Africa; 1400–1800. A Study in Ethnocentrism," Isis, 49 (1958), 62–72.
22. Francis Moore, Travels into the Inland Parts of Africa: Containing a Description of the Several Nations for the Space of Six Hundred Miles up the River Gambia . . . (London, 1738), 131.
23. Nathaniel Uring, A History of the Voyages and Travels of Capt. Nathaniel Uring . . . (London, 1726), 40–41. Also Behn, Oroonoko, 136; John Barbot, A Description of the Coasts of North and South-Guinea; and of Ethiopia Inferior, Vulgarly Angola . . . , in Churchill, comps., Voyages, V, 100; William Snelgrave, A New Account of Some Parts of Guinea, and the Slave-Trade . . . (London, 1734), 40–41; Moore, Travels into the Inland Parts, 29–30, 214.

this time, the development of the slave trade to America was beginning to transform the Negro's color from a marvel into an issue. In what was surely a remarkable complaint for the master of a slaving vessel, Captain Thomas Phillips wrote in 1694 that he could not "imagine why they should be despis'd for their colour, being what they cannot help, and the effect of the climate it has pleas'd God to appoint them. I can't think there is any intrinsick value in one colour more than another, nor that white is better than black, only we think it so because we are so, and are prone to judge favourably in our own case, as well as the blacks, who in odium of the colour, say, the devil is white, and so paint him." [24] During the eighteenth century the Negro's color was to come into service as an argument for "diversitarian" theories of beauty; [25] Europe's discovery of "blacks" and "tawnies" overseas helped nurture a novel relativism. More important so far as the Negro was concerned, his color was to remain for centuries what it had been from the first, a standing problem for natural philosophers.

2. THE CAUSES OF COMPLEXION

Black human beings were not only startling but extremely puzzling. The complexion of Negroes posed problems about its nature, especially its permanence and utility, its cause and origin, and its significance. Although these were rather separate questions, there was a pronounced tendency among Englishmen and other Europeans to formulate the problem in terms of causation alone, for if that nut could be cracked the other answers would be readily forthcoming; if the cause of human blackness could be explained, then its nature and significance would follow.

Not that the problem was completely novel. The ancient Greeks had touched upon it without ever really coming to grips with it. The story of Phaëton's driving the chariot sun wildly through the heavens apparently served as an explanation for the Ethiopian's blackness even before written records, and traces of this ancient fable were still drifting about during the seventeenth century.

> The Æthiopians then were white and fayre,
> Though by the worlds combustion since made black
> When wanton Phaeton overthrew the Sun.[26]

24. Phillips, *Journal*, in Churchill, comps., *Voyages*, VI, 219.
25. Sypher, *Guinea's Captive Kings*, 51.
26. R. Warwick Bond, ed., *The Poetical Works of William Basse (1602–1653)* (London, 1893), 279; Conway Zirkle, "The Early History of the Idea of the

Less fancifully, Ptolemy had made the important suggestion that the Negro's blackness and woolly hair were caused by exposure to the hot sun and had pointed out that people in northern climates were white and those in temperate areas an intermediate color.[27] Aristotle, Antigonus, Pliny, and Plutarch, an impressive battery of authorities, had passed along the familiar story of a black baby born into a white family (telltale trace of some Ethiopian ancestor), but this was scarcely much help as to original cause. The idea that black babies might result from maternal impressions during conception or pregnancy found credence during the Middle Ages and took centuries to die out, if indeed it ever has entirely.[28] Before the fifteenth century, though, the question of the Negro's color can hardly be said to have drawn the attention of Englishmen or indeed of Europeans generally.

The opening of West Africa and the development of Negro slavery, which for the first time brought Englishmen frequently into firsthand contact with really black Negroes, made the question far more urgent and provided an irresistible playground for awakening scientific curiosity. The range of possible answers was rigidly restricted, however, by the virtually universal assumption, dictated by church and Scripture, that all mankind stemmed from a single source. Giordano Bruno's statement in 1591 that "no sound thinking person will refer the Ethiopians to the same protoplast as the Jewish one" was unorthodox at best. Indeed it is impossible fully to understand the various efforts at explaining the Negro's complexion without bearing in mind the strength of the tradition which in 1614 made the chronicler, the Reverend Samuel Purchas, proclaim vehemently: "the tawney Moore, blacke Negro, duskie Libyan, ash-coloured Indian, olive-coloured American, should with the whiter European become *one sheep-fold,* under *one great Sheepheard,* till *this mortalitie being swallowed up of Life,* wee may all *be one, as he and the father are one . . .* without any more distinction of Colour,

Inheritance of Acquired Characters and of Pangenesis," American Philosophical Society, *Transactions,* New Ser., 35 (1945–46), Pt. ii, 145. The original story of Phaëton is in Thomas Bulfinch, *Bulfinch's Mythology* (N. Y.: Modern Library, n.d.), 36–42; Edith Hamilton, *Mythology* (N. Y.: Mentor, 1953), 131–34.

27. [Claudius] Ptolemy, *Tetrabiblos,* trans. and ed. F. E. Robbins (Cambridge, Mass., and London, 1940), 121–25, 439.

28. Conway Zirkle, "The Knowledge of Heredity before 1900," L. C. Dunn, ed., *Genetics in the 20th Century: Essays on the Progress of Genetics during Its First 50 Years* (N. Y., 1951), 42; Thorndike, "De Complexionibus," *Isis,* 49 (1958), 400; Don Cameron Allen, *The Legend of Noah: Renaissance Rationalism in Art, Science, and Letters* (Urbana, 1949), 119. For an interesting modification, Browne, "Of the Blackness of Negroes," Sayle, ed., *Works of Browne,* II, 375–76.

Nation, Language, Sexe, Condition, all may bee *One* in him that is One, *and onely blessed for ever.*" [29]

In general, the most satisfactory answer to the problem was some sort of reference to the action of the sun, whether the sun was assumed to have scorched the skin, drawn the bile, or blackened the blood. People living on the Line had obviously been getting too much of it; after all, even Englishmen were darkened by a little exposure. How much more, then, with the Negroes who were "so scorched and vexed with the heat of the sunne, that in many places they curse it when it riseth." [30] The sun's heat was itself sometimes described as a curse—a not unnatural reaction on the part of those Englishmen who visited the West African coast where the weather was "of such putrifying qualitie, that it rotted the coates of their backs." [31] This association of the Negro's color with the sun became a commonplace in Elizabethan literature; as the Prince of Morocco apologized, "Mislike me not for my complexion,/ The shadow'd livery of the burnish'd sun,/ To whom I am a neighbour and near bred." [32]

Unfortunately this theory ran headlong into a stubborn fact of nature which simply could not be overridden: if the equatorial inhabitants of Africa were blackened by the sun, why not the people living on the same line in America? Logic required them to be the same color. As Ptolemy's formidably authoritative *Geographia* stated this logic, "Reason herself asserts that all animals, and all plants likewise, have a similarity under the same kind of climate or under similar weather conditions, that is, when under the same parallels, or when situated at the same distance from either pole." [33]

29. T[homas] Bendyshe, "The History of Anthropology," *Anthropological Society of London, Memoirs,* 1 (1863–64), 355; Samuel Purchas, *Purchas his Pilgrimage. Or Relations of the World and the Religions Observed in All Ages and Places Discovered, from the Creation unto This Present,* 2d ed. (London, 1614), 656.

30. "Second Voyage to Guinea," Hakluyt, *Principal Navigations,* VI, 167; Cawley, *Voyagers and Elizabethan Drama,* 88–89, 159–60. A remarkably early suggestion that sun-blackened skin afforded protection against the sun "as if naturaliz'd" was made by John Ogilby, *Africa: Being an Accurate Description of the Regions of Ægypt, Barbary, Lybia, and Billedulgerid, the Land of Negroes, Guinee, Æthiopia, and the Abyssines . . . Collected and Translated from Most Authentick Authors, and Augmented with Later Observations* (London, 1670), 445.

31. "The First Voyage to Guinea and Benin" (1553), Hakluyt, *Principal Navigations,* VI, 148.

32. *The Merchant of Venice,* II, i, 1–3; also Ben Jonson, "Masque of Blackness," Gifford, ed., *Works of Jonson,* VII, 12.

33. Edward L. Stevenson, trans. and ed., *Geography of Claudius Ptolemy* (N. Y., 1932), 31–32.

Yet by the middle of the sixteenth century it was becoming perfectly apparent that the Indians living in the hottest regions of the New World could by no stretch of the imagination be described as black. They were "olive" or "tawny," and moreover thay had long hair rather than the curious wool of Negroes; clearly they were a different sort of men. Peter Martyr, the official Spanish court chronicler whose accounts Richard Eden translated in 1555, made the point as early as 1516, a trifle over-enthusiastically to be sure: "in all that navigation, he [Columbus] never wente oute of the paralelles of Ethiope. . . . [Yet] the Ethiopians are all blacke, havinge theyr heare curld more lyke wulle then heare. But these people [in America] . . . are whyte, with longe heare, and of yellowe colour." Fortunately it did not take long to calm down this entrancing, overly Nordic presentation of the Indian. Toward the end of the century Richard Hakluyt picked up Eden's own account of a voyage of 1554 which had carefully noted that the Indians were "neither blacke, nor with curlde and short wooll on their heads, as they of Africke have, but of the colour of an Olive, with long and blacke heare on their heads." [34] Clearly the method of accounting for human complexion by latitude just did not work. The worst of it was that the formula did not seem altogether wrong, since it was apparent that in general men in hot climates tended to be darker than in cold ones. The tenacity of the old logic was manifest in many writers who clung to the latitudinal explanation and maintained stoutly that for one or many reasons the actual climate on the ground was more temperate in America than in Guinea and men accordingly less dark.[35]

Another difficulty with the climatic explanation of skin color arose as lengthening experience augmented knowledge about Negroes. If the heat of the sun caused the Negro's blackness, then his removal to cold northerly countries ought to result in his losing it; even if he did not himself surrender his peculiar color, surely his descendants must. By mid-seventeenth century it was becoming increasingly apparent that this expectation was ill founded: Negroes in Europe

34. Martyr, *Decades of Newe Worlde*, trans. Eden, 88, 387–88; "Second Voyage to Guinea," Hakluyt, *Principal Navigations*, VI, 176.

35. Both Martyr and Hakluyt did so in the preceding passages; James Spedding, Robert L. Ellis, Douglas D. Heath, eds., *The Works of Francis Bacon . . . ,* 14 vols. (London, 1857–74), II, 473; John Selden's notes in *Works of Michael Drayton*, II, 675; John Ovington, *A Voyage to Suratt, in the Year 1869*, ed. H. G. Rawlinson (London, 1929), 285. For a more general statement of the influence of climate on complexion, Matthew Hale, *The Primitive Origination of Mankind, Considered and Examined According to the Light of Nature* (London, 1677), 200–201.

and northern America were simply not whitening up very noticeably. Still, the evidence on this matter was by no means entirely definite, and some observers felt that it was not yet all in hand. Though they conceded that lightening of black skin by mixture with Europeans should be ruled out of the experiment, these writers thought they detected a perceptible whitening of the unmixed African residing in colder climates, and they bolstered their case by emphasizing how long it was going to take to whiten up the African completely.[36]

From the beginning, however, many Englishmen were certain that the Negro's blackness was permanent and innate and that no amount of cold was going to alter it. There was good authority in Jeremiah 13:23; "Can the Ethiopian change his skin/ or the leopard his spots?" Elizabethan dramatists used the stock expression "to wash an Ethiop white" as indicating sheer impossibility.[37] In 1578 a voyager and speculative geographer, George Best, announced that "I my self have seene an Ethiopian as blacke as cole brought into England, who taking a faire English woman to wife, begat a sonne in all respects as blacke as the father was . . . whereby it seemeth this blacknes proceedeth rather of some natural infection of that man, which was so strong, that neither the nature of the Clime, neither the good complexion of the mother concurring, coulde any thing alter, and therefore, wee cannot impute it to the nature of the Clime." The blackness of the Negroes, Best decided, "proceedeth of some naturall infection of the first inhabitants of that country, and so all the whole progenie of them descended, are still polluted with the same blot of infection." [38] The well-known physician Sir Thomas Browne put the matter this way in 1646:

If the fervour of the Sun, or intemperate heat of clime did solely occasion this complexion, surely a migration or change thereof might cause a sensible, if not a total mutation; which notwithstanding[,] experience will not admit. For *Negroes* transplanted, although into cold and phlegmatick habitations, continue their hue both in themselves, and also their generations; except they mix with different complexions; whereby notwithstanding there only succeeds a remission of their tinctures; there remaining

36. A widely popular work, [Thomas Burnet], *The Theory of the Earth . . . the First Two Books . . .*, 2d ed. (London, 1691), 191, bk. II, chap. 2, announced that "after some generations they become altogether like the people of the Country where they are." Ovington, *Voyage to Suratt*, ed. Rawlinson, 285, was at pains to deny this "current Opinion."

37. Cawley, *Voyagers and Elizabethan Drama*, 87–88.

38. "Experiences and reasons of the Sphere, to proove all partes of the worlde habitable, and thereby to confute the position of the five Zones," Hakluyt, *Principal Navigations*, VII, 262–63.

unto many descents a strong shadow of their Originals; and if they preserve their copulations entire, they still maintain their complexions. . . . And so likewise fair or white people translated in hotter Countries receive not impressions amounting to this complexion.

Browne was certain that blackness was permanent and that it was transmitted in the sperm ("even their abortions are also dusky"), but he was far from sure why this should have been so. One possible explanation, he suggested in a display of intellectual daring, was that Negroes had always been black, a possibility which, Browne noted, raised the troublesome problem of how animals got to America and many other questions on the origin of things. This was as far as he dared go, but he had firmly set forth a case for the innateness of blackness with a quasi-genetic explanation which confirmed the permanence of the color without, unfortunately, doing anything to explain its original cause.[39]

Similar views were forwarded by a number of writers during the next hundred years. An essayist in 1695 declared that "for time out of mind" there had been black men with woolly hair and that it was "plain, their colour and wool are innate, or seminal from their first beginning"—precisely when that "beginning" had occurred the writer evidently did not care to say. Some points, however, seemed to him clear: "This colour (which appears to be as ingenite, and as original, as that in whites) could not proceed from any accident; because, when animals are accidentally black, they do not procreate constantly black ones, (as the negroes do)." "A negroe will always be a negroe," he concluded firmly, "carry him to Greenland, give him chalk, feed and manage him never so many ways." [40] By the first half of the eighteenth century the majority of writers were certain blackness in man was permanent. As an account published in the Churchills' *Voyages* in 1732 declared briskly, "Some suppose the reason [why Negroes are black] to be, because those people live betwixt the *tropicks* in the *torrid zones,* where the perpetual scorching heat of the sun blackens them, as it does the earth in some parts, which makes it look as if burnt by fire. But this vanishes presently, if we consider that *Europeans* living within the *tropicks,* tho' ever so long, will never turn black or sooty; and that *Blacks* living many years in *Europe,* will always breed black or sooty children. Besides

39. Browne, "Of the Blackness of Negroes," Sayle, ed., *Works of Browne,* II, 368–80.
40. *Two Essays, Sent in a Letter from Oxford, to a Nobleman in London. The First Concerning Some Errors About the Creation, General Flood, and the Peopling of the World . . . By L. P. Master of Arts. 1695,* in Walter Scott, ed., *Somers Tracts,* XII, 2d ed. (London, 1814), 27–28.

the *Americans* and *East-Indians,* tho' inhabiting the same parallel zones, are not black." [41] Even as late as 1735 few men were willing to press the matter of causation so far as John Atkins, a naval surgeon, who declared bluntly that "tho' it be a little Heterodox, I am persuaded the black and white Race have, *ab origine,* sprung from different-coloured first Parents." [42] To call this position "a little Heterodox" was like calling water a little wet.

The logical complement to the question of the Negro's change in color was whether the European by removing to a torrid climate would become darker or even black. Something of a consensus on this point emerged in the seventeenth century, since understandably Englishmen did not relish the prospect of turning into Negroes by prolonged residence in their expanding tropical empire. By the eighteenth century it was generally understood that European complexions would be darkened by tropical sun and weather, but that a return to cooler climates would restore the original color; even European children born in hot climates would be thoroughly white at first. [43]

There was an alternative to these naturalistic explanations of the Negro's blackness. Some writers felt that God's curse on Ham (Cham), or upon his son Canaan, and all their descendants was entirely sufficient to account for the color of Negroes. This could be an appealing explanation, especially for men like George Best who wished to stress the "natural infection" of blackness and for those who hoped to incorporate the Negro's complexion securely within the accepted history of mankind. The original story in Genesis 9 and 10 was that after the Flood, Ham had looked upon his father's nakedness as Noah lay drunk in his tent, but the other two sons, Shem and Japheth, had covered their father without looking upon him; when Noah awoke he cursed Canaan, son of Ham, saying that he would be a "servant of servants" unto his brothers. Given this

41. Barbot, *Description of the Coasts,* Churchill, comps., *Voyages,* V, 8.

42. John Atkins, *A Voyage to Guinea, Brasil, and the West-Indies; In His Majesty's Ships, the Swallow and Weymouth* . . . (London, 1735), 39.

43. For representative opinions, *The Works of the Right Reverend Joseph Hall, D. D., Bishop of Exeter and Afterwards of Norwich,* 10 vols. (Oxford, 1863), I, 126; [John Watts], *A True Relation of the Inhuman and Unparalleled Actions, and Barbarous Murders, of Negroes or Moors: Committed on Three Englishmen in Old Calabar in Guiney* . . . [1672], in Thomas Osborne, *A Collection of Voyages and Travels* . . . , 2 vols. (London, 1745), II, 515; Godwyn, *Negro's and Indians Advocate,* 22; *Two Essays,* Scott, ed., *Somers Tracts,* XII, 28; George Roberts, *The Four Years Voyages of Capt. George Roberts; Being a Series of Uncommon Events, Which Befell Him in a Voyage to the Islands of the Canaries, Cape de Verde, and Barbadoes, from Whence He Was Bound to the Coast of Guiney* . . . (London, 1726), 180–81.

text, the question becomes why a tale which logically implied slavery but absolutely nothing about skin color should have become an autonomous and popular explanation of the Negro's blackness. Probably, over the very long run, this development was owing partly to the ancient association of heat with sensuality and with the fact that some Ethiopians had been enslaved by Europeans since ancient times.

What is more arresting, there did exist a specific textual basis for utilizing the curse as an explanation for blackness—but it was a specifically Jewish rather than a Christian one. The writings of the great church fathers such as St. Jerome and St. Augustine referred to the curse in connection with slavery but not with Negroes. They casually accepted the assumption that Africans were descended from one or several of Ham's four sons, an assumption which became universal in Christendom despite the obscurity of its origins. They were probably aware, moreover, that the term *Ham* originally connoted both "dark" and "hot," yet they failed to seize this obvious opportunity to help explain the Negro's complexion. In contrast the approximately contemporaneous Talmudic and Midrashic sources contained such suggestions as that "Ham was smitten in his skin," that Noah told Ham "your seed will be ugly and dark-skinned," and that Ham was father "of Canaan who brought curses into the world, of Canaan who was cursed, of Canaan who darkened the faces of mankind," of Canaan "the notorious world-darkener."

While it probably is not possible to trace a direct line of influence, it seems very likely that these observations affected some Christian writers during the late Medieval and Renaissance years of reviving Christian interest in Jewish writings. It is suggestive that the first Christian utilizations of this theme came during the sixteenth century—the first great century of overseas exploration. As should become clear in this chapter, there was reason for restless Englishmen to lay hold of a hand-me-down curse which had been expounded originally by a people who had themselves restlessly sought a land of freedom.[44]

When the story of Ham's curse did become relatively common in the seventeenth century it was utilized almost entirely as an explanation of color rather than as justification for Negro slavery and as

44. The quotations are from I. Epstein *et al.*, trans., *The Babylonian Talmud*, 35 vols. (London, 1935–60), *Sanhedrin*, II, 745; H. Freedman and Maurice Simon, trans., *Midrash Rabbah*, 10 vols. (London, 1939), I, 293; Harry Sperling and Maurice Simon, trans., *The Zohar*, 5 vols. (London, 1931), I, 246–47.

such it was probably denied more often than affirmed.[45] Sir Thomas Browne, the first Englishman to discuss the Negro's color in great detail, ruled out Ham's curse as well as simple climatic causation after explaining that these two explanations were the only ones "generally received." Yet Peter Heylyn was letting Ham's curse into court just when Browne was tossing it out: in three successive editions of his grandiose *Microcosmus* he ignored the story in 1621, called a slightly altered version of it a "foolish tale" in 1627, and repeated his denial in 1666 but at the last moment conceded that "possibly enough the Curse of God on *Cham* and on his posterity (though for some cause unknown to us) hath an influence on it."[46]

The extraordinary persistence of this idea in the face of centuries of incessant refutation was probably sustained by a feeling that blackness could scarcely be anything *but* a curse and by the common need to confirm the facts of nature by specific reference to Scripture. In contrast to the climatic theory, God's curse provided a satisfying purposiveness which the sun's scorching heat could not match until the eighteenth century. The difficulty with the story of Ham's indiscretion was that extraordinarily strenuous exegesis was required in order to bring it to bear on the Negro's black skin. Faced with difficulties in both the climatic and Scriptural explanation, some seekers after truth threw up their hands in great humility and accounted blackness in the African another manifestation of God's omnipotent providence. This was Peter Heylyn's solution (at least in 1627).

45. For affirmations, Richard Jobson, *The Golden Trade: Or, a Discovery of the River Gambra, and the Golden Trade of the Aethiopians* (1623), ed. Charles G. Kingsley (Teignmouth, Devonshire, 1904), 65–66; Thomas Herbert, *Some Years Travels into Divers Parts of Africa, and Asia the Great, Describing More Particularly the Empires of Persia and Industan . . .* [4th ed.] (London, 1677), 16. The only monograph on the subject mistakenly attributes the idea to Lutherans particularly and offers 1677 as the date of the first explicit statement; Albert Perbal, "La Race Nègre et la Malédiction de Cham," *Revue de l'Université d'Ottawa*, 10 (1940), 157–59. It was denied in 1583, perhaps as early as 1566, by John Bodin, *Method for the Easy Comprehension of History*, trans. Beatrice Reynolds (N. Y., 1945), 87. Allen, *Legend of Noah*, 119, shows that the idea was not unknown in the 16th century and suggests that it may have existed prior to the Renaissance. An important 14th-century English legal treatise referred to the curse on Ham in connection with slavery but not the Negro; Andrew Horne, *The Mirror of Justices . . .* , ed. William C. Robinson (Washington, D. C., 1903), 123–24.
46. Browne, "Of the Blackness of Negroes," Sayle, ed., *Works of Browne*, II, 368–85; H[eylyn], *Microcosmus*, 403; Heylyn, ΜΙΚΡΌΚΘΣΜΘΣ (1627), 771; Peter Heylyn, *Cosmographie, in Four Books. Containing the Chorographie and Historie of the Whole World . . .* , 3d ed. (London, 1666), 1016.

The inhabitants (though a great part of this country [America] lieth in the same parallell with *Ethiopia, Lybia,* and *Numidia*) are of a reasonable faire complexion, and very little (if at all) inclining to blacknesse. So that the extraordinary and continuall vicinity of the Sunne, is not (as some imagine) the efficient cause of blacknesse: though it may much further such a colour: as wee see in our country lasses, whose faces are alwaies exposed to winde and weather. Others, more wise in their owne conceite, though this conceit know no confederate; plainely conclude the generative seed of the *Africans* to be blacke, but of the *Americans* to be white: a foolish supposition, and convinced not only out of experience, but naturall Philosophie. As for that foolish tale of *Cham's* knowing his wife in the Arke. whereupon by divine curse his son *Chus* with all his posterity, (which they say are *Africans*) were all blacke: it is so vaine, that I will not endeavour to retell it. So that we must wholy refer it to Gods peculiar will and ordinance.[47]

Fair enough perhaps, but this was scarcely an explanation to stand the test of centuries; the cause of the Negro's color was to remain a confusing mystery. Even Sir Thomas Browne's admirably ingenious and manful efforts at resolution, which were far in advance of his contemporaries', faltered badly once he had finished explaining what was *not* the cause of the Negro's blackness.

In the long run, of course, the Negro's color attained greatest significance not as a scientific problem but as a social fact. Englishmen found blackness in human beings a peculiar and important point of difference. The Negro's color set him radically *apart* from Englishmen. It also served as a highly visible label identifying the natives of a distant continent which for ages Christians had known as a land of men radically defective in religion.

3. DEFECTIVE RELIGION

While distinctive appearance set Africans over into a novel category of men, their religious condition set them apart from Englishmen in a more familiar way. Englishmen and Christians everywhere were sufficiently acquainted with the concept of heathenism that they confronted its living representatives without puzzlement. Certainly the rather sudden discovery that the world was teeming with heathen people made for heightened vividness and urgency in a long-standing problem; but it was the fact that this problem was already well formulated long before contact with Africa which proved important in shaping English reaction to the Negro's defective religious condition.

47. Heylyn, ΜΙΚΡΌΚΟΣΜΟΣ (1627), 771.

In one sense heathenism was less a "problem" for Christians than an exercise in self-definition: the heathen condition defined by negation the proper Christian life. In another sense, the presence of heathenism in the world constituted an imperative to intensification of religious commitment. From its origin Christianity was a universalist, proselytizing religion, and the sacred and secular histories of Christianity made manifest the necessity of bringing non-Christians into the fold. For Englishmen, then, the heathenism of Negroes was at once a counter-image of their own religion and a summons to eradicate an important distinction between the two peoples.

The interaction of these two facets of the concept of heathenism made for a peculiar difficulty. On the one hand, to act upon the felt necessity of converting Negroes would have been to eradicate the point of distinction which Englishmen found most familiar and most readily comprehensible. Yet if they did not act upon this necessity, continued heathenism among Negroes would remain an unwelcome reminder to Englishmen that they were not meeting their obligations to their own faith—nor to the benighted Negroes. Englishmen resolved this implicit dilemma by doing nothing.

Considering the strength of the Christian tradition, it is almost startling that Englishmen failed to respond to the discovery of heathenism in Africa with at least the rudiments of a campaign for conversion. Although the impulse to spread Christianity seems to have been weaker in Englishmen than, say, in the Catholic Portuguese, it cannot be said that Englishmen were indifferent to the obligation imposed upon them by the overseas discoveries of the sixteenth century. While they were badly out of practice at the business of conversion (again in contrast to the Portuguese) and while they had never before been faced with the practical difficulties involved in Christianizing entire continents, they nonetheless were able to contemplate with equanimity and even eagerness the prospect of converting the heathen. Indeed they went so far as to conclude that converting the natives in America was sufficiently important to demand English settlement there. As it turned out, the well-publicized English program for converting Indians produced very meager results, but the avowed intentions certainly were genuine. It was in marked contrast, therefore, that Englishmen did not avow similiar intentions concerning Africans until the late eighteenth century. Fully as much as with skin color, though less consciously, Englishmen distinguished between the heathenisms of Indians and of Negroes.

The suggestive congruence of these twin distinctions between

Negroes and Indians is not easy to account for. On the basis of the travelers' reports there was no reason for Englishmen to suppose Indians inherently superior to Negroes as candidates for conversion. While in the sixteenth and seventeenth centuries the Englishmen who had first-hand contact with Africans were not, unlike many of the Portuguese, engaged in missionary efforts, the same may be said of most English contact with Indians. On the other hand, America was not Africa. Englishmen contemplated settling in America, where voyagers had established the King's claim and where supposedly the climate was temperate; in contrast, Englishmen did not envision settlement in Africa, which had quickly gained notoriety as a graveyard for Europeans and where the Portuguese had been first on the scene. Certainly these very different circumstances meant that Englishmen confronted Negroes and Indians in radically different social contexts and that Englishmen would find it far easier to contemplate converting Indians than Negroes. Yet it remains difficult to see why Negroes were not included, at least as a secondary target, by extension from the program actually directed at the Indians. The fact that English contact with Africans so frequently occurred in a context of slave dealing does not entirely explain the omission of Negroes, since in that same context the Portuguese and Spanish did sometimes attempt to minister to the souls of Negroes (somewhat perfunctorily, to be sure) and since Englishmen in America enslaved Indians when good occasion arose. Given these circumstances, it is hard to escape the conclusion that the distinction which Englishmen made as to conversion was at least in some small measure modeled after the difference they saw in skin color.

Although Englishmen failed to incorporate Negroes into the proselytizing effort which was enjoined by the Christian heritage, that heritage did much to shape the English reaction to Negroes as a people. Paradoxically, Christianity worked to make Englishmen think of Negroes as being both very much like themselves and very different. The emphasis on similarity derived directly from the emphatic Christian doctrine which affirmed that mankind was one. The Old Testament, most notably the book of Genesis, seemed absolutely firm on this point: all men derived from the same act of creation and had at first shared a common experience. So too the New Testament declared all nations to be of one blood. The strength of this universalist strain in Christianity was evident in the assurances offered by a number of English travelers in Africa that they had discovered rudiments of the Word among the most barbarous heathens. In 1623 Richard Jobson exclaimed that "they have a wonderous reference, to the leviticall law, as it is in our holy Bible related; the principalls whereof they are not ignorant in, for they do report concerning *Adam* and *Eve,* whom they call *Adama* and *Evahaha,* talking of *Noahs* flood, and of *Moses,* with many other things our sacred History makes mention of." Another commentator hinted at covert Calvinism in the jungle: "They keep their *Fetissoes* [Fetish] day, one day in seven, and that Tuesday (a Sabbath it seems is natural) more solemnly and stricktly than the *Hollanders* do their Sunday." [48] To call the Sabbath "natural" among heathens was an invitation to the missionary to harvest the seed planted everywhere by God. Such a description also serves to demonstrate how powerfully the Christian tradition operated to make Englishmen and other Europeans consider the new peoples of the freshly opened world as being inherently similar to themselves.

At the same time, Christianity militated against the unity of man. Because Englishmen were Christians, heathenism in Negroes was a fundamental defect which set them distinctly apart. However much Englishmen disapproved of Popery and Mahometanism, they were accustomed to these perversions. Yet they were not accustomed to dealing face to face with people who appeared, so far as many travelers could tell, to have no religion at all.[49] Steeped in the legacy and trappings of their own religion, Englishmen were ill prepared to see any legitimacy in African religious practices. Judged by Christian cosmology, Negroes stood in a separate category of men.

Perhaps the ambivalence inherent in Christian assessment of heathenism played a part in muting the importance of the Negro's heathenism in the eyes of Englishmen. Probably the increasingly Protestant character of English religious belief also had the same effect, for the Portuguese and Spanish seem to have found the heathenism of Negroes and Indians a more salient and distinct quality than the English did; in the seventeenth and eighteenth centuries this differing reaction among Protestants and Catholics was to become still more obvious upon the slave plantations of the Americas. At any rate, it is clear that during the early period of contact with Africa heathenism was far from being *the* critical attribute which caused Englishmen to view Negroes as a separate kind of people.

Indeed the most important aspect of English reaction to Negro

48. Jobson, *Golden Trade,* ed. Kingsley, 78 (probably there was good basis for Jobson's contention since the Negroes he referred to were Muslims) ; *The Golden Coast,* 80.

49. For example, Hakluyt, *Principal Navigations,* VI, 144.

heathenism was that Englishmen evidently did not regard it as separable from the Negro's other attributes. Heathenism was treated not so much as a specifically religious defect but as one manifestation of a general refusal to measure up to proper standards, as a failure to be English or even civilized. There was every reason for Englishmen to fuse the various attributes they found in Africans. During the first century of English contact with Africa, Protestant Christianity was an important element in English patriotism; especially during the struggle against Spain the Elizabethan's special Christianity was interwoven into his conception of his own nationality, and he was therefore inclined to regard the Negroes' lack of true religion as part of theirs. Being a Christian was not merely a matter of subscribing to certain doctrines; it was a quality inherent in oneself and in one's society. It was interconnected with all the other attributes of normal and proper men: as one of the earliest English accounts distinguished Negroes from Englishmen, they were "a people of beastly living, without a God, lawe, religion, or common wealth" [50]—which was to say that Negroes were not Englishmen. Far from isolating African heathenism as a separate characteristic, English travelers sometimes linked it explicitly with barbarity and blackness. They already had in hand a mediating term among these impinging concepts—the *devil*. As one observer declared, Negroes "in colour so in condition are little other than Devils incarnate," and, further, "the Devil . . . has infused prodigious Idolatry into their hearts, enough to rellish his pallat and aggrandize their tortures when he gets power to fry their souls, as the raging Sun has already scorcht their cole-black carcasses." [51] "Idolatry" was indeed a serious failing, but English travelers in West Africa tended to regard defect of true religion as an aspect of the Negro's "condition." In an important sense, then, heathenism was for Englishmen one inherent characteristic of savage men.

4. SAVAGE BEHAVIOR

The condition of savagery—the failure to be civilized—set Negroes apart from Englishmen in an ill-defined but crucial fashion. Africans were *different* from Englishmen in so many ways: in their clothing, huts, farming, warfare, language, government, morals, and (not least important) in their table manners. Englishmen were fully aware that Negroes living at different parts of the coast were not all alike; it was not merely different reactions

50. "Second Voyage to Guinea," *ibid.*, 167.
51. Herbert, *Some Years Travels*, 10, 7.

in the observers which led one to describe a town as "marveilous artificially builded with mudde walles . . . and kept very cleane as well in their streetes as in their houses" and another to relate how "they doe eate" each other "alive" in some places but dead in others "as we wolde befe or mutton." [52] No matter how great the actual and observed differences among Negroes, though, none of these black men seemed to live like Englishmen.

To judge from the comments of voyagers, Englishmen had an unquenchable thirst for the details of savage life. Partly their curiosity was a matter of scientific interest in the "natural productions" of the newly opened world overseas. To the public at large, the details of savage behavior appealed to an interest which was not radically different from the scientist's; an appetite for the "wonderful" seems to have been built into Western culture. It is scarcely surprising that civilized Englishmen should have taken an interest in reports about cosmetic mutilation, polygamy, infanticide, ritual murder and the like—of course *English* men did not really *do* any of these things themselves. Finally, reports about savages began arriving at a time when Englishmen very much needed to be able to translate their apprehensive interest in an uncontrollable world out of medieval, religious terms. The discovery of savages overseas enabled them to make this translation easily, to move from miracles to verifiable monstrosities, from heaven to earth.

As with skin color, English reporting of African customs constituted an exercise in self-inspection by means of comparison. The necessity of continuously measuring African practices with an English yardstick of course tended to emphasize the differences between the two groups, but it also made for heightened sensitivity to instances of similarity. Thus the Englishman's ethnocentrism tended to distort his perception of African culture in two opposite directions. While it led him to emphasize differences and to condemn deviations from the English norm, it led him also to seek out similarities (where perhaps none existed) and to applaud every instance of conformity to the appropriate standard. Though African clothing and personal etiquette were regarded as absurd, equivalents to European practices were at times detected in other aspects

52. Both seem to be eyewitness reports. "Voyage of Thomas Candish," Hakluyt, *Principal Navigations*, XI, 293; anonymous author on Hawkins' third voyage quoted in James A. Williamson, *Sir John Hawkins: The Time and the Man* (Oxford, 1927) , 509. There is an interesting description of (almost certainly) the now well-known symbiotic relationship between Negroes and Pygmies in *The Golden Coast*, 66–67, "I have not found so much faith, nor faithfulness, no not in Israel."

of African culture. Particularly, Englishmen were inclined to see the structures of African societies as analogous to their own, complete with kings, counselors, gentlemen, and the baser sort. Here especially they found Africans like themselves, partly because they knew no other way to describe a society and partly because there was actually good basis for such a view in the social organization of West African communities.[53]

Most English commentators seem to have felt that Negroes would behave better under improved circumstances; a minority thought the Africans naturally wicked, but even these observers often used "natural" only to mean "ingrained." (English accounts of West Africa did not emphasize ingrained stupidity in the natives; defect of "Reason" was seen as a function of savagery.) [54] Until well into the eighteenth century there was no debate as to whether the Negro's non-physical characteristics were inborn and unalterable; such a question was never posed with anything like sufficient clarity for men to debate it. There was no precise meaning in such statements about the Africans as, "Another (as it were) innate quality they have [is] to Steal any thing they lay hands of, especially from Foreigners . . . this vicious humor [runs] through the whole race of Blacks," or in another comment, that "it would be very surprizing if upon a scrutiny into their Lives we should find any of them whose perverse Nature would not break out sometimes; for they indeed seem to be born and bred Villains: All sorts of Baseness having got such sure-footing in them, that 'tis impossible to lye concealed." [55] These two vague suggestions concerning innate qualities in the Negro were among the most precise in all the English accounts of West Africa. It was sufficient to depict and describe. There might be disagreement as to the exact measure of tenacity with which the African clung to his present savage character, but this problem would yield to time and accurate description.

Despite the fascination and self-instruction Englishmen derived from expatiating upon the savage behavior of Africans, they never

53. An early instance is in Clements R. Markham, ed., *The Hawkins' Voyages during the Reigns of Henry VIII, Queen Elizabeth, and James I (Works Issued by the Hakluyt Soc., 1st Ser., 57 [1878])*, 19.

54. For example, H[eylyn], *Microcosmus*, 379. But compare a later and precursively environmentalist argument that culturally dictated lack of mental and moral exercise had literally weakened the African brain: John Atkins, *The Navy Surgeon . . . and Physical Observations on the Coast of Guiney*, 2d ed. (London, 1742), 366–67; also his *Voyage to Guinea*, 80–88.

55. Ogilby, *Africa*, 452; William Bosman, *A New and Accurate Description of the Coast of Guinea, Divided into the Gold, the Slave, and the Ivory Coasts . . .* , trans. from the Dutch (London, 1705), 117.

felt that savagery was as important a quality in Africans as it was in the American Indians. Two sets of circumstances made for this distinction in the minds of Englishmen. As was the case with heathenism, contrasting social contexts played an important role in shaping the English response to savagery in the two peoples. Inevitably, the savagery of the Indians assumed a special significance in the minds of those actively engaged in a program of bringing civilization into the American wilderness. The case with the African was different: the English errand into Africa was not a new or a perfect community but a business trip. No hope was entertained for civilizing the Negro's steaming continent, and Englishmen lacked compelling reason to develop a program for remodeling the African natives. The most compelling necessity was that of pressing forward the business of buying Negroes from other Negroes. It was not until the slave trade came to require justification, in the eighteenth century, that some Englishmen found special reason to lay emphasis on the Negro's savagery.

From the beginning, also, the importance of the Negro's savagery was muted by the Negro's color. Englishmen could go a long way toward expressing their sense of being different from Negroes merely by calling them black. By contrast, the aboriginals in America did not have the appearance of being radically distinct from Europeans except in religion and savage behavior. English voyagers placed much less emphasis upon the Indian's color than upon the Negro's, and they never permitted the Indian's physiognomy to distract their attention from what they regarded as his essential quality, his savagery. Even in the eighteenth century, when the savages of the world were being promoted to "nobility" by Europeans as an aid to self-scrutiny and reform at home, the Negro was not customarily thought of as embodying all the qualities of the noble savage. Certainly he never attained the status of the Indian's primitive nobility. It was not merely that Negroes had by then become pre-eminently the slaves of Europeans in the Americas. The Negro's appearance remained a barrier to acceptance as the noble type. In one of the earliest attempts to dramatize the nobility of the primitive man (1688), Aphra Behn described her hero Oroonoko in terms which made clear the conditions under which the Negro could be admitted as a candidate for admiration:

The most famous Statuary could not form the Figure of a Man more admirably turn'd from Head to Foot. His Face was not of that brown rusty Black which most of that Nation are, but a perfect Ebony, or polished Jet. His Eyes were the most aweful that could be seen, and very piercing; the

White of 'em being like Snow, as were his Teeth. His nose was rising and *Roman*, instead of *African* and flat: His Mouth the finest shaped that could be seen; far from those great turn'd Lips, which are so natural to the rest of the Negroes. The whole Proportion and Air of his Face was so nobly and exactly form'd, that bating his Colour, there could be nothing in Nature more beautiful, agreeable and handsome.[56]

As this description makes clear, the Negro might attain savage nobility only by approximating (as best he could) the appearance of a white man.

It would be a mistake, however, to slight the importance of the Negro's savagery, since it fascinated Englishmen from the very first. English observers in West Africa were sometimes so profoundly impressed by the Negro's deviant behavior that they resorted to a powerful metaphor with which to express their own sense of difference from him. They knew perfectly well that Negroes were men, yet they frequently described the Africans as "brutish" or "bestial" or "beastly." The hideous tortures, the cannibalism, the rapacious warfare, the revolting diet (and so forth page after page) seemed somehow to place the Negro among the beasts. The circumstances of the Englishman's confrontation with the Negro served to strengthen this feeling. Slave traders in Africa handled Negroes the same way men in England handled beasts, herding and examining and buying. The Guinea Company instructed Bartholomew Haward in 1651 "to buy and put aboard you so many negers as yo'r ship can cary, and for what shalbe wanting to supply with Cattel, as also to furnish you with victualls and provisions for the said negers and Cattel." [57] Africa, moreover, teemed with strange and wonderful animals, and men that killed like tigers, ate like vultures, and grunted like hogs seemed indeed to merit comparison with beasts. In making this instinctive analogy, Englishmen unwittingly demonstrated how powerfully the African's different culture—for Englishmen, his "savagery"—operated to make Negroes seem to Englishmen a radically different kind of men.

5. THE APES OF AFRICA

If Negroes were likened to beasts, there was in Africa a beast which was likened to men. It was a strange and eventually

56. Behn, *Oroonoko*, 136. For later developments especially, see Philip D. Curtin, *The Image of Africa: British Ideas and Action, 1780–1850* (Madison, Wis., 1964).
57. Elizabeth Donnan, ed., *Documents Illustrative of the History of the Slave Trade to America*, 4 vols. (Washington, D. C., 1930–35), I, 129.

tragic happenstance of nature that the Negro's homeland was the habitat of the animal which in appearance most resembles man. The animal called "orang-outang" by contemporaries (actually the chimpanzee) was native to those parts of western Africa where the early slave trade was heavily concentrated. Though Englishmen were acquainted (for the most part vicariously) with monkeys and baboons, they were unfamiliar with tailless apes who walked about like men.[58] Accordingly, it happened that Englishmen were introduced to the anthropoid apes and to Negroes at the same time and in the same place. The startlingly human appearance and movements of the "ape"—a generic term though often used as a synonym for the "orang outang"—aroused some curious speculations.

In large measure these speculations derived from traditions which had been accumulating in Western culture since ancient times. Medieval bestiaries contained rosters of strange creatures who in one way or another seemed disturbingly to resemble men. There were the *simia* and the *cynocephali* and the *satyri* and the others, all variously described and related to one another, all jumbled in a characteristic amalgam of ancient reports and medieval morality. The confusion was not easily nor rapidly dispelled, and many of the traditions established by this literature were very much alive during the seventeenth century.

The section on apes in Edward Topsell's *Historie of Foure-Footed Beastes* (1607) serves to illustrate how certain seemingly trivial traditions and associations persisted in such form that they were bound to affect the way in which Englishmen would perceive the natives of Africa.[59] Topsell, who built principally upon the work of the great Swiss naturalist Konrad von Gesner (1516–65), was

58. H. W. Janson, *Apes and Ape Lore in the Middle Ages and the Renaissance* (London, 1952), chap. 11; also Robert M. and Ada W. Yerkes, *The Great Apes: A Study of Anthropoid Life* (New Haven, 1929), 1–26; John C. Greene, *The Death of Adam: Evolution and Its Impact on Western Thought* (Ames, Iowa, 1959), chap. 6. I have oversimplified the confused state of terminology concerning simians; see M. F. Ashley Montagu, *Edward Tyson, M. D., F. R. S., 1650–1708, and the Rise of Human and Comparative Anatomy in England; A Study in the History of Science* (Phila., 1943), 228, 244–49. By 1600 "baboons," "marmosets," "monkies," "apes" were common in literature; several (probably baboons) were on show in London. Yet a foreign visitor in 1598 did not list any sort of "apes" in the Tower menagerie, though there were lions there. W. Strunk, Jr., "The Elizabethan Showman's Ape," *Modern Language Notes*, 32 (1917), 215–21; Emma Phipson, *The Animal-Lore of Shakespeare's Time . . .* (London, 1883), 5.

59. Edward Topsell, *The Historie of Foure-Footed Beastes . . . Collected out of All the Volumes of Conradus Gesner, and All Other Writers to This Present Day* (London, 1607), 2–20.

careful to distinguish tailless apes from monkeys. They were to be found in three regions: south of the Caucasus, India, and *"Lybia and all that desart Woods betwixt Egypt, Æthiopia and Libia."* When he came to describe the various kinds of "apes," however, Topsell was far less definite as to location than as to their general character: above all else, "apes" were venerous. In India the red apes were "so venerous that they will ravish their Women." Baboons were "as lustful and venerous as goats"; a baboon which had been "brought to the French king . . . above all loved the companie of women, and young maidens; his genitall member was greater than might match the quantity of his other parts." Pictures of two varieties of apes, a "Satyre" and an "Ægopithecus," graphically emphasized the "virile member."

In addition to stressing the "lustful disposition" of the ape kind, Topsell's compilation contained suggestions concerning the character of simian facial features. "Men that have low and flat nostrils," readers were told in the section on apes, "are Libidinous as Apes that attempt women, and having thicke lippes the upper hanging over the neather, they are deemed fooles, like the lips of Asses and Apes." This rather explicit association was the persistent connection made between apes and devils. In a not altogether successful attempt to distinguish the "Satyre-apes" from the mythical creatures of that name, Topsell straightened everything out by explaining that it was "probable, that Devils take not any dænomination or shape from Satyres, but rather the Apes themselves from Devils whome they resemble, for there are many things common to the Satyre-apes and devilish Satyres." Association of apes and/or satyrs with devils was common in England: James I linked them in his *Daemonology* (1597).[60] The inner logic of this association derived from uneasiness concerning the ape's "indecent likenesse and imitation of man"; it revolved around evil and sexual sin; and, rather tenuously, it connected apes with blackness.

Given this tradition and the coincidence of contact, it was virtually inevitable that Englishmen should discern similarity between the man-like beasts and the beast-like men of Africa.[61] A few commentators went so far as to suggest that Negroes had sprung from the generation of ape-kind or that apes were themselves the

60. G. B. Harrison, ed., *King James the First Daemonologie (1597)* . . . (London, 1924), 19.

61. Jobson, *Golden Trade*, ed. Kingsley, 186; Thomas Herbert, *A Relation of Some Yeares Travaile, Begunne Anno 1626. Into Afrique and the Greater Asia, Especially the Territories of the Persian Monarchie . . .* (London, 1634), 16–17; Herbert, *Some Years Travels* (1677), 16–17.

offspring of Negroes and some unknown African beast.[62] These contentions were squarely in line with the ancient tradition that Africa was a land "bringing dailie foorth newe monsters" because, as Aristotle himself had suggested, many different species came into proximity at the scarce watering places. Jean Bodin, the famous sixteenth-century French political theorist, summarized this wisdom of the ages with the categorical remark that "promiscuous coition of men and animals took place, wherefore the regions of Africa produce for us so many monsters." [63] Despite all these monsters out of Africa, the notion that Negroes stemmed from beasts in a literal sense did not receive wide credence; even the writers who advanced it did not suggest that the Negro himself was now a beast.

Far more common and persistent was the notion that there sometimes occurred "a beastly copulation or conjuncture" between apes and Negroes, and especially that apes were inclined wantonly to attack Negro women.[64] The very explicit idea that apes assaulted female human beings was not new; Negroes were merely being asked to demonstrate what Europeans had known for centuries. Englishmen seemed ready to credit the tales about bestial connections, and even as late as the 1730's a well-traveled, intelligent naval surgeon, John Atkins, was not at all certain that the stories were false: "At some Places the *Negroes* have been suspected of Bestiality with them [apes and monkeys], and by the Boldness and Affection they are known under some Circumstances to express to our Females; the Ignorance and Stupidity on the other side, to guide or control Lust; but more from the near resemblances are sometimes met to the Human Species would tempt one to suspect the Fact." Atkins went on to voice the generally received opinion that if offspring were ever produced by such mixtures they would themselves be infertile: "Altho' by the way, this, like other *Hebridous* Productions, could never go no farther; and as such a monstrous

---

62. Herbert, *Some Years Travels*, 18; Zirkle, "Knowledge of Heredity," Dunn, ed., *Genetics in the 20th Century*, 39–40.

63. Quotation from Alexander B. Grosart, ed., *The Complete Works of Thomas Nashe*, 6 vols. (London and Aylesbury, 1883–85), I, 160; Aristotle, *Historia Animalium*, trans. D'Arcy W. Thompson, in J. A. Smith and W. D. Ross, eds., *The Works of Aristotle*, IV (Oxford, 1910), 606b; Bodin, *Method for Easy Comprehension of History*, 105.

64. Quotation from Herbert, *Some Years Travels*, 18. Montagu, *Edward Tyson*, 250–52; John Locke, *An Essay Concerning Human Understanding*, 2 vols. in 1 (London, 1721), II, 53 (Bk. III, chap. 6, sec. 23); Phillips, *Journal*, Churchill, comps., *Voyages*, VI, 211; William Smith, *A New Voyage to Guinea . . .* (London, 1744), 52; Zirkle, "Knowledge of Heredity," Dunn, ed., *Genetics in the 20th Century*, 39–40; Janson, *Apes and Ape Lore*, 267–76.

Generation would be more casual and subject to Fatality, the Case must be uncommon and rare." [65]

By the time Atkins addressed himself to this evidently fascinating problem, some of the confusion arising from the resemblance of apes to men had been dispelled. In 1699 the web of legend and unverified fact was disentangled by Edward Tyson, whose comparative study of a young "orang-outang" was a masterwork of critical scientific investigation. Throughout his dissection of the chimpanzee, Tyson meticulously compared the animal with human beings in every anatomical detail, and he established beyond question both the close relationship and the non-identity of ape and man. [66] Here was a step forward; the question of the ape's proper place in nature was now grounded upon much firmer knowledge of the facts. Despite their scientific importance, Tyson's conclusions did nothing to weaken the vigorous tradition which linked the Negro with the ape. The supposed affinity between apes and men had as frequently been expressed in sexual as in anatomical terms, and his findings did not effectively rule out the possibility of unnatural sexual unions. Tyson himself remarked that orangs were especially given to venery. [67]

The sexual association of apes with Negroes had an inner logic which kept it alive without much or even any factual sustenance. [68] Sexual union seemed to prove a certain affinity without going so far as to indicate actual identity—which was what Englishmen really thought was the case. By forging a sexual link between Negroes and apes, furthermore, Englishmen were able to give vent to their feeling that Negroes were a lewd, lascivious, and wanton people.

6. LIBIDINOUS MEN

It was no accident that this affinity between Negroes and apes was so frequently regarded as sexual, for undertones of sexu-

65. Atkins, *Voyage to Guinea*, 108; also his *Navy Surgeon*, 369.
66. Edward Tyson, *Orang-Outang, Sive Homo Sylvestris: Or, the Anatomy of a Pygmie Compared with That of a Monkey, an Ape, and a Man. To Which is Added, A Philological Essay Concerning the Pygmies, the Cynocephali, the Satyrs, and Sphinges of the Ancients. Wherein It will Appear That They Are All Either Apes or Monkeys; and Not Men, As Formerly Pretended* (London, 1699) ; Montagu, *Edward Tyson*, 225–321.
67. Tyson, *Orang-Outang*, 42.
68. Perhaps there was some slight basis in fact for the association, for certain kinds of sexual contact (though surely not consummation) between apes and human beings are known to be possible and even likely under some circumstances. Earnest Hooton, *Man's Poor Relations* (Garden City, N. Y., 1942) , 19, 84–85.

ality run throughout many English accounts of West Africa. To liken Africans—any human beings—to beasts was to stress the animal within the man. Indeed the sexual connotations embodied in the terms *bestial* and *beastly* were considerably stronger in Elizabethan English than they are today, and when the Elizabethan traveler pinned these epithets upon the behavior of Negroes he was frequently as much registering a sense of sexual shock as describing swinish manners: "They are beastly in their living," young Andrew Battell wrote, "for they have men in women's apparel, whom they keep among their wives." [69]

Lecherousness among the Negroes was at times merely another attribute which one would expect to find among heathen, savage, beast-like men. A passage in Samuel Purchas's collection makes evident how closely interrelated all these attributes were in the minds of Englishmen: "They have no knowledge of God; those that traffique and are conversant among strange Countrey people are civiller then the common sort of people, they are very greedie eaters, and no lesse drinkers, and very lecherous, and theevish, and much addicted to uncleanenesse: one man hath as many wives as hee is able to keepe and maintaine." [70] Sexuality was what one expected of savages.

Clearly, however, the association of Africans with potent sexuality represented more than an incidental appendage to the concept of savagery. Long before first English contact with West Africa, the inhabitants of virtually the entire continent stood confirmed in European literature as lustful and venerous. About 1526 Leo Africanus (a Spanish Moroccan Moor converted to Christianity) supplied the most authoritative and influential description of the little-known lands of "Barbary," "Libya," "Numedia," and "Land of Negroes"; and Leo was as explicit as he was imaginative. In the English translation (*ca.* 1600) readers were informed concerning the "Negros" that "there is no Nation under Heaven more prone to Venery." Having reduced the "Numedians" to being "principally addicted unto Treason, Treacherie, Murther, Theft and Robberie"

69. Ernest George Ravenstein, ed., *The Strange Adventures of Andrew Battell of Leigh, in Angola and the Adjoining Regions. Reprinted from "Purchas His Pilgrimes"* (*ca.* 1607) (*Works Issued by the Hakluyt Soc.*, 2d Ser., 6 [London, 1901]), 18. The term *bestiality* was first used to denote sexual relations with animals early in the 17th century; it was thus used frequently only for about 150 years!

70. "A Description . . . of Guinea . . ." in Samuel Purchas, *Hakluytus Posthumus or Purchas His Pilgrimes, Contayning a History of the World in Sea Voyages and Lande Travells by Englishmen and Others*, 20 vols. (Glasgow, 1905-07), VI, 251.

and the inhabitants of Libya to living a "brutish kind of life" destitute of "any Religion, any Lawes, or any good form of living," Leo went on to disclose that "the Negroes likewise leade a beastly kind of life, being utterly destitute of the use of reason, of dexteritie of wit, and of all arts. Yea, they so behave themselves, as if they had continually lived in a Forrest among wild beasts. They have great swarmes of Harlots among them; whereupon a man may easily conjecture their manner of living." [71] Nor was Leo Africanus the only scholar to elaborate upon the classical sources concerning Africa. In a highly eclectic work first published in 1566, Jean Bodin sifted the writings of ancient authorities and concluded that heat and lust went hand in hand and that "in Ethiopia . . . the race of men is very keen and lustful." Bodin announced in a thoroughly characteristic sentence, "Ptolemy reported that on account of southern sensuality Venus chiefly is worshiped in Africa and that the constellation of Scorpion, which pertains to the pudenda, dominates that continent." [72]

Depiction of the Negro as a lustful creature was not radically new, therefore, when Englishmen first met Negroes face to face. Seizing upon and reconfirming these long-standing and apparently common notions about Africa, Elizabethan travelers and literati spoke very explicitly of Negroes as being especially sexual. Othello's embraces were "the gross clasps of a lascivious Moor." Francis Bacon's New Atlantis (ca. 1624) referred to "an holy hermit" who "desired to see the Spirit of Fornication; and there appeared to him a little foul ugly Æthiop." Negro men, reported a seventeenth-century traveler, sported "large Propagators." [73] In 1623 Richard Jobson, a sympathetic observer, reported that Mandingo men were "furnisht with such members as are after a sort burthensome unto them"; it was the custom in that tribe not to have intercourse during pregnancy so as not to "destroy what is conceived." During this abstinence, Jobson explained, the man "hath allowance of other women, for necessities sake," though this was not to be considered "overstrange" since in the twenty-third chapter of Ezekiel two incontinent sisters were "said to doate upon those people

71. Leo Africanus, History and Description of Africa, trans. Pory, ed. Brown, I, 180, 187. Leo continues concerning the Negroes, "except their conversation perhaps bee somewhat more tolerable, who dwell in the principall Townes and Cities: for it is like that they are somewhat more addicted to Civilitie." Leo's work was available to Englishmen in Latin from 1556.
72. Bodin, Method for Easy Comprehension of History, 103–6, 143.
73. Rice, Turk, Moor, and Persian, 401; Othello, I, i, 127; Spedding, Ellis, and Heath, eds., Works of Francis Bacon, III, 152; Ogilby, Africa, 451.

whose members were as the members of Asses." Jobson's explanation for the unusual size of these men was incorporated neatly into the context of Scriptural anthropology. "Undoubtedly," he wrote, "these people originally sprung from the race of *Canaan*, the sonne of *Ham*, who discovered his father *Noahs* secrets, for which *Noah* awakening cursed *Canaan* as our holy Scripture testifieth[;] the curse as by Scholemen hath been disputed, extended to his ensuing race, in laying hold upon the same place, where the originall cause began, whereof these people are witnesse." [74]

The neatness of Jobson's exegesis was unusual, but his initial observation was not. Another commentator, the anonymous author of *The Golden Coast* (1665), thought Negroes "very lustful and impudent, especially, when they come to hide their nakedness, (for a *Negroes* hiding his Members, their extraordinary greatness) is a token of their Lust, and therefore much troubled with the Pox." [75] By the eighteenth century a report on the sexual aggressiveness of Negro women was virtually *de rigueur* for the African commentator. By then, of course, with many Englishmen actively participating in the slave trade, there were pressures making for descriptions of "hot constitution'd Ladies" possessed of a "temper hot and lascivious, making no scruple to prostitute themselves to the *Europeans* for a very slender profit, so great is their inclination to white men." [76] And surely it was the Negro women who were responsible for lapses from propriety: "If they can come to the Place the Man sleeps in, they lay themselves softly down by him, soon wake him, and use all their little Arts to move the darling Passion." [77]

While the animus underlying these and similar remarks becomes sufficiently obvious once Englishmen began active participation in the slave trade, it is less easy to see why Englishmen should have fastened upon Negroes a pronounced sexuality virtually upon first sight. Certainly the ancient notions distilled in the alembics of Bodin and Leo Africanus must have helped pattern initial English perceptions. Yet it is scarcely possible that these notions were fully responsible for the picture of Negro sexuality which developed so rapidly and in such explicit terms in the sixteenth and early seventeenth centuries.

Another tradition was of possible relevance—the curse upon

74. Jobson, *Golden Trade*, ed. Kingsley, 65–67.
75. *The Golden Coast*, 75–76.
76. Smith, *New Voyage to Guinea*, 146; Barbot, *Description of the Coasts*, Churchill, comps., *Voyages*, V, 34.
77. Smith, *New Voyage to Guinea*, 221–22, clearly based on Bosman, *New and Accurate Description*, 206–7.

Ham's son Canaan. According to the Scriptural account Ham's offense was that he had "looked upon the nakedness of his father." To the post-Freudian ear this suggests castration. To early Jewish commentators it suggested not merely castration but other sexual offenses as well. The Hebraic literature of *ca.* 200–600 A.D. which saw the posterity of Ham and Canaan as smitten in the skin speculated as to whether Ham's offense was (variously) castrating his father Noah (described in the Midrash Rabbah as Noah's saying "You have prevented me from doing something in the dark"), and (in the same source) as copulating "in the Ark," and (again) copulating "with a dog . . . therefore Ham came forth black-skinned while the dog publicly exposes its copulation." The depth and diffuse pervasiveness of these explosive associations are dramatized in the mystic Zohar of the thirteenth century, where Ham, it was said, "represents the refuse and dross of the gold, the stirring and rousing of the unclean spirit of the ancient serpent."

What is especially striking in these commentaries is that for centuries they remained peculiar though not secret to Jewish scholars. Although some Christian writers in the early centuries of the church seem to have been aware of sexual connotations in Ham's offense, they appear never to have dilated upon them. With the onset of European expansion in the sixteenth century, some Christian commentators, or rather some commentators who were Christians, suddenly began speaking in the same mode which Jews had employed a thousand years and more before. Though the genealogy of Noah's descendants was always somewhat tangled, Ham always represented for the ancient Jews the southward peoples *including* the Canaanites, whom the Jews drove from the promised land and upon whom they fastened the millstone of sexual offenses which are repeatedly and so adamantly condemned and guarded against in the Pentateuch. More than two thousand years later a similar disquietude seems to have come over Europeans and Englishmen as they embarked upon a program of outward migration and displacement and exploitation of other peoples. The curse upon Ham's posterity took on for Christian Englishmen a potential immediacy and relevance which it could never have had if Englishmen had not as a people been undergoing an experience which they half sensed was in some measure analogous to that of the ancient special people of God's word.[78]

78. I hope to discuss this complex matter more fully on another occasion and in the meantime cite only the sources directly quoted. Freedman and Simon, trans., *Midrash Rabbah*, I, 293; Sperling and Simon, trans., *Zohar*, I, 246.

The measure of influence exerted upon English commentators by these Hebraic traditions is problematical, but it is certain that the presumption of heightened sexuality in black men was far from being an incidental or casual association in the minds of Englishmen. How very deeply this association operated is obvious in *Othello*, a drama which loses most of its power and several of its central points if it is read with the assumption that because the black man was the hero English audiences were friendly or perhaps indifferent to his blackness.[79] Shakespeare was writing both about and to his countrymen's feelings concerning physical distinctions between kinds of people; the play is shot through with the language of blackness and sex. Iago goes out of his way to soliloquize upon his own motives: "I hate the Moor,/ And it is thought abroad that 'twixt my sheets/ He has done my office." Later, he becomes more direct, "For that I do suspect the lusty Moor hath leaped into my seat." It was upon this so obviously absurd suspicion that Iago based his resolve to "turn her virtue into pitch." Such was his success, of course, that Othello finally rushes off "to furnish me with some means of death for the fair devil." With this contorted denomination of Desdemona, Othello unwittingly revealed how deeply Iago's promptings about Desdemona's "own clime, complexion, and degree" had eaten into his consciousness. Othello was driven into accepting the premise that the physical distinction *matters:* "For she had eyes," he has to reassure himself, "and chose me." Then, as his suspicions give way to certainty, he equates her character with his own complexion:

> Her name, that was as fresh,
> As Dian's visage, is now begrim'd and black
> As mine own face.

This important aspect of Iago's triumph over the noble Moor was a subtly inverted reflection of the propositions which Iago, hidden in darkness, worked upon the fair lady's father. No one knew better than Iago how to play upon hidden strings of emotion. Not content with the straight-forward crudity that "your daughter and the Moor

79. See Philip Mason, *Prospero's Magic: Some Thoughts on Class and Race* (London, 1962), chap. 3. The following quotations from *Othello* may be found in I, i, 88–89, 111–12, 117–18, 143; I, ii, 66, 69–71; I, iii, 101, 392–94; II, i, 307–8; II, iii, 369; III, iii, 189, 230, 387–89, 478–79; V, ii, 128–29, 155, 161–62. Shakespeare's play was based on an Italian drama in which Iago told "the Moor" that Desdemona had committed adultery, partly because she was tired of the Moor's color: Kenneth Muir, *Shakespeare's Sources: Comedies and Tragedies* (London, 1957), 124.

are now making the beast with two backs," Iago told the agitated Brabantio that "an old black ram/ Is tupping your white ewe" and alluded politely to "your daughter cover'd with a Barbary horse." This was not merely the language of (as we say) a "dirty" mind: it was the integrated imagery of blackness and whiteness, of Africa, of the sexuality of beasts and the bestiality of sex. And of course Iago was entirely successful in persuading Brabantio, who had initially welcomed Othello into his house, that the marriage was "against all rules of nature." Brabantio's first reaction betrayed a lurking fear: "This accident is not unlike my dream." Then, as he pondered the prospect, he could only conclude that witchcraft—the unnatural—was responsible; he demanded of Othello what other cause could have brought a girl "so tender, fair, and happy"

> To incur a general mock
> Run from her guardage to the sooty bosom
> Of such a thing as thou.

Altogether a curious way for a senator to address a successful general.

These and similar remarks in the play *Othello* suggest that Shakespeare and presumably his audiences were not totally indifferent to the sexual union of "black" men and "white" women. Shakespeare did not condemn such union; rather, he played upon an inner theme of black and white sexuality, showing how the poisonous mind of a white man perverted and destroyed the noblest of loves by means of bringing to the surface (from the darkness, whence Iago spoke) the lurking shadows of animal sex to assault the whiteness of chastity. Never did "dirty" words more dramatically "blacken" a "fair" name. At the play's climax, standing stunned by the realization that the wife he has murdered was innocent, Othello groans to Emilia, " 'Twas I that killed her"; and Emilia responds with a torrent of condemnation or, rather, of expulsive repudiation: "O! the more angel she,/ And you the blacker devil." Of Desdemona: "She was too fond of her filthy bargain." To Othello: "O gull! O dolt!/ As ignorant as dirt!" Shakespeare's genius lay precisely in juxtaposing these two pairs: inner blackness and inner whiteness. The drama would have seemed odd indeed if his audiences had felt no response to this cross-inversion and to the deeply turbulent double meaning of black *over* white.

It required a very great dramatist to expose some of the more inward biocultural values which led—or drove—Englishmen to accept readily the notion that Negroes were peculiarly sexual men.

Probably these values and the ancient reputation of Africa upon which they built were of primary importance in determining the response of Englishmen to Negroes. Whatever the importance of biologic elements in these values—whatever the effects of long northern nights, of living in a cool climate, of possessing light-colored bodies which excreted contrasting lumps of darkness—these values by Shakespeare's time were interlocked with the accretions of English history and, more immediately, with the circumstances of contact with Africans and the social upheaval of Tudor England.[80]

The most obvious of these circumstances was that Englishmen were unaccustomed to West African standards concerning suitable public attire. Many Negroes were (or perhaps merely appeared to trousered Englishmen) utterly "naked." [81] Fully as important were African matrimonial practices, which in fact frequently failed to match the accepted norm for Christian Englishmen. It may be that Englishmen found Negroes free in a primitive way and found this freedom somehow provocative; many chroniclers made a point of discussing the Negro women's long breasts and ease of

80. The power of these values may be seen in Thomas Adams, *The White Devil, or the Hypocrite Uncased* . . . (London, 1614), 1–2: "A Devill he was, blacke within and full of rancour, but white without, and skinned over with hypocrisie; therefore to use *Luthers* word, wee will call him the white *Devill.*"
There seem to be no cross-cultural studies of the meaning of color. It clearly would be a mistake to take the English valuations as representing responses to northern (versus Mediterranean) climate or to assume that these valuations were peculiarly Judeo-Christian.

> On the Day when
> Some faces will be (lit up
> With) white, and some faces
> Will be (in the gloom of) black:
> To those whose faces
> Will be black, (will be said) :
> "Did ye reject Faith
> After accepting it?
> Taste then the Penalty
> For rejecting Faith."
>
> But those whose faces
> Will be (lit with) white,—
> They will be in (the light
> Of) God's mercy: therin
> To dwell (for ever).

Abdullah Yusuf Ali, trans., *The Holy Qur-an* (Lahore, 1937), Sûrah III, 106–7, where the (Muslim) editor comments, "The 'face' (*wajh*) expresses our Personality, our inmost being. . . . Black is the colour of darkness, sin, rebellion, misery; removal from the grace and light of God."
81. "The First Voyage Made by Master William Towrson . . ." (1555), Hakluyt, *Principal Navigations*, VI, 184; "A voyage to Benin . . . Written by James Welsh . . ." (1589), *ibid.*, 457.

childbearing.[82] The life of "savages" had attractions, even if civilized white men were not entirely aware what these attractions
were. No doubt these differences between the two colliding cultures
helped support the notion that Africans were highly sexed; yet
Europeans have not everywhere and always made so much of nudity
and polygamy among other peoples, and it seems necessary to inquire briefly concerning certain qualities of thought and feeling in
Tudor England which may help account for what seems an unusual
hypersensitivity to another people's sexuality.

7. THE BLACKNESS WITHIN

The Protestant Reformation in England was a complex
development, but certainly it may be said that during the century
between Henry VIII and Oliver Cromwell the content and tone of
English Christianity were altered in the direction of Biblicism,
personal piety, individual judgment, and more intense self-scrutiny
and internalized control. Many pious Englishmen, not all of them
"Puritans," came to approach life as if conducting an examination
and to approach Scripture as if peering in a mirror. As a result,
their inner energies were brought unusually close to the surface,
more frequently into the almost rational world of legend, myth, and
literature. The taut Puritan and the bawdy Elizabethan were not
enemies but partners in this adventure which we usually think of in
terms of great literature—of Milton and Shakespeare—and social
conflict—of Saints and Cavaliers. The age was driven by the twin
spirits of adventure and control, and while "adventurous
Elizabethans" embarked upon voyages of discovery overseas, many
others embarked upon inward voyages of discovery. Some men, like
William Bradford and John Winthrop, were to do both.
    Given this charged atmosphere of (self-) discovery, it is scarcely
surprising that Englishmen should have used peoples overseas as
social mirrors and that they were especially inclined to discover
attributes in savages which they found first but could not speak of
in themselves.
    Nowhere is the way in which certain of these cultural attributes
came to bear upon Negroes more clearly illustrated than in a
passage by George Best, an Elizabethan adventurer who sailed with
Martin Frobisher in 1577 in search of the Northwest Passage. In his
discourse demonstrating the habitability of all parts of the world,

82. An early example is "First Voyage by William Towrson" (1555), *ibid.*, 187.

Best veered off to the problem of the color of Negroes. The cause of their blackness, he decided, was explained in Scripture. Noah and his sons and their wives were "white" and "by course of nature should have begotten . . . white children. But the envie of our great and continuall enemie the wicked Spirite is such, that as hee coulde not suffer our olde father Adam to live in the felicitie and Angelike state wherein he was first created, . . . so againe, finding at this flood none but a father and three sons living, hee so caused one of them to disobey his fathers commandment, that after him all his posteritie should bee accursed." The "fact" of this "disobedience," Best continued, was this: Noah "commanded" his sons and their wives to behold God "with reverence and feare," and that "while they remained in the Arke, they should use continencie, and abstaine from carnall copulation with their wives: . . . which good instructions and exhortations notwithstanding his wicked sonne Cham disobeyed, and being perswaded that the first childe borne after the flood . . . should inherite . . . all the dominions of the earth, hee . . . used company with his wife, and craftily went about thereby to dis-inherite the off-spring of his other two brethren." To punish this "wicked and detestable fact," God willed that "a sonne should bee born whose name was Chus, who not onely it selfe, but all his posteritie after him should bee so blacke and lothsome, that it might remain a spectacle of disobedience to all the worlde. And of this blacke and cursed Chus came all these blacke Moores which are in Africa." [83]

The inner themes running throughout this extraordinary exegesis testify eloquently to the completeness with which English perceptions could integrate sexuality with blackness, the devil, and the judgment of a God who had originally created man not only "Angelike" but "white." These running equations lay embedded at a deep and almost inaccessible level of Elizabethan culture; only occasionally do they appear in complete clarity, as when evil dreams

. . . hale me from my sleepe like forked Devils,
Midnight, thou Æthiope, Empresse of Black Soules, Thou general Bawde to the whole world.[84]

But what is still more arresting about George Best's discourse is the shaft of light it throws upon the dark mood of strain and control in

83. *Ibid.*, VII, 263–64. Best's discourse was published separately in 1578.
84. John Day, *Law-Tricks or, Who Would Have Thought It* (London, 1608), Act V, scene i.

Elizabethan culture. In an important sense, Best's remarks are not about Negroes; rather they play upon a theme of external discipline exercised upon the man who fails to discipline himself. The linkages he established—"disobedience" with "carnall copulation" with something "black and lothsome"—were not his alone; the term *dirt* first began to acquire its meaning of moral impurity, of smuttiness, at the very end of the sixteenth century. Perhaps the key term, though, is "disobedience"—to God and parents—and perhaps, therefore, the passage echoes one of the central concerns of Englishmen of the sixteenth and early seventeenth centuries. Tudor England was undergoing social ferment, generated by an increasingly commercialized economy and reflected in such legislative monuments as the Statute of Apprentices and the Elizabethan vagrancy and poor laws. Overseas mercantile expansion brought profits and adventure but also a sense, in some men, of disquietude. One commentator declared that the merchants, "whose number is so increased in these our daies," had "in times past" traded chiefly with European countries but "now in these daies, as men not contented with these journies, they have sought out the east and west Indies, and made now and then suspicious voiages." [85] Literate Englishmen generally (again not merely the Puritans) were concerned with the apparent disintegration of social and moral controls at home; they fretted endlessly over the "masterless men" who had once had a proper place in the social order but who were now wandering about, begging, robbing, raping. They fretted also about the absence of a spirit of due subordination—of children to parents and servants to masters. They assailed what seemed a burgeoning spirit of avariciousness, a spirit which one social critic described revealingly as "a barbarous or slavish desire to turne the penie." [86] They decried the laborers who demanded too high wages, the masters who would squeeze their servants, and the landed gentlemen who valued

85. [William Harrison], *An Historicall Description of the Iland of Britaine* . . . (1577), in *Holinshed's Chronicles of England, Scotland, and Ireland,* 6 vols. (London, 1807–08), I, 274. A similar sense of the necessity of ordering and controlling the spreading migrations of peoples underlay Sir Walter Raleigh's revealing notation that "first, we are to consider that the world after the flood was not planted by imagination, neither had the children of *Noah* wings, to fly from *Shinaar* to the uttermost border of *Europe, Africa,* and *Asia* in haste, but that these children were directed by a wise father, who knew those parts of the world before the flood, to which he disposed his children after it, and sent them not as discoverers, or at all adventure, but assigned and allotted to every son, and their issues, their proper parts." Sir Walter Raleigh, *The History of the World, in Five Books,* 11th ed., 2 vols. (London, 1736), I, 75–76.

86. [Harrison], *Historicall Description of Britaine* (1577), in *Holinshed's Chronicles,* I, 276.

sheep more than men—in short, the spirit of George Best's Cham, who aimed to have his son "inherite and possesse all the dominions of the earth."

It was the case with English confrontation with Negroes, then, that a society in a state of rapid flux, undergoing important changes in religious values, and comprised of men who were energetically on the make and acutely and often uncomfortably self-conscious of being so, came upon a people less technologically advanced, markedly different in appearance and culture. From the first, Englishmen tended to set Negroes over against themselves, to stress what they conceived to be radically contrasting qualities of color, religion, and style of life, as well as animality and a peculiarly potent sexuality. What Englishmen did not at first fully realize was that Negroes were potentially subjects for a special kind of obedience and subordination which was to arise as adventurous Englishmen sought to possess for themselves and their children one of the most bountiful dominions of the earth. When they came to plant themselves in the New World, they were to find that they had not entirely left behind the spirit of avarice and insubordination. Nor does it appear, in light of attitudes which developed during their first two centuries in America, that they left behind all the impressions initially gathered of the *Negro* before he became preeminently the *slave*.

II UNTHINKING DECISION

Enslavement of Negroes in America to 1700

AT THE START OF ENGLISH SETTLEMENT IN AMERICA, NO one had in mind to establish the institution of Negro slavery. Yet in less than a century the foundations of a peculiar institution had been laid. The first Negroes landed in Virginia in 1619, though very, very little is known about their precise status during the next twenty years. Between 1640 and 1660 there is evidence of enslavement, and after 1660 slavery crystallized on the statute books of Maryland, Virginia, and other colonies. By 1700 when African Negroes began flooding into English America they were treated as somehow deserving a life and status radically different from English and other European settlers. The Negro had been debased to a condition of chattel slavery; at some point, Englishmen in America had created a legal status which ran counter to English law.

Unfortunately the details of this process can never be completely reconstructed; there is simply not enough evidence (and very little chance of more to come) to show precisely when and how and why Negroes came to be treated so differently from white men, though there is just enough to make historians differ as to its meaning. Concerning the first years of contact especially we have very little information as to what impression Negroes made upon English settlers: accordingly, we are left knowing less about the formative years than about later periods of American slavery. That those early years were crucial ones is obvious, for it was then that the cycle of Negro debasement began; once the Negro became fully the slave it is not hard to see why white men looked down upon him. Yet precisely because understanding the dynamics of these early years is so important to understanding the centuries which followed, it is necessary to bear with the less than satisfactory data and to attempt to reconstruct the course of debasement undergone by Negroes in

[44]

seventeenth-century America. In order to comprehend it, we need first of all to examine certain social pressures generated by the American environment and how these pressures interacted with certain qualities of English social thought and law that existed on the eve of settlement, qualities that even then were being modified by examples set by England's rivals for empire in the New World.

1. THE NECESSITIES OF A NEW WORLD

When Englishmen crossed the Atlantic to settle in America, they were immediately subject to novel strains. In some settlements, notably Jamestown and Plymouth, the survival of the community was in question. An appalling proportion of people were dead within a year, from malnutrition, starvation, unconquerable diseases, bitter cold, oppressive heat, Indian attacks, murder, and suicide. The survivors were isolated from the world as they had known it, cut off from friends and family and the familiar sights and sounds and smells which have always told men who and where they are. A similar sense of isolation and disorientation was inevitable even in the settlements that did not suffer through a starving time. English settlers were surrounded by savages. They had to perform a round of daily tasks to which most were unaccustomed. They had undergone the shock of detachment from home in order to set forth upon a dangerous voyage of from ten to thirteen weeks that ranged from unpleasant to fatal and that seared into every passenger's memory the ceaselessly tossing distance that separated him from his old way of life.[1]

Life in America put great pressure upon the traditional social and economic controls that Englishmen assumed were to be exercised by civil and often ecclesiastical authority. Somehow the empty woods seemed to lead much more toward license than restraint. At the same time, by reaction, this unfettering resulted in an almost pathetic social conservatism, a yearning for the forms and symbols of the old familiar social order. When in 1618, for example, the Virginia Company wangled a knighthood for a newly appointed governor of the colony the objection from the settlers was not that this artificial elevation was inappropriate to wilderness conditions but that it did not go far enough to meet them; several planters petitioned that a governor of higher rank be sent, since some settlers had "only Reverence of the Comanders Eminence, or Nobillitye

---

1. There is an eloquent revivification by William Bradford, *Of Plymouth Plantation, 1620–1647*, ed. Samuel Eliot Morison (N. Y., 1952), 61–63.

(whereunto by Nature everye man subordinate is ready to yeild a willing submission without contempt, or repyning) ." [2] English social forms were transplanted to America not simply because they were nice to have around but because without them the new settlements would have fallen apart and English settlers would have become men of the forest, savage men devoid of civilization.

For the same reason, the communal goals that animated the settlement of the colonies acquired great functional importance in the wilderness; they served as antidotes to social and individual disintegration. The physical hardships of settlement could never have been surmounted without the stiffened nerve and will engendered by commonly recognized if sometimes unarticulated purposes. In New England lack of articulation was no problem. The Puritans knew precisely who they were (the chosen of God, many of them) and that they were seeking to erect a Godly community. Though that community (eventually) eluded them, they retained their conviction that they manned a significant outpost of English civilization. As Cotton Mather grandly told the Massachusetts governor and General Court in 1700, "It is no Little Blessing of God, that we are a part of the *English nation*." [3] A similar deep sense of self-transplantation buttressed the settlements in Virginia and Maryland. While there was less talk than in New England about God's special endorsement, virtually every settler knew that Englishmen were serving His greater glory by removing to Virginia and by making a prosperous success of the project. They recognized also that their efforts at western planting aggrandized English wealth and power and the cause of reformed Christianity. As Richard Hakluyt summarized these purposes, "This enterprise may staye the spanishe kinge ["the supporter of the great Antechriste of Rome"] from flowinge over all the face of that waste firme of America, yf wee seate and plante there in time." [4] For Englishmen planting in America, then, it was of the utmost importance to know that they were Englishmen, which was to say that they were educated (to a degree suitable to their station), Christian (of an appropriate Protestant variety), civilized, and (again to an appropriate degree) free men.

2. Susan M. Kingsbury, ed., *Records of the Virginia Company of London*, 4 vols. (Washington, D.C., 1906–35), III, 216–19, 231–32.

3. Cotton Mather, *A Pillar of Gratitude* . . . (Boston, 1700), 32–33.

4. From his own "Discourse on Western Planting" (1584), in E. G. R. Taylor, ed., *The Original Writings and Correspondence of the Two Richard Hakluyts* (*Works Issued by the Hakluyt Soc.*, 2d Ser., 76–77 [1935]), II, 314–15. See Perry Miller, "Religion and Society in the Early Literature of Virginia," in his *Errand into the Wilderness* (Cambridge, Mass., 1956), 99–140.

It was with personal freedom, of course, that wilderness conditions most suddenly reshaped English laws, assumptions, and practices. In America land was plentiful, labor scarce, and, as in all new colonies, a cash crop desperately needed. These economic conditions were to remain important for centuries; in general they tended to encourage greater geographical mobility, less specialization, higher rewards, and fewer restraints on the processes and products of labor. Supporting traditional assumptions and practices, however, was the need to retain them simply because they were familiar and because they served the vital function of maintaining and advancing orderly settlement. Throughout the seventeenth century there were pressures on traditional practices which similarly told in opposite directions.

In general men who invested capital in agriculture in America came under fewer customary and legal restraints than in England concerning what they did with their land and with the people who worked on it. On the other hand their activities were constrained by the economic necessity of producing cash crops for export, which narrowed their choice of how they could treat it. Men without capital could obtain land relatively easily: hence the shortage of labor and the notably blurred line between men who had capital and men who did not. Men and women in England faced a different situation. A significant amount of capital was required in order to get to America, and the greatest barrier to material advancement in America was the Atlantic Ocean.

Three major systems of labor emerged amid the interplay of these social and economic conditions in America. One, which was present from the beginning, was free wage labor, in which contractual arrangements rested upon a monetary nexus. Another, which was the last to appear, was chattel slavery, in which there were no contractual arrangements (except among owners). The third, which virtually coincided with first settlement in America, was temporary servitude, in which complex contractual arrangements gave shape to the entire system. It was this third system, indentured servitude, which permitted so many English settlers to cross the Atlantic barrier. Indentured servitude was linked to the development of chattel slavery in America, and its operation deserves closer examination.

A very sizable proportion of settlers in the English colonies came as indentured servants bound by contract to serve a master for a specified number of years, usually from four to seven or until age twenty-one, as repayment for their ocean passage. The time of service to which the servant bound himself was negotiable property, and he might be sold or conveyed from one master to another at any time up to the expiration of his indenture, at which point he became a free man. (Actually it was his *labor* which was owned and sold, not his *person*, though this distinction was neither important nor obvious at the time.) Custom and statute law regulated the relationship between servant and master. Obligation was reciprocal: the master undertook to feed and clothe and sometimes to educate his servant and to refrain from abusing him, while the servant was obliged to perform such work as his master set him and to obey his master in all things. This typical pattern, with a multitude of variations, was firmly established by mid-seventeenth century. In Virginia and Maryland, both the legal and actual conditions of servants seem to have improved considerably from the early years when servants had often been outrageously abused and sometimes forced to serve long terms. Beginning about 1640 the legislative assemblies of the two colonies passed numerous acts prescribing maximum terms of service and requiring masters to pay the customary "freedom dues" (clothing, provisions, and so forth) at the end of the servant's time.[5] This legislation may have been actuated partly by the need to attract more immigrants with guarantees of good treatment, in which case underpopulation in relation to level of technology and to natural resources in the English colonies may be said to have made for greater personal freedom. On the other hand, it may also have been a matter of protecting traditional freedoms threatened by this same fact of underpopulation which generated so powerful a need for labor which would not be transient and temporary. In this instance, very clearly, the imperatives enjoined by settlement in the wilderness interacted with previously acquired ideas concerning personal freedom. Indeed without some inquiry into Elizabethan thinking on that subject, it will remain impossible to comprehend why Englishmen became servants in the plantations, and Negroes slaves.

2. FREEDOM AND BONDAGE IN THE ENGLISH TRADITION

Thinking about freedom and bondage in Tudor England was confused and self-contradictory. In a period of social dislocation there was considerable disagreement among contempo-

5. William Waller Hening, ed., *The Statutes at Large Being a Collection of All the Laws of Virginia*, 13 vols. (Richmond, N.Y., and Phila., 1809–23), I, 257, 435, 439–42, II, 113–14, 240, 388, III, 447–62; *Archives of Maryland*, 69 vols. (Baltimore, 1883—), I, 53, 80, 352–53, 409–10, 428, 443–44, 453–54, 464, 469, II, 147–48, 335–36, 527.

rary observers as to what actually was going on and even as to what ought to be. Ideas about personal freedom tended to run both ahead of and behind actual social conditions. Both statute and common law were sometimes considerably more than a century out of phase with actual practice and with commonly held notions about servitude. Finally, ideas and practices were changing rapidly. It is possible, however, to identify certain important tenets of social thought that served as anchor points amid this chaos.

Englishmen lacked accurate methods of ascertaining what actually was happening to their social institutions, but they were not wrong in supposing that villenage, or "bondage" as they more often called it, had virtually disappeared in England. William Harrison put the matter most strenuously in 1577: "As for slaves and bondmen we have none, naie such is the privilege of our countrie by the especiall grace of God, and bountie of our princes, that if anie come hither from other realms, so soone as they set foot on land they become so free of condition as their masters, whereby all note of servile bondage is utterlie remooved from them." [6] Other observers were of the (correct) opinion that a few lingering vestiges— bondmen whom the progress of freedom had passed by—might still be found in the crannies of the decayed manorial system, but everyone agreed that such vestiges were anachronistic. In fact there were English men and women who were still "bond" in the mid-sixteenth century, but they were few in number and their status was much more a technicality than a condition. In the middle ages, being a villein had meant dependence upon the will of a feudal lord but by no means deprivation of all social and legal rights. In the thirteenth and fourteenth centuries villenage had decayed markedly, and it may be said not to have existed as a viable social institution in the second half of the sixteenth century.[7] Personal freedom had become the normal status of Englishmen. Most contemporaries welcomed this fact; indeed it was after about 1550 that there began to develop in England that preening consciousness of the peculiar glories of English liberties.

6. [Harrison], *Historicall Description of Britaine*, in *Holinshed's Chronicles*, I, 275.

7. The best place to start on this complicated subject is Paul Vinagradof, *Villainage in England: Essays in English Mediaeval History* (Oxford, 1892). The least unsatisfactory studies of vestiges seem to be Alexander Savine, "Bondmen under the Tudors," Royal Historical Society, *Transactions*, 2d Ser., 17 (1903), 235–89; I. S. Leadam, "The Last Days of Bondage in England," *Law Quarterly Review*, 9 (1893), 348–65. William S. Holdsworth, *A History of English Law*, 3d ed., 12 vols. (Boston, 1923), III, 491–510, explodes the supposed distinction between villeins *regardant* and *gross*.

How had it all happened? Among those observers who tried to explain, there was agreement that Christianity was primarily responsible. They thought of villenage as a mitigation of ancient bond slavery and that the continuing trend to liberty was animated, as Sir Thomas Smith said in a famous passage, by the "perswasion . . . of Christians not to make nor keepe his brother in Christ, servile, bond and underling for ever unto him, as a beast rather than as a man." [8] They agreed also that the trend had been forwarded by the common law, in which the disposition was always, as the phrase went, *in favorem libertatis,* "in favor of liberty." Probably they were correct in both these suppositions, but the common law harbored certain inconsistencies as to freedom which may have had an important though imponderable effect upon the reappearance of slavery in English communities in the seventeenth century.

The accreted structure of the common law sometimes resulted in imperviousness to changing conditions. The first book of Lord Coke's great *Institutes of the Laws of England* (1628), for example, was an extended gloss upon Littleton's fifteenth-century treatise on *Tenures* and it repeatedly quoted the opinions of such famous authorities as Bracton, who had died in 1268. When Bracton had described villenage, English law had not yet fully diverged from the civil or Roman law, and villenage actually existed. Almost four hundred years later some legal authorities were still citing Bracton on villenage without even alluding to the fact that villenage no longer existed. The widely used legal dictionary, Cowell's *Interpreter* (1607 and later editions), quoted Bracton at length and declared that his words "expresse the nature of our villenage something aptly." [9] Anyone relying solely on Cowell's *Interpreter* would suppose that some Englishmen in the early seventeenth century were hereditary serfs. Thus while villenage was actually extinct, it lay unmistakably fossilized in the common law. Its survival in that rigid form must have reminded Englishmen that there existed a sharply differing alternative to personal liberty. It was in this vague way that villenage seems to have been related to the development of chattel slavery in America. Certainly villenage was not the forerunner of slavery, but its survival in the law books meant that a possibility which might have been foreclosed was not. Later, after Negro slavery had clearly emerged, English lawyers were inclined to

8. Thomas Smith, *De Republica Anglorum: A Discourse on the Commonwealth of England,* ed. L. Alston (Cambridge, Eng., 1906), 133.

9. Coke's section on villenage is Lib. II, cap. XI; see John Cowell, *The Interpreter: Or Booke Containing the Signification of Words . . .* (Cambridge, Eng., 1607), "villein."

think of slavery as being a New World version of the ancient tenure described by Bracton and Cowell and Coke.

That the common law was running centuries behind social practice was only one of several important factors complicating Tudor thought about the proper status of individuals in society. The social ferment of the sixteenth century resulted not only in the impalpable mood of control and subordination which seems to have affected English perception of Africans but also in the well-known strenuous efforts of Tudor governments to lay restrictions on elements in English society which seemed badly out of control. From at least the 1530's the countryside swarmed with vagrants, sturdy beggars, rogues, and vagabonds, with men who could but would not work. They committed all manner of crimes, the worst of which was remaining idle. It was an article of faith among Tudor commentators (before there were "Puritans" to help propound it) that idleness was the mother of all vice and the chief danger to a well-ordered state. Tudor statesmen valiantly attempted to suppress idleness by means of the famous vagrancy laws which provided for houses of correction and (finally) for whipping the vagrant from constable to constable until he reached his home parish. They assumed that everyone belonged in a specific social niche and that anyone failing to labor in the niche assigned to him by Providence must be compelled to do so by authority.

Some experiments in compulsion ran counter to the trend toward personal liberty. In 1547, shortly after the death of Henry VIII, a parliamentary statute provided that any able-bodied person adjudged a vagabond upon presentment to two justices of the peace should be branded with a "V" on the chest and made a "slave" for two years to the presenter who was urged to give "the saide Slave breade and water or small dryncke and such refuse of meate as he shall thincke mete [and] cause the said Slave to worke by beating cheyninge or otherwise in such worke and Labor how vyle so ever it be." Masters could "putt a rynge of Iron about his Necke Arme or his Legge for a more knowledge and suretie of the keepinge of him." A runaway "slave" convicted by a court was to be branded on the cheek or forehead and adjudged "to be the saide Masters Slave for ever." These provisions reflected desperation. Fully as significant as their passage was their repeal three years later by a statute which frankly asserted in the preamble that their "extremitie" had "byn occation that they have not ben putt in ure [use]." [10]

10. *The Statutes of the Realm*, 11 vols. ([London], 1810–28), 1 Edw. VI. c. 3; 3 and 4 Edw. VI. c. 16. A standard treatment is Frank Aydelotte, *Elizabethan Rogues and Vagabonds* (Oxford, 1913).

Englishmen generally were unwilling to submit or subscribe to such debasement. Despite a brief statutory experiment with banishment "beyond the Seas" and with judgment "perpetually to the Gallyes of this Realme" in 1598,[11] Tudor authorities gradually hammered out the legal framework of a labor system which permitted compulsion but which did not permit so total a loss of freedom as lifetime hereditary slavery. Apprenticeship seemed to them the ideal status, for apprenticeship provided a means of regulating the economy and of guiding youth into acceptable paths of honest industry. By 1600, many writers had come to think of other kinds of bound labor as inferior forms of apprenticeship, involving less of an educative function, less permanence, and a less rigidly contractual basis. This tendency to reason from apprenticeship downward, rather than from penal service up, had the important effect of imparting some of the very strong contractualism in the master-apprentice relationship to less formal varieties of servitude. There were "indentured" servants in England prior to English settlement in America. Their written "indentures" gave visible evidence of the strong element of mutual obligation between master and servant: each retained a copy of the contract which was "indented" at the top so as to match the other.

As things turned out, it was indentured servitude which best met the requirements for settling in America. Of course there were other forms of bound labor which contributed to the process of settlement: many convicts were sent and many children abducted.[12] Yet among all the numerous varieties and degrees of non-freedom which existed in England, there was none which could have served as a well-formed model for the chattel slavery which developed in America. This is not to say, though, that slavery was an unheard-of novelty in Tudor England. On the contrary, "bond slavery" was a memory trace of long standing. Vague and confused as the concept of slavery was in the minds of Englishmen, it possessed certain fairly consistent connotations which were to help shape English perceptions of the way Europeans should properly treat the newly discovered peoples overseas.

3. THE CONCEPT OF SLAVERY

At first glance, one is likely to see merely a fog of inconsistency and vagueness enveloping the terms *servant* and *slave* as

11. *Statutes of the Realm*, 39 Eliz. c. 4.
12. The "standard" work on this subject unfortunately does not address itself to the problem of origins: Abbot Emerson Smith, *Colonists in Bondage: White Servitude and Convict Labor in America, 1607–1776* (Chapel Hill, 1947).

they were used both in England and in seventeenth-century America. When Hamlet declaims "O what a rogue and peasant slave am I," the term seems to have a certain elasticity. When Peter Heylyn defines it in 1627 as "that ignominious word, *Slave;* whereby we use to call ignoble fellowes, and the more base sort of people," [13] the term seems useless as a key to a specific social status. And when we find in the American colonies a reference in 1665 to "Jacob a negro slave and servant to Nathaniel Utye," [14] it is tempting to regard slavery as having been in the first half of the seventeenth century merely a not very elevated sort of servitude.

In one sense it was, since the concept embodied in the terms *servitude, service,* and *servant* was widely embracive. *Servant* was more a generic term than *slave.* Slaves could be "servants"—as they were eventually and ironically to become in the ante-bellum South—but servants *should not* be "slaves." This injunction, which was common in England, suggests a measure of precision in the concept of slavery. In fact there was a large measure which merits closer inspection.

First of all, the "slave's" loss of freedom was complete. "Of all men which be destitute of libertie or freedome," explained Henry Swinburne in his *Briefe Treatise of Testaments and Last Willes* (1590), "the slave is in greatest subjection, for a slave is that person which is in servitude or bondage to an other, even against nature." "Even his children," moreover, ". . . are infected with the Leprosie of his father's bondage." Swinburne was at pains to distinguish this condition from that of the villein, whom he likened to the *Ascriptitius Glebæ* of the civil law, "one that is ascrited or assigned to a ground or farme, for the perpetuall tilling or manuring thereof." "A villeine," he insisted, "howsoever he may seeme like unto a slave, yet his bondage is not so great." [15] Swinburne's was the prevailing view of bond slavery; only the preciseness of emphasis was unusual. At law, much more clearly than in literary usage, "bond slavery" implied utter deprivation of liberty.

Slavery was also thought of as a perpetual condition. While it had not yet come invariably to mean lifetime labor, it was frequently thought of in those terms. Except sometimes in instances of punishment for crime, slavery was open ended; in contrast to servitude, it did not involve a definite term of years. Slavery was perpetual also in the sense that it was often thought of as hereditary. It was these

13. *Hamlet,* II, ii; Heylyn, ΜΙΚΡΌΚΟΣΜΟΣ, 175.
14. *Archives of Maryland,* XLIX, 489.
15. Henry Swinburne, *A Briefe Treatise of Testaments and Last Willes . . .* (London, 1590), 43.

dual aspects of perpetuity which were to assume such importance in America.

So much was slavery a complete loss of liberty that it seemed to Englishmen somehow akin to loss of humanity. No theme was more persistent than the claim that to treat a man as a slave was to treat him as a beast. Almost half a century after Sir Thomas Smith had made this connection a Puritan divine was condemning masters who used "their servants as slaves, or rather as beasts" while Captain John Smith was moaning about being captured by the Turks and "all sold for slaves, like beasts in a market-place."[16] No analogy could have better demonstrated how strongly Englishmen felt about total loss of personal freedom.

Certain prevalent assumptions about the origins of slavery paralleled this analogy at a different level of intellectual construction. Lawyers and divines alike assumed that slavery was impossible before the Fall, that it violated natural law, that it was instituted by positive human laws, and, more generally, that in various ways it was connected with sin. These ideas were as old as the church fathers and the Roman writers on natural law. In the social atmosphere of pre-Restoration England it was virtually inevitable that they should have been capsulated in the story of Ham. The Reverend Jeremy Taylor (an opponent of the Puritans) explained what it was "that brought servitude or slavery into the world": God had "consigned a sad example that for ever children should be afraid to dishonour their parents, and discover their nakedness, or reveal their turpitude, their follies and dishonours." Sir Edward Coke (himself scarcely a Puritan) declared, "This is assured, That Bondage or Servitude was first inflicted for dishonouring of Parents: For Cham the Father of Canaan . . . seeing the Nakedness of his Father Noah, and shewing it in Derision to his Brethren, was therefore punished in his Son Canaan with Bondage." [17]

The great jurist wrote this in earnest, but at least he did offer another description of slavery's genesis. In it he established what was perhaps the most important and widely acknowledged attribute

16. William Gouge, *Of Domesticall Duties Eight Treatises* (London, 1622), 690; Edward Arber, ed., *Travels and Works of Captain John Smith . . .* , 2 vols. (Edinburgh, 1910) , II, 853.

17. *The Whole Works of the Right Rev. Jeremy Taylor . . .* , 10 vols. (London, 1850–54) , X, 453; Sir Edward Coke, *The First Part of the Institutes of the Laws of England: or, a Commentary upon Littleton . . .* , 12th ed. (London, 1738) , Lib. II, Cap. XI. For the long-standing assumption that slavery was brought about by man's sinfulness see R. W. and A. J. Carlyle, *A History of Medieval Political Theory in the West,* 6 vols. (Edinburgh and London, 1903–36) , I, 116–24, II, 119–20.

of slavery: at the time of the Flood "all Things were common to all," but afterward, with the emergence of private property, there "arose battles"; "then it was ordained by Constitution of Nations . . . that he that was taken in Battle should remain Bond to his taker for ever, and he to do with him, all that should come of him, his Will and Pleasure, as with his Beast, or any other Cattle, to give, or to sell, or to kill." This final power, Coke noted, had since been taken away (owing to "the Cruelty of some Lords") and placed in the hands only of kings.[18] The animating rationale here was that captivity in war meant an end to a person's claim to life as a human being; by sparing the captive's life, the captor acquired virtually absolute power over the life of the man who had lost the power to control his own.

More than any other single quality, *captivity* differentiated slavery from servitude. Although there were other, subsidiary ways of becoming a slave, such as being born of slave parents, selling oneself into slavery, or being adjudged to slavery for crime, none of these were considered to explain the way slavery had originated. Slavery was a power relationship; servitude was a relationship of service. Men were "slaves" to the devil but "servants" of God. Men were "galley-slaves," not galley servants. Bondage had never existed in the county of Kent because Kent was "never vanquished by [William] the Conquerour, but yeelded it selfe by composition." [19]

This tendency to equate slavery with captivity had important ramifications. Warfare was usually waged against another people; captives were usually foreigners—"strangers" as they were termed. Until the emergence of nation-states in Europe, by far the most important category of strangers was the non-Christian. International warfare seemed above all a ceaseless struggle between Christians and Turks. Slavery, therefore, frequently appeared to rest upon the "perpetual enmity" which existed between Christians on the one hand and "infidels" and "pagans" on the other.[20] In the sixteenth and seventeenth centuries Englishmen at home could read scores of accounts concerning the miserable fate of Englishmen and other Christians taken into "captivity" by Turks and Moors and

18. Coke, *Institutes*, Lib. II, Cap. XI.
19. William Lambard[e], *A Perambulation of Kent* . . . (London, 1576), 11. The notion of selling oneself into slavery was very much subsidiary and probably derived from the Old Testament. Isaac Mendelsohn, *Slavery in the Ancient Near East* . . . (N. Y., 1949), 18, points out that the Old Testament was the only ancient law code to mention voluntary slavery and self-sale.
20. The phrases are from Michael Dalton, *The Countrey Justice* . . . (London, 1655), 191.

oppressed by the "verie worst manner of bondmanship and slav-erie." [21] Clearly slavery was tinged by the religious disjunction.

Just as many commentators thought that the spirit of Christianity was responsible for the demise of bondage in England, many divines distinguished between ownership of Christian and of non-Christian servants. The Reverend William Gouge referred to "such servants as being strangers were bond-slaves, over whom masters had a more absolute power than others." The Reverend Henry Smith declared, "He which counteth his servant a slave, is in error: for there is difference betweene beleeving servants and infidell servants." [22] Im-plicit in every clerical discourse was the assumption that common brotherhood in Christ imparted a special quality to the master-servant relationship.

Slavery did not possess that quality, which made it fortunate that Englishmen did not enslave one another. As we have seen, however, Englishmen did possess a *concept* of slavery, formed by the cluster-ing of several rough but not illogical equations. The slave was treated like a beast. Slavery was inseparable from the evil in men; it was God's punishment upon Ham's prurient disobedience. Enslave-ment was captivity, the loser's lot in a contest of power. Slaves were infidels or heathens.

On every count, Negroes qualified.

4. THE PRACTICES OF PORTINGALS AND SPANYARDS

Which is not to say that Englishmen were casting about for a people to enslave. What happened was that they found thrust before them not only instances of Negroes being taken into slavery but attractive opportunities for joining in that business. English-men actually were rather slow to seize these opportunities; on most of the sixteenth-century English voyages to West Africa there was no dealing in slaves. The notion that it was appropriate to do so seems to have been drawn chiefly from the example set by the Spanish and Portuguese.

Without inquiring into the reasons, it can be said that slavery had persisted since ancient times in the Iberian peninsula, that prior to the discoveries it was primarily a function of the religious wars against the Moors,[23] that Portuguese explorers pressing down the

21. *The Estate of Christians, Living under the Subjection of the Turke* . . . (London, 1595) , 5.

22. Gouge, *Domesticall Duties*, 663; *The Sermons of Master Henry Smith* . . . (London, 1607) , 40.

23. The complex situation is set forth by Charles Verlinden, *L'Esclavage dans L'Europe Médiévale. Vol. I, Péninsule Ibérique-France* (Brugge, 1955) . The still

coast in the fifteenth century captured thousands of Negroes whom they carried back to Portugal as slaves, and that after 1500, Portuguese ships began supplying the Spanish and Portuguese settlements in America with Negro slaves. By 1550 European enslavement of Negroes was more than a century old, and Negro slavery had become a fixture of the New World.

For present purposes there is no need to inquire into the precise nature of this slavery except to point out that in actual practice it did fit the English concept of bond slavery. The question which needs answering pertains to contemporary English knowledge of what was going on. And the answer may be given concisely: Englishmen had easily at hand a great deal of not very precise information.

The news that Negroes were being carried off to forced labor in America was broadcast across the pages of the Hakluyt and Purchas collections. While only one account stated explicitly that Negroes "be their slaves during their life," it was clear that the Portuguese and Spaniards treated Negroes and frequently the Indians as "slaves." [24] This was the term customarily used by English voyagers and by translators of foreign accounts and documents. Readers of a lament about the treatment of Indians in Brazil by an unnamed Portuguese could hardly mistake learning that slavery there was a clearly defined condition: Indians held "a title of free" but were treated as "slaves, all their lives," and when masters died the poor Indians "remaine in their wils with the name of free, but bound to serve their children perpetually . . . as if they were lawful slaves." The same author objected to unjust wars mounted against Indians in "the hope of the profit that is offered them, of getting of slaves . . . to serve themselves perpetually." [25] Repeatedly the language employed in these widely read books gave clear indication of how the Negro was involved. William Towrson was told by a Negro

---

prevalent state of enmity becomes clear in Franklin L. Baumer, "England, the Turk, and the Common Corps of Christendom," *American Historical Review*, 50 (1944–45) , 26–48; Chew, *The Crescent and the Rose.*

24. Hakluyt, *Principall Navigations* (1589) , 572; see also the comment, "It is good traffiking with the people of Guinea, specialy with such as are not over ruled and opprest by the Portingales, which take the people, and make them slaves, for which they are hated," in *John Huigen van Linschoten. His Discours of Voyages into the Easte and West Indies . . .*, trans. William Phillip (London, [1598]) , 198.

25. Purchas, *Purchas His Pilgrimes*, XVI, 513–15, 506. See also the early translation of a famous Spanish condemnation of the abuse of Indians in which they were said to be held in "an absolute, perpetuall, forced, and unwilling bondage." Bartolomé de las Casas, *The Spanish Colonie, or Briefe Chronicle of the Actes and Gestes of the Spaniardes in the West Indies . . .* (London, 1583) , 4 and *passim.*

in 1556 "that the Portingals were bad men, and that they made them slaves, if they could take them, and would put yrons upon their legges." There were "rich trades" on that coast in Negroes "which be caried continually to the West Indies." The Portuguese in the Congo "have divers rich Commodities from this Kingdome, but the most important is every yeere about five thousand Slaves, which they transport from thence, and sell them at good round prices in . . . the West Indies." In the New World the Spaniards "buy many slaves to follow their husbandry" and had "Negros to worke in the mynes." As for the Negroes, according to an Englishman they "doe daily lie in waite to practice their deliverance out of that thraldome and bondage, that the Spaniards do keepe them in"; according to a Spanish official, "there is no trust nor confidence in any of these Negros, and therefore we must take heede and beware of them, for they are our mortall enemies." [26] By 1600 the European demand for slaves in Africa had altered the character of West African slavery, which for the most part had been a household institution very different from the chattel slavery practiced in America. A description of Guinea by an unnamed Dutchman explained that "in this Warre whosoever is taken Prisoner they make him a slave all his life long"; the "Kings of the Townes have many Slaves, which they buy and sell, and get much by them; and to be briefe, in those Countries there are no men to be hired to worke or goe of any errand for money, but such as are Slaves and Captives, which are to spend their dayes in slaverie." [27]

Some Englishmen decided that there might be profit in supplying the Spanish with Negroes, despite the somewhat theoretical prohibition of foreigners from the Spanish dominions in the New World. John Hawkins was first; in the 1560's he made three voyages to Africa, the islands, and home. The first two were very successful; the third met disaster at San Juan de Ulua when the Spanish attacked his ships, took most of them, and turned the captured English seamen over to the Inquisition. [28] This famous incident, which thoroughly provoked a young captain on the expedition, Francis Drake, may have done something to discourage English slave trading in favor of other maritime activities. English vessels were not again active frequently in the slave trade until the next century.

26. Hakluyt, *Principal Navigations*, VI, 200, VII, 98, VI, 110, X, 445, IX, 430, X, 149.
27. Purchas, *Purchas His Pilgrimes*, VI, 306, 341–42.
28. Well told by Rayner Unwin, *The Defeat of John Hawkins: A Biography of His Third Slaving Voyage* (N. Y., 1960).

As assiduously collected by Richard Hakluyt, the various accounts of the Hawkins voyages did not state explicitly that English seamen were making "slaves" of Negroes. They scarcely needed to do so. On the first voyage in 1562 Hawkins learned at the Canary Islands "that Negroes were very good marchandise in Hispaniola, and that store of Negroes might easily be had upon the coast of Guinea." At Sierra Leone Hawkins "got into his possession, partly by the sword, and partly by other meanes . . . 300. Negroes at the least." Thereupon, "with this praye" he sailed westwards where he "made vent of" the Negroes to the Spaniards. On his second voyage he was able to get hold of Negroes from one tribe which another tribe "tooke in the warres, as their slaves," and he attacked the town of Bymba where the "Portingals" told him "hee might gette a hundreth slaves." On the third voyage, in 1567, Hawkins agreed with an African chief to join in attacking another town "with promise, that as many Negroes as by these warres might be obtained, as well of his part as ours, should be at our pleasure." Eventually the English "obtained betweene 4. and 500. Negroes, where with we thought it somewhat reasonable to seek the coast of the West Indies, and there, for our Negroes, and other our merchandise, we hoped to obtaine . . . some gaines." [29] Gain they did until a Spanish admiral caught up with them.

The Hawkins voyages were the principal but not the only instances where Englishmen had direct contact with the sixteenth-century trade in Negroes. George Fenner, who was offered "Negroes for ware" by some Portuguese on his way out to Guinea in 1566, sold five Negroes to a Portuguese vessel on his way back. In 1592 off the Isle of Dominica William King captured "a shippe of an hundred tunnes come from Guiny, laden with two hundred and seventy Negros." [30] Long before English settlement in the New World, there were English merchants who knew the prices Negroes were bringing there. At the Admiralty Court hearing after the third Hawkins voyage, William Fowler, who had not been with Hawkins, was called in to testify concerning the value of the Negroes lost at San Juan de Ulua. Fowler deposed "that the best trade in those places is of Negroes: the trade whereof he hath used, and hath sold Negroes at the said places; and seen other merchants likewise sell their Negroes there, divers times." [31]

29. Hakluyt, *Principal Navigations*, X, 7–8, 17–18, 21–22, 64–66.
30. *Ibid.*, VI, 277, 284, X, 191.
31. Edward Arber, ed., *An English Garner: Ingatherings from Our History and Literature*, 8 vols. ([London], 1877–96), V, 228–29.

By the end of the first quarter of the seventeenth century it had become abundantly evident in England that Negroes were being enslaved on an international scale. A century before, Leo Africanus had referred frequently to "Negro-slaves" in North Africa. By 1589 Negroes had become so pre-eminently "slaves" that Richard Hakluyt gratuitously referred to five Africans brought temporarily to England as "black slaves." [32] Readers of Hakluyt, Purchas, and other popular accounts were informed that the Dutch had "Blacks (which are Slaves)" in the East Indies; that Greeks ventured "into Arabia to steale Negroes"; that the "blacks of Mozambique" were frequently taken as "slaves" to India, and, according to George Sandys, that near Cairo merchants purchased "Negroes" (for "slavery") who came from the upper Nile and were "descended of *Chus,* the Sonne of cursed *Cham;* as are all of that complexion." [33]

As suggested by Sandys's remark, an equation had developed between African Negroes and slavery. Primarily, the associations were with the Portuguese and Spanish, with captivity, with buying and selling in Guinea and in America. While the Negro's exact status in America was not entirely clear, neither was it conceived as an off-brand of apprenticeship or servitude: Hawkins assumed as his crest a "demi-Moor" (plainly Negroid) "captive and bound." [34] Nor was Portuguese or Spanish slavery regarded as being of a mild, protective sort:

The Portugals doe marke them as we doe Sheepe with a hot Iron, which the Moores call Crimbo, the poore slaves stand all in a row . . . and sing Mundele que sumbela he Carey ha belelelle, and thus the poore rogues are beguiled, for the Portugals make them beleeve that they that have not the marke is not accounted a man of any account in Brasil or in Portugall, and thos they bring the poore Moores to be in a most damnable bondage under the colour of love.[35]

Englishmen had no special wish to emulate their rivals in these cruelties, unless like Hawkins they could silently profit by raiding some villages and furnishing transportation. There is no reason to suppose Englishmen eager to enslave Negroes, nor even to regard

32. Leo Africanus, *The History and Description of Africa,* trans. Pory, ed. Brown, I, 76–77, II, 309, 482, III, 724, 780, 791, 835; Hakluyt, *Principall Navigations* (1589), 97.

33. Purchas, *Purchas His Pilgrimes,* IV, 519; Hakluyt, *Principal Navigations,* V, 301–2; Burnell and Tiele, *Voyage of Linschoten,* I, 275; [George Sandys], *A Relation of a Journey Begun An: Dom: 1610 . . . ,* 2d ed. (London, 1621), 136, which was reprinted by Purchas, *Purchas His Pilgrimes,* VI, 213.

34. Markham, ed., *The Hawkins' Voyages,* xi; see also Donnan, ed., *Documents of the Slave Trade,* I, 44–71.

35. Purchas, *Purchas His Pilgrimes,* XVI, 269.

Richard Jobson eccentric in his response to a chief's offer to buy some "slaves": "I made answer, We were a people, who did not deale in any such commodities, neither did wee buy or sell one another, or any that had our owne shapes." [36] By the seventeenth century, after all, English prejudices as well as English law were *in favorem libertatis.*

When they came to settle in America, Englishmen found that things happened to liberty, some favorable, some not. Negroes became slaves, partly because there were social and economic necessities in America which called for some sort of bound, controlled labor. The Portuguese and Spanish had set an example, which, however rough in outline, proved to be, at very least, suggestive to Englishmen. It would be surprising if there had been a clear-cut line of influence from Latin to English slavery.[37] Elizabethans were not in the business of modeling themselves after Spaniards. Yet from about 1550, Englishmen were in such continual contact with the Spanish that they could hardly have failed to acquire the notion that Negroes could be enslaved. Precisely what slavery *meant,* of course, was a matter of English preconceptions patterning the information from overseas, but from the first, Englishmen tended to associate, in a diffuse way, Negroes with the Portuguese and Spanish. The term *negro* itself was incorporated into English from the Hispanic languages in mid-sixteenth century and *mulatto* a half century later. This is the more striking because a perfectly adequate term, identical in meaning to *negro,* already existed in English; of course *black* was used also, though not so commonly in the sixteenth century as later.

The fashion in which this absorption of foreign values took place may be illustrated by a remarkable passage in a book by a well-known Puritan theologian, Paul Baynes, who died in 1617, two years before the first Negroes arrived in the English colonies. Except for the four words set here in italics, his remarks were commonplace.

Now servants are either more slavish, or else more free and liberall: the first are such whose bodies are perpetually put under the power of the

36. Jobson, *The Golden Trade,* ed. Kingsley, 112.
37. The *clearest* instance of *direct* influence in America is probably the experience of Christopher Newport who was in Virginia five times between 1607 and 1611 and who had commanded a voyage in 1591 to the West Indies on which, as a member of his company reported, "wee tooke a Portugall ship . . . from Gunie . . . bound for Cartagena, wherein were 300. Negros young and olde." The English mariners took the prize to Puerto Rico and sent a Portuguese merchant ashore because "he hoped to help us to some money for his Negros there." Hakluyt, *Principal Navigations,* X, 184–85.

Master, *as Blackmores with us;* of which kinds servants are made sometime forcibly, as in captivity: sometime voluntarily, as when one doth willingly make himselfe over: sometime naturally, as the children of servants are borne the slaves of their Masters; and this [following type] was the most frequent kinde of service, wherein parties are upon certaine termes or conditions for a certaine time onely under the power of a man: such are our Apprentises, Journeymen, maideservants, etc.[38]

Here, Negroes were incorporated casually into a thoroughly conventional discussion of age-old categories of servitude. His use of Negroes to illustrate a traditional category of bound labor would not have been possible much earlier. Baynes knew, as everyone did, that the "more slavish" variety of servitude had disappeared in England.

Actually, it is possible that someone else added the "Blackmores" to Baynes's remarks after his death in 1617. In this period sermons were sometimes published with the speaker's original notes as the only basis for the final text, and the colossal tome which contains this passage was not published until the early 1640's. It is possible, therefore, that "as Blackmores with us" reflected more than an accidental spark struck off by English contact with the Hispanic world. For by 1640 it was becoming apparent that in many of the new colonies overseas the English settlers had obtained Negroes and were holding them, frequently, as hereditary slaves for life.

In considering the development of slavery in various groups of colonies, the above passage of (if not by) Paul Baynes can serve as a summary of the most essential features of the Negro's status as a slave. As the passage suggests, that status was at first distinguished from servitude more by duration than by onerousness; the key term in this and in many other early descriptions of the Negro's condition was *perpetual.* Negroes served "for ever" and so would their children. Englishmen did not do so. Despite his conflation of the terms *servant* and *slave,* Baynes clearly differentiated the two statuses, and in this his thinking was typical. Servitude, no matter how

38. Paul Bayne[s], *An Entire Commentary upon the Whole Epistle of the Apostle Paul to the Ephesians* . . . (London, 16[41–]43), 694–95 (italics mine). Too late for incorporation in the text, I came across a discussion published in 1627 which described five varieties of "servants." The author, a minister, used that term except for one category, the *"servi belli,* as these that are taken slaves in the wars." In this context he explained that "this curse to be a servant was laid, first upon a disobedient sonne *Cham,* and wee see to this day, that the *Moores, Chams* posteritie, are sold like slaves yet." This passage suggests how clearly defined a condition slavery was for Englishmen and that they associated it with Negroes, but of course it fails to disclose *who* is selling Negroes as slaves "yet." John Weemse [i.e., Weemes], *The Portraiture of the Image of God in Man* . . . (London, 1627), 279.

long, brutal, and involuntary, was not the same thing as perpetual slavery. Servitude comprehended alike the young apprentice, the orphan, the indentured servant, the redemptioner, the convicted debtor or criminal, the political prisoner, and, even, the Scottish and Irish captive of war who was sold as a "slave" to New England or Barbados. Yet none of these persons, no matter how miserably treated, served for life in the colonies, though of course many died before their term ended.[39] Hereditary lifetime service was restricted to Indians and Negroes. Among the various English colonies in the New World, this service known as "slavery" seems first to have developed in the international cockpit known as the Caribbean.

5. ENSLAVEMENT: THE WEST INDIES

The Englishmen who settled the Caribbean colonies were not very different from those who went to Virginia, Bermuda, Maryland, or even New England. Their experience in the islands, however, was very different indeed. By 1640 there were roughly as many English in the little islands as on the American continent. A half century after the first settlements were established in the 1620's, the major islands—Barbados, St. Kitts and the other Leeward Islands—were overcrowded. Thousands of whites who had been squeezed off the land by burgeoning sugar plantations migrated to other English colonies, including much larger Jamaica which had been captured from the Spanish in 1655. Their places were taken by Negro slaves who had been shipped to the islands, particularly after 1640, to meet an insatiable demand for labor which was cheap to maintain, easy to dragoon, and simple to replace when worked to death. Negroes outnumbered whites in Barbados as early as 1660. This rapid and thorough commitment to slavery placed white settlers under an ever-present danger of slave rebellion (the first rising came in 1638 on Providence Island), and whereas in the very early years authorities had rightly been fearful of white servant revolt, by the 1670's they were casting about desperately for means to attract white servants as protection against foreign and servile attack. Negro slavery matured hothouse fashion in the islands.

This compression of development was most clearly evident in the Puritan colony on the tiny island of Providence 150 miles off the coast of Central America, first settled in 1629 though not a going

---

39. Smith, *Colonists in Bondage*, 171, said flatly that "there was never any such thing as perpetual slavery for any white man in any English colony." To my knowledge, he was correct.

concern for several years. During the brief period before the Spanish snuffed out the colony in 1641 the settlers bought so many Negroes that white men were nearly outnumbered, and in England the Providence Company, apprehensive over possible Negro uprisings (with good reason as it turned out), drew up regulations for restricting the ratio of slaves to white men, "well knowing that if all men be left at Libty to buy as they please no man will take of English servants." [40] Not only were Negroes cheaper to maintain but it was felt that they could legitimately be treated in a different way from Englishmen—they could be held to service for life. At least this was the impression prevailing among officials of the Providence Company in London, for in 1638 they wrote Governor Nathaniel Butler and the Council, "We also think it reasonable that wheras the English servants are to answer XX [pounds of tobacco] per head the Negros being procured at Cheaper rates more easily kept as perpetuall servants should answer 40 [pounds of tobacco] per head. And the rather that the desire of English bodyes may be kept, we are depending upon them for the defence of the Island. We shall also expect that Negroes performe service in the publique works in double proporcon to the English." [41]

In Barbados this helpful idea that Negroes served for life seems to have existed even before they were purchased in large numbers. In 1627 the ship bearing the first eighty settlers captured a prize from which ten Negroes were seized, so white men and Negroes settled the island together.[42] Any doubt which may have existed as to the appropriate status of Negroes was dispelled in 1636 when Governor Henry Hawley and the Council resolved "that *Negroes* and *Indians,* that came here to be sold, should serve for Life, unless a Contract was before made to the contrary." [43] Europeans were not treated in

40. Earl of Holland, John Pym, Robert Warwick, and others to Governor and Council, London, July 3, 1638, Box 9, bundle: 2d and last portion of List no. 3, *re* Royal African Co. and Slavery Matters, 17, Parish Transcripts, New-York Historical Society, New York City. For Providence, see Arthur P. Newton, *The Colonising Activities of the English Puritans: The Last Phase of the Elizabethan Struggle with Spain* (New Haven, 1914); for further details on early slavery in the English West Indies and New England, Winthrop D. Jordan, "The Influence of the West Indies on the Origins of New England Slavery," *William and Mary Quarterly*, 3d Ser., 18 (1961), 243–50.

41. Earl of Holland and others to Governor and Council, July 3, 1638, Box 9, bundle: 2d and last portion of List no. 3, *re* Royal African Co. and Slavery Matters, 17, Parish Transcripts, N.-Y. Hist. Soc.

42. Vincent T. Harlow, *A History of Barbados, 1625–1685* (Oxford, 1926), 4.

43. [William Duke], *Memoirs of the First Settlement of the Island of Barbados and Other the Carribbee Islands, with the Succession of the Governors and Commanders in Chief of Barbados to the Year 1742* . . . (London, 1743), 20.

this manner: in 1643 Governor Philip Bell set at liberty fifty Portuguese who had been captured in Brazil and then offered for sale to Barbadians by a Dutch ship. The Governor seems to have been shocked by the proposed sale of Christian white men.[44] In the 1650's several observers referred to the lifetime slavery of Negroes as if it were a matter of common knowledge. "Its the Custome for a Christian servant to serve foure yeares," one wrote at the beginning of the decade, "and then enjoy his freedome; and (which hee hath dearly earned) 10£ Ster. or the value of it in goods if his Master bee soe honest as to pay it; the Negros and Indians (of which latter there are but few here) they and the generation are Slaves to their owners to perpetuity." The widely read Richard Ligon wrote in 1657: "The Iland is divided into three sorts of men, *viz*. Masters, Servants, and slaves. The slaves and their posterity, being subject to their Masters for ever, are kept and preserv'd with greater care then the servants, who are theirs but for five yeers, according to the law of the Iland." [45] Finally, one Henry Whistler described the people of the island delightfully in 1655:

The genterey heare doth live far better than ours doue in England: thay have most of them 100 or 2 or 3 of slaves apes whou they command as they pleas: hear they may say what they have is thayer oune: and they have that Libertie of contienc which wee soe long have in England foght for: But they doue abus it. This Island is inhabited with all sortes: with English, french, Duch, Scotes, Irish, Spaniards thay being Jues: with Ingones and miserabell Negors borne to perpetuall slavery thay and thayer seed: these Negors they doue alow as many wifes as thay will have, sume will have 3 or 4, according as they find thayer bodie abell: our English heare doth think a negor child the first day it is born to be worth 05[11], they cost them noething the bringing up, they goe all ways naked: some planters will have 30 more or les about 4 or 5 years ould: they sele them from one to the other as we doue shepe. This Illand is the Dunghill wharone England doth cast forth its rubidg: Rodgs and hors and such like peopel are those which are gennerally Broght heare.[46]

Dunghill or no dunghill, Barbados was treating her Negroes as slaves for life.

The rapid introduction of Negro slavery into the English islands

44. Alan Burns, *History of the British West Indies* (London, 1954), 232n.

45. "A Breife Discription of the Ilande of Barbados," Vincent T. Harlow, ed., *Colonising Expeditions to the West Indies and Guiana, 1623–1667 (Works Issued by the Hakluyt Soc.*, 2d Ser., 56 [1925]), 44–45; Richard Ligon, *A True and Exact History of the Island of Barbadoes . . .* (London, 1657), 43.

46. "Extracts from Henry Whistler's Journal of the West India Expedition," Charles H. Firth, ed., *The Narrative of General Venables, with an Appendix of Papers Relating to the Expedition to the West Indies and the Conquest of Jamaica, 1654–1655* (London, 1900), 146.

was accomplished without leaving any permanent trace of hesitation or misgivings. This was not the case in many of the continental colonies, both because different geographic and economic conditions prevailed there and because these conditions permitted a more complete and successful transplantation of English ways and values. This difference was particularly pronounced in New England, and it was therefore particularly ironic that the treatment accorded Negroes in New England seems to have been directly influenced by the West Indian model.

6. ENSLAVEMENT: NEW ENGLAND

Negro slavery never really flourished in New England. It never became so important or so rigorous as in the plantation colonies to the southwards. There were relatively few Negroes, only a few hundred in 1680 and not more than 3 per cent of the population in the eighteenth century; no one thought that Negroes were about to rise and overwhelm the white community.[47] Treatment of slaves in New England was milder even than the laws allowed: Negroes were not employed in gangs except occasionally in the Narragansett region of Rhode Island, and the established codes of family, congregation, and community mitigated the condition of servitude generally. Negroes were not treated very differently from white servants—except that somehow they and their children served for life.

The question with New England slavery is not why it was weakly rooted, but why it existed at all. No staple crop demanded regiments of raw labor. That there was no compelling economic demand for Negroes is evident in the numbers actually imported: economic exigencies scarcely required establishment of a distinct status for only 3 per cent of the labor force. Indentured servitude was adequate to New England's needs, and in fact some Negroes became free servants rather than slaves. Why, then, did New Englanders enslave Negroes, probably as early as 1638? Why was it that the Puritans rather mindlessly (which was not their way) accepted slavery for Negroes and Indians but not for white men?

The early appearance of slavery in New England may in part be explained by the provenance of the first Negroes imported. They

47. Lorenzo J. Greene, *The Negro in Colonial New England, 1620–1776* (N. Y., 1942) ; report by the Massachusetts governor, Box 4, bundle: The Royal African Co. of England, MS. relating to the Company's trade in Negroes (1672–1734/35) , 13, Parish Transcripts, N.-Y. Hist. Soc.

were brought by Captain William Peirce of the Salem ship *Desire* in 1638 from the Providence Island colony where Negroes were already being kept as perpetual servants.[48] A minor traffic in Negroes and other products developed between the two Puritan colonies, though evidently some of the Negroes proved less than satisfactory, for Governor Butler was cautioned by the Providence Company to take special care of "the cannibal negroes brought from New England." [49] After 1640 a brisk trade got under way between New England and the other English islands, and Massachusetts vessels sometimes touched upon the West African coast before heading for the Caribbean. Trade with Barbados was particularly lively, and Massachusetts vessels carried Negroes to that bustling colony from Africa and the Cape Verde Islands. As John Winthrop gratefully described the salvation of New England's economy, "it pleased the Lord to open to us a trade with Barbados and other Islands in the West Indies." [50] These strange Negroes from the West Indies must surely have been accompanied by prevailing notions about their usual status. Ship masters who purchased perpetual service in Barbados would not have been likely to sell service for term in Boston. Then too, white settlers from the crowded islands migrated to New England, 1,200 from Barbados alone in the years 1643–47.[51]

No amount of contact with the West Indies could have by itself created Negro slavery in New England; settlers there had to be willing to accept the proposition. Because they were Englishmen, they were so prepared—and at the same time they were not. Characteristically, as Puritans, they officially codified this ambivalence in 1641 as follows: "there shall never be any bond-slavery, villenage or captivitie amongst us; unless it be lawfull captives taken in just warrs, and such strangers as willingly sell themselves, or are solde to us: and such shall have the libertyes and christian usages which the law of God established in Israell concerning such persons doth morally require, provided, this exempts none from servitude who shall be judged thereto by Authoritie." [52] Here were the wishes of the General Court as expressed in the Massachusetts

48. John Winthrop, *Winthrop's Journal: "History of New England,"* *1634–1649*, ed. James K. Hosmer, 2 vols. (N. Y., 1908), I, 260.

49. Newton, *Colonising Activities of the English Puritans*, 260–61.

50. Winthrop, *Journal*, ed. Hosmer, II, 73–74, 328; Donnan, ed., *Documents of the Slave Trade*, III, 4–5, 6, 9, 10, 11–14.

51. Harlow, *Barbados*, 340.

52. Max Farrand, ed., *The Laws and Liberties of Massachusetts* (Cambridge, Mass., 1929), 4. See the very good discussion in George H. Moore, *Notes on the History of Slavery in Massachusetts* (N. Y., 1866).

Body of Liberties, which is to say that as early as 1641 the Puritan settlers were seeking to guarantee in writing their own liberty without closing off the opportunity of taking it from others whom they identified with the Biblical term, "strangers." It was under the aegis of this concept that Theophilus Eaton, one of the founders of New Haven, seems to have owned Negroes before 1658 who were "servants forever or during his pleasure, according to Leviticus, 25: 45 and 46." [53] ("Of the children of the strangers that do sojourn among you, of them shall ye buy, and of their families . . . : and they shall be your possession. And ye shall take them as an inheritance for your children . . . ; they shall be your bondmen for ever: but over your brethren the children of Israel, ye shall not rule one over another with rigor.") Apart from this implication that bond slavery was reserved to those not partaking of true religion nor possessing proper nationality, the Body of Liberties expressly reserved the colony's right to enslave convicted criminals. For reasons not clear, this endorsement of an existing practice was followed almost immediately by discontinuance of its application to white men. The first instance of penal "slavery" in Massachusetts came in 1636, when an Indian was sentenced to "bee kept as a slave for life to worke, unles wee see further cause." Then in December 1638, ten months after the first Negroes arrived, the Quarter Court for the first time sentenced three white offenders to be "slaves"—a suggestive but perhaps meaningless coincidence. Having by June 1642 sentenced altogether some half dozen white men to "slavery" (and explicitly releasing several after less than a year) the Court stopped.[54] Slavery, as had been announced in the Body of Liberties, was to be only for "strangers."

The Body of Liberties made equally clear that captivity in a just war constituted legitimate grounds for slavery. The practice had begun during the first major conflict with the Indians, the Pequot War of 1637. Some of the Pequot captives had been shipped aboard the *Desire*, to Providence Island; accordingly, the first Negroes in New England arrived in exchange for men taken captive in a just war! That this provenance played an important role in shaping views about Negroes is suggested by the first recorded plea by an

53. Simeon E. Baldwin, "Theophilus Eaton, First Governor of the Colony of New Haven," New Haven Colony Historical Society, *Papers*, 7 (1908) , 31.

54. Nathaniel B. Shurtleff, ed., *Records of the Governor and Company of the Massachusetts Bay in New England*, 5 vols. in 6 (Boston, 1853–54) , I, 181, 246; John Noble and John F. Cronin, eds., *Records of the Court of Assistants of the Colony of the Massachusetts Bay, 1630–1692*, 3 vols. (Boston, 1901–28) , II, 78–79, 86, 90, 94, 97, 118.

Englishman on the North American continent for the establishment
of an African slave trade. Emanuel Downing, in a letter to his
brother-in-law John Winthrop in 1645, described the advantages:
"If upon a Just warre [with the Narragansett Indians] the Lord
should deliver them into our hands, wee might easily have men
woemen and children enough to exchange for Moores, which wilbe
more gaynefull pilladge for us then wee conceive, for I doe not see
how wee can thrive untill wee get into a stock of slaves sufficient to
doe all our buisiness, for our children's children will hardly see this
great Continent filled with people, soe that our servants will still
desire freedome to plant for themselves, and not stay but for verie
great wages. And I suppose you know verie well how wee shall
mayneteyne 20 Moores cheaper than one Englishe servant." [55]

These two facets of justifiable enslavement—punishment for
crime and captivity in war—were closely related. Slavery as punishment probably derived from analogy with captivity, since presumably a king or magistrates could mercifully spare and enslave a man
whose crime had forfeited his right to life. The analogy had not
been worked out by commentators in England, but a fairly clear
linkage between crime and captivity seems to have existed in the
minds of New Englanders concerning Indian slavery. In 1644 the
commissioners of the United Colonies meeting at New Haven decided, in light of the Indians' "proud affronts," "hostile practices,"
and "protectinge or rescuinge of offenders," that magistrates might
"send some convenient strength of English and, . . . seise and
bring away" Indians from any "plantation of Indians" which persisted in this practice and, if no satisfaction was forthcoming, could
deliver the "Indians seased . . . either to serve or be shipped out
and exchanged for Negroes." [56] Captivity and criminal justice
seemed to mean the same thing, slavery.

It would be wrong to suppose that all the Puritans' preconceived
ideas about freedom and bondage worked in the same direction.
While the concepts of difference in religion and of captivity worked
against Indians and Negroes, certain Scriptural injunctions and
English pride in liberty told in the opposite direction. In Massachusetts the magistrates demonstrated that they were not about to
tolerate glaring breaches of "the Law of God established in Israel"
even when the victims were Negroes. In 1646 the authorities ar-

55. Donnan, ed., *Documents of the Slave Trade*, III, 8.
56. Nathaniel B. Shurtleff and David Pulsifer, eds., *Records of the Colony of
New Plymouth in New England*, 12 vols. (Boston, 1855–61), IX, 70–71. See also
Ebenezer Hazard, comp., *Historical Collections; Consisting of State Papers, and
Other Authentic Documents* . . . , 2 vols. (Phila., 1792–94), II, 63–64.

rested two mariners, James Smith and Thomas Keyser, who had carried two Negroes directly from Africa and sold them in Massachusetts. What distressed the General Court was that the Negroes had been obtained during a raid on an African village and that this "haynos and crying sinn of man stealing" had transpired on the Lord's Day. The General Court decided to free the unfortunate victims and ship them back to Africa, though the death penalty for the crime (clearly mandatory in Scripture) was not imposed.[57] More quietly than in this dramatic incident, Puritan authorities extended the same protections against maltreatment to Negroes and Indians as to white servants.

Only once before the eighteenth century was New England slavery challenged directly, and in that instance the tone was as much bafflement as indignation. This famous Rhode Island protest perhaps derived from a diffuse Christian equalitarianism which operated to extend the English presumption of liberty to non-Englishmen. The Rhode Island law of 1652 actually forbade enslavement.

Whereas, there is a common course practised amongst English men to buy negers, to that end they may have them for service or slaves forever; for the preventigge of such practices among us, let it be ordered, that no blacke mankind or white being forced by covenent bond, or otherwise, to serve any man or his assignes longer than ten yeares, or untill they come to bee twentie four yeares of age, if they bee taken in under fourteen, from the time of thier cominge within the liberties of this Collonie. And at the end or terme of ten yeares to sett them free, as the manner is with the English servants. And that man that will not let them goe free, or shall sell them away elsewhere, to that end that they may bee enslaved to others for a long time, hee or they shall forfeit to the Collonie forty pounds.

Perhaps it was Rhode Island's tolerance of religious diversity and relatively high standard of justice for the Indian which led to this attempt to prevent Englishmen from taking advantage of a different people.[58]

57. Donnan, ed., *Documents of the Slave Trade*, III, 6–9. Exodus 21:16: "And he that stealeth a man, and selleth him, or if he be found in his hand, he shall surely be put to death." Compare with Deuteronomy 24:7: "If a man be found stealing any of his brethren of the children of Israel, and maketh merchandise of him, or selleth him; then that thief shall die; and thou shalt put evil away from among you."

58. John R. Bartlett, ed., *Records of the Colony of Rhode Island and Providence Plantations, in New England*, 10 vols. (Providence, 1856–65) , I, 243. The act passed during the Coddington secession; only two of the four towns, Providence and Warwick, were represented. Roger Williams was in England, and it seems likely Samuel Gorton pressed passage. The absence of the two southern towns (where trading in Negroes must have centered) suggests a strangely prophetic division of opinion. See Charles M. Andrews, *The Colonial Period of American History*, 4 vols. (New Haven, 1934–38) , II, 29–30.

The law remained a dead letter. The need for labor, the example set in the West Indies, the condition of Negroes as "strangers," and their initial connection with captive Indians combined to override any hesitation about introducing Negro bond slavery into New England. Laws regulating the conduct of Negroes specifically did not appear until the 1690's.[59] From the first, however, there were scattered signs that Negroes were regarded as different from English people not merely in their status as slaves. In 1639 Samuel Maverick of Noddles Island attempted, apparently rather clumsily, to breed two of his Negroes, or so an English visitor reported: *"Mr. Maverick was desirous to have a breed of Negroes, and therefore seeing [that his "Negro woman"] would not yield by persuasions to company with a Negro young man he had in his house; he commanded him will'd she nill'd she to go to bed to her which was no sooner done but she kickt him out again, this she took in high disdain beyond her slavery."* In 1652 the Massachusetts General Court ordered that Scotsmen, Indians, and Negroes should train with the English in the militia, but four years later abruptly excluded Negroes, as did Connecticut in 1660.[60] Evidently Negroes, even free Negroes, were regarded as distinct from the English. They were, in New England where economic necessities were not sufficiently pressing to determine the decision, treated differently from other men.

7. ENSLAVEMENT: VIRGINIA AND MARYLAND

In Virginia and Maryland the development of Negro slavery followed a very different course, for several reasons. Most obviously, geographic conditions and the intentions of the settlers quickly combined to produce a successful agricultural staple. The deep tidal rivers, the long growing season, the fertile soil, and the absence of strong communal spirit among the settlers opened the way. Ten years after settlers first landed at Jamestown they were on the way to proving, in the face of assertions to the contrary, that it was possible "to found an empire upon smoke." More than the

59. *The Acts and Resolves, Public and Private, of the Province of the Massachusetts Bay* . . . , 21 vols. (Boston, 1869–1922) , I, 130, 154, 156, 325, 327; J. Hammond Trumbull and Charles J. Hoadly, eds., *The Public Records of the Colony of Connecticut*, 15 vols. (Hartford, 1850–90) , IV, 40. For treatment of servants see Lawrence W. Towner, "'A Fondness for Freedom': Servant Protest in Puritan Society," *Wm. and Mary Qtly.*, 3d Ser., 19 (1962) , 201–19.

60. John Josselyn, *An Account of Two Voyages to New-England* . . . , 2d ed. (London, 1675) , reprinted in Massachusetts Historical Society, *Collections*, 3d Ser., 3 (1833) , 231; Shurtleff, ed., *Records of Massachusetts Bay*, III, 268, 397, IV, Pt. i, 86, 257; *Acts and Resolves Mass.*, I, 130; Trumbull and Hoadly, eds., *Recs. Col. Conn.*, I, 349.

miscellaneous productions of New England, tobacco required labor
which was cheap but not temporary, mobile but not independent,
and tireless rather than skilled. In the Chesapeake area more than
anywhere to the northward, the shortage of labor and the abundance of land—the "frontier"—placed a premium on involuntary
labor.

This need for labor played more directly upon these settlers' ideas
about freedom and bondage than it did either in the West Indies or
in New England. Perhaps it would be more accurate to say that
settlers in Virginia (and in Maryland after settlement in 1634)
made their decisions concerning Negroes while relatively virginal,
relatively free from external influences and from firm preconceptions. Of all the important early English settlements, Virginia had
the least contact with the Spanish, Portuguese, Dutch, and other
English colonies. At the same time, the settlers of Virginia did not
possess either the legal or Scriptural learning of the New England
Puritans whose conception of the just war had opened the way to
the enslavement of Indians. Slavery in the tobacco colonies did not
begin as an adjunct of captivity; in marked contrast to the Puritan
response to the Pequot War the settlers of Virginia did *not* generally
react to the Indian massacre of 1622 with propositions for taking
captives and selling them as "slaves." It was perhaps a correct
measure of the conceptual atmosphere in Virginia that there was
only one such proposition after the 1622 disaster and that that one
was defective in precision as to how exactly one treated captive
Indians.[61]

In the absence, then, of these influences which obtained in other
English colonies, slavery as it developed in Virginia and Maryland
assumes a special interest and importance over and above the fact
that Negro slavery was to become a vitally important institution
there and, later, to the southwards. In the tobacco colonies it is
possible to watch Negro slavery *develop*, not pop up full-grown
overnight, and it is therefore possible to trace, very imperfectly, the
development of the shadowy, unexamined rationale which supported it. The concept of Negro slavery there was neither borrowed
from foreigners, nor extracted from books, nor invented out of
whole cloth, nor extrapolated from servitude, nor generated by
English reaction to Negroes as such, nor necessitated by the exigencies of the New World. Not any one of these made the Negro a
slave, but all.

61. Kingsbury, ed., *Recs. Virginia Company*, III, 672–73, 704–7.

In rough outline, slavery's development in the tobacco colonies seems to have undergone three stages. Negroes first arrived in 1619, only a few days late for the meeting of the first representative assembly in America. John Rolfe described the event with the utmost unconcern: "About the last of August came in a dutch man of warre that sold us twenty Negars." [62] Negroes continued to trickle in slowly for the next half century; one report in 1649 estimated that there were three hundred among Virginia's population of fifteen thousand—about 2 per cent.[63] Long before there were more appreciable numbers, the development of slavery had, so far as we can tell, shifted gears. Prior to about 1640, there is very little evidence to show how Negroes were treated—though we will need to return to those first twenty years in a moment. After 1640 there is mounting evidence that some Negroes were in fact being treated as slaves, at least that they were being held in hereditary lifetime service. This is to say that the twin essences of slavery—the two kinds of perpetuity—first become evident during the twenty years prior to the beginning of legal formulation. After 1660 slavery was written into statute law. Negroes began to flood into the two colonies at the end of the seventeenth century. In 1705 Virginia produced a codification of laws applying to slaves.

Concerning the first of these stages, there is only one major historical certainty, and unfortunately it is the sort which historians find hardest to bear. There simply is not enough evidence to indicate with any certainty whether Negroes were treated like white servants or not. At least we can be confident, therefore, that the two most common assertions about the first Negroes—that they were slaves and that they were servants—are *unfounded*, though not necessarily incorrect. And what of the positive evidence?

Some of the first group bore Spanish names and presumably had been baptized, which would mean they were at least nominally Christian, though of the Papist sort. They had been "sold" to the English; so had other Englishmen but not by the Dutch. Certainly these Negroes were not fully free, but many Englishmen were not. It can be said, though, that from the first in Virginia Negroes were set apart from white men by the word *Negroes*. The earliest Virginia census reports plainly distinguished Negroes from white men, often giving Negroes no personal name; in 1629 every commander of the

62. Arber, ed., *Travels of John Smith*, II, 541.

63. *A Perfect Description of Virginia* . . . (London, 1649) , reprinted in Peter Force, ed., *Tracts* . . . , 4 vols. (N. Y., 1947) , II, no. 8.

several plantations was ordered to "take a generall muster of all the inhabitants men woemen and Children as well *Englishe* as Negroes." [64] A distinct name is not attached to a group unless it is regarded as distinct. It seems logical to suppose that this perception of the Negro as being distinct from the Englishman must have operated to debase his status rather than to raise it, for in the absence of countervailing social factors, the need for labor in the colonies usually told in the direction of non-freedom. There were few countervailing factors present, surely, in such instances as in 1629 when a group of Negroes were brought to Virginia freshly captured from a Portuguese vessel which had snatched them from Angola a few weeks earlier.[65] Given the context of English thought and experience sketched in this chapter, it seems probable that the Negro's status was not ever the same as that accorded the white servant. But we do not know for sure.

When the first fragmentary evidence appears about 1640 it becomes clear that *some* Negroes in both Virginia and Maryland were serving for life and some Negro children inheriting the same obligation.[66] Not all Negroes, certainly, for Nathaniel Littleton had released a Negro named Anthony Longoe from all service whatsoever in 1635, and after the mid-1640's the court records show that other Negroes were incontestably free and were accumulating property of their own. At least one Negro freeman, Anthony Johnson, himself owned a Negro. Some Negroes served only terms of usual length, but others were held for terms far longer than custom and statute permitted with white servants.[67] The first fairly clear indication that slavery was practiced in the tobacco colonies appears in 1639, when a Maryland statute declared that "all the Inhabitants of this Province being Christians (Slaves excepted) Shall have and enjoy all such rights liberties immunities priviledges and free customs within this Province as any naturall born subject of England." Another Maryland law passed the same year provided that "all

64. Henry R. McIlwaine, ed., *Minutes of the Council and General Court of Colonial Virginia, 1622–1632, 1670–1676* (Richmond, 1924), 196. Lists and musters of 1624 and 1625 are in John C. Hotten, ed., *The Original Lists of Persons of Quality . . .* (N. Y., 1880), 169–265.

65. Philip A. Bruce, *Economic History of Virginia in the Seventeenth Century . . .*, 2 vols. (N. Y., 1896), II, 73.

66. Further details are in Winthrop D. Jordan, "Modern Tensions and the Origins of American Slavery," *Journal of Southern History*, 28 (1962), 18–30.

67. Susie M. Ames, *Studies of the Virginia Eastern Shore in the Seventeenth Century* (Richmond, 1940), 99; John H. Russell, *The Free Negro in Virginia, 1619–1865* (Baltimore, 1913), 23–39; and his "Colored Freemen As Slave Owners in Virginia," *Journal of Negro History*, 1 (1916), 234–37.

persons being Christians (Slaves excepted)" over eighteen who were imported without indentures would serve for four years.[68] These laws make very little sense unless the term *slaves* meant Negroes and perhaps Indians.

The next year, 1640, the first definite indication of outright enslavement appears in Virginia. The General Court pronounced sentence on three servants who had been retaken after absconding to Maryland. Two of them, a Dutchman and a Scot, were ordered to serve their masters for one additional year and then the colony for three more, but "the third being a negro named John Punch shall serve his said master or his assigns for the time of his natural life here or else where." No white servant in any English colony, so far as is known, ever received a like sentence. Later the same month a Negro (possibly the same enterprising fellow) was again singled out from a group of recaptured runaways; six of the seven culprits were assigned additional time while the Negro was given none, presumably because he was already serving for life.[69]

After 1640, when surviving Virginia county court records began to mention Negroes, sales for life, often including any future progeny, were recorded in unmistakable language. In 1646 Francis Pott sold a Negro woman and boy to Stephen Charlton "to the use of him . . . forever." Similarly, six years later William Whittington sold to John Pott "one Negro girle named Jowan; aged about Ten yeares and with her Issue and produce duringe her (or either of them) for their Life tyme. And their Successors forever"; and a Maryland man in 1649 deeded two Negro men and a woman "and all their issue both male and Female." The executors of a York County estate in 1647 disposed of eight Negroes—four men, two women, and two children—to Captain John Chisman "to have hold occupy posesse and injoy and every one of the afforementioned Negroes forever." [70] The will of Rowland Burnham of "Rapahanocke," made in 1657, dispensed his considerable number of Negroes and white servants in language which clearly differentiated between the two by specifying that the whites were to serve for their "full terme of tyme" and the Negroes "for ever." [71] Noth-

68. *Archives Md.*, I, 41, 80, also 409, 453–54.

69. "Decisions of the General Court," *Virginia Magazine of History and Biography*, 5 (1898), 236–37.

70. For these four cases, Northampton County Deeds, Wills, etc., no. 4 (1651–54), 28 (misnumbered 29), 124, Virginia State Library, Richmond; *Archives Md.*, XLI, 261–62; York County Records, no. 2 (transcribed Wills and Deeds, 1645–49), 256–57, Va. State Lib.

71. Lancaster County Loose Papers, Box of Wills, 1650–1719, Folder 1656–1659, Va. State Lib.

ing in the will indicated that this distinction was exceptional or novel.

Further evidence that some Negroes were serving for life in this period lies in the prices paid for them. In many instances the valuations placed on Negroes (in estate inventories and bills of sale) were far higher than for white servants, even those servants with full terms yet to serve. Higher prices must have meant that Negroes were more highly valued because of their greater length of service. Negro women may have been especially prized, moreover, because their progeny could also be held perpetually. In 1643, for example, William Burdett's inventory listed eight servants, with the time each had still to serve, at valuations ranging from 400 to 1,100 pounds of tobacco, while a "very anntient" Negro was valued at 3,000 and an eight-year-old Negro girl at 2,000 pounds, with no time remaining indicated for either. In the late 1650's an inventory of Thomas Ludlow's estate evaluated a white servant with six years to serve at less than an elderly Negro man and only one half of a Negro woman.[72] Similarly, the labor owned by James Stone in 1648 was evaluated as follows:

	lb tobo
Thomas Groves, 4 yeares to serve	1300
Francis Bomley for 6 yeares	1500
John Thackstone for 3 yeares	1300
Susan Davis for 3 yeares	1000
Emaniell a Negro man	2000
Roger Stone 3 yeares	1300
Mingo a Negro man	2000 [73]

The 1655 inventory of Argoll Yeardley's estate provides clear evidence of a distinction between perpetual and limited service for Negroes. Under the heading "Servants" were listed "Towe Negro men, towe Negro women (their wifes) one Negro girle aged 15 yeares, Item One Negro girle aged about teen yeares and one Negro child aged about sixe moneths," valued at 12,000 pounds, and under the heading "Corne" were "Servants, towe men their tyme three months," valued at 300 pounds, and "one Negro boye ["about three yeares old"] (which by witness of his godfather) is to bee free att twenty foure yeares of age and then to have towe cowes given him,"

72. Northampton County Orders, Deeds, Wills, etc., no. 2 (1640–45), 224; York County Deeds, Orders, Wills, etc. (1657–62), 108–9; in 1645 two Negro women and a boy sold for 5,500 lbs. of tobacco, York County Records, no. 2, 63; all Va. State Lib.

73. York County Records, no. 2, 390, Va. State Lib.

valued at 600 pounds.[74] Besides setting a higher value on Negroes, these inventories failed to indicate the number of years they had still to serve, presumably because their service was for an unlimited time.

Where Negro women were involved, higher valuations probably reflected the facts that their issue were valuable and that they could be used for field work while white women generally were not. This latter discrimination between Negro and white women did not necessarily involve perpetual service, but it meant that Negroes were set apart in a way clearly not to their advantage. This was not the only instance in which Negroes were subjected to degrading distinctions not immediately and necessarily attached to the concept of slavery. Negroes were singled out for special treatment in several ways which suggest a generalized debasement of Negroes as a group. Significantly, the first indications of this debasement appeared at about the same time as the first indications of actual enslavement.

The distinction concerning field work is a case in point. It first appears on the written record in 1643, when Virginia almost pointedly endorsed it in a tax law. Previously, in 1629, tithable persons had been defined as "all those that worke in the ground of what qualitie or condition soever." The new law provided that *all* adult men were tithable and, in addition, *Negro* women. The same distinction was made twice again before 1660. Maryland adopted a similar policy beginning in 1654.[75] This official discrimination between Negro and other women was made by men who were accustomed to thinking of field work as being ordinarily the work of men rather than women. As John Hammond wrote in a 1656 tract defending the tobacco colonies, servant women were not put to work in the fields but in domestic employments, "yet som wenches that are nasty, and beastly and not fit to be so employed are put into the ground." [76] The essentially racial character of this discrimination stood out clearly in a law passed in 1668 at the time slavery was taking shape in the statute books:

Whereas some doubts, have arisen whether negro women set free were still to be accompted tithable according to a former act, *It is declared by this*

74. Nora Miller Turman and Mark C. Lewis, eds., "Inventory of the Estate of Argoll Yeardley of Northampton County, Virginia, in 1655," *Va. Mag. of Hist. and Biog.*, 70 (1962), 410–19.

75. Hening, ed., *Statutes Va.*, I, 144, 242, 292, 454; *Archives Md.*, I, 342, II, 136, 399, 538–39, XIII, 538–39.

76. John Hammond, *Leah and Rachel, or, the Two Fruitfull Sisters Virginia, and Mary-land: Their Present Condition, Impartially Stated and Related* . . . (London, 1656), 9.

grand assembly that negro women, though permitted to enjoy their Free-dome yet ought not in all respects to be admitted to a full fruition of the exemptions and impunities of the English, and are still lyable to payment of taxes.[77]

Virginia law set Negroes apart from all other groups in a second way by denying them the important right and obligation to bear arms. Few restraints could indicate more clearly the denial to Negroes of membership in the white community. This first fore-shadowing of the slave codes came in 1640, at just the time when other indications first appeared that Negroes were subject to special treatment.[78]

Finally, an even more compelling sense of the separateness of Negroes was revealed in early reactions to sexual union between the races. Prior to 1660 the evidence concerning these reactions is equiv-ocal, and it is not possible to tell whether repugnance for intermix-ture preceded legislative enactment of slavery. In 1630 an angry Virginia court sentenced "Hugh Davis to be soundly whipped, before an assembly of Negroes and others for abusing himself to the dishonor of God and shame of Christians, by defiling his body in lying with a negro," but it is possible that the "negro" may not have been female. With other instances of punishment for interracial union in the ensuing years, fornication rather than miscegenation may well have been the primary offense, though in 1651 a Maryland man sued someone who he claimed had said "that he had a black bastard in Virginia." (The court recognized the legitimacy of his complaint, but thought his claim for £20,000 sterling somewhat

77. Hening, ed., *Statutes Va.*, II, 267.

78. *Ibid.*, I, 226; for the same act in more detail, "Acts of General Assembly, Jan. 6, 1639-40," *Wm. and Mary Qtly.*, 2d Ser., 4 (1924), 147. In Bermuda, always closely connected with Virginia, the first prohibition of weapons to Negroes came in 1623, only seven years after the first Negro landed. The 1623 law was the first law anywhere in English specifically dealing with Negroes. After stressing the insolence of Negroes secretly carrying "cudgells and other weapons and working tools, very dangerous and not meete to be suffered to be carried by such vassalls," it prohibited (in addition to arms) Negroes going abroad at night, trespassing on other people's lands, and trading in tobacco without permission of their masters. Unfortunately the evidence concerning lifetime service for Negroes is much less definite in the scanty Bermuda sources than in those for Maryland and Virginia; the first known incident suggestive of the practice might reasonably be placed anywhere from 1631 to 1656. Later evidence shows Bermuda's slavery and proportion of Negroes similar to Virginia's, and it seems unlikely that the two colonies' early experience was radically different. Henry C. Wilkinson, *The Adventurers of Bermuda; A History of the Island from Its Discovery until the Dissolution of the Somers Island Company in 1684* (London, 1933), 114; J. H. Lefroy, comp., *Memorials of the Discovery and Early Settlement of the Bermudas or Somers Islands, 1515-1685* . . . , 2 vols. (London, 1877-79), I, 308-9, 505, 526-27, 633, 645, II, 34-35, 70. But Negroes were to be armed at times of alarm (*ibid.*, II, 242, 366, 380 [1666-73]): Bermuda was exposed to foreign attack.

overvalued his reputation and awarded him 1500 pounds "of Tobacco and Cask.") [79] There may have been no racial feeling involved when in 1640 Robert Sweet, a gentleman, was compelled "to do penance in church according to laws of England, for getting a negroe woman with child and the woman whipt." [80] About 1650 a white man and a Negro woman were required to stand clad in white sheets before a congregation in lower Norfolk County for having had relations, but this punishment was sometimes used in cases of fornication between two whites. [81] A quarter century later in 1676, however, the emergence of distaste for racial intermixture was unmistakable. A contemporary account of Bacon's Rebellion caustically described one of the ringleaders, Richard Lawrence, as a person who had eclipsed his learning and abilities "in the darke imbraces of a Blackamoore, his slave: And that in so fond a Maner, . . . to the noe meane Scandle and affrunt of all the Vottrisses in or about towne." [82]

Such condemnation was not confined to polemics. In the early 1660's when slavery was gaining statutory recognition, the assemblies acted with full-throated indignation against miscegenation. These acts aimed at more than merely avoiding confusion of status. In 1662 Virginia declared that "if any christian shall committ Fornication with a negro man or woman, hee or shee soe offending" should pay double the usual fine. (The next year Bermuda prohibited all sexual relations between whites and Negroes.) Two years later Maryland banned interracial marriages: "forasmuch as divers freeborne English women forgettfull of their free Condicion and to the disgrace of our Nation doe intermarry with Negro Slaves by which alsoe divers suites may arise touching the Issue of such woemen and a great damage doth befall the Masters of such Negros for prevention whereof for deterring such freeborne women from such shamefull Matches," strong language indeed if "divers suites" had been the only problem. A Maryland act of 1681 described marriages of white women with Negroes as, among other things, "always to the Satisfaccion of theire Lascivious and Lustfull desires, and to the disgrace not only of the English butt allso of many other

---

79. Hening, ed., *Statutes Va.*, I, 146. (The term "negro woman" was in very common use.) *Archives Md.*, X, 114–15.

80. Hening, ed., *Statutes Va.*, I, 552; McIlwaine, ed., *Minutes Council Va.*, 477.

81. Bruce, *Economic History of Va.*, II, 110.

82. "The History of Bacon's and Ingram's Rebellion, 1676," in Charles M. Andrews, ed., *Narratives of the Insurrections, 1675–1690* (N. Y., 1915), 96. Cf. the will of John Fenwick (1683), *Documents Relating to the Colonial, Revolutionary and Post-Revolutionary History of the State of New Jersey . . .* [New Jersey Archives], 1st Ser. (Newark, etc., 1880–1949), XXIII, 162.

Christian Nations." When Virginia finally prohibited all interracial liaisons in 1691, the Assembly vigorously denounced miscegenation and its fruits as "that abominable mixture and spurious issue." [83]

From the surviving evidence, it appears that outright enslavement and these other forms of debasement appeared at about the same time in Maryland and Virginia. Indications of perpetual service, the very nub of slavery, coincided with indications that English settlers discriminated against Negro women, withheld arms from Negroes, and—though the timing is far less certain—reacted unfavorably to interracial sexual union. The coincidence suggests a mutual relationship between slavery and unfavorable assessment of Negroes. Rather than slavery causing "prejudice," or vice versa, they seem rather to have generated each other. Both were, after all, twin aspects of a general debasement of the Negro. Slavery and "prejudice" may have been equally cause and effect, continuously reacting upon each other, dynamically joining hands to hustle the Negro down the road to complete degradation. Much more than with the other English colonies, where the enslavement of Negroes was to some extent a borrowed practice, the available evidence for Maryland and Virginia points to less borrowing and to this kind of process: a mutually interactive growth of slavery and unfavorable assessment, with no cause for either which did not cause the other as well. If slavery caused prejudice, then invidious distinctions concerning working in the fields, bearing arms, and sexual union should have appeared *after* slavery's firm establishment. If prejudice caused slavery, then one would expect to find these lesser discriminations preceding the greater discrimination of outright enslavement. Taken as a whole, the evidence reveals a process of debasement of which hereditary lifetime service was an important but not the only part.

White servants did not suffer this debasement. Rather, their position improved, partly for the reason that they were not Negroes. By the early 1660's white men were loudly protesting against being made "slaves" in terms which strongly suggest that they considered slavery not as wrong but as inapplicable to themselves. The father of a Maryland apprentice petitioned in 1663 that "he Craves that his daughter may not be made a Slave a tearme soe Scandalous that if admitted to be the Condicon or tytle of the Apprentices in this

---

83. Hening, ed., *Statutes Va.*, II, 170, III, 86–87; *Archives Md.*, I, 533–34, VII, 204; Lefroy, comp., *Memorials Bermudas*, II, 190 (a resolution, not a statute). Some evidence suggests miscegenation was not taken as seriously in 17th-century Bermuda as on the mainland: *ibid.*, I, 550, II, 30, 103, 141, 161, 228, 314.

Province will be soe distructive as noe free borne Christians will ever be induced to come over servants." [84] An Irish youth complained to a Maryland court in 1661 that he had been kidnapped and forced to sign for fifteen years, that he had already served six and a half years and was now twenty-one, and that eight and a half more years of service was "contrary to the lawes of God and man that a Christian Subject should be made a Slave." (The jury blandly compromised the dispute by deciding that he should serve only until age twenty-one, but that he was now only nineteen.) Free Negro servants were generally increasingly less able to defend themselves against this insidious kind of encroachment. [85] Increasingly, white men were more clearly free because Negroes had become so clearly slave.

Certainly it was the case in Maryland and Virginia that the legal enactment of Negro slavery followed social practice, rather than vice versa, and also that the assemblies were slower than in other English colonies to declare how Negroes could or should be treated. These two patterns in themselves suggest that slavery was less a matter of previous conception or external example in Maryland and Virginia than elsewhere.

The Virginia Assembly first showed itself incontrovertibly aware that Negroes were not serving in the same manner as English servants in 1660 when it declared "that for the future no servant comeing into the country without indentures, of what christian nation soever, shall serve longer then those of our own country, of the like age." In 1661 the Assembly indirectly provided statutory recognition that some Negroes served for life: "That in case any English servant shall run away in company with any negroes who are incapable of makeing satisfaction by addition of time," he must serve for the Negroes' lost time as well as his own. Maryland enacted a closely similar law in 1663 (possibly modeled on Virginia's) and in the following year, on the initiative of the lower house, came out with the categorical declaration that Negroes were to serve "Durante Vita." [86] During the next twenty-odd years a succession of acts

84. *Archives Md.*, I, 464.

85. *Ibid.*, XLI, 476–78, XLIX, 123–24. Compare the contemporary difficulties of a Negro servant: William P. Palmer *et al.*, eds., *Calendar of Virginia State Papers* . . . , 11 vols. (Richmond, 1875–93), I, 9–10.

86. Hening, ed., *Statutes Va.*, I, 539, II, 26; *Archives Md.*, I, 449, 489, 526, 533–34. The "any negroes who are incapable" suggests explicit recognition that some were free, but in several sources the law as re-enacted the next year included a comma between "negroes" and "who," as did the Maryland act of 1663. See *The Lawes of Virginia Now in Force: Collected out of the Assembly Records* . . . (London, 1662), 59.

in both colonies defined with increasing precision what sorts of persons might be treated as slaves.[87] Other acts dealt with the growing problem of slave control, and especially after 1690 slavery began to assume its now familiar character as a complete deprivation of all rights.[88] As early as 1669 the Virginia Assembly unabashedly enacted a brutal law which showed where the logic of perpetual servitude was inevitably tending. Unruly servants could be chastened by sentences to additional terms, but "WHEREAS the only law in force for the punishment of refractory servants resisting their master, mistris or overseer cannot be inflicted upon negroes, nor the obstinacy of many of them by other then violent meanes supprest," if a slave "by the extremity of the correction should chance to die" his master was not to be adjudged guilty of felony "since it cannot be presumed that prepensed malice (which alone makes murther Felony) should induce any man to destroy his owne estate." [89] Virginia planters felt they acted out of mounting necessity: there were disturbances among slaves in several areas in the early 1670's.[90]

By about 1700 the slave ships began spilling forth their black cargoes in greater and greater numbers. By that time, racial slavery and the necessary police powers had been written into law. By that time, too, slavery had lost all resemblance to a perpetual and hereditary version of English servitude, though service for life still seemed to contemporaries its most essential feature.[91] In the last quarter of the seventeenth century the trend was to treat Negroes more like property and less like men, to send them to the fields at younger ages, to deny them automatic existence as inherent members of the community, to tighten the bonds on their personal and civil freedom, and correspondingly to loosen the traditional restraints on the master's freedom to deal with his human property as he saw fit.[92] In 1705 Virginia gathered up the random statutes of a whole generation and baled them into a "slave code" which would not have been out of place in the nineteenth century.[93]

87. Hening, ed., *Statutes Va.*, II, 170, 270, 283, 490–91, III, 137–40, 447–48; *Archives Md.*, VII, 203–5, XIII, 546–49, XXII, 551–52.

88. Especially Hening, ed., *Statutes Va.*, II, 270–71, 481–82, 493, III, 86, 102–3; *Archives Md.*, XIII, 451–53, XIX, 167, 193, XXII, 546–48, XXVI, 254–56.

89. Hening, ed., *Statutes Va.*, II, 270; compare law for servants, I, 538, II, 118.

90. *Ibid.*, II, 299.

91. Robert Beverley, *The History and Present State of Virginia*, ed. Louis B. Wright (Chapel Hill, 1947), 271–72.

92. For illustration, Hening, ed., *Statutes Va.*, II, 288, 479–80 (Negro *children* taxed from age 12, white *boys* from 14), III, 102–3; *Archives Md.*, VII, 76 (county courts required to register births, marriages, burials of all "Except Negroes Indians and Molottos").

93. Hening, ed., *Statutes Va.*, III, 447–62.

8. ENSLAVEMENT: NEW YORK AND THE CAROLINAS

While the development of Negro slavery followed a different pattern in the tobacco colonies than in New England, and while, indeed, there were distinctive patterns of development in each of the English colonies, there were also factors which made for an underlying similarity in the slavery which emerged. The universal need for labor, the common cultural background and acceptance of English law, and the increasing contacts among the various colonies all worked eventually to make Negro slavery a roughly similar institution from one colony to the next, especially where economic and demographic conditions did not differ markedly. In each of the colonies which England acquired after the Restoration of Charles II, slavery developed in a distinctive fashion, yet by 1700 New York's slavery was much like New England's and Carolina's much like Virginia's.

In 1664, at about the time slavery was being written into law in the tobacco colonies, the English took over a Dutch colony which had been in existence for over forty years. New York was already a hodgepodge of nationalities—Dutch, English, Walloons, French, Negroes and others. The status of Negroes under Dutch rule lies enshrouded in the same sort of fog which envelops the English colonies. It is clear, however, that the early and extensive Dutch experience in the international slave trade must have had some influence on the treatment of Negroes in New Amsterdam. There were Negroes in the colony as early as 1628. In that year (perhaps by coincidence) came the colony's first minister, the Reverend Jonas Michaëlius, who had previously been on the West African coast. Yet the first clearly indicated status of any Negroes was freedom, in the 1640's; indeed it remains possible that Negroes were not slaves in New Netherland until the 1650's.[94] In 1650 two sparring pamphleteers disagreed as to whether some Negroes were actually slaves.[95] Within a very few years, though, the records show indisputably that certain colonists were actively interested in the African slave trade. Possibly this interest may have been stimulated by Jacob Steendam, a poet who had resided at a Dutch fort in Guinea before coming to New Amsterdam about 1652.[96]

94. Ellis Lawrence Raesly, *Portrait of New Netherland* (N. Y., 1945), 161–62, 201–2.

95. J. Franklin Jameson, ed., *Narratives of New Netherland, 1609–1664* (N. Y., 1909), 329–30, 364.

96. Raesly, *New Netherland*, 160–62, 269–84.

So far as their response to Negroes is concerned, the cultural
background of Dutchmen was not very different from Englishmen.
They shared a similar commercial orientation and large portions of
religious and intellectual heritage. One of Steendam's poems, addressed to his legitimate mulatto son in Africa, lamented (in translation) :

> Since two bloods course within your veins,
> Both Ham's and Japhet's intermingling;
> One race forever doomed to serve,
> The other bearing freedom's likeness.[97]

Certainly there is no evidence of friction concerning slave-owning
when Englishmen took over the Dutch colony in 1664. The first
English code (the "Duke's Laws"), adopted in 1665 by an assemblage composed largely of New Englanders who had migrated to
Long Island and presided over by the newly appointed English
governor, specifically recognized the practice of service for life in a
proviso patterned after the Massachusetts Bay law of 1641.[98] During
the remaining years of the century Negro slavery flourished, and
New York eventually came to have a higher proportion of Negroes
than any other colony north of Delaware. In New York more than
anywhere else, Negro slavery seems to have grown Topsy fashion.

By contrast, in the Carolinas Negro slavery was deliberately
planted and cultivated. In the 1660's a group of enterprising gentlemen in Barbados, well acquainted with perpetual slavery, proposed
removal with some Negroes to the new mainland colony; their
agreement with the proprietors in England clearly distinguished
between white servants and Negro slaves. Barbadian influence remained strong in South Carolina throughout the seventeenth century. The establishment of slavery in the Carolinas was the more
easily accomplished because after 1660 traditional controls over
master-servant relations were breaking down rapidly in England
itself. Since the state in England was abdicating some of its traditional responsibilities for overseeing the relationship between land-
lords and tenants at home, it felt little solicitude for the relations
between planters and Negroes in far-off plantations. Besides, a good
supply of sugar was enough to bury any questions about its production. It was a telling measure of how far this process had advanced

97. *Ibid.*, 276. Quoted by permission of the Columbia University Press.
98. Colonial Office Papers, 5/1142, f. 33v., Public Record Office, London.

in the English-speaking world that the famous Fundamental Constitutions of Carolina (1669) should have granted each freeman of the colony "absolute power and authority over his negro slaves, of what opinion or religion soever." English civil authorities offered little or no resistance to the growth of this new idea of uncontrolled personal dominion in the colonies; they knew perfectly well what was going on and were inclined to welcome it, for, as the Council for Foreign Plantations exclaimed happily in 1664, "Blacks [are] the most useful appurtenances of a Plantation and perpetual servants." [99] For their part, the planters demanded that their legislative assemblies regulate Negro slavery, but what they wanted and got was unfettering of their personal power over their slaves and the force of the state to back it up. In the 1690's the South Carolina Assembly borrowed from the already mature slave code of Barbados in an effort to maintain control over the growing masses of slaves.[100] Negroes were given virtually none of the protections accorded white servants, protections which were in fact designed to encourage immigration of white men to counterbalance the influx of Negroes. A requirement that "all slaves shall have convenient clothes, once every year," the only right accorded slaves by an act of 1690, was dropped in 1696. Perhaps it would have comforted slaves had they known that anyone killing a slave "cruelly or willfully" (death or dismemberment during punishment specifically excepted) was liable to a fine of five hundred pounds.[101] By the end of the seventeenth century the development of rice plantations and the Barbadian example had combined to yield in South Carolina the most rigorous deprivation of freedom to exist in institutionalized form anywhere in the English continental colonies.

9. THE UN-ENGLISH: SCOTS, IRISH, AND INDIANS

In the minds of overseas Englishmen, slavery, the new tyranny, did not apply to any Europeans. Something about Negroes, and to lesser extent Indians, set them apart for drastic exploitation,

99. William L. Saunders, ed., *The Colonial Records of North Carolina*, 10 vols. (Raleigh, 1886–90), I, 41, 86–89, 204; William Noël Sainsbury, ed., "Virginia in 1662–1665," *Va. Mag. of Hist. and Biog.*, 18 (1910), 420.

100. Conclusive evidence of Barbadian influence is in M. Eugene Sirmans, "The Legal Status of the Slave in South Carolina, 1670–1740," *Jour. Southern Hist.*, 28 (1962), 462–66.

101. Thomas Cooper and David J. McCord, eds., *Statutes at Large of South Carolina*, 10 vols. (Columbia, 1836–41), VII, 343, 393 (1696 code misdated 1712).

oppression, and degradation. In order to discover why, it is useful to turn the problem inside out, to inquire why Englishmen in America did not treat any other peoples like Negroes. It is especially revealing to see how English settlers looked upon the Scotch (as they frequently called them) and the Irish, whom they often had opportunity and "reason" to enslave, and upon the Indians, whom they enslaved, though only, as it were, casually.

In the early years Englishmen treated the increasingly numerous settlers from other European countries, especially Scottish and Irish servants, with condescension and frequently with exploitive brutality. Englishmen seemed to regard their colonies as exclusively *English* preserves and to wish to protect English persons especially from the exploitation which inevitably accompanied settlement in the New World. In Barbados, for example, the assembly in 1661 denounced the kidnapping of youngsters for service in the colony in a law which applied only to "Children of the *English* Nation." [102] In 1650 Connecticut provided that debtors were not to "bee sould to any but of the English Nation." [103]

While Englishmen distinguished themselves from other peoples, they also distinguished *among* those different peoples who failed to be English. It seems almost as if Englishmen possessed a view of other peoples which placed the English nation at the center of widening concentric circles each of which contained a people more alien than the one inside it. On occasion these social distances felt by Englishmen may be gauged with considerable precision, as in the sequence employed by the Committee for Trade and Foreign Plantations in a query to the governor of Connecticut in 1680: "What number of English, Scotch, Irish or Forreigners have . . . come yearly to . . . your Corporation. And also, what Blacks and Slaves have been brought in." Sometimes the English sense of distance seems to have been based upon a scale of values which would be thought of today in terms of nationality. When the Leeward Islands encouraged immigration of foreign Protestants the Assembly stipulated that the number of such aliens "shall not exceed the One Fourth of *English, Scotch, Irish,* and *Cariole* [Creole] Subjects." Jamaica achieved a finer discrimination: the colony offered a bounty of £18 in time of war, £14 in peace, for importing English, Welsh, Scots, or residents of *"Jersey, Gernsey,* or *Man,"* and lower bounties of £15 and £12 for Irish. Maryland placed a discriminatory duty on

---

102. Hening, ed., *Statutes Va.,* I, 161; *Acts of Assembly, Passed in the Island of Barbadoes, from 1648, to 1718* (London, 1721), 22.
103. Trumbull and Hoadly, eds., *Recs. Col. Conn.,* I, 510.

Irish servants while Virginia did the same with all servants not born in England or Wales.[104]

At other times, though, the sense of foreignness seems to have been explicitly religious, as instanced by Lord William Willoughby's letter from Barbados in 1667: "We have more than a good many Irish amongst us, therefore I am for the down right Scott, who I am certain will fight without a crucifix about his neck." [105] It is scarcely surprising that hostility toward the numerous Irish servants should have been especially strong, for they were doubly damned as foreign and Papist. Already, for Englishmen in the seventeenth century, the Irish were a special case, and it required more than an ocean voyage to alter this perception. In the 1650's, while Cromwell was wielding the sword of Protestantism in Ireland and while Puritan factions held sway in Virginia, Maryland, and Bermuda, the Virginia Assembly assigned Irish servants arriving without indentures somewhat longer terms than other Europeans (the previous blanket act "being only [for] the benefitt of our own nation") and then extended this discrimination to "all aliens." With re-establishment of royal control in 1660 the assembly repealed these laws, terming them full of "rigour and inconvenience" and a discouragement to immigration of servants, and declared with finality "that for the future no servant comeing into the country without indentures, of what christian nation soever, shall serve longer then those of our own country, of the like age." [106]

As time went on Englishmen began to absorb the idea that their settlements in America were not going to remain exclusively English preserves. In 1671 Virginia began encouraging naturalization of legal aliens, so that they might enjoy "all such liberties, priviledges, immunities whatsoever, as a naturall borne Englishman is capable of," and Maryland accomplished the same end with private natural-

---

104. *Ibid.*, III, 293 (an inquiry also sent other governors) ; *Acts of Assembly, Passed in the Charibbee Leeward Islands, from 1690, to 1730* (London, 1734) , 127; *Acts of Assembly, Passed in the Island of Jamaica; From 1681, to 1737, Inclusive* (London, 1738) , 100; also *Montserrat Code of Laws: from 1668, to 1788* (London, 1790) , 19; Hening, ed., *Statutes Va.*, III, 193; Thomas Bacon, ed., *Laws of Maryland at Large, 1637–1763* (Annapolis, 1765) , 1715, chap. xxxvi, 1717, chap. x, 1732, chap. xxii. The Maryland laws aimed at Irish Papists.

105. Willoughby quoted in C. S. S. Higham, *The Development of the Leeward Islands under the Restoration, 1660–1688; A Study of the Foundations of the Old Colonial System* (Cambridge, Eng., 1921) , 170n.

106. Hening, ed., *Statutes Va.*, I, 257, 411, 471, 538–39. In Barbados *ca.* 1660 there was apprehension concerning the "turbulent and dangerous" Irish; William Noël Sainsbury *et al.*, eds., *Calendar of State Papers, Colonial Series* (London, 1860—) , *America and West Indies, 1574–1660*, 481, 483, 487.

ization acts that frequently included a potpourri of French, Dutch, Swiss, Swedes, and so forth.[107]

The necessity of peopling the colonies transformed the long-standing urge to discriminate among non-English peoples into a necessity. Which of the non-English were sufficiently different and foreign to warrant treating as "perpetual servants"? The need to answer this question did not mean, of course, that upon arrival in America the colonists immediately jettisoned their sense of distance from those persons they did not actually enslave. They discriminated against Welshmen and Scotsmen who, while admittedly "the best servants," were typically the servants of Englishmen. There was a considerably stronger tendency to discriminate against Papist Irishmen, those "worst" servants, but never to make slaves of them.[108] And here lay the crucial difference. Even the Scottish prisoners taken by Cromwell at Worcester and Dunbar—captives in a just war!—were never treated as slaves in England or the colonies. Certainly the lot of those sent to Barbados was miserable, but it was a different lot from the African slave's. In New England they were quickly accommodated to the prevailing labor system, which was servitude. As the Reverend Mr. Cotton of the Massachusetts Bay described the situation to Oliver Cromwell in 1651,

The Scots, whom God delivered into you hand at Dunbarre, and whereof sundry were sent hither, we have been desirous (as we could) to make their yoke easy. Such as were sick of the scurvy or other diseases have not wanted physick and chyrurgery. They have not been sold for slaves to perpetuall servitude, but for 6 or 7 or 8 yeares, as we do our owne; and he that bought the most of them (I heare) buildeth houses for them, for every 4 an house, layeth some acres of ground thereto, which he giveth them as their owne, requiring 3 dayes in the weeke to worke for him (by turnes) and 4 dayes for themselves, and promisteth, as soone as they can repay him the money he layed out for them, he will set them at liberty.[109]

Here was the nub: captive Scots were men "as our owne." Negroes were not. They were almost hopelessly far from being of the English nation. As the Bermuda legislature proclaimed in 1663, even such Negroes "as count themselves Free because no p.ticler masters clay-

107. Hening, ed., *Statutes Va.*, II, 289–90, 464–65; for one of many in Maryland, *Archives Md.*, II, 205–6.

108. The designations are a prominent planter's, quoted in Higham, *Development of the Leeward Islands*, 169, also 170n.

109. Boston, July 28, 1651, W. H. Whitmore and W. S. Appleton, eds., *Hutchinson Papers*, 2 vols. (Prince Society, *Publications* [Albany, 1865]) , I, 264–65. For prisoners to Barbados see Smith, *Colonists in Bondage*, 152–59.

meth their servies, in our judgments are not Free to all nationall priviledges." [110]

Indians too seemed radically different from Englishmen, far more so than any Europeans. They were enslaved, like Negroes, and so fell on the losing side of a crucial dividing line. It is easy to see why: whether considered in terms of complexion, religion, nationality, savagery, bestiality, or geographical location, Indians were more like Negroes than like Englishmen. Given this resemblance the essential problem becomes why Indian slavery never became an important institution in the colonies. Why did Indian slavery remain numerically insignificant and typically incidental in character? Why were Indian slaves valued at much lower prices than Negroes? Why were Indians, as a kind of people, treated like Negroes and yet at the same time very differently?

Certain obvious factors made for important differentiations in the minds of the English colonists. As was the case with first confrontations in America and Africa, the different contexts of confrontation made Englishmen more interested in converting and civilizing Indians than Negroes. That this campaign in America too frequently degenerated into military campaigns of extermination did nothing to eradicate the initial distinction. Entirely apart from English intentions, the culture of the American Indians probably meant that they were less readily enslavable than Africans. By comparison, they were less used to settled agriculture, and their own variety of slavery was probably even less similar to the chattel slavery which Englishmen practiced in America than was the domestic and political slavery of the West African cultures. But it was the transformation of English intentions in the wilderness which counted most heavily in the long run. The Bible and the treaty so often gave way to the clash of flintlock and tomahawk. The colonists' perceptions of the Indians came to be organized not only in pulpits and printshops but at the bloody cutting edge of the English thrust into the Indians' lands. Thus the most pressing and mundane circumstances worked to make Indians seem very different from Negroes. In the early years especially, Indians were in a position to mount murderous reprisals upon the English settlers, while the few scattered Negroes were not. When English-Indian relations did not turn upon sheer power they rested on diplomacy. In many instances the colonists took assiduous precautions to prevent abuse of Indians belong-

110. Lefroy, comp., *Memorials Bermudas*, II, 190–91.

ing to friendly tribes. Most of the Indians enslaved by the English had their own tribal enemies to thank. It became a common practice to ship Indian slaves to the West Indies where they could be exchanged for slaves who had no compatriots lurking on the outskirts of English settlements.[111] In contrast, Negroes presented much less of a threat—at first.

Equally important, Negroes had to be dealt with as individuals —with supremely impartial anonymity, to be sure—rather than as nations. Englishmen wanted and had to live with their Negroes, as it were, side by side. Accordingly their impressions of Negroes were forged in the heat of continual, inescapable personal contacts. There were few pressures urging Englishmen to treat Indians as integral constituents in their society, which Negroes were whether Englishmen liked or not. At a distance the Indian could be viewed with greater detachment and his characteristics acknowledged and approached more coolly and more rationally. At a distance too, Indians could retain the quality of nationality, a quality which Englishmen admired in themselves and expected in other peoples. Under contrasting circumstances in America, the Negro nations tended to become Negro people.

Here lay the rudiments of certain shadowy but persistent themes in what turned out to be a multi-racial nation. Americans came to impute to the braves of the Indian "nations" an ungovernable individuality (which was perhaps not merited in such exaggerated degree) and at the same time to impart to Negroes all the qualities of an eminently governable sub-nation, in which African tribal distinctions were assumed to be of no consequence and individuality unaspired to. More immediately, the two more primitive peoples rapidly came to serve as two fixed points from which English settlers could triangulate their own position in America; the separate meanings of *Indian* and *Negro* helped define the meaning of living in America. The Indian became for Americans a symbol of their American experience; it was no mere luck of the toss that placed the profile of an American Indian rather than an American Negro on the famous old five-cent piece. Confronting the Indian in America

111. Hening, ed., *Statutes Va.*, II, 299. A good study of Indian slavery is needed, but see Almon Wheeler Lauber, *Indian Slavery in Colonial Times within the Present Limits of the United States* (N. Y., 1913). In 1627 some imported Carib Indians proved unsalable in Virginia and were turned over to the colony; the General Court decided that, since the Caribs had stolen goods, attempted murder, tried to run away to the Virginia Indians, and might prove the downfall of the whole colony, the best way to dispose of the problem was to hang them: McIlwaine, ed., *Minutes Council Va.*, 155.

was a testing experience, common to all the colonies. Conquering the Indian symbolized and personified the conquest of the American difficulties, the surmounting of the wilderness. To push back the Indian was to prove the worth of one's own mission, to make straight in the desert a highway for civilization. With the Negro it was utterly different.

10. RACIAL SLAVERY: FROM REASONS TO RATIONALE

And *difference,* surely, was the indispensable key to the degradation of Negroes in English America. In scanning the problem of *why* Negroes were enslaved in America, certain constant elements in a complex situation can be readily, if roughly, identified. It may be taken as given that there would have been no enslavement without economic need, that is, without persistent demand for labor in underpopulated colonies. Of crucial importance, too, was the fact that for cultural reasons Negroes were relatively helpless in the face of European aggressiveness and technology. In themselves, however, these two elements will not explain the enslavement of Indians and Negroes. The pressing exigency in America was labor, and Irish and English servants were available. Most of them would have been helpless to ward off outright enslavement if their masters had thought themselves privileged and able to enslave them. As a group, though, masters did not think themselves so empowered. Only with Indians and Negroes did Englishmen attempt so radical a deprivation of liberty—which brings the matter abruptly to the most difficult and imponderable question of all: what was it about Indians and Negroes which set them apart, which rendered them *different* from Englishmen, which made them special candidates for degradation?

To ask such questions is to inquire into the *content* of English attitudes, and unfortunately there is little evidence with which to build an answer. It may be said, however, that the heathen condition of the Negroes seemed of considerable importance to English settlers in America—more so than to English voyagers upon the coasts of Africa—and that heathenism was associated in some settlers' minds with the condition of slavery.[112] This is not to say that

112. See above, chap. 1, sec. 3. Also John C. Hurd, *The Law of Freedom and Bondage in the United States,* 2 vols. (Boston, 1858–62), I, 159–60; Horne, *The Mirror of Justices,* ed. Robinson, 124; Marcus W. Jernegan, *Laboring and Dependent Classes in Colonial America, 1607–1783; Studies of the Economic, Educational, and Social Significance of Slaves, Servants, Apprentices, and Poor Folk* (Chicago, 1931), 24–26; Helen T. Catterall, ed., *Judicial Cases Concerning Ameri-*

the colonists enslaved Negroes because they were heathens. The most clear-cut positive trace of such reasoning was probably unique and certainly far from being a forceful statement: in 1660 John Hathorne declared, before a Massachusetts court in partial support of his contention that an Indian girl should not be compelled to return to her master, that "first the law is undeniable that the indian may have the same distribusion of Justice with our selves: ther is as I humbly conceive not the same argument as amongst the negroes[,] for the light of the gospell is a begineing to appeare amongst them—that is the indians." [113]

The importance and persistence of the tradition which attached slavery to heathenism did not become evident in any positive assertions that heathens might be enslaved. It was not until the period of legal establishment of slavery after 1660 that the tradition became manifest at all, and even then there was no effort to place heathenism and slavery on a one-for-one relationship. Virginia's second statutory definition of a slave (1682), for example, awkwardly attempted to rest enslavement on religious difference while excluding from possible enslavement all heathens who were not Indian or Negro.[114] Despite such logical difficulties, the old European equation of slavery and religious difference did not rapidly vanish in America, for it cropped up repeatedly after 1660 in assertions that slaves by becoming Christian did not automatically become free. By about the end of the seventeenth century, Maryland, New York, Virginia, North and South Carolina, and New Jersey had all passed laws reassuring masters that conversion of their slaves did not necessitate manumission.[115] These acts were passed in response to occasional

---

can Slavery and the Negro, 5 vols. (Washington, 1926–37), I, 55n. Data in the following pages suggest this. The implication that slavery could last only during the heathen state is in Providence Company to Gov. Philip Bell, London, Apr. 20, 1635, Box 9, bundle: List no. 7, 2d portion, MS. relating to the Royal African Co. and Slavery matters, 43, Parish Transcripts, N.-Y. Hist. Soc.: ". . . a Groundless opinion that Christians may not lawfully keepe such persons in a state of Servitude during their strangeness from Christianity." In 1695 Gov. John Archdale of South Carolina prohibited sale of some Indians, captured by his own Indian allies, as slaves to the West Indies and freed them because they were Christians: John Archdale, A New Description of That Fertile and Pleasant Province of Carolina . . . (London, 1707), in Alexander S. Salley, Jr., ed., Narratives of Early Carolina, 1650–1708 (N. Y., 1911), 300.

113. Records and Files of the Quarterly Courts of Essex County Massachusetts, 1636–1683, 8 vols. (Salem, 1911–21), II, 240–42.

114. Hening, ed., Statutes Va., II, 490–92.

115. Archives Md., I, 526, 533 (1664), II, 272; "Duke's Laws," C. O. 5/1142, f. 33v., P. R. O., a portion of the section of "Bondslavery" omitted from the standard New York printed sources which reads "And also provided that This Law shall

pleas that Christianity created a claim to freedom and to much more frequent assertions by men interested in converting Negroes that nothing could be accomplished if masters thought their slaves were about to be snatched from them by meddling missionaries.[116] This decision that the slave's religious condition had no relevance to his status as a slave (the only one possible if an already valuable economic institution was to be retained) strongly suggests that heathenism was an important component in the colonists' initial reaction to Negroes early in the century.

Yet its importance can easily be overstressed. For one thing, some of the first Negroes in Virginia had been baptized before arrival. In the early years others were baptized in various colonies and became more than nominally Christian; a Negro woman joined the church in Dorchester, Massachusetts, as a full member in 1641.[117] With some Negroes becoming Christian and others not, there might have developed a caste differentiation along religious lines, yet there is no evidence to suggest that the colonists distinguished consistently between the Negroes they converted and those they did not. It was racial, not religious, slavery which developed in America.

Still, in the early years, the English settlers most frequently contrasted themselves with Negroes by the term *Christian*, though they also sometimes described themselves as *English*;[118] here the explicit religious distinction would seem to have lain at the core of English reaction. Yet the concept embodied by the term *Christian* embraced so much more meaning than was contained in specific doctrinal affirmations that it is scarcely possible to assume on the basis of this

---

not extend to sett at Liberty Any Negroe or Indian Servant who shall turne Christian after he shall have been bought by Any Person." (This unpublished Crown Copyright material is reproduced by permission of the Controller of H. M. Stationery Office.) *The Colonial Laws of New York from the Year 1664 to the Revolution* . . . , 5 vols. (Albany, 1894–96), I, 597–98 (1706); Hening, ed., *Statutes Va.,* II, 260 (1667); Saunders, ed., *Col. Recs. N. C.,* I, 204 (1670), II, 857; Cooper and McCord, eds., *Statutes S. C.,* VII, 343 (1691), 364–65; *Anno Regni Reginae Annae . . . Tertio;* [*The Acts Passed by the Second Assembly of New Jersey in December, 1704*] ([N. Y., 1704]), 20, an act which was disallowed for other reasons.

116. For example, in 1652 a mulatto girl pleaded Christianity as the reason why she should not be "a perpetuall slave" (Lefroy, comp., *Memorials Bermudas,* II, 34–35, also 293–94), and in 1694 some Massachusetts ministers asked the governor and legislature to remove that "wel-knowne Discouragement" to conversion of slaves with a law denying that baptism necessitated freedom (*Acts and Resolves Mass.,* VII, 537).

117. Winthrop, *Journal,* ed. Hosmer, II, 26.

118. These statements on prevailing word usage are based on a wide variety of sources, many of them cited in this chapter; some passages already quoted may serve to amplify the illustrations in the following paragraphs.

linguistic contrast that the colonists set Negroes apart because they were heathen. The historical experience of the English people in the sixteenth century had made for fusion of religion and nationality; the qualities of being English and Christian had become so inseparably blended that it seemed perfectly consistent to the Virginia Assembly in 1670 to declare that "noe negroe or Indian though baptised and enjoyned their owne Freedome shall be capable of any such purchase of christians, but yet not debarred from buying any of their owne nation." Similarly, an order of the Virginia Assembly in 1662 revealed a well-knit sense of self-identity of which Englishness and Christianity were interrelated parts: "ME-TAPPIN a Powhatan Indian being sold for life time to one Elizabeth Short by the king of Wainoake Indians who had no power to sell him being of another nation, *it is ordered* that the said Indian be free, he speaking perfectly the English tongue and desiring baptism." [119]

From the first, then, vis-à-vis the Negro the concept embedded in the term *Christian* seems to have conveyed much of the idea and feeling of *we* as against *they:* to be Christian was to be civilized rather than barbarous, English rather than African, white rather than black. The term *Christian* itself proved to have remarkable elasticity, for by the end of the seventeenth century it was being used to define a species of slavery which had altogether lost any connection with explicit religious difference. In the Virginia code of 1705, for example, the term sounded much more like a definition of race than of religion: "And for a further christian care and usage of all christian servants, *Be it also enacted, by the authority aforesaid, and it is hereby enacted,* That no negroes, mulattos, or Indians, although christians, or Jews, Moors, Mahometans, or other infidels, shall, at any time, purchase any christian servant, nor any other, except of their own complexion, or such as are declared slaves by this act." By this time "Christianity" had somehow become intimately and explicitly linked with "complexion." The 1705 statute declared "That all servants imported and brought into this country, by sea or land, who were not christians in their native country, (except Turks and Moors in amity with her majesty, and others that can make due proof of their being free in England, or any other christian country, before they were shipped, in order to transportation hither) shall be accounted and be slaves, and as such be here bought and sold notwithstanding a conversion to christianity after-

119. Hening, ed., *Statutes Va.,* II, 281 (1670), 155 (1662).

wards." [120] As late as 1753 the Virginia slave code anachronistically defined slavery in terms of religion when everyone knew that slavery had for generations been based on the racial and not the religious difference.[121]

It is worth making still closer scrutiny of the terminology which Englishmen employed when referring both to themselves and to the two peoples they enslaved, for this terminology affords the best single means of probing the content of their sense of difference. The terms *Indian* and *Negro* were both borrowed from the Hispanic languages, the one originally deriving from (mistaken) geographical locality and the other from human complexion. When referring to the Indians the English colonists either used that proper name or called them *savages,* a term which reflected primarily their view of Indians as uncivilized, or occasionally (in Maryland especially) *pagans,* which gave more explicit expression to the missionary urge. When they had reference to Indians the colonists occasionally spoke of themselves as *Christians* but after the early years almost always as *English.*

In significant contrast, the colonists referred to *Negroes* and by the eighteenth century to *blacks* and to *Africans,* but almost never to Negro *heathens* or *pagans* or *savages.* Most suggestive of all, there seems to have been something of a shift during the seventeenth century in the terminology which Englishmen in the colonies applied to themselves. From the initially most common term *Christian,* at mid-century there was a marked drift toward *English* and *free.* After about 1680, taking the colonies as a whole, a new term appeared—*white.*

So far as the weight of analysis may be imposed upon such terms, diminishing reliance upon *Christian* suggests a gradual muting of the specifically religious element in the Christian-Negro disjunction in favor of secular nationality: Negroes were, in 1667, "not in all respects to be admitted to a full fruition of the exemptions and impunities of the English." [122] As time went on, as some Negroes became assimilated to the English colonial culture, as more "raw Africans" arrived, and as increasing numbers of non-English Europeans were attracted to the colonies, the colonists turned increas-

120. *Ibid.,* III, 447–48 (1705), also 283, V, 547–48, VI, 356–57. Lingering aftereffects of the old concept cropped up as late as 1791, when *Negro* was still contradistinguished by *Christian:* Certificate of character of Negro Phill, Feb. 20, 1791, Character Certificates of Negroes, Papers of the Pennsylvania Abolition Society, Historical Society of Pennsylvania, Philadelphia.

121. Hening, ed., *Statutes Va.,* VI, 356–57.

122. *Ibid.,* II, 267.

ingly to the striking physiognomic difference. By 1676 it was possible in Virginia to assail a man for "eclipsing" himself in the "darke imbraces of a Blackamoore" as if "Buty consisted all together in the Antiphety of Complections." In Maryland a revised law prohibiting miscegenation (1692) retained *white* and *English* but dropped the term *Christian*—a symptomatic modification. As early as 1664 a Bermuda statute (aimed, ironically, at protecting Negroes from brutal abandonment) required that the "last Master" of senile Negroes "provide for them such accomodations as shall be convenient for Creatures of that hue and colour untill their death." By the end of the seventeenth century dark complexion had become an independent rationale for enslavement: in 1709 Samuel Sewall noted in his diary that a "Spaniard" had petitioned the Massachusetts Council for freedom but that "Capt. Teat alledg'd that all of that Color were Slaves." [123] Here was a barrier between "we" and "they" which was visible and permanent: the Negro could not become a white man. Not, at least, as yet.

What had occurred was not a change in the justification of slavery from religion to race. No such justifications were made. There seems to have been, within the unarticulated concept of the Negro as a different sort of person, a subtle but highly significant shift in emphasis. Consciousness of the Negro's heathenism remained through the eighteenth and into the nineteenth and even the twentieth century, and an awareness, at very least, of his different appearance was present from the beginning. The shift was an alteration in emphasis within a single concept of difference rather than a development of a novel conceptualization. The amorphousness and subtlety of such a change is evident, for instance, in the famous

123. "History of Bacon's and Ingram's Rebellion," Andrews, ed., *Narratives of the Insurrections*, 96; *Archives Md.*, XIII, 546–49; Lefroy, comp., *Memorials Bermudas*, II, 216; *Diary of Samuel Sewall, 1674–1729* (Mass. Hist. Soc., *Collections*, 5th Ser. 5–7 [1878–82]) , II, 248. In 1698 Gov. Francis Nicholson informed the Board of Trade that the "major part" of Negroes in Maryland spoke English: *Archives Md.*, XXIII, 499. For first use of "white" in statutes of various colonies, Bartlett, ed., *Recs. Col. R. I.*, I, 243 (1652) ; *Archives Md.*, VII, 204–5 (1681) ; Aaron Leaming and Jacob Spicer, eds., *The Grants, Concessions, and Original Constitutions of the Province of New Jersey* . . . , 2d ed. (Somerville, N. J., 1881), 236 (1683) ; *Col. Laws N. Y.*, I, 148 (1684) ; Cooper and McCord, eds., *Statutes S. C.*, VII, 343 (1691) ; Hening, ed., *Statutes Va.*, III, 86–87 (1691) ; *Acts of Assembly, Made and Enacted in the Bermuda or Summer-Islands, from 1690, to 1713–14* (London, 1719) , 12–13 (1690 or 1691) . West Indian assemblies used the term in the 1680's and 1690's, possibly earlier. Officials in England were using "whites" and "blacks" as early as 1670 in questionnaires to colonial governors: Hening, ed., *Statutes Va.*, II, 515; Trumbull and Hoadly, eds., *Recs. Col. Conn.*, III, 293.

tract, *The Negro's and Indians Advocate,* published in 1680 by the Reverend Morgan Godwyn. Baffled and frustrated by the disinterest of planters in converting their slaves, Godwyn declared at one point that "their *Complexion,* which being most obvious to the sight, by which the *Notion* of things doth seem to be most certainly conveyed to the Understanding, is apt to make no *slight* impressions upon rude Minds, already prepared to admit of any thing for *Truth* which shall make for Interest." Altering his emphasis a few pages later, Godwyn complained that "these two words, *Negro* and *Slave*" are "by custom grown Homogeneous and Convertible; even as *Negro* and *Christian, Englishman* and *Heathen,* are by the like corrupt Custom and Partiality made Opposites." [124] Most arresting of all, throughout the colonies the terms *Christian, free, English,* and *white* were for many years employed indiscriminately as metonyms. A Maryland law of 1681 used all four terms in one short paragraph! [125]

Whatever the limitations of terminology as an index to thought and feeling, it seems likely that the colonists' initial sense of difference from the Negro was founded not on a single characteristic but on a congeries of qualities which, taken as a whole, seemed to set the Negro apart. Virtually every quality in the Negro invited pejorative feelings. What may have been his two most striking characteristics, his heathenism and his appearance, were probably prerequisite to his complete debasement. His heathenism alone could never have led to permanent enslavement since conversion easily wiped out that failing. If his appearance, his racial characteristics, meant nothing to the English settlers, it is difficult to see how slavery based on race ever emerged, how the concept of complexion as the mark of slavery ever entered the colonists' minds. Even if the colonists were most unfavorably struck by the Negro's color, though, blackness itself did not urge the complete debasement of slavery. Other qualities—the utter strangeness of his language, gestures, eating habits, and so on—certainly must have contributed to the colonists' sense that he was very different, perhaps disturbingly so. In Africa these qualities had for Englishmen added up to *savagery;* they were major components in that sense of *difference* which provided the mental margin absolutely requisite for placing the European on the deck of the slave ship and the Negro in the hold.

The available evidence (what little there is) suggests that for Englishmen settling in America, the specific religious difference was

124. Godwyn, *The Negro's and Indians Advocate,* 20, 36.
125. *Archives Md.,* VII, 204.

initially of greater importance than color, certainly of much greater relative importance than for the Englishmen who confronted Negroes in their African homeland. Perhaps Englishmen in Virginia, living uncomfortably close to nature under a hot sun and in almost daily contact with tawny Indians, found the Negro's color less arresting than they might have in other circumstances. Perhaps, too, these first Virginians sensed how inadequately they had reconstructed the institutions and practices of Christian piety in the wilderness; they would perhaps appear less as failures to themselves in this respect if compared to persons who as Christians were *totally* defective. In this connection they may be compared to their brethren in New England, where godliness appeared (at first) triumphantly to hold full sway; in New England there was distinctly less contrasting of Negroes on the basis of the religious disjunction and much more militant discussion of just wars. Perhaps, though, the Jamestown settlers were told in 1619 by the Dutch shipmaster that these "negars" were heathens and could be treated as such. We do not know. The available data will not bear all the weight that the really crucial questions impose.

Of course once the cycle of degradation was fully under way, once slavery and racial discrimination were completely linked together, once the engine of oppression was in full operation, then there is no need to plead *ignoramus*. By the end of the seventeenth century in all the colonies of the English empire there was chattel racial slavery of a kind which would have seemed familiar to men living in the nineteenth century. No Elizabethan Englishman would have found it familiar, though certain strands of thought and feeling in Elizabethan England had intertwined with reports about the Spanish and Portuguese to engender a willingness on the part of English settlers in the New World to treat some men as suitable for private exploitation. During the seventeenth century New World conditions had exploited this predisposition and vastly enlarged it, so much so that English colonials of the eighteenth century were faced with full-blown slavery—something they thought of not as an institution but as a host of ever present problems, dangers, and opportunities.

Part Two

PROVINCIAL DECADES

1700—1755

III   ANXIOUS OPPRESSORS

Freedom and Control in a Slave Society

DURING THE FIRST QUARTER OF THE EIGHTEENTH CENTURY
Negro slaves poured into the English colonies on the American
continent in unprecedented numbers. This sudden enlargement of
the slave population meant for white men a thoroughgoing commitment to slavery; the institution rapidly thrust its roots deeply into a
maturing American society. For roughly the first sixty years of the
eighteenth century slavery itself grew without appreciable opposition, or even comprehension, gradually becoming barnacled with
traditions, folkways, and a whole style of life. Most important for
the future, unthinking acquiescence in the existence of slavery
resulted in unthinking acceptance of the presuppositions upon
which slavery rested. Slavery seemed a necessary response to conditions, a submission to the decrees of life in America.

Basic to the emergent pattern of master-slave relations was the
demographic pattern of European and African settlement in the
seaboard colonies. Despite the crucial and at times determinative
influence of this pattern, the varying degrees of rigor which slavery
exhibited in various regions did more than reflect population ratios;
in their enactment and application the laws of slavery reflected the
complex needs and responses of communities which for varying
reasons were both different and roughly similar to each other.
White reactions to manifestations of slave discontent, especially,
seem to have differed in ways which suggest that the measure of
communal integration among white men was crucial to the shape of
their response. In all the English settlements, though, colonials
faced common problems which turned around certain central
facts—that Negro slaves were property but also men, that they had
always to be governed and sometimes suppressed, that some Negroes
were not slaves, and that racial slavery existed in burgeoning settle-

ments which were characterized notably by personal freedom and
ethnic diversity.

1. DEMOGRAPHIC CONFIGURATIONS IN THE COLONIES

The influx of Negroes into the American colonies was
part of a more general development, the arrival of large numbers of
non-English peoples. It is impossible to say precisely when the flood
began, but the trend toward variegation of England's colonial peoples accelerated rapidly in the early years of the eighteenth century.
Three groups contributed most heavily to this novel diversity. The
Scotch-Irish (the lowland Scots who had migrated to Ulster) pushed
through to frontier regions where they rapidly established a reputation for bellicosity among themselves and toward the Indians. The
Germans flocked especially to Pennsylvania where by mid-century
they constituted a third of the population. Though most were
Protestant, their presence aroused some antagonism, for their large
numbers and tenacious devotion to their language and ways suggested to some colonists that Pennsylvania might be becoming New
Germany. In a famous outburst Benjamin Franklin asked petu-
lantly, "why should the Palatine Boors be suffered to swarm into
our Settlements, and by herding together establish their Language
and Manners to the Exclusion of ours? Why should Pennsylvania,
founded by the English, become a Colony of *Aliens,* who will
shortly be so numerous as to Germanize us instead of our Anglifying
them, and will never adopt our Language or Customs, any more
than they can acquire our Complexion." [1]

By far the most numerous (and surely the most distinctive in
"Complexion") of the three major non-English groups were the
Africans. Like Europeans, they differed among themselves in nationality and language, but they too shared, for the most part, a common culture.[2] Like most European immigrants, they clustered in
certain areas, without having anything to say in the matter. In the
eighteenth century Negroes were heavily concentrated on the seaboard of the southern half of the English territory along the Atlantic edge of the North American continent. From about 1730 almost
until the Revolution Negroes comprised at least one-third the total
population within the line of English settlement from Maryland to

1. "Observations Concerning the Increase of Mankind" (1751), Leonard W.
Labaree *et al.,* eds., *The Papers of Benjamin Franklin* (New Haven, 1959———) ,
IV, 234.

2. Though now challenged on many points, the single most important work on
the African background of American slaves remains Melville J. Herskovits, *The
Myth of the Negro Past* (N. Y. and London, 1941) .

South Carolina (and to Georgia after its firm establishment in mid-century). Within this area there were significant variations from colony to colony: North Carolina had only about 25 per cent Negroes, Maryland had over 30 per cent, Virginia about 40, and South Carolina probably over 60 per cent. The concentration of Negroes varied greatly within each colony, too, since usually the movement of slaves onto new lands lagged markedly behind the pace of western settlement. A similar lag occurred in representation of the white population in the assemblies, so that the areas with the heaviest slave populations were usually over-represented in the legislatures, a fact of some but probably not overriding importance concerning statutory regulation of slavery. From Pennsylvania northwards there were spots of Negro concentration in the bustling port cities: New York City's population was probably at least 15 per cent Negro, Newport's only slightly less so, Boston's roughly 8 per cent, and Philadelphia's appreciably less. The colony of New York contained the highest proportion of Negroes north of the plantations (14 per cent), with Rhode Island having slightly fewer although far more than the 3 per cent for New England as a whole. New Jersey and Pennsylvania had about 8 per cent.[3]

These figures are important only insofar as they made for important, even crucial differences in social atmosphere among various regions of the colonies. The tone and rhythm of life in an inland Connecticut village, where the only Negro to be seen was the minister's house servant, must have been rather different, to say the least, from that on a rice plantation in South Carolina where within a five-mile radius there were ten slaves for every white person, man, woman, and child. In the middle of the eighteenth century perhaps 200,000 white persons in the continental colonies lived in neighborhoods where Negroes outnumbered them. And the population of the colonies which later became the United States, taken as a whole, contained a higher proportion of Negroes in the period 1730–65 than at any other time in the nation's history. In many areas one of the major daily concerns of responsible men was the effective control of masses of slaves.

2. SLAVERY AND THE SENSES OF THE LAWS

As slavery rapidly entrenched itself in the plantation colonies during the early years of the eighteenth century, it forced

3. Sources for population figures are given in Essay on Sources, pp. 598–99.

the colonists to come to grips with novel problems which arose from
the very nature of the institution. Plainly, Negro slaves were property in a sense not thoroughly comprehended by traditional English
concepts and legal categories of bondage and servitude. Sometimes
this novelty produced legal confusion: representative assemblies in
America and colonial officials in England were trying to stuff a new
kind of property into old legal pigeonholes and were frequently
unable to achieve a very good fit. In various colonies slaves were
variously declared to be real or personal (chattel) property.[4] What
was to be done, for instance, when an estate administered for an
orphan during his minority lost value because of deaths, childless-
ness, and superannuation among the slaves? Could a slaveowner will
or deed Negroes not yet conceived, property which did not yet exist?
Should slaves be taxed by head or by value? These were vexing if
not crucial problems. Chattel slavery required, in common with
other manifestations of the commercialization of society, decisions
as to how the account books were to be kept.

Considered as men, slaves raised much more difficult problems.
The most pressing necessity was maintenance of discipline: hence
the famous slave codes. The older plantation colonies at first
adopted brief laws aimed at specific problems and later codified
them during the early years of the eighteenth century. The newer
colonies plunged in more directly: Georgia formulated in 1755 a
full-scale code based on South Carolina's.[5] The process of revision
and recapitulation continued throughout the eighteenth century,
but alterations in the statutory framework of slavery were in most
cases minor until the time of the Revolution. No English colony
remained without laws dealing specifically with the governance of
Negroes, though in England itself there were no such statutes. In
the northern colonies, laws concerning Negroes were less detailed,
more haphazard, and generally somewhat less harsh than to the
southwards. New Hampshire's regulations consisted of a 1686 law
prohibiting sale of strong drinks to Negroes and a special act of 1714
which curtailed their going out of doors after nine o'clock at night.
Elsewhere in the North restrictions on Negroes were considerably
more elaborate, probably most so in Boston, a community which

4. See particularly Sirmans, "The Legal Status of the Slave in South Carolina,"
Jour. Southern Hist., 28 (1962), 462–73.
5. Allen D. Candler, comp., *The Colonial Records of the State of Georgia*, 26
vols. (Atlanta, 1904–16), XVIII, 102–44; James Habersham and others to Benjamin Franklin, Savannah, May 19, 1768, Lilla M. Hawes, ed., "Letters to the
Georgia Colonial Agent, July, 1762 to January, 1771," *Georgia Historical Quarterly*, 36 (1952), 274.

had never shown itself backward when it came to legislating proper behavior.[6]

Except on occasions of panic, the punishments prescribed for Negro offenders in the North were considerably lighter than in the southern colonies where the traditional thirty-nine lashes (a number derived from Hebraic law) was the usual rule but by no means the limit of chastisement. The New England colonies, in momentary lapse from Scriptural exactitude, frequently limited the lawful prescription to twenty. Contemporaries recognized this progression of severity from northern to southern to West Indian colonies; as the famous lawyer Daniel Dulany of Maryland explained, "In proportion of the jealousy entertained of them [the slaves], or as they are considered to be formidable, the rigours and severities to which they are exposed, seem to rise, and the power of the magistrate or of the master, is more easily admitted." [7] In the North, the intimacy of contact between master and slave which obtained in so many instances sometimes resulted in a collapse of discipline. Slaves in a family—families were something one was "in," not born into—had excellent opportunity to exercise the leverage of a forceful or guileful personality. A surgeon in Albany discovered this to his cost: as he wrote to a friend, he was determined to sell one of his slaves even though "he is so likely a young Fellow and used to hard country work. His fault is, being born in the Family with me, he thinks I am not to use the same government with him as with one who wasnt, or at least he should be allowed as much priveliege as he chuses, and knowing my Disposition, that I cannot flog him, for the aforesaid Reason, he has at length got the upper hand of me, by the advice of a free Negro Wench who he woud have for his Wife, against my Will." [8] Thus the master might occasionally become the slave. None-

6. Albert S. Batchellor and Henry H. Metcalf, eds., *Laws of New Hampshire*, 5 vols. (Manchester, 1904–22), I, 117, II, 138–39; for Boston, especially the detailed ordinance of 1723 following some fires thought perhaps set by Negroes, Boston Record Commissioners, *Report*, 38 vols. (Boston, 1876–1908), VIII, 173–77.

7. Thomas Harris, Jr., and John M'Henry, eds., *Maryland Reports . . . Provincial Court and Court of Appeals . . .* , 4 vols. (N. Y., 1809–18), I, 560. The 39 lashes are in Deuteronomy 25:3; II Corinthians 11:24.

8. Samuel Stringer to Major Jellis Fonda, Albany, Mar. 2, 1770, MS. letter in New York–Albany Papers, 1770–1783, Stringer, New York Public Library. Rev. James MacSparran in Rhode Island found occasional flogging the only answer: once he gave his Hannibal "one or two Lashes" despite his wife's disapproval, but on another occasion she was so angered by Hannibal that she gave him a few lashes herself after her husband had finished; Daniel Goodwin, ed., *A Letter Book and Abstract of Out Services . . . by the Reverend James MacSparran . . .* (Boston, 1899), 29, 52, 54.

theless, crucial power remained in the hands of the white man; he could sell his masterful possession.

This unharnessed personal power was exemplified in the slave codes of the southern colonies, codes which varied in detail from one colony to another but displayed underlying similarities. Slaves were forbidden to wander off their plantation without a "ticket" from their master or overseer. They were never to be allowed to congregate in large numbers, carry clubs or arms, or strike a white person. Masters were given immunity from legal prosecution should their slave die under "moderate" correction. (One wonders what kind of moderation was envisaged in such cases, but eighteenth-century standards of physical punishment were also harsh for white men and women.) Many colonies found it necessary to provide compensation from the public treasury to owners of slaves executed for a crime or killed in process of capture, since otherwise owners would lie under great temptation to conceal their slaves' offenses. All white persons were authorized to apprehend any Negro unable to give a satisfactory account of himself. In areas of heavy slave concentration white men were required to serve in the slave "patrols" which were supposed to protect the community especially at night and on Sundays, though except in periods of special alarm the patrols were probably far more impressive on paper than in actuality. The critical importance of the numerical ratio of slaves to white men was evident in a South Carolina patrol law of 1740 which specifically exempted from its provisions those "townships lately laid out in this Province, the white inhabitants whereof are much superior in [numbers] to the negroes there, so that the riding patrol there may not be necessary." [9] Frequently the patrols were accorded powers of search and seizure in the slave quarters which American colonials later found so objectionable when applied against themselves.[10] In addition, slaves committing felonies were tried in specially constituted courts which typically consisted of a justice of the peace and two (other) slaveowners. Official punishments ranged from a specific number of stripes "well laid on" all the way to burning at the stake (often but not always after strangulation), a punishment not restricted to the southern colonies or to Negroes and not entirely abandoned for Negroes until the nineteenth century.[11]

9. Cooper and McCord, eds., *Statutes S. C.*, III, 571.
10. For example, Candler, comp., *Col. Recs. Ga.*, XVIII, 232–33.
11. Instances of burning are in Edward McCrady, "Slavery in the Province of South Carolina, 1670–1770," American Historical Association, *Annual Report* (1895), 659; Annapolis *Maryland Gazette*, May 6, 20, 1746; Jeffrey R. Brackett, "The Status of the Slave, 1775–1789," J. Franklin Jameson, ed., *Essays in the*

The codes devoted much attention to the most persistent and potentially dangerous problem of slave control—running away. Probably more time, money, and energy was expended on this problem by white slaveowners, legislators, constables, jailers, and newspaper printers than on any other aspect of administering the slave system. Getting the slaves to work efficiently was the owner's problem, but runaways affected the safety of everyone, the security of all movable property, and the very discipline upon which slavery rested.

Running away was of course not confined in America to Negro slaves; it reflected the inherent difficulty of binding any sort of labor when labor was in short supply. Virtually every issue of every newspaper published in the colonies contained advertisements of servants or slaves run away or taken up at the public jail. Indeed, the problem was as old as bound labor in America. Virginia, for example, had cracked down hard in 1643 by ordering that runaway servants should serve additional time twice the length of their absence and for a second offense be branded with an R (for rogue). The branding represented more than moralistic retribution; it served the same decidedly practical purpose which underlay the Virginia act of 1659 (entitled *"How to know a Runaway Servant"*) providing "that the master of everie such runaway shall cutt or cause to be cutt, the hair of all such runnawayes close above their ears, whereby they may be with more ease discovered and apprehended." [12] The magnitude of the runaway problem, which once the servant had absconded was a problem of identification, may be judged by the Virginia Assembly's passage of *ten* separate laws on the matter between 1661 and 1670. As one writer summarized the situation in 1708, " 'Tis supposed by the Planters, that all unknown Persons are run away from some Master." [13]

Constitutional History of the United States in the Formative Period, 1775–1789 (Boston and N. Y., 1889), 269; Saunders, ed., *Col. Recs. N. C.*, V, 976; Walter Clark, ed., *The State Records of North Carolina*, 26 vols. (Goldsboro, 1886–1907), XIII, 375–76; Jeffrey R. Brackett, *The Negro in Maryland; A Study of the Institution of Slavery* (Baltimore, 1889), 113; Hugh T. Lefler, ed., *North Carolina History Told by Contemporaries* (Chapel Hill, 1934), 263–64; John S. Bassett, *Slavery in the State of North Carolina* (Baltimore, 1899), 95–96; *Providence Gazette*, Apr. 9, 1763; *New-York Gazette*, Jan. 28, 1734.

12. Hening, ed., *Statutes Va.*, I, 254–55, 401, 517–18.

13. *Ibid.*, II, 21, 26, 35, 116–17, 187–88, 239, 266, 273–74, 277–79, 283–84; Eben[ezer] Cook[e], *The Sot-weed Factor: Or a Voyage to Maryland* . . . (London, 1708), 3n. South Carolina and Georgia prohibited teaching slaves to write (1740, 1755) largely in hopes of curtailing forged passes, and Georgia added teaching of reading in 1770: Cooper and McCord, eds., *Statutes S. C.*, VII, 413; Candler, comp., *Col. Recs. Ga.*, XVIII, 136, 685, XIX, Pt. i, 242–43, laws not always observed of course.

Negroes represented something of an answer to the problem of identification. Their distinctive appearance was one attribute which might initially have led masters to prefer Negroes as such to white servants, though this factor undoubtedly was of minor relevance to the growth of slave importations. Still, the Negro was readily identifiable as such; he was born branded, with a mark less definite but no less striking than R. His appearance was not without its disadvantages as an identifying mark, however, for the very distinctiveness of his features tended to overwhelm the white man's ability to discriminate among individuals: some descriptions of the faces of plantation Negroes in runaway advertisements sound as if they might well have fitted every fifth Negro in the region. Much more drastic, there were leaks in a system which logically should have been watertight; not all black men were slaves, a fact which badly weakened the practical effectiveness of blackness as the badge of slavery, as the constantly reiterated phrase "he may try to pass for a free man" so cogently indicated.

While the colonial slave codes seem at first sight to have been intended to discipline Negroes, to deny them freedoms available to other Americans, a very slight shift in perspective shows the codes in a different light: they aimed, paradoxically, at disciplining white men. Principally, the law told the white man, not the Negro, what he must do; the codes were for the eyes and ears of slaveowners (sometimes the law required publication of the code in the newspaper and that clergymen read it to their congregations).[14] It was the white man who was *required* to punish his runaways, prevent assemblages of slaves, enforce the curfews, sit on the special courts, and ride the patrols. Members of the assemblies, most of whom owned slaves, were attempting to enforce slave-discipline by the only means available, by forcing owners, individually and collectively, to exercise it. This surely was a novel situation. In England the King's government sought to keep the lower orders in check by requiring the local gentry to enforce the laws of the realm, but in policing the lowly these country gentlemen acted chiefly in their capacities as justices of the peace, that is, as officials of government. In America, the slaveholding gentry were coerced as individuals by the popularly elected legislatures toward maintenance of a private tyranny which was conceived to be in the community interest. In the community at large, effective maintenance of slavery depended to considerable degree on vigilance and force, and colonial governments

14. For example, Charleston *South-Carolina Gazette*, Apr. 5, 19, 1735; Hening, ed., *Statutes Va.*, IV, 134.

had at their direct command precious little force with which to be vigilant. The militia, which was at most a quasi-governmental organization, was available in emergency (Southern militia laws were transparently concerned with the danger from the internal enemy), but the effectiveness of the militia depended on the spirit of the populace. Thus the maintenance of slavery depended on mass consent among the white population, on widespread agreement that every master should, indeed had to maintain effective control. This situation, sensed but not thought out by white men, tended to highlight in the white slaveowner's mind the necessity and the nakedness of his personal power. The slave codes played a vital role in this process, for they were, in an important sense, public dialogues among masters and among white men generally, intended to confirm their sense of mastery over their Negro slaves—and over themselves. Here were the makings of a lockstep discipline.

The slave codes served white men in still another way by furnishing indirect justification for the severities of slavery. Even in the seventeenth century, a period not distinguished by public agonizing over human misery, it is possible to detect a slight sense of uneasiness over the rigorous restraints which Negroes seemed to require and over the complete absence of restraints on the individual master's power. In 1692 the Maryland legislature freed a mulatto girl whose master and mistress had cut off her ears; the master's claim was, significantly, that the girl was a thief and a runaway and that he had punished her "thinking that as his Slave, he might do with her as he pleased." [15] Probably this sense of uneasiness was palliated by spelling out the necessities of slavery on paper; a slaveowner might lash his slaves unmercifully, in full confidence that he was carrying out an obligation to society—and he had the written law to prove it. Getting slave regulations onto paper also provided opportunity for delineating the characteristics of Negroes in such terms as to leave no doubt that stringent measures with them were utterly necessary. Perhaps there was, after all, considerable basis in fact for the following preamble to the South Carolina code, first borrowed in 1696 from Barbados and reiterated as late as 1735.

WHEREAS, the plantations and estates of this Province cannot be well and sufficiently managed and brought into use, without the labor and service of negroes and other slaves; and forasmuch as the said negroes and other slaves brought unto the people of the Province for that purpose, are of barbarous, wild, savage natures, and such as renders them wholly unqualified to be governed by the laws, customs, and practices of this

15. *Archives Md.*, XIII, 292–307, 383, 390, 457; but see XXII, 446.

Province; but that it is absolutely necessary, that such other constitutions, laws and orders, should in this Province be made and enacted, for the good regulating and ordering of them, as may restrain the disorders, rapines and inhumanity, to which they are naturally prone and inclined; and may also tend to the safety and security of the people of this Province and their estates. . . .[16]

No matter how accurate or inaccurate this unflattering sketch of Negro slaves, the intensity of its tone suggests that legislators were expressing, indirectly, something more than the practical necessity of placing Negroes under different law than white men. In this South Carolina preamble, for example, one has only to substitute "English and other European settlers" for "negroes and other slaves" to achieve an almost classic description of the disintegration of civil society in the wilderness. It seems almost as if the Negro had become a counter image for the European, a vivid reminder of the dangers facing transplanted Europeans, the living embodiment of what they must never allow themselves to become. "Disorders, rapines, and inhumanity" were precisely those qualities which seemed to emerge all too readily when Europeans failed to discipline themselves in America.[17] Application of a distinctly different law to barbarous Negroes in itself afforded reassurance that Englishmen in America had not themselves lapsed into barbarism and had not lost their grip on the old standards.

3. SLAVE REBELLIOUSNESS AND WHITE MASTERY

In addition to clinging to "the laws, customs, and practices of this Province," the colonists were concerned about "the safety and security of the people." Fear of Negro slave rebellion, expressed as early as 1672 in Virginia,[18] was ever-present in the West Indies, the plantation colonies on the continent, and even, with less good reason, in some areas in the North. In many areas it was a

16. Cooper and McCord, eds., *Statutes S. C.*, VII, 352, 371, 385.
17. Compare with the language used by Rev. Charles Woodmason to describe whites in the S. C. back country in the 1760's: "detestable Practices contrary to the Principles of Humanity"; "Vice, Beggary, and Theft"; "Idleness. Lewdness, Theft, Rapine Violence"; "Robberies Thefts, Murders, Plunderings, Burglaries and Villanies of ev'ry Kind"; "Fighting, Brawling Gouging, Quarreling"; "Cunning; Rapine; Fraud and Violence." Richard J. Hooker, ed., *The Carolina Backcountry on the Eve of the Revolution; The Journal and Other Writings of Charles Woodmason, Anglican Itinerant* (Chapel Hill, 1953), 98, 101, 121, 122, 226.
18. Hening, ed., *Statutes Va.*, II, 299–300.

gnawing, gut-wringing fear, intermittently heightened by undeniable instances of servile discontent. Every planter knew that *the* fundamental purpose of the slave laws was prevention and deterrence of slave insurrection. In pleading for a strengthened law in 1710 Governor Alexander Spotswood reminded the Virginia Assembly that constant vigilance was the price of continued mastery:

I Would Willingly Whisper to You The Strength of Your Country and The State of Your Militia; Which on The foot it Now Stands is so Imaginary A Defence, That we Cannot too Cautiously Conceal it from our Neighbours and our Slaves, nor too Earnestly Pray That Neither The Lust of Dominion, nor The Desire of freedom May Stir those people to any Attempts The Latter Sort (I mean our Negro's) by Their Dayly Encrease Seem to be The Most Dangerous; And the Tryals of Last *Aprill* Court may shew that we are not to Depend on Either their Stupidity, or that Babel of Languages among 'em; freedom Wears a Cap which Can Without a Tongue, Call Togather all Those who Long to Shake of the fetters of Slavery and as Such an Insurrection would surely be attended with Most Dreadfull Consequences so I Think we Cannot be too Early in providing Against it, both by putting our Selves in a better posture of Defence and by Making a Law to prevent The Consultations of Those Negros.[19]

Freedom wore the red cap of bloody rebellion, and the colonists never doubted for a moment that their slaves might suddenly clap it to their heads. William Byrd, characteristically, was struck by the obvious analogy with classical slavery: "We have already at least 10,000 men of these descendants of Ham, fit to bear Arms, and these numbers increase every day, as well by birth, as by Importation. And in case there should arise a Man of desperate courage amongst us, exasperated by a desperate fortune, he might with more advantage than Cataline kindle a Servile War. Such a man might be dreadfully mischeivous before any opposition could be formed against him, and tinge our Rivers as wide as they are with blood." [20] This apprehensiveness was entirely genuine among the planters; in 1730, a year of alarm about slaves in Virginia, the governor and Council issued a proclamation ordering that "all persons repairing to their respective Churches or Chappells on Sundays or Holy Days do carry with them their arms to prevent any Surprize thereof in

19. Henry R. McIlwaine, ed., *Journals of the House of Burgesses of Virginia, 1619 . . . 1761,* 9 vols. (Richmond, 1908–15) , *1703–1712,* 240.

20. To Lord Egmont, Va., July 12, 1736, "Letters of the Byrd Family," *Va. Mag. of Hist. and Biog.,* 36 (1928) , 220–21. Denials of danger were rare; Byrd himself made one when tooting Virginia's virtues to a foreign correspondent, to Peter Beckford, Va., Dec. 6, 1735, *ibid.,* 121. For the same motivation, Hugh Jones, *The Present State of Virginia from Whence is Inferred a Short View of Maryland and North Carolina,* ed. Richard L. Morton (Chapel Hill, 1956) , 93.

their Absence when the Slaves are most at Liberty and have greatest Opportunity." [21]

Actual slave revolts were not common, but they did occur—often enough to confirm beyond question the horrifying conviction that they would occur again. A rumor of a poisoning in the next county, an outbreak of unexplained conflagrations, the too-large cluster of furtive Negroes discovered on some lonely road, the vivid memory of the woolly head spiked on a pole at the nearby crossroads (stark punctuation closing the last conspiracy), the image of sullen looks of black defiance which scudded across the impassive faces at today's whipping—only the blind could be free from fear, a chilling fear which even the rhythmic tedium of daily life could never entirely smother.

Whenever slaves offered violent resistance to the authority of white persons, the reaction was likely to be swift and often vicious even by eighteenth-century standards. The bodies of offenders were sometimes hanged in chains, or the severed head impaled upon a pole in some public place as a gruesome reminder to all passers-by that black hands must never be raised against white. These instructive tableaux were not invented by the colonists, for they had been common enough in England; the colonists thought of them as warnings to slaves, though of course they were also warning and counseling themselves by erecting tangible monuments to their own fears. These monuments were far more common than such directly purposeful, drastic methods of slave control as crippling incorrigible runaways by hamstringing or cutting off one foot.[22]

The line between public and private punishment of offending slaves was of course by no means distinct. Until 1722, slaveholders in South Carolina were *required,* under penalty of the law, to have any of their female slaves running away for the fourth time "severely whipped, . . . branded on the left cheek with the letter R, and her left ear cut off." [23] In that colony in 1732 a man named Charles Jones met resistance from a runaway Negro and killed him on the

21. Henry R. McIlwaine and Wilmer L. Hall, eds., *Executive Journals of the Council of Colonial Virginia*, 5 vols. (Richmond, 1925–45), IV, 228.

22. Cooper and McCord, eds., *Statutes S. C.*, VII, 360; *Acts Jamaica* (1738), 160. A famous description of a slave hanged in a cage is in [M. G. St. Jean de Crèvecoeur], *Letters from an American Farmer* . . . (London, 1782), 232–35. For several of the many instances of heads on poles, Savannah *Georgia Gazette*, June 6, 1765; "Punishment for Arson, By a Slave, 1780," *Va. Mag. of Hist. and Biog.*, 16 (1908), 95; and particularly the details in "How a Murder Was Punished in Colonial Days," *Tyler's Quarterly Historical and Genealogical Magazine*, 8 (1926–27), 61–64.

23. Cooper and McCord, eds., *Statutes S. C.*, VII, 360.

spot; Jones thereupon dutifully went to inform a justice of the peace of what he had done and was instructed to cut off the Negro's head and stick it up on a pole at the crossroads.[24] The owner of this now useless piece of property was of course entitled to compensation from the public treasury.

The degree to which slaves actually offered violent resistance to slavery has been the subject of considerable controversy. In the West Indies there were fairly frequent outbreaks, though they are hard to filter out from the steady flow of human violence in the islands. On the American continent, it now seems clear that there were many more rumors than revolts and that the number of actual revolts was small; if it takes a score of persons to make a "revolt" the number all-told before 1860 was probably not more than a dozen.[25] On the other hand, resistance on a small scale was common and widespread, demonstrably so. Probably there was considerable measure of truth in the following description by a mid-century English traveler (despite his consistent bias in favor of slaves) : "To be sure, a *new Negro,* if he must be broke, either from Obstinacy, or, which I am more apt to suppose, from Greatness of Soul, will require more hard Discipline than a young Spaniel: You would really be surpriz'd at their Perseverance; let an hundred Men shew him how to hoe, or drive a Wheelbarrow, he'll still take the one by the Bottom, and the other by the Wheel; and they often die before they can be conquer'd." [26] (The author might have made even more of his point about the hoe had he known it to be the chief agricultural tool in West Africa.) Traces of this sort of subtle sabotage are necessarily rare, but there can be no doubt about the runaways who sometimes banded together in swamps where they caused great alarm if not much actual danger to nearby settlements.[27] With some justification the colonists were unsettled by recurring instances of masters, mistresses, overseers, even whole families murdered by their slaves— variously strangled, clubbed, stabbed, burned, shot, or (most com-

24. Charleston *S.-C. Gaz.,* Jan. 29, 1732.
25. My count. The two most important in the 19th century: Gabriel (1800, Va.) , Nat Turner (1831, Va.) . Herbert Aptheker, *American Negro Slave Revolts* (N. Y., 1943) heavily stresses slave rebelliousness.
26. [Edward Kimber], ["Observations in Several Voyages and Travels in America"], *London Magazine,* [15] (1746) , 325.
27. There is a vivid description in J[ohn] F[erdinand] D. Smyth, *A Tour in the United States of America . . . ,* 2 vols. (London, 1784) , II, 101–2. See also Hening, ed., *Statutes Va.,* III, 210–11. There seems to have been what can only be called a crime wave among slaves in Caroline County, Va., 1761–64; David John Mays, *Edmund Pendleton, 1721–1803: A Biography,* 2 vols. (Cambridge, Mass., 1952) , I, 42–45.

monly the colonists felt) poisoned.[28] Some of these instances might perhaps be properly regarded as ordinary crimes, yet it is impossible to separate slave crime from resistance to slavery; slashing an overseer with an axe might stem from blind rage or a disordered mind, but it scarcely represented acquiescence in the role of slave. At very least, there can be no question that the colonists had considerable justification for regarding their slaves as dangerous.

Presumably the principal reason for the colonists' fear of slave insurrections was a pardonable distaste for having their throats cut. Plainly, however, their fears were exaggerated far beyond the proportions of the danger and were in part a response to more complicated anxieties. The spectre of Negro rebellion presented an appalling world turned upside down, a crazy nonsense world of black over white, an anti-community which was the direct negation of the community as white men knew it. As one Virginian put it, Negro insurrection threatened "their lives, liberties, properties, and every other human blessing." The proper ordering of society was at stake: a conspiracy in New Jersey was discovered when a Negro got drunk, started boasting to a white man of forthcoming exploits, and when reprimanded announced to the astounded white man that he was as good a man as himself. Abhorrence of Negro rule united all white men. In 1775 amid rumors of British proposals to arm the slaves a British traveler commented that such action would put an end to all quarreling between American patriots and Tories, for "in that case friends and foes will be all one." [29] Nearly universally, Negro conspiracies were regarded (and perhaps there was some real basis for the view) as aiming not only at freedom but Negro mastery. Slave conspirators were often said to have plotted taking over the entire locality for themselves and to have intended "utter Extirpation" of

28. For a few instances, Harry B. and Grace M. Weiss, *An Introduction to Crime and Punishment in Colonial New Jersey* (Trenton, 1960), 50–55, 75; William A. Whitehead, *Contributions to the Early History of Perth Amboy and Adjoining Country . . .* (N. Y., 1856), 318–19; Charleston *S.-C. Gaz.*, Aug. 25, 1733, Sept. 20, 1735, May 28, 1737, Apr. 15, 1738, June 28, 1742, July 30, 1744, Oct. 30, 1749, Jan. 24, 1761; Box 3, bundle: Minutes of the House of Burgesses (1750–51) and Minutes of the Council in Assembly (1751–53), 5–6, Parish Transcripts, N.-Y. Hist. Soc.; Cooper and McCord, eds., *Statutes S. C.*, VII, 422–23; John Bartram, "Diary of a Journey through the Carolinas, Georgia, and Florida . . . 1766," ed. Francis Harper, Amer. Phil. Soc., *Transactions*, New Ser., 33 (1942), Pt. i, 22.

29. Pinkney's Williamsburg *Virginia Gazette*, Aug. 31, 1775; *N.-Y. Gaz.*, Mar. 25, 1734; [Janet Schaw], *Journal of a Lady of Quality; Being the Narrative of a Journey from Scotland to the West Indies, North Carolina, and Portugal, in the Years 1774 to 1776*, ed. Evangeline Walker Andrews and Charles M. Andrews, 3d ed. (New Haven, 1939), 199.

most or all of the white people.[30] The colonists seemed incapable of envisaging a Negro revolt which would end with the blacks gaining freedom and nothing more. A successful insurrection loomed as total destruction, as the irretrievable loss of all that white men had won in America—which, of course, was America itself.

This vision of social revolution as wholly destructive derived from the very nature of slavery, and the fact that American slavery was based on racial distinctions merely aggravated a tendency common to all rigidly structured societies. Like the mid-nineteenth-century Russian aristocracy, American planters regarded their bound laborers as a very different kind of people, and the peculiar appearance of the Negro heightened that sense of difference rather than governed it. Certainly most American colonists did not regard their slaves as so different from themselves as to be content in bondage. There was little in the colonists' experience to suggest the existence of such a possibility; in the plantation colonies especially, the one reaction to slave conspiracies most notably lacking was *surprise*. In New York there was a distinctive and contrasting situation which needs to be described in a moment; but it remains the case that in general the colonists felt no need to claim that slavery was a happy arrangement (though it was useful and necessary) and had considerable reason to think that it was not.

This picture of the Negro as a potential insurrectionary was of course most vivid in the plantation colonies, though it was present in the North as well. Significantly, it cut two ways in its implications about Negroes in general. While it implied that the Negro shared with other men a common desire for freedom, it also underlined his difference from the white man by presupposing his natural antagonism. Freedom wore a cap which fitted the Negro and the white man alike, but, as one report said of a supposed conspirator in Charleston, he looked "upon every white Man he should meet as his declared Enemy."[31] Thus every insurrection reinforced both a sense of identity with the Negro and a sense of the gulf between him and his master.

Several of the most important slave uprisings in the colonial period may serve to illustrate some of these suggestions. The first one of serious proportions occurred on a fearful night in 1712 in

30. Quotation from Saunders, ed., *Col. Recs. N. C.*, II, 421.
31. *New-York Weekly Journal*, Sept. 28, 1741; also *Boston News-Letter*, Oct. 1, 1741. For a rare characterization of slaves as contented, James Glen to Board of Trade, S. C., Mar. 1751, Box 22, bundle: New York and South Carolina, 30–31, Parish Transcripts, N.-Y. Hist. Soc.

New York City when a group of some two dozen slaves calculatedly ignited a building, slaughtered nine white men, and wounded almost as many more as they came running to put out the fire. The city had already been set on edge four years earlier by the murder of a family of seven on Long Island (for which four slaves had been put to death with "all the torment possible for a terror to others"), and this new incident set the town in a panic.[32] There was general agreement that the city had narrowly escaped being almost entirely wiped out; as one report said, "had it not been for the Garrison there, that city would have been reduced to ashes, and the greatest part of the inhabitants murdered."[33] The conspirators were hunted down (several cut their own throats in preference to submission) and were quickly brought to trials that were conducted with overenthusiasm yet within the forms of the law; probably many of the Negroes executed were actually guilty. The methods of execution served notice to all Negroes that they would not be permitted to go about barbarously stabbing the civilized inhabitants of New York: thirteen slaves were hanged, one left to die in chains without sustenance, three burned, one burned over slow fire for eight to ten hours, and one left broken on the wheel. No group of white men in the English continental colonies ever received similar treatment.

The conspiracy of 1712 sent New York's frightened legislators scurrying about devising additional legal restraints on Negroes, as virtually every conspiracy did. New York had no more major difficulties for a generation, but then about 1740 the entire seaboard seemed to be shaken by a wave of slave unrest. Events in New York attained the dimensions of a major tragedy, for in the summer of 1741 the city fell into the vortex of a classic witch hunt.

There were many contributing factors. Great Britain was at war with Spain, and the inhabitants of New York were genuinely afraid that Spanish ships were about to descend upon the city at any moment. The winter of 1740–41 had been one of the coldest in memory, with ice choking the docks, and in the deep of the winter the city's bakers had ungraciously gone on strike. Wheat was at its highest price in a generation. A few months later across the river in

32. Kenneth Scott, "The Slave Insurrection in New York in 1712," *N.-Y. Hist. Soc. Quarterly*, 45 (1961), 43–74, a nearly definitive treatment. See particularly Lord Cornbury to Lords of Trade, N. Y., Feb. 10, 1708, E. B. O'Callaghan and Berthold Fernow, eds., *Documents Relative to the Colonial History of the State of New-York*, 15 vols. (Albany, 1853–87), V, 39; Gov. Robert Hunter to Lords of Trade, N. Y., June 23, 1712, *ibid.*, 341–42.

33. Quoted in Scott, "Insurrection in 1712," *N.-Y. Hist. Soc. Qtly.*, 45 (1961), 51.

Hackensack, two Negroes, perhaps exhilarated by the returning warmth of spring, generated some of their own by burning down several barns in one night. They were promptly executed.[34] New Yorkers already had reason to be edgy about Negro arsonists, and it was fire, appropriately, which set off the famous Negro "plot" of 1741. Whether the fires at the fort, chapel, barracks, governor's house, and several other buildings were actually set by Negroes will probably never be known. It is impossible now to tell surely whether there was *any* legitimate basis for suspecting a slave conspiracy, though clearly contemporary suspicions swelled out of all proportion to reality.[35] Many New Yorkers somehow managed to convince themselves that "so bloody and Destructive a Conspiracy was this, that had not the mercifull hand of providence interposed and Confounded their Divices, in one and the Same night the Inhabitants would have been butcher'd in their houses, by their own Slaves, and the City laid in ashes." [36]

Attention somehow fastened on some Negroes who had been seen in the vicinity of the fires, and the trail of investigation soon led to a tavern owned by an unsavory white couple who, it was alleged, catered to Negroes and served as a fence for goods stolen by them. Like other witch hunts the affair would never have blossomed fully without an imaginative informer, who turned up in the person of Mary Burton, a servant to the owners of the tavern and none too savory herself. With her memory joggled in the right direction by officials eager to ferret out the very last conspirator, she was able to

34. Files of *N.-Y. Weekly Jour.*; Richard B. Morris, *Government and Labor in Early America* (N. Y., 1946), 162–64; for New Jersey, *N.-Y. Weekly Jour.*, May 4, 1741; *Boston News-Letter*, May 14, 1741; O'Callaghan and Fernow, eds., *Docs. N.-Y.*, VI, 197; and an earlier instance of arson in Weiss, *Crime in New Jersey*, 45.

35. T. Wood Clarke, "The Negro Plot of 1741," *New York History*, 25 (1944), 167–81; also Aptheker, *Revolts*, 193n; Samuel McKee, Jr., *Labor in Colonial New York, 1664–1776* (N. Y., 1935), 156–66. Important contemporary sources are especially instructive: [Daniel Horsmanden], *A Journal of the Proceedings in the Detection of the Conspiracy Formed by Some White People, in Conjunction with Negro and Other Slaves, for Burning the City of New-York in America, and Murdering the Inhabitants . . .* (N. Y., 1744); and O'Callaghan and Fernow, eds., *Docs. N.-Y.*, VI, 187–88, 196–98, 201–3, VII, 528n; *Journal of the Votes and Proceedings of the General Assembly of the Colony of New York, 1691–1765*, 2 vols. (N. Y., 1764–66), I, 792–94, 806–7; *Col. Laws N. Y.*, III, 148–50; *Boston News-Letter*, Apr. 9, June 25, July 16, 23, Aug. 27, Oct. 8, 1741; *N.-Y. Weekly Jour.*, Mar. 23, Apr. 20, 27, June 15, 22, 29, July 20, Sept. 14, Oct. 18, 1741; Richard Charlton to the Secretary, Oct. 30, 1741, B9, no. 62, S.P.G. Manuscripts (transcripts), Lib. Cong.

36. Daniel Horsmanden to Cadwallader Colden, From on Board Admiral Winne near the Mouth of the Highlands, Aug. 7, 1741, *The Letters and Papers of Cadwallader Colden*, 9 vols. (N.-Y. Hist. Soc., *Collections*, 50–56 [1917–23]), II, 225.

recall that virtually any Negro brought before her had joined in furtive councils in the tavern concerning firing the town and slaughtering the white inhabitants. The court supplemented Mary Burton's evidence most effectively by calling on all Negroes who had participated in the awful conspiracy to save themselves from the stake by coming forward to confess their guilt. Convicted slaves standing at their place of execution were encouraged to name more names, a procedure so effective that one Negro, idling in a crowd gathered to enjoy still another hanging, immediately turned himself over to the constable when he heard his own name croaked by the victim at the stake.[37] As other Protestant Englishmen had done at other periods of social crisis, New York authorities detected in the plot the nefarious influence of Popery. A vagabond dance-master, John Ury, was arrested on suspicion that he was actually a disguised Spanish priest and had fomented the plot; Ury denied both the ecclesiastical elevation and any knowledge of the conspiracy and was therefore executed.

The grip of hysteria weakened as the exceptionally hot summer wore on and the jails become insupportably packed with frightened Negroes. More important in halting the proceedings, Mary Burton's triumphs entirely turned her head and she began alluding to gentlemen of such unimpeachable reputation that the authorities hastened to shut off her stream of accusations.[38] (An astute gentleman in Boston caustically remarked that a parallel development had "finished our Salem Witchcraft.") [39] The toll of this enormous social wreckage was four whites hanged, thirteen Negroes burned, eighteen hanged, and seventy shipped out of the colony.

The reaction of New Yorkers to what seemed a major slave conspiracy may best be characterized as one of thoroughly confused horror. In retrospect it is not the horror but the confusion which is revealing, for that confusion plainly demonstrated that New Yorkers had no firm framework of belief into which a major Negro uprising could be securely fitted. An absurd variety of self-conflicting explanations for the conspiracy were advanced. One of the participating judges, Daniel Horsmanden, published a lengthy justification of the court proceedings which variously treated the

37. N.-Y. Weekly Jour., July 6, 1741.
38. The reaction of one of the justices was confused at best: in his letter of Aug. 7 he wrote first that "it is almost incredible to Say, that great pains has been taken by Some amoung us, to bring a discredit upon Mary Burton the Original Witness" and then explained concerning her most recent revelations, "we could not but be Shockt, the persons mentioned being beyond Suspicion." Daniel Horsmanden to Cadwallader Colden, Colden Papers, II, 224–27.
39. Anon. to Colden, Province of the Massachusetts Bay, 1741, ibid., VII, 271.

conspiracy as a Roman Catholic plot, as a monstrous instance of ingratitude toward kindly white masters who had retrieved these Negroes from the heathen barbarism of Africa, as a conspiracy of normally loyal slaves duped by utterly depraved white people treasonous to their natural loyalties, as an example of the dangerous villainy of slaves in New York, and as a revelation of the inherent baseness of Negroes in general. As one would expect, it is difficult to tell whether the Negro conspirators were being blamed as Negroes or as slaves: Horsmanden, for example, pompously proclaimed he had written his book so "that those who have Property in Slaves, might have a lasting Memento concerning the Nature of them." There is no mistaking, though, the pregnant implications in a courtroom lecture addressed to a condemned Negro in which the uncomprehending fellow was told that in "many, it may be said most, of your complexion" there was "an Untowardness, as it would seem, in the very Nature and Temper of ye . . . , degenerated and debased below the Dignity of Humane Species . . . , *the Beasts of the People*" without so much loyalty as an ox or ass.[40]

The expressions of injured surprise that New York's Negroes had concocted such a horrible plot are especially suggestive in light of the virtual absence of such expressions following conspiracies in other colonies. New York's unique reaction points to a number of factors peculiar to that city. For one thing, New Yorkers rightly had less reason to expect slave uprisings than did plantation owners, for the city's Negroes (probably about 18 per cent of the population) did not work in large gangs but as household servants, assistants to craftsmen, gardeners, porters, and the like. On the other hand, the city had at least twice as large a proportion of Negroes as Philadelphia and Boston, a fact which might facilitate explanation of New York's unique record of actual and supposed conspiracies were it not for the fourth largest northern city, Newport, which had almost as high a proportion of Negroes as New York and apparently no conspiracies of any kind. It seems reasonable to suppose that the tragedy of 1741 in New York, including the confusion as to the nature of a Negro uprising, had roots in the social history of the city. Ever since Leisler's rebellion in 1689 the colony had been plagued by political factionalism which demonstrably affected the course of justice meted out to Negroes in 1712 and probably did so in 1741.[41] More basic still was the long-standing cosmopolitan character of the burgeoning city and its diversity of religious and national groups; from its early years New York had a relatively

40. [Horsmanden], *Journal of the Proceedings*, vi, 186.
41. Scott, "Insurrection in 1712," *N.-Y. Hist. Soc. Qtly.*, 45 (1961), 43–74.

stunted sense of community compared to Boston, Philadelphia, and considerably smaller Newport. Probably this relative lack of communal solidarity cut several ways as far as Negroes were concerned. Certainly it was conducive to just the sort of social explosion which occurred in the summer of 1741. More generally, while diversity of national backgrounds in New York might be thought to have created an atmosphere in which the Negro could be more readily accepted as an inherent member of the community, as merely one stranger among many, the resultant lack of social cohesiveness and sense of communal identity may have operated more powerfully toward generating an insecurity which could to some extent be palliated by turning viciously against the Negro. In New York exclusion of Negroes from the white community would by apposition provide—hopefully—solidarity among the remaining members. In many areas of the South this solidarity was less illusory; indeed where large numbers of slaves constituted a genuine threat it was almost palpable. Colonists in the South thus stood on far more solid vantage ground when viewing this threat than New Yorkers were able to attain.

The plot of 1741 was one of a series of disturbances by (or over) slaves which affected many colonies around 1740. That the disturbances coincided with the Great Awakening of religious excitement is suggestive of widespread heightening of diffuse social tensions throughout the colonies. Outside New York there seem usually to have been solid grounds for the alarms which were raised, though it is well to remember that two opposing parties are required to make an uprising and that the line between a real and an imaginary slave conspiracy cannot be drawn with precision. One or two reports or rumors of slave unruliness tended to break others loose and produce an avalanche. In 1739 the most serious outbreak of the colonial period occurred at Stono, South Carolina, when between fifty and a hundred slaves killed some white men and marched southwards "with Colours displayed, and two Drums beating" to join the Spanish in Florida. They were dispersed by the hastily summoned militia after a brief pitched battle "wherein one fought for Liberty and Life the other for their Country and every thing that was Dear to them"—a revealing characterization of an American slave rebellion.[42] Next year in South Carolina a plot revealed to

---

42. To the numerous citations in Aptheker, *Revolts*, 186–89, may be added "A Ranger's Report of Travels with General Oglethorpe, 1739–1742," Newton D. Mereness, ed., *Travels in the American Colonies* (N. Y., 1916), 222–23; [Alexander Hewat], *An Historical Account of the Rise and Progress of the Colonies of South Carolina and Georgia*, 2 vols. (London, 1779), II, 72–74.

authorities by a slave (faithful or traitorous according to one's lights) resulted in dozens of exemplary hangings.[43] Maryland, too, was the scene of slave rebelliousness in the late 1730's, and some frightened citizens of Prince George's County warned the Council of "a most wicked and dangerous Conspiracy having been formed by them the slaves to destroy his Majestys Subjects within this Province, and to possess themselves of the whole Country"—total destruction once again.[44] In Roxbury, Massachusetts, in July 1741 there occurred what can almost be described as a Negro lynching— perhaps the only such instance before the nineteenth century— when the *Boston News-Letter* reported "a very sorrowful Affair" in which "a Negro Man suspected of stealing some Money, was by divers Persons ty'd to a Tree and whip'd in order to bring him to confess the Fact; after which he was taken down and lying some Time upon the Grass was carried into his Masters House, but died soon after." [45] This was communal effort with a vengeance.

What was notably lacking in the reaction of the colonists to this wave of disturbances was the panic which struck New York. In South Carolina, the only colony seriously threatened, refractory slaves were not lectured and roasted but dispersed, whipped, and some hanged as examples. These hangings, in contrast to New York's, were preventative rather than retributive. South Carolinians, moreover, seemed under no compulsion to invent slave conspiracies; they were sufficiently acquainted with the real thing. In 1749, for example, an alarm was raised which might easily have led to panic. A man named James Akin ran breathlessly to the colony's officials warning of a combined revolt and runaway conspiracy revealed to him by some Negroes, including several of his own, who apparently hoped to be rewarded for their meritorious disclosures. According to Akin, the ringleader was a white man but most of the conspirators were Negroes. Instead of panicking, the authorities carefully interrogated several whites and a large number of Negroes. In a dramatic climax Governor James Glen himself examined a number of Negroes individually in his chambers, and several admitted that their accusations were baseless. The Governor then gathered his Council, which agreed that the conspiracy, which had once been "horrid," was merely "supposed" and that Akin had been too much taken in by several of his slaves—which he very obviously

43. Aptheker, *Revolts*, 189.

44. *Ibid.*, 191–92. There were some suspicions of Roman Catholic influence; *Archives Md.*, XL, 457, 460, 485, 486, 494.

45. *Boston News-Letter*, July 23, 1741. A white murderer caught red-handed was lynched in 1792: Norfolk *Virginia Chronicle*, Sept. 8, 1792.

had. The deluded planter was given no punishment, but several slaves were shipped out of the province. This sober and realistic handling of a potentially explosive incident seems to have come easily to people who were committed beyond recall to slavery as a way of life, and knew it. Fortunately, James Akin did not live in New York City, nor, one might add, a century later.[46]

4. FREE NEGROES AND FEARS OF FREEDOM

Because the colonists dreaded slave insurrections they were quick to excoriate persons they conceived to be potential fomenters of revolt. A chief source of danger, the colonists sometimes felt, was the Negro who was not a slave. Most of the laws restricting free Negroes claimed merely that they were given to receiving goods stolen by slaves and to harboring runaways. Yet Governor William Gooch of Virginia thought he detected a far more serious danger: as he said, "there had been a Conspiracy discovered amongst the Negros to Cutt off the English, wherin the Free-Negros and Mulattos were much Suspected to have been Concerned, (which will forever be the Case)." [47] While there may have been good grounds for the charges of theft and harboring runaways, there certainly were not for thinking that free Negroes encouraged slave conspiracies. *No* free Negro—with one possible exception—was clearly implicated in any conspiracy in the United States until 1822. One was imprisoned during the New York prosecutions of 1712 but was eventually tried and acquitted by a jury; in 1741 when panic-stricken New Yorkers were arresting and convicting Negroes on the flimsiest grounds imaginable, only six free Negroes were arrested, of which five were released and one transported out of the colony.[48] Plainly the fear of free Negroes rested on something more than the realities of the situation.

46. This affair, not mentioned by Aptheker, can be followed in Box 3, three bundles: Minutes of Council in Assembly (1747–48, 1748–49) including papers on the Negro conspiracy, Pts. i–iii, Parish Transcripts, N.-Y. Hist. Soc. For a similar instance of restraint, Charleston S.-C. Gaz., Aug. 15, 1741.

47. Emory G. Evans, ed., "A Question of Complexion: Documents Concerning the Negro and the Franchise in Eighteenth-Century Virginia," Va. Mag. of Hist. and Biog., 71 (1963), 414.

48. Scott, "Insurrection in 1712," N.-Y. Hist. Soc. Qtly., 45 (1961), 62–67; Horsmanden, Journal of the Proceedings, 151, appendix, 12–16. The exception was "James Booth, a free negroe, the Court finding he was knowing of the negroes Intentions of goeing away and likewise enterteyned diverse of them att his house, ordered that he receive twenty-nine Lashes upon his bare Back, well lay'd on—which was done accordingly. . . ." This "Late Dangerous Conspiracy" in Virginia in 1709 was largely a runaway plot, but evidently there were plans to kill if necessary. Palmer et al., Cal. Va. State Papers, I, 129–30.

The colonists' claim was grounded on a revealing assumption: that free Negroes were essentially more Negro than free, that in any contest between oppressed and oppressors free Negroes would side not with their brethren in legal status but with their brethren in color. The flowering of racial slavery had crowded out the possibility, which had once been perhaps close to an actuality, that some free Negroes would think of themselves as full members of the white community. Paralleling this assumption was the assured feeling that all white men would stand together in any final crisis. It was still possible for white men to imagine that a few traitors in their midst might join and lead the Negroes (much more possible than in 1859—John Brown was a foreign enemy), but the fear of white servants and Negroes uniting in servile rebellion, a prospect which made some sense in the 1660's and 70's, had vanished completely during the following half century. Significantly, the only rebellions by white servants in the continental colonies came before the firm entrenchment of slavery.[49]

The tendency toward barring *all* Negroes from full participation in the white man's world, the first faint signs of which had appeared in the southern colonies in 1640 with the beginning of the significant historical record concerning Negroes, became more and more pronounced until it had become a widespread pattern well before the American Revolution. The Virginia Assembly's declaration in 1668 that free Negroes "ought not in all respects to be admitted to a full fruition of the exemptions and impunities of the English" proved to be the guideline which in varying degrees was accepted in every colony.[50] On the other hand, no universal practices developed, no indications of complete consensus on the restrictions appropriate for free Negroes. Rather, the frequently random and miscellaneous character of these restrictions suggests merely a trend, the terminal point of which became completely clear only in the ante-bellum South.

Many colonies made efforts in the first half of the eighteenth century to prevent too many Negroes from becoming free. During the years between 1722 and 1740 South Carolina unabashedly required newly freed Negroes to leave the province unless permitted to remain by special act of assembly. During the same period North Carolina flatly barred freed slaves from remaining in the colony but in 1741 allowed them to remain if their manumission

---

49. For example, "The Servants' Plot of 1663," *Va. Mag. of Hist. and Biog.*, 15 (1907–08), 38–43.

50. Hening, ed., *Statutes Va.*, II, 267.

had been approved by a county court. Virginia in 1691 required manumitted Negroes to leave the colony, in 1705 dropped the requirement, but then in 1723 prohibited all manumissions except those specifically permitted by the governor and Council for "meritorious services." Not all the plantation colonies were so resolved, for Georgia placed no restrictions on manumission and in Maryland in 1715 a move by the Council to forbid manumission was blocked by the lower house which successfully pushed through a less drastic law fining free Negroes for harboring runaway slaves.[51] In the northern colonies, laws which set conditions on manumission, while calling free Negroes "idle and slothful," aimed chiefly at the difficulties created by masters freeing superannuated slaves so their support would fall upon the public purse.[52] In every colony, though, there was a steady trickle of private manumissions and in the southern colonies an occasional dramatic bestowal of freedom by the legislature upon a Negro who had revealed a conspiracy or compounded a remedy for syphilis or rattlesnake bite. No one suggested, as men were to do in the waning days of slavery, that free Negroes be re-enslaved. South Carolina and Georgia placed the burden of legal proof on free Negroes to show positively that they were not slaves, yet the North Carolina assembly, as well as Virginia's, took determined measures against "the Practice of Binding out Free Negroes and Mollottoes till they Come to thirty one years of Age Contrary to the Assent of the partys and to Law." [53]

Once free, whether born so or manumitted, Negroes were in many instances subjected to humiliating restrictions, though again no colony worked out a well-considered policy. It is suggestive that many of the acts liberating individual slaves in the plantation colonies extended to them "all the liberties, priviledges and immu-

51. Cooper and McCord, eds., *Statutes S. C.*, VII, 384 (lapsed 1740) ; Clark, ed., *State Recs. N. C.*, XXIII, 65, 107, 203–4; Hening, ed., *Statutes Va.*, III, 87–88, 447–62, IV, 132; *Archives Md.*, XXX, 16, 65–66, 177–79, 284. Maryland regulated the form of manumission (1752) but never made it drastically difficult; James M. Wright, *The Free Negro in Maryland, 1634–1860* (N. Y., 1921) , 24, 53–72.

52. For example, *Acts and Laws, of His Majesty's Colony of Rhode-Island, and Providence-Plantations, in America* (Newport, 1730) , 162–63; Trumbull and Hoadly, eds., *Recs. Col. Conn.*, IV, 375–76, 408, V, 233; *Col. Laws N. Y.*, I, 764–65, 922–23; Samuel Allinson, ed., *Acts of the General Assembly of the Province of New-Jersey . . . 1702 . . . 1776 . . .* (Burlington, 1776) , 20–21, 316; *Laws of the State of Delaware*, 4 vols. (New Castle and Wilmington, 1797–1816) , I, 214, 435–36.

53. Cooper and McCord, eds., *Statutes S. C.*, VII, 352, 371, 398; Candler, comp., *Col. Recs. Ga.*, XVIII, 104; quotation from Box 2, bundle: N. C. Minutes of Council in Assembly (1731–33, 1756–60) , Minutes of House of Burgesses (1756–60) , 9, Parish Transcripts, N.-Y. Hist. Soc.; Russell, *Free Negro in Va.*, 99.

nitys of or to a free negro belonging." [54] In the southern colonies
free Negroes were barred from testifying against white persons—a
disability which gave carte blanche to any unscrupulous white
man—but were themselves often the legitimate objects of testimony
by slaves, who under no circumstances could testify against whites.
By contrast, free Negroes in New York were immune from testimony
by slaves, and in New England slaves themselves could testify
against anyone. [55] In many colonies, North and South, free Negroes
were sometimes cavalierly included in certain provisions of the slave
codes. In Virginia, for example, where in 1680 slaves had been
forbidden to strike Christians, the Assembly in 1705 prohibited any
Negro, mulatto, or Indian, "bond or free," from lifting his hand in
opposition to "any christian, not being negro, mulatto, or
Indian." [56] Also, free Negroes were generally barred from sexual
relations with whites and occasionally (but by no means usually)
assigned more severe punishments than white men for the same
crime, taxed more heavily than whites, or prohibited from owning
real estate. [57] Many colonies passed laws excluding Negroes from the
militia, though on this matter the gulf between paper and practice
was especially large. Although this exclusion lay on the statute
books of all four New England colonies, Negroes served in New
England forces in every colonial war. New York at first legally
excluded all Negroes but later only slaves; New Jersey eventually
adopted the same policy; Pennsylvania and Delaware did not ex-

54. Hening, ed., *Statutes Va.*, III, 537–38 (1710); Cooper and McCord, eds., *Statutes S. C.*, VII, 419–20.

55. Hening, ed., *Statutes Va.*, III, 298, V, 245, VI, 107, XII, 182; Clark, ed., *State Recs. N. C.*, XXIII, 202–3, 262, 559; Candler, comp., *Col. Recs. Ga.*, XVIII, 111–12, 660, XIX, Pt. i, 218–19; Cooper and McCord eds., *Statutes S. C.*, VII, 401–2; *Archives Md.*, XXXIII, 111; Edwin Olson, "The Slave Code in Colonial New York," *Jour. Negro Hist.*, 29 (1944), 148, 150; Greene, *The Negro in New England*, 179–82.

56. Hening, ed., *Statutes Va.*, II, 481, III, 459, VI, 110; and other instances in *Acts and Resolves Mass.*, I, 578; Bartlett, ed., *Recs. Col. R. I.*, III, 492; Trumbull and Hoadly, eds., *Recs. Col. Conn.*, V, 52–53; Greene, *Negro in New England*, 299; Wright, *Free Negro in Md.*, 31; Cooper and McCord, eds., *Statutes S. C.*, VII, 402, 407; Candler, comp., *Col. Recs. Ga.*, XVIII, 112–13, 660–61, XIX, Pt. i, 219–21.

57. For sexual relations, see chap. 4; for punishments, previous note and *Col. Laws N. Y.*, I, 764; *Laws Del.*, I, 306; Hening, ed., *Statutes Va.*, III, 276; for taxes, Ralph B. Flanders, "The Free Negro in Ante-bellum Georgia," *North Carolina Historical Review*, 9 (1932), 251–52 (after 1768); Clark, ed., *State Recs. N. C.*, XXIII, 72, 106, 345, discrimination which elicited protest from several groups of white men in the 1760's and early 1770's (Saunders, ed., *Col. Recs. N. C.*, V, 295, VI, 902, 982–83, IX, 97–98, 146); for real estate, *Col. Laws N. Y.*, I, 764; repealed 18 years later, II, 682–83, 687–88; [*Acts N. J. in 1704*], 20; Allinson, ed., *Acts N. J.*, 20; Greene, *Negro in New England*, 312–13.

clude Negroes; Maryland did, but Virginia allowed them to serve without arms; North Carolina required all freemen to serve, while South Carolina and Georgia mustered in some Negroes both free and slave. In Boston, where private citizens had rarely been left in doubt concerning their public duties, free Negroes were liable to service repairing the public roads because they did not serve in the trained bands.[58]

A similar trend, again not attaining the dimensions of a universal pattern, was evident in the common exclusion of free Negroes from the polls. It is enormously difficult to discover what sorts of people even among the white population actually voted, and the best that may be said concerning Negroes is that in the northern colonies and probably North Carolina a few free Negroes occasionally did vote. Significantly, in the early years of the eighteenth century, opinion in North and South Carolina had not yet hardened sufficiently to keep a few free Negroes from coming forward at the polls, but just as significantly, the fact that a few Negroes actually voted is known today only because there were several indignant protests against their doing so. Both colonies officially prohibited Negro voting about 1715, but North Carolina did not continue the prohibition after the 1730's—not the only instance of North Carolina's deviation on matters concerning the Negro. Georgia restricted the suffrage to white men in 1761. Until the Revolution Maryland and the northern colonies did not officially bar Negroes from the polls, but it seems fairly certain that they were usually barred by local custom. The Virginia Assembly left no doubt on the matter, for in 1705 it declared Negroes ineligible for public office (a prohibition which suggests the possibility that a Negro may have occupied one) and in 1723 excluded Negroes from the polls.[59]

58. Benjamin Quarles, *The Negro in the American Revolution* (Chapel Hill, 1961), 8–9; Greene, *Negro in New England*, 126–28, 187–90; *Col. Laws N. Y.*, I, 506, II, 91, IV, 776; [*Acts N. J. in 1704*], 5; *The Laws, and Acts of the General Assembly of His Majesties Province of Nova Caesarea or New-Jersey* . . . ([N. Y.], 1717), 17; Allinson, ed., *Acts N. J.*, 140; Edward R. Turner, *The Negro in Pennsylvania, Slavery—Servitude—Freedom, 1639–1861* (Washington, 1911), 179; *Laws Del., passim*; Bacon, ed., *Laws Md., 1715*, chap. 43, no. 7; *Archives Md.*, VII, 56, 190, XIII, 556, XXII, 564, XXVI, 271, XXX, 279; Russell, *Free Negro in Va.*, 94–96; Hening, ed., *Statutes Va.*, VI, 533; Saunders, ed., *Col. Recs. N. C.*, II, 197; Clark, ed., *State Recs. N. C.*, XXIII, 29, 244, 518, 596; Charleston *S.-C. Gaz.*, Oct. 31, 1748; Cooper and McCord, eds., *Statutes S. C.*, VII, 347–51, 422; Candler, comp., *Col. Recs. Ga.*, XVIII, 7, 16–17, 38–46; Boston Record Commissioners, *Report*, XI, 60, 72–74, 115–16, 137–38, 144, 166–67, 210, 232–33, XIII, 8–9, 42–43, 59–60, 82–83, 106, 109–10, 145, XV, 135, 251, XVII, 29, 68, XIX, 103–4, 195–96, 240, XX, 218, 236, 257; and perhaps other Massachusetts towns also: *Acts and Resolves Mass.*, I, 606–7.

59. The best treatment, avowedly incomplete, is Emil Olbrich, *The Development of Sentiment on Negro Suffrage to 1860* (Madison, Wis., 1912); see also

This Virginia provision of 1723 came immediately after a slave conspiracy and represented one kind of reflex action to slave rebellion. Freemen in America—*Negro* freemen—lost their franchise because Negro slaves alarmed their white masters. Already traditional English liberties were being altered in the New World. A dozen years later the Virginia provision was challenged by colonial authorities in England (nowhere near a record in delay) who asked pointedly why free Negroes and mulattoes were excluded from elections. Governor William Gooch, a popular man with Virginians and rapidly becoming a Virginian himself, hastened to straighten out his ivory-towered superiors with a polite but firm lecture on the realities of life in the plantations.

[The] Assembly thought it necessary, not only to make the Meetings of Slaves very Penal, but to fix a perpetual Brand upon Free Negros and Mulattos by excluding them from that great Priviledge of a Freeman, well knowing they always did, and ever will, adhere to and favour the Slaves. And 'tis likewise said to have been done with design, which I must think a good one, to make the free Negros sensible that a distinction ought to be made between their offspring and the Descendants of an Englishman, with whom they never were to be Accounted Equal. This, I confess, may Seem to carry an Air of Severity to Such as are unacquainted with the Nature of Negros, and Pride of a manumitted Slave, who looks on himself imediately On his Acquiring his freedom to be as good a Man as the best of his Neighbours, but especially if he is descended of a white Father or Mother, lett them be of what mean Condition soever; and as most of them are the Bastards of some of the worst of our imported Servants and Convicts, it seeems no ways Impolitick, as well for discouraging that kind of Copulation, as to preserve a decent Distinction between them and their Betters, to leave this mark on them, until time and Education has changed the Indication of their spurious Extraction, and made some Alteration in their Morals.[60]

Though they comprehended the economics of slavery well enough, officials in England did not really quite understand, at least during the first third of the century, this logic of the racial situation in the

Albert E. McKinley, *The Suffrage Franchise in the Thirteen English Colonies in America* (Phila., 1905) ; Stephen B. Weeks, "The History of Negro Suffrage in the South," *Political Science Quarterly*, 9 (1894) , 671–703; Greene, *Negro in New England*, 300–303; Turner, *Negro in Pa.*, 172–73. For the laws and protests, Clark, ed., *State Recs. N. C.*, XXIII, 12–13, 208; Saunders, ed., *Col. Recs. N. C.*, II, 214–15, 903, 908, IV, 251; McKinley, *Suffrage*, 137–38; Cooper and McCord, eds., *Statutes S. C.*, III, 3, 136, 657, IV, 99; Candler, comp., *Col. Recs. Ga.*, XVIII, 465–66; Hening, ed., *Statutes Va.*, III, 250–51, IV, 133–34, VII, 519.

60. To Alured Popple, May 18, 1736, Evans, ed., "Question of Complexion," *Va. Mag. of Hist. and Biog.*, 71 (1963) , 414. William Gooch to [Board of Trade], Va., May 18, 1736, Box 1, bundle: Virginia Historical Documents relating to Negroes and Slavery, 1699–1760, 73–74, Parish Transcripts, N.-Y. Hist. Soc. See also McIlwaine, ed., *Jours. House Burgesses Va., 1712–26*, 360.

New World. In 1717, for instance, the Crown's attorney-general advised the Council of Trade and Plantations that it was reasonable that a free Christian Negro should be admitted to the same privileges as other freemen.[61] Planters in America were better attuned to their own convictions.

5. RACIAL SLAVERY IN A FREE SOCIETY

These convictions became evident not merely in legal restrictions on free Negroes but in various ways which suggest a trend toward exclusion of all Negroes from full participation in the white community. The trend was least obvious in the arena of human activity within which the relation between the two races was most completely rationalized—work. Slavery itself operated on an exclusionary principle, so that when the Negro was considered in his role as a laboring machine he appeared sufficiently separated from the white community. As a laborer in the colonies, the Negro slave did not arouse widespread hostility among white men. This fact attains additional importance in light of the widespread use of Negroes not merely as agricultural laborers but as seamen and porters, as coachmen and house servants; a considerable number were trained to skilled trades, everything from cooper and carpenter to baker and blacksmith, both in towns and on the plantations. There were, however, some expressions of resentment against the use of slaves in certain areas and occupations. Protests against Negro slave competition were slanted principally at the employment of Negroes as skilled craftsmen, porters, and boat pilots; these protests cropped up particularly in urban centers, where competition was most obvious and protest most easily organized.[62] Significantly, it is

61. Sainsbury *et al.*, eds., *Calendar of State Papers, America and West Indies, 1716–17*, 286.

62. Boston Record Commissioners, *Report*, VII, 5; Greene, *Negro in New England*, 112; Trumbull and Hoadly, eds., *Recs. Col. Conn.*, XIV, 329; *Minutes of the Common Council of the City of New York, 1675–1776*, 8 vols. (N. Y., 1905), I, 179; Box 1, bundle: New York, Minutes of Council in Assembly, Minutes of House of Burgesses (1688–93, 1705, 1743–60), 1, Parish Transcripts, N.-Y. Hist. Soc.; Candler, comp., *Col. Recs. Ga.*, I, 58, XIII, 276, XVIII, 277–82, XIX, Pt. ii, 23–30, XXIII, 442–47; Francis Moore, *A Voyage to Georgia . . . 1735 . . .* (London, 1744) (Georgia Historical Society, *Collections*, 1 [1840]), 96–97; Charles Z. Lincoln, ed., *State of New York. Messages from the Governors . . .*, 11 vols. (Albany, 1909), I, 260. And the best secondary account, Morris, *Government and Labor*, 182–88, 524. The usual pattern of employment is suggested by an advertisement for "a WHITE CARPENTER, capable of superintending a few Negro Carpenters, either in Town or Country." Charleston *Gazette of the State of South-Carolina*, July 8, 1784.

often impossible to ascertain from the language of these protests whether they aimed only at slave labor or at free Negro labor as well. Indignant petitions deplored the "Great Confusion and Irregularity [which] daily Insue from the Insolent and Turbilent disposition and behaviour" of Negro competitors whose presence debarred "the Petitioners from being employed, to the utter Ruin of themselves and Families" or would lead "to the great discouragement of [the immigration of] Your Majestys white Subjects." [63] In fact the presence of large numbers of Negro slaves in the South did discourage white immigration, and colonial officials occasionally responded to these over-tearful laments with ordinances restricting the entry of free and slave Negroes into various employments. What is impressive about the evidence of resentment over economic competition, however, is its occasional character. In Williamsburg, for instance, white and Negro craftsmen seem to have felt no sense of racial competition.[64] Only in Charleston was there evidence of widespread and continuing resentment, and there distaste for the Negro as a job competitor was closely linked to fear that South Carolina was running dangerously short of white men.[65] No important movement for restricting Negroes to chores of servile drudgery developed,[66] and of course no one tried to claim that Negroes were incapable of engaging in skilled crafts—a notion concocted after the abolition of slavery.[67] What happened in the South instead was that white workers became reluctant to labor in the fields as employees of another man. As the Earl of Egmont recounted the views of a Carolina merchant in 1740, "He said that where there are Negroes, a white

63. An amalgam from quotations in Saunders, ed., *Col. Recs. N. C.*, IX, 803–4; Cheesman A. Herrick, *White Servitude in Pennsylvania; Indentured and Redemption Labor in Colony and Commonwealth* (Phila., 1926), 88; Donnan, ed., *Documents Slave Trade*, IV, 288–89.

64. Thad W. Tate, Jr., *The Negro in Eighteenth-Century Williamsburg* (Charlottesville, Va., 1966), 70.

65. Donnan, ed., *Documents Slave Trade*, IV, 288–89; Charleston *S.-C. Gaz.*, Nov. 8, 1742, July 9, 1750, supplement, Nov. 1, 1760; Warren B. Smith, *White Servitude in Colonial South Carolina* (Columbia, 1961), 34–36; Richard Walsh, *Charleston's Sons of Liberty: A Study of the Artisans, 1763–1789* (Columbia, 1959), 23–25, 49, 57–58, 109–10, 124–27; Carl Bridenbaugh, *Cities in Revolt: Urban Life in America, 1743–1776* (N. Y., 1955), 88–89, 274, 286; Jernegan, *Laboring Classes in America*, 20–21.

66. In 1750 the South Carolina lower house "humbly proposed that all white persons who will accept of any servile Labour such as Porters etc. shall have the preference to all Jobbs that offer, and be intitled to additional hire per diem." Box 3, bundle: S. C., Minutes of House of Burgesses (1749–50), 14, Parish Transcripts, N.-Y. Hist. Soc.

67. And exploded by Leonard Price Stavisky, "Negro Craftsmanship in Early America," *Amer. Hist. Rev.*, 54 (1948–49), 315–25.

Man despises to work, saying, *what, will you have me a Slave and work like a Negroe?* Nevertheless, if such white Man had Negroes of his own, he would work in the field with them." [68]

Absence of widespread resentment against Negro competition reflected the prevailing shortage of all kinds of labor in America. Employers wanted Negroes because they were cheaper to buy and keep than white men and perhaps, as one contemporary claimed, because Negroes of both sexes could be put to work in the fields while white women could not.[69] Then, too, a white craftsman could never tell when he might want to hire or buy a Negro of his own. For men on the make, Negroes afforded additional leverage for pulling oneself up by the bootstraps.

Apart from the sphere of work, though, slavery did much less to structure the Negro's role in the white man's mind, and accordingly white men were under greater pressure to elaborate upon their sense of distinctness from Negroes. This pressure operated with all Negroes, slave almost as much as free. On occasion slaves were criticized for dressing too finely, though on this score gentlemen had been having trouble with all their inferiors ever since landing in America.[70] In the 1730's in New York some Negroes were reported to have had "the Impudence to assume the Stile and Title of FREE MASONS, in Imitation of a Society here; which was looked upon to be a gross Affront to the Provincial Grand Master and Gentlemen of the Fraternity . . . and was very ill ACCEPTED." In 1721, a Boston newspaper's account of a grand Negro wedding, in which the happy pair "went to Church in a Sley; where an Englishman stood as a Father to give the Woman in Marriage," failed to show much appreciation of this interracial harmony and suggested that such a public display might have been concocted to ridicule the government. In 1745, Massachusetts expressly prohibited Negroes from participating in a government lottery, presumably to preclude the off-chance that some Negro might win it. More revealing was Dela-

68. Candler, comp., *Col. Recs. Ga.*, V, 476. For similar expressions, "An Impartial Inquiry into the State and Utility of the Province of Georgia. London: 1741," Ga. Hist. Soc., *Collections*, 1 (1840), 172; Saunders, ed., *Col. Recs. N. C.*, II, 310; "Colonel William Byrd on Slavery and Indentured Servants, 1736, 1739," *Amer. Hist. Rev.*, 1 (1895–96), 88–89.

69. [Thomas Nairne], *A Letter from South Carolina; Giving an Account of the Soil, Air, Product, Trade, Government, Laws, Religion, People, Military Strength, etc. of That Province* . . . (London, 1710), 59.

70. Phila. *American Weekly Mercury*, Aug. 10, 1738; Cooper and McCord, eds., *Statutes S. C.*, VII, 396; Charleston *S.-C. Gaz.*, Nov. 5, 1744.

ware's law of 1770 which forbade employing Negroes to administer corporal punishment to white offenders.[71]

This tendency to hold Negroes at arm's length amounted to something very different from modern "segregation." Much later, something resembling the twentieth-century practice developed in the ante-bellum North, but in the South segregation did not come into general existence with legal support until after (often long after) the Civil War.[72] "Segregation," as a mechanism for maintaining social distance and control, was for the most part unnecessary and almost meaningless in the period when most Negroes were slaves, for slavery was very effective segregation—at least in the mind, where it counted. Until the latter part of the eighteenth century, moreover, there was no explicit racist doctrine in existence which could have served as rationale for separate public water pumps. Then too, life in the colonies was characterized by less travel, less schooling, and less urban concentration, that is, by few of the focal points of twentieth-century controversy. Indeed there were only two or three points at which whites and Negroes were likely to come together in a social context which might have implied equality and hence have threatened the white man's security. Specifically these were the church and the burying ground and to less extent the schools.

It may be said generally that some Negroes often attended regular church services, were sometimes accepted into full membership, and occasionally even invited to address largely white congregations.[73]

71. [Horsmanden], *Journal of the Proceedings*, 26; Boston *New-England Courant*, Dec. 25, 1721 (an anti-government paper); *Acts and Resolves Mass.*, XIII, 431; *Laws Del.*, I, 479.

72. Leon F. Litwack, *North of Slavery: The Negro in the Free States, 1790–1860* (Chicago, 1961); C. Vann Woodward, *The Strange Career of Jim Crow*, 2d rev. ed. (N. Y., 1966).

73. The records of many New England churches show Negroes as full members. For some instances of membership and attendance in various colonies, Wilkins Updike, *A History of the Episcopal Church in Narragansett, Rhode Island, Including a History of Other Episcopal Churches in the State*, ed. Daniel Goodwin, 2d ed., 3 vols. (Boston, 1907), III, 63, 65, 66, 75, 77; Edgar Legare Pennington, "Thomas Bray's Associates and Their Work Among the Negroes," American Antiquarian Society, *Proceedings*, New Ser., 48 (1938), 359, 388, 390; Henry J. Cadbury, "Negro Membership in the Society of Friends," *Jour. Negro Hist.*, 21 (1936), 152–53, 184–210; Richard I. Shelling, "William Sturgeon, Catechist to the Negroes of Philadelphia and Assistant Rector of Christ Church, 1747–1766," *Historical Magazine of the Protestant Episcopal Church*, 8 (1939), 388; Morgan Edwards, "History of the Baptists in Delaware," *Pennsylvania Magazine of History and Biography*, 9 (1885), 206; James B. Lawrence, "Religious Education of the Negro in the Colony of Georgia," *Ga. Hist. Qtly.*, 14

They were usually seated in a distinct section of the church,[74] a seemingly flagrant instance of "segregation" which was actually in large measure an expression of eighteenth-century ideas about people in general rather than Negroes in particular. The pattern of seating in most colonial churches was partly governed (whether formally or not) by accepted social distinctions; the town drunk did not occupy a prominent pew even when sober. The meaner sort of people accepted seats at the back or in the gallery, and Negroes, even Negroes who owned some property, were patently of the meaner sort. Here lay the makings but not the actuality of a radical separation.

The temptation to categorize the orders of men extended literally to the grave. In the northern cities and towns at least, Negroes were often, probably usually, interred in a separate section of the burial ground, and in this matter alone separation was occasionally written into law.[75] Graveyards have always served as drawing boards upon which the community can plot its hopes for stratifying itself in the world to come.[76] Even the early Quakers, who with customary

---

(1930), 49, 51; also next note and chap. 5, below. Perhaps most typical was the experience of Rev. Ezra Stiles, who had 7 Negroes among his 80 communicants (Newport, 1772) but who also held separate meetings for Negroes, and of the itinerant Rev. Francis Asbury, who preached to both racially mixed and separate groups: Franklin B. Dexter, ed., *The Literary Diary of Ezra Stiles, D.D., LL.D., President of Yale College*, 3 vols. (N. Y., 1901), I, 39, 204, 247–48; Elmer T. Clark *et al.*, eds., *The Journal and Letters of Francis Asbury*, 3 vols. (London and Nashville, 1958), 9–10, 57, 89, 200, 221, 351, 355, 441, 473. For Negroes addressing whites, *ibid.*, I, 328, 336; Saunders, ed., *Col. Recs. N. C.*, VII, 164; Goodwin, ed., *Letter Book of James MacSparran*, 26–27.

74. Cadbury, "Negro Membership in Society of Friends," *Jour. Negro Hist.*, 21 (1936), 168; Clark *et al.*, eds., *Journal of Asbury*, I, 223; Charles C. Jones, *The Religious Instruction of the Negroes in the United States* (Savannah, 1842), 36; Writers' Program of the Work Projects Administration in the State of Virginia, *The Negro in Virginia* (N. Y., 1940), 98; *Archives Md.*, LXIV, 375–76; Greene, *Negro in New England*, 280–84.

75. Boston Record Commissioners, *Report*, VIII, 176, XIII, 263, XIV, 53, XVII, 120; *Boston News-Letter*, Mar. 12, 1741; Goodwin, ed., *Letter Book of James MacSparran*, 85n; Bernard C. Steiner, *History of Slavery in Connecticut* (Baltimore, 1893), 20; Greene, *Negro in New England*, 284; [David] Humphreys, *An Account of the Endeavours Used by the Society for the Propagation of the Gospel in Foreign Parts, to Instruct the Negroe Slaves in New York . . .* (London, 1730), 7; *Minutes of Common Council, N. Y. C.*, V, 416; Townsend Ward, "The Germantown Road and Its Associations," *Pa. Mag. of Hist. and Biog.*, 6 (1882), 131; Peter D. Keyser, "A History of the Upper Germantown Burying-Ground . . .," *Pa. Mag. of Hist. and Biog.*, 8 (1884), 419; Turner, *Negro in Pa.*, 47; Candler, comp., *Col. Recs. Ga.*, XVIII, 568–69. See, too, John Luffman, *A Brief Account of the Island of Antigua . . .* (London, 1789), 109–10.

76. For this generally W. Lloyd Warner, *The Living and the Dead; A Study of the Symbolic Life of Americans* (New Haven, 1959), chap. 9.

literal-mindedness wiped the slate clean at death by erecting no marking stones in their burying grounds, usually marked off a separate plot for Negroes.[77]

The only other places where whites and Negroes might have rubbed shoulders on terms of equality were the schools. Occasionally one or two Negroes attended school with a group of white children,[78] but the vast majority of Negroes, slave and free, grew old and died with very little formal education or indeed any education at all. What little schooling was available to Negroes came by way of the churches. More often than not Negroes were catechized in exclusively Negro groups at an hour appointed by the catechist, though there must have been many exceptions to this practice. The scattered short-lived schools sponsored by missionary groups connected with the Church of England sometimes admitted Negroes with white children but more often Negroes alone.[79] This general pattern derived in large part from the fact that teaching Negroes presented rather special problems; Negro and white children came, after all, from what are now termed different socio-economic backgrounds. Nonetheless, racially mixed school classes in the colonies occasionally raised hackles and objections which have a startlingly modern ring. A Mr. Bolton was arraigned in Philadelphia for teaching Negroes in his school, though he successfully defended this practice before the grand jury.[80] Some teachers in North Carolina refused to teach Negroes and whites together when the idea was proposed by an English missionary group. And in Virginia the Reverend Adam Dickie reported that he had to conduct separate catechizing sessions "because White People thought it a Mighty

77. Thomas E. Drake, *Quakers and Slavery in America* (New Haven, 1950), 16.

78. W. H. Morse, "Lemuel Haynes," *Jour. Negro Hist.*, 4 (1919), 22–23; Esther B. Carpenter, "Negro Slavery in the Colony of Rhode Island," in her *South County Studies . . . of Narragansett* (Boston, 1924), 202; Carl Bridenbaugh, *Cities in the Wilderness: The First Century of Urban Life in America, 1625–1742*, [2d ed.] (N. Y., 1955), 446.

79. Goodwin, ed., *Letter Book of James MacSparran*, xxiv, 10, 13, 24; Updike, *Church in Narragansett*, III, 90; Carter G. Woodson, *The History of the Negro Church*, 2d ed. (Washington, 1921), 17; Pennington, "Bray's Associates," Amer. Antiq. Soc., *Proceedings*, New Ser., 48 (1938), 387; William W. Kemp, *The Support of Schools in Colonial New York by the Society for the Propagation of the Gospel in Foreign Parts* (N. Y., 1913), 241, 246, 249; Shelling, "William Sturgeon," *Hist. Mag. Prot. Eps. Church*, 8 (1939), 390–93; David D. Wallace, *The History of South Carolina*, 4 vols. (N. Y., 1934), I, 194; H. A. Scomp, "Georgia—The Only Free Colony," *Magazine of American History*, 22 (1889), 304.

80. Charleston *S.-C. Gaz.*, July 18, 1740.

Scandal to have their Children repeat the Catechism with Negroes." [81]

Mightily scandalized or not, the colonists in general seemed wary of opening their society to Negroes, even to those who were legally free and whose ancestors may have been free (by 1760) for three or four generations. This exclusionary trend, if not principle, stood out all the more sharply in a society which by European standards was wide open to all comers. In committing themselves to a slavery whose logic rested, in the final analysis, on racial differences, the colonists may in fact have enhanced the fluidity of the American social structure above the racial line. For the firmness of Negro exclusion may have served as a bedrock of assured but inexpressible confidence that the structure of the community was indeed as firmly ordered as it should be, thus permitting the revolutionary new social mobility among white persons to develop without the crippling apprehensiveness that proper social ordering was going entirely by the board. Paradoxically too, while slavery served as a working model of social subordination, it was one that could be applied only to Negroes, and thus the status of slave became the very model of what white Americans could *never* be.

As for the free Negro's position in the community, the association of slavery with race had transformed a free black man into a walking contradiction in terms, a social anomaly, a third party in a system built for two. Not only did free Negroes provide an "evil example" [82] to slaves but, much worse, their presence imposed a question mark on the rationale of slavery. In retrospect it is easy to see that their presence constituted an invitation to development of a new rationale which would tell white men who they were and where they stood in the community—the rationale of racial superiority. At the time, it seems ironic that many of the anxieties connected with slavery should have derived from what little fluidity remained in the caste system, from the fact that a few slaves had and could still slip over into freedom.

The importance and impact of certain of these paradoxes and ironies were not nearly so great, or at least so apparent, in the long years when slavery remained a largely unexamined fact of life in the colonies as they were to become at the time of the American Revolution and after. The sustained debate over natural rights and British

81. Pennington, "Bray's Associates," Amer. Antiq. Soc., *Proceedings*, New Ser., 48 (1938), 343, 352.

82. *Laws Del.*, I, 214, 435; also James T. Mitchell *et al.*, eds., *Statutes at Large of Pennsylvania from 1682 to 1809*, 18 vols. (Harrisburg, 1896–1915), IV, 61.

tyranny at the time of the Revolution not only brought into question the laws of slavery but altered the context in which Americans contemplated the facts of slave rebelliousness and Negro freedom. While in the years prior to the Revolutionary era slavery and growing freedom existed side by side without apparent strain, it would be a mistake to suppose that freedom and slavery were not at issue for colonial Englishmen. As cultural heirs of Elizabethans and Puritans they were acutely attuned—on the wave lengths which carry such messages—to urgent human problems of liberty and discipline, of license and control. The development of biracial slavery in America, with its concomitant themes of license and discipline, did nothing to quiet among colonial Englishmen the mood of taut adventurousness and control which had done so much to make England a restless navigating, discovering, trafficking, planting nation. Rather, the new freedom and the new slavery in America acted together to vivify this mood, to raise practical problems which agitated it, and to rake toward the surface certain of its energies which had somehow to be dealt with. For intimately related with economic exploitation, exclusion of free Negroes from the white community, slave unrest, and daily discipline in America was another kind of restlessness, discipline, exploitation, and exclusion. That this kind should have operated in such a way as to leave abundant traces in contemporary source materials suggests how salient and dynamic it was at the time and how important and persistent in America it was to become.

IV   FRUITS OF PASSION

The Dynamics of Interracial Sex

WHEN EUROPEANS MET AFRICANS IN AMERICA THE RESULT was slavery, revolt, the sociability of daily life, and, inevitably, sexual union. The blending of black and white began almost with the first contact of the two peoples and has far outlasted the institution of chattel slavery. It became, in some English colonies, almost an institution in itself. It rivaled the slave revolt as a source of tension. It may even have equaled the pressure of daily contact as a mechanism of cultural fusion. Most important, however, was the reticular complex of tensions which arose concerning interracial mixture.

These tensions may be viewed in several interrelated ways. The Englishmen who came to America brought with them not merely a prevalent social mood but also certain specific sexual mores and certain more or less definite ideas about African sexuality. Many of them came with more or less explicit intentions as to the proper character of the communities they wished to establish in the wilderness. These intentions were not always, or perhaps ever, fully realized; they were deflected—again sometimes more, sometimes less—by conditions in the New World. One of the most important deflectors was the development of a racial slavery which itself became one of the New World's "conditions," though of course the character of this condition was not everywhere the same. Presumably all Englishmen would have had similar reactions (allowing for enormous and significant variations among individuals and groups) to the attributes which set the Negro apart if they had perceived these attributes in similar contexts. But of course the Negro was encountered in very different contexts in the various English colonies. Particularly important in making for such differences was the demographic pattern which matured during the first quarter of the eighteenth century; variations in the numbers of the races and of the sexes in the English colonies may be shown to be almost determinative in shaping certain attitudes. These attitudes did not of course spring full blown from demographic tables, but demographic conditions did do a great deal to shape attitudes by imparting to racial intermixture distinct social functions and meanings in various regions. Within these varying social contexts, moreover, English colonials acted and reacted in revealing ways which serve to expose how powerfully and pervasively the most basic human biological and psychic energies were in operation and how, too, these energies affected the character of the emergent English communities in America.

1. REGIONAL STYLES IN RACIAL INTERMIXTURE

Miscegenation was extensive in all the English colonies, a fact made evident to contemporaries by the presence of large numbers of mulattoes. It is impossible to ascertain how much intermixture there actually was, though it seems likely there was more during the eighteenth century than at any time since.[1] Although miscegenation was probably most common among the lower orders, white men of every social rank slept with Negro women.[2] The colonists, as well as European travelers in the colonies, frequently pointed to this facet of American life.

No one thought intermixture was a good thing. Rather, English colonials were caught in the push and pull of an irreconcilable conflict between desire and aversion for interracial sexual union. The perceptual prerequisite for this conflict is so obvious as to be too easily overlooked: desire and aversion rested on the bedrock fact that white men perceived Negroes as being *both alike and different* from themselves. Without perception of similarity, no desire and no widespread gratification was possible. Without perception of difference, on the other hand, no aversion to miscegenation nor tension concerning it could have arisen. Without perception of difference,

1. My own impression and that of Edward B. Reuter, *The Mulatto in the United States; Including a Study of the Role of Mixed-Blood Races throughout the World* (Boston, 1918), 112. An interesting but over-eager world-wide treatment is Joel A. Rogers, *Sex and Race; Negro-Caucasian Mixing in All Ages and All Lands,* 3 vols. (N. Y., 1940–44).

2. Explicit references to gentlemen fathering mulattoes were uncommon in the continental colonies; for example, Samuel Thornely, ed., *The Journal of Nicholas Cresswell, 1774–1777* (N. Y., 1924), 164–65; Thomas Anburey, *Travels through the Interior Parts of America,* 2 vols. (Boston, 1923), II, 223.

of course, the term *miscegenation* had no meaning. Given the simultaneous feelings of desire and aversion, it seems probable that of the two the latter is more demanding of explanation. The sexual drive of human beings has always, in the long run, overridden even the strongest sense of difference between two groups of human beings and, in some individuals, has even overridden the far stronger sense which men have of the difference between themselves and animals. What demands explanation, in short, is why there was any aversion among the white colonists to sexual union with Negroes. More than desire, aversion was a manifestation of cultural rather than biological patterns, so that the answers may be looked for in the qualities of the various cultural settings which were emerging in English America and to the prevailing patterns of miscegenation which constituted important elements in New World cultural styles.

In most colonies virtually all the offspring of these unions were illegitimate, but legally sanctified interracial marriages did occur, especially though not exclusively in New England. Miscegenation in colonial America, as has been true since, typically involved fornication between white men and Negro women, though the inverse combination was common, far more common than is generally supposed. Probably a majority of interracial marriages in New England involved Negro men and white women of "the meaner sort." [3] In the plantation colonies, though there were occasional instances of white women marrying Negroes, legitimization of this relationship was unusual. Yet white men were sometimes left to

---

3. Greene, *Negro in New England*, 200–202. For intermarriages involving white women elsewhere, Anne Grant, *Memoirs of an American Lady; With Sketches of Manners and Scenes in America As They Existed Previous to the Revolution*, ed. James Grant Wilson, 2 vols. (N. Y., 1901), I, 86; Arthur W. Calhoun, *A Social History of the American Family from Colonial Times to the Present*, 3 vols. (Cleveland, 1917–19), I, 211; Catterall, ed., *Judicial Cases*, II, 11; Duc de La Rochefoucauld-Liancourt, *Travels through the United States of North America . . . 1795, 1796, and 1797 . . .* , 2 vols. (London, 1799), I, 602; Annapolis *Md. Gaz.*, July 31, 1794. For this combination outside marriage, see extracts from Box 16, bundle: Court of General Sessions of the Peace [Suffolk Co., Mass.], Apr. 4, 1704, Oct. 2, 1705, Apr. 6, 1708, July 4, 1710, Apr. 6, 1714, Parish Transcripts, N.-Y. Hist. Soc.; Morse, "Lemuel Haynes," *Jour. Negro Hist.*, 4 (1919), 22; [Horsmanden], *Journal of the Proceedings*, 2, 4; *Boston News-Letter*, June 25, 1741; Calhoun, *Family*, I, 211; Catterall, ed., *Judicial Cases*, I, 89–91, II, 12, IV, 28, 32; Annapolis *Md. Gaz.*, Aug. 19, 1746; James H. Johnston, Race Relations in Virginia and Miscegenation in the South, 1776–1860 (unpubl. Ph.D. diss., University of Chicago, 1937), 199–202; John H. Franklin, *The Free Negro in North Carolina, 1790–1860* (Chapel Hill, 1943), 37, 39; Saunders, ed., *Col. Recs. N. C.*, II, 704; Klaus G. Loewald, Beverly Starika, and Paul S. Taylor, trans. and eds., "Johann Martin Bolzius Answers a Questionnaire on Carolina and Georgia," *Wm. and Mary Qtly.*, 3d Ser., 14 (1957), 235.

ponder indignities such as that suffered (and in return imposed) by a Maryland man who advertised in 1759 that he would no longer be responsible for his wife's debts because *"Mary Skinner,* my Wife, has, after all the Love and Tenderness which could possibly be shown by Man to a Woman, polluted my Bed, by taking to her in my Stead, her own Negro Slave, by whom she hath a Child, which hath occasioned so much Disgrace to me and my Family, that I have thought proper to forbid her my Sight any more." [4]

Public feeling about miscegenation was strong enough to force itself over the hurdles of the legislative process into the statute books of many English continental colonies. As early as the 1660's the Maryland and Virginia assemblies had begun to lash out at miscegenation in language dripping with distaste and indignation. By the turn of the century it was clear in many continental colonies that the English settlers felt genuine revulsion for interracial sexual union, at least in principle. About 1700 the Chester County Court in Pennsylvania ordered a Negro "never more to meddle with any white woman more uppon paine of his life." [5] Statutory prohibitions roughly similar to those of the tobacco colonies and Bermuda were adopted by Massachusetts in 1705, North Carolina in 1715, South Carolina in 1717, Pennsylvania in 1726, and by Georgia when Negroes were admitted to the colony in 1750. Delaware enacted no outright prohibition but prescribed heavier fines for interracial bastardy cases than for such cases involving two white persons. Thus two northern and all the plantation colonies legally prohibited miscegenation.[6] Community feeling was of course not monolithically arrayed against interracial union: in 1699 several citizens petitioned the Virginia Council for repeal of the intermarriage prohibition, and as late as 1755 the North Carolina Assembly responded favorably to a petition by inhabitants from several counties asking repeal of the laws in which "free Negroes and Mulatto's

4. Annapolis *Md. Gaz.*, Oct. 12, 1769, also Apr. 22, 1773.
5. Turner, *Negro in Pa.*, 30n.
6. Hening, ed., *Statutes Va.*, II, 170, III, 86–87, 452–54; *Archives Md.*, I, 533–34, VII, 204–5, XIII, 546–49, XXII, 552, XXVI, 259–60, XXX, 289–90, XXXIII, 112, XXXVI, 275–76; Lefroy, comp., *Memorials Bermudas*, II, 190; *Acts and Resolves Mass.*, I, 578–79; Clark, ed., *State Recs. N. C.*, XXIII, 65, 106, 160, 195; Cooper and McCord, eds., *Statutes S. C.*, III, 20; Mitchell *et al.*, eds., *Statutes Pa.*, IV, 62–63; Candler, comp., *Col. Recs. Ga.*, I, 59–60; *Laws Del.*, I, 105–9. For circumstances surrounding the Massachusetts and Pennsylvania acts, *Diary of Sewall*, II, 143; Herrick, *White Servitude in Pennsylvania*, 92. The 18th-century laws barred all licit unions, illicit unions involving white women, and in most cases illicit unions involving white men, but Maryland and Virginia arrived at this position by different routes, Maryland at first barring only interracial fornication and Virginia only interracial marriage.

Intermarrying with white women are obliged to pay taxes for their wives and families." [7] In general, though, the weight of community opinion was set heavily against the sexual union of white and black, as the long-standing statutory prohibitions indicated. Even in South Carolina, where interracial liaisons were less carefully concealed than elsewhere on the continent, a grand jury in 1743 publicly condemned "THE TOO COMMON PRACTICE of CRIMINAL CONVERSATION with NEGRO and other SLAVE WENCHES IN THIS PROVINCE, as an Enormity and Evil of general Ill-Consequence." In significant contrast, none of the West Indian assemblies prohibited extramarital miscegenation and only one took the probably unnecessary step of banning racial intermarriage.[8]

In the West Indian colonies especially, and less markedly in South Carolina, the entire pattern of miscegenation was far more inflexible than in the other English settlements. White women in the islands did not sleep with Negro men, let alone marry them. Nor did white men actually marry Negroes or mulattoes: as one usually temperate planter declared, "The very idea is shocking." [9] Yet white men commonly, almost customarily, took Negro women to bed with little pretense at concealing the fact. Colored mistresses were kept openly. "The Planters are in general rich," a young traveler wrote, "but a set of dissipating, abandoned, and cruel people. Few even of the married ones, but keep a Mulatto or Black Girl in the house or at lodgings for certain purposes." [10] Edward Long of Jamaica described the situation more vividly: "He who should presume to shew any displeasure against such a thing as simple fornication, would for his pains be accounted a simple blockhead; since not one in twenty can be persuaded, that there is either sin; or shame in cohabiting with his slave." [11] Negro concubinage was an integral part of island life, tightly interwoven into the social fabric.

It is scarcely necessary to resort to speculation about the influence

7. Henry R. McIlwaine, ed., *Legislative Journals of the Council of Colonial Virginia*, 3 vols. (Richmond, 1918–19), I, 262; Box 2, bundle: N. C., Minutes of Council in Assembly (1732–55), Minutes of House of Burgesses (1733–46), 19, Parish Transcripts, N.-Y. Hist. Soc.

8. Charleston *S.-C. Gaz.*, Mar. 28, 1743. For the West Indies, Jordan, "American Chiaroscuro: The Status and Definition of Mulattoes in the British Colonies," *Wm. and Mary Qtly.*, 3d Ser., 19 (1962), 194–95. The one West Indian law (Montserrat's) was probably disallowed: CO 391/69, 51, P.R.O.

9. Edwards, *History of British West Indies*, II, 26.

10. Thornely, ed., *Journal of Nicholas Cresswell*, 39. There is a vivid picture of an overseer's life in the West Indies in O. A. Sherrard, *Freedom from Fear: The Slave and His Emancipation* (London, 1959), chap. 9.

11. [Edward Long], *The History of Jamaica . . .*, 3 vols. (London, 1774), II, 328.

of tropical climate in order to explain this situation, for life in the islands was in large degree shaped by the enormous disproportion of Negroes to white settlers and characterized by the concomitant brutal nakedness of planter domination over the slaves. In the West Indian islands and to less extent South Carolina, racial slavery consisted of unsheathed dominion by relatively small numbers of white men over enormous numbers of Negroes, and it was in these colonies that Negro men were most stringently barred from sexual relations with white women. Sexually as well as in every other way, Negroes were utterly subordinated. White men extended their dominion over their Negroes to the bed, where the sex act itself served as ritualistic re-enactment of the daily pattern of social dominance. In New England, at the other extreme, white men had no need for aggressive assertion of their dominance in order to sustain slavery on a major scale and hence in New England Negro men were accorded some measure of sexual freedom.

Congruent to these regional differences in slavery and interracial relationships were the bedrock demographic facts which so powerfully influenced, perhaps even determined, the kind of society which emerged in each colony. With Negroes overwhelmingly outnumbering white men in the various islands (ten to one in Jamaica), and with white men outnumbering Negroes everywhere on the continent except South Carolina, it was inevitable that radically dissimilar social styles should have developed in the two areas. As a French traveler perceptively epitomized this dissimilarity in 1777, when it had become so evident in the pattern of revolt against Great Britain: "In the colonies of the Antilles, most of the colonists are people who have left their homeland with the intention of rebuilding their fortunes. Far from settling in the islands, they look upon them merely as a land of exile, never as a place where they plan to live, prosper, and die. On the other hand, the Anglo-American colonists are permanent, born in the country and attached to it; they have no motherland save the one they live in; and, although London formerly was so considered, they have clearly proved that they held it in less esteem than they did the prosperity, tranquility, and freedom of their own country." [12] The West Indian planters were lost not so much in the Caribbean as in a sea of blacks. They found it impossible to re-create English culture as they had known it. They were corrupted by living in a police state, though not themselves the

12. Edward D. Seeber, trans., *On the Threshold of Liberty: Journal of a Frenchman's Tour of the American Colonies in 1777* (Bloomington, Ind., 1959), 123–24.

objects of its discipline. The business of the islands was business, the production of agricultural staples; the islands were not where one really lived, but where one made one's money. By contrast, the American colonists on the continent maintained their hold upon their English background, modifying it less for accommodating slavery than for winning the new land. They were sufficiently numerous to create a new culture with a self-evident validity of its own, complete with the adjustments necessary to absorb non-English Europeans. Unlike the West Indian planters, they felt no need to be constantly running back to England to reassure themselves that they belonged to civilization. Because they were conscious of having attained a large measure of success in transplanting their own society, they vehemently rejected any trespass upon it by a people so alien as the Negroes. The islanders could hardly resent trespass on something which they did not have. By sheer weight of numbers their society was black and slave.

It was precisely this difference which made the Negro seem so much more alien on the continent than on the islands and miscegenation accordingly less common. For a West Indian to have declared, with Samuel Sewall of Boston, that Negroes "cannot mix with us and become members of society, . . . never embody with us, and grow up into orderly Families, to the Peopling of the Land" would have been false by reason of the extensive blending of the races in the islands and meaningless because the "peopling" of the islands had already been accomplished—by Negroes. Americans on the continent stood poised for a destiny of conquering a vast wilderness while Englishmen in the little crowded islands looked forward down a precipice of slave rebellion or at best a slippery slope of peaceful but inevitable defeat. It was geography rather than culture which in the last analysis placed South Carolina closer to Massachusetts than to the islands. Certainly the bustling communities on the continent had good reason to feel that they had successfully established a beachhead of English civilization in America. They possessed optimism, self-confidence, and a well-defined sense of Englishness, a sense which came automatically to bear when they were confronted with peoples who for whatever reason seemed appreciably dissimilar. When large numbers of very dissimilar people threatened the identity of the continental colonists, their response was rejection of those people in the mind and a tendency to perceive them as being more dissimilar than ever. For the sense of dissimilarity fed on itself: once the cycle was started, the differences between

Americans and "others," which first sparked anxiety and rejection, loomed progressively larger and generated further anxiety and rejection.

Certainly many Americans on the continent became convinced that the American people were not intended to be Negroes. Benjamin Franklin, who was as fully attuned to American destiny as anyone, nervously expressed this feeling in his famous *Observations Concerning the Increase of Mankind* (1751), where one of his main purposes was demonstration that the American continent was of all regions upon the globe the most conducive to population growth. After throwing querulous aspersions at the Germans in Pennsylvania, he pointed out (as has been frequently pointed out since) that "the Number of purely white People in the World is proportionably very small." Even most Europeans, including the Germans, he declared, "are generally of what we call a swarthy Complexion." The Saxons and the English "make the principal Body of White People on the Face of the Earth." And though Benjamin Franklin plainly felt awkward in expressing the idea and consequently presented it in fanciful terms, he was convinced that America should belong to the "White People." "I could wish their Numbers were increased. And while we are, as I may call it, *Scouring* our Planet, by clearing America of Woods, and so making this Side of our Globe reflect a brighter Light to the Eyes of Inhabitants in Mars or Venus, why should we in the Sight of Superior Beings, darken its People? Why increase the Sons of Africa, by Planting them in America, where we have so fair an Opportunity, by excluding all Blacks and Tawneys, of increasing the lovely White and Red? But perhaps I am partial to the Complexion of my Country," he concluded with his usual self-conscious good sense, "for such Kind of Partiality is natural to Mankind." With all his puns and despite his apologetics, Franklin was expressing an important feeling, one which a famous Virginian, William Byrd, expressed more directly: "They import so many Negros hither, that I fear this Colony will some time or other be confirmd by the Name of New Guinea." [13]

It was more than a matter of colonial Americans not wanting to give their country over to the Africans. Miscegenation probably did not seem so much a matter of long-term discoloration as an immediate failure to live up to immemorial standards. Here again, the

13. Samuel Sewall, *The Selling of Joseph, a Memorial* (Boston, 1700), 2; Labaree *et al.*, eds., *Papers of Franklin*, IV, 225–34; William Byrd to Lord Egmont, Virginia, July 12, 1736, "Colonel William Byrd on Slavery and Indentured Servants," *Amer. Hist. Rev.*, 1 (1895), 88–89.

intentions which drove English overseas expansion were of crucial importance. The colonists' conviction that they must sustain their civilized condition wherever they went rendered miscegenation *ipso facto* a negation of the underlying plan of settlement in America. Simply because most Negroes were chattel slaves, racial amalgamation was stamped as irredeemably illicit; it was irretrievably associated with loss of control over the baser passions, with weakening of traditional family ties, and with breakdown of proper social ordering. Judge Sewall's "orderly Families" were rendered a mockery by fathers taking slave wenches to bed.

At the same time it would be absurd to suppose that the status of Negroes in itself aroused American aversion to intermixture and that the physical difference in Negroes was of slight importance. Without that difference there could never have developed well-formulated conceptions about sexual relations between Africans and Europeans in America. Although perhaps there was some feeling that the laws which prevented racial intermingling helped prevent Negroes, as one astute foreign observer put it, "from forming too great opinions of themselves," the underlying reason for their passage was that these mixtures were "disagreeable" to white men. Probably it was this feeling which prompted the prominent Boston merchant, James Bowdoin, to ship one of his Negroes to the West Indies in exchange for produce or another Negro boy, explaining that "my Man Caesar has been engaged in an amour with some of the white ladies of the Town." When Mrs. Anne Grant recalled her early years in the colony of New York she daintily reported that the citizens of Albany possessed a particular "moral delicacy" on one point: "they were from infancy in habits of familiarity with these humble friends [the Negroes], yet being early taught that nature had placed between them a barrier, which it was in a high degree criminal and disgraceful to pass, they considered a mixture of such distinct races with abhorrence, as a violation of her laws." [14]

2. MASCULINE AND FEMININE MODES IN CAROLINA AND AMERICA

While the "laws" of nature seem to have appeared in abundant clarity in Albany, New York, they were very dimly per-

---

14. Adolph B. Benson, trans. and ed., *The America of 1750: Peter Kalm's Travels in North America. The English Version of 1770*, 2 vols. (N. Y., 1937) , I, 209; James Bowdoin to George Scott, Boston, Oct. 14, 1763, Bowdoin-Temple Papers, XXVIII, 56, Massachusetts Historical Society, Boston; Grant, *Memoirs*, ed. Wilson, I, 85.

ceived in Charleston, South Carolina, where white persons were surrounded by so many more "humble friends." On the face of things it seems paradoxical that the one region on the continent which had become demographically most like a new Guinea should have been the one in which white men seemed least anxious about interracial sexual activity. While permanent unions between persons of the two races normally were quiet or secretive affairs elsewhere on the continent, in South Carolina and particularly in Charleston they were not. It was the only city worthy of the name in the plantation colonies. It was an elegant, gay, extravagant city, where men took advantage of certain of their opportunities in more overt, more relaxed, and probably more enterprising fashion than in the colonies to the northward. They possessed an abundance of Negro women. The result may best be described in the words of two travelers from different backgrounds. As young Josiah Quincy of Boston reported on his tour through North and South Carolina, "The enjoyment of a negro or mulatto woman is spoken of as quite a common thing: no reluctance, delicacy or shame is made about the matter." [15] A visiting merchant from Jamaica, where the atmosphere surrounding interracial sex was so utterly different from New England, wrote from Charleston in 1773, "I know of but one Gentleman who professedly keeps a Mulatto Mistress and he is very much pointed at: There are swarms of Negroes about the Town and many Mulattoes, and by the Dress of the Girls, who mostly imitate their Mistresses, I have no doubt of their Conversations with the whites, but they are carried on with more privacy than in our W. India Islands." (Josiah Quincy would scarcely have appreciated the niceness of the distinction.) "As I travell'd further North," the Jamaican visitor continued, concerning his trip from Charleston to North Carolina, "there were fewer Negroes about the Houses, and these taken less notice of, and before I finish'd my Journey North, I found an empty House, the late Tenant of which had been oblig'd by the Church Wardens to decamp on Account of his having kept a Black Woman. Dont suppose Fornication is out of Fashion here," he added reassuringly about North Carolina, "more than in other Places, No! the difference only is, that the White Girls monopolize it." [16]

Here was an important regional difference in social "fashion."

15. Mark Anthony De Wolfe Howe, ed., "Journal of Josiah Quincy, Junior, 1773," Mass. Hist. Soc., *Proceedings*, 49 (1915–16), 463.
16. G. Moulton to ?, Charles Town, Jan. 23, 1773, Additional Manuscripts, 22677, 75, British Museum, London. For reference to this letter I am indebted to Pitman, *British West Indies, 1700–1763*, 28.

Charleston was the only English city on the continent where it was at all possible to jest publicly concerning miscegenation. In 1732 the *South-Carolina Gazette* published a verse which touched off a round robin on the subject.

The CAMELEON LOVER

If what the *Curious* have observ'd be true,
That the *Cameleon* will assume the *Hue*
Of all the Objects that approach its *Touch;*
No Wonder then, that the *Amours* of *such*
Whose *Taste* betrays them to a close Embrace
With the *dark* Beauties of the *Sable* Race
(Stain'd with the Tincture of the *Sooty* Sin,)
Imbibe the *Blackness* of their *Charmer's* Skin.[17]

This "little smattering of Wit" greatly offended one serious-minded citizen who, pointedly signing himself "ALBUS", declared that he was "one of those, who are not a little fired at any Instance of this Kind." "ALBUS" caustically admitted that "it is too well known, that I need not be under any great Apprehension of pointing at *One* Man only. Were that the Case, he would not be worth our Notice, and we might silently contemn both the *Offence* and the *Offender.* But it is too shocking to see an *Evil* of this *Kind,* spreading it self among us. Too gross to be suffered to pass in Silence!" Unfortunately, the impact of Albus's lengthy admonition was somewhat dampened by the presence of a poem defending miscegenation in the very same issue of the *Gazette.*[18] And four years later the paper published some frank advice to the bachelors and widowers of Charleston ostensibly from some ladies newly arrived from Bermuda: "that if they are in a Strait for Women, to wait for the next Shipping from the Coast of Guinny. Those African Ladies are of a strong, robust Constitution: not easily jaded out, able to serve them by Night as well as Day. When they are Sick, they are not costly, when dead, their funeral Charges are but *viz* an old Matt, one Bottle Rum, and a lb. Sugar[.] The cheapness of a Commo-di-ty becomes more taking when it fully Answers the end, or T——l." Next week another writer replied in obvious determination not to be outdone in indelicacy of expression: "in my Opinion, our Country-Women are full as capable for Service either night or day as any African Ladies whatsoever, unless their native Constitution is much

17. Charleston *S.-C. Gaz.,* Mar. 11, 1732.
18. *Ibid.,* Mar. 18, 1732.

alter'd. In all Companies wheresoever I have been, my Country-Women have always the praise for their Activity of Hipps and humoring a Jest to the Life in what Posture soever their Partners may fancy, which makes me still hope that they'll have the Preference before the black Ladies in the Esteem of the Widowers and Batchelors at C————town." Next week the *Gazette* published still another verse.[19]

If these contributions to the *South-Carolina Gazette* were a trifle raw by the standards of a modern family newspaper, they reflected more than eighteenth-century literary frankness about sex. Newspapers elsewhere on the continent did not publish similar discussions of interracial sex, though everywhere (including Boston) they published some none-too-delicate pieces concerning sexual matters. Only in Charleston was it possible to debate publicly, "Is sex with Negroes right?" In other colonies the topic was not looked upon as being open.

The reasons for this distinctiveness are apparent in the mosaic of South Carolina's economic and social history. The original colonization of South Carolina had been intimately linked with the English experience in the Caribbean islands. Although staple crops (rice and indigo) and large plantations in the low country made for aristocratic control along the Virginia pattern, the presence of Charleston, which served as entrepôt for the back country as well as the social and commercial center of the low country, made for less political responsibility, for more absenteeism on the plantations, and for a gayer, less serious-minded style of life among the aristocracy.[20] More important, the preponderance of slaves in the low country tended to give white men a queasy sense that perhaps they were marooned, a feeling that their society was irrevocably committed to Negro slavery and that somehow their mere Englishness had lost its savor in the shuffle for plantation prosperity. The effect of this uneasiness was to make men feel like both fleeing and embracing Negro slavery all at once: hence the common annual flights from the plantations to Charleston and from South Carolina to northern cities and England, the negation of cherished traditional liberties in the slave codes, the importation of more and more slaves, the continual efforts to encourage white immigration, and not least, the simultaneous embracing of Negro women and rejection of the ensuing offspring. Caught as they were in powerful crosscurrents, it is

19. *Ibid.*, July 17, 24, 31, 1736.
20. The best introduction is Carl Bridenbaugh, *Myths and Realities: Societies of the Colonial South* (Baton Rouge, La., 1952), chap. 2.

no wonder that white men in Charleston joked nervously about their sexual abandon.

For white women the situation was different, and here again the Charleston area seems to have been characterized by attitudes somewhere mid-way between those of the West Indies and further north. In the islands, where English settlers were most thoroughly committed to a Negro slave society and where strenuous attempts to attract more white settlers had been unavailing, white women were, quite literally, the repositories of white civilization. White men tended to place them protectively upon a pedestal and then run off to gratify their passions elsewhere. For their part white women, though they might propagate children, inevitably held themselves aloof from the world of lust and passion, a world which reeked of infidelity and Negro slaves. Under no circumstances would they have attempted, any more than they would have been allowed, to clamber down from their pedestal to seek pleasures of their own across the racial line. In fact white women in the West Indies tended to adhere rigidly to the double sexual standard which characterized English sexual mores and to refrain more than in the continental colonies from infidelity with white men.[21] The oppressive presence of slavery itself tended to inhibit the white woman's capacity for emotional, sexual, and intellectual commitment. She served principally an ornamentive function, for everything resembling work was done by Negro slaves. Visitors to the islands were almost universally agreed in describing her life as one of indolence and lassitude, though some were impressed by a formal, superficial gaiety. Her choices were to withdraw from the world or to create an unreal one of her own. She withdrew from the colored race and, perhaps not entirely because of prevailing notions about health, scrupulously shielded her face from the darkening effects of the tropic sun.[22] A tanned skin implied an affinity which she had to deny.

The white women of the Charleston area were less tightly hemmed in. Nevertheless, they rarely if ever established liaisons with Negro men, as happened in the South Carolina back country.

21. Stated emphatically, for example, by Luffman, *Brief Account of Antigua,* 37, also 168–70. For sexual mores in England, see Keith J. Thomas, "The Double Standard," *Journal of the History of Ideas,* 20 (1959), 195–216.

22. John Singleton, *A General Description of the West-Indian Islands . . .* (Barbados, 1767), 146–51; [Schaw], *Journal of a Lady of Quality,* eds. Andrews, 114–15, 123–24; [Long], *Jamaica,* II, 413; Luffman, *Brief Account of Antigua,* 35. For this in the southern colonies, John Lawson, *A New Voyage to Carolina . . .* (London, 1709), 84; entry of June 22, 1781, in Military Journal of William Feltman, May 26, 1781, to Apr. 25, 1782, Hist. Soc. Pa.

Some visitors to the city were struck by their dessicated formality, which seems now to betray the strains imposed by the prevailing pattern of miscegenation. A New Jersey lawyer who moved to Charleston just after the Revolution described his initial impressions of aristocratic circles there in the following terms:

It is hard that hospitality should thus want its most essential part (sociability) and that a person cannot be made an object of politeness without being also made an object of formality. The ladies carry formality and scrupulosity to a considerable extreme; a stranger makes his female acquaintance by slow gradations interspersed with niceties and punctilios which often disconcert the forward and intimidate the bashful. The maxims of the country have taught them and custom has forced them to almost consider a sociability on their part with gentlemen as an unbecoming forwardness—and they are by this means circumscribed within such narrow bounds as exclude the frankness and care which are necessary to put people on the most agreeable footing and constitutes the principal charms of Society.

The gentlemen are more sociable and I must confess as agreeable as any I have ever seen after a person has made an acquaintance with them. But they are generally very dissipated, little inclined to study and less to business.[23]

The dissipation of the white gentleman was as much a tragedy for his white lady as for him. A biracial environment warped her affective life in two directions at once, for she was made to feel that sensual involvement with the opposite sex burned bright and hot with unquenchable passion and at the same time that any such involvement was utterly repulsive. Accordingly, as the above passage suggests so clearly, she approached her prospective legitimate sexual partners as if she were picking up a live coal in one hand and a dead rat in the other.

If women were particularly affected by the situation in South Carolina, white persons of both sexes in *all* the English colonies were affected in a more general way by the tensions involved in miscegenation. Though these tensions operated in white men rather differently than in white women, it seems almost self-evident that the emergent attitudes toward Negroes possessed a unity which transcended differences between the two sexes. Put another way, out of a pattern of interracial sexual relationships which normally placed white men and white women in very different roles, there arose a common core of belief and mythology concerning the Negro which belonged to neither sex but to white American culture as a

23. Joseph W. Barnwell, ed., "Diary of Timothy Ford, 1785–1786," *South Carolina Historical and Genealogical Magazine,* 13 (1912), 190–91.

whole. The emergence of common beliefs out of divergent experiences was of course principally a function of the homogenizing effect of culture upon individual experience, but it is important to bear in mind that the functional significance of beliefs about the Negro may have been very different for white women than for white men even when the beliefs themselves were identical. Since the English and colonial American cultures were dominated by males, however, sexually-oriented beliefs about the Negro in America derived principally from the psychological needs of men and were to a considerable extent shaped by specifically masculine modes of thought and behavior. This is not to say that American attitudes toward the Negro were *male* attitudes but merely that when one talks about *American* attitudes toward anything (the frontier, the city, money, freedom, the Negro) one is using a shorthand for attitudes common to both sexes but predominantly male in genesis and tone.[24]

3. NEGRO SEXUALITY AND SLAVE INSURRECTION

As for these ideas or beliefs about the Negro, many seem startlingly modern. Least surprising, perhaps, was the common assumption that Negro women were especially passionate, an idea which found literary or at least literate expression especially in the *South-Carolina Gazette* and in West Indian books. The Negro woman was the sunkissed embodiment of ardency:

> Next comes a warmer race, from sable sprung,
> To love each thought, to lust each nerve is strung;
> The Samboe dark, and the Mullattoe brown,
> The Mestize fair, the well-limb'd Quaderoon,
> And jetty Afric, from no spurious sire,
> Warm as her soil, and as her sun—on fire.
> These sooty dames, well vers'd in Venus' school,
> Make love an art, and boast they kiss by rule.[25]

If such amiable assessments could find their way into public print, one can imagine what tavern bantering must have been like. There may well have been, of course, objective basis in fact for this

24. A closely related problem is discussed by David M. Potter, "American Women and the American Character," *Stetson University Bulletin*, 62 (1962), 1–22.

25. *Jamaica, a Poem, in Three Parts . . .* (London, 1777), 22–23. Also, "The Sable Venus; An Ode," in Edwards, *History of British West Indies*, II, 32–38.

assessment of Negro women, for just as the white woman's experience tended to inhibit sexual expression, so the Negro woman's very different situation may have encouraged it. Yet plainly white men were doing more than reporting pleasant facts. For by calling the Negro woman passionate they were offering the best possible justification for their own passions. Not only did the Negro woman's warmth constitute a logical explanation for the white man's infidelity, but, much more important, it helped shift responsibility from himself to her. If she was *that* lascivious—well, a man could scarcely be blamed for succumbing against overwhelming odds. Further reinforcement for this picture of the Negro woman came from the ancient association of hot climates with sexual activity,[26] a tradition which persists today despite the introduction of central heating. Operating less strongly in the same direction was the old equation of barbarism with sexual abandonment: Negro women seemed more natural and were sometimes described, for instance, as giving birth more easily than white women.[27]

Attitudes toward the Negro male were more complex and potentially far more explosive. The notion that Negro men were particularly virile, promiscuous, and lusty was of course not new in the eighteenth century, but the English colonists in America showed signs of adding a half-conscious and revealingly specific corollary: they sometimes suggested that Negro men lusted after white women. Again there was probably some objective basis for the charge, since sexual intercourse with a white woman must in part have been for Negro men an act of retribution against the white man. For different reasons there was also good basis for the common feeling that only the most depraved white woman would consent to sleep with a Negro,[28] since white women of the lowest class had the least to lose in flouting the maxims of society and the most reason to hate them. No matter how firmly based in fact, however, the image of the sexually aggressive Negro was rooted even more firmly in deep strata of irrationality. For it is apparent that white men projected their own desires onto Negroes: their own passion for Negro women was

26. J. W. Johnson, " 'Of Differing Ages and Climes,' " *Jour. Hist. Ideas,* 21 (1960) , 474–75.

27. For example, [Long], *Jamaica,* II, 380. Apparently this notion about parturition is incorrect: Julian H. Lewis, *The Biology of the Negro* (Chicago, 1942) , chap. 6. Negro wet nurses for white babies, and objections to the practice, are noted in Luffman, *Brief Account of Antigua,* 36; Julia C. Spruill, *Women's Life and Work in the Southern Colonies* (Chapel Hill, 1938) , 55–57; *Works of James Houstoun, M.D.* (London, 1753) , 293–94; "Letters of Rev. Jonathan Boucher," *Maryland Historical Magazine,* 7 (1912) , 6.

28. For example, [Horsmanden], *Journal of the Proceedings,* 2.

not fully acceptable to society or the self and hence not readily admissible. Sexual desires could be effectively denied and the accompanying anxiety and guilt in some measure assuaged, however, by imputing them to others. It is not we, but others, who are guilty. It is not we who lust, but they. Not only this, but white men anxious over their own sexual inadequacy were touched by a racking fear and jealousy. Perhaps the Negro better performed his nocturnal offices than the white man. Perhaps, indeed, the white man's woman really wanted the Negro more than she wanted him.

Significantly, these tensions tended to bubble to the surface especially at times of interracial crisis when the colonists' mundane control over their Negroes appeared in jeopardy. During many scares over slave conspiracies, for instance, reports circulated that the Negroes had plotted killing all white persons except the young women, whom they "intended to reserve for themselves." [29] In fact these charges were ill-founded at best, for there is no evidence that any Negroes in revolt ever seized any white women for their "own use," even though rebellious slaves certainly had opportunity to do so during the successful insurrections in the West Indies and also at Stono in South Carolina. It is especially striking that in the eighteenth century, reports of sexual aims were confined to the continental colonies; in the seventeenth century, that is before the institutionalization of miscegenation in the West Indian islands, these reports circulated during two insurrections on Barbados, revealing a tension there which later remitted as Barbadians relaxed into an amiable attitude toward interracial sex and gradually accepted the fact that the island had been utterly given over to masses of slaves.[30] In the continental colonies there was a revealing overeagerness in

---

29. N.-Y. Gaz., Mar. 25, 1734; Stephen Bordley to Matt Harris, Annapolis, Jan. 30, 1739 [/40], Stephen Bordley's Letterbook, 1738–1740, Maryland Historical Society, Baltimore; [Horsmanden], Journal of the Proceedings, passim, especially p. 42 when the New York jury was told that "the White Men should be all killed, and the Women become a Prey to the rapacious Lust of these Villains!"; N.-Y. Weekly Jour., June 15, 1741; Phila. American Weekly Mercury, June 18, 1741; Charleston S.-C. Gaz., July 30, 1741; Box 3, bundle: Minutes of Council in Assembly (1748–49), Including Papers on the Negro Conspiracy, [Pt. ii], 30, Parish Transcripts, N.Y. Hist. Soc.

30. Great Newes from the Barbadoes. Or, a True and Faithful Account of the Grand Conspiracy of the Negroes against the English . . . (London, 1676), 10; [John Oldmixon], The British Empire in America . . . , 2 vols. (London, 1708), II, 47, re a conspiracy ca. 1687. Estimated proportion of Negroes in Barbados: 14% in 1643, 47% in 1655, 64% during last quarter of 17th century, 75% in 1724. In the 18th century there was one such report in the West Indies (the leader of a Jamaican revolt said to have wanted the lieutenant-governor's wife as his concubine) by a belligerently anti-Negro writer: [Long], Jamaica, II, 457n.

the way the press in distant cities picked up the idea that Negro insurrectionaries in a certain locality had aimed at acquisition of white women. In 1757 the *London Magazine* published an account describing how the "ring-leaders" of a 1730 insurrection in South Carolina were "executed, after confessing the conspiracy, and each of them declaring whose wife, daughter, or sister he had fixed on for his future bedfellow," even though the only widely circulated contemporary on-the-scene account failed to mention any sexual aim on the part of the conspirators.[31] Still more striking are the remarks of a Hessian officer who included an historical account of South Carolina in his diary kept during the siege and capture of Charleston in 1780. Captain Johann Hinrichs wrote in the most explicit terms about a major Negro conspiracy which he set at August 1736, though in all probability his account was based on eighth-hand information about the Stono insurrection of 1739, for there are no records of any conspiracy on the earlier date. In any case, his summation of the affair indicates clearly which direction, over a period of forty years, the exaggerations and distortions about a Negro conspiracy were likely to take: "The entire Negro population, at least the greater part, had conspired to assault their masters on a certain night, massacre all the [male] white population, make the women either their slaves or use them to gratify their desires, and sacrifice the rest." [32] No such conspiracy had ever been discovered in South Carolina.

From these indications it seems more than likely that fears of Negro sexual aggression during periods of alarm over insurrection did not represent direct response to actual overt threat, but rather a complex of reactions in the white man. Any group faced with a real threat of serious proportions is inclined to sense, even on a conscious level, a sexual element in the opponents' aggressiveness—as many have identified Communism with free love. Any Negro insurrection, furthermore, threatened the white man's dominance, including his valuable sexual dominance, and hence the awful prospect of being overthrown was bound to assume a sexual cast. Although the white man's sexual anxiety focused on the Negro male, it could easily spill over into resentful suspicion of the supposed objects of the Negro's lust, as in a Maryland planter's sarcastic coda

31. *London Mag.*, 26 (1757), 330–31. The lone account was a letter from South Carolina published only in *Boston News-Letter*, Oct. 22, 1730; and *Boston Gazette*, Oct. 26, 1730. See Aptheker, *Revolts*, 180–81.

32. "Diary of Captain Johann Hinrichs," Bernhard A. Uhlendorf, trans. and ed., *The Siege of Charleston . . . Diaries and Letters of Hessian Officers . . .* (Ann Arbor, 1938), 323.

to his remarks on the folly of a white woman who had heard from her slave of a forthcoming revolt and who had done nothing to inquire into an affair which could have led to her death—"but perhaps She had a mind for a black husband." [33] And finally, white men anxious and guilty over their own sexual aggressiveness were quick to impute it to others especially at a time of interracial crisis. One has only to imagine the emotions flooding through some planter who had been more or less regularly sleeping with some of his slave wenches when he suddenly learned of a conspiracy among their male counterparts; it was virtually inevitable that his thoughts turn in a torrent of guilt to the "safety" of his wife.

4. DISMEMBERMENT, PHYSIOLOGY, AND SEXUAL
   PERCEPTIONS

The white man's fears of Negro sexual aggression were equally apparent in the use of castration as a punishment in the colonies. This weapon of desperation was not employed by angry mobs in the manner which became familiar after Emancipation. In a few instances, particularly in the West Indies, individual planters emasculated their slaves, sometimes in outbursts of sadism involving hideous tortures which planter society deplored but did not effectively control until the latter part of the eighteenth century.[34] Far more significant, castration was dignified by specific legislative sanction as a lawful punishment in Antigua, the Carolinas, Bermuda, Virginia, Pennsylvania, and New Jersey.[35] It was sometimes prescribed for such offenses as striking a white person or running away: until 1722 South Carolina legally required masters of slaves running away for the fourth time to have them castrated, and in 1697

33. Stephen Bordley to Matt Harris, Annapolis, Jan. 30, 1739 [/40], Stephen Bordley's Letterbook, 1738–1740, Md. Hist. Soc.

34. Hans Sloane, A Voyage to the Islands Madera, Barbados, Nieves, S. Christophers and Jamaica, with the Natural History . . . , 2 vols. (London, 1707–25), I, lvii; Sainsbury, ed., Cal. State Papers, 1708–09, 470, 520, 1724–25, 56; James Ramsay, An Essay on the Treatment and Conversion of African Slaves in the British Sugar Colonies (London, 1784), 86, 282; Purdie and Dixon's Wmsbg. Va. Gaz., Dec. 23, 1773.

35. Acts Leeward Islands (1734), 136 (1702—unspecific, allowing "any Member cut off" for injuring a white person); Cooper and McCord, eds., Statutes S. C., VII, 360 (1696); Clark, ed., State Recs. N. C., XXIII, 489 (1758); Sainsbury, ed., Cal. State Papers, 1704–05, 506–9 (1704, Bermuda); Hening, ed., Statutes Va., III, 461 (1705); Mitchell et al., eds., Statutes Pa., II, 79 (1700); [Acts of N. J. in 1704], 18–20. The Virginia act provided for "dismembring," a term which seems usually to have been taken to mean castration but which may occasionally have encompassed punishments such as severing toes.

the Assembly ordered castration of three Negroes who had attempted to abscond to the Spanish in St. Augustine. Employed in this way, castration was a not irrational method of slave control, closely akin to a South Carolina penalty for the fifth offense, hamstringing, and to the Jamaica law which authorized severing one foot of a runaway.[36] (When a member of an early Baptist church in South Carolina castrated one of his runaway slaves he caused an unseemly row among his brethren which was patched up with the aid of advice from a Baptist congregation in England in which his action was cautiously endorsed.) [37] As time went on, gradually rising standards of humane treatment for all human beings tended to limit the use of castration as slave punishment. Georgia's first slave code of 1755 specifically prohibited owners from maiming or emasculating their slaves, and Virginia almost entirely abandoned castration as a lawful punishment in 1769. Yet as late as 1758 North Carolina authorized its use, and until repeal in 1764 the colony was paying jailers for performing official castrations and reimbursing masters whose slaves failed to survive.[38]

Yet castration was not simply another of the many brands of hideous cruelty which graced the colonial criminal codes: it was reserved for Negroes and occasionally Indians. Pennsylvania was the only colony to authorize castration of white men (in 1700 in an effort to curtail capital punishments) ; and significantly, the novel penalty was reserved for grave sexual offenses such as sodomy, bestiality, second offense of rape, and perhaps incest, and apparently was never applied.[39] In some colonies, laws authorizing castration were worded so as to apply to all Negroes whether free or slave. As a legal punishment castration was a peculiarly American experiment, for there was no basis for it in English law. Indeed colonial officials in England were shocked and outraged at the idea. It was a measure

36. Cooper and McCord, eds., *Statutes S. C.*, VII, 360, and ff. for ensuing codes; *Acts Jamaica* (1738) , 160; for the three Negroes, A. S. Salley, ed., *Journals of the Commons House of Assembly of South Carolina for the Two Sessions of 1697* (Columbia, 1913) , 20.

37. William G. McLoughlin and Winthrop D. Jordan, eds., "Baptists Face the Barbarities of Slavery in 1710," *Jour. Southern Hist.*, 29 (1963) , 495–501.

38. Candler, comp., *Col. Recs. Ga.*, XVIII, 132–33; Hening, ed., *Statutes Va.*, VIII, 358; Clark, ed., *State Recs. N. C.*, XXIII, 489, 656; and for 16 slaves castrated (1 died and 1 executed) , *ibid.*, XXII, 819, 825, 830, 831, 834, 837, 839, 843, 850; and Saunders, ed., *Col. Recs. N. C.*, VI, 740, 742.

39. Mitchell *et al.*, eds., *Statutes Pa.*, II, 7–8. Lawrence H. Gipson, "Crime and Its Punishment in Provincial Pennsylvania; A Phase of the Social History of the Commonwealth," *Pennsylvania History*, 2 (1935) , 3–16, cites no incidents of legal castration. But in Connecticut a Negro who castrated his master's son was castrated after trial: Phila. *Amer. Weekly Mercury*, Jan. 18, 1744.

of the gulf between Americans and Englishmen created by America's racial slavery that such laws should be passed in America and vehemently disallowed in England. In towering indignation, English officials called castration "inhumane and contrary to all Christian Laws," "a punishment never inflicted by any Law [in any of] H.M. Dominions," and "such as never was allowed by or known in the Laws of this Kingdom." [40] Some Americans thought the practice necessary to restrain a lecherous and barbarous people; Englishmen thought the barbarity was on the other side.

Castration of Negroes clearly indicated a desperate, generalized need in white men to persuade themselves that they were really masters and in all ways masterful, and it illustrated dramatically the ease with which white men slipped over into treating their Negroes like their bulls and stallions whose "spirit" could be subdued by emasculation. In some colonies, moreover, the specifically sexual aspect of castration was so obvious as to underline how much of the white man's insecurity vis-à-vis the Negro was fundamentally sexual. Significant regional distinctions suggest this strongly. In the West Indian islands and South Carolina, legally authorized castration of slaves occurred infrequently and seems to have ended earlier than in other colonies.[41] Furthermore, in the islands and South Carolina castration seems to have been employed with cool rationality as a method of slave control, as one method among many. Following a slave uprising in Barbados in 1693, the colony paid ten guineas to Alice Mills for castrating forty-two Negroes (an episode which says a good deal about Barbados and something about Alice Mills) .[42] In the more northerly colonies, by contrast, where the pattern of interracial sex was less stable and less rigidly structured, white men were

40. The castration provisions of three colonies (Pa., Bermuda, N. J., 1704–09) were disallowed and not re-enacted: Sainsbury, ed., *Cal. State Papers, 1704–05*, 277, 280, 506, 507, 509; *Documents N. J.*, III, 473–74; O'Callaghan and Fernow, eds., *Docs. N.-Y.*, V, 157. For omission of castration in later acts in sources not already given, *Acts Bermuda*, Allinson, ed., *Acts N.-J.* Although apparently castration was dead in English law by 1700, it was not unknown in medieval England; Henry I closed a monetary investigation with 90 emasculations: James W. Thompson and Edgar N. Johnson, *An Introduction to Medieval Europe, 300–1500* (N. Y., 1937), 444n.

41. The only statutory authorization I have found (Antigua, 1702, and unspecific at that) was nullified in 1723 by a law, as the governor explained, "to prevent the inhumane murdering, maiming and castrating of slaves by cruel and barbarous persons (as has been too much practiced by laying a fine on those that shall be guilty of such crueltys." *Acts Leeward Islands* (1734), 216; Gov. John Hart to Council of Trade and Plantations, St. Christophers, Mar. 11, 1724, Sainsbury, ed., *Cal. State Papers, 1724–25*, 56.

42. Minutes of Council of Barbadoes, Jan. 24, 1693, Sainsbury, ed., *Cal. State Papers, 1693–96*, 5.

accordingly less sure of themselves and more likely to exact specifically sexual retribution against sexual aggression by Negro males. The Pennsylvania and New Jersey laws passed early in the eighteenth century (and quickly disallowed) prescribed castration of Negroes as punishment for one offense only, attempted rape of a white woman. Still more strikingly, Virginia's provision for castration of Negroes, which had been on the books for many years and permitted castration ("dismemberment") for a variety of serious offenses, was repealed in 1769 for humanitarian reasons, but the repealing statute specifically declared that it might still be inflicted for one particular offense—rape or attempted rape of a white woman. (In the eyes of the law, of course, there was really no such thing as one slave raping another.) [43]

There were limits to the colonists' need to impose drastic sexual retribution. Even in Virginia, Negro rape of a white girl did not necessarily result in massive sexual retaliation, and North Carolina's seven-year experiment with castration seems to have been merely an attempt to save the colony the cost of paying for executed slaves. In New York a Negro convicted of two attempts at raping white women was simply burned alive.[44] The fact remains, however, that certain groups of colonial assemblymen conceived of writing sexual retaliation into law, and this fact is undeniably suggestive of fairly widespread and strong feeling on the "protection" of white women. The nature of that feeling may be easily ascertained from the

43. Only one little island seems to have provided otherwise: *Acts of the Legislature of the Island of Tobago; from 1768, to 1775, Inclusive* (London, 1776), 107–8. I have come across only one instance of prosecution of a slave for raping another, though there must have been others: Robert Carter (of Nomini Hall) to Gov. Patrick Henry, June 3, 1778, Letter Book III (June 1775–May 1780), Carter Papers, Duke University Library, Durham, N. C. (microfilm at Colonial Williamsburg, Williamsburg, Va.).

44. A free Negro convicted in Isle of Wight Co. Court of attempting to rape a seven-year-old white girl was punished by one hour in the pillory (where he was "much pelted by the Populace"), 29 lashes, and temporary servitude for payment of fees: Wmsbg. *Va. Gaz.*, Aug. 26, 1737. The North Carolina law (1758) prescribed mandatory castration for all first capital offenses by male slaves *except* murder and rape (which continued to require execution): Clark, ed., *State Recs. N. C.*, XXIII, 489; Bassett, *Slavery in N. C.*, 31–32; *N.-Y. Gaz.*, Jan. 28, 1734. Negro rape of a white woman meant death in Maryland, loss of both ears in Delaware, and branding, whipping, and transportation in Rhode Island: *Archives Md.*, XL, 93, XLVI, 618; *Laws Del.*, I, 104; *Acts and Laws of the English Colony of Rhode-Island and Providence-Plantations* . . . (Newport, 1767), 195–96. For much lighter penalties in Massachusetts, Superior Court of Judicature, Bristol Co., Sept. 14, 1708, Box 16, bundle: Miscellaneous—Negroes; Petition of James Fosdick, Apr. 7, 1721, Box 16, bundle: Mass. Petitions, Parish Transcripts, N.-Y. Hist. Soc.

following instructive item in the *Boston News-Letter* of March 3, 1718.

From New-London [Connecticut], Feb. 20th past. By certain Information from a Gentleman we are assured, that some Weeks ago to the Westward of that place, a very remarkable thing fell out, (which we here relate as a caveat for all Negroes medling for the future with any white Women, least they fare with the like Treatment,) and it is this, A Negro Man met abroad an English Woman, which he accosted to lye with, stooping down, fearing none behind him, a Man observing his Design, took out his Knife, before the Negro was aware, cut off all his unruly parts smack and smooth, the Negro Jumpt up roaring and run for his Life; the Black now an Eunuch is alive and like to recover of his Wounds and doubtless cured from any more such Wicked Attempts.

Doubtless a cure, but for whom?

The concept of the Negro's aggressive sexuality was reinforced by what was thought to be an anatomical peculiarity of the Negro male. He was said to possess an especially large penis. The idea was considerably older even than the exegesis on Ham's offense against his father offered by the West African traveler Richard Jobson in 1623. Indeed the idea without question antedated the settlement of America and possibly even the Portuguese explorations of the West African coast. Several fifteenth-century cartographers decorated parts of Africa with little naked figures which gave the idea graphic expression, and in due course, in the seventeenth century, English accounts of West Africa were carefully noting the "extraordinary greatness" of the Negroes' "members." [45] By the final quarter of the eighteenth century the idea that the Negro's penis was larger than the white man's had become something of a commonplace in European scientific circles.[46] Whether it was a commonplace in popular

45. Andrea Bianco, Map of the World, 1436, in Adolf E. Nordenskiöld, *Periplus: An Essay on the Early History of Charts and Sailing-Directions*, trans. Francis A. Bather (Stockholm, 1897); The "Cantino" Planisphere, 1502, in Armando Corteseão and Avelino Teixeira Da Mota, *Portugaliae Monumenta Cartographica* (Lisbon, 1960——), I, plate 5. Similar depictions of a 14th-century Negro king, Mansa Musa, are noted by E. W. Bovill, *The Golden Trade of the Moors* (London, 1958), 92n, who cites particularly the planisphere of Jayme Bertrand, 1482. For the English accounts, Jobson, *Golden Trade*, ed. Kingsley, 52; *The Golden Coast*, 75–76; Ogilby, *Africa*, 451.

46. In a work notorious as a collection of commonplaces, Oliver Goldsmith represented Linnaeus as having shown that the Negro's "penis was longer and much wider"; *An History of the Earth, and Animated Nature*, 8 vols. (London, 1774), II, 228. See also Johnson, "'Of Differing Ages and Climes,'" *Jour. Hist. Ideas*, 21 (1960), 475. The astonishing degree to which the constructs of the interracial sexual complex filtered into Europe, where they presumably had far less functional value, may be illustrated by this comment from a pre-eminent anthropologist (a German) in 1795: "It is generally said that the penis in the

circles in the English colonies is more difficult to ascertain, since it was scarcely the sort of assertion likely to find its way into print even if a great many people talked about it. Certainly the idea was not unheard of, for as an officer in the First Pennsylvania Regiment commented pointedly in his journal about the Negro boys waiting on Virginia dinner tables: "I am surprized this does not hurt the feelings of this fair Sex to see these young boys of about Fourteen and Fifteen years Old to Attend them. these whole nakedness Expos'd and I can Assure you It would Surprize a person to see these d—d black boys how well they are hung." [47]

If this belief concerning the Negro had some currency in the English continental colonies, as seems probable, it might easily be regarded as early evidence of a now classic instance of the influence of sexual insecurity upon perception. On the other hand, there may have been genuine basis in fact for the white man's perception, for the few modern studies of the subject have indicated that the penis of the Negro is on average larger than that of the white man, though of course not enough larger to explain entirely what is now almost an article of faith for millions of white men.[48] Whatever the objective facts of the matter, the belief blended flawlessly with the white man's image of the Negro. If a perceptible anatomical difference did in fact exist, it fortuitously coincided with the already firmly established idea of the Negro's special sexuality; it could only have served as striking confirmation of that idea, as salt in the wounds of the white man's envy.

Neatly dovetailing with these various elements in the racial complex was the common belief that Negroes were lustily promiscuous

Negro is very large. And this assertion is so far borne out by the remarkable genitory apparatus of an Æthiopian which I have in my anatomical collection. Whether this prerogative be constant and peculiar to the nation I do not know. It is said that women when eager for venery prefer the embraces of Negroes to those of other men. On the other hand, that Ethiopian and Mulatto women are particularly sought out by Europeans. The cause of this preference may be various, but I do not know what it is." Thomas Bendyshe, trans. and ed., *The Anthropological Treatises of Johann Friedrich Blumenbach* . . . (London, 1865) , 249.

47. Entry of June 22, 1781, Military Journal of Lt. William Feltman, May 26, 1781 to Apr. 25, 1782, Hist. Soc. Pa., a passage deleted in a published version, Hist. Soc. Pa., *Collections*, 1 (1853) , 303-48.

48. William Montague Cobb, "Physical Anthropology of the American Negro," *American Journal of Physical Anthropology*, 29 (1942) , 158-59, cites five studies indicating greater size and says his own observations substantiate this. See, too, Carleton S. Coon, Stanley M. Garn, and Joseph B. Birdsell, *Races: A Study of the Problems of Race Formation in Man* (Springfield, Ill., 1950) , 63, 91; Lewis, *Biology of the Negro*, 77. Social scientists, on the other hand, have almost universally assumed that this notion has little or no basis in fact.

among themselves.[49] Here there was solid foundation in fact. By the colonists' standards, the sexual morality of the slaves was so low as to be out of sight. As for the slaves, their standards were utterly confused. Wrenched from the integral cultures of their homelands, under favorable circumstances in America they tended to adopt the values of their masters. Yet slavery as such was scarcely a very favorable circumstance under which to make the difficult transition, for slavery recognized no permanent human relationship other than master and slave. Though there were a host of exceptions in practice, even in the plantation colonies, the law of slavery blandly eradicated traditional family relationships. As a prominent Maryland lawyer explained, "slaves are bound by our criminal laws generally, yet we do not consider them as the objects of such laws as relate to the commerce between the sexes. A slave has never maintained an action against the violator of his bed. A slave is not admonished for incontinence, or punished for fornication or adultery." [50] In fact, anything *but* promiscuity among slaves represented tenacious cultural conservatism or, more significant in the long run, a triumph of cultural adaptivity.

Most planters in the eighteenth century did little to discourage this promiscuity. It was not that planters thought they were breeding slaves. Slaveowners acquired valuable young Negroes not by forcing their slaves to mate (clear instances of this being very rare) but by doing little to interfere with a system which gave every encouragement to early and frequent sexual intercourse among slaves. In their widespread failure to institutionalize restraints on slave sexual activity, planters could scarcely have been unaware that the result would be more slaves. The most important reason for the planters' failure, however, was that the logic of slavery demanded it. The more temperate contemporary critics of slavery recognized this, for they usually charged that masters *allowed* sexual excesses among the Negroes; these critics decried not the encouragement of promiscuity among slaves but the lack of zeal among white men in sup-

49. A few examples are Elias Neau to John Chamberlayne, N. Y., [ca. May 1711], Robert Jenney to [David Humphreys], Rye, N. Y., Nov. 19, 1725, S.P.G. Manuscripts (Transcripts), A6, no. 87, B1, no. 78, Lib. Cong.; Frank J. Klingberg, ed., *The Carolina Chronicle of Dr. Francis Le Jau, 1706–1717* (Berkeley and Los Angeles, 1956), 41–42, 60, 93–94; "Extracts from Henry Whistler's Journal," Firth, ed., *Narrative of General Venables*, 146; Sloane, *Voyage to the Islands*, I, xlviii; Griffith Hughes, *The Natural History of Barbados* (London, 1750), 16; Edwards, *History of British West Indies*, II, 97–98. An exceptional contrary assessment was Ligon, *True History of Barbadoes*, 47.

50. Harris and M'Henry, eds., *Maryland Reports*, I, 563. In New England the situation was very different: Greene, *Negro in New England*, chap. 8.

pressing it by active imposition of the standards of English morality.[51] In the long run, especially after the Revolution, slaveowners
succumbed to the implications embedded in the fact that they had
enslaved men and not animals, and, working against the logic of
slavery, planters tended increasingly to recognize and even to encourage permanent familial relationships among their slaves.[52] Despite this gradual cultural assimilation, though, the implications of
Negro promiscuity sank deeply into the white man's mind and
provided further confirmation of the Negro's special sexuality.

The sexual leitmotif in the relations between the two races was
further emphasized and sustained by a simple fact of mundane life:
slaves often wore little clothing, sometimes very little. Africans had
somewhat different standards from Europeans as to what parts of
the body required a covering of modesty; most slaves lived in warm
or tropical climates, and any clothing worn by slaves had to be paid
for by their masters. The result was sometimes an atmosphere of
semi-nudity. Many Negroes coming off the slave ships were clad only
in breech cloths and some were not clad at all. The men (and
occasionally women) who purchased these nearly naked Africans
were, of course, particularly interested in physical attributes, and it
behooved them to investigate before investing.[53] As one foreign
traveler prissily described a slave market, "If negresses are put up,
scandalous and indecent questions and jests are permitted." [54] "Permitted" scarcely seems the appropriate term. On southern plantations slaves were usually clothed in a long shirt or in trousers made
of "negro cloth." More surprising, it was apparently common practice for partially or fully matured Negro boys to wait upon dinner
tables wearing only a shirt not always long enough to conceal their
private parts.[55] Vistors commented upon the casualness with which

51. *An Extract of the Journals of Mr. Commissary Von Reck . . .* (London,
1734), in Force, ed., *Tracts*, IV, no. 5. The only clear-cut case found was a
famous one in Massachusetts, 1639: Josselyn, *Voyages to New-England*, Mass.
Hist. Soc., *Collections*, 3d Ser., 3 (1833), 231.

52. Even in the islands: in 1798 the Leeward Islands legislature declared
Negroes should be encouraged to have only one wife, though without formal
marriage. To this end, white men were prohibited from cohabiting with any
female slave having such nominal husband. *The Laws of the Island of Antigua:
Consisting of the Acts of the Leeward Islands . . . [1690–1798]; and the Acts of
Antigua [1668–1804] . . . ,* 2 vols. (London, 1805), I, 31–32.

53. See particularly [Kimber], ["Observations in America"], *London Mag.,* [15]
(1746), 325n.

54. Johann David Schoepf, *Travels in the Confederation (1783–1784),* trans.
and ed. Alfred J. Morrison, 2 vols. (Phila., 1911), II, 148.

55. *Ibid.,* I, 357; entry of June 22, 1781, Military Journal of Lt. William
Feltman, May 26, 1781, to Apr. 25, 1782, Hist. Soc. Pa.; Marquis de Chastellux,

this exposure was taken by their hosts, male and female; and probably this casualness was entirely genuine, for whenever nudity is
customary it soon ceases to shock. No matter how customary or
casually regarded, however, semi-nudity among the Negroes must
have strengthened the sexual undertones in the daily relationships
between the races.

Precisely because these relationships were structured by daily contact, Negroes seemed more highly sexed to the colonists than did the
American Indians. The magnitude of the differentiation they made
between the two aboriginal peoples on this score was so great as to
suggest that it reflected not merely the immediate circumstances in
which the colonists found themselves but the entirety of English
historical experience since the beginning of expansion overseas. For
it is arresting that the colonists did not consider Indians as being in
any sense pale replicas of Negroes. Rather, they set up Indians
against Negroes. They assumed the two uncivilized peoples nursed
inveterate hostility toward each other.[56] Far from finding Indians
lusty and lascivious, they discovered them to be notably deficient in
ardor and virility.[57] (Eventually and almost inevitably a European

Travels in North America, in the Years, 1780, 1781 and 1782, trans. and ed.
Howard C. Rice, Jr., 2 vols. (Chapel Hill, 1963), II, 585 (Grieve's note);
Luffman, *Brief Account of Antigua*, 52–53. For nakedness more generally,
[Charles Leslie], *A New History of Jamaica, from the Earliest Accounts, to the
Taking of Porto Bello by Vice-Admiral Vernon . . .*, [2d ed.] (London, 1740),
34–35; W. J. Hinke, trans. and ed., "Report of the Journey of Francis Louis
Michel from Berne, Switzerland, to Virginia, October 2, 1701—December 1, 1702,"
Va. Mag. of Hist. and Biog., 24 (1916), 116–17; Charleston *S.-C. Gaz.*, Jan. 31,
June 5, 12, 1736; John Brickell, *The Natural History of North-Carolina . . .*
(Dublin, 1737), 276; Lawrence, "Religious Education of Negro in Georgia," *Ga.
Hist. Qtly.*, 14 (1930), 45; Thornely, ed., *Journal of Nicholas Cresswell*, 36;
William Beckford, *Remarks upon the Situation of Negroes in Jamaica . . .*
(London, 1788), 7; Lida T. Rodman, ed., *Journal of a Tour to North Carolina,
by William Attmore, 1787* (Chapel Hill, 1922), 44; Edwards, *History of British
West Indies*, II, 151–52; Fred Shelley, ed., "The Journal of Ebenezer Hazard in
Virginia, 1777," *Va. Mag. of Hist. and Biog.*, 62 (1954), 410; John Henry, *A New
and Accurate Map of Virginia . . .* (London, 1770); William Duane, trans.,
Thomas Balch, ed., *The Journal of Claude Blanchard . . . 1780–1783* (Albany,
1876), 163.

56. For instances of this assumption, Jones, *Present State of Virginia*, ed.
Morton, 50; Brickell, *Natural History*, 263, 273; Grant, *Memoirs*, ed. Wilson, I,
134; [George Milligen-Johnston], *A Short Description of the Province of South-
Carolina* (London, 1770), in Chapman J. Milling, ed., *Colonial South Carolina;
Two Contemporary Descriptions . . .* (Columbia, 1951), 136; Box 3, bundle:
Minutes of Council in Assembly (1755), 3, Parish Transcripts, N.-Y. Hist. Soc.;
Kenneth W. Porter, "Relations between Negroes and Indians within the Present
Limits of the United States," *Jour. Negro Hist.*, 17 (1932), 298–306, 322–27.

57. William Byrd thought Indians had "Constitutions untainted by Lewdness"; William K. Boyd, ed., *William Byrd's Histories of the Dividing Line
betwixt Virginia and North Carolina* (Raleigh, N. C., 1929), 3. John Lawson

commentator announced that the Indian's penis was smaller than the European's.) [58] And the colonists developed no image of the Indian as a potential rapist: their descriptions of Indian attacks did not include the Indians "reserving the young women for themselves." In fact the entire interracial sexual complex did not pertain to the Indian.[59] In the more settled portions of the colonies, Englishmen did not normally take Indian women to bed, but neither did an aura of tension pervade the sexual union of red and white. Of the various laws which penalized illicit miscegenation, none applied to Indians, and only North Carolina's (and Virginia's for a very brief period) prohibited intermarriage.[60] On the contrary, several colonists were willing to allow, even advocate, intermarriage with the Indians—an unheard of proposition concerning Negroes.[61] Patrick Henry pushed a bill through two readings in the Virginia House which offered bounties (if that is the proper term) for children of Indian-white marriages. It is suggestive, too, that Virginia's statutory definition of mulattoes extended the taint of Negro ancestry through three generations and of Indian ancestry through only one.[62]

---

found Indians promiscuous but not lascivious, and in speaking of physical attributes declared "the *Indian* Men are not so vigorous and impatient in their Love as we are." Lawson, *Voyage to Carolina*, 34–36, 183–84, 186.

58. [Cornelis] de P[auw], *Recherches Philosophiques sur les Américains . . .*, 3 vols. (London and Berlin, 1770), I, 32–44, III, 16–20. A number of Europeans, notably De Pauw, Lord Kames, Buffon, and William Robertson, eagerly seized upon this supposed deficiency in Indians for disparaging the new Americans. Gilbert Chinard, "Eighteenth Century Theories on America as a Human Habitat," Amer. Phil. Soc., *Proceedings*, 91 (1947), 27–57; Antonello Gerbi, *La Disputa del Nuovo Mondo; Storia di una Polemica, 1750–1900* (Milan and Naples, 1955), chaps. 1, 3.

59. For illustration, the catalog of sins attributed to Indian slaves in the preamble to a 1712 act prohibiting their importation; *Acts and Resolves Mass.*, I, 698.

60. Clark, ed., *State Recs. N. C.*, XXIII, 65, 160, but see 106; Hening, ed., *Statutes Va.*, III, 86–87, 453–54. Though in Massachusetts Samuel Sewall had to get "the Indians out of the Bill" which became the 1705 act, and they were included in 1786; *Diary of Sewall*, II, 143; *Acts and Laws of the Commonwealth of Massachusetts (1780–1805)*, 13 vols. (Boston, 1890–98), IV, 10.

61. Boyd, ed., *Byrd's Histories of the Dividing Line*, 3–4, 120; Beverley, *The History of Virginia*, ed. Wright, 38–39; Lawson, *Voyage to Carolina*, 185, 237–38; James Oglethorpe to the Trustees, Frederica, Apr. 24, 1736, "Letters from General Oglethorpe to the Trustees of the Colony and Others, from October 1735 to August 1744," Ga. Hist. Soc., *Collections*, 3 (1873), 32; also, James Fontaine, *Memoirs of a Huguenot Family . . .*, trans. and ed. Ann Maury (N. Y., 1872), 350; A. A. Luce and T. E. Jessop, eds., *The Works of George Berkeley, Bishop of Cloyne*, 9 vols. (London, 1948–57), VII, 122. Royal officials directed encouragement of intermarriage with Indians (never with Negroes) in only one colony, Nova Scotia: Leonard W. Labaree, ed., *Royal Instructions to British Colonial Governors, 1670–1776*, 2 vols. (N. Y. and London, 1935), II, 470.

62. Albert J. Beveridge, *The Life of John Marshall*, 4 vols. (N. Y., 1916–19), I, 239n; Hening, ed., *Statutes Va.*, III, 252.

5. THE SECULARIZATION OF REPRODUCTION

The problem of ancestry was the inescapable concomitant of interracial sex. Before turning to examine the way the colonists conceived and handled the problem, it is important to notice certain logical implications embedded within it. For there are, and have been in human history, other modes of considering human heredity than one that is entirely enmeshed in the facts and vocabulary of the sex act and physiognomic reproduction and physical parenthood. In a century when civil magistrates were still reminded that they were "nursing fathers" of the churches and when the "rising generation" was urged to cultivate the "seed" of grace, it is apparent that men spoke of interracial sex in a mode which was explicitly and pronouncedly biological. That there could exist such a phenomenon as *interracial* sex meant that a *physical* rather than a religious (i.e., a cultural) distinction was being made. The fruits of such unions were distinctive especially by reason of their physiognomy. From time immemorial Englishmen had been born to a status, to a cultural role; now they were being born to an appearance, to a physical condition, as well. When the legislative assemblies of Maryland and South Carolina condemned sexual intimacies between white persons and Negroes as "unnatural and inordinate Copulations," [63] they underlined the sheerly physical aspects of these relationships. That copulation between human beings should have been "unnatural" and that the resultant offspring could be described, as they were, as "mixt," "spurious," and "mungril" [64] suggests that white men had come to think of interracial union as contradicting the laws of nature—which is to say that in America strange things had happened to the concept of natural law.

It was scarcely a step from these assertions to formulation of an equation between the superior physical beauty of white persons, the

63. *Archives Md.*, XXII, 552, XXVI, 260, XXX, 290; Cooper and McCord, eds., *Statutes S. C.*, III, 20.

64. For example, Clark, ed., *State Recs. N. C.*, XXIII, 160; Hening, ed., *Statutes Va.*, III, 86–87; *Archives Md.*, XIII, 307; [Long], *Jamaica*, II, 327; [Thomas Tryon], *Friendly Advice to the Gentlemen-Planters of the East and West Indies* . . . ([London], 1684), 127; William Logan to Lord Granville, London, Aug. 13, 1761, Logan Papers, XI, 60, Hist. Soc. Pa.; E[benezer] C[ooke], *Sotweed Redivivus: or the Planters Looking-Glass. In Burlesque Verse. Calculated for the Meridian of Maryland* (Annapolis, 1730), iv; Singleton, *General Description*, 152; James Otis, *The Rights of the British Colonies Asserted and Proved* (Boston, 1764), 24.

wickedness of racial intermixture, and the evident intention of the Creator to foster order and distinct complexions among His human creatures. At least such an equation was evident in the words of an indignant South Carolinian who fired off in the *South-Carolina Gazette* what he apparently supposed to be a withering blast at "the *scandalous Offence*" which "must surely rouse against it the Resentment of every Man, who has the least Sense of the Obligation he lies under to his *Creator,* for that *Form* and *Complexion* he has thought fit to bestow upon us." For just as we have been "most peculiarly indebted to him for all the Blessings of human Nature" and for "the indulgent *Affluence* of his Bounty," this anonymous critic declared, "so may we . . . with no less Reason imagine, that this Distinction of Colour, in our Complexion, from that other Part of his human Creatures, of the opposite Hue, may be a concurrent Instance of his Favour." What are we to think, then, of all those who "dare to subvert and deface the *Order* and *Beauty,* which this our *All-wise Creator* has discovered to us through all his works?" Growing increasingly vehement with every stroke of his pen, the writer seized eagerly upon a minor outbreak of the dreaded smallpox in Charleston: "I scarce know which ought to be most dreaded, the *Infection* of the *Epidemical Disease* we are at present alarm'd with, or of *this other.* Tho' I declare had I a Child in danger of either. I should choose rather to loose him by the *natural* Distemper, than the *unnatural* One." [65] This was scarcely the first time in Western culture that sexual intercourse was held to be against nature, but it *was* new that this concept of nature was grounded on physiological distinctions between groups of human beings. Nowhere was the magnitude of this shift from the spirit to the flesh more poignantly expressed than in Samuel Sewall's assertion that "there is such a disparity in their Conditions, Colour and Hair, that they can never embody with us and grow up into orderly Families, to the Peopling of the Land: but still remain in our Body Politick as a kind of extravasat Blood." [66] Here, if ever, was a novel Puritan interpretation of community.

The final term in Sewall's exclusionary principle—and he was writing *against* slavery and the slave trade—presaged a significant tendency. The use of "blood" in connection with miscegenation represented, especially before the advent of knowledge about genetics, much more than a convenient metaphor. For blood was the essence

65. Charleston *S.-C. Gaz.*, Mar. 18, 1732.
66. Sewall, *Selling of Joseph*, 2.

of man, the principle of life. More important, at least from the time
of the Greeks it had been intimately and explicitly linked with the
concept of human generation: some writers assumed that the
mother's blood actually ebbed into the fetus and most authorities
agreed that male semen was a distillation, "the office of the Testes
. . . [being] to separate the seed from the blood." [67] (Herodotus had
maintained that the semen of the Negro was black, but Aristotle
had set that matter straight and Herodotus's erroneous but not illogical notion had cropped up again only occasionally.) [68] Thus the
term *blood* implied for the colonists a deep inherency and permanence through the generations, and when they called sexual union
between Negroes and whites a mixture of bloods they were expressing a strong sense of radical distinction between the two kinds of
people. The fact that the difference between the two bloods was not
conceived very literally or explicitly does not detract from the importance of the distinction being made: in 1785 a South Carolina
woman went to the trouble of obtaining an affidavit (duly recorded
in the county clerk's office) that she was believed "to be an English
woman and clar of any Negro blood Indian or Mulatoo." [69] Unions
of two Negroes or of two white persons were *never* called mixtures
of two kinds of blood. And though this concept had not yet attained
the proportions of an article of faith, in retrospect it is easy to see an
embryonic significance in such complaints as that miscegenation

67. See "seed" and "blood" in *Oxford English Dictionary;* F. J. Cole, *Early
Theories of Sexual Generation* (Oxford, 1930) ; Conway Zirkle, "Early History of
Inheritance," Amer. Phil. Soc., *Transactions,* New Ser., 35 (1945–46), Pt. ii,
119–45; Richard B. Onians, *The Origins of European Thought about the Body,
the Mind, the Soul, the World, Time, and Fate; New Interpretations of Greek,
Roman and Kindred Evidence, Also of Some Basic Jewish and Christian Beliefs*
(Cambridge, Eng., 1951) , 109n, 121. For references in the colonies to mixing of
racial bloods, Petition of the Welsh and Pennsylvanians Settled upon Peede
River, S. C., July 7, 1739, Box 2, bundle: S. C., Minutes of Council in Assembly
(1737/38, 1739) , 11, Parish Transcripts, N.-Y. Hist. Soc.; Phila. *Pennsylvania
Journal,* Oct. 1, 1747; Charleston *S.-C. Gaz.,* Mar. 14, 1748; Herbert Aptheker, ed.,
A Documentary History of the Negro People in the United States (N. Y., 1951) ,
13. For idea of national "blood," *Works of James Houstoun,* 1–5.

68. Aristotle, *De Generatione Animalium,* trans. Arthur Platt, in Smith and
Ross, eds., *Works of Aristotle,* V, 736a; Aristotle, *Historia Animalium,* trans.
Thompson, in *ibid.,* IV, 523a; [Vincentius Rumpf], *On the Human Inhabitants
of Our Globe Who Are of One and the Same Species and Origin,* 2d ed.
(Hamburg, 1738) , trans. Thomas Bendyshe in his "History of Anthropology,"
Anthro. Soc. of London, *Memoirs,* 1 (1863–64) , 410. Bodin said men had for a
long time "ridiculed" Herodotus's idea; Bodin, *Method for Easy Comprehension
of History,* trans. Reynolds, 87.

69. H. M. Henry, *The Police Control of the Slave in South Carolina* (Emory,
Va., 1914) , 196.

had "polluted the blood of many amongst us," and had "smutted our blood." [70]

6. MULATTO OFFSPRING IN A BIRACIAL SOCIETY

If miscegenation resulted in smutted blood, it also resulted in children. Somehow they had to be accommodated to a system of racial slavery whose strictest logic their existence violated. How were mulattoes to be treated? Were they to be free or slave, acknowledged or denied, white or black? The ways in which American colonials answered these questions are profoundly revelatory. The questions arose, of course, in the cultural matrix of purpose, accomplishment, self-conception, and social circumstances of settlement in the New World. The social identification of children requires self-identification in the fathers. Inevitably the fruits of interracial sex, fully as much as the generative seeds of passion, grew differently in different contexts of self-identification.

All European colonists in the Americas faced the problem of racially mixed offspring. In the Portuguese and Spanish colonies there rapidly developed a social hierarchy structured according to degrees of intermixture of Negro and European blood, replete with a complicated battery of terminology to facilitate definition. In contrast the English colonists in Maryland, Virginia, and the Carolinas created no such system of ranking. Although cultural differences among the colonizing nations may have done something to effect this divergence, it is significant that the English reaction to racially mixed offspring was not everywhere the same, that men bearing the same cultural baggage reacted differently when dealing with radically different conditions in the New World.

As far as the continental colonies were concerned, it is easy to detect a pattern which has since become so familiar to Americans that they rarely pause to think about it or to question its logic and inevitability. The word *mulatto* is not frequently used in the United States. It is customarily reserved for biological contexts, and for social purposes a mulatto is termed a *Negro*. Americans lump together both socially and legally all persons with perceptible admixture of Negro ancestry, thus making social definition without regard to genetic logic; white blood becomes socially advantageous only in overwhelming proportion. This peculiar bifurcation seems to have existed almost from the beginning of English contact with

70. Fontaine, *Memoirs of a Huguenot Family*, trans. and ed. Maury, 350.

Negroes. The word *mulatto,* borrowed from the Spanish, was in English usage from about 1600 and was probably first used in Virginia records in 1666.[71] Thereafter laws dealing with Negro slaves began to add "and mulattoes," presumably to make clear that mixed blood did not confer exemption from slavery. From the first, every English continental colony lumped mulattoes with Negroes in their slave codes and in statutes governing the conduct of free Negroes: the law was clear that mulattoes and Negroes were not to be distinguished for different treatment.

If mulattoes were to be considered Negroes, logic required some definition of mulattoes, some demarcation between them and white men. Law is not always the embodiment of logic, however, and throughout the colonial period only Virginia and North Carolina grappled with the question raised by continuing intermixture. In 1705 the Virginia Assembly defined a mulatto as "the child, grand child, or great grand child of a negro"; North Carolina wavered on the matter but generally pushed the taint of Negro ancestry from one-eighth to one-sixteenth.[72] There is no reason to suppose that these two colonies were atypical, and in all probability similar rules operated in the other continental colonies. What the matter came down to, of course, was visibility. Anyone whose appearance discernibly connected him with the Negro was held to be such. The line was drawn with regard to practicalities rather than logic. Daily practice supplied logic enough.

Another indication of the refusal of the English continental colonists to separate the "mixed breed" from the African was the absence of terminology which could be used to define a hierarchy of status. The colonists did, of course, seize upon a separate word to describe those of mixed blood. They were forced to do so if they were to deal with the problem at all, even if they merely wished, as they did, to lump "mulattoes" with Negroes. If, however, an infusion of white blood had been regarded as elevating status, then the more white blood the higher the social rank. Had such ranking existed, descriptive terminology would have been required with which to handle shades of distinction. Yet no such vocabulary developed in the continental colonies. Only one word besides *mulatto* was used to describe those of mixed ancestry. The term *mustee*

71. S.v. "mulatto," *OED;* "The Randolph Manuscript," *Va. Mag. of Hist. and Biog.,* 17 (1909), 232; also *Archives Md.,* VII, 76.

72. Hening, ed., *Statutes Va.,* III, 252; Clark, ed., *State Recs. N. C.,* XXIII, 106, 160, 262, 345, 526, 559, 700, 882, XXIV, 61, XXV, 283, 445; Saunders, ed., *Col. Recs. N. C.,* VII, 605, 608, 645.

(with its variant spellings) was used to describe a mixture which was in part Indian, usually Indian-Negro but occasionally Indian-white. The term came into common usage only in the Carolinas, Georgia, and to some extent New York, that is, in those colonies where such crosses occurred with some frequency. Its use rested upon the colonists' feeling that Indians and Negroes were not the same kind of people. Yet while the colonists thus distinguished persons of some Indian ancestry by a separate word, they included these mustees with mulattoes and Negroes in their slave codes.

In addition to this statutory homogenization of all persons with Negro ancestry, mulattoes do not seem to have been accorded higher status than Negroes in actual practice. Whatever the case in other countries or in later centuries, mulattoes seem generally to have been treated no better than unmixed Africans. The diaries, letters, travel accounts, and newspapers of the period do not indicate any pronounced tendency to distinguish mulattoes from Negroes, any feeling that their status was higher and demanded different treatment. These sources give no indication, for instance, that mulattoes were preferred as house servants or concubines. There may well have been a relatively high proportion of mulattoes among manumitted slaves, but probably this was owing to the not unnatural desire of some masters to liberate their own offspring. It seems likely that the relatively few mulattoes given favored treatment were favored for literally paternal reasons.

A single exception to these generalizations stands out sharply from the mass of colonial legislation. In 1765 the colony of Georgia not only undertook to encourage immigration of free colored persons (itself a unique step) but actually provided that free mulatto and mustee immigrants might be naturalized as white men by the legislature and be endowed with "all the Rights, Priviledges, Powers and Immunities whatsoever which any person born of British parents" could have, except the right to vote and sit in the Commons House of Assembly.[73] Thus a degree of citizenship was begrudgingly extended to free mulattoes. That Georgia should so distinguish herself from her northern neighbors was a measure of the colony's weak and exposed condition. A small population with a mounting proportion of slaves and perpetual danger from powerful Indian tribes made Georgians eager to attract men who might be counted as white and who would thereby strengthen the colony's defenses against her foreign and domestic enemies. The legislature went to

---

73. Candler, comp., *Col. Recs. Ga.*, XVIII, 659.

extraordinarily great lengths in its search—perhaps too far for its
own tastes, for it never naturalized anyone under the terms of the
1765 law.

Throughout the colonial period the status of mulattoes, as distinguished from Negroes, rarely received attention from literate Americans. Mulattoes were so fixed in station that their position did not
attract or merit attention. The subject did come up once in the
South-Carolina Gazette, yet even then it was raised tangentially in
connection with an entirely different matter. In 1735 an anonymous
contributor tendered some strictures on Carolina's *nouveaux riches,*
the "half Gentry," and lustily assailed their imitative and snobbish
behavior. For illustration he turned to the character of the mulatto.

> It is observed concerning the Generation of *Molattoes,* that they are
> seldom well belov'd either by the Whites or the Blacks. Their Approach
> towards Whiteness, makes them look back with some kind of Scorn upon
> the Colour they seem to have left, while the Negroes, who do not think
> them better than themselves, return their Contempt with Interest: And the
> Whites, who respect them no Whit the more for the nearer Affinity in
> Colour, are apt to regard their Behaviour as too bold and assuming, and
> bordering upon Impudence. As they are next to Negroes, and but just
> above 'em, they are terribly afraid of being thought Negroes, and therefore
> avoid as much as possible their Company or Commerce: and Whitefolks
> are as little fond of the Company of *Molattoes.*[74]

The point here was, of course, not that mulattoes were in fact
superior to Negroes, but that they alone thought they were. Apparently mulattoes thought white blood to be a source of social elevation, a proposition which whites (and Negroes as well) were quick
to deny. White blood secured one's status only if undiluted.

A somewhat different aspect of this problem came up in 1784
when it was forced on the attention of a Savannah merchant, Joseph
Clay. As executor of a will Clay found himself responsible for the
welfare of two young mulattoes, very possibly the children of his
deceased friend. Because the young people were both free, Clay's
letter to a gentleman in Ireland helps to indicate what a combination of personal freedom and some white ancestry afforded in the
way of social position in Georgia. "These young Folks are very
unfortunately situated in this Country," Clay wrote, "their descent
places them in the most disadvantageous situation, as Free persons
the Laws protects them—but they gain no rank in Life[;] White
Persons do not commonly associate with them on a footing of
equality—so many of their own Colour (say the mixt breed) being

74. Charleston *S.-C. Gaz.,* Mar. 22, 1735.

Slaves, they too naturally fall in with them, and even the Negro Slaves claim a right to their acquaintance and Society." For Joseph Clay the situation was one of unrelieved gloom, even of horror: "Thus a little reflection will present to you what their future Prospects here must be—neglected by the most respectable Class of Society, [they] are forced to intermix with the lowest, and in what that must end—we woud wish to draw a Veil—all the Care that can be taken of them cant prevent it, it arrises from our peculiar situation in regard to these people." Clay went on to recommend as "the most eligible plan" that the youngsters be sent to Europe if his correspondent would accept them as wards. "The Boy might be Bound to some business . . . and the Girl might make a very good Wife to some honest Tradesman." It was essential that they cross the Atlantic: "This alone can save them . . . I think they might both be made usefull Members of Society no such distinctions interfere with their happiness on your side the Water." Clay noted finally that several of his friends endorsed his proposal.[75] Evidently America afforded little opportunity for blacks to become whites through intermixture. American society, wedded as it was to Negro slavery, drew a rigid line which did not exist in Europe: this was indeed "our peculiar situation in regard to these people."

The existence of a rigid barrier between whites and those of Negro ancestry necessarily required a means by which the barrier could on occasion be passed. Some accommodation had to be made for those persons with so little Negro blood that they appeared to be white, for one simply could not go around calling apparently white persons Negroes. Once the stain was washed out visibly it was useless as a means of identification. Thus there developed the silent mechanism of "passing." Such a device would have been unnecessary if those of mixed ancestry and appearance had been regarded as midway between white and black. It was the existence of a broad chasm which necessitated the sudden leap which passing represented.

Fortunately it is possible to catch a glimpse of this process as it operated in the colonial period by following the extraordinary career of a family named Gibson in South Carolina. In 1731 a member of the Commons House of Assembly announced in the chamber that several free colored men with their white wives had immigrated from Virginia with the intention of settling on the

75. Joseph Clay to John Wright, Savannah, Feb. 17, 1784, "Letters of Joseph Clay, Merchant, of Savannah, 1776–1793 . . . ," Ga. Hist. Soc., *Collections*, 8 (1913), 203–4.

Santee River. Free Negroes were undesirable enough, but white wives made the case exceptionally disturbing. "The house apprehending [this prospect] to be of ill Consequence to this Province," appointed a committee to inquire into the matter. Governor Robert Johnson had already sent for what seemed to be the several families involved, and the committee asked him to report his findings to the house.

"The people lately come into the Settlements having been sent for," Johnson duly reported, "I have had them before me in Council and upon Examination find that they are not Negroes nor Slaves but Free people, That the Father of them here is named Gideon Gibson and his Father was also free, I have been informed by a person who has lived in Virginia that this Gibson has lived there Several Years in good Repute and by his papers that he has produced before me that his transactions there have been very regular, That he has for several years paid Taxes for two tracts of Land and had seven Negroes of his own, That he is a Carpenter by Trade and is come hither for the support of his Family." This evident respectability so impressed the governor that he allowed the Gibson family to remain in the colony. "The account he has given of himself," Johnson declared, "is so Satisfactory that he is no Vagabond that I have in Consideration of his Wifes being a white woman and several White women Capable of working and being Serviceable in the Country permitted him to Settle in this Country upon entering into Recognizance for his good behaviour which I have taken accordingly." [76]

The meaning of Johnson's statement that "they are not Negroes nor Slaves but Free people" is not entirely clear. Certainly Gideon Gibson himself was colored; it seems likely that he was mulatto rather than Negro, but it is impossible to tell surely. At any rate Gideon Gibson prospered very nicely: by 1736 either he or a son of the same name owned 450 acres of Carolina land. He continued to own Negroes, and in 1757 he was described as owning property in two widely separated counties. By 1765 the status of Gideon Gibson (by this time unquestionably the son of the original carpenter) was such that he was appointed administrator of an estate.[77] His sister married a wealthy planter, and there is no evidence to indicate that

76. Box 2, bundle: S. C., Minutes of House of Burgesses (1730–35) , 9, Parish Transcripts, N.-Y. Hist. Soc.

77. Charleston *S.-C. Gaz.*, Aug. 29, 1743, supplement, Nov. 26, Dec. 10, 1750, Mar. 3, 1757, supplement; "Abstracts of Records of the Proceedings in the Court of Ordinary, 1764–1771," *S. C. Hist. and Geneal. Mag.*, 22 (1921) , 97, 127; 23 (1922) , 35; [Prince Frederick Parish], *The Register Book for the Parish Prince Frederick, Winyaw* (Baltimore, 1916) , 15, 20, 32, 34.

Gibson himself was regarded by his neighbors as anything but white.[78] In 1768 he was leading a band of South Carolina Regulators almost to battle. The commander dispatched to arrest Gibson was a planter and colonel in the militia, George Gabriel Powell, who ignominiously resigned his commission when his men sided with the Regulators.[79] This latter worthy, apparently a kind master to his own Negroes, sought vindication by attacking Gibson's ancestry. The exact nature of the attack is unclear, but the matter came up on the floor of the Commons, of which Powell was a member. The prominent merchant-patriot of Charleston, Henry Laurens, described the incident some years later when writing from England concerning his own belief that slavery ought to be brought to an end.

Reasoning from the colour carries no conviction. By perseverance the black may be blanched and the "stamp of Providence" effectually effaced. Gideon Gibson escaped the penalties of the negro law by producing upon comparison more red and white in his face than could be discovered in the faces of half the descendants of the French refugees in our House of Assembly, including your old acquaintance the Speaker. I challenged them all to the trial. The children of this same Gideon, having passed through another stage of whitewash were of fairer complexion than their prosecutor George Gabriel [Powell].—But to confine them to their original clothing will be best. They may and ought to continue a separate people, may be subjected by special laws, kept harmless, made useful and freed from the tyranny and arbitrary power of individuals; but as I have already said, this difficulty cannot be removed by arguments on this side of the water.[80]

Laurens showed both sides of the coin. He defended an individual's white status on the basis of appearance and at the same time expressed the conviction that colored persons "may and ought to continue a separate people." Once an Ethiopian always an Ethiopian, unless he could indeed change his skin.

Gideon Gibson's success in hurdling the barrier was exceptional. Unfortunately there is no way of telling how many other persons were effectively transformed into white men. Passing was difficult but not impossible, and it stood as a veiled, unrecognized and ironic

78. Alexander Gregg, *History of the Old Cheraws*, [2d ed.] (Columbia, 1905), 72n.

79. *Ibid.*, 73–74, 139–56; Hooker, ed., *Carolina Backcountry*, 176–77. Biographical information on Powell is in A. S. Salley, ed., "Diary of William Dillwyn during a Visit to Charles Town in 1772," *S. C. Hist. and Geneal. Mag.*, 36 (1935), 35, and note.

80. Henry Laurens to William Drayton, Feb. 15, 1783, in David Duncan Wallace, *The Life of Henry Laurens; With a Sketch of the Life of Lieutenant-Colonel John Laurens* (N. Y. and London, 1915), 454. The speaker was Peter Manigault.

monument to the American ideal of a society open to all comers. One Virginia planter advertised in the newspaper for his runaway mulatto slave who he stated might try to pass for free or as a "white man." An English traveler reported calling upon a Virginia lawyer who was "said to be" and who looked like a mulatto.[81] But the problem of evidence is insurmountable. The success of the passing mechanism depended upon its operating in silence. Passing was a conspiracy of silence not only for the individual but for a biracial society which had drawn a rigid color line based on visibility. Unless a white man was a white man, the gates were open to endless slander and confusion.

That the existence of such a line in the continental colonies was not predominantly the effect of the English cultural heritage is suggested by even a glance at the English colonies in the Caribbean. The social accommodation of mixed offspring in the islands followed a very different pattern from that on the continent. It was regarded as improper, for example, to work mulattoes in the fields—a fundamental distinction. Apparently they were preferred to Negroes as tradesmen, house servants, and especially as concubines.[82] John Luffman wrote that mulatto slaves "fetch a lower price than blacks, unless they are tradesmen, because the purchasers cannot employ them in the drudgeries to which negroes are put too; the colored men, are therefore mostly brought up to trades or employed as house slaves, and the women of this description are generally prostitutes."[83] Though the English in the Caribbean thought of their society in terms of white, colored, and black, they employed a complicated battery of names to distinguish persons of various racial mixtures. This terminology was borrowed from the neighbor-

81. Rind's Wmsbg. *Va. Gaz.*, Apr. 23, 1772; Smyth, *Tour in the United States,* I, 123. Possibly some of the Gibson clan were unable to clear the barrier: the Charleston *South-Carolina Gazette; And Country Journal*, May 19, 1767, carried notice that Edward Gibson, "*(a Mulatto) a stout well-set Man, with short black curly Hair,*" had escaped prison with four other men (apparently white). Reliance upon color as the mark of slavery brought confusion into the courts at a later period, for lawyers were trapped between two kinds of evidence: current appearance and documented ancestry. See Hudgins *v.* Wrights (1806) in *Virginia Reports, Jefferson—33 Grattan, 1730–1880,* annotated by Thomas J. Michie, vol. 1, 2, 3, and 4 Hening and Mumford (Charlottesville, 1903), 71–75.

82. [Tryon], *Friendly Advice*, 140–41; Singleton, *General Description*, 152–53; [Schaw], *Journal of a Lady of Quality*, eds. Andrews, 112; [Long], *Jamaica*, II, 328–30, 332–35; William Beckford, *A Descriptive Account of the Island of Jamaica . . .* , 2 vols. (London, 1790), II, 322; Edwards, *History of British West Indies*, II, 18–31. Institutionalized mulatto concubinage developed in only one place in the United States, New Orleans, where the influence of the Spanish and of French refugees from the West Indies was strong.

83. Luffman, *Brief Account of Antigua*, 115.

ing Spanish, but words are never acquired unless they fulfill a need. While the English settlers on the continent borrowed one Spanish word to describe all mixtures of black and white, the islanders borrowed at least four—*mulatto, sambo, quadroon,* and *mestize*—to describe differing degrees.[84] And some West Indians were prepared to act upon the logic which these terms implied. The respected Jamaican historian, Bryan Edwards, actually proposed extension of civil privileges to mulattoes in proportion to their admixture of white blood.[85] Such a proposition was unheard of on the continent.

The connection between the status of mulattoes and the prevailing pattern of miscegenation is obvious. Mulattoes in the West Indies were products of accepted practice, something they assuredly were not in the continental colonies. In the one area they were the fruits of a desire which society tolerated and almost institutionalized; in the other they represented an illicit passion which public morality unhesitatingly condemned. On the continent, unlike the West Indies, mulattoes represented a practice about which men could only feel guilty. To reject and despise the productions of one's own guilt was only natural.

Although the most important factor making for divergence in social atmosphere among the English colonies was the proportion of Negroes to Europeans, another demographic distinction may have affected the development of attitudes toward miscegenation and mulattoes. In the seventeenth century the ratio of men to women had been high in America and higher still in the West Indies, where in 1675 the ratio averaged about three to two, or, as the sex ratio is usually expressed, 150 (males per 100 females). In the following century it dropped drastically. New England's sex ratio went below 100 as a result of emigration which was as usual predominantly male, a fact which may help explain why white women in New England were occasionally willing actually to marry Negroes. Elsewhere on the continent the bounding birth rate came near to erasing the differential: in 1750, except on the edge of the frontier (where Negroes were even scarcer than women), the sex ratio was probably no more than 110 and in most places less. The same numerical feminization occurred in most of the English islands;

84. *Mulatto* meant one-half white; *sambo,* one-fourth white; *quadroon,* three-fourths white; and *mestize* (which did not imply Indian mixture as it did on the continent), seven-eighths white. [Long], *Jamaica,* II, 260–61; Edwards, *History of British West Indies,* II, 18; J[ohn] G. Stedman, *Narrative of a Five Years' Expedition, against the Revolted Negroes of Surinam, in Guiana . . . ,* 2 vols. (London, 1796), II, plate opposite p. 98; *Jamaica, a Poem,* 22–23.

85. Edwards, *History of British West Indies,* II, 24n.

emigration sapped their male strength until Barbados had a sex ratio in the 80's and the various Leeward Islands were balanced in the neighborhood of 100. A significant exception was Jamaica, where in mid-eighteenth century a plentiful supply of land helped maintain a nearly two-to-one disproportion of men.[86]

Male numerical predominance must surely have been conducive to development of a system of Negro concubinage and, concomitantly, to widespread acceptance of such a system—at least by its participants, which meant a major proportion of white men in the West Indies. As for white women there, a kind of psycho-sexual Gresham's law tended to drive them out of circulation. And while a high sex ratio must have contributed to the acceptability of miscegenation, it may by extension have enhanced the acceptability of mulatto offspring.

Certainly it is striking that Jamaica, the only major English colony where the sex ratio continued high, was the only one to give legislative countenance to the social ascent of mulattoes. In 1733 the legislature provided that "no Person who is not above Three Degrees removed in a lineal Descent from the Negro Ancestor exclusive, shall be allowed to vote or poll in Elections; and no one shall be deemed a Mulatto after the Third Generation, as aforesaid, but that they shall have all the Privileges and Immunities of His Majesty's white Subjects of this Island, provided they are brought up in the Christian Religion." [87] By contrast, in this same period Barbados was barring any person "whose original Extract shall be proved to have been from a Negro" from voting and from testifying against white persons.[88] One English traveler reacted most unfavorably to the white inhabitants of Jamaica as compared to those of Barbados: "The very Propriety and Accent of the *English* Language were quite corrupted in this Island [Jamaica], by conversing so much with *Mulatoes* and *Negros;* for they were so very closely intermixed, that

86. These figures apply, of course, only to the white population. Among Negroes in the islands there was considerable preponderance of males, a situation which must have further aggravated sexual rivalry between the races.

87. *Acts Jamaica* (1738), 260–61; also [Long], *Jamaica*, II, 261, 321. This definition was retained in 1780: *Acts of Assembly, Passed in the Island of Jamaica; from 1770, to 1783, Inclusive* (Kingston, 1786), 174.

88. *Acts Barbadoes* (1721), 112, 153, 171, 213, 226, 267; Richard Hall, comp., *Acts, Passed in the Island of Barbados. From 1643, to 1762, Inclusive* (London, 1764), 256. According to a source dated 1813, free mulattoes but not free Negroes in one of the Leeward Islands, Antigua, were permitted to vote: Elsa V. Goveia, *Slave Society in the British Leeward Islands at the End of the Eighteenth Century* (New Haven and London, 1965), 82.

they suckled, eat, drank, and lay together; wherefore their Tempers and Manners may be very easily accounted for." [89]

Beginning in the 1730's the Jamaican legislature passed numerous private acts conferring upon the colored offspring and sometimes the colored mistress of such and such a planter the rights and privileges of white persons, especially the right to inherit the planter's estate. This blanching of mulattoes met some stiff opposition, for in 1761 the Assembly restricted the amount of property a planter might leave to his mulatto children, declaring that "such bequests tend greatly to destroy the distinction requisite, and absolutely necessary to be kept up in this island, between white persons and negroes, their issue and offspring." The law failed to destroy the widespread acceptance of the practice, however, for the private acts continued. [90] It was in Jamaica, too, that Bryan Edwards called for extension of civil privileges to mulattoes. And Edward Long, in his history of the island, noted that those beyond the third generation were "called English, and consider themselves as free from all taint of the Negroe race" and then went on to declare that all mulattoes ought to be regarded more highly than the blacks, "above whom (in point of due policy) they ought to hold some degree of distinction." [91] Thus Jamaica, which had the highest sex ratio of all the English colonies as well as the highest proportion of Negroes, was unique in its practice of publicly transforming Negroes into white men.

The colonist on the American continent refused to make this extension of privilege. He remained firm in his rejection of the mulatto, in his categorization of mixed-bloods as belonging to the lower caste. It was an unconscious decision dictated perhaps in large part by the weight of Negroes on his community, heavy enough to be a burden, yet not so heavy as to make him abandon all hope of maintaining his own identity, physically and culturally. Interracial propagation was a constant reproach that he was failing to be true

89. *Works of James Houstoun*, 293.

90. *Acts of Assembly, Passed in the Island of Jamaica, from the Year 1681 to the Year 1769 Inclusive*, 2 vols. in 1, with an *Appendix: Containing Laws Respecting Slaves* (Kingston, 1787), II, 36–39. For the private acts, the Table of Acts in *ibid.*; in *Acts Jamaica* (1786); and in *Acts of Assembly, Passed in the Island of Jamaica, from the Year 1784 to the Year 1788 Inclusive* (Kingston, 1789). Also Edwards, *History of British West Indies*, II, 22–23; [Long], *Jamaica*, II, 320–23.

91. [Long], *Jamaica*, II, 332–35. This general picture is borne out by a work on a later period: Philip D. Curtin, *Two Jamaicas: The Role of Ideas in a Tropical Colony, 1830–1865* (Cambridge, Mass., 1955), chaps. 1–3.

to himself. Sexual intimacy strikingly symbolized a union he wished
to avoid. If he could not restrain his sexual nature, he could at least
reject its fruits and thus solace himself that he had done no harm.
Perhaps he sensed as well that continued racial intermixture would
eventually undermine the logic of the racial slavery upon which his
society was based. For the separation of slaves from free men depended on a clear demarcation of the races, and the presence of
mulattoes blurred this essential distinction. Accordingly he made
every effort to nullify the effects of racial intermixture. By classifying the mulatto as a Negro he was in effect denying that intermixture had occurred at all.

V   THE SOULS OF MEN

The Negro's Spiritual Nature

DESPITE THEIR INTIMATE CONTACTS WITH NEGROES, THE American colonists generally made little conscious effort to assess the nature of the people they enslaved and took to bed. They felt no pressing need for assessment because both the Negro and slavery were, by and large, self-explanatory. Negroes were people from Africa bought for the purpose of performing labor. What fact could be more obvious and natural, less demanding of explanation?

There were strains, of course, beneath this calm surface of placid acceptance. Even when the colonists did not "think" about the Negro, they felt the tug of two opposing ways of looking at his essential nature. One view derived from his uniquely base status in colonial society. In all societies men tend to extrapolate from social status to actual inherent character, to impute to individuals characteristics suited to their social roles. As one member of a much older slave society put it, some men were "slaves by nature." In the face of Aristotle's contention, the societies in the Western tradition have always minimized this tendency and have emphasized the contrary idea that all individuals possess inherently the same fundamental nature. This emphasis originally drew much of its strength from the doctrines of Christianity, and still in the seventeenth century any assertion of human unity was bound to be made in religious terms. No matter in what terms asserted, though, the deep sense of the oneness of humanity clashed head on with the sense that the lowly members of society must necessarily be possessed of low nature. Inevitably then, the introduction of chattel slavery by Europeans into their American settlements was an invitation to conflict. There were inherent conflicts and tensions long before the abolition movement, the Civil War, and more recent crises. Perhaps it is a credit to Western culture, however, that there was any tension at all.

[179]

1. CHRISTIAN PRINCIPLES AND THE FAILURE OF
CONVERSION

Indications of internal stress bubbled quickly to the surface because the Christian tradition demanded that the souls of
men be given spiritual care while still on earth; not just some souls
but all, for Christianity was on this point firmly universalist. The
obligation of English Christians to convert Indians and Negroes
was as obvious and undeniable in the eighteenth century as it had
been two hundred years earlier. Yet many of the Englishmen who
settled in America proved reluctant or downright unwilling to meet
this obligation. In part their failure was owing to practical considerations arising from the exigencies of plantation management.
Inescapably, however, since conversion was the necessary outward
manifestation of the assumption of inner sameness in all men, any
opposition to conversion—even when grounded on "necessity"—
represented direct denial of inner similarity between the master
and his lowly slave. Furthermore, by allowing slaves to remain un-
converted, masters were perpetuating the outward differences between the two peoples, and thus in an important sense opposition
to conversion fed upon itself.

Not only is it extremely difficult to sort out the practical considerations underlying opposition to conversion of Negroes from more
subtle sources of hostility, but it is impossible to determine just how
much opposition there actually was. Most of the evidence of opposition derives from indignant assertions by men keenly interested in
seeing conversion accomplished. These men, usually members of the
clergy, can scarcely be regarded as disinterested observers. It is
possible, however, to infer from their reports a good deal about the
attitudes of slaveowners: amid the blare of trumpets rallying Christians to the work of God one can easily detect the shuffle of dragging
feet.

The first hurdle in the path of conversion was the vague but
persistent notion that no Christian might lawfully hold another
Christian as a slave. Unless something was done to clear up this
matter, missionaries to the Negroes were going to run into insurmountable opposition at every turn. For roughly half a century
after 1660, legislative assemblies in the colonies, colonial officials in
England, the Society for the Propagation of the Gospel in Foreign
Parts (the S.P.G.), the Church of England, and ministers of colonial churches cooperated in stuffing this somewhat amorphous but

inconveniently persistent notion into the trash can.[1] Long before 1729, when the Crown's attorney-general and solicitor-general clapped on the lid with an official pronouncement, all southern and two northern colonies had enacted laws declaring that baptism of slaves did not necessitate their manumission.[2] Unfortunately, these strenuous and charitable statutory reassurances were not followed by waves of conversion among the Negroes.[3] It rapidly became clear that the planters' reluctance to join in the cause was not owing entirely to fear of losing their valuable property.

Many slaveholders felt that no matter how much conversion might benefit the Negroes' souls, it could only make them worse slaves. Occasionally they went so far as to charge that efforts at conversion fostered rebellion rather than piety.[4] The famous evangelist George Whitefield was accused (by an S.P.G. missionary, no less) of having given "great countenance" to the New York plot of 1741 by "his imprudence and indiscretion" in a pamphlet urging conversion published the previous year.[5] In 1737 the *South-Carolina Gazette* published a letter from Antigua which declared that many leaders of a recent slave conspiracy on the island were Christians, were able to read and write, and that rebellion was just what was to be expected when Negroes were converted. An indignant citizen of South Carolina replied, however, saying that to baptize Negroes was

1. Among many sources are Frank J. Klingberg, *Anglican Humanitarianism in Colonial New York* (Phila., 1940), 127; Frank J. Klingberg, *An Appraisal of the Negro in Colonial South Carolina: A Study in Americanization* (Washington, 1941), 14; Cotton Mather, *The Negro Christianized. An Essay to Excite and Assist that Good Work, the Instruction of Negro-Servants in Christianity* (Boston, 1706), 25–28; [Edmund Gibson], *Two Letters of the Lord Bishop of London: The First, to the Masters and Mistresses . . . Abroad. . . . The Second, to the Missionaries There; Directing Them to Distribute the Said Letter, and Exhorting Them to Give Their Assistance towards the Instruction of the Negroes . . .* (London, 1727). Conversion of Negroes is discussed by Jernegan, *Laboring Classes in America*, chap. 2.

2. See chap. 2, n.115; and for the well-known pronouncement, which actually pertained only to slaves brought from the colonies into Great Britain, Hurd, *Law of Freedom and Bondage*, 185n. Cf. Earl of Bellomont to the Lords of Trade, N. Y., Apr. 27, 1699, O'Callaghan and Fernow, eds., *Docs. N.-Y.*, IV, 510–11.

3. But see an S.P.G. missionary's exceptional and prematurely optimistic claim of good effects from the New York law; Kemp, *Support of Schools*, 239.

4. Charleston *S.-C. Gaz.*, Apr. 24, 1742; Gov. William Gooch to the Bishop of London, Williamsburg, May 28, 1731, G. McLaren Brydon, ed., "The Virginia Clergy; Governor Gooch's Letters to the Bishop of London, 1727–1749," *Va. Mag. of Hist. and Biog.*, 32 (1924), 322–23; Box 3, bundle: Minutes of Council in Assembly (1747–48), Including Papers on the Negro Conspiracy, [Pt. i], 34, Parish Transcripts, N.-Y. Hist. Soc.

5. Richard Charlton to the Secretary, N. Y., Oct. 30, 1741, S.P.G. MSS. (Transcripts) B9, no. 62, Lib. Cong.

a duty and a kindness and that to maintain that conversion fostered revolt was a calumny on the Christian religion.[6]

Most commonly, though, planters voiced the less specific objection that Christianizing the slaves made them "more perverse and untractable," less amenable to discipline, more discontented with their lot—which may well have been true.[7] A group of slaveholders who migrated from the West Indies to Georgia were said to have claimed that a slave was "ten times worse than a Xn, than in his State of Paganism." [8] Entirely aside from these objections, it seems fair to suppose that one of the major barriers to conversion was unwillingness to put forth the requisite effort. It was a great deal easier simply to forget the slaves on Sunday than to round them up to listen to a sermon. As one S.P.G. missionary reported, "in those that have Negroes I find littel or no Disposition to have them baptised; But on the contrary an Aversion to it in some, and in most an Indifference." [9]

Much of the opposition to conversion of Negroes was pervaded by a revealing anxiety. A "common Objection," declared the Reverend Thomas Bacon in a sermon addressed to Negroes and published for white men, is "that your being baptized only makes you more proud and saucy." Bacon reassured slaves that he would help smooth their arduous pathway to Christ: "I rejoice indeed, to see you growing more regular, and honestly joining in Marriage;—and whatever foolish Jesting there may be at your being asked in Church, whatever thoughtless Objection may be made by silly, proud People at your being treated like Christians, and your Banns published, and you and your Children baptized at the same Time, and in the same Manner, with White People, be assured, that I will stand firmly your Friend." [10] An Anglican minister in Virginia explained, "as for baptizing Indians and Negroes, several of the people disapprove of it; because they say it often makes them proud, and not so good servants." Similarly, an S.P.G. missionary reported that many people thought baptism "hurt [slaves] by giving them better Notions of

6. Charleston S.-C. Gaz., Apr. 23, July 30, 1737.

7. Good evidence lies in the assertions of two Anglican ministers, in William Stevens Perry, ed., Historical Collections Relating to the American Colonial Church, 5 vols. in 4 (Hartford, 1870–78), II, 184, V, 48.

8. Joseph Ottolenghe quoted in Lawrence, "Religious Education of the Negro in Georgia," Ga. Hist. Qtly., 14 (1930), 45–46.

9. Robert Jenney to [David Humphreys], Nov. 19, 1725, Rye, N. Y., S.P.G. MSS. (Transcripts), B1, no. 78, Lib. Cong.

10. [Thomas Bacon], Two Sermons, Preached to a Congregation of Black Slaves, at the Parish Church of S.P. in the Province of Maryland (London, 1749), 64–65.

themselves than is consistent with their state of Slavery and their duty to their Masters." [11] In a tract straightforwardly entitled *The Duty of Christians to Propagate Their Religion Among Heathens, Earnestly Recommended to the Masters of Negroe Slaves in Virginia,* the Reverend Samuel Davies undertook to refute the hypothetical objection, "That christianizing the Negroes makes them proud and saucy, and tempts them to imagine themselves upon an Equality with white People?" Still more directly, the Reverend Francis Le Jau reported from South Carolina that a lady had inquired of him, "Is it possible that any of my slaves could go to Heaven and must I see them there?" and that "a young gentleman had said sometime before that he is resolved never to come to the Holy Table while slaves are received there." Perhaps the best assessment of objection to Christian instruction of Negroes came from the astute Swedish visitor to America, Peter Kalm, who wrote that opposition arose "partly by the conceit of its being shameful to have a spiritual brother or sister among so despicable people; partly by thinking that they would not be able to keep their negroes so subjected afterwards; and partly through fear of the negroes growing too proud on seeing themselves upon a level with their masters in religious matters." [12]

What the colonists feared, of course, was the dimly recognized challenge to their distinct status and the mental differentiation upon which it rested. For by Christianizing the Negro, by proffering to him even the meager crumbs of religious instruction which were prerequisite to baptism, the colonist was making the Negro just so much more like himself.[13] The Negro's inevitable acquisition of the white settler's language and manners was having precisely this effect. It was virtually inevitable, too, that the colonists should have abhorred the prospect that Negroes might come to resemble them. For if the Negro were like themselves, how could they enslave him? How explain the bid on the block, the whip on the back?

11. Jones, *Present State of Virginia,* ed. Morton, 99; Robert Jenney to [David Humphreys], Nov. 19, 1725, Rye, N. Y., S.P.G. MSS. (Transcripts), B1, no. 78, Lib. Cong.

12. Samuel Davies, *The Duty of Christians to Propagate Their Religion Among Heathens, Earnestly Recommended to the Masters of Negro Slaves in Virginia . . .* (London, 1758), 37; Le Jau quoted in Klingberg, *Negro in S. C.,* 23; Benson, trans. and ed., *Peter Kalm's Travels,* I, 209. See also Klingberg, *Negro in S. C.,* 89; Thomas Bacon, *Four Sermons, upon the Great and Indispensable Duty of All Christian Masters and Mistresses to Bring up Their Negro Slaves in the Knowledge and Fear of God . . .* (London, 1750), 81–101.

13. A point made felicitously by Klingberg, *Anglican Humanitarianism in N. Y.,* 122–23.

Slavery could survive *only* if the Negro were a man set apart; he simply had to be different if slavery was to exist at all.

For the most part slaveholders in the English colonies were unwilling to put these half-conscious feelings into words. To come right out and deny the age-old obligation to convert the heathen was to deny the undeniable, the more so because denial would imply that settlement of America rested on a sandy foundation of hypocrisy. Yet in some colonies, particularly before the campaign for conversion gathered full momentum in the second quarter of the century, men were willing to assert that Christianization of Negroes was an impossible task. In 1699 the Virginia House of Burgesses replied to official English requests for passage of a law facilitating conversion by claiming "that Negroes borne in this Country are generally baptized and brought up in the Christian Religion but for Negroes Imported hither the Gros Barbarity and rudeness of their manners, the variety and Strangeness of their Languages and the weakness and Shallowness of their minds renders it in a manner impossible to attain to any Progress in their Conversion." [14] The Burgesses' language made manifest their determination not to attempt the "impossible."

Probably there was considerable validity in the Burgesses' distinction between the two groups of Negroes. Teaching African-born Negroes even the simplest points of Christian doctrine must have been difficult under any circumstances. In the plantation colonies, continuing large-scale importation of Negroes meant that there were always a sizable number who, as the runaway advertisements noted, spoke "no English." [15] The Burgesses failed to mention, however, the one circumstance which had greatest effect on the pace at which conversion proceeded. Wherever there were large numbers of slaves on large plantations, with swarms of new Negroes staggering off the slave ships every year, Christianization was bound to seem difficult and, in light of the ever-present problem of slave control, downright dangerous.

It is not surprising, therefore, that the most frequent and strident objection to conversion of slaves came from the West Indies and to less extent South Carolina. As early as 1681 the Barbados Assembly

14. H. R. McIlwaine, ed., *Jours. House of Burgesses Va., 1695–1702*, 174; see also Lefroy, comp., *Memorials Bermudas*, II, 569.

15. Between one-fourth and one-third of the runaways advertised in the Savannah *Ga. Gaz.* in 1765 were described as speaking "no English," but of course the proportion among runaways may well have differed from that among the total slave population. Many of the sources cited in this chapter refer to language as a barrier to conversion.

piously demurred: "We are ready to do anything for the encouragement of Christian servants," it assured the governor, "but as to making the negroes Christians, their savage brutishness renders them wholly incapable. Many have endeavoured it without success. If a good expedient could be found, the Assembly and people would be ready to promote it." [16] Plainly the Assembly was less than eager to go running about looking for a "good expedient." Some gentlemen in Barbados were still more frank when humbly delivering their advice to the Committee of Trade and Plantations in 1680:

They declare that the Conversion of their Slaves will not only destroy their Property, but endanger the Safety of the Island, in as much as such Negroes as are converted usualy grow more perverse and intractable than others and will not bee soe fit for labor and sale as others, and that as there is a great disproportion of Blacks to Whites they have noe greater Security than the diversity of their Languages as they are brought from several Countries [.] And that in order to their being made Christians It will bee necessary to teach them all English which gives them an opportunity and facility of combining together against their Masters and of destroying them.

That they are a sort of People soe averse to Learning that they will rather hang themselves or run away than submit to it and that their Conversion will very much impair their value and price which will much affect the African Company who are their first Masters.[17]

It was characteristic of this West Indian situation that the only clergyman in the English colonies to speak out against conversion was a resident of Nevis. The Reverend William Smith declared flatly that "when a Slave is once Christened, he conceits that he ought to be upon a level with his Master, in all other respects." And it was equally characteristic that the only newspaper on the continent to publish a forthright denunciation of slave Christianization was the *South-Carolina Gazette*. In reply to an appeal written probably by two clergymen, an anonymous contributor in 1742 lashed out at the danger that some designing person might gather cabals of Negroes under guise of religious instruction "and instead of teaching them the *Principles* of *Christianity*, filling their heads with a Parcel of *Cant-Phrases, Trances, Dreams, Visions,* and *Reve-*

16. Sainsbury *et al.*, eds., *Cal. State Papers, 1681–1685*, 25. See also J. Harry Bennett, Jr., "Of the Negroes Thereon," Frank J. Klingberg, ed., *Codrington Chronicle: An Experiment in Anglican Altruism on a Barbados Plantation, 1710–1834* (Berkeley and Los Angeles, 1949), 93–95, 98.

17. Box 9, bundle: New England, Virginia, West Indies, New Jersey—ca. 1670–ca. 1710, Parish Transcripts, 19, N.-Y. Hist. Soc.; a paraphrase is available in Sainsbury *et al.*, eds., *Cal. State Papers, 1677–1680*, 611.

lations, and something still *worse,* and which Prudence forbids to name." [18]

Yet even in South Carolina some planters were favorably disposed toward conversion and gave active encouragement to work which was enormously more difficult than in the northern colonies, where Negroes were fewer and in every way less menacing to the white man's emotional and physical security. In the tobacco colonies, as one would expect, the clergy reported finding a broad spectrum of opinion among the planters; and, of course, some clergymen approached their work with more enthusiasm than others. When Commissary Jacob Henderson gathered a group of Anglican ministers at Oxford on Maryland's eastern shore in 1731, for example, his request for reports on the religious instruction of Negroes in each parish elicited the following replies:

Mr. Fletcher said his parishioners were generally so brutish that they would not suffer their Negroes to be instructed, catechized, or baptized. The commissary, upon this, advised him to take care that this be true, for that the account would go to the Lord Bishop of London, and it would be of Ill consequence to misrepresent them; but he persisted in it that he had often preached up the necessity of instructing them, that he had conversed frequently with them about it, and warned them of the danger of neglecting it, but all to no purpose, that their answer was, that it made them the greater Rogues and villains, and they would not suffer it.

Mr. Wye says his people are better disposed; they are generally willing to have their Negroes instructed and baptized; that there are in his parish a dozen Negroes, Communicants; that he is but of short standing in the parish, but resolves to pursue that good work.

Mr. Thompson says he has taken pains to convince the people of the necessity of having their Negroes instructed, but 'tho he has baptized several, yet he finds them generally very remiss.

Mr. Airey finds the people of his parish very inclined to have their Negro's instructed, but they will not be at the pains and trouble of it.

Mr. Dell lately come, but says he resolves to attend to that good work.

Mr. Manadier has often pressed on his people their obligation to instruct their Negroes, but yet they are very remiss and neglectful.

Mr. Nichols says his custom has always been to catechise the Youth of this parish on all holidays. He has from the Pulpit and in conversation been Instant with his Parishioners to instruct their Negroes, in order to their being made Christians; but that the best answer he can get, even from the best people, is that they are very sorry, and Lament that they cannot comply with it.

Mr. Cox has urged the necessity of instructing the negroes, but 'tho his Parishioners allow it to be a good thing, yet they generally Excuse themselves as thinking it to be impracticable.

18. William Smith, *A Natural History of Nevis, and the Rest of the English Leeward Charibee Islands* . . . (Cambridge, Eng., 1745), 230; Charleston *S.-C. Gaz.,* Apr. 17, 24, 1742.

Mr. Williamson says that, by the Pains he has taken in instructing the negroes of his parish, he finds them to be of 3 sorts, the first whereof are so grossly Ignorant, that there is no possibility of Instructing them in the principles of Christianity; the 2d are capable of instruction, and learn the answers to the questions of the church Catechism, but are so egregiously wicked as to render Baptism ineffectual. The 3rd are duly qualified, and of Exemplary Lives, some of whom are baptised, and others are soon to be Baptized, so that he has good hopes to succeed with the latter sort, Especially their Masters and Mistresses being assistant.[19]

2. THE QUESTION OF NEGRO CAPACITY

The concluding testimony by Mr. Williamson that some Negroes were "so grossly Ignorant" as to preclude their acquiring even the first principles of true religion glanced upon an issue concerning the Negro which has become far more important in retrospect than it was at the time. To the relatively lettered English colonists, Negroes must indeed have seemed ignorant and often downright stupid. As Cotton Mather wrote in his hortatory *The Negro Christianized*, "Indeed their *Stupidity* is a *Discouragement*. It may seem, unto as little purpose, to *Teach*, as to *wash an AEthiopian*." Yet Mather regarded this defect as a challenge rather than a permanent obstacle: "But the greater their *Stupidity*, the greater must be our *Application*." In fact many proponents of conversion were entirely willing to concede that Negroes were ignorant, stupid, unteachable, barbarous, stubborn, and deficient in understanding. One antislavery advocate was willing to go still further, so early as 1733: "Now altho' the Negroes might not have the Understanding that some other Nations have, then I do believe there is the less required [of them], and if they do but as well as they know, I do believe it is well with them." [20] More frequently, many advocates of conversion felt called upon to assert with considerable vehemence that Negroes possessed the same capacities as Europeans and wanted only the opportunity of improvement in order to develop them. Even before the beginning of the eighteenth century one writer insisted repeatedly that Negroes were "endued with equal Faculties,

19. Perry, ed., *Historical Collections Colonial Church*, IV, 304–5. Other reports of mixed reaction to conversion are in *ibid.*, I, 261–318, IV, 190–231; "The Letters of Hon. James Habersham, 1756–1775," Ga. Hist. Soc., *Collections*, 6 (1904), 99–102, 135–36, 238–43; Stanley Pargellis, ed., "An Account of the Indians in Virginia," *Wm. and Mary Qtly.*, 16 (1959), 242. See Jerome W. Jones, "The Established Virginia Church and the Conversion of Negroes and Indians, 1620–1760," *Jour. of Negro Hist.*, 46 (1961), 12–23.

20. Mather, *Negro Christianized*, 25; Elihu Colman, *A Testimony against That Antichristian Practice of Making Slaves of Men . . .* ([Boston], 1733), 10.

both *Sensitive* and *Intellectual*," and in 1711 the Bishop of London reminded masters in the plantations that their slaves were "equally the Workmanship of God, with themselves; endued with the same Faculties, and intellectual Powers." [21] By mid-century these assertions had become almost commonplace in pleas for conversion. The Reverend Samuel Davies, shortly to become president of the College of New Jersey (Princeton), went out of his way to lecture Virginia slaveowners on the subject. "Your Negroes may be ignorant and stupid as to divine Things," Davies wrote emphatically in a published sermon, "not for Want of Capacity, but for Want of Instruction; not through their Perverseness, but through your Negligence. From the many Trials I have made, I have Reason to conclude, that making Allowance for their low and barbarous Education, their imperfect Acquaintance with our Language, their having no Opportunity for intellectual Improvements, and the like, they are generally as capable of Instruction, as the white People." It was not much of a step to extend this argument beyond the bounds of strictly religious capability, as the Reverend Griffith Hughes of Barbados did in 1750: "The Capacities of their Minds in the common Affairs of Life," Hughes wrote in his history of the island, "are but little inferior, if at all, to those of the *Europeans*. If they fail in some Arts, it may be owing more to their Want of Education, and the Depression of their Spirits by Slavery, than to any Want of natural Abilities; for an higher Degree of improved Knowledge in any Occupation would not much alter their Condition [as slaves] for the better." [22]

What these arguments were groping toward, of course, was the proposition that the Negro's stupidity, far from being inherent, was caused by his condition, and that this condition of slavery had been imposed by white men. By the time of the Revolution, the point at issue had become abundantly clear. In 1770, for instance, a prominent Georgia merchant who was greatly interested in promoting the cause of conversion referred to "the barren, because too generally unimproved Capacities of these poor Creatures," and then hastened to explain himself: "I say unimproved Capacities, as some ignorant people would *foolishly* insinuate, that they are scarcely reasonable

21. [Tryon], *Friendly Advice*, 90, 114–17, 120, 188–89; Bishop William Fleetwood's sermon reprinted in Klingberg, *Anglican Humanitarianism in N. Y.*, 203.
22. Davies, *Duty of Christians*, 34; Hughes, *Natural History of Barbados*, 16. Complaints of the uneducability of Negroes were sometimes voiced by S.P.G. missionaries, though rarely publicly; Thomas Crauford to the Secretary, Dover Hundred, Kent Co., Pa., Aug. 31, 1708, S.P.G. MSS. (Transcripts), A4, no. 71, Lib. Cong.; Klingberg, *Anglican Humanitarianism in N. Y.*, 20n, 131.

Creatures, and not capable of being instructed in the divine Thruths of Christianity; an absurdity too obvious to deserve any refutation." [23]

The ominous implications embedded in these refutations—and they were refutations, despite the disclaimer by the Georgia merchant—may be readily detected. Proponents of conversion would never have felt compelled to declare that the Negro was inherently as intelligent as the European unless they had encountered insinuations to the contrary. To affirm positively that the Negro was the mental equal of the white man was to affirm by indirection that some people thought the Negro was not. In light of later developments in the United States, these affirmations appear to be the first faint rumblings of a long-distant dispute.

It is essential, however, that developments not be read backwards. For one thing, eighteenth-century ideas about human intelligence are almost disconcertingly imprecise when set alongside the presuppositions which underlie modern intelligence tests. The bewildering variety of words then used to denote what we call intelligence was symptomatic of an underlying vagueness about the abilities in men which, it was half-recognized, were inborn rather than acquired. "Capacity," "faculty," and "understanding" generally indicated mental (and sometimes emotional and manual) abilities which were "natural," that is, what we would call "innate." Yet these terms were applied indiscriminately to abilities which could not be changed and those that could. Just as with the early reports of European travelers in West Africa it is impossible to determine precisely what the secretary of the S.P.G. had in mind when he reported that a missionary in New York was "labouring earnestly to accomodate his Discourse to their Capacities." [24] In the early eighteenth century the concept of intelligence had not yet become disassociated from the idea of capacity for religious experience or even from the idea of wisdom. [25] The attribute which we frequently term "I.Q." did not then appear distinct from attributes which we might term "spirituality," "disposition," and "learnedness." The amorphous fluidity and overlapping of these potentially separable concepts was nowhere more evident than in Cotton Mather's charge

23. James Habersham to the Rev. Thomas Broughton, Secretary of the Society for Promoting Christian Knowledge, Savannah, Dec. 1, 1770, "Letters of James Habersham," Ga. Hist. Soc., *Collections*, 6 (1904), 100–101. He became acting governor of Georgia in 1771.

24. Humphreys, *Endeavors by the S.P.G. in New York*, 8.

25. Cf. Eugene F. Rice, Jr., *The Renaissance Idea of Wisdom* (Cambridge, Mass., 1958).

that "poor *Negro's* especially are kept Strangers to the *way of Life*" because their masters made "pretense" that they were "dull." "They are kept only as *Horses* or *Oxen,* to do our Drudgeries," Mather went on, "but their *Souls,* which are as white and good as those of other Nations, their *Souls* are not look'd after, but are *Destroyed for lack* of *Knowledge.* This is a desperate Wickedness. But are they *dull?* Then *instruct* them the *rather;* That is the Way to *sharpen* them." [26] This absence of clearcut distinctions and interlacing of mental capacity with spiritual grace also becomes manifest in the fact that the issue of the Negro's mental ability first arose historically out of doubts concerning his ability to participate in the experiences of conversion. So long as men thought of themselves as primarily spiritual creatures, no one could possibly talk about innately inferior intelligence in the sense the concept is used today. Later in the century, however, the separation of mental from spiritual abilities was clearly underway, as was to become especially obvious after the Revolution.

Paradoxically, the vagueness of the demarcation between inherent and acquired attributes in men itself helped pave the way for later assertions of inherent Negro stupidity. To realize this, it is only necessary to consider the way some white men must have been talking in the first half of the eighteenth century. The cultural gulf between the two peoples was enormous, and Negroes fresh from Africa and even their children must have seemed very stupid indeed. As with any quality in other people which seems extreme, the Negro's stupidity must at times have seemed downright irredeemable, as hopelessly rooted in his essential character; from there it was no step at all to calling him casually a naturally stupid brute. And because there existed no clear demarcation between inborn and acquired characteristics, it became easy enough to slip into thinking that the Negro's natural and inveterate stupidity was "innate," without, however, imparting much precision or meaning to the notion.

3. SPIRITUAL EQUALITY AND TEMPORAL SUBORDINATION

It is no wonder that men interested in the cause of Negro conversion were at pains to strike down any such insinuations. These men rightly recognized, however, that the chief obstacle in the path of their program was the slaveholder's fear that conversion might weaken his dominion over his slaves. Accordingly they went

26. Cotton Mather, *Small Offers towards the Tabernacle in the Wilderness* (Boston, 1689), 58.

out of their way to stress that Christianizing Negroes would make them much better slaves, not worse. As outlined by Dean George Berkeley in 1725, the problem was to convince American planters "that it would be of Advantage to their Affairs, to have Slaves who should *obey in all Things their Masters according to the Flesh, not with Eye-service as Men-pleasers, but in Singleness of Heart as fearing God:* That Gospel Liberty consists with temporal Servitude; and that their Slaves would only become better Slaves by being Christians." [27] Two years later the bishop of London composed a public letter *To the Masters and Mistresses of Families in the English Plantations Abroad* urging baptism of slaves and expounding the nature of true religion and the kind of freedom it implied.

Christianity, and the embracing of the Gospel, does not make the least Alteration in Civil Property, or in any of the Duties which belong to Civil Relations; but in all these Respects, it continues Persons just in the same State as it found them. The Freedom which Christianity gives, is a Freedom from the Bondage of Sin and Satan, and from the Dominion of Mens Lusts and Passions and inordinate Desires; but as to their *outward* Condition, whatever that was before, whether bond or free, their being baptiz'd, and becoming Christians, makes no manner of Change in it. . . . And so far is Christianity from discharging Men from the Duties of the Station and Condition in which it found them, that it lays them under stronger Obligations to perform those Duties with the greatest Diligence and Fidelity.[28]

By embracing the Gospel, then, the Negro was to obtain protection from his own "Lusts" and "inordinate Desires," though not, as the good bishop made evident, from the white man's. These clergymen had been forced by the circumstance of racial slavery in America into propagating the Gospel by presenting it as an attractive device for slave control. As the Reverend Hugh Jones of Virginia put it, "Christianity encourages and orders them to become more humble and better servants, and not worse, than when they were heathens." The Reverend Thomas Bacon felt no hesitation in telling slaves that they must obey their masters in all things, even when cruelly abused: "your *Masters* and *Mistresses,*" he explained glowingly, "are God's Overseers." [29]

After laying down this doctrine of absolute obedience, Thomas

27. *A Proposal for the Better Supplying of Churches in Our Foreign Planta-tions* . . . (London, 1725) , in Luce and Jessop, eds., *Works of George Berkeley*, VII, 346.
28. [Gibson], *Two Letters*, 11.
29. Jones, *Present State of Va.*, ed. Morton, 99; [Bacon], *Two Sermons to Black Slaves*, 30–38, also 68–74; and for further illustration, Benjamin Fawcett, *A Compassionate Address to the Christian Negroes in Virginia, and Other British Colonies in North America* . . . , 2d ed. (Salop, Eng., 1756) , 10–12, 15–18; Davies, *Duty of Christians*, 27–29; [Hewat], *Account of S. C. and Ga.*, II, 102–3.

Bacon added a highly significant afterthought. Obedience was not required of anyone, Bacon said, if he were commanded to commit a sinful act. This exception, which had long been stressed in Christian and particularly Protestant political thought, was symptomatic of the enormously important fact that the idea of Christian liberty could not be strictly confined to matters of the spirit. Theologians tried manfully to maintain the disjunction between spiritual freedom and temporal bondage, but any emphasis on the former was potentially explosive. As an English Puritan wrote concerning servitude early in the seventeenth century, *"those who are over us, have no power, but over the bodies and outward man of us . . .* all that a Magistrate can doe, either as a Magist[r]ate or Christian, it is but to the body, as to bring us to that outward conformitie, to keepe the tongue from swearing, to debarre open things, prophaning the Sabbath: therefore as we are the servants of men, so we are not, we are bodily, but free in spirit. . . . Which is comfortable to servants." [30] The trouble was that sometimes servants forgot which was the proper realm of comfort. Especially after the Protestant Reformation, enthusiasm for equality in Christ tended to spill over into an alarming enthusiasm for equality in temporal condition. Any evidence of this tendency was bound to cause consternation in many quarters; the slaveholder's distaste for slave conversion was a new version of an old fear, similar to Luther's horror at the great peasant revolt his doctrines helped foment and to Cromwell's denunciation of the budding democrats in his New Model Army. Because Christianity had always leveled the souls of men before God, it was potentially corrosive of the world's social hierarchies.

The process of reasoning from spiritual to earthly status was most likely to occur at times when economic and social changes were undermining traditional concepts of social order. Often these changes became manifest in catastrophic upheavals, as in the English Civil War, yet in an important sense the major social revolutions themselves were symptoms of an underlying and steady current of change which was sweeping the Western world. This current was especially swift in the American colonies, where social leveling went on rapidly yet without cataclysm because it never became dammed up by powerful institutional and intellectual resistance. The firm ideas of the early settlers concerning due social subordination were eroded by the abrasive conditions of life in the New World and by certain tendencies embedded in the ideas themselves. In 1631, for example, a Massachusetts court degraded a man "from

30. Bayne[s], *Commentary upon Paul,* 697.

the title of a gentleman," [31] but a century later the concept of "gentleman" was already showing signs of the growing elasticity which has ended with "gents" meaning only that "ladies" should use the other door. The complementary concept of subordination in servitude suffered such extensive erosion that it began to dissipate after the Revolution. To realize the enormity of this change, we have only to realize that seventeenth-century settlers regarded due subordination as the mortar of the social and indeed the cosmic order. In 1666, for instance, a tract promoting settlement in Maryland explained the indisputable obligations of servants in terms of a larger hierarchy.

> As there can be no Monarchy without the Supremacy of a King and Crown, nor no King without Subjects, nor any Parents without it be by the fruitful off-spring of Children; neither can there be any Masters, unless it be by the inferior Servitude of those that dwell under them, by a commanding enjoynment: And since it is ordained from the original and superabounding wisdom of all things, That there should be Degrees and Diversities amongst the Sons of men, in acknowledging of a Superiority from Inferior to Superiors; the Servant with a reverent and befitting Obedience is as liable to this duty in a measureable performance to him whom he serves, as the loyalest of Subjects to his Prince.[32]

Had it been offered a century later, this statement would have seemed, at very least, an overstatement. By then, indeed, thousands of runaway servants had successfully flouted this principle, and the American colonies as a whole were evincing an obstreperous disregard for due subordination to their King. As yet few Americans felt like proposing that every man was as good as his neighbor, but without realizing it they had thoroughly loosened the bolts which held the ideal of social hierarchy together.

4. THE THIN EDGE OF ANTISLAVERY

With the other hand, however, Americans had tightened the bolts which held the Negro in a unique and extreme condition of social subordination. There was bound to be difficulty when Americans came to recognize the shabby inconsistency in their social construction. Until the Revolutionary era, however, very few colonists saw any inconsistency because they were unaware of what was happening; moreover, the few men who did object to the enslavement of Negroes were no more aware than anyone of the subtle

---

31. Winthrop, *Journal*, ed. Hosmer, I, 68.
32. George Alsop, *A Character of the Province of Mary-land* . . . (London, 1666), 27–28.

process of social leveling. Early objection to the Negro's subordination derived not from ideas about earthly equality but from the
concept of equality before God. Viewed in the broadest terms, then,
early antislavery was an application of a religious idea to social
practice, an application made possible by the unrecognized gradual
weakening of old ideas about natural and inevitable social hierarchy.

Certainly it was no accident that early antislavery pronouncements came largely from members of a religious group which had
originated at a time of social upheaval. The Society of Friends arose
out of the social and religious turmoil of the English Civil War in
the mid-seventeenth century and underwent years of persecution
partly for doctrinal heresy and partly for their stubborn persistence
in pushing the religious principle of equality into areas which
nearly everyone else regarded as of purely temporal concern. The
twin Quaker doctrines of the inner light (which eliminated all
intermediaries between men and God) and of the brotherhood of
man gave renewed emphasis to the strong streak of equalitarianism
which had always run through Christian thought. Just how easy it
was to slip from talking of the liberty of the spirit to liberty of the
body was made apparent by George Fox's public letters of admonition to Quakers in the West Indies. In 1657 he urged that the
Gospel be preached to everyone, including slaves, because it was
"the power that giveth liberty and freedom, and is glad tidings to
every captivated creature under the whole heaven." [33] After visiting
Barbados, Fox was more than ever convinced that the principle of
equality must be applied to the poor Negro slaves. "And so now
consider," he wrote in 1676, "do not slight them, to wit, the *Ethyopians,* the *Blacks* now, neither any Man or Woman upon the Face
of the Earth, in that *Christ* dyed for all, both *Turks, Barbarians,
Tartarians,* and *Ethyopians;* he dyed for the *Tawnies* and for the
Blacks, as well as for you that are called *whites.*" From this universalism it was no step at all to a final, more pregnant suggestion. "It
will doubtless be very acceptable to the Lord, if so be that Masters
of Families here would deal so with their Servants, the *Negroes* and
Blacks, whom they have bought with their Money, to let them go
free after a considerable Term of Years, if they have served them
faithfully; and when they go, and are made free, *let them not go
away empty-handed.*" [34]

33. Quoted in Drake, *Quakers and Slavery,* 5.
34. G[eorge] F[ox], *Gospel Family-Order, Being a Short Discourse Concerning
the Ordering of Families, Both of Whites, Blacks and Indians* ([London], 1676),
13–14, 16.

Although by the eighteenth century Quakerism already showed signs of losing its crusading fervor and settling down into a comfortable and sometimes plush social conservatism, a few Quakers pressed the logic of their equalitarianism to the point which George Fox had so nearly reached. There were at least fifteen known written condemnations of slavery in the English colonies before 1750, almost all by Quakers.[35] With deep conviction they struck with almost childlike directness at the moral wrong of slavery, at the "*making Slaves* of them who bear the Image of God, *viz.* their fellow,-Creature, Man." The word of God, revealed alike by Scripture and by the Inner Light, declared all men to be one family, brothers in the bosom of the Christ who died "for all mankind, they being a part, though yet ungathered." Brotherhood demanded love, the brotherly love "which excepts not nor despises any for their Complections." And the demands of love were obvious: "Is there any that would be done or handled at this manner? viz., to be sold or made a slave for all the time of his life? . . . Now, though they are black, we cannot conceive there is more liberty to have them slaves, as it is to have other white ones. There is a saying, that we should do to all men like as we will be done ourselves; making no difference of what generation, descent, or colour they are." [36]

One of the most notable early antislavery tracts was written not by a Quaker but by Judge Samuel Sewall of Boston in 1700. As befitted a good Puritan, Sewall ranged through the Old and New Testament with an easy familiarity, gathering ammunition with which to riddle every conceivable justification for enslaving Negroes. In defense of equality, liberty, and property, he assailed the practice of making property of men. "It is most certain that all Men, as they are the Sons of *Adam,* are Coheirs; and have equal Right unto Liberty, and all other outward Comforts of Life. GOD *hath given the Earth* (with all its Commodities) unto the *Sons of* Adam, *Psal* 115. 16. *And hath made of One Blood, all Nations of*

35. All the Quaker protests and one by George Keith's schismatic "Christian Quakers" are cited in Drake, *Quakers and Slavery,* chaps. 1–2. See Samuel Sewall's tract cited below; the attack on the slave trade (perhaps by Sewall), *Boston News-Letter,* June 10, 1706; *A Letter from a Merchant at Jamaica to a Member of Parliament in London, Touching the African Trade. To Which Is Added, a Speech Made by a Black of Gardaloupe, at the Funeral of a Fellow-Negro* (London, 1709).

36. The four quotations are from John Hepburn, *The American Defence of the Christian Golden Rule, or an Essay to Prove the Unlawfulness of Making Slaves of Men* (n.p., 1715), preface, p. [1]; H. J. Cadbury, ed., "An Early Quaker Anti-Slavery Statement," *Jour. Negro Hist.,* 22 (1937), 492; Ralph Sandiford, *A Brief Examination of the Practice of the Times . . .* ([Phila.], 1729), 23–24; and the famous Germantown protest of 1688, in Albert B. Hart, ed., *American History Told by Contemporaries,* 4 vols. (N. Y., 1898–1908), II, 291.

Men, for to dwell on all the face of the Earth." Sewall concluded by reminding his readers that color was no indication of dubious ancestry: "These *Ethiopians,* as black as they are; seeing they are the Sons and Daughters of the First *Adam,* the Brethren and Sisters of the Last ADAM, and the Offspring of GOD; They ought to be treated with a Respect agreeable." Sewall's indictment, though tougher and more highly seasoned with Scripture, was essentially the same as those made by Quakers.[37]

Certainly these antislavery authors were high-minded men, utterly sincere in their pioneering efforts for a noble cause. In virtually every case, however, their opposition to slavery was not based exclusively on moral considerations. Some Quakers pointed to the danger of insurrections (in Pennsylvania in 1688, no less), though of course with pacifist Quakers this danger was moral as well as practical.[38] One need not debate the nature of altruism to detect even clearer instances of Quaker self-interest at work. Ownership of Negro slaves threatened the Quaker's spiritual purity, or at least a few Quakers thought it did: as one uneducated Friend mused, "If I Should have a bad one of them, that must be Corrected, Or would Run away, Or when I went from home, and Leave him with a women or Maid, and he Should desire or Seek to Comitt wickedness." [39] What then was a loving slaveholder to do? As time went on, it became clear that a major reason for growing Quaker distaste for slavery was that ownership of slaves by members of the Society was becoming a source of most unseemly dissension within meetings.[40] Nothing could have disturbed Friends more. One of the early Quaker abolitionists, an outright fanatic on the subject, specifically disclaimed any special love for Negroes as such.[41] For virtually all the antislavery advocates, the Negro's color was not a mark of brotherhood but a defect which brotherhood must ignore. For Samuel Sewall particularly, Negro slavery was an abomination not only because it involved enslavement but because it involved Negroes. "As many Negro men as there are among us," Sewall warned, "so

37. Sewall, *Selling of Joseph* (Sewall's brackets changed to parentheses). His decision to write the tract is in *Diary of Sewall,* II, 16.
38. Hart, ed., *American History,* II, 292; Cadbury, ed., "Anti-Slavery Statement," *Jour. Negro Hist.,* 22 (1937), 492; also H. J. Cadbury, ed., "Another Early Quaker Anti-Slavery Document," *Jour. Negro Hist.,* 27 (1942), 213n.
39. Thomas E. Drake, ed., "Cadwalader Morgan, Antislavery Quaker of the Welsh Tract," *Friends' Intelligencer,* 98 (1941), 575–76.
40. Drake, *Quakers and Slavery,* chaps. 1–2.
41. Sandiford, *Brief Examination,* 27–28.

many empty places there are in our Train Bands, and the places taken up of Men that might make Husbands for our Daughters." After announcing on the first page of his little tract that God *"hath made of One Blood, all Nations of Men,"* Sewall declared on page two that Negroes could never mix with "us" but would "remain in our Body Politick as a kind of extravasat Blood." [42] It was the old shell game: now you see the identity of all men, now you don't.

The gravamen of all the early antislavery arguments, including Sewall's, served to confirm that the Negro's essential nature was equal to the white man's. Compared to the campaign for conversion of Negroes, however, the early antislavery voices were crying in the wilderness. Indeed the two programs diverged rapidly despite their common genesis in Christian equalitarianism. Both the Society of Friends and the Church of England started in the seventeenth century urging conversion and better treatment of slaves, yet the Quakers ended in condemning slavery and the Anglican clergy in supporting it. An original identity of purpose was splintered by the rock-hard institution of slavery in America. Just how drastically far apart slavery had split the stream of equalitarianism may be gathered from a letter from Daniel Burton, secretary of the S.P.G. in London, to the Quaker Anthony Benezet who by 1768 had become the foremost American critic of slavery. Benezet had written the Society requesting its support, and Burton replied that the Society had considered his request:

I am directed to assure you, that they have a great esteem for you on account of the tenderness and humanity which you express for the Negro Slaves, and are extremely desirous that they should be treated with the utmost care and kindness, both with regard to Temporals and Spirituals.—That their Labour should be made easy to them in all Respects, that they should be provided with proper conveniences and accomodations to render their situations comfortable; and especially that they should be regularly instructed in the principles of the Christian Religion [.] . . . But they cannot condemn the Practice of keeping Slaves as unlawful, finding the contrary very plainly implied in the precepts given by the Apostles, both to Masters and Servants, which last were for the most part Slaves; and if the doctrine of the unlawfulness of Slavery should be taught in our Colonies, the Society apprehend that Masters, instead of being convinced of it, will grow more suspicious and cruel, and much more unwilling to let their Slaves learn Christianity; and that the poor Creatures themselves, if they come to

---

42. Sewall, *Selling of Joseph*. For a similar approach—"The Whites Strengthens and Peoples the Country, others do not."—see *Boston News-Letter*, Mar. 10, 1718.

look on this doctrine, will be so strongly tempted by it to rebel against their Masters, that the most dreadful consequences to both will be likely to follow; And therefore tho' the Society is fully satisfied that your intention in this matter is perfectly good, yet they most earnestly beg you not to go further in publishing your Notions, but rather to retract them, if you shall see cause, which they hope you may on further consideration.[43]

The Society seemed unaware that it was no longer possible to segregate the souls of men from their social conditions. Pathetically it attempted to decry the fact that the City of God was becoming the home of social reformers.

5. INCLUSION AND EXCLUSION IN THE PROTESTANT CHURCHES

The endorsement of slavery by many, though by no means all, proponents of conversion represented the most obvious but clearly not the most important failure of the equalitarian Christian tradition. For the most disastrous failing of the churches in America was embodied in the *kind* of slavery they were at least willing to put up with if not endorse. The slavery which the S.P.G. defended in 1768 was marked by complete deprivation of rights; despite the S.P.G.'s somewhat guarded plea for kind treatment and adequate food and clothing for slaves, neither the S.P.G. nor other proponents of conversion put up much of a fight against the many hideous manifestations of the commercial slavery which deprived Negroes of status as human beings. Despite traditional Christian concern for the sanctity of the family, for example, the churches in the plantation colonies made little serious effort to procure for slaves the right to maintain permanent familial relationships. The failure of the churches in the English colonies is the more striking because the Catholic Church in the Spanish and Portuguese colonies was apparently both more insistent and more successful in guarding a residue of rights for slaves. That Negro slavery in the Latin colonies was of significantly if perhaps not greatly different character from slavery in the English colonies was not owing entirely to the influence of the Catholic Church, but the outstanding rigidity and rigor of English plantation slavery and the eventual appearance of virulent racism in Anglo-America does raise the question whether the English Protestant churches were in some measure responsible.[44]

Because these churches varied appreciably in doctrine and institu-

43. Abington Street, Westminster, Feb. 3, 1768, printed in George S. Brookes, *Friend Anthony Benezet* (Phila., 1937), 417–18.

44. There have been numerous discussions of this matter, often suffering from imprecision as to the character of English Protestantism. See especially Frank

tional structure, they varied in their posture toward slavery and the Negro. Yet all the Protestant sects, including the Quakers, shared in common a low-church English Protestantism strongly tinged by Calvinism; many of the qualities of mind and temperament which are usually described as Puritan were shared by Anglicans and Baptists and by Quakers as well. The similarities among the Protestant sects were fully as important as the differences.

As far as *the* Puritans were concerned, slavery was simply not a problem. The Puritans who settled in colonies where slavery became a firmly established institution accepted the subordination of the Negro without protest yet without any special eagerness, and the same was true in Puritan-dominated New England. The Puritans' fondness for the Old Testament and their stress on the depravity of man and the selectivity of salvation might at first sight seem to have led them toward embracing racial slavery with open arms. In the first instance, however, the Old Testament was sufficiently vague on the subject of bond service in ancient Israel that new Israelites could either deny or affirm the legitimacy of Negro slavery by appealing to Scripture. The only forthright defense of slavery in the continental colonies until the time of the Revolution was made in direct reply to Samuel Sewall's antislavery attack. John Saffin, a merchant of Boston, tangled with Sewall in a confused quarrel over the promised manumission of Saffin's slave (whose name, inappropriately to Scripture at least, was Adam). Saffin successfully marshaled chapter and verse in support of enslaving heathen Negroes, which was no trick at all. More significant was the implication in his smattering of versified invective entitled "The Negroes Character."

> Cowardly and cruel are those *Blacks* Innate,
> Prone to Revenge, Imp of inveterate hate.
> He that exasperates them, soon espies
> Mischief and Murder in their very eyes.
> Libidinous, Deceitful, False and Rude,

Tannenbaum, *Slave and Citizen: The Negro in the Americas* (N. Y., 1947), 82–103; Stanley M. Elkins, *Slavery: A Problem in American Institutional and Intellectual Life* (Chicago, 1959), 68–77; also Donald Pierson, *Negroes in Brazil; A Study of Race Contact at Bahia* (Chicago, 1942), 193–94; Gilberto Freyre, *The Masters and the Slaves: A Study in the Development of Brazilian Civilization*, trans. Samuel Putnam, 2d Eng. ed. rev. (N. Y., 1956), 30–31; Arnold J. Toynbee, *A Study of History*, 2d ed., 10 vols. (London, 1935), I, 211–16; Cf. I. D. MacCrone, *Race Attitudes in South Africa; Historical, Experimental and Psychological Studies* (London, 1937), 125–36; C. R. Boxer, *Race Relations in the Portuguese Colonial Empire, 1415–1825* (Oxford, 1963), esp. chap. 3. Also this book's Essay on Sources.

The spume Issue of Ingratitude.
The Premises consider'd all may tell,
How near good *Joseph* they are parallel.[45]

Despite the casual but ominous way in which John Saffin hitched
slavery to the Negro's "Character," Puritans generally made no such
connection. On the contrary, some of the strongest assertions of the
Negro's fundamental identity with the white man came from prominent Puritans. In England in 1673 the influential Richard Baxter
addressed a vigorous reminder to owners of slaves in the plantations: "Remember that they are of as good a kind as you; that is,
They are reasonable Creatures, as well as you; and born to as much
natural liberty. If their sin have enslaved them to you, yet Nature
made them your equals. Remember that they have immortal souls,
and are equally capable of salvation with yourselves."[46] Puritans in
New England were generally uninterested in the Negro as such, but
that godly man, Cotton Mather, issued stern warnings to the citizens
of Massachusetts. (Mather wrote on the Negro because he wrote on
everything.) He briskly slapped down the notion that the Negro's
blackness made him base, that his lowly position in this world made
him unfit for participation in the possibility of salvation in the
next. There were as many precious souls among the blacks, Mather
announced, as among their white masters. In an orgy of alliteration
he admonished those who had Negroes in their households that they
possessed a glorious opportunity,

an Opportunity to try, Whether you may not be the Happy *Instruments,*
of Converting, the *Blackest* Instances of *Blindness* and Baseness, into
admirable *Candidates* of Eternal Blessedness . . . . make a Trial, Whether
by your Means, the most *Bruitish* of Creatures upon Earth [may perhaps
be saved.] . . . Suppose these Wretched *Negroes,* to be the Offspring of
Cham (which yet is not so very certain,) yet let us make a Trial, Whether the
CHRIST who *dwelt in the Tents of Shem,* have not some of His Chosen
among them; Let us make a Trial, Whether they that have been Scorched
and Blacken'd by the Sun of *Africa,* may not come to have their Minds
Healed by the more Benign *Beams* of the *Sun of Righteousness.*[47]

45. John Saffin, *A Brief and Candid Answer to a Late Printed Sheet, Entitled,
the Selling of Joseph* ([Boston], 1701) , reprinted in Moore, *Notes on Slavery in
Massachusetts,* 251–56 (italics reversed) ; Abner C. Goodell, Jr., "John Saffin and
His Slave Adam," Col. Soc. Mass., *Publications,* 1 (1895), 85–112; *Acts and
Resolves Mass.,* VIII, 266–71.

46. Richard Baxter, *A Christian Directory: Or, a Summ of Practical Theologie,
and Cases of Conscience . . .* (London, 1673) , 557.

47. Mather, *Negro Christianized,* 2–3. Also Mather, *Theopolis Americana. An
Essay on the Golden Street of the Holy City . . .* (Boston, 1710) , 21–23; Mather,

Despite his dreadful punning on the Negro's color, Mather was completely decided on the Negro's essential nature. His indecision concerning the Negro's descent from Ham indicated that any answer to that question would be compatible with spiritual equality. That old idea of Ham's curse floated ethereally about the colonies without anyone's seeming to attach great importance to it; one Anglican minister asserted that Negroes were indeed descended from Ham upon whom had fallen Noah's curse of slavery, but much more often the idea was mentioned by antislavery advocates for purposes of refutation.[48] No one attempted to connect the idea with inherent depravity. No matter how easy it was to pluck passages from Scripture which seemed to endorse perpetual slavery, the Christian tradition demanded acceptance of Negroes into the community of men. Though of course Cotton Mather exhorted Negroes (and white servants) to remain obedient and content in their bondage, he never minced words on the obligations of their masters: "You deny your *Master in Heaven*," he wrote in *The Negro Christianized*, "if you do nothing to bring your *Servants* unto the Knowledge and Service of that glorious *Master*." Nor was Mather alone. The Reverend Samuel Willard was equally definite on the injunctions of pure religion. "Members in a Family are therin equal," Willard declared in 1703, "in that they have Souls equally capable of being saved or lost: And the Soul of a Slave is, in its nature, of as much worth, as the Soul of his Master, having the same noble Faculties and Powers, and being alike Immortal; and being alike

---

Rules for the Society of Negroes, 1693 (Boston, [1706–13?]) , reprinted in Thomas J. Holmes, *Cotton Mather: A Bibliography of His Works*, 3 vols. (Cambridge, Mass., 1940) , III, 936; and *Diary of Cotton Mather, 1681–1724* (Mass. Hist. Soc., *Collections*, 7th Ser., 7–8 [1911–12]) , I, 564–65; Henry W. Haynes, "Cotton Mather and His Slaves," Amer. Antiq. Soc., *Proceedings*, New Ser., 6 (1890) , 191–95. Mather once described a man grown accustomed to a sinful life as "an *Ethiopian* in Wickedness," citing Jeremiah 13:23. *Tremenda* . . . (Boston, 1721) , 8, 23.

48. Jones, *Present State of Virginia*, ed. Morton, 49–50, 52, opposite p. 130; also William Byrd to Earl of Egmont, Va., July 12, 1736, "Colonel William Byrd on Slavery," *Amer. Hist. Rev.*, 1 (1895–96) , 88–89. Refutations were made either of the fact of descent or of the applicability of an ancient curse to American slavery: Sewall, *Selling of Joseph*, 2; William Edmundson's undated letter "For Friends in Maryland, Virginia, and other parts of America," printed in *A Brief Statement of the Rise and Progress of the Testimony of the Religious Society of Friends, against Slavery and the Slave Trade. Published by Direction of the Yearly Meeting, Held in Philadelphia* . . . (Phila., 1843) , 7; Hepburn, *American Defence*, 30–31; Sandiford, *Brief Examination*, 4–5; Coleman, *Testimony*, 9–10; and for a detailed discussion of the idea, Jacob Bryant to Granville Sharp, Cypenham, Oct. 20, 1772, Letters to Granville Sharp, 1768–73, B. V. Sec. Slavery, N.-Y. Hist. Soc.

Precious to Christ, who paid as great a Price for the Redemption of the Soul of *this* Person, as of the *other*." [49]

The equality of all souls before God was so very real, so axiomatic, and so important to the Puritans that they were virtually precluded from thinking that the Negro was an inherently inferior being. They always found spiritual equality perfectly compatible with pronounced distinctions in outward condition and abilities. The remarkable poise which the Puritans achieved when contemplating the worldly distinctions among men was dramatically demonstrated, for instance, during the inoculation controversy of 1721. A terrible visitation of smallpox in Boston was followed by an outbreak of acrimonious argument about inoculation; the ministers of the town generally supported the new untested procedure and most of the physicians opposed it. The most eminent proponent of inoculation was Cotton Mather, a man incapable of withholding from the public the enormous benefit of his own advice. Mather claimed to have learned of the strange procedure from his African slave, Onesimus, before he heard of its use in Europe. Mather personally was happy to credit the testimony of Negroes that inoculation had been used with success in Africa, but he was less than confident that Negro-evidence would be accepted by his audience in the town of Boston. He must have sensed that the Negroes' boorishness would raise doubts concerning their testimony, for he attempted to turn this characteristic into a weapon in his own hand. Mather recommended to Boston the experience of Africa in the following manner:

> There is at this Time a considerable Number of *Africans* in this Town, who can have no Conspiracy or Combination to cheat us. No body has instructed them to tell their Story. The more plainly, brokenly, and blunderingly, and like Ideots, they tell their Story, it will be with reasonable Men, but the much more credible. For *that these* all agree in *one* Story; 'That abundance of poor Negro's die of the *Small Pox*, till they learn this *Way*; that People take the Juice of the *Small Pox*, and *Cut the Skin*, and put in a drop; then by'nd by a little *Sick*, then few *Small Pox*; and no body dye of it: no body have *Small Pox* any more'.
> Here we have a clear Evidence, that in *Africa*, where the Poor Creatures dye of the *Small Pox* in the common way like Rotten Sheep, a Merciful GOD has taught them a *wonderful Preservative*.
> It is a *Common Practice,* and is attended with *Success.* I have as full Evidence of this, as I have that there are *Lions* in *Africa.* And I don't know why 'tis more unlawful to learn of *Africans,* how to help against the *Poison*

49. Mather, *Negro Christianized,* 5; Samuel Willard, *A Compleat Body of Divinity* . . . (Boston, 1726), 616.

of the *Small Pox*, than it is to learn of our *Indians,* how to help against the *Poison* of a *Rattle-Snake*.[50]

Much the same story was offered by the Reverend Benjamin Colman. Unlike Mather, though, Colman was apparently not intimately acquainted with the lions of Africa and allowed himself to backpedal on the worthiness of Negro testimony. "I believe I shall be scoff'd at for telling this *Simple* story," he wrote, and then added somewhat weakly, "whosoever seeks the Truth and desires to be informed will not despise it. And he that has learnt any thing as he ought, has this—to be willing to learn of the poorest *Slave* in the Town." [51]

Colman's hesitancy was soon justified, for several critics of inoculation poured ridicule on the evidence of Africans. Mather noted with pain in his diary that a "Lieutenant of a Man of War, whom I am a Stranger to, designing to putt an Indignity upon me, has called his *Negro-Slave* by the Name of COTTON MATHER." [52] The most outspoken opponent of inoculation, Dr. William Douglass, took up Mather and his cohorts on the point of Negro boorishness and then proceeded to run the argument directly into the ground. "Their second Voucher is an Army of half a Dozen or half a Score *Africans,*" Douglass wrote caustically, "by others call'd Negroe Slaves, who tell us now (tho' never before) that it is practised in their own Country. The more blundering and Negroish they tell their Story, it is the more credible says *C. M; a paradox in Nature;* for all they say true or false is after the same manner. There is not a Race of Men on Earth more *False Lyars,* etc. Their Accounts of what was done in their Country was never depended upon till now for Arguments sake." [53] All that Mather could do in reply was to marshal the Negro's speech under the head of ingenuous verisimilitude. In stressing this quality Mather made the first attempt to reproduce in writing the Negro's peculiar English speech. On reca-

50. [Cotton Mather], *Some Account of What Is Said of Inoculating or Transplanting the Small Pox* . . . (Boston, 1721) , 9 (Evans no. 2206) . For the entire ⌐ontroversy, George L. Kittredge, "Some Lost Works of Cotton Mather," Mass. Hist. Soc., *Proceedings,* 45 (1911–12) , 418–79; Otho T. Beall, Jr., and Richard H. Shryock, *Cotton Mather: First Significant Figure in American Medicine* (Baltimore, 1954) , chap. 7; Perry Miller, *The New England Mind: From Colony to Province* (Cambridge, Mass., 1953) , chap. 21; John B. Blake, *Public Health in the Town of Boston, 1630–1822* (Cambridge, Mass., 1959) , chap. 4.

51. [Benjamin] Colman, *Some Observations on the New Method of Receiving the Small-Pox by Ingrafting or Inoculating* . . . (Boston, 1721) , 15–16.

52. *Diary of Cotton Mather,* II, 663.

53. [William Douglass], *Inoculation of the Small Pox as Practised in Boston, Consider'd in a Letter to A—S— M. D. & F.R.S. in London* (Boston, 1722) , 6–7.

pitulating his Negro-evidence Mather sought to strengthen the "One Story" of the "Africans" by having them relate how "in their Countrey *grandy-many* dy of the *Small-Pox*" and how they *"Cutty-skin,* and Putt in a Drop; then by'nd by a little *Sicky, Sicky."* [54] Far from conceding stupidity or mendacity in the Negro, Mather maintained that their primitive traits were evidence of an admirable genuineness. Obviously Mather was arguing a case upon which he had staked his reputation as a scientist, yet even his opponents made no attempts to claim that Negroes were inherently incapable of making a medical discovery. The depth of William Douglass's vilification of Negroes was no greater than if he had been talking about white servants poaching on the private preserves of professional medical gentlemen. Most significant of all, no one suggested that a medical procedure which would work with Negroes might not work with white men.

While there can be no doubt that Puritan theology required that the Negro be regarded as possessing the same nature as the white man, certain ways in which Puritan theology operated in the community may have tended toward exclusion of Negroes from full participation. Embedded in New England Puritanism was a certain tribalism, a sense of being a folk set apart.[55] The Puritans' concern for God was matched by an equally intensive concern about themselves. The rigorous introspectiveness of individual Puritans was matched by intense self-scrutiny on the part of the Puritan community. Their sense of the special character of their religion was matched by a feeling that they were a special people.

Historically considered, this introspective style was of course neither exclusively New England nor exclusively Puritan; rather, it was an especially loud and persistent reverberation of the theme of adventure and control which had been so important an aspect of Tudor-Stuart England. It was not merely that the Godly saints of New England sought to avoid contamination from graceless riffraff who inevitably seeped (or flooded) into their wilderness Zion. At home Englishmen who became Puritans in the late sixteenth and early seventeenth century were frequently as "tribal" as the most provincial settlers of the Massachusetts Bay. Well before Puritans

54. Intended for publication but never published, Mather's MS. Angel of Bethesda is in the Amer. Antiq. Soc., Worcester; the quotation being from chap. 20, p. 134, as quoted by Kittredge, "Lost Works of Mather," Mass. Hist. Soc., *Proceedings,* 45 (1911–12), 431–32.

55. A fact emphasized by Edmund S. Morgan; see particularly his *The Puritan Family: Religion and Domestic Relations in Seventeenth-Century New England,* rev. ed. (N. Y., 1966).

on either side of the Atlantic had first hand contact with Negroes, their discussions of "Godly Families" were thoroughly pervaded by an exclusionary spirit. In 1612, without reference to Negroes, two Puritan tractarians asked, "Will one deale thus [use tree cuttings and animals of an inferior sort] for his Orchyard, and for his Sheepe? and should he not likewise consider, in the planting of his familie, when he takes a servant into his fold, out of what pasture comes he? hath he bin brought up in a rotten ground? in a place of disorder, of riot, of swearing, of breaking the Sabbath, and such like? and hath he a rotten bleate? will he sweare? will he lie? will he speake filthilie? doth he looke like a ruffian? and will you yet venture on him? then you are a foolish master." Masters were further admonished to "bee careful to take none into their family, but Christians." It was not Mahometans and heathens who were being ruled out—merely "wicked persons, teltales, proud persons, and swaggerers, such as have great looks and no grace."[56]

Migration to an isolated corner of the world certainly did nothing to diminish feelings of specialness and exclusiveness, and in some New England Puritans these feelings grew to such proportions that they overrode justice and charity and common sense. Yet tribalism was not peculiar to New England, nor to Puritans; in varying measure it pervaded all the Protestant sects in the English colonies. Indeed the sectarian character of Protestantism fostered a spirit of tribalism, since sectarianism meant emphasis on distinctiveness from others and virtual, though inadmissible, abandonment of the ideal of Christian universality. For those sects which bore scars from old wounds of civil persecution, a sense of exclusive virtue was a soothing balm. Even the state church, the Church of England, was not lacking a history of martyrdom at the hands of the Papists. All Protestant history was the history of some people differentiating themselves from others.

While the spirit of tribalism in Protestantism was probably in some measure responsible for the exclusion of Negroes from the community, the notion that Calvinist belief in predestination led Puritans to think that Negroes were damned and white men were not is so unbelievably crude as to be utterly incorrect.[57] A Negro

56. John Dod and Robert Cleaver, *A Plaine and Familiar Exposition of the Ten Commandments . . .* , 17th ed. (London, 1628) , 213–15.

57. But see the curious secondhand report of this assertion "by a Calvinist, and, to my astonishment a man of understanding above the common level," in "Thoughts upon the Enfranchisement of the Negroes," *United States Magazine,* 1 (1779) , 487.

woman was accepted into full membership in a Massachusetts church in 1641, only three years after the first Negroes are thought to have arrived in the colony.[58] Protestant doctrine called upon the English settlers to bring strangers into the fold; it was something in the style and spirit of Protestantism as it operated in the community which whispered, "not so fast."

What drastically sapped the energy of Protestant equalitarianism as applied to the Negro was not so much this feeling of exclusiveness as certain glaring institutional weaknesses in the structure of the Protestant churches in America. In New England, of course, the Puritan churches operated from a position of strength. Even in the eighteenth century the New England clergy and the members of the individual churches remained in a position to influence, though not dictate, the treatment of Negroes and to affect subtly the way in which Negroes were regarded by the entire community. In New England, however, there were not many Negroes. In the southern continental colonies the churches at best were in a weak position to dictate to slaveholders and in some times and places were virtually nonexistent. The burden of sustaining the Christian equalitarian tradition in the face of chattel slavery fell chiefly upon the Anglican Church, which remained predominant, particularly among wealthy slaveholders, in the coastal regions where there was heavy slave concentration. The Anglican Church was "established" in the five southern colonies, though the establishment was particularly shaky in North Carolina and Georgia. In Virginia the Church's position was relatively firm, but even there it could scarcely be termed a powerful institution; some of Virginia's parishes lacked ministers and many ministers lacked sanctity and leverage in the community.

The institutional weaknesses of the Church of England were still more glaringly apparent in the context of the Empire as a whole. During the eighteenth century the Church was far from militant in England and even further from it in America. The attempt to transplant England's established church to the New World was, on the whole, a resounding failure, partly owing to weaknesses at home but much more because the American social and geographical envi-

58. Winthrop, *Journal*, ed. Hosmer, II, 26; *New Englands First Fruits* . . . (London, 1643), reprinted in Samuel Eliot Morison, *The Founding of Harvard College* (Cambridge, Mass., 1935), 425. This was, however, an unusual case; in 1680 the governor of Massachusetts reported *re* Negroes: "none baptized that I ever heard of"; Box 4, bundle: The Royal African Company of England, MS. relating to the company's trade in Negroes (1672–1734/5), also some miscellaneous papers relating to Negroes and slaves (1676–1743), 13, Parish Transcripts, N.-Y. Hist. Soc.

ronment proved unfavorable to an episcopal establishment. Responsibility for governance of the Anglican churches in America fell into the lap of the bishop of London (as if London was not enough of a problem) and stayed there; accordingly, the Anglican Church in America remained an organizational monstrosity—an episcopal church without a bishop. Every prospective Anglican clergyman in the colonies had to traipse back to England to secure ordination. As a stopgap measure commissaries were appointed for Maryland, Virginia, the Carolinas and several other colonies, but this fact in itself suggests the difficulty the hierarchical organization was having in heaving its ponderous weight across the Atlantic. English colonial officials tried to help, but they were having difficulties of their own in maintaining imperial authority.[59] The failure of the English church to transmit its institutional structure to America resulted in a strange paradox: in the area of greatest Anglican strength, Virginia, the individual churches were as independent and as subject to lay control as most of the individual churches in New England. The Anglican churches of Virginia were in fact more congregational than the ostensibly congregational churches of Connecticut. By the beginning of the eighteenth century, control of the parish churches in Virginia had fallen into the hands of the vestry, and more often than not the vestrymen told the local cleric what to do rather than vice versa. It almost seems unnecessary to point out that the vestrymen were normally the leading planters of the parish.[60] The established Anglican Church of Virginia, the one institution which might best have implemented the equalitarianism of Christianity and which might at very least have welcomed Negroes into its own house, was in large measure dominated by slaveholders.

Outside Virginia and Maryland the Church of England was in a different condition but no better able to insist that Negroes be regarded and treated as God's own. In the three southernmost colonies the Church had more than enough to do just trying to meet the needs of the English population and totally lacked the resources and energy required for protecting Negroes in body and spirit. Churchmen in England, however, tried to meet the lack. It was thoroughly characteristic of the relationship of the Christian churches with the Negro in the English colonies that the principal agency concerned with conversion of Negroes was English, not

59. Labaree, ed., *Royal Instructions*, II, 505–6.
60. William H. Seiler, "The Anglican Parish in Virginia," in James Morton Smith, ed., *Seventeenth-Century America: Essays in Colonial History* (Chapel Hill, 1959), 119–42.

American. One of the initial purposes of the Society for the Propagation of the Gospel was to bolster the faltering Church in the colonies against inroads by secularism and the sects; Virginia and Maryland were felt to be in fairly sound condition, but scores of S.P.G. missionaries plunged dauntlessly into the spiritual deserts in other continental colonies.[61] (It seems instructive that the Church of England had to regard major, well-established English colonies as requiring *missionary* endeavors.) The S.P.G. had a second, no less important goal—conversion of the heathen, though at times the two purposes seemed indistinguishable; an S.P.G. agent in South Carolina declared that the white settlers "were making near approach to that heathenism which is to be found among negroes and Indians." [62] The bona fide heathen in hand, however, was the Negro, and he received more attention than the Indian.

S.P.G. missionaries achieved some success in baptizing Negroes but very little in raising masters' opinions of their slaves. The history of the S.P.G. and of its ally, the bishop of London, at times seems to consist largely of a series of hortatory sermons, instructions, pamphlets, reports, and letters of admonition. What is most revealing about these efforts is that Englishmen were far more eager to convert Negroes than Americans were. Clerical authorities in England never really understood that racial slavery had created an enormous gulf between England and her colonies, and when English bishops called upon masters in the plantations to treat their slaves as brothers by bringing them to a knowledge of Christ they showed themselves naïvely unaware of the facts of life in the plantations. The misconception in England of the racial situation in America at times became monumental. The bishop of London, for instance, referred to Negroes as "truly a Part of our own Nation"—which was just what the colonists were sure Negroes were not.[63] In 1771 the English authors of a geographical work offered a suggestion which must have seemed totally incomprehensible to many Americans.

But it would certainly be more consistent with justice, with the laws of humanity, and with the spirit of the Christian religion, to suffer these negroes, who have from their good behaviour, and the benevolence of their masters, obtained their freedom, to become planters; to become united to

61. Numbers are in C[harles] F. Pascoe, *Two Hundred Years of the S.P.G.:* . . . *1701–1900*, 2 vols. (London, 1901) , I, 86. A more recent general account is Henry P. Thompson, *Into All Lands: The History of the Society for the Propagation of the Gospel in Foreign Parts, 1701–1950* (London, 1951) .
62. Pascoe, *Two Hundred Years,* I, 13.
63. Humphreys, *Endeavours by the S.P.G. in New York,* 19.

the Christians by the bands of friendship, and by mutual good offices; and to be allowed all the advantages of freemen. The prospect of such a reward might have a happy effect on the slaves, by making obedience and fidelity the guides to liberty, wealth, and honour; and the strongest defence of the whites, by having a number of the blacks firmly united in the same interest with them.[64]

Proposals of this sort failed to recognize that in the colonies the revolutionary new division of men arising from racial slavery was not simply one of temporal condition.

Efforts to convert slaves frequently struck the planters as meddling by outsiders in affairs which only insiders could fully understand. In one sense, this reaction to English missionary work among the Negroes was merely one facet of a generalized determination, so characteristic of American colonials, to keep their affairs in their own hands. Yet although the widespread opposition in the colonies to establishment of an American episcopate arose mainly from larger religious and political considerations,[65] at least in the South this opposition must have been stiffened by apprehension that a bishop in America might adopt a tough line with planters on the matter of conversion. Viewed more generally, American resistance to transplantation of the English church, most of it passive but very effective, derived from a burgeoning American feeling of independence and divergence from England. One aspect of this divergence was that Americans faced a racial problem.

It was virtually inevitable that Americans should grow to resent any interference with their handling of this problem and that Englishmen should develop a remarkably durable self-righteousness which seemed to Americans flagrantly holier-than-thou. An incident in Georgia immediately before the outbreak of the Revolution may serve as illustration. The Countess of Huntingdon, who owned Negroes in Georgia, joined the Savannah merchant James Habersham in encouraging a Christian Negro named David to preach to his fellow Negroes. David had been in England, and Habersham was apprehensive "that the kind notice, he has met with in England will make him think too highly of himself." Perhaps Habersham was right, for in Charleston David failed to confine himself to

64. D[aniel] Fenning and J. Collyer, *A New System of Geography: Or, a General Description of the Whole Known World* . . . [2d? ed.], 2 vols. (London, 1771), II, 672 (bk. iv, chap. 3, sec. 8). For other indications of the gulf, [Gibson], *Two Letters, passim;* Bishop Joseph Butler's S.P.G. sermon (1739), quoted in Klingberg, *Anglican Humanitarianism in N. Y.,* 23–24.

65. Arthur L. Cross, *The Anglican Episcopate and the American Colonies* (N. Y., 1902); Carl Bridenbaugh, *Mitre and Sceptre: Transatlantic Faiths, Ideas, Personalities, and Politics, 1689–1775* (N. Y., 1962).

preaching up spiritual liberty and dropped some "unguarded Expressions" concerning a more immediate kind of freedom. Some irate citizens threatened to hang him, and a grand jury indicted a white man who had offered him encouragement. When Habersham discreetly shipped David back to England he wrote the Countess's agent in London, carefully explaining why David's mission had failed and politely expounding the realities of life in the plantations. "His Business was to preach a Spiritual Deliverance to these People, not a temporal one, but he is, if I am not mistaken, very proud, and very superficial, and conceited, and I must say it's a pity, that any of these People should ever put their Feet in England, where they get totally spoiled and ruined, both in Body and Soul, through a mistaken kind of compassion because they are black, while many of our own colour and Fellow Subjects, are starving through want and Neglect. We know these People better than you do." [66] Habersham's concluding claim, of course, was to roll echoing down the corridors of southern history.

This divergence of opinion between the mother country and the colonies demonstrated how completely the Church of England failed to implement its injunctions concerning the fundamental equality of Negroes with their masters. While Anglican doctrine, in common with all Protestant doctrine, spoke for equality and inclusion, the organizational weakness of the Anglican Church in America meant that the tendencies toward inequality and exclusion inherent in racial slavery were allowed to develop without effective check. By contrast, in all the European colonies in America where the leading Christian church was in a position to enforce its demands upon slaveholders, the Negro's position was more secure. Particularly was this true in the Catholic colonies, but it was to some extent true also where one Protestant sect was in a sufficiently authoritative position to enforce its demands, as with the Quakers and the early Puritans. The more genuinely authoritarian and powerful the church, apparently, the more protection afforded the Negro.

The Protestant sects were also distinguished from the Catholic Church by a notably different conception of the morphology of conversion, a conception intimately linked with the doctrines, spirit of exclusiveness, and institutional structures of the Protestant churches. The Protestant emphasis on individual piety external to

66. Habersham to the Countess of Huntingdon, Savannah, Apr. 19, 1775; and to Robert Keen, Savannah, May 11, 1775, "Letters of James Habersham," Ga. Hist. Soc., *Collections*, 6 (1904), 238–44.

the rituals of the church, on the directness of the individual's relationship with God, and on the importance of Scripture all made for the view that conversion to Christianity was an arduous and exacting process. All Protestants felt that true conversion required a transformation of the spirit which could not possibly be accomplished by running the heathen through a mill of sacramental rites. As one caustic New Englander put the matter concerning the Indians in 1647, "if wee would force them to baptisme (as the Spaniards do . . . , having learnt them a short answer or two to some Popish questions) or if wee would hire them to it by giving them coates and shirts, to allure them to it as some others have done, wee could have gathered many hundreds, yea thousands it may bee by this time, into the name of Churches; but wee have not learnt as yet that art of coyning Christians, or putting Christs name and Image upon copper mettle." [67] For Protestants generally, true converts were nurtured, not minted.

The tedious process of nurturing souls kept great numbers of slaves out of the churches: on technical grounds alone, Protestantism was exclusionary. Of course the sects varied considerably as to how much religious knowledge and sophistication they required of the convert. While the Negro woman who joined in full communion with a church in Massachusetts Bay in 1641 must have been not only very pious but very clever, the Anglican Church in the eighteenth century required merely some rough knowledge of Christian principles before baptism, often the Apostles' Creed, the Lord's Prayer, and the Ten Commandments.[68] Yet with all the Protestant sects, converting heathens required instructing them first. Especially during the early years of slavery's rapid growth in the eighteenth century, there were mountainous practical difficulties. An Anglican minister in Virginia replied in 1724 to an official query concerning the "infidels" in his parish (which measured 40 x 8 miles) saying, "A great many Black bond men and women infidels that understand not our Language nor me their's: not any free. The Church is open to them; the word preached, and the Sacraments administered with circumspection." [69] Always, everywhere, there was circumspection. It was characteristic of the entire program for Negro conversion that one of the S.P.G. missionary's principal duties was to

67. [Thomas Shepard?], *The Day-Breaking If Not the Sun-Rising of the Gospel with the Indians in New-England* (London, 1647) , 15.

68. *New Englands First Fruits*, 425, is very instructive; for an example of the Anglican approach, Pascoe, *Two Hundred Years*, I, 16, 17.

69. Perry, ed., *Historical Collections Colonial Church*, I, 283.

"catechise" Negroes.[70] This typically Protestant feeling that conversion was a slow and difficult educational experience, that it was a process rather than an act, served not only to emphasize the separation of the races in men's minds but also to make Christianizing slaves seem almost like a process of tribal adoption. Men hesitated to welcome Negroes into their religious club, perhaps because the initiation procedure was so thorough and so patently adoptive that anyone who went through it could scarcely be denied the status and privileges of full membership.

6. RELIGIOUS REVIVAL AND THE IMPACT OF CONVERSION

On the other hand, the pronounced strain of individualism in Protestantism which helped make conversion such a hurdle contained implications which operated directly against the obvious tendency toward exclusion. For the most part, these implications remained dormant in the colonies until about 1740, when with remarkable suddenness a wave of religious revivals brought them to life. The spirit of the Great Awakening tended toward a greater emphasis on intensity of religious conviction, often at the cost of religious knowledge. Whatever its effect upon white men, it is clear that the spirit of revivalism virtually beckoned Negroes to participate. Schisms ripped through many of the well-established sects, to the benefit particularly of the Baptists and later the Methodists and to the detriment of formalism and orderly procedures of admission. Almost by definition a religious revival was inclusive; itinerant preachers aimed at gathering every lost sheep, black as well as white. The revivals tended to break down the traditional structures of clerical control and emphasize once again the priesthood of all believers. Religious enthusiasm elbowed aside religious sophistication as the criterion of true piety. Nothing could make this tendency more evident than the remarks of one of the foremost critics of the Great Awakening, the Reverend Charles Chauncy of Boston, who lamented the appearance of "so many *Exhorters*," of totally unqualified persons preaching the gospel. As Chauncy described them, "They are *chiefly* indeed young *Persons*, sometimes *Lads*, or rather *Boys:* Nay, *Women* and *Girls;* yea, *Negroes,* have taken upon them to do the Business of *Preachers.*" [71]

Nowhere had Negroes previously taken on such a business; in-

70. Two organizations allied with the S.P.G. (the Society for Promoting Christian Knowledge, and the Bray Associates) aimed primarily at education. See especially Pennington, "Thomas Bray's Associates," Amer. Antiq. Soc., *Proceedings*, New Ser., 48 (1938), 311–403.

71. Charles Chauncy, *Seasonable Thoughts on the State of Religion in New-England* (Boston, 1743), 226.

deed in the southern colonies the great masses of slaves stood altogether outside the fold of Christianity. Probably the Reverend John Brunskill, who had resided in Virginia for eight years, correctly described the situation when he wrote in 1724 that while the white people were Christians "the Negroes who are slaves to the whites cannot, I think, be said to be of any Religion." After 1740, Negroes began entering the churches in much larger and accelerating numbers. They joined the Baptist and later the Methodist churches especially, though they were to be found in virtually every denomination. George Whitefield and numerous lesser-known evangelists rode doggedly across the length and breadth of the colonies preaching the Gospel to crowds of blacks and whites. The response was often gratifying: leaving Philadelphia in 1740 Whitefield reported that "near fifty negroes came to give me thanks for what God had done to their souls." He had seen Negroes, he wrote, who had been "exceedingly wrought upon under the Word preached." [72] One of the most characteristic scenes of the long-reverberating revival in the southern colonies was a tableau of Protestant enthusiasm—a meetinghouse brought to life by an itinerant preacher in the pulpit, scores of people from far and near stuffed hip-to-hip in the pews and crammed toe-to-heel in the aisles, boys perched on the rafters, and a still larger crowd outside jostling for a position close enough to the open windows to hear the groaning, whining, wheedling message of repentance and salvation. Many of the faces which pressed eagerly toward the windows and the open door were black. With doctrinal niceties and orderly catechism frequently going by the board, moreover, the way was open for any Negro, even a slave, who found Christ in his heart and a good tongue in his head to deliver his own message. In many localities certain Negroes gained considerable reputation as preachers to their own people and in several cases to whites as well. One Negro converted by Whitefield was reported to have "preached to crouded audiences." [73] The equalitarian implications in Protestant Christianity were never more apparent; if it was difficult for Negroes to become men of affairs in this world, it became increasingly easy, after the watershed of the Great Awakening, for them to become men of God.[74]

72. Perry, ed., *Historical Collections Colonial Church*, I, 277; *George Whitefield's Journals*, new ed. (Guildford and London, 1960), 422.

73. *Boston Gaz.*, Apr. 29, 1765.

74. One of the best sources is the Rev. Francis Asbury's journal, available in various editions. The Great Awakening was only the beginning; at the time of the Revolution most Negroes were not Christians, at least by prevailing definitions. See Dexter, ed., *Diary of Ezra Stiles*, I, 213–14; [Hewat], *Account of S. C. and Ga.*, II, 100.

The effects of the Great Awakening on American feelings about the Negro rippled slowly through colonial society. By clearing an avenue down which Negroes could crowd into an important sector of the white man's community, the Awakening gradually forced the colonists to face more squarely the fact that Negroes were going to participate in their American experience. Realization of this fact did not necessarily mean that the Negro would be welcomed; Landon Carter thought that Virginia's slaves "are grown so much worse" from imbibing New Light ideas.[75] In the long run, indeed, this realization could easily lead to strenuous efforts to find some novel and effective means of barring the Negro from the white community now that heathenism was no longer serving the purpose. More immediately, the Awakening may well have given impetus to the slowly gathering movement for more humane treatment of slaves and perhaps even to the broader trend of eighteenth-century humanitarianism; put flatly, a spiritual brother deserved, at very least, a measure of kindness. Most important of all, however, the Great Awakening re-emphasized the axiomatic spiritual equality of Negroes with white men. It demonstrated once again the staying power and profound influence of the equalitarian strain in Christianity. In 1740 George Whitefield was lecturing slaveholders in terms almost identical with those used by Richard Baxter in 1673 and Cotton Mather in 1706: "Think you," Whitefield asked the planters of the southern colonies in a widely circulated pamphlet, that your children "are any way better by Nature than the poor Negroes? No, in no wise. Blacks are just as much, and no more, conceived and born in Sin, as White Men are. Both, if born and bred up here, I am persuaded, are naturally capable of the same [religious] improvement." Although in the long run revivalism proved a hothouse for the growth of antislavery, its immediate emphasis lay on spiritual equality: Whitefield affirmed the legitimacy of slavery in a private letter to John Wesley in 1751 but stressed particularly how gladly he welcomed the presence of Negroes in Georgia as an opportunity "for breeding up their posterity in the nurture and admonition of the Lord." [76]

75. Jack P. Greene, ed., *The Diary of Colonel Landon Carter of Sabine Hall, 1752–1778*, 2 vols. (Charlottesville, Va., 1965), I, 378.

76. *Three Letters from the Reverend Mr. G. Whitefield . . . Letter III. To the Inhabitants of Maryland, Virginia, North and South-Carolina, Concerning Their Negroes* (Phila., 1740), 15; printed also in Boston *New-England Weekly Journal*, Apr. 29, 1740; Whitefield to Wesley, Bristol, Mar. 22, 1751, in L. Tyerman, *The Life and Times of the Rev. John Wesley, M.A., Founder of the Methodists*, 3 vols. (London, 1870–71), II, 132.

This central theme of religious equalitarianism, that Negroes were "by Nature" the equals of white men because they possessed immortal souls, fenced the thinking of every colonist in America. It may be argued that in the long run Christian principles prevailed, not merely in the sense that Negroes were eventually brought into the churches in increasing numbers, but also in the sense that the Christian reservoir of insistence on equality could still be drawn upon even when it became less specifically Christian. Yet the men who insisted upon this equality were always compelled either to disregard or to belittle the fact that however much the Negro's soul might resemble the white man's, his skin did not. In the eighteenth century it became increasingly difficult to ignore the Negro's complexion. Some evangelical ministers were perhaps not fully conscious of the way they fused the imagery of Scripture and their perceptions of human complexion, as Freeborn Garrettson did in 1777 when he recounted the "precious moments" he had had in preaching to the blacks: "while many of their sable faces were bedewed with tears, their withered hands of faith were stretched out, and their precious souls made white in the blood of the lamb." [77] This accommodation of complexion to revealed religion was a suggestive but less important development than another tendency among men less fully committed than Garrettson to affairs of the spirit. Increasingly, many men were turning their attention from the spiritual condition of mankind to the place of man in an ordered creation of natural beings. As is true with all aspects of the process of secularization in Western culture, this change was complicated, but however it operated it was bound to make the sheerly physical attributes of Negroes assume a novel importance.

77. *The Experience and Travels of Mr. Freeborn Garrettson, Minister of the Methodist-Episcopal Church in North-America* (Phila., 1791), 70. Cf. Revelation 7:13–14.

VI THE BODIES OF MEN
The Negro's Physical Nature

THE AVALANCHE OF NAVIGATIONS AND GEOGRAPHICAL DIS-
coveries beginning in the fifteenth century had created an increasingly pressing problem for European thought. Old ideas about the
natural world were almost buried by a mounting pile of information about distant lands and strange plants, animals, and even men.
By the eighteenth century it was obvious that this mass of information had to be squeezed into some logical framework if men were to
continue to make sense of the world. The tension created by the
undigested raw data of the explorers was so great that anyone
capable of bringing order out of chaos was bound to be welcomed as
a heroic deliverer. The brilliant successes of Newton and Linnaeus
brought clamorous acclamation; they also inspired imitation by
many lesser and lesser-known intellectuals.

Success in conceptual and technological manipulation of their
natural environment led Europeans increasingly to ponder their
own place in Nature's scheme. Unless man was a disembodied
spirit, it was essential that mankind be included in any assessment
of the handiwork of God. By the eighteenth century, moreover,
many men no longer fastened their eyes steadfastly upon the drama
of salvation. Many intellectuals were ripe for a new center of
interest which would bear the weight of their energy and curiosity;
and their curiosity had been whetted by the flood of reports about
strange-looking men in all quarters of the globe. During the sixteenth and early seventeenth centuries, the strange appearance of
Indians and Negroes and (somewhat later) Malays and Lapps had
of course attracted attention. So had their heathenism and their
savagery, and these attributes continued to merit the interest especially of clergymen and political reformers. Yet gradually, as men
became more interested in themselves as natural creatures, the

[216]

purely physical differences among men acquired heightened significance and greater relative importance. Viewed in the broadest terms, this growing interest in the physical distinctions among human beings was one aspect of the secularization of Western society. Secularization did not simply happen, of course; one of the myriad, interrelated causes of the process was the relatively sudden discovery that various groups of men looked very different from each other.

1. CONFUSION, ORDER, AND HIERARCHY

From the first, this fact had demanded explanation and had stimulated discussion of such subjects as the effects of climate and the behavior of Noah's sons. In the eighteenth century more than any other, though, Europeans were inclined to feel that the best way of explaining anything was to arrange relevant data into some meaningful order. Naturalists particularly reacted to reports from overseas much like a good housewife trying to tidy up after the movers had dumped everything helter-skelter into the new house. Newton had explained the arrangement of the universe with such brilliance as to cast a spell over generations. In unfortunate contrast, when natural philosophers set about arranging animals and men, they found their materials inherently less easy to manage than the steadily orbiting planets and their findings more liable to unleash disturbing religious and social questions. In the face of these difficulties they nonetheless remained determined to impose order as firmly on the motley variations of men as on all living things. It became apparent in the eighteenth century, however, that there were various ways in which order could be imposed.

The simplest method was to fasten upon one characteristic in which men differed and to group them accordingly. The first European to take this approach with all mankind, François Bernier in 1684, ran smack into the obvious difficulty of choosing a characteristic; although he discussed a variety of features such as hair, stature, and shape of nose and lips, when he came down to making his "Nouvelle Division de la Terre" he relied more upon color than anything else in chopping mankind into four (or possibly, Bernier thought, five or six) categories, the Europeans, Africans, Orientals, Lapps ("wretched animals"), and perhaps American Indians and Hottentots.[1] Bernier's classification was prophetic not only in its

1. [François Bernier], "Nouvelle Division de la Terre, par les Differentes Especes ou Races d'Hommes qui l'Habitent . . . ," *Journal des Sçavans*

stress on color but in its basic aim of dividing all mankind into discrete groups on the basis of physical attributes. This approach was, in fact, revolutionary.

Without a broader sweep of explanation, however, classifying the various sorts of men was going to remain a game for armchair travelers. It was Linnaeus who first fully transformed the game into a science. In the 1730's he took the fateful step of classifying mankind as an integral part of the animal creation, thereby dramatically underlining the fact that man was, after all, a physical being. In his great *Systema Naturae* which rolled majestically through twelve editions during his lifetime, Linnaeus began his catalog of all living things with "MAMMALIA: Order I. Primates" and included in this category the simians, the sloth, and "HOMO." [2] Certainly the assumptions underlying this decision were not entirely new, for they had guided the dissecting knife which Edward Tyson had wielded on his "Orang-outang" in 1701. But to throw man into the same "Order" with the "SIMIA" was to make a bald case for regarding man as subject to the same kind of scrutiny as other animals.

Linnaeus's almost prescriptive influence in the eighteenth century did not derive from this classification of men with simians but from his general predilection for descriptive classification. Here was a new tool with which order could be hammered into the natural world, and it was as eagerly grasped in America as anywhere. Linnaeus himself gave proof of its power by describing and classifying thousands of plants and extending his system into the animal kingdom. He began to classify diseases, and other men took up this task; even clouds eventually fell under the spell of the Linnaean impulse to classification. The trick was merely to seize upon certain physical characteristics common to some specimens and not to others; the criteria might then be applied to any specimen in hand, and membership in a certain group neatly followed. While Linnaeus himself was vague and indecisive when he came to classifying var-

---

[Amsterdam], 12 (1684), 148–55; a translation is in Bendyshe, "History of Anthropology," Anthro. Soc. of London, *Memoirs*, 1 (1863–64), 360–64, cited in this chapter as Bendyshe, "History of Anthropology." A less sophisticated attempt at division was made by Richard Bradley, *A Philosophical Account of the Works of Nature* . . . (London, 1721), 169, which Bendyshe reprints, pp. 358–59.

2. Available in English as Sir Charles Linné, *A General System of Nature* . . . , trans. William Turton, 7 vols. (London, 1802–06). The sections in the various editions pertaining to man are reproduced and discussed in Bendyshe, "History of Anthropology," 421–48.

ious kinds of men, nothing in his approach indicated that mankind should not be subject to this same sort of categorization.

Linnaean classification was not, however, the only attractive method of making nature dance to the natural philosopher's tune. An ancient concept with roots deep in classical Greece was reaching full flower in the seventeenth and eighteenth centuries, a concept which had the merit of systematizing all creation and even the Creator himself. The idea of the Great Chain of Being possessed all the power and all the weaknesses of any gigantic synthesis. The Chain of Being, as usually conceived, commenced with inanimate things and ranged upwards through the lowliest forms of life, through the more intelligent animals until it reached man himself; but it did not stop with man, for it continued upward through the myriad ranks of heavenly creatures until it reached its pinnacle in God. By definition a chain was without gaps, the more so with the Great Chain forged by the Creator. The gradations between ranks on the scale were merely subtle alterations, so that the assembled hierarchy always remained a harmonious whole. Man, the middling creature on this scale, was carefully suspended between the heavenly and brute creation. As Edward Tyson explained in the course of comparing simian and human anatomy, *"Man* is part a *Brute,* part an *Angel;* and is that *Link* in the *Creation,* that joyns them both together."[3] Or, as man's position was expounded by the poet who did so much to popularize the concept of the Chain,

> Plac'd on this isthmus of a middle state,
> A Being darkly wise, and rudely great:
> With too much knowledge for the Sceptic side,
> With too much weakness for the Stoic's pride,
> He hangs between; in doubt to act, or rest:
> In doubt to deem himself a God, or Beast.[4]

Understandably, the beings between man and God on the Great Scale received less attention than man himself and the beings below him. It was essential that the various ranks of heavenly beings be posited, however, if man was to retain his traditionally dual nature. It was this necessity which in 1728 led Benjamin Franklin (then in

3. Tyson, *Orang-Outang,* 55.
4. Alexander Pope, *An Essay on Man* (1732–34), Epistle II, lines 3–8; see also I, 173–294, II, 1–18, III, 1–26, 109–18. The standard work is Arthur O. Lovejoy, *The Great Chain of Being; A Study of the History of an Idea* . . . (Cambridge, Mass., 1936); see also Eustace M. W. Tillyard, *The Elizabethan World Picture* (London, 1943).

a period of youthful theological instability but never a man to daydream about archangels) to declare that "I believe that Man is not the most perfect Being but One, rather that as there are many Degrees of Beings his Inferiors, so there are many Degrees of Beings superior to him." [5] Considered in the long term, reiterated simultaneous assertions of human arrogance and humility were precisely what one would expect to characterize the centuries of transition between helpless Faith and all-mastering Technology: "for man is of a middle between the beasts and Angels, transcending the one, and yet not worthy to equalize the other." [6]

As these formulations suggest, the "idea" of the Chain functioned at several levels of thought. To summarize baldly for the moment: it served to dramatize the Christian view of man as a creature with a divine soul; it served to formulate men's vague sense of the beast within themselves and their capacity for rising above bestiality; it served to satisfy the eighteenth century's ravenous appetite for hierarchical principles in the face of social upheaval; and it served as a powerful means of organizing the facts of the natural world. As should become plain in this and later discussions, no one of these functions was unrelated to any other.

As a means of conceptualizing the differences among the creatures of the natural world, the Great Chain of Being differed appreciably from the method forged by Linnaeus. It was one thing to classify all living creation and altogether another to arrange it in a single great hierarchy; and when Linnaeus undertook the first of these tasks he was not thereby forced to attempt the latter. In the many editions of the *Systema Naturae* he duly cataloged the various kinds of men, yet never in a hierarchic manner. In 1758 his arrangement of "Homo" was as follows:

Sapiens.—1. H. diurnus; *varying by culture, situation.*
Wild Man four-footed, mute, hairy. . . .
American. a. red, choleric, erect.
  Hair black, straight and thick; *Nostrils* wide; *Face* freckled; *Beard* scanty. *Obstinate,* content, free. *Paints* himself with fine red lines. *Regulated* by habit.
European. β. white, sanguine, brawny.

5. From his MS. "Articles of Belief and Acts of Religion," in Labaree *et al.,* eds., *Papers of Franklin,* I, 102. For the same idea, John Locke, *An Essay Concerning Human Understanding* (1690), bk. 3, chap. 6, sec. 12. The edition used in this chapter is, 2 vols. in 1 (London, 1721). The common belief in superior beings in "other worlds" was in part a function of this necessity.
6. John Swan, *Speculum Mundi or a Glasse Representing the Face of the World* . . . (Cambridge, Eng., 1635), 428.

Hair abundantly flowing. *Eyes* blue. *Gentle,* acute, inventive. *Covered* with close vestments. *Governed* by customs.

Asiatic. γ. yellow, melancholy, rigid.
 Hair black. *Eyes* dark. *Severe,* haughty, covetous. *Covered* with loose garments. *Governed* by opinions.

African. δ. black, phlegmatic, relaxed.
 Hair black, frizzled. *Skin* silky. *Nose,* flat. *Lips* tumid. *Women's* bosom a matter of modesty, *Breasts* give milk abundantly. *Crafty,* indolent, negligent. *Anoints* himself with grease. *Governed* by caprice.

Monstrosus. ε. by himself (*a*) by art (*b, c*).
 a. Alpine small, active, timid.
  Patagonian large, indolent.
 b. Single-testicled, so less fertile: Hottentots.
  Rush-like girls with narrowed stomach: in Europe.
 c. Long-headed, head conic: Chinese.
  Slant-headed, head compressed in front: Canadians.

Troglodytes 2. H. nocturnus.[7]

Linnaeus's categories were not hierarchical; they were merely confusing. Although his student, Hoppius, referred to the great distance which separated the cultivated European from Hottentots and wild boys, he referred also to lack of education in such savages and made no attempt to embed the differences among men in their physical characteristics. Certainly for both Linnaeus and Hoppius man was clearly a "higher" creation. They could scarcely think otherwise. The manner in which Linnaeus inaugurated his classification of all living things with "HOMO" and then "SIMIA" was suggestive of the principle of ranking, and although the four "anthropomorpha" which Hoppius discussed at length were not really ranked, Hoppius spoke of one as most "nearly related" to men and another the least so.[8] Thus while there were hints of ranking in the Linnaean approach, the concept of hierarchy was never really developed. It is of the greatest significance that Linnaeus seems never to have expounded the metaphysics of the Chain of Being and that he was able to employ the traditional phrase "one chain of universal being" in a manner which completely robbed it of its traditional meaning. "If we consider the generation of animals," he wrote in 1754, "we find that each produces an offspring after its own kind . . . so that all living things, plants, animals, and even mankind

7. Translated from the Latin, reprinted in Bendyshe, "History of Anthropology," 424–26.
8. Christianus Emmanuel Hoppius, "Anthropomorpha" (Upsaliae, 1760), in *Caroli Linnaei, Amoenitates Academicae,* 10 vols. (Leiden, 1749–90), VI, 63–76, which has interesting plates. I have followed Bendyshe's translation in his "History of Anthropology," 448–58.

themselves, form one chain of universal being from the beginning to the end of the world. Of all the species originally formed by the Deity, not one is destroyed." [9] This was not a hierarchic chain but a simple connective, running through time.

To find Linnaeus outside the tradition of the Great Chain of Being is actually far from surprising, since achievement of the primary goal of describing and classifying all species of life precluded the possibility of ranking them. To obtain criteria for ranking all creatures on a single scale was virtually impossible. In fact the Great Chain of Being could stand in its traditional form only if the myriad kinds of creation were not viewed in very specific terms. The concept of the Chain had always been in difficulty the moment men got down to cases. When natural philosophers tried to decide whether the ape, the parrot, or the elephant was next below man, for instance, the grand Chain began to look like an unprepossessing pile of ill-assorted links. If anyone ever got down to cases it was Linnaeus. Any sharp increase in detailed knowledge of the multitude of species was bound to make hierarchical construction impossible even for the most masterful craftsman. How was one going to rank thousands of species of plants in exact order? It seems clear that Linnaeus could not have utilized the hierarchic element in the traditional Chain of Being, except for the residual suggestion that men came first and apes were next to them. It is equally clear, too, that Linnaeus was under no temptation to rank the various kinds of men.[10]

The Linnaean approach passed on into modern anthropology by way of Johann Friedrich Blumenbach, the great physiologist and comparative anatomist who is often called the founder of anthropology. Although a great admirer of Linnaeus, Blumenbach rightly saw Linnaeus's categories to be crude and inadequate. While politely palliating these defects by pointing to the lack of information available to Linnaeus, Blumenbach deliberately undertook a major revision of the categories of men. In 1775, in the first edition of his *De Generis Humani Varietate Nativa* he described four varieties, then in 1781 five, and in 1795 introduced some badly needed precise terminology, including the inept but remarkably adhesive term *Caucasian*. In each of his enlarging editions Blumenbach came down hard on his major point: all men belonged to the same

9. Preface to *Museum Regis Adolphi Friderici* (Upsaliae, 1754), quoted in Bendyshe, "History of Anthropology," 435.
10. Cf. Oscar Handlin, *Race and Nationality in American Life* (Garden City, N. Y., 1957), chap. 4 ("The Linnaean Web"), especially pp. 57–59.

species, and his groupings were merely varieties. The differences among men, he insisted, were not nearly so great as those which separated men from apes. Far from framing this point in religious terms, Blumenbach approached men and simians physiologically, scrupulously examining in turn such chacteristics as stature, carriage, skull, hair, skin color, and so on. In most or all of these respects, he concluded, the varieties of men differed from each other, yet still more from the apes. Nonetheless, Blumenbach was not without his preferences, for he argued that the original type of man was Caucasian. Yet at this critical juncture he made no attempt to seize the obvious opportunity for constructing a hierarchy of variations; he explained that mankind diverged "in both directions into two, most remote and very different from each other; on the one side, namely, into the Ethiopian, and on the other into the Mongolian." He went on to place "the American [Indian] between the Caucasian and Mongolian; the Malay between the same Caucasian and Ethiopian." [11] The white man was the "primeval" type and stood at the center; but there was no indication that he was on top.

While Linnaeus and Blumenbach were able to impose order without hierarchy, many natural philosophers were tempted by the synthesizing power of the Great Chain of Being. Clearly mankind was formed not in one image but in many. Clearly men were not equal in energy, talent, manner, and elegance of form. If all other created beings were ranked upon a grand scale, why not man? Could it be that the Creator had graded mankind from its noblest specimens to its most brutal savages? The possibilities were there for any European who paused to compare his own society with the newly discovered ones overseas.

The Chain of Being was a powerful means of comprehending the distinctions which Europeans saw. It was entirely possible, however, to derive satisfaction from the idea of hierarchy as applied to men without having need or thought of degrading any individual or group. The Swiss naturalist Charles Bonnet, for instance, who distinguished himself in 1763 by actually working the "ÉCHELLE des etres naturels" into pictorial form, announced happily that "there is a prodigious number of continued links between the most perfect man and the ape." He went on to contrast the men of various European nations with the Africans, Hurons, and Hottentots; but

---

11. *On the Natural Variety of Mankind* (1795), in Bendyshe, trans. and ed., *Treatises of Blumenbach*, 264–65, and for his remarks on Linnaeus, 150–53. Bendyshe translates portions of the 1781 edition and the 1775 and 1795 editions in entirety.

he referred also to the gradations between *individual* men. Compare Newton, he said, with a Scottish peasant. Compare indeed! Obviously Bonnet's use of the Chain was characterized more by love for a philosophical construct than by intellectual precision.[12] A similar capitulation of intellect to impulse was apparent in a disquisition "On the Chain of Universal Being" written in mid-century by Soame Jenyns, the English author and politician. "In the same manner" that vegetable life blends into animal, Jenyns declared as if merely acceding to reality, "this animal life rises from this low beginning in the shell-fish, through innumerable species of insects, fishes, birds, and beasts to the confines of reason, where, in the dog, the monkey, and chimpanzè it unites so closely with the lowest degree of that quality in man, that they cannot easily be distinguished from each other. From this lowest degree in the brutal Hottentot, reason, with the assistance of learning and science, advances, through the various stages of human understanding, which rise above each other, till in a Bacon or a Newton it attains the summit." [13]

This confusion whether the Chain was to be applied to groups of men or to individuals was symptomatic of the vagueness of the concept and of its function as a mystical, almost allegoric, cosmology. If both individuals *and* groups were to be ranked, it was going to be necessary to say that the Indian and African kings (who occasionally showed up in London) occupied a lower rank than the most cloddish Scottish peasant. Given eighteenth-century admiration for royalty, this was simply not a possibility. If the concept of the Chain was going to be applied with any exactitude, moreover, some single criterion for ranking was essential. While Isaac Newton might easily be conceded to be the most intelligent of men, he was not necessarily nor actually the most handsome.

What happened, almost inevitably, was that the ranks of men came increasingly to be conceived in terms of physiognomy. Sir William Petty, one of the founders of the Royal Society in mid-seventeenth century, was the first to emphasize the gradation among groups of men on the basis of physical distinctions. Though there existed "those differences between [individual] Man and man," Petty wrote thoughtfully,

12. C[harles] Bonnet, *The Contemplation of Nature*, 2 vols. (London, 1766), 68ff.; *Oeuvres d'Histoire Naturelle et de Philosophie de Charles Bonnet . . .* , 8 vols. (Neuchatel, 1779–83) , especially I, xxxiii, IV, 1.
13. Soame Jenyns, "Disquisitions on Several Subjects; Disquisition I: On the Chain of Universal Being," *The Works of Soame Jenyns . . .* , 2 vols. (Dublin, 1790) , II, 133.

there bee others more considerable, that is, between the Guiny Negroes and the Middle Europeans; and of Negros between those of Guiny and those who live about the Cape of Good Hope [the Hottentots], which last are the Most beastlike of all the Souls [? Sorts] of Men with whom our Travellers are well acquainted. I say that the Europeans do not onely differ from the aforementioned Africans in Collour, which is as much as white differs from black, but also in their Haire . . . [and] in the shape of their Noses, Lipps and cheek bones, as also in the very outline of their faces and the Mould of their skulls. They differ also in their Naturall Manners, and in the internall Qualities of their Minds.[14]

Petty was undecided which animal was next below man on the great scale; on the basis of appearance, the ape nearest resembled man, and on basis of voice, the parrot. But the elephant possessed the greatest intellectual capacities of any animal, and Petty was inclined to award the elephant the rank just below man, though he conceded that most writers preferred the ape. Despite this indirect confession of his inability to arrange even a handful of creatures on the scale and despite his preference for intelligence as the criterion for ranking, Petty's discussion of the ranks of men was prophetic of developments in the eighteenth century. For in explaining the vast differences among men, Petty had chosen Europeans and Negroes as representing the extremities of diversity and had based this decision primarily on physiognomic traits. Only after he had finished with the Negro's features was he able to tack on an inherently different temperament and mind. As men turned more and more toward regarding themselves as natural creatures, analysis of physiognomic and eventually anatomical traits became the only logical method of determining who ranked where on Nature's scale. Edward Tyson's dissection of a chimpanzee showed the way. In mid-century the renowned Comte de Buffon flirted with the idea that the elephant's intelligence placed him next to man and then joined the almost universal consensus that the creature most like man was the ape.[15] The work of the Dutch anatomist Peter Camper in the 1770's finally showed where the ideal of hierarchy was leading. It was Camper who pioneered the idea of the "facial angle" (roughly, a measure of prognathism) and who found in his collection of skulls a regular gradation from apes, through Negroes, to Europeans. "It is amusing to contemplate," he wrote, "an arrangement of these [skulls], placed

14. Henry W. Lansdowne, ed., *The Petty Papers; Some Unpublished Writings of Sir William Petty*, 2 vols. (London, 1927), II, 31. The "[? Sorts]" is the editor's.

15. Georges [Louis Leclerc, Comte de] Buffon, *Natural History, General and Particular . . .* , trans. William Smellie, 9 vols. (London, 1781–85) , VI, 1–2, VIII, 64ff.

in a regular succession: apes, orangs, negroes, the skull of an Hottentot, Madagascar, Celebese, Chinese, Moguller, Calmuck, and divers
Europeans. It was in this manner that I arranged them upon a shelf
in my cabinet." [16] In the long run, this sort of laboratory pastime
was more than amusing.

In the even longer run, however, this application of the principle
of gradation to the facts of anatomy was bound to collapse of its
own weight. When examined rigorously the anatomical differences
among men (both fossilized and living) simply cannot be forced
into a single continuum. If, for example, amount of hair had been
chosen as the criterion of ranking, the Negro would have come out
on top, the Indian in the middle, and the white man at the bottom,
next to the ape. It is clear that when Europeans set about to rank
the varieties of men, their decision that the Negro was at the bottom
and the white man at the top was not dictated solely by the facts of
human biology.

While it is easy to see why the European was firmly seated at the
top, it is less obvious why Negroes, of all the world's peoples, should
have been relegated to the bottom. Several ways of thinking about
the world's savage nations were in operation all at once. Color was
one means by which people overseas could be categorized, but there
were others. Drawing upon a classical tradition, Europeans tended
to regard savagery as a function of extreme temperatures. By this
logic the cold-ridden natives of Lapland and Nova Zembla were as
radically different from civilized Europeans as were the blacks of
tropical Guinea. At the same time Europeans were not blind to
observable distinctions among the societies they discovered; on the
basis of direct observation in the field they usually decided that the
Hottentots were the most appallingly barbarous of men, though
other peoples were darker and lived in worse climates. Sometimes
the peoples of the polar regions were chosen to share honors with
the Hottentots,[17] and this lack of unanimity in itself suggests that
several standards were being used and that Europeans were driven
more by need to select *some* lowest man than by the available facts
of anthropology. If the question of savagery had come to a vote,
however, the Hottentot would have won the prize by a wide margin.

16. T. Cogan, trans., *The Works of the Late Professor Camper, on the
Connexion between the Science of Anatomy and the Arts of Drawing, Painting,
Statuary* . . . (London, 1794) , 50, see also p. 9 and *passim*.
    17. Buffon, *Natural History*, III, 57–64, VIII, 64ff.; Voltaire quoted in Margaret
Sherwood Libby, *The Attitude of Voltaire to Magic and the Sciences* (N. Y.,
1935) , 202; Charleston *S.-C. Gaz.*, Aug. 12, 1732.

Linnaeus even mulled over the possibility that the Hottentots were not men but apes, though he rejected the idea.[18]

Although the Hottentot was generally regarded as more bestial than the Negro, Europeans often associated the two, probably in large part because of geographical proximity and a certain affinity in appearance. John Ovington's *Voyage to Suratt, in the Year 1689,* one of the most accurate early accounts of the Hottentots, was revelatory of this tendency. Ovington thought that "of all People they are the most Bestial and sordid" and that "they are the very Reverse of Human kind . . . so that if there's any medium between a Rational Animal and a Beast, the *Hotantot* lays the fairest Claim to that Species." His description of the Negroes of West Africa was not nearly so unflattering, yet in contrasting the appearance of the two groups he was definite on their affinity. The Hottentots, he wrote, "are more Tawny than the *Indians* [of India], and in Colour and Features come nearest the *Negroes* of any People, only they are not quite so Black, nor is their Cottony Hair so Crisp, nor their Noses altogether so flat." [19] Classifiers like Blumenbach usually treated the Hottentot as a particularly bestial off-brand of Negro. In this sense, then, the West African "true Negro" was the unlucky victim of a casually conceived association with a people who were, measured by the standards of modern anthropology, probably the most primitive of all the aborgines well known to Europeans prior to the second half of the eighteenth century.

Despite this association, Hottentots ordinarily were not slaves to Europeans, and Negroes were. Here, surely, was a crucial factor making for the burial of the Negro at the bottom of mankind. Though other peoples, most notably the Indians, were enslaved by Europeans, slavery was typically a Negro-white relationship. This fact in itself inevitably meant that the Negro would not be accorded a high place when Europeans set about arranging the varieties of men on a grand scale. No one thought of the Great Chain of Being as originating in differences in power or social status between human groups; to do so would have been to blaspheme the Creator. However, this did not prevent the idea of the Chain of Being from being applied to social relationships, and a historian of Jamaica was able to employ the rhetoric of the Chain in discoursing on proper social distinctions in the island without the slightest sense of incon-

18. In a note in the 10th (1758) edition of *Systema Naturae*, quoted in Bendyshe, "History of Anthropology," 429.

19. Ovington, *Voyage to Suratt,* ed. Rawlinson, 284–89, and for Negroes, 28–56. Originally published [London, 1696].

gruity. Like most West Indians, Edward Long thought that mulattoes should be held in higher esteem than the blacks, "above whom (in point of due policy) they ought to hold some degree of distinction. They would then form the centre of connexion between the two extremes, producing a regular establishment of three ranks of men, dependent on each other, and rising in a proper climax of subordination, in which the Whites would hold the highest place." [20]

As this passage suggests, the popularity of the concept of the Chain in the eighteenth century derived in large measure from its capacity to universalize the principle of hierarchy. It was no accident that the Chain of Being should have been most popular at a time when the hierarchical arrangement of society was coming to be challenged. No "idea," no matter how abstract or intricately structured, exists in isolation from the society in which it flourishes.

2. NEGROES, APES, AND BEASTS

It is equally a truism that an "idea" such as the Chain of Being can exert enormous leverage on social relationships and the way in which they are perceived. One of the most important and enduring influences of the concept of the Chain was its principle of continuity, a principle which operated particularly to emphasize the close affinity of men with beasts. It was virtually impossible, in fact, to discuss gradations of men without stressing the closeness of the lowest men to the highest animals. Because the principle of continuity ran counter to the Christian emphasis on the uniqueness of man, moreover, proponents of the Chain were driven to especially strenuous defense of this affinity. They hammered away to prove that the Chain's weakest conceptual link was, after all, as strong as any other. In 1713, for instance, the prominent physician Sir Richard Blackmore elaborated the "surprizing and delightful" principle of continuity in this way:

As Man, who approaches nearest to the lowest Class of Celestial Spirits (for we may justly suppose a Subordination in that excellent Order) being half Body and half Spirit, becomes the *Æquator,* that divides in the Middle the whole Creation, and distinguishes the Corporeal from the Invisible Intellectual World; so the Ape or Monkey, that bears the greatest Similitude to Man, is the next Order of Animals below him. Nor is the Disagreement between the basest Individuals of our Species and the Ape or

20. [Long], *Jamaica,* II, 333. Cf. "On the Use and Abuse of Negro Slaves," *New American Magazine,* 2 (1760), 25.

Monkey so great, but that were the latter endow'd with the Faculty of Speech, they might perhaps as justly claim the Rank and Dignity of the human Race, as the Salvage *Hotentot,* or stupid Native of *Nova Zembla.*[21]

Plainly any elaboration of the Chain of Being was going to associate some group of human beings with the ape.

By sheer accident, an appalling one in retrospect, Negroes and apes had already been linked together. European explorers had stumbled across Negroes and the most man-like of the apes simultaneously. The tendency to associate the two flowed in part from certain presuppositions which underlay the idea of the Chain of Being, but the careful exposition and popularity of that idea came more than a half-century after the tales about Negroes and apes began cropping up in the accounts of European travelers. Of course the relationship between the travelers' tales and the concept of the Chain was reciprocal: the "fact" that Negroes and apes sometimes had "a beastly copulation or conjuncture" served to demonstrate the affinity of men and beasts; conversely, the Chain of Being was an admirable way of explaining this "fact." The chance tales of travelers interlocked with the concept of the Chain of Being to transform the fortuitous geographical proximity of Negroes and apes into an association of cosmic significance. Almost certainly that fortuitous proximity played a crucial role in shaping the eighteenth century's consensus that on the Great Scale of Beings the place just above the ape was occupied by the Negro.

This consensus was as frequently revealed by denial as by affirmation, for the implications of the association of the Negro with the ape were profoundly disturbing to faithful Christians and men of good will. As early as 1680 the Reverend Morgan Godwyn announced that a "disingenuous and unmanly *Position* hath been formed; and privately (*and as it were in the dark*) handed to and again, which is this, That the *Negro's,* though in their Figure they carry some resemblances of Manhood, yet are indeed *no Men.*" From Godwyn's Christian point of view, Negroes were men because they possessed rationality and particularly a soul, but he was happy to buttress his argument by reference to physical features. Negroes were men and nothing else, Godwyn declared, and "the consideration of the shape and figure of our *Negro's* Bodies, their Limbs and Members; their Voice and Countenance, in all things according with other Mens; together with their *Risibility* and *Discourse*

21. [Richard Blackmore], *The Lay-Monastery. Consisting of Essays, Discourses, &c. Published Singly under the Title of Lay-Monk,* 2d ed. (London, 1714), no. 5, pp. 28–29.

(Man's *peculiar* Faculties) should be a sufficient Conviction." [22] Blumenbach, looking at Negroes from a very different standpoint a century later, roundly denounced those who claimed that the Negro was closer to the ape than other men. By the latter part of the eighteenth century the association had achieved such currency that Johann Gottfried von Herder felt called upon to announce that the Indian and the Negro were the European's brothers and the ape was not.[23] Even many of the natural philosophers who were attracted by the systematizing powers of the Great Chain became wary of the conclusions which might be drawn from the elaboration of a human hierarchy based on physical features. Peter Camper, gazing upon his "amusing" arrangement of skulls (in which a Negro's stood next to an orang-outang's), emphatically denied that this proximity implied any inferiority in the Negro. Just what it did imply, Camper did not say. To call the Negro a man and the ape a beast was in effect to shatter the Great Chain, though adherents of that concept could never admit it. It was impossible for scientists not to sense an enormous gulf between man, who was rational and immortal, and an ape, who was neither. Buffon, in his enormously popular *Histoire Naturelle*, acknowledged the difficulty in separating men from apes but concluded (using the Hottentot and the orang-outang for illustration) that the faculties of thought and speech and the possession of a soul did indeed make a great separation between the two. It was ominous, however, that when discussing the orang-outang, he could not resist calling Negroes "almost equally wild, and as ugly as these apes." [24]

It was in such half-hedged similes as Buffon's that the strains operating within the Negro-ape connection showed themselves. The importance of recognizing these strains has been heightened by frequent assertions in the twentieth century that white men in the eighteenth thought Negroes were beasts, for these assertions are incorrect, and they are obtuse to eighteenth-century assumptions about the nature of man. Everyone knew—then—that man possessed a soul and rationality. By these twin criteria even the wisest elephant and the most eloquent parrot failed admission to humankind. Virtually everyone knew, moreover, that by these criteria

22. Godwyn, *Negro's and Indians Advocate*, 3, 13. He devoted the entire first chapter to this fundamental point. His book was aimed primarily at the West Indies and has frequently been read too literally.

23. Blumenbach, *Natural Variety* (1795), 271; Herder quoted in Arthur Lovejoy, "Some Eighteenth Century Evolutionists," *Popular Science Monthly*, 65 (1904), 335.

24. Buffon, *Natural History*, VIII, 39–132, also III, 208–300.

Negroes were men. It seems very likely that the handful of assertions to the contrary were not advanced seriously. The Christian tradition created a rock-hard shelf below which the Negro could not fall. In the seventeenth century Sir Thomas Herbert, a traveler, author, and royalist hanger-on, tried to hammer his way through the barrier and succeeded only in reaching a position of absurd unorthodoxy. Herbert decided that Negroes might really stand midway between men and beasts: "Now what Philosophers alledge concerning the function of the Soul may be made applicable to these Animals [the Negroes], that the Soul of Man is gradually differenced from the Souls of Beasts." [25] This was not only heretical; it was nonsense.

It was not the ridiculous assertions of the Herberts but rather the protests of the friends of the Negro in the plantations which fully revealed the strains at work. Beginning about the time of Morgan Godwyn's *The Negro's and Indians Advocate* (1680), men interested in converting Negroes and alleviating the brutality of slavery began to advance the charge that the planters thought their slaves were beasts.[26] Usually the accusation was shaped in the simile that the planters regarded and treated their slaves *like* beasts or *as* other men did their cattle. Given the character of slavery, these advocates may be excused some exaggeration. What they *were* saying, in fact, was that the planters were neither treating nor regarding their slaves as human beings ought to be treated and regarded, which was perfectly true. The charge that planters treated Negroes like beasts was particularly effective precisely because the idea that any creatures so obviously human were regarded as animals was profoundly shocking in an age which drew a broad, clear line between men and all other living creatures. The charge represented a shorthand method for making the point that the Negro was being treated as if he had no soul; sometimes, indeed, this indictment was made ex-

---

25. Herbert, *Some Years Travels,* 18.
26. For a sampling of these charges, Godwyn, *Negro's and Indians Advocate;* Baxter, *Christian Directory,* 558; Davies, *Duty of Christians,* 26; Klingberg, ed., *Carolina Chronicle of Le Jau,* 55; William Gooch to Edmund Gibson (Bishop of London), Williamsburg, May 28, 1731, Brydon, ed., "Gooch's Letters," *Va. Mag. of Hist. and Biog.,* 32 (1924), 323; Pennington, "Thomas Bray's Associates," Amer. Antiq. Soc., *Proceedings,* New Ser., 48 (1938), 382; *Letter from a Merchant at Jamaica,* 4; *Three Letters from G. Whitefield,* 13; Levi Hart, *Liberty Described and Recommended; in a Sermon, Preached to the Corporation of Freemen in Farmington . . .* (Hartford, 1775), 17–18; [Crèvecoeur], *Letters from an American Farmer,* 217; and for the same *re* white servants, Carl T. Eben, trans., *Gottleib Mittelberger's Journey to Pennsylvania in the Year 1750 and Return to Germany in the Year 1754 . . .* (Phila., 1898), 27, 39–40.

plicitly.[27] Of the same order, until later in the century, was the accusation that the planters considered their Negroes "another Species." [28] All these protests represented humanitarianism's and particularly Christianity's recognition that the degradation of men in this world had gone too far.

This recognition was accorded to a very real, not an imaginary situation. American colonials no more thought Negroes were beasts than did European scientists and missionaries; if they had *really* thought so they would have sternly punished miscegenation for what it would have been—buggery. Yet the charge that white men treated Negroes as beasts was entirely justified if not taken literally. Equalitarian defenders of the Negro were laying bare an inherent tendency of slavery with the only terms they knew how to employ. It was recognition of this tendency which moved Samuel Sewall to try (unsuccessfully) "to prevent Indians and Negros being Rated with Horses and Hogs" by the Massachusetts legislature.[29] Chattel slavery in America *did* lead to a mode of thinking about the basest members of society which in its emphasis was novel in Western culture. Certain aspects of the revolutionary new racial slavery pushed the colonists toward thinking about their Negroes as primarily and merely physical creatures.

The bestial characteristics of Negroes which had been duly recorded in the English accounts of West Africa did not go unnoticed when Negroes began pouring into the plantations: "The most of them," Richard Ligon wrote of the slaves in Barbados in 1657, "are as neer beasts as may be, setting their souls aside." The Negro's initial barbarity was highlighted by the problem of slave control in the colonies where the Negroes' "Barbarous, Wild, and Savage Natures" took on an immediate and practical importance.[30] The urge to rebellion, however, was an undeniably human attribute; cattle did not ordinarily conspire to kill their owners and fire the

27. Humphreys, *Endeavours by the S.P.G. in New York*, 5, 8; Mather, *Negro Christianized*, 23; *The Athenian Oracle: Being an Entire Collection of All the Valuable Questions and Answers in the Old Athenian Mercuries . . .* , 4 vols. (London, 1703–?) , II, 462; [Hewat], *Account of S. C. and Ga.*, II, 101.

28. [Tryon], *Friendly Advice*, 88; the S.P.G. Anniversary Sermon (1732) in Luce and Jessop, eds., *Works of George Berkeley*, VII, 122; *American Magazine and Historical Chronicle*, 3 (1746) , 80; "On the Use and Abuse of Negro Slaves," *New American Magazine*, 2 (1760) , 25; Andrew Burnaby, *Travels through the Middle Settlements in North-America, in the Years 1759 and 1760 . . .* (London, 1775) , 18.

29. *Diary of Sewall*, III, 87.

30. Ligon, *True History of Barbadoes*, 47; *Acts Barbadoes* (1721) , 137; see also Frank J. Klingberg, ed., "As to the State of Jamaica in 1707," *Jour. Negro Hist.*, 27 (1942) , 291–92.

town. It was especially the day-to-day business of commercial slavery which placed a premium on the Negro's purely physical qualities. New slaves off the ships were described as "well-fleshed," "strong-limbed," "lusty," "sickly," "robust," "healthy," "scrawny," "unblemished." [31] In South Carolina, Georgia, and the West Indies, slaves were sometimes branded by their owners with a hot iron, usually with the owner's initials.[32] (Advertisements revelatory of this practice in South Carolina became much less frequent after about 1740: perhaps most of the branding stopped or perhaps owners became reluctant to admit their business-like practice publicly.) The everyday buying and selling and deeding and trading of slaves underscored the fact that Negroes, just like horses, were walking pieces of property: the Leeward Islands provided public compensation for "all Damage or Hurt, that shall happen to any Slave or Beast imployed on the Highways" and the governor of Grenada appointed a "Superintendant of all the Negroes and Mules or Horses which are furnished for His Majesty's Service in this Island." [33] Then, too, the discouragingly expensive mortality among the Negroes, especially in the West Indies and also in the rice swamps of South Carolina,[34] tended to make Negroes seem almost nonhuman. Even in an age thoroughly accustomed to the hovering omnipresence of early death, the enormous toll of Negro life must have caused many white men to withdraw in silent horror, to refuse to admit identity with a people they were methodically slaughtering year after year. The cruelties of slavery inevitably produced a sense of disassociation. To the horrified witness of a scene of torture, the victim becomes a "poor devil," a "mangled creature." He is no longer a man. He can no longer be human because to credit him with one's own human attributes would be too horrible.[35]

31. Donnan, ed., *Documents Slave Trade, passim.*

32. Charleston *S.-C. Gaz.*, May 25, June 22, 1734, Mar. 5, 19, 26, Nov. 5, 1737, Feb. 9, Mar. 30, Dec. 21, 1738, May 7, 1753, May 19, 1759; Candler, comp., *Col. Recs. Ga.*, XVIII, 120; Frank J. Klingberg, "British Humanitarianism at Codrington," *Jour. Negro Hist.*, 23 (1938), 463–64; Edwards, *History of British West Indies*, II, 154n.

33. *Acts Charibbee Leeward Islands*, 226; William L. Leyborne, Governor of Granada, Proclamations (1771–1776), West Indies, 50, N. Y. Pub. Lib. Also Savannah *Ga. Gaz.*, May 30, 1765.

34. Charleston *S.-C. Gaz.*, July 21, 1733; Anthony Stokes, *A View of the Constitution of the British Colonies . . .* (London, 1783), 414–15; Smyth, *Tour in the United States*, I, 205; Schoepf, *Travels in the Confederation*, trans. and ed. Morrison, II, 220. In this respect the West Indies were notorious: see the comparison with Virginia in [Edmund Burke], *An Account of the European Settlements in America . . .* , 2 vols. (London, 1757), II, 210.

35. Instances are in [Schaw], *Journal of a Lady of Quality*, eds. Andrews, 127; *Archives Md.*, XLI, 205.

It was easy enough, then, for white men to slip into a mode of thinking about the Negro which operated with a vocabulary and imagery which had previously been confined to thought about the beasts that perished. Even a gentlewoman traveling through the back settlements of Connecticut in 1704 could slip into complaining about the "too great familiarity" accorded Negroes by the white inhabitants who allowed Negroes "to sit at Table and eat with them, (as they say to save time,) and into the dish goes the black hoof as freely as the white hand." [36]

Yet it is just as significant that some humble folk in the villages of Connecticut were undisturbed by Negroes fishing around in the common supper dish. Even in the plantations, the Negro walked and hoed and talked and propagated like other men. No matter how much slavery degraded the Negro, every daily event in the lives and relationships of Negroes and white men indicated undeniably that the Negro was a human being. White man feared their slaves' desires for freedom, they talked with their Negroes, and they slept with them. These were human relationships, continually driving home the common humanity of all.

3. RATIONAL SCIENCE AND IRRATIONAL LOGIC

The unremitting pressure generated by social contact worked with religious doctrine and conscious benevolence to separate Negroes from beasts. In addition, certain scientific beliefs of the eighteenth century strongly supported the assumption that there was a pronounced dividing line between men and animals. Though there were many doubters, especially before mid-century, *species* were generally regarded as fixed in number and in kind— stable, that is, through time. This conception of species had been enshrined by the early pronouncements of Linnaeus: *Nullae species novae,* there existed now as many species as God had created in the beginning. Individual species did not vary beyond distinctly defined limits, else how could one species be distinguished from another? It was generally agreed also that the best test of species was interfertility. If union between two creatures could produce fertile offspring, then those two creatures belonged to the same species. The mule, the unfertile progeny of the horse and the ass, served as the most

36. Sarah Kemble Knight, *The Journal of Madam Knight,* ed. George Parker Winship (N. Y., 1935), 38.

popular illustration. Any variations of kind within a species were just that, *varieties* and not species.[37]

This scientific framework formed an effective counter to the tendency to associate Negroes with beasts. No matter what the Negro appeared to be, no matter how bestial and prognathous, the Negro belonged to the species of man. There was no doubt that he could mate with other varieties of mankind and that the off-spring were themselves fertile: a multitude of reports from the international ethnological laboratory in America provided irrefutable proof.

Yet there were three weak strands in this rope which bound the Negro with the rest of mankind, and their intertwining left the Negro in a precarious position. In the first place, the conceptualism propounded by John Locke tended to transform "species" from real categories existing in nature into subjective and almost inconvenient categories imposed by the mind: *"the Boundaries of the Species, whereby Men sort them, are made by Men."* [38] This conceptualism powerfully reinforced the principle of continuity and found its way into the thought of many naturalists, notably Buffon, who wavered on the objective reality of species. Secondly, some natural philosophers were not convinced of the stability of species; various experiments with hybridization raised the distinct possibility, even probability, that two species could be crossed to produce a third which would in turn be fertile. Finally, it was not completely certain that the Negro was unable to breed with the ape or that the Negro had not sprung from some mixture with that animal. The reports from Africa had done their work.

One interrelationship between these strands of thought may be illustrated by Locke's casual use of hybridization in the anthropoid order to support his conceptualistic destruction of "species": "And I imagine, none of the Definitions of the Word *Man*, which we yet have, nor Descriptions of that sort of Animal, are so perfect and exact, as to satisfy a considerate inquisitive Person; much less to obtain a general Consent, and to be that which Men would every where stick by, in the Decision of Cases, and determining of Life and Death, Baptism and no Baptism, in Productions that might

37. Of the many discussions, perhaps the best introduction is Bentley Glass, Oswei Temkin, and William L. Straus, Jr., eds., *Forerunners of Darwin, 1745–1859* (Baltimore, 1959). A third term, *genera*, was more vaguely and less often used to describe groups of species.

38. Locke, *Human Understanding*, bk. 3, chap. 6.

happen." [39] The key interrelationship with these strands of thought, however, was between hybridization of supposedly real species and the myth of the Negro-ape connection. It became most apparent in the poignantly expressed doubts of Linnaeus when in the 1750's he came to realize that hybridization of species actually occurred. Originally a firm advocate of the fixity of species, Linnaeus was able to accept a hybrid plant in his own garden without alarm. Applied to higher animals, however, the notion of hybridization was little short of appalling to a man who was as good a Christian as he was a scientist. "It is said," he wrote with heartfelt caution in his *Metamorphosis Plantarum* (1755), "that Réaumur caused a rabbit to fertilize a hen. The eggs produced chickens which were exactly like ordinary fowls except that they were covered, not with feathers, but with fine hair. This experiment is admittedly relevant up to a point, but we dare not draw any general conclusion from such cases. The most frightful conclusions could in fact be drawn from this; as far as mankind is concerned one would have reason to think that the Moors [i.e., the Negroes] had a rather strange origin—something that I for my part, however, am unwilling to ascribe to them." [40] No wonder Linnaeus backed away. Abandonment of the fixity of species had led him toward what were, in fact, "the most frightful conclusions."

Linnaeus's choice of the Negro to illustrate how frightful the conclusions might be was in itself frightening. That he chose the Negro from all the peoples of the globe revealed how widespread the association of the Negro with the ape had become. The casual tales of credulous travelers, originally calculated for titillating equally credulous readers at home, had become thoroughly cemented into Western thought. Linnaeus was not alone. Even without hybridization in mind, some natural philosophers accepted the idea. The normally sensible Buffon casually referred to the orangoutang as "equally ardent for women as for its own females" and to Negresses who had forced or voluntary intercourse with apes. [41] Lord Monboddo, an eccentric Scot who made something of a name for himself by contending that apes could speak and were actually a variety of men, airily announced that orang-outangs copulated with human females and almost certainly fathered offspring in this man-

39. *Ibid.*, bk. 3, chap. 6, sec. 27. See the intriguing novel: Vercors [pseud.], *You Shall Know Them*, trans. Rita Barisse (Boston, 1953).

40. Quoted in Knut Hagberg, *Carl Linnaeus*, trans. Alan Blair (London, 1952), 199. Hagberg correctly indicates that "Moors" meant Negroes.

41. Buffon, *Natural History*, VIII, 40, 66; also Hoppius, "Anthropomorpha," as translated by Bendyshe, "History of Anthropology," 453.

ner. Monboddo clearly had no desire to degrade the Negro; he wanted merely to elevate the orang-outang. At no time did he suggest that *only* Negroes could have intercourse with apes; but, as it turned out, all his illustrations came from reports about Africa! [42]

The measure to which the association had filtered into the interstices of Western thinking became evident also in denials of physiographic affinity between apes and Negroes. As Peter Camper explained by way of refutation, "The striking resemblance between the race of Monkies and of Blacks, particularly upon a superficial view, has induced some philosophers to conjecture that the race of blacks originated from the commerce of the whites with orangs and pongos; or that these monsters, by gradual improvements, finally become men." [43] It is apparent, however unpalatable the apparency may be, that certain superficial physical characteristics in the West African Negro helped sustain (and perhaps helped initiate) the popular connection with the ape. By the latter part of the century, Bryan Edwards, a thoroughly good-hearted man, thought it necessary to discuss the apparent resemblance in the Ibo tribe.

I cannot help observing too, that the conformation of the face, in a great majority of them, very much resembles that of the baboon. I believe indeed there is, in most of the nations of Africa, a greater elongation of the lower jaw, than among the people of Europe; but this distinction I think is more visible among the Eboes, than in any other Africans. I mean not however to draw any conclusion of natural inferiority in these people to the rest of the human race, from a circumstance which perhaps is purely accidental, and no more to be considered as a proof of degradation than the red hair and high cheek bones of the Natives of the North of Europe.[44]

Once again, the Negro was the victim of a fortuitous circumstance: the white man's strange notion was furnished with a visual handle which was all too easy to seize with eagerness.

Considered from a different vantage point, the significance of the association of the Negro with the ape was its existence on a bewildering variety of levels of mental construction. At one ex-

42. James Burnett, Lord Monboddo, *Of the Origin and Progress of Language,* 6 vols. (Edinburgh, 1774–92), I, especially bk. 2, chaps. 3–5. Cf. James Lind, *An Essay on Diseases Incidental to Europeans in Hot Climates . . . ,* 3d ed. (London, 1777), 44n.

43. "Extracts from Henry Whistler's Journal," in Firth, ed., *The Narrative of General Venables,* 146; Cogan, trans., *Works of Camper,* 32. See also Camper's "De l'Orang-Outang, et de Quelques Autres Expèces de Singes," in H. J. Jansen, ed., *Oeuvres de Pierre Camper, Qui Ont pour Objet l'Histoire Naturelle, la Physiologie et l'Anatomie Comparée,* 3 vols. (Paris and Bordeaux, 1803), I, 1–196, which seems to have been printed originally in Amsterdam as *Natuurkundige Verhandeling over den Orang-Outang* in 1782 or possibly earlier.

44. Edwards, *History of British West Indies,* II, 89.

treme, it appeared in a technical treatise by Linnaeus, the pre-eminent naturalist of the eighteenth century. The old classical allusions were still alive: the Reverend Charles Woodmason exclaimed that "Africk never more abounded with New Monsters, than Pennsylvania does with New Sects." At a rather different level of formulation, it cropped up as a crude joke in 1734 when someone inserted an advertisement in the *South-Carolina Gazette* for a runaway baboon: "Whereas a stately *Baboon* hath lately slipp'd his Collar and run away; He is big-bon'd, full in Flesh, and has learn'd to walk very erect on his two Hind-Legs, he grins and chatters much, but will not bite, he plays Tricks impudently well, and is mightily given to clambering, whereby he often shews his A___. If any one finds him, or will send any news of him to _____ Office, in _____ street, shall be rewarded proportionably to the Merit of the Creature." [45] Still less (self-) conscious was a traveler's much earlier offhand observation in 1655 that the "genterey" of Barbados "have most of them 100 or 2 or 3 of slaves apes whou they command as they pleas." The sum of these remarks speaks for itself. No one thought that the Negro was an ape, but then there was always the old tale about . . . and so on.

The extraordinarily pervasive and enduring character of this notion was in itself an indication of the diverse functions it served. The notion had scientific value: it forged a crucial link in the Chain of Being and helped explain the Negro's and the ape's prognathism. On a less rational level the notion gave expression to men's half-conscious realization that they were linked to beasts and bestiality. And just as the concept of the Chain ordered every being on a vertical scale, the association of the Negro with the ape ordered men's deep, unconscious drives into a tightly controlled hierarchy. The association was usually conceived in sexual terms, no matter whether remarks about the physical resemblance between Negroes and apes were tacked on. The "beastly copulation" and "unnatural mixture" which described the association was vague in one sense and highly specific in another, despite and because of the utter lack of reliable reports about such conjunctures. The specific element in the association is profoundly revealing. The sexual union of apes and Negroes was *always* conceived as involving *female Negroes* and *male apes!* Apes had intercourse with Negro *women*. The aggressors were literally beasts; the sexual drive was conceived as thrusting

45. Hooker, ed., *The Carolina Backcountry*, 78; Charleston *S.-C. Gaz.*, May 4, 1734, quoted in entirety.

upwards from below. The Negro-ape association was an allegory of the nature of man.[46]

It was a good deal else too. The association functioned also as a means of expressing the social distance between the Negro and the white man. It was this function which was bound to appeal particularly to men with experience in America. Given any crisis over slavery, any sense that the white man's superiority was in danger, the association would be bound to attract the eye of men willing to go to the extreme, but before the Revolution the English colonists generally felt no need to expound or even mention the Negro-ape connection.

4. INDIANS, AFRICANS, AND THE COMPLEXION OF MAN

One important reason was that they were at work on a dual anthropological problem. Europeans living on both sides of the Atlantic were not equally interested in or knowledgeable about all the world's peoples, and their attention fastened particularly upon the two primitive peoples with whom they had most intimate contact. Indians and Negroes raised questions of a pressing nature, though of course the questions were not in both cases the same. By reason of their original geographical separation, their dissimilarity in culture and appearance, and the very different ways they had to be treated by advancing Europeans, the Indian and the Negro remained what they had been from the first—distinctively different intellectual problems. By very reason of their own intention to plant themselves in America, Englishmen had from the first been under pressure to describe the Indian's complexion in terms which would render the prospect of settlement in the New World an attractive one. One promotional sermon of 1610 claimed the favorable climate as one of the many reasons for planting in Virginia and went on to explain that although Virginia and Spain were on the same latitude the former was far more temperate. As evidence, an Indian brought from Virginia to England was cited: though he had gone naked most of his life his complexion "was so farre from a

46. A similar half-conscious conceptualization of sexuality may be seen in the remark of a virulently anti-Negro writer: "The lower class of women in *England,* are remarkably fond of the blacks, for reasons too brutal to mention; they would connect themselves with horses and asses, if the laws permitted them." [Edward Long], *Candid Reflections upon the Judgement Lately Awarded by the Court of King's Bench, in Westminster-Hall, on What Is Commonly Called the Negro-Cause, By a Planter* (London, 1772), 48–49.

Moores or East or West *Indians,* that it was little more blacke or tawnie, then one of ours would be if he should goe naked in the South of *England.* And to that experience added a better, namely of *our brethren in Virginea,* who some of them have been there many yeeres, and doe not complaine of any alteration caused by distemper of the Climate." [47]

The presence of the Indian in America posed the intriguing question of how he got there in the first place. No difficulty would have existed had it not been for the underlying assumption with which Europeans approached all the new peoples, that all men were descended from the original pair created by God. The Bible was equally explicit about Noah and his three sons, who served as inspiration for several attempts to classify all known peoples of the earth into three categories.[48] How, though, had any of Noah's descendants reached America? All other persons had been destroyed in the Flood, and the Ark had unquestionably landed in the Old World. It was a long swim to the New. The most widely accepted answer was the one accepted today: the Indian came from Asia. Natural philosophers reached this conclusion without knowing much about the Bering Straits or about Asiatics and Indians; they plumped for it because it seemed the best way out of the awkward situation arising from the premise of common parenthood. There were dissenters: some maintained that men had crossed from Europe by a northern route running through Greenland. A daring few came out for the thoroughly heretical idea that the Indians had sprung from an independent creation in the New World.[49] Whatever decision was made, however, the question which the Indian raised in European minds was that of his point of origin.

The Negro presented an entirely different puzzle. There was no difficulty over how he had arrived at his homeland in Africa, but there was a great deal of long-standing difficulty as to the cause of his peculiar appearance. In the eighteenth century the problem had

47. William Crashaw, *A Sermon Preached in London before the Right Honorable Lord Lawarre, Lord Governour and Captaine Generall of Virginea* . . . (London, 1610), fol. E2.

48. Jones, *Present State of Virginia,* ed. Morton, 49–52; Thomas Pownall, *The Administration of the Colonies,* 2d ed. (London, 1765), 155–56.

49. Notably Bernard Romans, *A Concise Natural History of East and West Florida* . . . (N. Y., 1775), 38; and Henry Homes, Lord Kames, *Sketches on the History of Man,* 2d ed., 4 vols. (Edinburgh, 1778), III, 134–44. See Justin Winsor, ed., *Narrative and Critical History of America,* 8 vols. (Boston and N. Y., 1884–89), I, 369–71; Allen, *The Legend of Noah,* 119–32; Barnard G. Sharrow, British Colonial Conceptions of American Indian Origins (unpubl. M.A. thesis, Columbia University, 1947); also Charleston *S.-C. Gaz.,* Aug. 11, Oct. 6, 1758.

become more pressing than previously because men were increasingly disposed to think of themselves as an integral part of the natural world of plants and animals. To some extent the riddle of complexion was posed by all the newly discovered peoples, but the Negro became the focal point of attempts at solution. He was nearer at hand than the Asian (and in Europe, though not in America, the Chinese were being lionized for purposes which had little to do with the cultivation of natural philosophy). His appearance was probably the most arresting of all, and without question his color was the most strikingly different from the white man's.

This contrast in color presented a handle by which natural philosophers could grasp the entire problem of physiognomic differences among men. The Negro's complexion seemed more important than the Indian's not only because the Indian was less dark but because with the Indian attention was focused primarily on the question of origin. Indeed both in Europe and America white men belittled the importance of the Indian's "tawny" complexion or used it merely as a foil for proving certain points about the Negro's blackness. Most writers, moreover, saw the Indian as naturally and innately lighter than he was in fact. Of the "five Sorts of Men," wrote the botanical systematist Richard Bradley in 1721, "the *White Men . . .* are *Europeans,* that have Beards; and a sort of *White Men* in *America* (as I am told) that only differ from us in having no *Beards.*" A Maryland promotional tract of 1666 set forth folk beliefs about the Indians which were still commonplace a century and a half later: "Their skins are naturally white, but altered from their originals by the several dyings of Roots and Barks, that they prepare and make useful to metamorphize their hydes into a dark Cinnamon brown. The hair of their head is black, long and harsh, but where Nature hath appointed the situation of it any where else, they divert it (by an antient custom) from its growth, by pulling it up hair by hair by the root in its primitive appearance." [50] There was little dissent to the commonplace assertion that the Indians' tawny color resulted wholly or in part from their custom of daubing themselves with bear grease, oils, or the like from a well-stocked cabinet of natural cosmetics.[51] When less

50. Bradley, *The Works of Nature,* 169, in Bendyshe, "History of Anthropology," 358–59; Alsop, *Character of Mary-land,* 59.

51. Purchas, *Hakluytus Posthumus,* XVIII, 325; Cook[e], *The Sot-weed Factor,* 8; Lawson, *Voyage to Carolina,* 171; Archdale, *New Description of Carolina,* 7; Brickell, *Natural History of N. C.,* 294–95; Mark Catesby, *The Natural History of Carolina, Florida and the Bahama Islands . . . ,* 2 vols. (London, 1731–43), II, viii; Eben, ed., *Gottlieb Mittelberger's Journey,* 83; [Michel G. St. Jean] de

fanciful explanations of the Indian's darkish color were advanced, they usually proved to be corollaries of conclusions already reached concerning the Negro. The eclectic Dutch author, Cornelis De Pauw, for instance, wrote an entire chapter on the color of the Indians in which the burden of his argument, and half the space of the chapter, was devoted to the color of Negroes.[52] White men seemed to want to sweep the problem of the Indian's color under the rug. The question of the color of man was pre-eminently the question of the color of the Negro.

During the seventeenth century there had been little progress on the scientific problem of the Negro's blackness, and the reigning mood at the beginning of the eighteenth century was one of puzzlement, eclecticism, and shotgun explanation. One popular writer disposed of the matter in the following illuminating manner:

Q. *What is the reason that some Men are black, some tawny, and some white, in the same Climate, as in* India?
A. We shall endeavour a satisfaction by shewing the diversity of Opinions about this matter, and by advancing an Hypothesis of our own, chargeable with as little absurdity as we can. Some have believed that *Cain's Mark* was black, and therefore his Successors Colour might be alter'd from what *Adam's* was, and so by new Marriages and Intermixtures, the World might be diversely coloured. Some say *Lot's* Daughters having, upon their flight from *Sodom,* an Idea of the Smoke and Flames they left behind them, might very probably, in the act of Generation with their Father, fix a similitude of Colour upon Conception, by the power of their imaginary faculty. Some, that the nearness of distance of the Sun, may have an Effect upon the Skin, as the *Portuguese* are more tawny than the *English,* or Northern Climates. We shall give you one instance more, and then lay down that we conceive to be the reason. One Mr. *Briggins,* now a Captain of a Privateer, who is yet alive, and may be heard of at the *Tower,* mentions in his Journals, that they toucht upon an Island of Blacks [where the king] . . .

Crèvecoeur, *Sketches of Eighteenth Century America; More "Letters from an American Farmer,"* ed. Henri L. Bourdin, Ralph H. Gabriel, and Stanley T. Williams (New Haven, 1925), 110; these examples may be multiplied almost indefinitely. Romans, *Florida,* 42, thought Indians were born white but soon darkened. So late as 1750 one writer conceived it necessary to explain that Indians were not mixtures of white and black people; Hughes, *Natural History of Barbados,* 14n. For an exceptional view of the Indian's color as thoroughly innate, J[onathan] Carver, *Travels through the Interior Parts of North-America* . . . (London, 1778), 223–24. For earlier reaction to color of Indians, Cawley, *Voyagers and Elizabethan Drama,* 351–53.

52. De P[auw], *Recherches Philosophiques sur les Américains,* I, 175–207. Though there was great interest in Western Europe (not in America) concerning the Chinese, no one seemed interested in their appearance. In George Anson, *A Voyage round the World, in the Years MDCCXL, I, II, III, IV,* comp. Richard Walter, 4th ed. (London, 1748), there are numerous and frequently derogatory reflections on the Chinese but none concerning their physical characteristics.

told them that he had one Rarity in his Court, a white Child born of two of his Subject Blacks, that had neither of 'em seen a white Man or Woman in all their Lives, and then caused the Child to be brought forth, which in its Skin (not its Physiognomy) resembled a fair *English* Child. From which last Example we affirm, That 'tis more than barely probable that the first change of *Colours* in Persons came from such an Instance as this; and where such an Instance happened, the news or sight of it would form an Idea in others, which in the Act of Generation would have the same Effect, the Imaginary power being stronger than the Generative, both in Women and other *Creatures*. We have frequent Examples of the first, and want not some in the last, particularly in *Jacob*'s Policy of transferring *Laban*'s Flocks into his: See *Gen.* 30. v. 37, 38, 39. Now a Colour being once changed, it naturally follows that Intermarriages, Transplantations, and Commixtures of such Persons must produce variety of Colours, though we must allow a great Cause in the nearness or distance of the Sun.[53]

It was thoroughly characteristic of the early years of the century that such a mixed bag of Scripture, observation, and speculation was advanced to explain the Negro's color.

As time went on, the theologically oriented explanations, notably the curse on Ham, gradually lost their popularity. Most philosophers inclined instead to the naturalistic idea that the heat of the sun was the essential agent, though some talked vaguely of accidental alterations or maternal impressions. With the passage of time, moreover, there was more evidence available concerning the effects of living in a cold climate on the Negroes' complexion. Buffon, for one, still thought that they would become perceptibly lighter by the eighth or tenth or twelfth generation, but Americans generally did not see much improvement.[54] Their opinions were epitomized by Peter Kalm, a pupil of Linnaeus, after his visit to America in mid-century:

The negroes have therefore been upwards of a hundred and thirty years in this country. As the winters here, especially in New England and New York, are as severe as our Swedish winter, I very carefully inquired whether the cold had not been observed to affect the color of the negroes, and to change it, so that the third or fourth generation from the first that came hither became less black than their ancestors. But I was generally answered that there was not the slightest difference of color to be perceived; and that a negro born here of parents who were likewise born in this country, and whose ancestors, both men and women had all been blacks born in this country, up to the third or fourth generation, was not at all different in color from those negroes, who were brought directly from Africa. Hence many people concluded that a negro or his posterity did not change color,

53. *The Athenian Oracle,* I, 2d ed. (London, 1704) , 29–30.
54. Buffon, *Natural History,* III, 163–65, 201, VII, 394–95.

though they continued ever so long in a cold climate; but the union of a white man with a negro woman, or of a negro man with a white woman had an entirely different result.[55]

A *very* different result, as Americans had reason to know.

The source of the confusion over the Negro's color becomes clearer when the problem is considered in modern terms. Eighteenth-century speculation was based on the assumption that an acquired characteristic (blackness from the heat of the sun) could be transmitted to progeny.[56] Yet this process just did not seem to work in the climatological laboratory: children of white men in the tropics did not inherit the darkened complexion of their parents. The converse situation with Negroes in northern climates did not work even for the first generation, let alone the children. The problem was insoluble, of course, unless men were willing to distort the facts or until development of the idea of natural selection operating over an unbelievably long period of time.

Only two European naturalists seem to have come close to detecting the true importance of accidental variation in an hereditary trait. In the middle of the eighteenth century Pierre Louis Moreau de Maupertuis, a prominent scientist possessing a highly original turn of mind, and Henry Baker, a naturalist, poet, and fellow of the Royal Society, both saw that an accidental abnormality in one individual might become the source of an entire race of men bearing that abnormality. Significantly, both men arrived at this conclusion after studying cases of startling human deformities, polydactylism for Maupertuis and a peculiar prickly skin for Baker. Maupertuis advanced his conclusions much further than Baker, but Baker's profoundly simple idea was also far ahead of his time. The most amazing thing about this prickly man, Baker reported, was that all the man's six children had the same peculiar condition. "It appears therefore past all doubt," Baker went on, "that a race of people may be propagated by this man, having such rugged coats or coverings as himself: and, if this should ever happen, and the accidental original be forgotten, 'tis not improbable they might be deemed a different species of mankind: a consideration, which would almost lead one to imagine, that if mankind were all produced from one and the same stock, the black skins of the negroes, and many other differences of the like kind, might possibly have been originally owing to

55. Benson, ed., *Peter Kalm's Travels*, I, 209.
56. See the survey by Zirkle, "Early History of Inheritance," Amer. Phil. Soc., *Transactions*, New Ser., 35 (1946), Pt. ii, 91–151.

some such accidental cause." [57] No other commentators picked up these suggestions. Even in America, few writers so much as suggested that the Negro's color might afford protection against the sun.[58]

It was perfectly possible to explain the Negro's complexion by predicating separate creations of men in distinct colors, but few men wished to crawl so far out the limb of unorthodoxy. Lord Kames, the Scottish philosopher and man of letters, set out to demonstrate that men were created in different species or races from the beginning, but having pointed out how the Mosaic account disagreed with his historical facts in every particular, he tried to resolve sacred and secular history by saying that upon the dispersion following the Tower of Babel, the constitutions of men were changed to fit their respective climates. Having denied Scripture, he turned and embraced it.[59] His original denial, however, raised a chorus of denunciation.

It was also possible to approach the problem of the Negro's color from a different vantage point, whence the investigator could advance without fear of embroilment with touchy guardians of holy writ. After the middle of the seventeenth century some writers foresook the larger question to delve into the more palpable problem of the physiology of skin color. In his *Account of Two Voyages to New-England* (1674), for example, John Josselyn self-consciously ruled out the larger problem before reporting the results of his probing into a living Negro's skin: "It is the opinion of many men, that the blackness of the *Negroes* proceeded from the curse upon *Cham's* posterity, others again will have it to be the property of the

57. It is suggestive that Baker singled out the Negro's color as needing explanation. Henry Baker, "A Supplement to the Account of a Distempered Skin, Published in the 424th Number of the Philosophical Transactions [in 1732 by John Machin]," Royal Society, *Philosophical Transactions*, 49 (1755), 21–24; see L. S. Penrose, "The Porcupine Man," *The Listener*, May 9, 1957; and Bentley Glass, "Maupertuis, Pioneer of Genetics and Evolution," Glass, Temkin, Straus, eds., *Forerunners of Darwin*, 51–83.

58. One writer thought the Negro's woolly hair a defense against the sun, another that his complexion afforded protection against disease, and a third that an oily substance oozing from the skin and not blackness accounted for Negroes' ability to withstand heat. See, respectively, ["Mr. Morgan"], *A Plan for the Abolition of Slavery in the West Indies* (London, 1772), 5; [Benjamin Rush], *An Address to the Inhabitants of the British Settlements, on the Slavery of the Negroes in America. The Second Edition. To Which Is Added, A Vindication of the Address* . . . (Phila., 1773), 33–34; Anburey, *Travels through the Interior*, II, 222–23.

59. Kames, *History of Man*, I, 3–84, esp. 72–84; and also Romans, *Florida*, 54–55.

climate where they live. I pass by other philosophical reasons and skill, only render you my experimental knowledge." [60]

From the time of the pioneering work in microscopic anatomy by Marcello Malpighi (1628–94), the most common view seems to have been that the Negro's skin contained a black fluid. The only difficulty here was that reputable eighteenth-century investigators were unable actually to find such a substance. Among them was Dr. John Mitchell of Urbanna, Virginia, whose thoroughgoing analysis was unique in the colonies. Americans were seemingly not much disposed to investigate a question that to them was loaded with implications extraneous to science. Actually, in common with a number of men living in America, Mitchell was more a European than an American, and he always identified himself with the European scientific community.[61] It would therefore be wrong to take Mitchell's investigations (and the fact that he made them) as indicating the temper of the American colonists. Still, Mitchell's conclusions in 1745 represented the views of an able and respected scientist who had considerable contact with Negroes. Like so many scientists in America, he published his remarks in the widely read pages of the *Philosophical Transactions* of the Royal Society.[62]

Mitchell attempted to bring order to the confusing question of the Negro's color by stretching it out upon the procrustean bed of Newtonian optics. The Negro's skin, he announced, was not different in kind from the white man's; it was merely thicker and denser, and contained more particles. The tawny peoples possessed skin of intermediate nature. Proudly brandishing citations to Newton's *Opticks* (1704) which showed white to be all colors and black to be none, Mitchell threw out the fluid theory and aligned all peoples on a single spectrum. The effect of his reasoning was to emphasize the

60. Josselyn, *Voyages to New-England*, 335–36.
61. The best account of Mitchell is Theodore Hornberger, "The Scientific Ideas of John Mitchell," *Huntington Library Quarterly*, 10 (1947), 277–96. He was later described as "an English physician, who resided a number of years in Virginia"; Samuel Miller, *A Brief Retrospect of the Eighteenth Century* . . . , 2 vols. (N. Y., 1803), I, 498.
62. "An Essay upon the Causes of the Different Colours of People in Different Climates; by John Mitchell, M. D. Communicated to the Royal Society by Mr. Peter Collinson, F. R. S.," Royal Society, *Phil. Transactions*, 43 (1744–45), 102–50. Examples of the anatomical approach in Europe are Jean Nicholas Pechlin, *De Habitu et Colore Æthiopium* (Kiel, 1677); [Claude Nicolas] Le Cat, *Traité de la Couleur de la Peau Humaine en Général, de Celle des Negres en Particulier, et de la Métamorphose d'une de ces Couleurs en l'Autre, Soit de Naissance, Soit Accidentellement* (Amsterdam, 1765). See also MS. Journal Book of the Royal Society, Dec. 9, 1696, Library of the Royal Society, London, which is quoted in Montagu, *Edward Tyson*, 212–13.

fundamental sameness of men of the most diverse appearances. "Negroes, *Indians,* and white People," he declared, differed from one another "only in the Degree of one and the same Colour." The causes of these "different Colours" were "uniform and alike, agreeable to the exact Symmetry of Nature . . . ; so that, however different, and opposite to one another, these two Colours of Black and White may appear to be to the Unskilful, yet they will be found to differ from one another only in Degree." Whiteness was "all Colours" and blackness was none. "And hence it is," Mitchell concluded,

that one of these Colours is more easily changed into the other, than to any other Colour; and where any Body loses its white Colour, it of course turns black, without any other Cause concurring, but a bare Loss of its Whiteness . . . . From whence we may justly infer, 1. That there is not so great, unnatural, and unaccountable a Difference between Negroes and white People, on account of their Colours, as to make it impossible for both ever to have been descended from the same Stock, as some People, unskilled in the Doctrine of Light and Colours, are very apt too positively to affirm, and, without any Scruple, to believe, contrary to the Doctrine (as it seems to be) of the Sacred Pages.[63]

By this reasoning black and white were merely two aspects of the same thing, and anyone who thought otherwise was no true scientist. John Mitchell had wrestled an apparently enormous distinction into conformity with "the exact Symmetry of Nature." His explication of human colors provided a physiological basis for the unity of man.

It is suggestive that this unusual erasure of distinctions in color should have come from a scientist living in America. Possibly John Mitchell half recognized that contrary conclusions might have tragic repercussions in an area seemingly far removed from natural philosophy, an area of human concern to which a man living in Virginia would have been far more sensitive than any closet philosopher in Europe. Certainly it is striking that Mitchell should have reached the highly unusual conclusion that the original color of man was not white but tawny. And it scarcely seems coincidental that the only other scientists in America to speculate at length on the Negro's color reached the same conclusion in striking contrast to the consensus among philosophers in Europe. Actually, very few Americans seemed to want to delve into the subject. Dr. William Douglass of Boston raised the matter briefly in 1749 but only got as

---

63. Mitchell, "Essay upon Different Colours of People," Royal Society, *Phil. Transactions,* 43 (1744–45), 130–31.

far as stating all the difficulties involved; Douglass plainly did not know what to think.[64] John Winthrop IV, safely ensconsed as Hollis Professor of Mathematics and Natural Philosophy at Harvard, was more definite in a lengthy private reply in 1759 to an inquiry on the matter by the Reverend Ezra Stiles. Winthrop was inclined to think that climatic differences had caused human variations in color and also in hair, stature, and features. "It has long seemd most probable to me," Winthrop wrote, "that the original complexion of mankind, considering the climate they lived in, was swarthy or tawny . . . and that our color and that of the Africans are equal deviations from this primitive color towards the opposite extremes of whiteness and blackness." [65] Among able scientists of international reputation, this was a most unusual view.

By far the most common assumption was that the original color of man was white, an assumption which gave special sharpness to the question why the Negro was black. It was not so much a matter of why the Negro was black as why the Negro had become the very negation of white. Many commentators treated the Negro's blackness as a degeneration from original color.[66] It was Oliver Goldsmith (author of *She Stoops to Conquer*) who first pressed this self-comforting conception to its logical conclusion. White, Goldsmith announced, was the natural color of man; after all, children everywhere were born fair. The variations of the human figure, he continued, "are actual marks of the degeneracy in the human form; and we may consider the European figure and colour as standards to which to refer all other varieties, and with which to compare them. In proportion as the Tartar or American approaches nearer to European beauty, we consider the race as less degenerated; in proportion as he differs more widely, he has made greater deviations from his original form. That we have all sprung from one common parent, we are taught, both by reason and religion, to believe; and we have good reason also to think that the Europeans resemble him more than any of the rest of his children." [67] The secret was out: Adam was a white man.

The concept of degeneration from primitive whiteness was seem-

64. William Douglass, *A Summary, Historical and Political, of . . . the British Settlements in North-America*, 2 vols. (Boston, 1749–51), I, 158n.

65. John Winthrop to Ezra Stiles, Cambridge, July 19, 1759, Isabel M. Calder, ed., *Letters and Papers of Ezra Stiles, President of Yale College, 1778–1795 . . .* (New Haven, 1933), 5–8.

66. In the 18th century the term *degeneration* carried the precise connotation of movement away from true and original type; the term was usually, though *not* always, to some degree pejorative.

67. Goldsmith, *History of the Earth*, II, 232–42. Goldsmith admitted that other races thought it was the European who had degenerated.

ingly confirmed by a curious phenomenon: Negro babies are born considerably lighter than they shortly become, a fact which many eighteenth-century writers noted with almost gleeful interest.[68] Once again, a fact of physiology confirmed the predispositions of the white man. A few men, particularly in the West Indies, were so intent on distinguishing Negroes from whites that they proceeded to invent the facts they were unable to discover; they claimed, variously, that the Negro's blood, brains, and skull were black.[69] Cornelis de Pauw announced in 1770 that the Negro had dark brains, blood, and semen, and he even seized upon the latter long-discredited notion to announce triumphantly that the mulatto's intermediate color was caused by blending of dark and white seminal liquors. Edward Long, true to form, proclaimed that the lice carried by Negroes were black rather than white.[70]

Still another curious phenomenon tended to confirm the widespread feeling that black was not a natural color for a human being. For just when Europeans had become adjusted to the fact that some men were black, reports began sifting in from Africa and America that some black men were white. "Leucoaethiopes" had been reported by such ancient authorities as Pliny and Ptolemy and therefore duly noted by Jean Bodin, but Europeans had never before been presented with such definite and reliable information.[71] Before the beginning of the eighteenth century, travelers' accounts

68. Sloane, *Voyage to the Islands*, I, liii; Smith, *Natural History of Leeward Islands*, 231; Le Cat, *Traité de la Couleur de la Peau*, 91; Romans, *Florida*, 111; John Hunter, *An Inaugural Dissertation . . .* (Edinburgh, 1775), trans. Bendyshe, in his *Treatises of Blumenbach*, 372; Blumenbach, *Natural Variety* (1795), in *ibid.*, 211; Buffon, *Natural History*, trans. [Smellie], III, 200; Jansen, ed., *Oeuvres de Pierre Camper*, II, 469–70; Stedman, *Narrative of Expedition, against the Negroes*, II, 253. These assertions placed the newborns' color at anything from absolutely white to darkish grey or brown; several mentioned that the genitals and/or cuticles of the nails were dark from the beginning. One writer reversed colors by saying Negroes were born black except for their "privities" and a small circle about the nails, an assertion still current today; "The Modern Part of an Universal History . . . ," *Critical Review*, 9 (1760), 82.

69. Most notably *re* blood by Dr. Thomas Towns in a letter dated Barbadoes, Mar. 26, 1675 submitted by a Mr. Lister to the Royal Society, Royal Society, *Phil Transactions*, 10 (1675), 400. Buffon, *Natural History*, trans. [Smellie] III, 201–2, was inclined to believe this; but [Leslie], *New History of Jamaica*, 312, was certain that Negro blood was "equally fair with" European and expressed surprise to see the contrary asserted in the *Philosophical Transactions*. See also Romans, *Florida*, 55; De P[auw], *Recherches Philosophiques sur les Americains*, II, 27, 45–46; and for a refutation of the claim by Johann Friedrich Meckel, Jansen, ed., *Oeuvres de Pierre Camper*, II, 457–59. See also Ramsay, *Treatment and Conversion of African Slaves*, 214–15.

70. De P[auw], *Recherches Philosophiques sur les Americains*, I, 179–82; [Long], *Jamaica*, II, 352.

71. Pearson, Nettleship, and Usher, *Monograph on Albinism*, I, 11–12; Bodin, *Method for Easy Comprehension of History*, trans. Reynolds, 89.

of white or dappled Negroes had become sufficiently numerous and reliable to remove them from the category of reports about men with heads between their shoulders. The English traveler Andrew Battell reported in the first decade of the seventeenth century that in Africa the blacks sometimes bore "white children" who "are as white as any white man." In 1697 William Byrd, the first Virginian to be elected Fellow of the Royal Society, communicated "An Account of a Negro-Boy that is dappel'd in several places of his Body with White Spots" and assured the Society that "his Father and Mother were both perfect Negroes," that the lad had been a perfect Negro at first and only at age three had begun to break out with spreading white spots. Byrd refused to speculate as to the cause of this remarkable transformation, though he was certain the boy was not sick in any usual sense. Ten years later Hans Sloane, then secretary of the Royal Society, reported seeing "Mr. *Birds*" boy in England.[72] In 1699 Lionel Wafer published a first-hand, level-headed description of the white Indians of Panama, whose descendants still live in the same remote area.[73] Apart from Wafer's account and several vague references to these Indians by other writers, however, albinism in man was known only as it occurred in the Negro.

In describing "white negroes," European observers knew they were not dealing with light-skinned mulattoes, for they often referred to them as white children born of perfectly black parents. Their allusions to squint-eyed sensitivity to sunlight, moreover, make it certain that they were in fact dealing with true albinos. These white black men aroused interest which ranged all the way from scientific speculation to side-show curiosity. Maupertuis's important investigation of the patterns of heredity was first stimulated by a white Negro who turned up in Paris.[74] Reports from America on white or spotted Negroes quickly found their way to Europe,

72. Ravenstein, ed., *Strange Adventures of Andrew Battell*, 48, 81; William Byrd, "An Account of a Negro-Boy That Is Dappel'd in Several Places of His Body with White Spots," Royal Society, *Phil. Transactions*, 19 (1695–97), 781–82; Sloane, *Voyage to the Islands*, I, liii. Sloane's confusion was evident in his report on the same page of seeing a white girl with Negroid features and hair who had white parents and whose mother related that she had previously borne a white girl of a black father.

73. Lionel Wafer, *A New Voyage and Description of the Isthmus of America*, ed. L. E. Elliott Joyce (*Works Issued by Hakluyt Soc.*, 2d Ser., 73 [1934]), 80–82; D. B. Stout, "Further Notes on Albinism among the San Blas Cuna, Panama," *Amer. Jour. Physical Anthro.*, New Ser., 4 (1946), 483–90; Richard Oglesby Marsh, *White Indians of Darien* (N. Y., 1934).

74. [Pierre Louis Moreau de Maupertuis], *Venus Physique, Contenant Deux Dissertations, l'Une, sur l'Origine des Hommes et des Animaux: et l'Autre, sur l'Origine des Noirs* (La Haye, 1746), 129–50.

sometimes followed by the living evidence.[75] If there was one kind of profit in exhibiting white Negroes to the Royal Society, there was another to be had by showing them to the public: in 1765 an advertisement in a New York newspaper announced, "That there is to be seen, at the House of Mr. Edward Bardon in the Fields, at the Sign of the King's-Arms, a white Girl, aged 13 Years, born of black Parents, who has all the Resemblance of a Negro Wench, the Colour excepted. N.B. She is to be seen from 6 to 10 o'Clock, every Afternoon. Price to each 6d." At least two other completely white Negroes were similarly exhibited in the colonies before the Revolution.[76]

There was general agreement that these white Negroes did not constitute a separate race of people. Voltaire, who examined the same white Negro as Maupertuis, claimed to have found a new race of men, but few people agreed.[77] How could these strange individuals belong to a distinct race when they were born of black parents and bore black children? Some commentators felt that whiteness in a Negro was nothing less than a disease and bolstered their case by pointing to the general debility of white Negroes, at least in the daytime.[78] Other writers saw a whitened Negro as an instance of the same kind of degeneration which had long ago transformed some men from white to black, which came very close to saying that white Negroes were reverting to original color.[79] Frequently no attempt was made to explain this thoroughly puzzling prodigy of nature.

What is most revealing in the approach of Europeans to this problem is that for many years no one seems to have made the obvious connection between white Negroes and European albinos. Though it is probable that albinism was more common in West

75. James Bate, "An Account of the Remarkable Alteration of Colour in a Negro Woman [in Maryland] . . . ," Royal Society, *Phil. Transactions*, 51 (1759), Pt. 1, 175–78; James Parsons, "An Account of the White Negro Shewn before the Royal Society . . . ," *ibid.*, 55 (1765), 45–53. Many travelers and compilers reported on white Negroes, and these reports circulated widely. Bate's account, for instance, was picked up by the *Gentleman's Magazine*, 30 (1760), 361–62, and by the *Annual Register*, [3] (1760), 75–76.

76. *New-York Gazette; or the Weekly Post-Boy*, Mar. 14, 1765, supplement; *Boston News-Letter*, June 30, 1743, Aug. 9, 1764.

77. Libby, *Voltaire and the Sciences*, 199–200.

78. For example Stedman, *Narrative of Expedition against the Negroes*, II, 251.

79. Goldsmith, *History of the Earth*, II, 240–42; [Maupertuis], *Venus Physique*, 142–50 (who accepted the old idea that white parents sometimes had black babies but who claimed this occurred very rarely). At one point Buffon treated the phenomenon as a degenerative defect and at another as a reversion to original color; Buffon, *Natural History*, III, 180–82, VII, 404–5.

Africa than in Europe, it is certain that there were albinos among
the native peoples of England and the Continent.[80] These albino
white persons seem to have aroused little interest. Still, it is strongly
suggestive of the power of ethnocentrism that for years no one
connected the two phenomena by recognizing that they represented
a single physiological peculiarity. Maupertuis recognized the connection between anomalously white crows and blackbirds and white
Negroes in the 1740's, but it was not until 1766 that anyone linked
white Negroes to albino Europeans. In that year Buffon, discussing
this strange whiteness as a form of degeneration, mentioned its
appearance among both Negroes and whites as well as among
various animals. In 1775 Blumenbach pointed out that this "disease" appeared in all varieties of man. Two years later Buffon
returned to the subject, saying that albinism was more widely
spread among mankind than he had thought; there was probably
no race of men, he decided, which did not include individuals with
this bizarre degeneration.[81] Yet his discussion was strangely casual;
he gave no indication that he had hit upon anything new. And still
more strangely, despite Buffon's widespread influence, some writers
failed to take up his idea and continued to treat the white Negro in
isolation.[82] Evidently for some men the Negro seemed so distinct
from the white man that a change in the Negro's color could not
easily be equated with a similar change among whites. Certainly the
alteration in the Negro was the more startling, but it does seem
likely that a connection would have been made and widely accepted
much earlier if the Negro and his color had not been perceived as
utterly distinct.

5. THE VALUATION OF COLOR

The fact remained, however, that most Negroes were
black. In many ways this was a useful color. For classifiers of
mankind, the Negro's blackness was in itself sufficient reason for

80. An epitaph cited in Pearson, Nettleship, and Usher, *Albinism in Man*, I,
12*n*, indicates existence of an English albino boy prior to 1632; for living cases,
Benedict Duddell, *A Supplement to the Treatise of the Diseases of the Horny-
coat and Cataract of the Eye, and Its Appendix* (London, 1736), 19–20; John
Hunter, *Observations on Certain Parts of the Animal Œconomy* . . . [1786], ed.
Richard Owen (Phila., 1840), 290–91.

81. [Georges Louis Leclerc], Comte de Buffon, *Histoire Naturelle, Générale et
Particulière* . . . , 36 vols. (Paris, 1749–88), XIV [1766], 324–35, Supplement IV
[1777], 556ff.; Blumenbach, *Natural Variety* (1775), 133–40.

82. Thomas Jefferson, *Notes on the State of Virginia*, ed. William Peden
(Chapel Hill, 1955), 70–71. De P[auw], *Recherches Philosophiques*, II, 12, 41–42,
thought albinos existed only among the black and brown races of the torrid
zone.

placing him in a distinct category. For Europeans in general, the Negro's blackness afforded a fixed polar position from which they could calculate the colors of all the peoples of the globe. Probably as much as any single factor, the Negro's blackness lay at the root of the eventual European predilection for dividing the world's population into "white men" and "colored," a predilection more recently acquired by the "colored" peoples themselves. Even in the eighteenth century, no matter how one wished to describe the majority of men (tawny, copper, yellow, olive, brown), Negroes were black and Europeans, happily, were white. Black remained the opposite of white. Newton's *Opticks* had shown black for what it was—a deprivation. No one was lighter than Europeans, a fact that when joined to a consciousness of cultural superiority could produce the most extraordinary thoughts in the minds of Europeans. For on the spectrum of human colors they were at one end, and it was very tempting, especially for light-skinned residents of the British Isles, to place them at the top.

David Hume, the great Scottish philosopher, put the matter more baldly than anyone. Hume was convinced that the peoples near the poles and in the tropics were essentially inferior to those in the temperate zones, a conviction which can be traced historically back through European thought to the Greeks—who also lived in a temperate climate. What Hume did in 1748, though, was to go ancient philosophers one better by hitching superiority to complexion.

I am apt to suspect the negroes, and in general all the other species of men (for there are four or five different kinds) to be naturally inferior to the whites. There never was a civilized nation of any other complexion than white, nor even any individual eminent either in action or speculation. No ingenious manufactures amongst them, no arts, no sciences. On the other hand, the most rude and barbarous of the whites, such as the ancient GERMANS, the present TARTARS, have still something eminent about them, in their valour, form of government, or some other particular. Such a uniform and constant difference could not happen, in so many countries and ages, if nature had not made an original distinction betwixt these breeds of men. Not to mention our colonies, there are NEGROE slaves dispersed all over EUROPE, of which none ever discovered any symptoms of ingenuity; tho' low people, without education, will start up amongst us, and distinguish themselves in every profession. In JAMAICA indeed they talk of one negroe as a man of parts and learning; but 'tis likely he is admired for very slender accomplishments, like a parrot, who speaks a few words plainly.[83]

83. From a footnote added in the 1753-54 edition of his essay "Of National Characters," first published in 1748; I have used David Hume, *Essays: Moral, Political, and Literary*, eds. T. H. Green and T. H. Grose, 2 vols. (London, 1875), I, 252.

Here, indeed, was the white man's burden of superiority. There was a certain logic (not to say attractiveness) in this self-congratulation. Oliver Goldsmith, in his eight-volume, indiscriminately eclectic *History of the Earth* (1774), first decided who was going to be admitted to his sodality and then expatiated glowingly on the virtues of its members.

The sixth and last variety of the human species, is that of the Europeans, and the nations bordering on them. In this class we may reckon the Georgians, Circassians, and Mingrelians, the inhabitants of Asia Minor, and the northern parts of Africa, together with a part of those countries which lie north-west of the Caspian sea. The inhabitants of these countries differ a good deal from each other; but they generally agree in the colour of their bodies, the beauty of their complexions, the largeness of their limbs, and the vigour of their understandings. Those arts which might have had their invention among the other races of mankind, have come to perfection there.[84]

By and large, Europeans were a marvelous race.

The shadings of human color were of special value to Englishmen and Americans. For if Europeans were white, some were whiter than others. In an age infused with the presuppositions of the Chain of Being, it was fatally easy to envision Europeans and the rest of mankind as constituting a Great Chain of Color. While David Hume thought the distinctions which had been drawn between southern and northern peoples of the temperate climates were "uncertain and fallacious," others were not so sure. Benjamin Franklin, for instance, disgusted with the Germanization of Pennsylvania, wistfully explained his preferences in terms of complexion. "The Number of purely white People in the World is proportionably very small. All Africa is black or tawny. Asia chiefly tawny. America (exclusive of the new Comers) wholly so. And in Europe, the Spaniards, Italians, French, Russians and Swedes [!], are generally of what we call a swarthy Complexion; as are the Germans also, the Saxons only excepted, who with the English, make the principal Body of White People on the Face of the Earth. I could wish their Numbers were increased." A similar mode of thinking cropped up occasionally under a variety of provocations. In 1742 a writer in the *South-Carolina Gazette* referred angrily to the French as "swarthy brethren" of the Indians. Driven by a different fear, an historian of Jamaica warned stridently that admitting Negroes into England would result in a contaminated mixture "till the whole nation resembles the *Portuguese* and *Moriscos* in complexion of skin and

84. Goldsmith, *History of the Earth*, II, 230–31.

baseness of mind." From an opposite point of view, an antislavery writer in the *Virginia Gazette* described the hazards lurking in a hierarchy of complexions: "If Negroes are to be Slaves on Account of Colour, the next Step will be to enslave every Mulatto in the Kingdom, then all the Portuguese, next the French, then the brown complexioned English, and so on till there be only one free Man left, which will be the Man of the palest Complexion in the three Kingdoms!" [85]

The questions concerning the Negro's place in creation and of his color were played out upon an international stage. They were not peculiarly American problems, although their formulation was based partly on information from America. To the extent that these questions were "scientific," they were necessarily international. Scientists belonged to an international fraternity, and trans-Atlantic communications, slow as they were in the eighteenth century, enabled natural philosophers in America to make claim to membership.

There were some matters concerning the Negro's physical nature, though, which depended so heavily upon intimate daily experience with Negroes that the problems involved were peculiarly American. The American colonists had more reason than Europeans, for instance, to find ways to express the social distance between Negroes and themselves. Yet slavery, which created this need, also answered it, for slavery served admirably as a means of categorization. Americans showed less need than Europeans to place the Negro in an ordered creation because slavery firmly fixed his position in their own immediate social world. On the other hand, American colonials had greater reason to emphasize the physical differences between themselves and Negroes in order to confirm the validity of their social order. It is clear, certainly, that in regard to physical distinctions Americans far more than Europeans were subject to powerful stresses arising from their intimate social relationships with Negroes. It is equally clear that these stresses arose from extremely diverse sources.

One sort of stress arose from emotional turmoil within individuals, and here it is possible to gain an occasional glimpse into the deepest, least rational *meaning* of human blackness for white men. Negroes have scarcely been the only group in history to be used as

85. "Observations Concerning the Increase of Mankind" (1751), Labaree *et al.*, eds., *Papers of Franklin*, IV, 234; Charleston *S.-C. Gaz.*, Aug. 23, 1742; [Long], *Candid Reflections upon the Negro Cause*, 49; Purdie and Dixon's Wmsbg. *Va. Gaz.*, Aug. 20, 1772.

objects of the psychological difficulties of others, but the Negro's appearance, his blackness, seems to have served certain deep-seated unconscious needs of at least some white men. There are sufficient indications of this fact in colonial America to make ignoring it difficult. Sexual intermixture was frequently referred to as "staining" the white population. Robert Pyle of Pennsylvania, an early antislavery Quaker, included the following fantasy in his argument against slavery:

I considered the motion that rose in me to buy off them whether it was not self,—knowing hitherto by my moderate and honest indevors I have not wanted food nor rayment, theyrwith be content, saith the Apostle; being exercised upon my mind for many dayes considering those things as I was lieng upon my bed as in a sleep I saw myself and a friend going on a road, and by the roadside I saw a black pott. I took it up, the friend said give mee part, I said no, I went a little farther and I saw a great ladder standing exact upright, reaching up to heaven up which I must go to heaven with the pott in my hand intending to carry the black pott with me, but the ladder standing so upright, and seeing no man holding of it up, it seemed that it would fall upon mee; at which I steps down and laid the pot at the foot of the ladder, and said them that will take it might, for I found work enough for both hands to take hold of this ladder.

When he awoke this good Quaker considered the matter and decided firmly, in an astonishing phrase, "self must bee left behind, and to lett black negroes or pots alone." And years later an Englishman who traveled widely in the colonies expressed his disgust after spending a most uncomfortable night in a tiny cabin with an overseer and six Negroes by calling the Negroes "a parcel of nasty black devils." [86]

On another, and not necessarily disconnected level, was the

86. H. J. Cadbury, ed., "An Early Quaker Anti-Slavery Statement," *Jour. Negro Hist.*, 22 (1937), 492–93; Smyth, *Tour in the United States*, I, 76. See also the gratuitous intrusion in the baboon advertisement cited previously. Some readers will find this paragraph incomprehensible or suppositious; they may ask themselves why. If these materials have no particular psychological significance, a whole generation of American mothers has been hoodwinked by Dr. Benjamin Spock on the subject of toilet training. There is voluminous scholarly and clinical literature which does not of course support any single interpretation of the symbols and "meaning" of these fantasies but which also does not permit us to pronounce them meaningless or unconnected with an important function of the body. There are many kinds of "pots" (not all of them "black") but only one which could have been associated with such "motion" and with the obligation to leave part of the "self," i.e., selfishness, "behind." There is an interesting treatment of some historical aspects of this matter in Norman O. Brown, *Life Against Death: The Psychoanalytical Meaning of History* (N. Y., 1959). I am grateful to Dr. Robert Coles, Research Psychiatrist at the Harvard University Health Services and a Consultant to the Southern Regional Council, for assuring me that I have not misread these materials.

widely circulated notion that Negroes emitted a rank and fetid odor.[87] The trustees of Georgia were most reassuring about the use of Negroes in silk culture: "For, upon Trial, it appears there is not the least Ground for the Apprehension, some People have had, that the Smell from the Negroes would be offensive to the Worms." [88] Whether there was factual basis for these assertions is hard to tell.

Considered in a broader cultural context, it was the Negro's blackness which proved his most important characteristic. When he was not called a "negroe" he was called by the indigenous term, a "black." Although the evidence from language and ideals of beauty in Elizabethan England suggests that the English response to blackness may not have been entirely a matter of associating a physical characteristic with social inferiority, the fact was that from the beginning white Englishmen met black Negroes on a footing of inequality. And although the fantasy of Robert Pyle in 1698 suggests that repulsion for blackness may in some individuals have derived from deep levels in the personality which were associated with or perhaps even dependent upon purely physiological processes, the fact remains that Pyle perceived Negro blackness in a specific and derogatory social context. So the historian, rather like the modern student of race-awareness in very young children, must remain tentative and indeed baffled as to whether white men originally responded adversely to the Negro's color because of strictly accidental prior cultural valuation of blackness *per se,* instinctual repulsion founded on physiological processes or perhaps fear of the night which may have had adaptive value in human evolution, the association of dirt and darkened complexion with the lower classes in Europe, or association of blackness with Negroes who were inferior in culture or status.

Certainly by the eighteenth century, the latter mechanism was in full operation. Blackness was eminently functional in a slave society where white men were masters. It served as an easily grasped symbol

87. Instances are in Mitchell, "Essay upon Different Colours of People," Royal Society, *Phil. Transactions*, 43 (1744–45), 143–44; Ligon, *True History of Barbadoes*, 28; Catesby, *Natural History of Carolina*, II, viii; Jonathan Boucher quoted in Pennington, "Thomas Bray's Associates," Amer. Antiq. Soc., *Proceedings*, New Ser., 48 (1938), 358; Alexander Macraby quoted in Bridenbaugh, *Cities in Revolt*, 285; [Long], *Jamaica*, II, 352–53, 425–26; Goldsmith, *History of the Earth*, II, 226; Kames, *History of Man*, I, 25; Schoepf, *Travels in the Confederation*, trans. and ed. Morrison, I, 357; Edwards, *History of British West Indies*, II, 73; Charleston S.-C. Gaz., July 17, 1736; Smyth, *Tour in the United States*, I, 39.
88. Unpublished Colonial Records of Georgia (typescript copy in State Department of Archives and History, Atlanta), XXXIII, 574.

of the Negro's baseness and wickedness. The S.P.G. missionary Elias
Neau, always one to exaggerate in a good cause, claimed that "I
have been told that the negroes bear on their foreheads the marks of
the reprobation and that their color and their condition confirms
that opinion." [89] Cotton Mather, among others, went out of his way
to denounce the idea that it would have any meaning in the next
world: "Their *Complexion* sometimes is made an Argument," he
wrote in *The Negro Christianized*, "why nothing should be done
for them. A *Gay* sort of argument! As if the great God went by the
Complexion of Men, in His Favours to them! As if none but *Whites*
might hope to be Favoured and Accepted with God! . . . Away with
such Trifles! The God who *looks on the Heart,* is not moved by the
colour of the *Skin;* is not more propitious to one *Colour* than
another." [90] In fact the literature of conversion and antislavery was
shot through with apologies and extenuations of the Negro's color
and with insistence on its irrelevance to his status as a man. Blackness had become so thoroughly entangled with the basest status in
American society that at least by the beginning of the eighteenth
century it was almost indecipherably coded into American language
and literature. Enslavement of blacks in a bright land of promise
immensely complicated the meaning of color. It is easy to understand the drama of *Othello;* it is less easy to comprehend the
cryptogram of a great white whale.

So as not to leapfrog centuries it seems well to epitomize the state
of inquiry into the meaning of blackness at the beginning of the
eighteenth century with a passage from a highly miscellaneous series
of brief, chatty, and highly revealing disquisitions which were popular in both England and America.

Quest. *Whether Negroes shall rise so at the last Day?*
Answ. The Pinch of the Question only lies—Whether *White* or *Black* is
the *better Colour?* For the Negroes won't be persuaded but their Jett is
finer and more beautiful than our Alabaster. If we Paint the Devil black,
they are even with us, for they Paint him *White,* and no doubt are as much
in the right on't as we; none amongst them, who are legitimate, being born
white, but such as are a kind of *Leprous Persons.* And they boast of an
Emperor of *Rome,* one of the best of 'em, ('twas *Severus*) and Saints,
Fathers, and Martyrs without Number, who have been of that Colour.—But after all, unless we are very partial, there is something natural
in't. Black is of the Colour of Night, Frightful, Dark and Horrid; but

---

89. Quoted in Klingberg, *Anglican Humanitarianism in N. Y.,* 132.

90. Pp. 24–25. For a similar argument, [Tryon], *Friendly Advice,* 115–16; and
for a description of the popular interest aroused when a white and a black man
hanging dead in public apparently exchanged colors, [Horsmanden], *A Journal
of the Proceedings,* 123.

White of the Day and Light, refreshing and lovely. Taking then this Blackness of the Negro to be an accidental imperfection . . . I conclude thence,
that he shall not arise with that Complexion, but leave it behind him in
the Darkness of the Grave, exchanging it for a brighter and a better, at his
return again into the World.[91]

It is possible here to sense our past as very distant and at the same
time very close. In twentieth-century America few people remember
the emperors of Rome, but few people have to be told (though
incessantly everyone is) that whiteness is "lovely" and "refreshing."
In the latter part of the eighteenth century, moreover, as becomes
apparent after the Revolution, Americans would find pressing reason to regard their own whiteness as integral to their emergence as
an enlightened nation, into "a brighter and a better" though a less
spiritual "World."

6. NEGROES UNDER THE SKIN

Although many aspects of the Negro's appearance afforded white men means by which they could capsulate and convey
their sense of social distance from him, they regarded his physical
appearance as in one sense superficial. Most men acquainted with
Negroes refused to extrapolate from outward appearance to inward
physical dissimilarity. Those who did so—for the most part West
Indians—simply borrowed the Negro's color and tarred the elements of life within him (blood, brains, and semen) and thereby
rendered themselves ridiculous. Reputable scientists either ignored
or summarily dismissed these absurdities. Even when investigators
like John Josselyn and Dr. John Mitchell found the Negro's skin
structurally different from the white man's, they made no attempt
to suggest that the Negro's internal organs might also be different.
The Negro was so clearly a man that his physiological processes
were assumed to be like other men's. Significantly, white men failed
to seize the opportunity for saying that the Negro was susceptible to
different diseases than the white man. Disease was fundamental, it
touched man's very core, and almost no one was prepared to say
that the Negro was different in such a fundamental way. Writers on
medical subjects, particularly, were not the sort to take a special
interest in degrading the Negro; by their very nature the healing
arts demanded universal application. During the great debate on

91. *The Athenian Oracle* . . . , I, 2d ed. (London, 1704), 435–36; but see II
(London, 1703), 389. The common 18th-century idea that the more brutish
people in any country were darker complexioned presents similar difficulties.

smallpox inoculation in Boston in 1721 the ministers who advocated the procedure assumed without question that God's visitation might touch anyone, regardless of color, and of course no one challenged their assumption that Negroes and whites would have the same reactions to inoculation. Throughout the colonial period in fact, speculation about Negroes' diseases was extremely offhand and not very common. Not even a generally received medical opinion developed on the subject. Many medical works, even those on tropical diseases, scarcely mentioned the Negro, though it was recognized, of course, that men living in the tropics were susceptible to peculiarly tropical complaints. Occasionally physicians casually suggested that a particular disease was especially common among Negroes or among Europeans; often they recognized that certain disorders such as yaws, leprosy, and skin-worms had originated in Africa.[92] Even before 1760 a few men offered an environmentalist explanation for the commonness of some diseases among the slaves,[93] thereby presaging the endorsements of the antislavery cause by many American physicians in the latter part of the century.

Though the American colonists generally thought of the Negro as internally a similar physiological being to the white man, at times they were disposed to feel that the Negro was far better suited to arduous labor in hot climates. Especially when the institution of slavery was in any way challenged, they were likely to respond that Negroes could do the necessary work and white men could not.

92. Probably coincidentally, these diseases manifested themselves in the outer flesh. Some writers thought yaws a venereal disease, which it is not, though the organism causing yaws is similar to that causing syphilis. Hans Sloane described a disorder in a Negro woman which can only have been leprosy and speculated that it "might come from some peculiar indisposition of their black skin." Sloane, *Voyage to the Islands*, I, cvi. My statements are based mainly on about 35 contemporary medical works; for the continental colonies, see Francisco Guerra, comp., *American Medical Bibliography, 1639–1783* . . . (N. Y., 1962). The most persistent and consistent assertions of racial differences in susceptibility are in [James Grainger], *An Essay on the More Common West-India Diseases; and the Remedies Which That Country Itself Produces. To Which Are Added, Some Hints on the Management, etc. of Negroes. By a Physician in the West Indies* (London, 1764). John Mitchell did mention several diseases he regarded as peculiar either to whites or to Negroes because of cutaneous differences, but he failed to develop his suggestions; "Essay upon Different Colours of People," Royal Society, *Phil. Transactions*, 43 (1744–45), 144–45. See also Lionel Chalmers, *An Account of the Weather and Diseases of South-Carolina*, 2 vols. in 1 (London, 1776), I, 37, 70, 219. The broadest modern treatment is Lewis, *Biology of the Negro*.

93. William Hillary, *Observations on the Changes of the Air, and the Concomitant Epidemical Diseases in the Island of Barbadoes* . . . *With Notes by Benjamin Rush*, [3d? ed.] (Phila., 1811), 164–65; [Leslie], *New History of Jamaica*, 312.

There were few signs, however, of anyone's attempting to ground slavery in physiological necessity and hence in the natural order; the widespread belief in the Negro's suitability for labor in hot climates was convenient but formless and imprecise.[94] For one thing, slavery ordinarily did not require justification; it constituted an unquestioned aspect of the American social system. For another, the suitability (vaguely conceived) of men to the climates in which they lived was an idea much older than American Negro slavery. It was in the context of this tradition that one English traveler who was disgusted by Negro slavery in the colonies declared that "they are the most awkward, ungain Wretches, in cold Weather, that can be met with, and if not stirr'd up, will sit whole Days shivering in a Corner without moving Hand or Foot: They seem to be form'd only for the sultry Climate they were born in, and those they are principally apply'd to the Use of; tho' when inur'd to a cold one long, they bear it tolerably well." [95] It is especially suggestive that one of the most forthright endorsements of slavery on climatic grounds in the eighteenth century was made not by an American but by Montesquieu, famous for his elaboration of the influence of climate upon government. Though Montesquieu was opposed to slavery he felt that "there are countries where the excess of heat enervates the body, and renders men so slothful and dispirited that nothing but the fear of chastisement can oblige them to perform any laborious duty: slavery is there more recognizable to reason." [96]

When the American colonists came to elaborate the climatic theory of slavery they frequently confused what are in fact two very different ideas—that the plantations which developed in the warmer colonies in response to the need for a staple crop required many laborers, and that Negroes were better fitted physiologically to labor in the sun. The confusion was apparent in the Reverend Alexander Hewat's explanation for the need for Negroes in South Carolina and Georgia.

94. The most precise attempt to embed the belief in the Negro's physiology was by Benjamin Franklin to John Lining, London, June 17, 1758, Labaree *et al.*, eds., *Papers of Franklin*, VIII, 108–12; see also Mitchell, "Essay upon Different Colours of People," Royal Society, *Phil. Transactions*, 43 (1744–45), 142–43, 146.

95. [Kimber], ["Observations in America"], *London Mag.*, [15] (1746), 127. See also Benson, trans. and ed., *Peter Kalm's Travels*, I, 207; [Anthony Benezet], *A Short Account of That Part of Africa, Inhabited by the Negroes* . . . (Phila., 1762), 6.

96. *Spirit of the Laws*, bk. 15, sec. 7; I have used Thomas Nugent, trans., with an intro. by Franz Neumann, *The Spirit of the Laws by Baron de Montesquieu*, 2 vols. in 1 (N. Y., 1949), I, 240.

The utter inaptitude of Europeans for the labour requisite in such a climate and soil, is obvious to every one possessed of the smallest degree of knowledge respecting the country; white servants would have exhausted their strength in clearing a spot of land for digging their own graves, and every rice plantation would have served no other purpose than a burying ground to its European cultivators. The low lands of Carolina, which are unquestionably the richest grounds in the country, must long have remained a wilderness, had not Africans, whose natural constitutions were suited to the clime and work, been employed in cultivating this useful article of food and commerce.[97]

Like Montesquieu, Hewat was opposed to slavery on principle. Only when slavery came into open question on the eve of the Revolution did antislavery advocates realize that the theory needed refutation.[98]

On only one occasion did the comparative suitability of whites and Negroes for labor in a hot climate become the subject of outright debate, and happily the arguments were advanced in such a way as to reveal with striking clarity the social and economic pressures behind development of the climatic theory. When the colony of Georgia was founded in the 1730's the English trustees were anxious to establish a bulwark against the Spanish in Florida as well as to create a haven for debtors and the poor. The trustees and their representatives in Georgia felt strongly that Negro slaves would weaken the colony by taking the places of white workers and by rebelling against their masters in alliance with the Spanish. On the basis of this racial Gresham's law, Negroes were banned from the colony. All very well, but by the time Georgia was fairly settled, the settlers began to clamor for Negroes, whom they described "as essentially necessary to the cultivation of Georgia, as axes, hoes, or any other utensil of agriculture." [99] Some of the malcontents declared that it was "simply impossible to manufacture the rice by white men"; they described the labor of cultivation as being so

97. [Hewat], *Account of S. C. and Ga.*, I, 120.

98. Stokes, *Constitution of the British Colonies*, 415; [Benjamin Rush], *An Address to the Inhabitants of the British Settlements in America upon Slave-Keeping* (Phila., 1773), 8–9; John Wesley, *Thoughts upon Slavery* (Phila., 1774), 41–44; Granville Sharp's MS. marginal notes in [Long], *Candid Reflections upon the Negro-Cause*, 14, the copy in the Yale University Library. In fact, Negroes seem probably to have slightly greater tolerance for hot, moist climates, though there is no good evidence that white men cannot work and survive in the tropics, not to say Georgia. An experimental study is reported by Paul T. Baker, "Racial Differences in Heat Tolerance," *Amer. Jour. Physical Anthro.*, New Ser., 16 (1958), 287–305; compare this with A. Grenfell Price, with additional notes by Robert G. Stone, *White Settlers in the Tropics* (N. Y., 1939), 29–32; chap. 12.

99. [Thomas Stephens], *A Brief Account of the Causes That Have Retarded the Progress of the Colony of Georgia . . .* (London, 1743), reprinted in Ga. Hist. Soc., *Collections*, 2 (1842), 93.

severe that in other colonies "many hundreds of" Negroes " (notwithstanding all the care of their masters) yearly lose their lives by that necessary work." [100] An incessant theme in these complaints (and in many other assertions of the climatic theory) was that white men could not do such literally killing work, or rather that they preferred killing Negroes to killing themselves. The Earl of Egmont virtually admitted the validity of this argument when he airily commented, "the labour of rice growing is only proper for Negroes: but it is not designed that rice should be followed in Georgia." [101] Planters countered that Negroes were requisite for easing "the white servants from *those* labours that are most fatal to a *British constitution.*" [102]

The trustees received support from the colony of Salzburgers settled at Ebenezer. On the whole, these Germans seemed more opposed to Negroes than to slavery as such, but in any event they came out in opposition to the climatic theory. "We were told by several People, after our Arrival," they said in a petition in 1739, "that it proves quite impossible and dangerous for White People to plant and manufacture any Rice, being a Work only for Negroes, not for European People; but having Experience of the contrary, we laugh at such a Talking, seeing that several People of us have had, in the last Harvest, a greater Crop of Rice than they wanted for their own Consumption." [103] The disaffected planters reiterated, however, that the Negro and only the Negro was capable of the "more Laborious parts of Culture," especially clearing the land and cultivating rice in the heat of the Georgia sun.[104] As one group put their case, with a trace of exaggeration:

The falling of timber was a task very unequal to the strength and constitution of white servants; and the hoeing the ground, they being exposed to the sultry heat of the sun, insupportable; and it is well known, that this labour is one of the hardest upon the Negroes, even though their constitutions are much stronger than white people, and the heat no way disagreeable nor hurtful to them; but in us it created inflammatory fevers of various kinds both continued and intermittent; wasting and tormenting fluxes, most excruciating cholicks, and dry belly-aches; tremors, vertigoes, palsies, and a long tra[i]n of painful and lingring nervous distempers, which brought on to many a cessation both from work and life. . . .[105]

100. Clarence L. Ver Steeg, ed., *A True and Historical Narrative of the Colony of Georgia; by Pat. Tailfer and Others; With Comments by the Earl of Egmont* (Athens, Ga., 1960), 139.
101. *Ibid.*, 139.
102. *Ibid.*, 103.
103. Candler, comp., *Col. Recs. Ga.*, III, 429.
104. *Ibid.*, XXII, Pt. ii, 412.
105. Ver Steeg, ed., *Narrative of Georgia*, 50.

Evidently there was nothing hard work and the Georgia sun would not do to a white man.

That no one during the Georgia debate linked the supposed differences between Negroes and whites to specific physiological features does not detract from the fact that an important point concerning physical difference was being made. The trustees finally gave way of course, in 1750, though their retreat was forced not by argument but by sheer necessity. Eventually, too, the climatic argument took on more definite form and precision. In 1790, for instance, a man who had been in Jamaica for some years explained: "An European, who would be almost dissolved were he to work beneath the vertical ardours of a tropic sun, does not always consider, when he expresses his surprise that the negroes should be obliged to labour in such an intensity of heat, that the climate is congenial to their natural feelings, and that the careful benevolence of Providence has thickened their skins, to enable them to bear what would otherwise be insufferable." [106] For an earlier generation, there had been no need for such precision on the Negro's constitution nor for shoring up slavery with the "benevolence of Providence."

By 1790, though, a great many things had changed. Americans had been transformed into a free people, dwelling in an open land under an ordered government constructed on principles which were the antithesis of hierarchical. The pronounced trend during the eighteenth century toward regarding mankind as pre-eminently a species of the natural creation was accelerated by a revolution waged in favor of the Creator's endowments upon all natural men. Republican scholarship was anxious to advance the study of natural philosophy and especially to explain to hostile or uncomprehending Europeans the nature of men and of nature in America. In an era of nation-building, the character—perhaps even the complexion—of the American population was bound to come under consideration. Most immediately, of course, a revolution carried forward in the name of liberty and equality was bound to intensify and reshape the thinking of Americans concerning men who were not free and, perhaps, not equal with white men. When American colonials "awoke," as John Adams put it, to their rights, they awakened to the character of their new society. Any major shift in the way in which white Americans regarded themselves and their own society

106. Beckford, *Descriptive Account of Jamaica,* II, 65–66. Also [Long], *Candid Reflections upon the Negro-Cause,* 13–21.

was bound to affect their views of the Negro. Human self-conception is always changing and enormously complex, but it is clear that a change in self-conception of major proportions began in America just after mid-century. In this sense, as should become clear, the American Revolution was profoundly revolutionary. And of course its reverberations are not done.

Part Three

THE REVOLUTIONARY ERA

1755-1783

VII SELF-SCRUTINY IN THE
REVOLUTIONARY ERA

A GLANCE AT THE COLONISTS' THOUGHTS IN MID-eighteenth century suggests an awakening to changes which had hitherto passed without conscious assessment. It was almost as if American colonials had drifted for years down a river without noticing that they were being carried into a new country. After the Great Awakening of the early 1740's they began to evince manifestations of growing awareness that the American continent was not merely a corner of the world. When Thomas Paine inquired in 1775 whether an island should rule a continent, he played upon a sense of special destiny which had first been formulated twenty-five years earlier by the most self-conscious of Americans, Benjamin Franklin. With "One Million English Souls in North-America," Franklin predicted, the population would double every twenty-five years, and "in another Century . . . the greatest Number of Englishmen will be on this Side the Water. What an Accession of Power to the British Empire by Sea as well as Land! What Increase of Trade and Navigation! What Numbers of Ships and Seamen!" Franklin seized the opportunity to lecture imperial authorities on their obligations. "How important an Affair then to Britain, is the present Treaty for settling the Bounds between her Colonies and the French, and how careful should she be to secure Room enough, since on the Room depends so much the Increase of her People?" This self-congratulatory mood achieved new heights after stunning victories over the French in the late 1750's. The conquest of Canada, the Reverend Ezra Stiles proclaimed proudly to his congregation, suggested that divine providence was "making way for the planting and Erection in this land the best policied Empire that has yet appeared in the World. In which Liberty and property will be secured." Stiles predicted this empire would afford the manifold

[269]

blessings of "Liberty civil and religious," "apostolic purity" among the churches, and renown "for Science and Arts."

Americans were becoming conscious, also, of the diversity which characterized their communities. Religious groups had proliferated after the Great Awakening. Boatloads of immigrants were arriving from Germany, Africa, and the countries of the British Isles. Owing to the pattern of migration and settlement, religious and ethnic diversity among white men was greatest in Pennsylvania and the southern back country. For a time, Franklin fretted about the future of Pennsylvania where "the Palatine Boors" were crowding out "the English." But the greater threat was, as Franklin said and most Americans must have sensed, that importation of slaves had "blacken'd half America." [1]

The growth of American self-awareness formed an important theme during the gathering political crisis prior to the Revolution. Indeed the Revolution has been said to have been primarily a revolution in American consciousness. If this was the case in the realm of politics, it was even more so in the shadowy realm of communal intellect and self-identification. But it is impossible to separate completely the two realms, and their inseparability becomes apparent in the development of antislavery during the Revolutionary era. Indeed the assumption of heightening self-awareness in America serves to tie together apparently disparate developments in the period. Americans came to realize that they were no longer Englishmen; at the same time they grew conscious of their own "prejudices" concerning Negroes. As they began to question slavery, they began to see that there was a race problem in America and that it was necessary to assert the fundamental equality of Negroes with white men and to combat suggestions to the contrary. In doing so they embraced a mode of thought which for a half century was to serve the purposes of those who sought to achieve a viable national community. Environmentalism became an engine in the hands of republicans asserting their independence from the Old World. It was an integral aspect of the ideology of the Revolution, which itself was rooted in ideas about property and liberty and in the concept of equality. During the Revolution interesting transformations revealed themselves in *that* ancient concept: equality was naturalized, legalized, politicized, and nationalized. Perhaps these barbarisms do something to summarize what

1. "Observations Concerning the Increase of Mankind" (1751), Labaree *et al.*, eds., *Papers of Franklin*, IV, 232–34; Edmund S. Morgan, *The Gentle Puritan: A Life of Ezra Stiles, 1727–1795* (New Haven and London, 1962), 213–14.

happened to attitudes toward Negroes in the Revolutionary era if they are set in the context of awakening self-consciousness in America.

1. QUAKER CONSCIENCE AND CONSCIOUSNESS

The rapid growth of antislavery began before the onset of the political crisis, but it remained confined to one religious sect until Americans began protesting against certain imperial measures. Significantly, the rapid spread of antislavery sentiments among the Quakers occurred at a time when the Society, especially in Pennsylvania, was painfully reappraising its position in a predominantly non-Quaker colony. When war broke out against the French in 1754, the ravaging Indian assaults on frontier settlements were soon translated into private struggles within both the Society of Friends and the minds of individual Quakers. The eruption of violence threatened the purity of pacifist principles and hence the very existence of Quaker political control in Pennsylvania; and finally some Friends withdrew from the Assembly rather than vote for military measures. Connected with this withdrawal was an outbreak of revivalistic self-searching among Quakers.[2] As they examined their moral condition they found slaveholding to be one of their most crying faults; feeling against the practice developed so rapidly that in 1758 the Philadelphia Yearly Meeting, citing the "desolating calamities of war and bloodshed," formally recorded its hope that Friends would set their slaves at liberty and ruled that any Friend buying or selling slaves should be excluded from the business affairs of Meetings. From 1758 until 1776, antislavery activists in the most important Quaker jurisdiction in America labored and dealt with members "to do the thing that was right." Finally, several months after adoption of the Declaration of Independence, the Philadelphia Yearly Meeting noted that "many there are in membership with us who, notwithstanding the labor bestowed, still continue to hold these people as slaves" and ordered that Monthly Meetings disown Friends who resisted all persuasion to the Truth.[3] In slower but equally characteristic fashion the other four Yearly Meetings moved progressively first against members' dealing in slaves and then against ownership. By the end of the war the

2. Sydney V. James, *A People Among Peoples: Quaker Benevolence in Eighteenth-Century America* (Cambridge, Mass., 1963), chaps. 8–12.

3. Drake, *Quakers and Slavery*, 61, 69, 72. See also Darold D. Wax, "Quaker Merchants and the Slave Trade in Colonial Pennsylvania," *Pa. Mag. of Hist. and Biog.*, 86 (1962), 143–59.

Society had advanced a long way toward being clear of the sin of making slaves of other men. Although well-known Quaker publicists like Anthony Benezet spread antislavery principles among the world's people until the end of the Revolutionary War the Quaker antislavery crusade aimed first and foremost at ridding the Society of Friends of the moral taint of slaveholding.

This Quaker concentration on slaveholding as a fault in themselves arose partly from the nature of Quakerism. As a people set apart from others they were inclined to dwell introspectively on their own peculiarities. Certainly the strong equalitarian strain in Quakerism as well as mounting humanitarian sentiment within and without the Society guided their introspection toward sympathy with the oppressed. Yet their tribalistic concentration on their own condition, which was intensified and channeled by their peculiar ecclesiastical organization, meant that Quaker opposition to slavery was for many years a distinct strand in American antislavery thought, constantly interacting but never quite coalescing with other elements in the antislavery movement. Eventually, Quakers were to become a quiet voice of conscience to the nation.

At the same time, Quaker concentration on the inward sin of degrading Negroes was not totally unconnected with the increased self-awareness which characterized so much of colonial thought from the Great Awakening onward. Nowhere is this fact so clear as in the writings of John Woolman, the man who as much as any other galvanized the Quakers into action. Woolman is usually admired as the founding father of Quaker antislavery and as typically, even archetypically, embodying the Quaker spirit of brotherhood and the fellowship of man. Unfortunately, his very saintliness—and he was a saint without being a martyr about it—has distracted attention from his perceptive intellect and the astonishingly thorough fashion in which he presaged America's awakening to its racial problem. For it was John Woolman who first clearly exposed the tangle of difficulties which had overgrown the path toward abolition of Negro slavery. By the beginning of the war many Americans who shared his aims but not his religious convictions had discovered the same tangle by means of a similar process of self-evaluation.

In 1743, as if struck by lightning, Woolman suddenly recognized his aversion to human slavery when he was asked to write a bill of sale for a Negro. Three years after this conversion, upon returning to New Jersey from a trip through Maryland and Virginia, he jotted down thoughts on the subject which were published as two pamphlets in 1754, one under his own name and the other as the widely circulated Yearly Epistle of the Philadelphia Yearly Meeting.[4] His overwhelming sense of empathy, which with Woolman was both a character trait and a religious principle, led him to explore the feelings of the oppressed: "let us calmly consider their Circumstance; and, the better to do it, make their Case ours."

Suppose then, that our Ancestors and we had been exposed to constant Servitude, in the more servile and inferior Employments of Life; that we had been destitute of the Help of Reading and good Company; that amongst ourselves we had had few wise and pious Instructors; that the Religious amongst our Superiors seldom took Notice of us; that while others, in Ease, have plentifully heaped up the Fruit of our Labour, we had receiv'd barely enough to relieve Nature, and being wholly at the Command of others, had generally been treated as a contemptible, ignorant Part of Mankind: Should we, in that Case, be less abject than they now are? Again, if Oppression be so hard to bear, that a wise Man is made mad by it, Eccl. vii. 7, then a Series of those Things, altering the Behaviour and Manners of a People, is what may reasonably be expected. . . . These and other Circumstances, rightly considered, will lessen that too great Disparity which some make between us and them.

In addition to recognizing the crushing effects of slavery upon the enslaved, Woolman realized that oppression was a two-way street. If we can cut through his religious terminology to his inner meaning, we can see him groping toward a new cognizance of the effects of slavery upon white men: "being concerned with a People so situated that they have no Voice to plead their own Cause, there's Danger of using ourselves to an undisturbed Partiality, till, by long Custom, the Mind becomes reconciled with it, and the Judgment itself infected." Woolman was of course most concerned with slavery's propagation of an unseemly pride within the slaveholder; his concern was similar to Thomas Jefferson's a generation later. "And if Children are not only educated in the Way of so great Temptation," Woolman wrote, "but have also the Opportunity of lording it over their Fellow Creatures, and being Masters of Men in their Childhood, how can we hope otherwise than that their tender Minds will be possessed with Thoughts too high for them?" "For while the Life of one," he summarized aphoristically, "is made grievous by the Rigour of another, it entails Misery on both."[5]

In the years after publication of his pamphlet and Yearly Epistle,

4. Janet Whitney, *John Woolman: American Quaker* (Boston, 1942), chap. 21.
5. John Woolman, *Some Considerations on the Keeping of Negroes. Recommended to the Professors of Christianity of Every Denomination* (Phila., 1754), reprinted in Amelia Mott Gummere, ed., *The Journal and Essays of John Woolman* . . . (N. Y., 1922), 338–39, 342–43.

Woolman became more active in visiting Friends to persuade them to Truth. He journeyed through Virginia again in 1757. Evidently he encountered more than passive resistance to his persuasion, for his next antislavery tract (1762) was intended in part as a gentle reproof to proslavery arguments. At considerable length he tried to show that Scripture, far from supporting Negro slavery, required kind treatment and manumission. He quoted long passages from accounts of the slave trade in Africa to demonstrate dramatically both its inhumanity and utter wrongfulness—an antislavery technique then being brought to perfection by another Quaker, Anthony Benezet. Most important, he thought through more carefully than before the effects of Negro slavery upon white men and the consequent difficulty of achieving abolition. If most of his points had been mentioned incidentally by friends of the Negro in earlier years, Woolman's compendium showed such a greater depth of self-awareness as to be revolutionary.

Perhaps his most important insight was recognition of the interactive relationship between the Negro's debased status and the debasement of Negroes in the eyes of white men. The very system of slavery, Woolman insisted, inculcated a pride which was corruption and the reverse of brotherhood. "Placing on Men the ignominious Title, SLAVE, dressing them in uncomely Garments, keeping them to servile Labour, in which they are often dirty, tends gradually to fix a Notion in the Mind, that they are a Sort of People below us in Nature, and leads us to consider them as such in all our Conclusions about them." For Woolman, only charity could overcome the spirit of oppression: "The Blacks seem far from being our Kinsfolks; . . . They have neither Honours, Riches, outward Magnificence nor Power; their Dress coarse, and often ragged; their Employ Drudgery, and much in the Dirt: they have little or nothing at Command; but must wait upon and work for others to obtain the Necessaries of Life: so that, in their present Situation, there is not much to engage the Friendship, or move the Affection of selfish men." By looking upon the hearts of men, Woolman had linked the Negro's outward condition with the white man's inner corruption; wrongful enslavement of Negroes, he wrote in a telling phrase, "deprave[s] the Mind in like Manner, and with as great Certainty, as prevailing Cold congeals Water."

Woolman was acutely conscious of the racial element at the root of this individual and social corruption. "Through the Force of long Custom," he wrote with his customary, almost oblique mildness, "it appears needful to speak in Relation to Colour." White children, "born of Parents of the meanest Sort," were never considered candidates for a lifetime in slavery. "This is owing chiefly to the Idea of Slavery being connected with the Black Colour, and Liberty with the White: and where false Ideas are twisted into our Minds, it is with difficulty we get fairly disentangled." Thus Woolman laid bare the dynamic which made racial slavery different from any other. In much the same manner as Cotton Mather, he denied that color was in any way relevant to justice, but unlike Mather, Woolman was alive to the workings of the psychological mechanism he was dealing with. As a Quaker he necessarily described it in terms of *self*-interest, the obverse of charity: "Selfishness being indulged, clouds the Understanding; and where selfish Men, for a long Time, proceed on their Way without Opposition, the Deceivableness of Unrighteousness gets so rooted in their Intellects, that a candid Examination of Things relating to Self-interest is prevented; and in this Circumstance, some who would not agree to make a Slave of a Person whose Colour is like their own, appear easy in making Slaves of others of a different Colour, though their Understandings and Morals are equal to the Generality of Men of their own Colour." The essential difficulty was, as Woolman explained in more familiar language, that "the Ideas of *Negroes* and Slaves are so interwoven in the Mind." [6]

In retrospect, the importance of John Woolman's insights lay in the fact that they rapidly became commonplace. Partly this was owing to his direct influence. His pamphlet of 1762 was his last published work bearing directly upon slavery, but he remained a key figure in suffusing antislavery principles among Friends until his death ten years later. Anthony Benezet, less persuasive in person but more prolific on paper, had almost certainly been affected by personal conversation with Woolman when he wrote, also in 1762, that Negroes "are constantly employed in servile Labour, and the abject Condition in which we see them, from our Childhood, has a natural Tendency to create in us an Idea of a Superiority over them, which induces most People to look upon them as an ignorant and contemptible Part of Mankind." [7] As the campaign to cleanse the Quaker fellowship of slaveholding became increasingly successful, Quaker writers began to speak of the basic problem of racial

---

6. John Woolman, *Considerations on Keeping Negroes; Recommended to the Professors of Christianity, of Every Denomination. Part Second* (Phila., 1762), reprinted in Gummere, ed., *Journal and Essays of Woolman,* 353, 363, 366–68, 380.

7. [Benezet], *Short Account of Africa,* 51.

slavery as if it were a universal social law more than a failure of charity within their Society. "The power of prejudice," David Cooper of Burlington, New Jersey, declared in 1772, "over the minds of mankind is very extraordinary; hardly any extreams too distant, or absurdities too glaring for it to unite or reconcile, if it tends to promote or justify a favourite pursuit. It is thus we are to account for the fallacious reasonings and absurd sentiments used and entertained concerning negroes, and the lawfulness of keeping them slaves. The low contempt with which they are generally treated by the whites, lead children from the first dawn of reason, to consider people with a black skin, on a footing with domestic animals, form'd to serve and obey." [8]

2. THE DISCOVERY OF PREJUDICE

This recognition that Americans were "prejudiced" toward Negroes was by no means confined to Quakers. Indeed the concept of "prejudice" toward social groups—the very term itself!—came suddenly into wide currency in the years after 1760. Principally, of course, the concept pertained to the white man's reaction to the Negro. Samuel Hopkins, the prominent New Divinity minister of Newport, asked why Americans saw Negroes as "fit for nothing but slaves." The reason, he explained, was that "we have been used to look on them in a mean, contemptible light; and our education has filled us with strong prejudices against them, and led us to consider them, not as our brethren, or in any degree on a level with us; but as quite another species of animals, made only to serve us and our children; and as happy in bondage, as in any other state. . . . If we could only divest ourselves of these strong prejudices, which have insensibly fixed on our minds, and consider them as, by nature, and by right, on a level with our brethren and children, and those of our neighbors." [9] This novel introspection into "prejudices" was not confined to the problem of the Negro's condition. In a famous pamphlet assailing the wanton massacre of some friendly Indians in Pennsylvania, Benjamin Franklin pointed out the logical absurdities which underlay all racial categorization.

8. [David Cooper], *A Mite Cast into the Treasury: Or, Observations on Slave-Keeping* (Phila., [1772]), iii (Evans no. 12322).

9. [Samuel Hopkins], *A Dialogue Concerning the Slavery of the Africans; Shewing It To Be the Duty and Interest of the American Colonies to Emancipate All Their African Slaves . . .* (Norwich, Conn., 1776), 34. See also [Nathaniel Appleton], *Considerations on Slavery. In a Letter to a Friend* (Boston, 1767), 14-15.

If an *Indian* injures me, does it follow that I may revenge that Injury on all *Indians?* It is well known, that *Indians* are of different Tribes, Nations and Languages, as well as the White People. In *Europe,* if the *French,* who are White People, should injure the *Dutch,* are they to revenge it on the *English* because they too are White People? The only Crime of these poor Wretches seems to have been, that they had a reddish-brown Skin, and black Hair; and some people of that Sort, it seems, had murdered some of our Relations. If it be right to kill Men for such a Reason, then, should any Man, with a freckled Face and red Hair, kill a Wife or Child of mine, it would be right for me to revenge it, by killing all the freckled red-haired Men, Women and Children, I could afterwards anywhere meet with.[10]

Nor were attacks upon "prejudice" necessarily confined to the problem of disengaging men from their color. Nicholas Cresswell, a young and delightfully candid Englishman who traveled in America with a ready pen and an unusually open mind, decided that distaste for peoples of another culture was also an instance of "prejudice." His gratitude toward some gentlemen for various kindnesses, he said, gave him pause for a particular reason: they were "all Scotchmen, to which nation I had a particular dislike, owing to the prejudice of my education." Yet he had always liked the ones he met, and he wished therefore to "most heartily condemn this pernicious system of education by which we are taught to look upon the inhabitants of a different nation, language or complexion, as a set of beings far inferior to our own. This is a most illiberal and confined sentiment, for human nature is invariably the same throughout the whole human species, from the sooty Africans down to the fair European, allowance being made for their different customs, manners and education." [11] By this logic, all differences among men were individual; all groupings of men were "illiberal." What mattered was human membership, as individuals, in the human species.

This suddenly heightened awareness about social attitudes resulted in part from and in turn affected certain long-term developments in eighteenth-century thought, among them a decline of religious intensity in many quarters, the search for universal and frequently rather mechanistic principles of human motivation, the apotheosis of "reason," and fascination with the natural environment. In America one of the most compelling of these interrelated elements was the ethnic diversity which characterized the colonies. If they for a moment paused to examine carefully their relations

10. *A Narrative of the Late Massacres . . . ,* in Albert Henry Smyth, ed., *The Writings of Benjamin Franklin,* 10 vols. (N. Y., 1905–07) , IV, 298.
11. Thornely, ed., *Journal of Nicholas Cresswell,* 205.

with Indians on the frontier and particularly with Negroes in their families and plantations, Americans could hardly help but recognize that these relations were affected by perceptible physical differences. The physiognomic distinction would not down. Nor has it today: Franklin's little speech about red hair is still used for the same purpose. Cresswell also sensed the intransigence of the central difficulty, for after starting out with a condemnation of cultural "prejudices" he ended up by talking about "sooty Africans" and "fair Europeans."

Amidst the protests against British encroachments upon their liberties in the 1760's and 1770's, some Americans came to realize, in far sharper terms than ever before, that they had on their hands a color problem. At first, despite Woolman's formulation of the problem, recognition came haltingly in the form of ridicule or indignant denial that blackness was any justification for slavery. This line of argument had been advanced long before by proponents of Negro conversion, but ironically and perhaps appropriately, it was first advanced in connection with slavery by a European. The colonists picked up Montesquieu's remarks in the *Spirit of the Laws* (1748) and passed them around the increasingly active antislavery circuit. Erratic young James Otis, delivering one of the opening barrages in defense of colonial rights in 1764, derided the logic of slavery based on color: "The Colonists are by the law of nature free born, as indeed all men are, white or black. No better reasons can be given, for enslaving those of any color than such as baron Montesquieu has humorously given. . . . Does it follow that tis right to enslave a man because he is black? Will short curl'd hair like wool, instead of christian hair, as tis called by those, whose hearts are as hard as the nether millstone, help the argument? Can any logical inference in favour of slavery, be drawn from a flat nose, a long or a short face." [12] Antislavery writers took up the theme and played it vigorously. One conjectured that some oppressors of the Negro "perhaps may conceive from their colour that they are of an inferiour species and that they may be oppressed without guilt." Another mocked the claim of the slaveholder: "But they are black, and ought to obey; we are white and ought to rule." A third declared that "Some have been so grossly stupid as to assign colour as a mark for servitude. This, if it could prove any thing would prove too much. It would establish it, that all complexions but the fairest should be, in some degree deprived of liberty. That all black

12. Otis, *Rights of the British Colonies*, 29. Montesquieu's remarks may be found in Nugent, trans., *Spirit of the Laws*, I, 238–39 (bk. 15, sec. 5).

persons should be slaves, says Montesquieu, is as ridiculous as that law of a certain country, that all red-haired persons should be hanged." [13]

Taken at face value, these statements seem to be only slightly more explicit versions of previous assertions of the irrelevance of color to men's proper spiritual condition. The staying power of traditional Christian equalitarianism was evident in admonitions given by the Reverend Andrew Eliot in 1774. "We are all children of the same Father," he insisted; "one God hath created us; and he hath, in the essential part of our constitution, fashioned our souls alike. We ought, therefore, to treat one another as brethren. This we may do, and yet a suitable distinction be preserved.—The meanest slave hath a soul as good by nature as your's, and possibly by grace it is better. A dark complection may cover a fair and beautiful mind." [14] What was new about this line of argument was that it achieved wide currency in an atmosphere where slavery seemed not merely wrong but at variance with American professions of attachment to liberty. The logic of color seemed to run counter to the logic of English liberties. If this wedge of an argument were driven very far home, however, it was bound to split open and expose the fundamental problem: extending liberty to Negroes was enormously difficult simply because they did not look like other Americans. As antislavery advocates hammered away, the popular assignment of "the colour as a mark for servitude" was bound to become not only "grossly stupid" but a major impediment to emancipation. What was at first perceived as a logical absurdity was gradually recognized to be the rock upon which slavery was founded.

At an early stage, Woolman's sensitivity to the feelings of his opponents permitted him to recognize the association of color with slavery as an obstacle to right action rather than to mistake it for a mere absurdity to be dismissed by reference to red-headed men. After about 1770 others came to the same realization. An

13. Charles Crawford, *Observations upon Negro-Slavery* (Phila., 1784), 4; [David Cooper], *A Serious Address to the Rulers of America, on the Inconsistency of Their Conduct Respecting Slavery: Forming a Contrast between the Encroachments of England on American Liberty, and, American Injustice in Tolerating Slavery* (Trenton, 1783), 8 (Evans no. 17839); "Thoughts upon the Enfranchisement of the Negroes," *United States Mag.*, 1 (1779), 487–88; see also *Observations on the Slavery of the Negroes, in the Southern States, Particularly Intended for the Citizens of Virginia* (N. Y., 1785), 9.

14. Andrew Eliot, *Twenty Sermons* (Boston, 1774), 49–50.

anonymous West Indian critic of slavery wrote concerning the planters, "The ideas of laziness, vice, blackness and slavery, are so blended, so twisted together in their minds, that they may be supposed as utterly incapable of separating them." [15] The concept was pressed into startlingly modern shape by Jonathan Boucher, an Anglican minister in Maryland who became a courageous and astute critic of American resistance to imperial authority. "Thus much, however, I may be permitted to observe," Boucher wrote, "that, in no other country was slavery so well regulated as it is in the British colonies. In some respects I hope it is on a better footing than it ever was, or is, any where else: but it is surely worse in this, that here, in one sense, it never can end. An African slave, even when made free, supposing him to be possessed even of talents and of virtue, can never, in these colonies, be quite on terms of equality with a free white man. Nature has placed insuperable barriers in his way. This is a circumstance of great moment; though, I think, it has not often been adverted to by popular writers." More boldly, the Marquis de Chastellux, visiting in the best American circles toward the end of the war, directly contrasted non-racial slavery with the novel institution which had sprung up in America. Not enough distinction had been made, Chastellux declared, between the ancient and the modern institutions: slaves in Greece and Rome could, when freed, embody with their onetime masters. "But in the present case, it is not only the slave who is beneath his master, it is the Negro who is beneath the white man. No act of enfranchisement can efface this unfortunate distinction." [16]

Most antislavery writers failed to see the matter so clearly because their vision was blurred by devotion to their cause. For if blackness meant that slavery could never really end, as Boucher said, then their efforts were tinged with futility. If blackness was indeed intrinsic to slavery, then slavery could never be completely abolished without erasing the Negro's color. Few men, as yet, held any hope that the Ethiopian could change his skin. And the strength of antislavery principles had not yet been fully tested. The hope that the Negro could be freed discouraged concentration on the worst of obstacles to freedom.

15. ["Morgan"], *Abolition of Slavery in the West Indies*, 8–9; see also [Cooper], *Serious Address on Slavery*, 7.

16. Jonathan Boucher, *A View of the Causes and Consequences of the American Revolution; in Thirteen Discourses, Preached in North America between the Years 1763 and 1775: with an Historical Preface* (London, 1797), 40; Chastellux, *Travels in North America*, ed. Rice, II, 440.

3. ASSERTIONS OF SAMENESS

The eyes of antislavery advocates tended to fall, therefore, upon problems which were sensed to be more tractable than the Negro's complexion. With the institution of slavery being brought into question by Revolutionary ideology, moreover, antislavery writers were canvassing about for effective arguments in favor of abolition. Though they could not easily defend the Negro's color, they found that they could—and had to—defend his character. They discovered many discreditable human qualities which were associated with Negroes by the "prejudices" of the popular mind, but if Negroes were "brutish, ignorant, idle, crafty, treacherous, bloody, thievish, mistrustful, and superstitious," [17] perhaps they might be reformed. Better still, these unlovely characteristics in the Negro afforded standing arguments for his emancipation. What better way to reform a man than to free him from the bondage of chattel slavery? Escape from the bondage of sin into the liberty of the Christian had always worked wonders. The logic was particularly effective in that it completely inverted a major justification for slavery: the Negro's immorality and ignorance could be completely transformed by saying that these qualities were not a reason for but the result of enslavement. If the Negro's failings resulted from the very nature of oppression, then all that was required was that oppression be brought to an end. Reform would follow.

Inversion of the causal sequence of vice and slavery was easily accomplished. Dr. Benjamin Rush didactically explained the proper relation between the two conditions: "Slavery is so foreign to the human mind, that the moral faculties, as well as those of the understanding are debased, and rendered torpid by it. All the vices which are charged upon the Negroes in the southern colonies and the West-Indies, such as Idleness, Treachery, Theft, and the like, are the genuine offspring of slavery, and serve as an argument to prove that they were not intended, by Providence for it." William Dillwyn, a perceptive Quaker from Burlington, elaborated this inversion in a private letter: "If the Negroes are generally '*unprincipled and vicious,*'" Dillwyn asked (apparently quoting a Dr. Chandler), "is it not the natural Consequence of a State of Slavery? Can we reasonably expect their Morals or Manners will equal those of Freemen, until they are cultivated with the same Degree of Care, in

17. [Long], *Jamaica*, II, 354.

an equally extensive Field of Action, and with the same Encouragement? Were a Number of *Whites* treated just as they are . . . who
will venture to assert that it would not occasion a like Depression of
Spirit, and consequent Depravity of Manners?" By this reasoning,
abolition of slavery was a kindness, a duty, and an impressive act of
reformation.[18]

Advocates of abolition found this argument from the poisonous
environment of slavery an essential weapon for combatting suggestions that Negroes were deficient in understanding. That such
suggestions were fairly common is made evident by the early and
persistent efforts of the antislavery people to refute them.
Antislavery advocates had to deal as best they could with the
ill-defined, rarely articulated feeling of many Americans, especially
in the South, that Negroes were inherently stupid and unfeeling. As
a young New Englander visiting in the Carolinas complained, rather
too strongly, "The Africans are said to be inferior in point of
sense and understanding, sentiment and feeling, to the Europeans
and other white nations. Hence the one infer a right to enslave the
other." [19]

Given the not very elevated level of learning among Negro slaves
it was not an easy task to transform the Negro into the mental peer
of the white man. As early as 1762 Anthony Benezet explained that
he was quoting extensively from the narratives of travelers in
Guinea to prove "that the *Negroes* are generally sensible, humane
and sociable, and that their Capacity is as good, and as capable of
Improvement, as that of the White People." By the 1770's outright
denials of Negro mental inferiority had become common. Benjamin
Franklin thought Negroes "not deficient in natural Understanding," though Alexander Hamilton seemed less certain
when he remarked that "their natural faculties are ~~perhaps~~ probably as good as ours." [20]

18. [Rush], *Address upon Slave-Keeping*, 2–3, also 22; William Dillwyn to John
Mehelm, Burlington, Feb. 16, 1774, Miscellaneous Manuscripts-D, N.-Y. Hist. Soc.
19. Howe, ed., "Journal of Josiah Quincy, Jr.," Mass. Hist. Soc., *Proceedings*, 49
(1915–16), 463.
20. [Benezet], *Short Account of Africa*, 8 (a constant theme in his writings);
Franklin to the Marquis de Condorcet, London, Mar. 20, 1774, Smyth, ed.,
Writings of Franklin, VI, 222; Hamilton to John Jay, [Middlebrook, N. J., Mar.
14, 1779], Harold C. Syrett and Jacob E. Cooke, eds., *The Papers of Alexander
Hamilton* (N. Y., 1961—), II, 17–18. See also Benjamin Colman in Newburyport,
Mass., *Essex Journal*, Mar. 8, 1776; James Swan, *A Dissuasion to Great-Britain
and the Colonies, from the Slave Trade to Africa* . . . (Boston, [1772]), 58, 69;
Wesley, *Thoughts upon Slavery*, 47.

More effective than denial was application of the environmental-ist argument in either of two ways. On the one hand, the Negro's supposed mental inferiority could be dismissed as a figment of the white man's imagination turned febrile by the "prejudices" engen-dered by the institution of slavery. Anthony Benezet, for one, stated that on the basis of his experience with children in his Negro school he could "with Truth and Sincerity declare . . . that the notion entertained by some, that the Blacks are inferior to the Whites in their capacities, is vulgar prejudice, founded on the Pride or Igno-rance of their lordly Masters, who have kept their Slaves at such a distance, as to be unable to form a right judgment of them." Alexander Hewat, Presbyterian minister in Charleston, presented a similar argument showing that "the inhabitants of Africa have the same faculties with those of Europe." The alternative method of appealing to environment was somewhat more popular. Current weakness of understanding in the Negro could be readily conceded and then laid to the noxious effects of slavery. As John Wesley declared succinctly in 1774, "Their stupidity therefore in our plan-tations is not natural; otherwise than it is the natural effect of their condition." Samuel Hopkins suggested the same principle by re-marking that "a state of slavery has a mighty tendency to sink and contract the minds of men." Benjamin Rush characteristically tried to take every tack at once by saying that travelers had shown the Negroes in Africa to be ingenious and humane, "equal to the Europeans, when we allow for the diversity of temper and genius which is occasioned by climate," and that American slavery had "debased" the "faculties" of the Negroes' "understanding." [21]

Equalitarian antislavery advocates were so anxious to find tangi-ble evidence for their contentions concerning mental equality that they almost trampled each other in rushing to acclaim the first exemplar of Negro literary talent. A French official living in Amer-ica during the war took surprised and rather bemused note of the sudden appearance of this remarkable prodigy, "one of the strangest creatures in the country and perhaps in the whole world." "Phyllis is a negress," wrote the Marquis de Barbé-Marbois, "born in Africa, brought to Boston at the age of ten, and sold to a citizen of that city. She learned English with unusual ease, eagerly read and reread the

21. [Anthony Benezet], *Short Observations on Slavery, Introductory to Some Extracts from the Writing of the Abbe Raynal, on that Important Subject* ([Phila., 1781]), 11–12; [Hewat], *Account of S. C. and Ga.*, II, 101; Wesley, *Thoughts upon Slavery*, 47; [Hopkins], *Dialogue Concerning Slavery*, 44; [Rush], *Address upon Slave-Keeping*, 2.

Bible, the only book which had been put in her hands, became
steeped in the poetic images of which it is full, and at the age of
seventeen published a number of poems in which there is imagination, poetry, and zeal, though no correctness nor order nor interest.
I read them with some surprise. They are printed, and in the front
of the book there are certificates of authenticity which leave no
doubt that she is its author." [22] The poems were indeed by Phyllis
Wheatley and were first published in London in 1773. The publication of five editions before 1800 and their widespread circulation
testified to the importance of the author's race. The poems themselves were written in the effusive, coupleted style so popular in the
eighteenth century. One, for example, descanted "On the Death of
the Rev. Mr. George Whitefield. 1770."

> Hail, happy saint, on thine immortal throne,
> Possest of glory, life, and bliss unknown;
> We hear no more the music of thy tongue,
> Thy wonted auditories cease to throng.
> Thy sermons in unequall'd accents flow'd,
> And ev'ry bosom with devotion glow'd;
> Thou didst in strains of eloquence refin'd
> Inflame the heart, and captivate the mind.
> Unhappy we the setting sun deplore,
> So Glorious once, but ah! it shines no more.[23]

If lines like these are not well suited to modern tastes, their appearance admirably suited the needs of antislavery advocates. Phillis
Wheatley could scarcely have been better for their purposes. She
was young, raised in Africa, enslaved, untutored, and a girl to boot.
If a Negro laboring under this load of disabilities could write such
acceptable poems, how much greater genius might someday be
expected to appear among "the sable generation." Phillis Wheatley,
"the negro poetess," became antislavery's most prized exhibit, her
name virtually a household term for the Negro's mental equality.[24]

22. Eugene P. Chase, trans., and ed., *Our Revolutionary Forefathers; The
Letters of François, Marquis de Barbé-Marbois during His Residence in the
United States as Secretary of the French Legation, 1779–1785* (N. Y., 1929),
84–85.

23. Phillis Wheatley, *Poems on Various Subjects, Religious and Moral* (London, 1773), 22.

24. Or, as she is so delightfully labeled in one recent book, "the negress poet."
[Rush], *Address upon Slave-Keeping*, 2n; Phila. *Pennsylvania Packet*, May 24,
1773; New Haven *Connecticut Journal*, Apr. 1, 1774; John Rogers Williams,
ed., *Philip Vickers Fithian: Journal and Letters, 1767–1774*, 2 vols. (Princeton,
1900–34), I, 118; *Letters of the Late Ignatius Sancho, an African. To Which Are*

In far-off Goettingen, Blumenbach triumphantly proclaimed her poems "a collection which scarcely any one who has any taste for poetry could read without pleasure." [25]

The handful of public opponents of Negro equality were disgusted by this lionizing. One of them twitted Benjamin Rush for peddling "a single example of a negro girl writing a few silly poems, to prove that the blacks are not deficient to us in understanding." Bernard Romans, a capable but unorthodox natural philosopher, claimed that "against the Phillis of Boston (who is the *Phaenix* of her race) i could bring at least twenty well known instances of the contrary effect of education on this sable generation." Edward Long, a judge who resided in Jamaica for a dozen years before returning to England, ridiculed the popular favor accorded these Negro achievements:

> What woeful stuff this madrigal would be
> In some starv'd, hackney sonneteer, or me!
> But let a *Negroe* own the happy lines,
> How the wit brightens! How the Style refines!
> Before his sacred name flies ev'ry fault,
> And each exalted stanza teems with thought!

From the very first, Negro literature was chained to the issue of racial equality.[26]

Proponents of Negro equality could scarcely rest their entire case on the poems of a little Negro girl. No matter how successful they were in demonstrating that talent could blossom amidst the weeds of slavery, moreover, equalitarians faced the task of explaining away the embarrassingly barbarous condition of unenslaved Negroes in Africa. If the Negro was naturally the equal of the white man, why was he so notoriously barbarous in his natural state?

Prefixed Memoirs of His Life, 2 vols. (London, 1782) , I, 175–76; Crawford, *Observations upon Negro Slavery,* 5*n;* John C. Fitzpatrick, ed., *The Writings of George Washington . . . 1745–1799,* 39 vols. (Washington, 1931–44) , IV, 360–61; Dixon and Hunter's Wmsbg. *Va. Gaz.,* Mar. 30, 1776; Boston *Independent Chronicle,* Jan. 29, 1778; Benjamin Franklin to Jonathan Williams, London, July 7, 1773, Smyth, ed., *Writings of Franklin,* VI, 96; Edwards A. Park, *Memoir of the Life and Character of Samuel Hopkins, D. D.,* 2d ed. (Boston, 1854) , 137–38; Edward D. Seeber, "Phillis Wheatley," *Jour. Negro Hist.,* 24 (1939) , 259–62.

25. John Friedrich Blumenbach, "Contributions to Natural History. Part 1" (Goettingen, 1806) , in Bendyshe, trans., *Treatises of Blumenbach,* 310 and note.

26. [Richard Nisbet], *Slavery Not Forbidden by Scripture . . .* (Phila., 1773) , 23*n.* (original entirely italics) ; Romans, *Florida,* 105; [Long], *Jamaica,* II, 484. Long was actually referring to her less famous West Indian counterpart, Francis Williams, *ibid.,* II, 475–85; and also Ramsay, *Treatment and Conversion of African Slaves,* 238–39.

Happily for the antislavery people, there were several routes around
this difficulty. Some writers, notably Anthony Benezet, pooh-poohed
the alleged barbarism of the Africans. Eagerly thumbing through
reports by European travelers in West Africa, they managed sometimes to portray the life of Negroes unmolested by Europeans as one
of idyllic simplicity. This Eden-like picture afforded the further
advantage of enabling the writer to entail upon the slave trade all
the current manifestations of barbarity in Africa. Thus a dual
purpose was served: the trade stood condemned as responsible for
barbaric tribal warfare and enslavement, and the Negroes became
the innocent victims of European brutality.[27] It had to be admitted
that Africans were at a different stage of civilization, but antislavery
advocates announced that they were no more savage than the "Ancient *Britains*" had been before their translation into their undeniably preferable present state. The natives of Africa, furthermore, had
never been exposed to the inestimably civilizing influence of Christianity, though no one was able to explain precisely why.[28]

One of the surest reliances for the antislavery people was the
African climate; it was easy to fall back on the time-worn principle
of Western anthropology that climate made the man. This argument from natural environment was a highly versatile means of
conveying the principle of Negro equality, since it could be steered
in any direction. It could be easily utilized to confirm the innocence
of the African natives in the face of rapacious slave traders: "the
Africans are an harmless people," wrote Nathaniel Appleton, "having never gone beyond their own bounds, to trouble mankind; and
but for the interruption from white people might enjoy all the
sweets of a rural life; being bless'd with a fine fruitful soil, which
yields with small labour all the necessaries of life." [29] In similar
fashion, it could be used to explain away African barbarism. Did
the natives of Africa enslave each other? Excessive heat had depraved them. Did the natives live in ease and peaceful indolence?
Their tropical surroundings made exertion unnecessary, since nature readily yielded up its fruits without the strenuous human
exertions required in colder climates.

More than anyone, Benjamin Rush, a benevolent physician and a

27. [Benezet], *Short Account of Africa*; Anthony Benezet, *Some Historical
Account of Guinea, Its Situation, Produce and the General Disposition of Its
Inhabitants. With an Inquiry into the Rise and Progress of the Slave-Trade, Its
Nature and Lamentable Effects* . . . (Phila., 1771).
28. For example, Benezet, *Historical Account of Guinea*, 68–69; Swan, *Dissuasion from the Slave Trade*, 57–58; Hopkins, *Dialogue Concerning Slavery*, 7.
29. [Appleton], *Considerations on Slavery*, 5.

firm patriot, rode the crest of this argument toward the goal of fundamental equality. "I shall allow," he wrote disarmingly in 1773, "that many of them are inferior in Virtue, Knowledge, and the love of Liberty to the Inhabitants of other parts of the World: but this may be explained from *Physical* causes." The vast and forbidding expanses of uninhabited territory which separated the various African nations, Rush continued, had prevented stimulating conquests and the erection of great empires; thus the arts of civilization had been stunted. "The Heat of the Climate in Africa," Rush continued, "by bringing on Indolence of Mind, and Body, exposes them at all Times to Slavery, while the Fertility of the Soil renders the Want of Liberty a less Evil to them, than it is to the Inhabitants of Northern, or less Warm and fruitful Countries." Rush drew himself up for a sweeping summary: "Human Nature is the same in all Ages and Countries; and all the difference we perceive in its Characters in respect to Virtue and Vice, Knowledge and Ignorance, may be accounted for from Climate, Country, Degrees of Civilization, form of Government, or other accidental causes." [30] Writing in 1773 as the eye of the Revolutionary storm passed overhead, Rush epitomized the newly intense concentration of Americans upon their environment.

4. ENVIRONMENTALISM AND REVOLUTIONARY IDEOLOGY

No line of reasoning—one might almost say no expression of faith—could have better typified the changed pattern of thought in the Revolutionary era. Indeed, the flowering of environmentalism was one of the major historical developments of the second half of the eighteenth century. It did not of course appear out of nowhere, but because environmentalism was not an idea but a way of thinking it is difficult to trace its development. Certainly the notion that men were powerfully molded by their surroundings was intertwined with other important, long-term trends of thought. Perhaps most important of all was the gradual decomposition of old religious beliefs. Traditionally, the soul of man had to be transformed, not his surroundings. As men paid less attention to the inner drama of salvation, they paid more to their earthly stage. Perhaps the most important intellectual support was provided by John Locke's psychology, which denied the existence of innate ideas and rendered man's mind utterly dependent on sensations of the external world received through the senses. And it seems clear that

30. [Rush], *Address on Slavery of the Negroes*, 24-26.

development of an environmentalist outlook was hastened by the discoveries of savage peoples in the far reaches of the world. For if savage and heathen men were men at all, they simply had to possess capacity for improvement. To assume that savages could be nothing but savage forever implied that God had created some men basically different from others—which was not a possibility. The same discoveries helped impart a naturalistic cast to environmentalism. The axiomatic fact that human beings belonged to a single natural species created by God necessitated the assumption that variations within the species derived from some less august sponsorship. Men seemed to vary by locale. What was more natural than for European intellectuals to scan the peculiar natural features of various localities for clues to the variability of man? Certainly during the eighteenth century both the corruptions and virtues in men had come to look less like rigid functions of their immutable nature and more like elicited responses to their "situation." This view did not presuppose a pervasive goodness in man merely awaiting to be unfettered by a more beneficent environment; human nature still usually seemed dangerously corrupt. It was not malleable; it was an unstable constant, in the sense that human beings possessed enormous potentialities for both egregiously barbarous and admirably civilized behavior. Man's environment functioned, then, as a stimulus to performance—what kind of performance would depend on the environment.

Environmentalism was especially attractive to Americans in the Revolutionary era for a number of reasons. They had always lived in close dependence upon America's natural advantages. In 1760 a people awakening to the inestimable advantages of living on a vast and virgin continent (now providentially cleared, to the north and west, of foreign control) were bound to delight in their surroundings. Then, as the political crisis mounted, they developed a more pressing interest in their habitat. Since they thought of themselves as colonial Englishmen and yet were undergoing an unwelcome estrangement from England, they were compelled to ask what made the child different from the parent, the New World different from the Old, the continent different from the island.

As the Revolutionary logic unfolded, as Americans talked increasingly of the rights of "man"—natural rights—they were impelled to take an environmentalist approach to the differences among men. For if all men everywhere possessed the same rights and were in this sense really created equal, then distinctions among groups of men stood in another category—created not by the Creator but by "accidental causes." After the formal break with England, moreover, the logic of governmental reconstruction and reform required the assumption that men were affected by their political and social environment. And environmentalism tended to feed on itself. Once men found that one aspect of their environment, such as "oppression," or "room," or "heat," affected man's behavior, they were the more inclined to scrutinize their surroundings for evidence of other external influences.

The environmentalist mode of thought presupposed that the differences among men were circumstantial, that they were alterable, and that the core of human nature was everywhere, as Benjamin Rush put it, "the same." This postulation of quintessential human nature formed the critical point of contact between environmentalist thinking and the political ideology of the Revolution. Of course the tendency to universalize men into "man" was not new in American political thought when it flowered into the eloquence of 1776. The concept of natural rights belonging to all who were by nature men had been superbly set forth by John Locke and by lesser successors well known to Americans. The concept served admirably to justify revolution. Locke's principles and the Glorious Revolution of 1688–89 itself served as the lodestar of American political thought when colonials began resistance to unpopular imperial measures. From the "liberties of Englishmen" it was an easy step to the universalist assertion that all men had a right to be free.

Natural rights theory argued strongly for an end to Negro slavery, and environmentalist antislavery was closely linked with the political philosophy which carried forward the Revolution. It was inevitable that when mankind was being described as naturally free and equal some men should think of the Negro's condition. Negroes were, as Anthony Benezet put it, "as free as we are by nature." [31] This widely shared presumption led inescapably to realization that Americans were indulging in a monstrous inconsistency. While Americans were claiming liberty for themselves they were denying it to a group of men in their midst. Hundreds of times the appalling gap between word and deed was called to the public's attention. In newspapers and pamphlets of the Revolutionary era, the charge was leveled with vehemence and telling accuracy. "How suits it with the glorious cause of Liberty," asked a correspondent to a Philadelphia newspaper in 1768, "to keep your fellow men in bondage, men equally the work of your great Creator, men formed for freedom as yourselves." A New Jersey man wrote in 1780 that "if after we have

31. "Letters of Anthony Benezet," *Jour. Negro Hist.*, 2 (1917), 83.

made such a declaration to the world, we continue to hold our fellow creatures in slavery, our words must rise up in judgement against us, and by the breath of our own mouths we shall stand condemned." [32] Even before the Declaration of Independence anti-slavery advocates were crying out the theme of inconsistency.

> Blush ye pretended votaries for freedom! ye trifling patriots! who are making a vain parade of being advocates for the liberties of mankind, who are thus making a mockery of your profession by trampling on the sacred rights and privileges of Africans; for while you are fasting, praying, nonim-porting, nonexporting, remonstrating, resolving, and pleading for a resto-ration of your charter rights, you at the same time are continuing this lawless, cruel, inhuman, and abominable practice of enslaving your fellow creatures.[33]

Even the Quakers, who felt rather different impulses concerning slavery, saw the power of this argument. The original articles of the Society for the Relief of Free Negroes Unlawfully Kept in Bondage (founded under predominantly Quaker auspices in Philadelphia in 1775) stated that this good work was patently incumbent on all professors of Christianity, "but more especially, at a time when Justice, Liberty, and the Laws of the Land are the general Topicks amongst most Ranks and Stations of Men." [34] The Quaker David Cooper played vigorously on this theme after quoting from the Declaration: "If these solemn *truths,* uttered at such an awful crisis, are *self-evident:* unless we can shew that the African race are not *men,* words can hardly express the amazement which naturally arises on reflecting, that the very people who make these pompous declarations are slave-holders, and, by their legislative conduct, tell us, that these blessings were only meant to be the *rights* of *white-men* not of all *men:* and would seem to verify the observation of an eminent writer; 'When men talk of liberty, they mean their own liberty, and seldom suffer their thoughts on that point to stray to their neighbours.' " Slavery was inconsistent with the premises of the Revolution. As Cooper wrote at the end of the war, "We need not now turn over the libraries of Europe for authorities to prove that blacks are born equally free with whites: it is declared and recorded as the sense of America." [35]

32. Phila. *Pennsylvania Chronicle, and Universal Advertiser,* Nov. 28, 1768; Trenton *New Jersey Gazette,* Sept. 20, 1780.

33. [John Allen], *The Watchman's Alarm to Lord N---h* . . . (Salem, Mass., 1774), 27.

34. In the Cox-Parrish-Wharton Papers, Hist. Soc. Pa.

35. [Cooper], *Serious Address on Slavery,* 12–13. See also Boston *Massachusetts Spy,* Jan. 28, 1773; Daniel Byrnes, *A Short Address to the English Colonies in North-America* (Wilmington, Del., 1775).

This devastating critique of slavery was bandied about so widely that Negro slaves, in the North at least, saw no danger in having a go at it themselves. One group in Massachusetts wrote pointedly in 1777 "that every principle from which America has acted in the course of her unhappy difficulties with Great-Britain, pleads stronger than a thousand arguments in favor of your Petitioners." [36] Another group in New Hampshire demonstrated a commendable—or alarming—acquaintance with the rhetoric of natural rights: "That the *God* of nature gave them life and freedom, upon the terms of the most perfect equality with other men; That freedom is an inherent right of the human species, not to be surrendered, but by consent, for the sake of social life; That private or public tyranny and slavery are alike detestable to minds conscious of the equal dignity of human nature; . . . they hold themselves in duty bound strenuously to exert every faculty of their minds to obtain that blessing of freedom, which they are justly entitled to from that donation of the beneficent Creator." [37] This swelling chorus of white and Negro indignation was augmented occasionally by strident blasts from British critics of rebellion: Ambrose Serle, secretary to Admiral Lord Howe, castigated Americans for treating Negroes "as a better kind of Cattle . . . while they are bawling about the Rights of *human Nature*." [38]

At one level, these protests against slavery merely projected American colonial liberties onto all men, including Negroes. The preamble of a Rhode Island law (1774) prohibiting slave importation noted simply: "Whereas, the inhabitants of America are generally engaged in the preservation of their own rights and liberties, among which, that of personal freedom must be considered as the greatest; as those who are desirous of enjoying all the advantages of liberty themselves, should be willing to extend personal liberty to others." [39] At a more dynamic level of logic, however, the semantics of Revolutionary protest gave special power to the argument from freedom for American colonials to freedom for Negroes. From the beginning of the Revolutionary agitation, the colonists had cried that ministerial tyranny tended to make "slaves" of freeborn Englishmen. This common contention that they were being reduced to a

---

36. Petition of Negro Slaves, 1777, Box 16, bundle: Mass. and R. I. bills, petitions, and cases, 18th century, 58, Parish Transcripts, N.-Y. Hist. Soc.

37. Quoted in Isaac W. Hammond, "Slavery in New Hampshire," *Mag. of Amer. Hist.*, 21 (1889), 63.

38. Edward H. Tatum, Jr., ed., *The American Journal of Ambrose Serle, Secretary to Lord Howe, 1776–1778* (San Marino, Calif., 1940), 249.

39. Bartlett, ed., *Recs. Col. R. I.*, VII, 251.

state of "slavery" was more than hyperbole; many colonists believed wholeheartedly that there was a conspiracy on foot to deprive them of their liberties.[40] Nor was this belief entirely the child of radical paranoia in New England. George Washington wrote in 1774, "the crisis is arrived when we must assert our rights, or submit to every imposition, that can be heaped upon us, till custom and use shall make us tame and abject slaves, as the blacks we rule over with such arbitrary sway." [41] Because Revolutionary fervor was pitted against this deprivation—which was "slavery"—it was the more easily transferred to the Negro's condition, which had long borne that now odious name. The Revolutionary struggle was hitched to the struggle against Negro slavery by a stout semantic link.

The reciprocality of this relationship suggests that the relationship between Revolutionary ideology and antislavery was a complex one and that antislavery sentiment was not simply a by-product or a species of escalation from the political agitation. For one thing, the crucial Quaker antislavery contributions began well before the imperial crisis. Certainly, Quaker writers later incorporated arguments concerning natural rights and American inconsistency, yet while Quakers like David Cooper frequently give the impression of borrowing ammunition against slavery from essentially external sources, other antislavery writers worked from inside the natural rights ideology. A number of antislavery pronouncements were integral parts of essentially political arguments for colonial rights. The most notable instance was James Otis's *The Rights of the British Colonies Asserted and Proved* (1764) in which he declared that "the Colonists are by the law of nature free born, as indeed all men are, white or black." [42] It is apparent from the content and tone of antislavery literature, moreover, that many if not most antislavery advocates were operating on a complex battery of impulses. Religious convictions came to bear on slavery from different directions and at different levels of intensity. A stronger feeling of humanitarian benevolence came into operation not only among the Quakers. And the ideology of the Revolution, despite its simplicity as an ideology, was itself entangled with humanitarianism and especially religious conviction, the more so when this ideology was applied to the rationale of Negro slavery.

40. Bernard Bailyn, ed., *Pamphlets of the American Revolution, 1750–1776* (Cambridge, Mass., 1965), I, esp. 60–89, 140–50.

41. To Bryan Fairfax, Mount Vernon, Aug. 24, 1774, Fitzpatrick, ed., *Writings of Washington*, III, 242.

42. Otis, *Rights of the British Colonies*, 29.

Revelatory of the interconnections among these strands of thought and feeling is the impossibility of getting them thoroughly disentangled in some of the most forceful antislavery statements. In the minutes of a conference of Methodists in Virginia in 1784, for example, this intermingling clearly represented more than calculated appeal to various segments of public opinion. "We are deeply conscious of the Impropriety of making new Terms of Communion for a religious Society already established," the conference resolved, "excepting on the most pressing Occasion: and such we esteem the Practice of holding our Fellow-Creatures in Slavery. We view it as contrary to the Golden Law of God on which hang all the Law and the Prophets, and the unalienable Rights of Mankind, as well as every Principle of the Revolution, to hold in the deepest Debasement, in a more abject slavery than is perhaps to be found in any Part of the World except America, so many souls that are capable of the Image of God." [43] Similarly, a theme of humanitarian empathy could easily accompany orthodox natural rights theory: the Africans, wrote the Reverend Alexander Hewat, "are by nature equally free and independent, equally susceptible of pain and pleasure, equally averse from bondage and misery, as Europeans themselves." Before the catastrophe brought upon them by the war, most Quakers could subscribe happily to the idea of natural rights and set it within the framework of reforming benevolence: "the Slave Trade is a very wicked and abominable Practice," one Friend wrote in 1767, "contrary to the natural Rights and Privileges of all mankind, and against the Golden Rule of doing to others as we would be done unto." [44]

The commingling of natural rights theory with religious affirmations of equality suggests that the two streams of thought were not incompatible. As John Wise wrote in a tract of 1717 that is widely regarded as typifying the transition from Puritan to Revolutionary political thought, "It follows as a Command of the Law of Nature, that every Man Esteem and treat another as one who is naturally his Equal, or who is a Man as well as he. There be many popular, or plausible Reasons that greatly Illustrate this Equality, *viz.* that we all Derive our Being from one stock, the same Common Father of

43. Albert Matthews, ed., "Notes on the Proposed Abolition of Slavery in Virginia in 1785," Col. Soc. of Mass., *Publications*, 6 (1900), 374. See also the 1779 petition by some Negroes to the Connecticut General Assembly, in Aptheker, ed., *Documentary History of the Negro*, 11.
44. [Hewat], *Account of S. C. and Ga.*, II, 92; Thomas Nicholson, MS. paper, On Keeping Negroes (1767), Society Miscellaneous Collection, Negroes, Box 11a, Hist. Soc. Pa.

humane Race." By the time of the Revolution the concept of natural rights was still suffused with religious feeling and, in its most common form, with explicitly religious ideas. The right to liberty was normally spoken of as God's gratuitous gift to mankind, as an endowment by the Creator. More important, all men partook of "natural" rights because, as Thomas Paine wrote in the preamble to Pennsylvania's abolition law of 1780, "all are the work of the Almighty Hand." [45]

5. THE SECULARIZATION OF EQUALITY

Within the framework of this orthodox doctrine there was an intellectual shift of major proportions. God had not been removed, but he had been pushed back from the arena of human events. Some men found His will better recorded in the book of Nature than in the Bible. Although a few antislavery contributors combed Scripture for ammunition against slavery, their arguments from chapter and verse had taken on the air of stale squabbling. The Reverend Levi Hart of Connecticut, for example, thought it more appropriate to denounce the slave trade as "a flagrant violation of the law of nature, of the natural rights of mankind" than as a violation of the Mosaic law against man-stealing.[46] The very term *natural* keynoted this shift in self-conception. For the depersonalization of God into the Author of Nature was *pari passu* a transformation of man into a natural species originally created by the Deity whom men found it increasingly hard to mention without using the definite article. All men, including Negroes, shared in "natural" rights because they were men, not because they were candidates for immortality.

The naturalization of man, so tightly linked with environmentalist thinking, had important ramifications in several arenas of thought which had relevance to Negroes. For one, a subtle alteration in thinking about the relations of men in society became apparent during the half-century after 1740. If the colonists talked of *natural* rights, these rights were in fact *political* in content, that is, of relevance chiefly to men's rightful claims in the face of human authority. Sometimes the colonists spoke very much as if they

---

45. John Wise, *Vindication of the Government of the New England Churches* (Boston, 1717), 40 (available in facsimile with intro. by Perry Miller, Gainesville, Fla., 1958); Philip S. Foner, ed., *The Complete Writings of Thomas Paine*, 2 vols. (N. Y., 1945), II, 21.
46. Hart, *Liberty Described and Recommended*, 16.

thought that elective assemblies, trial by jury, taxation by consent, and the other traditional institutions and practices of British government were eternal natural principles set down by the Almighty Hand. God had become less the judge and more the legislator, less the arbiter of human affairs and more the compiler of the rules of the game. And men stood in relation to each other no longer principally as members of a clearly defined religious fellowship, no longer so rigidly as members in extended family units or in small and tightly knit communities, but increasingly as participants in larger social units (the colonies and states, the empire and the nation) which were characterized by institutional forms and symbols which can only be described as political. Especially in the cities, brothers in Christ had become Sons of Liberty. Relationships among individual men and of all men to the larger community were increasingly governed by the sanctions of impersonal law and conducted in an atmosphere of litigation.

This shift toward a political, even legalistic, conception of proper social relations had the most far-reaching effects upon attitudes toward the Negro. It refocused attention from his inner condition as a human being with an imperiled soul to his outward condition as a constituent member in the political community of men. Whereas traditional Christian equalitarianism had demanded his right to participate equally in an eternal community, political equalitarianism threw into question his legal relationship with his master. At first this newer equalitarianism did little more than that, if for no other reason than that it was forced to tackle first things first. Negro slavery loomed as a flagrant violation of the new ideal of a society composed of equal and therefore free individuals and in which there was equality of contractual power among the constituent members of society.

By itself this legalistic view of men afforded dangerously weak leverage against such a massive institution as Negro slavery. For it was possible to argue, as some members of the Virginia Convention did in 1776, that Negro slaves were not constituent members of the body politic. After heated debate the Convention adopted an amended version of George Mason's original statement of natural rights (the crucial amendment appearing here in italics) : "That all men are by nature equally free and independent, and have certain inherent rights, of which, *when they enter into a state of society,* they cannot, by any compact, deprive or divest their posterity; namely, the enjoyment of life and liberty, with the means of acquiring and possessing property, and pursuing and obtaining happiness

and safety." [47] The far-reaching implications in this seemingly innocent phrase did not become truly apparent until after the Revolution.

What the emphasis on man as a political being did do during the
Revolutionary era was to channel the religious ideal of equality
toward reconsideration of the Negro's external legal status. Conversion of Negroes was suddenly after 1760 no longer the chief aim of
American equalitarians. Clergymen stopped preaching up the necessity of converting Negroes and began preaching the sinfulness of
enslaving them. It was no longer possible for American ministers to
urge Negro slaves to remain content as Christians in their bondage
when they were urging white members of their congregations to
resist oppression. The new emphasis on man as a political being
meant that churchmen were no longer willing to pay the price of
endorsing slavery in order to obtain Negro conversion. Slavery had
been altered by Revolutionary political agitation and Negro conversion by the Great Awakening.

Ironically the reverberations of a great revival of religion, which
gathered strength in the South in the 1760's, helped funnel the
energy of religious equalitarianism toward an assault upon the
Negro's temporal condition. Heightened interest in the Negro's
worldly status was not merely a function of the rationalism and
worldliness reactively stimulated by the excesses of the revival. For
the assumptions which drove the revival had gone a fair way toward
destroying the issue of Negro conversion. By re-emphasizing Christian universality, by venturing out into the highways and byways in
search of the unchurched, the bereft, and the lowly, the revival had
robbed the problem of converting Negroes of its distinctive character. Spreading the Gospel among slaves on great plantations had its
special problems, but so did the same good work in the hinterlands
of, say, North Carolina, where many of the unchurched were neither black nor red but white. The Methodist itinerant Francis
Asbury trudged up and down the length of the land for forty years
after 1770 preaching to whites and blacks, sometimes together,
sometimes separately, but always indiscriminately.[48] After the Great
Awakening and still more after slave importations were cut off by
the Revolution, more rapid acculturation of Negroes hastened this
process by which conversion of Negroes became less a separate task
in itself and more an integral part of the broader problem of main-

47. Mays, *Edmund Pendelton*, II, 120–22; Kate Mason Rowland, *The Life of
George Mason, 1725–1792*, 2 vols. (N. Y., 1892) , I, 240, 434, 438–39.
48. Clark *et al.*, eds., *Journal of Francis Asbury.*

taining faith in faltering brethren of whatever color. This radical transformation in the issue of Negro conversion helped midwife the birth of religious antislavery thought, for it permitted questioning of the Negro's temporal status without the distraction of wondering whether freeing Negroes would impede their conversion.

The transformation was rendered the more thorough by an important institutional change. The best tooled and best situated instrument for Negro conversion had always been the S.P.G. Its ministrations to Negroes were not much altered by the great revival except that S.P.G. missionaries now had a good deal of unprecedented and effective competition. In the late 1750's, owing largely to a change of personnel and strategy in London, the S.P.G. was put to the task of winning American sectarians to the Church of England. Heathen Negroes were not altogether abandoned, but they came near to being lost in the shuffle of ecclesiastic politics. Finally in the 1770's the S.P.G. was obliged to decamp from what was rapidly becoming rebel territory.

Its departure was gratifying especially to clergymen in New England, where the storm in the early 1760's over proposals to establish an Anglican bishop in America had been particularly intense.[49] The New England clergy also took an especially active part and at times assumed leadership in defending the political rights of the colonies. Many of them rose in their pulpits to defend all the rights claimed in the face of British tyranny, including the right to keep the fingers of British customs officials out of American pocketbooks. In one sense, their active involvement in defense of secular rights merely demonstrated their immersion in an intellectual tide which was carrying so many men toward a more worldly view of their existence. In another, though, they were evincing how easy—indeed how compelling—it was for the heirs of Puritans to fan the sparks of worldly liberty with concepts which derived from their fathers' sense of sin. To watch them pour new wine from old bottles is to watch one process of secularization.

The antislavery pronouncements of such New England ministers as Samuel Hopkins, Levi Hart, Elhanan Winchester, and also Deacon Benjamin Colman represented a complex fusion of religious and political modes of thought strongly tinged with the less lofty quality of opportunism. For these men as well as for many Americans, the enslavement of Negroes was sin. It was a peculiarly introspective view; it focused not on the miseries of the victims of slavery but on the wickedness of the victimizers. In the long run, painful

49. See Bridenbaugh, *Mitre and Sceptre*.

consciousness of wrongdoing was vital to the continued strength of antislavery. More immediately, the conception of slavery as sin enabled Americans to bring to bear against slavery both the natural rights philosophy and humanitarian benevolence in an intellectual context which, because it was old and familiar, greatly heightened their effectiveness. As an act of kindness or as a concession to the logic of natural rights, abolition of slavery was an impersonal stroke of social change, not the sort to which Americans had been accustomed. As an impressive demonstration of personal reformation, however, abolition of slavery was an altogether traditional step, novel in outward form but completely comprehensible as to inner meaning. As Samuel Hopkins said after acclaiming the ban on slave importations by the Continental Congress, abolition of slavery itself would constitute a "thorough reformation." [50] Getting rid of slavery involved the same procedures as with any sins, such as worldliness, lust, or drunkenness: first came acknowledgement, repentance, and then suitable change in outward behavior—a change which constituted prima-facie evidence of inward reformation.

The weight of the Puritan heritage was sufficiently evident in the manner in which American ministers collectivized the personal sin of slaveholding and thereby threw responsibility for reformation onto the entire community. Their rhetoric was virtually the same as that used by their grandfathers in warning of God's dealings with a faithless people; as Deacon Benjamin Colman of Newburyport declared in 1775, God might be expected to punish "a stubborn incorrigible people" for holding men as slaves.[51]

More important than this atavistic, generalized sense of slavery as a communal sin and of impending punishment was the way in which the clergy wove the sin of slaveholding into the fabric of the Revolutionary crisis. For men so familiar with the formula, it was no trick at all. Samuel Hopkins's *Dialogue Concerning the Slavery of the Africans* (1776), which was structured very much like a Puritan sermon, opened and closed on this note: "if the slavery in which we hold the blacks, is wrong; it is a very great and public sin; and therefore a sin which God is now testifying against in the calamities he has brought upon us, consequently must be reformed, before we

50. [Hopkins], *Dialogue Concerning Slavery*, 53.
51. Quoted in Joshua Coffin, *A Sketch of the History of Newbury, Newburyport, and West Newbury, from 1635 to 1845* (Boston, 1845), 341. Colman quarreled with his pastor over slavery and was suspended from the church in 1780; he was readmitted after the pastor's death and he conceded that he had urged his antislavery opinions "with excessive vehemence and asperity." Theophilus Parsons, [Jr.], *Memoir of Theophilus Parsons . . .* (Boston, 1859), 17.

can reasonably expect deliverance, or sincerely ask for it." Benjamin
Colman wielded this logic with an astounding precision by suggesting in 1775 that the port of Boston had been closed by British
authorities because Boston had been the first town to engage in the
slave trade! In Philadelphia the Reverend Francis Alison was more
specific about the relevant "calamities" when writing to Ezra Stiles
in 1768, "I am assured the Common father of all men will severely
plead a Controversy against these Colonies for Enslaving Negros,
and keeping their children[,] born British subjects, in perpetual
slavery—and possibly for this wickedness God threatens us with
slavery." [52] Effortlessly Alison had incorporated the natural rights
theory into the traditional Jeremiad; simply by playing upon the
word *slavery* he had transformed the colonies' political quarrels
with Great Britain into a terrible manifestation of Divine wrath
upon a slaveholding people! The inconsistency between American
ideology and practice concerning Negroes had been placed in the
context of a long-familiar religious formula and its appeal thereby
enormously enhanced. Nothing could make more plain how intricately the growth of antislavery was interwoven with the political
revolution.

Certainly the voices of Puritan ministers did not fall upon entirely uncomprehending ears, at least in the northern colonies. In
1774 the Danbury Town Meeting in Connecticut included in its
resolves the pious observation "that we have great reason to apprehend the enslaving the *Africans* is one of the crying sins of our land,
for which Heaven is now chastising us." In Norwich, Connecticut:
"A black Cloud Witnesseth against us, and our own Mouths condemn us." [53] Even Thomas Paine, only a few weeks after his arrival
in Philadelphia, was able to grasp the rudiments of this logic. "How
just," he exclaimed in a newspaper article in 1775, "how suitable to
our crime is the punishment with which providence threatens us?
We have enslaved multitudes . . . and now are threatened with the
same. And while other evils are confessed, and bewailed, why not
this especially, and publicly; than which no other vice . . . has

52. [Hopkins], *Dialogue Concerning Slavery*, 5, also 51–54; Colman in Coffin,
Newbury, 342; Francis Alison to Ezra Stiles, Phila., Oct. 20, 1768, Franklin B.
Dexter, ed., *Extracts from the Itineraries and Other Miscellanies of Ezra Stiles,
D.D., LL.D., 1755–1794, with a Selection from His Correspondence* (N. Y., 1916),
434.
53. Steiner, *Slavery in Connecticut*, 30; *Norwich Packet*, July 7, 1774. Cf. Perry
Miller, "From the Covenant to the Revival," in James Ward Smith and A.
Leland Jamison, eds., *The Shaping of American Religion*, in Smith and Jamison,
eds., *Religion in American Life*, I (Princeton, 1961), 322–50.

brought so much guilt on the land?" [54] Less frequently some abolitionist Quakers were similarly inclined to communalize the sin of slaveholding. Anthony Benezet was among the first to portray communal calamity as God's punishment on a slave-trading people: in 1759 he observed that the slave trade was a cause of the terrible disasters of the French and Indian War. Later Benezet and several Meetings decided that slave-dealing was well up on the list of transgressions which had provoked Divine vengeance in the form of the Revolutionary War.[55]

It is an arresting fact that this formula, this style, of antislavery reasoning was common in the North (especially New England) and uncommon in all parts of the South. At first sight this appears to mean that a sense of collective sin was impossible in regions where the institution of slavery was deeply entrenched, even though, as was to become clear after the war especially, there was vehement opposition to slavery in parts of the South. No doubt this was in some measure the case, but it would be wrong to see the pattern of antislavery thought as altogether governed by the circumstances of slavery. A closer look at individual writers suggests that the pattern was not so much regional as religious. It was men rooted in or deriving from a specifically *Puritan* tradition who advanced the equation of slavery and sin. One of the very few Virginians to attack slavery with the weapon of sinfulness was a Presbyterian minister.[56] Thus it was Presbyterians, Congregationalists, and to a lesser degree Quakers who spoke in this fashion, and the more explicit denunciations came from men whose intellectual backgrounds were most explicitly Calvinist, men like Samuel Hopkins and Benjamin Colman. Men less firmly rooted in Puritanism tended to be vague and sloppy with the formula. Benjamin Rush, whose background was Quakerish, Presbyterian, and half a dozen other "isms," framed the equation in terms which were familiar to all Christians in America. In summoning the clergy to action he admonished: "Remember that national crimes require national punishments, and without declaring what punishment awaits this evil, you may venture to

---

54. Foner, ed., *Writings of Paine*, II, 18.

55. [Anthony Benezet], *Observations on the Inslaving, Importing and Purchasing of Negroes* . . . (Germantown, 1759), 2–3; James, *A People Among Peoples*, 246, 257.

56. David Rice, *Slavery Inconsistent with Justice and Good Policy* . . . (Phila., 1792, reprinted London, 1793). One wonders about audience reaction to the words of a Massachusetts minister published as Elhanan Winchester, *The Reigning Abominations, Especially the Slave Trade, Considered as Causes of Lamentation; Being the Substance of a Discourse Delivered in Fairfax County, Virginia, December 30, 1774. And Now Published with Several Additions* (London, 1788).

assure them, that it cannot pass with impunity, unless God shall cease to be just or merciful." [57]

Planters were no doubt familiar with this sort of language but they were disinclined to use it. Indeed southerners were not disposed to regard slavery as resulting from their own wickedness. Virginians especially were prone to think that responsibility for slavery rested not with themselves but with the British. It was possible to reconcile this view with the Jeremiad, and the Meeting for Sufferings in Philadelphia actually did so toward the end of the war by saying that Britain's failure to subdue the rebellious colonies represented God's judgment against slave trading, which the British were seeking to continue but which the colonies had forsworn.[58] The Anglican planters of Virginia, however, by pointing to royal disallowances of several laws passed by the Assembly restricting the slave trade, were able to document their *innocence* rather than their guilt. Ignoring the fact that these laws had been passed because of planter indebtedness and fear of too many Negroes in Virginia, southerners generally, as well as many people in the North, gladly seized this opportunity to exculpate themselves.[59] This very different formula almost found its way into the Declaration of Independence, but it was deleted at the insistence of South Carolina and Georgia, who disliked the implication that participation in the slave trade called for extenuation, or even worse, self-condemnation. What seems to have been the only public pronouncement against slavery in the Lower South came from the Revolutionary Committee in Darien, a Georgia village settled by Scottish Presbyterians.[60]

When the storm of rebellion finally broke, the pressure of events acted for the most part to confirm and even implement the logic of

57. [Rush], *Address upon Slave-Keeping*, 30.

58. James, *A People Among Peoples*, 246.

59. "Address of the House of Burgesses to the King, 1772," in Donnan, ed., *Documents Slave Trade*, IV, 154–55; *Observations on the Slavery of the Negroes*, 10–11; Julian Boyd, ed., *The Papers of Thomas Jefferson* (Princeton, 1950—), I, 130, 338, 357, 378; Henry Laurens to John Laurens, Aug. 14, 1776, in Wallace, *Life of Henry Laurens*, 446; Mitchell *et al.*, eds., *Statutes Pa.*, X, 67–68. And well after the Revolution, too; Annapolis *Md. Gaz.*, Nov. 25, 1790.

60. Peter Force, comp., *American Archives . . .* , 4th Ser., 6 vols. (Washington, 1837–46), I, 1136. An outstanding exception was George Mason of Virginia: "They [slaves] bring the judgment of heaven on a country. As nations can not be rewarded or punished in the next world they must be in this. By an inevitable chain of causes and effects providence punishes national sins, by national calamities," Max Farrand, ed., *The Records of the Federal Convention of 1787*, rev. ed., 4 vols. (New Haven, 1937), II, 370.

secular equalitarianism. Despite the heel-dragging of the two southernmost states, antislavery sentiment had grown sufficiently strong
elsewhere to become a factor in political decision-making. The
prohibition of slave importations by the Continental Association of
1774 was aimed primarily at Parliament via the purses of British
merchants, but many delegates to the Continental Congress regarded it as a blow for the slave's freedom as well as their own.[61]
Before the war was over, Pennsylvania had passed a gradual emancipation act with a high-toned preamble written by Thomas Paine.[62]
Even the Negro's right to vote came under discussion during the
extended public debate over Massachusetts' proposed new constitution.[63]

In a more direct way, too, the tide of events during the Revolution moved in the Negro's favor. Some Negroes won their freedom
by fighting for the American cause. Despite the weight of tradition,
the fear of slave rebellion, and the uncomfortable feeling that
Negro slaves were not suitable recruits for an army engaged in a
struggle for liberty, the necessities of war eventually pulled both
slave and free Negroes into the armed forces, many of them clutching promises of freedom as their eventual reward for fighting for it.
An initial refusal to recruit Negroes into the Continental Army was
reversed because men were desperately needed to fill the ranks.
Rhode Island raised a separate battalion of Negroes. Significantly,
South Carolina and Georgia were alone in holding out to the end
against slave enlistments.[64] A proposal by John Laurens to authorize
formation of a battalion of Negro troops received "contemptuous
huzzas" in the South Carolina legislature. John Laurens's more
famous father, Henry, was virtually alone among South Carolinians
in expressing hope for the eventual disappearance of the institution
to which the state was so thoroughly committed.[65]

The participation of Negroes in the struggle for independence
seemed to imply that they possessed membership in the new republic. In general, however, Negroes were utilized rather than
welcomed. A scattering of Negroes in the army was scarcely the
fulcrum for elevating the status of Negroes throughout the country.

61. W. E. Burghardt DuBois, *The Suppression of the African Slave-Trade to
the United States of America, 1638–1870* (N. Y., 1896), 41–47.
62. Mitchell *et al.*, eds., *Statutes Pa.*, X, 67–73; Foner, ed., *Writings of Paine*,
II, 21–22.
63. Moore, *Notes on Slavery in Massachusetts*, 185–96.
64. The best treatment is Quarles, *Negro in the American Revolution*.
65. Wallace, *Life of Henry Laurens*, 446, 448–50.

The crust of long-accumulated attitudes was far too thick, as is suggested by the remark of a young Pennsylvanian concerning a well-disciplined contingent from Marblehead encamped outside of Boston, "But even in this regiment there were a number of Negroes, which, to persons unaccustomed to such associations, had a disagreeable, degrading effect." [66] Negro participation in the turmoil of Revolution could, in fact, militate against any feeling of identity with them. South Carolinians regarded putting guns in the hands of slaves as downright suicidal. Virginians seethed with anger when Lord Dunmore issued his infamous invitation from aboard a man-of-war in the York River. Hundreds of slaves actually responded to his promise of freedom, and Virginians were appalled and outraged at the loss of their property and at the prospect of humiliating skirmishes with blacks. [67] Dunmore had violated the rules of the game. When planter control over the slave population was seriously threatened, Virginians turned from talk of rights to ridicule and indignant protests. "We hear that lord Dunmore's *Royal Regiment of Black Fusileers* is already recruited, with runaway and stolen negroes, to the formidable number of 80 effective men, who, after doing the drudgery of the day (such as acting as scullions, etc. on board the fleet) are ordered upon deck to perform the military exercise; and, to comply with their *native* warlike genius, instead of the drowsy drum and fife, will be gratified with the use of the sprightly and enlivening *barrafoo,* an instrument peculiarly adapted to the martial tune of '*Hungry Niger parch'd Corn!*' and which from henceforward is to be styled, by way of eminence, the BLACKBIRD MARCH." [68]

Significantly, the storm over Dunmore's proclamation apparently did nothing to weaken the attachment of many Virginians to the cause of eventual abolition and may even have strengthened it in some quarters. At the end of the war James Madison sent his slave Billey, who had been recaptured after trying to join the British, to Pennsylvania as an indentured servant; Madison remarked that he did not wish to punish a slave "merely for coveting that liberty for which we have paid the price of so much blood, and have pro-

66. Quoted by Herbert Aptheker, "The Negro in the American Revolution," in his *Essays in the History of the American Negro* (N. Y., 1945) , 101.

67. Benjamin Quarles, "Lord Dunmore as Liberator," *Wm. and Mary Qtly.,* 15 (1958) , 494–507.

68. Purdie's Wmsbg. *Va. Gaz.,* Mar. 22, 1776. For similar resentment in North Carolina, Saunders, ed., *Col. Recs. N. C.,* X, 138a. See also Bartlett, ed., *Recs. Col. R. I. ,*VII, 361.

claimed so often to be the right, and worthy the pursuit, of every human being." [69] During the war Virginians were as busy as anyone trying to implement the natural rights philosophy in the realm of practical politics. The ideology of the Revolution was, in a very genuine sense, what white men in America were fighting for, and even the more socially conservative gentlemen throughout the new nation—and there were many—felt that slavery must somehow, someday, be brought to an end. Especially in view of the way their grandchildren were talking after 1830, it is important to bear in mind that during the Revolutionary War, despite the virtual absence of antislavery pronouncements in the Lower South and the cautiousness of Virginians on the subject, no one in the South stood up in public to endorse Negro slavery.

6. THE PROSLAVERY CASE FOR NEGRO INFERIORITY

In the North and in the West Indies, a few men did. For many reasons, including the preponderance of slaves and the exposed situation of the islands, English colonials in the West Indies never joined in the hue and cry after "rights" and "liberty." Rebellion was not their cup of tea. In the northern colonies, the few scattered proslavery writings came from the pens of a few disgruntled individuals, some or perhaps most of whom were transplanted West Indians. In most instances, these defenses of slavery were made in direct response to specific attacks on the institution. These defenses perhaps now seem more important than they actually were because they foretold an important future change. Their arguments are instructive because of this embryonic quality and, no less important, because they represented extreme statements of the inertial sentiment that antislavery advocates had to overcome.

Proslavery writers were for the most part unwilling or unable or afraid to challenge the philosophy of equal rights directly. One way to avoid doing so was to assert that the Negro was not the white man's equal. The most extreme attempt of this sort was by the anonymous author of *Personal Slavery Established,* published in the midst of a pamphlet debate over slavery in Philadelphia in 1773. Certain possibilities inhering in a naturalistic view of man became abundantly clear as he effortlessly wrote off the Negro's humanity merely by manipulating Linnaean categories. Of the species known as man, he wrote with caustic condescension, Africans were actually

69. Gaillard Hunt, ed., *The Writings of James Madison . . . ,* 9 vols. (N. Y., 1900–10) , II, 15.

"species of that *genus,* though utterly devoid of reason." He went on to "subdivide the Africans into five *classes,* arranging them in the order as they approach nearest to reason, as 1st, Negroes, 2d, Ourang Outangs, 3d, Apes, 4th, Baboons, and 5th, Monkeys. The opinion of their irrationality is so well supported by *facts,* that to those acquainted with them, I need advance very little on the subject." [70] Here was hierarchic classification with a vengeance. Amid controversy over slavery in America, two streams of scientific thought found their confluence. This unknown author took up the element of hierarchy in the Great Chain of Being and stamped it with the rigid specificity of Linnaean classification. Linnaeus would have been appalled had he ever looked upon this powerful engine of oppression.

Less dramatically but no less significantly, virtually all the writers intent on degrading the Negro became enmeshed in the logical thicket of environmentalism. With antislavery advocates laying all the Negro's admitted unattractive characteristics at the door of slavery or to the climate and mode of living in Africa, these frustrated writers could only protest that these characteristics were "natural" to Negroes. In doing so they helped to sharpen, just as the antislavery writers did, the concept of innate as opposed to acquired qualities in man. Refuting the environmentalist assertions of Negro equality, however, was rather like spearing an army of ants with a toothpick, since the Negro's environment was not one influence but thousands. Bernard Romans plainly came off second best when he declared in 1775, "Treachery, theft, stubbornness, and idleness . . . are such consequences of their manner of life at home [in Africa] as to put it out of all doubt that these qualities are natural to them and not originated by their state of slavery." [71] The Negro's "manner of life" in Africa had long since been claimed by the antislavery people as a portion of his environment.

One indication of the slippery strength of the environmentalist argument was the frustrated hyperbole of its opponents. The author of *Personal Slavery Established* plagiarized David Hume in order to combat the environmentalist contentions of Benjamin Rush. "There never was a civilized nation of any other complexion than *white;* nor ever any individual eminent either in action or speculation that was not rather inclining to the *fair.* Africa, except

70. *Personal Slavery Established, by the Suffrages of Custom and Right Reason. Being a Full Answer to the Gloomy and Visionary Reveries, of All the Fanatical and Enthusiastical Writers on that Subject* (Phila., 1773) , 18–19.

71. Romans, *Florida,* 105.

a small part of it, inhabited by those of our own colour, is totally overrun with Barbarism." Having reassured his readers that "the Europeans are blessed with reason, and therefore capable of improvement," he denied Rush's contention that Negroes possessed "genius." He was willing to admit their "docility," though, in "a few such instances" as West Indian Negro craftsmen and one remarkable fellow who could handle double-entry bookkeeping. A "mere *Lusus Naturae,*" however, was no evidence "of their being endued with reason." Everyone knew that "extraordinary instances of docility in brutes have naturally excited great admiration in all ages." Pliny, indeed, had described an African elephant who carried on the tinker's trade "with some reputation." The author concluded by baiting the antislavery writers with remarks about provisioning the West India islands with the bodies of slaves ("cured in pickle or smoak") who died on route from Africa or in the islands. "A considerable quantity of provision might be thus procured that would furnish a tolerable succedaneum for *pork* and hams." [72] Fortunately no one bothered to reply.

A far more effective tactic against the logic of environmentalism was to stay within the realm of known "facts" about the Negro and then to deal with the *probabilities* concerning his inherent nature. Richard Nisbet, an emotionally unstable West Indian living in Pennsylvania who later turned to the Negro's defense and closed his life in tragic insanity, undertook this task when assailing Benjamin Rush in 1773.[73] "It is impossible to determine, with accuracy," Nisbet wrote, "whether their intellects or ours are superior, as individuals, no doubt, have not the same opportunities of improving as we have." Having thus disarmed the environmentalists by admitting the validity of their first principles, Nisbet went on to appeal to evidence which is still used today for the same purpose. "However, on the whole," he wrote with becoming moderation, "it

72. *Personal Slavery Established,* 19–26. He seems to have thought of the Chinese as white people.
73. [Nisbet], *Slavery Not Forbidden by Scripture.* For Nisbet (variously, Nesbit or with two t's), Samuel Coates, Notebook on Cases of Insanity, Medical Library of the Pennsylvania Hospital, Phila.; an account based on this by George W. Corner, ed., *The Autobiography of Benjamin Rush; His "Travels Through Life" together with His Commonplace Book for 1789–1813* (Princeton, 1948), 83n; Susanna Dillwyn Emlen to William Dillwyn, Oxmead, July 11, 1795, Dillwyn Correspondence, 1770–1824, Library Company of Philadelphia. For his later views, see Richard Nisbet, *The Capacity of Negroes for Religious and Moral Improvement Considered . . .* (London, 1789); and his MS. The Notioniad. A Serio-Comic Poem. In Four Books. Fourteen Cantos, 29–114, Richard Nisbet Papers, Hist. Soc. Pa.

seems probable, that they are a much inferior race of men to the whites, in every respect. We have no other method of judging, but by considering their genius and government in their native country. Africa, except the small part of it inhabited by those of our own colour, is totally over-run with barbarism." With a nod to David Hume, Nisbet plunged on down the usual list of defects—the absence of great kingdoms, the despotism, the lack of any ideas concerning a supreme Being, the hopeless deficiency of friendship and gratitude. Africans, in short, were "utterly unacquainted with the arts, letters, manufactures, and every thing which constitutes civilized life. . . . A few instances may be found, of African negroes possessing virtues and becoming ingenius; but still, what I have said, with regard to their general character, I dare say, most people acquainted with them, will agree to." [74]

Nisbet's tract came closer than anyone's to joining the debate with the equalitarians. American antislavery advocates felt confident, however, in relying upon the power they saw in environmental influences; they remained certain that the equality of Negroes prescribed by benevolence, the natural rights philosophy, and the injunctions of religion would eventually be confirmed in actuality by appropriate alterations in the Negro's environment. Detailed exegesis of Scripture, so natural to Samuel Sewall, no longer seemed relevant to the main issue. The flurry of public discussion of slavery in 1773 in Philadelphia was capped by a piece in the *Pennsylvania Packet* which pretended to find in Genesis a passage indicating that Adam and his posterity had been granted dominion not only over fish, fowl, cattle, and all creeping things, "but likewise in a particular manner over the negroes of Africa." The cited passage was, indeed, most explicit: "And the beasts of Æthiopia shall bow down to thee, even they whose figure and speech are like unto thine own, and whose heads are covered like unto fine wool. They who dwell on the sea coast, shall serve thee, and thy seed after thee, even they who shall sojourn in the Islands afar off, where the sun hath his going down." Certainly this was a new way of bringing Scripture to bear on Negro slavery. [75] One turgid debate over slavery in the *Connecticut Journal*, probably stimulated by the pamphlet warfare of 1773 in Philadelphia, did indeed revolve dizzily around genuine chapter and verse, but both parties became bogged down in intricacies which, even in Connecticut, no longer held much fascina-

74. [Nisbet], *Slavery Not Forbidden by Scripture,* 21–23.
75. Winthrop D. Jordan, ed., "An Antislavery Proslavery Document?" *Jour. Negro Hist.,* 47 (1962) , 54–56.

tion. All that the anonymous proslavery writer had to say about Negroes as such was that they were descended from Ham and were "a race of men devoted to slavery." [76]

Many Americans were more alive to the real issues. At Harvard commencement in 1773 two students formally debating "The Legality of Enslaving the Africans" touched upon most of them. Both agreed that Negroes were "brethren" to the whites. The proslavery speaker declaimed that the "real character" of the Africans appeared to be a compound of "a child, an ideot," and "a madman." His opponent was at considerable pains to refute the charge of hopeless barbarism in Africa and to deprecate recent attempts to prove Negroes a different species.[77] As yet, however, the antislavery people were not fully alive to the dangerous flanking movement represented by the utilization of the Great Chain of Being in *Personal Slavery Established*.

7. THE REVOLUTION AS TURNING POINT

What is particularly impressive about the debate over the Negro's nature during the Revolutionary period is how much the fundamental issue of nature versus nurture had crystallized and yet at the same time how far removed it still was from its modern form. The increased self-consciousness about human behavior which characterized the period greatly sharpened men's sense of the dichotomy between themselves and their social and natural surroundings. With varying degrees of perceptiveness, the equalitarians utilized—and thereby reinforced—this dichtomy, and at the same time dimly recognized its dangers. For if environment was rigidly separated from innate nature, proponents of slavery could as easily grasp one as antislavery people the other. The risks involved in dueling with these weapons were not, of course, so apparent to equalitarians as they were later to become. Though as early as 1762 Anthony Benezet could quote an English antislavery advocate as protesting that men dealing in slaves possessed "a Kind of confused Imagination, or half formed Thought, in their Minds, that the

76. New Haven *Conn. Jour.*, Oct. 8, 1773, and subsequent issues; see also Romans, *Florida*, 108–10. Defenses of slavery were not necessarily anti-Negro: Tho. Thompson, *The African Trade for Negro Slaves, Shewn to be Consistent with Principles of Humanity, and with the Laws of Revealed Religion* (Canterbury, Eng., [1772]), copy in the Rutgers University Library, New Brunswick, N. J., with marginal comments by Benezet.

77. [Theodore Parsons and Eliphalet Pearson], *A Forensic Dispute on the Legality of Enslaving the Africans, Held at the Public Commencement in Cambridge, New-England . . .* (Boston, 1773), 7, 28–31, 35–45.

Blacks are hardly of the same Species with the white Men, but are Creatures of a Kind somewhat inferior," as late as 1784 James Ramsay, a prominent English opponent of slavery, thought it safe to conjecture that if "negroes are an inferior race; it is a conclusion that hitherto has lain hid and unobserved, and while it leads only to an abuse of power in the superior race, it is better concealed, than drawn out into notice. Perhaps Providence may keep it doubtful, till men be so far improved, as not to make an ill use of the discovery." [78] Just how ill a use some men could make of such a discovery Ramsay was to discover very shortly.

Nothing could illustrate more clearly the transitional character of Revolutionary thought on the question of Negro inferiority than the remarks of Arthur Lee. While studying in Edinburgh in 1764 the petulant young Virginian undertook an anonymous defense of the American colonists against Adam Smith, who had pointedly criticized the practice of slaveholding. Lee hated British criticism, but since he also hated slavery the only way he could get at Smith was to attack Smith's laudatory estimate of Negroes, drawing upon the Churchills' *Voyages* for ammunition. With volcanic energy Lee spewed forth a tirade of condemnation: African characteristics were "cruelty, cunning, perfidy, and cowardice"; their feeding habits were like those of "absolute brutes"; their religion was "the most gross idolatry," which entirely suited "the universal depravity and barbarism of their natures." [79] As Lee summarized his exhaustive roster of depravities, "We have seen that this his [Smith's] nation of heroes is a race the most detestable and vile that ever the earth produced. . . . Aristotle, long ago, declared, that slaves could have no virtue; but he knew not any who were so utterly devoid of any semblance of virtue as are the Africans; whose understandings are generally shallow, and their hearts cruel, vindictive, stubborn, base, and wicked." Then Lee crowned his diatribe with an astonishingly casual remark which to the modern reader comes as a perverse anti-climax: "Whether this proceeds from a native baseness that fits their minds for all villany; or that they never receive the benefit of

78. "Extracts from a Manuscript, Intituled, Two Dialogues on the Man-Trade. [by J. Philmore] Printed in London, in the Year 1760," [Benezet], *Short Account of Africa*, 31; Ramsay, *Treatment and Conversion of African Slaves*, 221.
79. [Arthur Lee], *An Essay in Vindication of the Continental Colonies of America, from a Censure of Mr. Adam Smith, in His Theory of Moral Sentiments. With Some Reflections on Slavery in General* (London, 1764), 11–13. Lee's antislavery was genuine; see Lee to Granville Sharp, n.p., n.d., 1773, and Benezet to Sharp, Phila., Nov. 8, 1772, Copies of Letters to Granville Sharp, 1768–73, B. V. Sec. Slavery, N.-Y. Hist. Soc.

education, I shall not presume to determine." [80] Fifty years earlier, Lee would have felt no need to express his hesitation; rather, he would have seen nothing to hesitate about. In 1764, however, he could roundly denounce the Negro and then calmly declare that he was uncertain whether the Negro's baseness was innate. He sensed the question which has since become so clear—and saw no pressing need to answer it.

On this fundamental question of nature versus nurture, as well as on so many related questions concerning the Negro, the Revolutionary era marked a critical turning point. From the Revolution on, the increasingly acrimonious debates on the Negro's nature were grounded in assumptions which, in contrast to those prevailing in pre-Revolutionary America, have a decidedly modern timbre. During this third quarter of the eighteenth century, many Americans awoke to the fact that a hitherto unquestioned social institution had spread its roots not only throughout the economic structure of much of the country but into their own minds. As they became conscious of this infiltration they came to recognize that enslavement of the Negro depended upon their assessment of him, that Negro slavery existed within themselves, within their "prejudices," particularly "in Relation to Colour." For equalitarians of whatever stripe, there were two possible ways of effecting a change in the white man's mind. Both necessarily involved an end to slavery, since slavery impaired the feeling of brotherhood within the white man and still more obviously presented an obstacle to the Negro's becoming the white man's equal in actuality. Appeal to environment provided an answer on both counts, and Americans plumped eagerly for a mode of thinking which afforded a prospect of dramatic change both in the Negro and within themselves.

This heightened self-consciousness with which environmentalist thinking was so closely connected was itself closely linked to the crisis known as the American Revolution. Indeed in an important sense the Revolution *was* a great awakening of English colonials in America. The radical change in Americans' thinking about the mother country was equally a change in thinking about themselves. The rise of antislavery sentiment also represented a process of self-evaluation, an integral part of what John Adams recalled as "this radical change in the principles, opinions, sentiments, and affections of the people." The "real American Revolution" involved

80. [Lee], *Essay in Vindication of America*, 30, 37–38.

a newly intense scrutiny of colonial society, including the peculiarly un-English institution of Negro slavery.

American thinking about the status of Negroes could never again be characterized by placid and unheeding acceptance. As a standing contradiction of age-old presuppositions about the equality of men, slavery cried out for a revival of public morality. As an inward sin, slavery invited the reform without which Americans could never expect success as an independent people. As a violation of the ideology of equal rights, slavery mocked the ideals upon which the new republic was founded.

In many ways the American Revolution was a revolution in the expectations of Americans concerning themselves, and the expectation that they would rid themselves of Negro slavery was not the least important. Other expectations made for contradiction, however, for Americans felt themselves to be embarked upon a grand experiment in republicanism, a feeling which sometimes generated mixed thoughts about Negro slavery. During the first years of the young republic, moreover, important economic changes were at work while citizens labored at the complex task of setting a new nation on foundations sufficiently firm to keep it from coming apart.

Part Four

SOCIETY AND THOUGHT
1783–1812

VIII THE IMPERATIVES OF ECONOMIC INTEREST AND NATIONAL IDENTITY

FOR THE POST-REVOLUTIONARY GENERATION OF AMERICANS, the most pressing political problem was formation of a viable national union. The existence of the United States of America was not —and it sometimes requires an effort of mind to remember this— inevitable. It is easy today to underestimate the centrifugal, disintegrative pressures that bore upon the union of ex-colonies forged by the necessity of uniting against British "tyranny." By examining these pressures, as well as the efforts made to resist them, it is possible to see how closely the primary political problem was interrelated with the presence of Negroes in America and with white men's thoughts about black.

The major factor making for sectional division in the United States was the proportion of Negroes in the population. By the 1790's it was clear that slavery was going to survive only in the area of high concentration of Negroes in the states south of Pennsylvania. Yet in the late eighteenth century sectional division lacked the clarity it was later to take on. The proportion of Negroes, despite a sharp break at the Mason-Dixon line, made for something of an achromatic spectrum—off-white in New Hampshire to dark grey in Georgia. Economic differences and the pattern of antislavery sentiment within the South also blurred the distinction between northern and southern states, since it was by no means definite that Virginia and Maryland would not become "northern" states by accomplishing general emancipation. Delaware was expected to abolish slavery and was usually classed with the North: hence the frequent contemporary allusions to five southern and eight northern states. To conceive of the ex-tobacco colonies as part of a monolithic South is to permit hindsight to remodel the facts. Despite the presence there of the twin factors which eventually proved determinative, slavery and a high proportion of Negroes, there was every reason to set off the upper "South" from the lower: proportion of Negroes, profitability of slavery, abolition sentiment—the very tone of society. North Carolina, moreover, served (as it had from the days of William Byrd) as a nebulous, anomalous borderland, characterized by diversified agriculture, a relatively low proportion of Negroes, and a culture which belonged, everyone agreed, almost in a class by itself. There was not one South but two and a half.[1]

While attending to these sectional realities and especially to economic changes which were working to solidify them, it is necessary to bear in mind that sectional discord over slavery depended on the existence of a national union and that existence of a union tended to make the presence of Negroes in America a national problem. Discussion of certain issues, especially in the national Congress after 1789, stirred up dormant hostilities without seeming to alter traditional ways of looking at the Negro. Yet of itself the rise of an independent American nation contained subtle and elusive implications for the Negro which were of far-reaching importance. For the task of building a new nation did not consist simply in laying down the bricks and mortar of national government; a rationale was needed to define the contents and purposes of the new structure. Without some sense of who and why Americans were a people and therefore a nation, work could not even begin. This necessity no less than the development of special sectional characteristics intensified what the Revolution had made the *problem* of Negroes in the American republic.

1. THE ECONOMICS OF SLAVERY

One incident capsulates the elements of sectionalism and national union and also a major aspect of the problem of the Negro in America. In the autumn of 1792, as the nation was girding its unanimity for re-election of General Washington as president of the United States, a tall young man from the rolling hill country of central Massachusetts found himself aboard ship bound for Savannah, Georgia. Fresh from Yale College, he was headed for a post as

1. For Delaware, [Philip Mazzei], *Recherches Historiques et Politiques sur les États-Unis de L'Amérique Septentrionale* . . . , 4 vols. (Colle, Italy, 1788), IV, 127; Farrand, ed., *Records Federal Convention, passim;* Jonathan Elliot, ed., *The Debates in the Several State Conventions, on the Adoption of the Federal Constitution* . . . , 2d ed., 5 vols. (Phila., 1896), I, 495, IV, 292. North Carolina was one of the two states, of course, to reject the federal Constitution.

tutor in a South Carolina family. Aboard the same vessel was a recent acquaintance, Mrs. Nathanael Greene, widow of the Rhode Island general, herself headed for the plantation which a grateful state of Georgia had conferred on her late husband. Upon docking in Savannah the young man found the tutor's post would pay only half what he had been led to expect, so he accepted Mrs. Greene's kind invitation to reside at her plantation. During that warm and pleasant winter he heard from gentlemen visiting the plantation of the need for some method of rendering upland cotton a feasible crop and learned that the difficulty lay in the laborious process of plucking out the seeds. The young man from Massachusetts possessed a penchant and, as it turned out, a talent for tinkering; he pieced together a machine, as so many men have before and since, without thought that he was shaping an economic revolution. By April Eli Whitney's machine was so efficient that one Negro could grind out fifty pounds of fiber in a day.[2]

The neatness of this incident has been compelling to later generations, especially when highlighted by statistics of cotton production. The nation harvested 6,000 bales in 1792; 17,000 in 1795; 73,000 in 1800; 146,000 in 1805; and 178,000 in 1810.[3] This enormous expansion has played upon the American imagination with such force as to make cotton sometimes appear both the foundation of American slavery and (presumably hence) the cause of Negro degradation. One modern social scientist has dated the origins of racial prejudice in America from the spring of 1793.[4] In fact, however, expansion of cotton production was by no means the midnight reprieve of a doomed institution, for in 1793 slavery was flourishing in the Lower South. Production of cotton was not new: the smooth-seed variety had been cultivated, and processed with the roller gin, before the Revolution. The war and postwar economic dislocation retarded expansion of cotton, but increasing amounts were grown for domestic use in the postwar period, taking up some of the slack caused by the decline of indigo. In the late 1780's sea-island cotton, a smooth-seed, long-staple variety, was introduced along the Georgia and South Carolina coast and enjoyed considerable popularity. Tobacco became important in the upland areas in the 1780's. Rice continued a major staple: exports from Charleston reached their peak in

2. Jeannette Mirsky and Allan Nevins, *The World of Eli Whitney* (N. Y., 1952), chaps. 4–6.

3. Lewis C. Gray, assisted by Esther Katherine Thompson, *History of Agriculture in the Southern United States to 1860*, 2 vols. (Washington, 1933), II, 1026; for helpful maps, II, 684.

4. Arnold Rose, "The Roots of Prejudice" in UNESCO, *The Race Question in Modern Science* (N. Y., 1956), 224.

1792–93, just as Whitney set to work. In short, as far as slave labor was concerned, there is every indication that expansion of cotton production in the 1790's merely whetted an existing appetite for slaves in the Lower South which was showing no signs of incipient satiation.[5]

Thus when South Carolina banned slave importations in 1787 the Assembly was not responding to lack of demand for slaves, nor of course to antislavery sentiment. For several years the economy of the entire country had been depressed, and many South Carolina planters had purchased more slaves than they could pay for, partly because of slaves lost owing to the British occupation. Indeed many South Carolinians were badly in debt because they had eagerly imported all manner of goods immediately after the war and had then been hit by three successive years of disastrous harvests. South Carolina's prohibition of slave imports in 1787, as remarks by contemporaries made evident, was a matter of men denying themselves what they wanted but could not afford.[6]

For sixteen years South Carolina stuck by its decision, gingerly extending the ban on imports for two or three years at a time. After 1794 members of the legislature had to face the unpleasant probability that reopening the trade would bring down the opprobrium of the nation on South Carolina for being the only state to permit slave importation. But the imperatives of expanding agriculture proved irresistible. South Carolina's ports were at last thrown open in 1803, though legislators comforted themselves that they were merely accommodating the law to actuality, since slaves had been illegally imported in large numbers. Significantly, demands for legalized importation came chiefly from the up country and opposition from the coastal region. The way west was to be paved with Negroes. Even after the federal prohibition of January 1, 1808,

5. For postwar economic developments in South Carolina, Gray, *Southern Agriculture*, II, 610–11, 674–86, 1023–24, 1030; Forrest McDonald, *We the People: The Economic Origins of the Constitution* (Chicago, 1958), 206–10; Charles G. Singer, *South Carolina in the Confederation* (Phila., 1941), chap. 1; Ulrich B. Phillips, "The South Carolina Federalists," *Amer. Hist. Rev.*, 14 (1908–09), 537–40; George C. Rogers, Jr., *Evolution of a Federalist: William Loughton Smith of Charleston (1758–1812)* (Columbia, S. C., 1962), 135–40.

6. Cooper and McCord, eds., *Statutes S. C.*, V, 38, VII, 430. For indebtedness as motive, *Charleston Evening Gazette*, Sept. 28, 1785; Donnan, ed., *Documents Slave Trade*, IV, 492–94; La Rochefoucauld-Liancourt, *Travels through the United States*, I, 574–75. Estimates on slaves lost to the British range from 5,000 to 30,000. Ironically, cotton cultivation killed off Negroes much more slowly than the rice swamps and thereby helped increase the supply of Negroes. See the comment in John Davis, *Travels of Four Years and a Half in the United States of America during 1798, 1799, 1800, 1801, and 1802*, ed. A. J. Morrison (N. Y., 1909), 93.

slave importation continued on a reduced scale as a smuggling operation.[7]

In the Upper South, the dynamics of economic development drove in a different direction. Virginia's principal crop, tobacco, recovered rapidly after the war but underwent no great expansion. Cotton was grown, but not in great quantity. Many tidewater planters, the riches of their soil robbed by tobacco, turned to more diversified farming and especially to grains such as wheat. It was in the tidewater region that Negroes were concentrated, left an ever-growing proportion of the eastern population by the tide of western settlement, since men of established wealth were reluctant to uproot themselves and head with their Negroes for a land that, beyond the piedmont, was not compellingly suited to slave agriculture. Far from wanting more slaves, many Virginians wanted to rid themselves of the ones they had. "It is demonstratively clear," George Washington wrote with customary bluntness, "that on this Estate (Mount Vernon) I have more working negros by a full moiety, than can be employed to any advantage in the farming system, and I shall never turn Planter [i.e., tobacco] thereon." In the 1790's a British traveler reported that Virginia's slave population was increasing rapidly; estates were "overstocked," a "circumstance complained of by every planter," though humanity prevented planters selling their slaves or casting them loose. A Virginia abolitionist dramatized the situation by noting that "since the cultivation of wheat has excited the attention of farmers in the northern neck of Virginia, the hoe has been exchanged for the plough, consequently the same number of hands are not now requisite, to work the same quantity of ground, as when tobacco was the chief crop." [8]

7. Cooper and McCord, eds., *Statutes S. C.*, VII, 431–36; Donnan, ed., *Documents Slave Trade*, IV, 500–502, also IV, 519–20; J. Franklin Jameson, ed., "Diary of Edward Hooker, 1805–1808," Amer. Hist. Assoc., *Annual Report* (1896), I, 878–80; *Debates and Proceedings in the Congress of the United States, 1789–1824* [*Annals of Congress*], 42 vols. (Washington, 1834–56), 8th Cong., 1st sess., 991–92, 1006. For clear evidence of illicit slave importations, Charleston *State Gazette of S.-C.*, Dec. 3, 1793; *Raleigh Register*, June 29, 1802; DuBois, *Suppression of the Slave-Trade*, 85–86, 109–12.

8. To Robert Lewis, Mount Vernon, Aug. 18, 1799, Fitzpatrick, ed., *Writings of Washington*, XXXVII, 338; Isaac Weld, Jr., *Travels through the States of North America, and the Provinces of Upper and Lower Canada . . . 1795, 1796, and 1797* (London, 1799), 85; *Minutes of the Proceedings of the Tenth American Convention for Promoting the Abolition of Slavery and Improving the Condition of the African Race: Assembled at Philadelphia* (Phila., 1805), 26, hereafter cited *Minutes Abolition Convention* (1805), and other years as explained chap. 9, note 5. See also John Parrish to William Dillwyn, Phila., Oct. 9, 1787, Misc. MSS.—Slavery, Box 2, N-O-P, no. 9, N.-Y. Hist. Soc. For Virginia agriculture, Gray, *Southern Agriculture*, II, 602–9, 614–17.

In Virginia the effects of agricultural change and the resulting
plethora of Negroes were profound. Slave importation never resumed after the war, not merely because it was forbidden by law but
because interest and morality had come to coincide.[9] It is too much
to say that lowered profitability caused the growth of antislavery
sentiment in Virginia, but in light of the situation in the Lower
South, the decline in profitability seems almost to have been a
precondition for public expression of such views. The economic
deterioration of slavery played a major role in making Maryland
and especially Virginia the antislavery South.

While the unprofitability of slavery pointed toward eventual
emancipation, it also suggested a more immediate and rewarding
remedy. Superfluous slaves could be transferred to regions where
they would no longer be superfluous, to Kentucky (especially if the
owner himself wished to remove) or, more commonly, to the southward. John J. Spooner reported in "A Topographical Description
of the County of Prince George, in Virginia, 1793" that "great
numbers" of slaves had been taken to Kentucky and to "the southern states."[10] While "motives of humanity" caused widespread reluctance to take advantage of this latter opportunity, the fact was
that slave dealers from the Lower South were buying and many
planters had every economic reason to sell. In 1804 a member of the
defunct Alexandria Abolition Society reported that slave dealers
from the Carolinas were purchasing Negroes in Maryland and
Virginia and were using Alexandria as "a place of deposit," a
noisome practice which had already been presented by the Alexandria grand jury. He was uncertain whether "the southern market is
now better supplied direct from Africa," but of late there had not
been so many slave dealers in evidence. As early as 1789 Oliver
Ellsworth of Connecticut had reported with malicious insinuation
that George Mason (actually a vigorous opponent of slavery)
owned "about three hundred slaves, and lives in Virginia, where it
is found by prudent management they can breed and raise slaves
faster than they want them for their own use, and could supply the
deficiency in Georgia and South Carolina."[11] Despite the hackles it
has always raised, the issue of slave-breeding was of peripheral
importance. The governing fact was that men in a region where
slavery was becoming less profitable found that an indispensable

---

9. Hening, ed., *Statutes Va.*, IX, 471–72, X, 307–8, XII, 182.
10. Mass. Hist. Soc., *Collections*, 1st Ser., 3 (1794), 92.
11. *Minutes Abolition Convention* (1805), 24–25; Ellsworth quoted by Frederic Bancroft, *Slave-Trading in the Old South* (Baltimore, 1931), 7.

social institution could be maintained well above the level of economic disaster by selling Negroes southwards. The price differential told the story: in 1797 prices for prime field hands ran about $300 in Virginia and $400 in Charleston; in 1803, over $400 in Virginia and somewhat under $600 in Charleston and Georgia; in 1808, $500 in Virginia and $550 in Charleston and Georgia.[12]

Thus by the turn of the century American slavery had taken on new dimensions. Eli Whitney's feat was impressive partly because it symbolized this change and underlined the nature of the new economy which was at once national and sectional. A New Englander obligingly fulfilled the South's technological need while New England ships (and English and southern too) supplied southerners with Negroes. Virginia was bonded to the system by the domestic slave traffic.

2. UNION AND SECTIONALISM

Even prior to these developments there had of course been sectional disagreements among the seaboard states. The first rumblings of sectional discord appeared with the first implementation of a tenuous "continental" union in 1774. Members of the Continental Congress argued over inclusion of Negroes in the army and whether slaves should be counted when taxes and requisitions were apportioned among the states.[13] After the war the slavery issue reappeared in novel form when Congress debated the future of the Northwest Territory. In 1784 a vote in the Congress to exclude slavery north of the Ohio River was lost for the inelegant reason that a New Jersey delegate was home sick in bed. The sectional pattern of voting was clear. Northern delegates were unanimous for exclusion, while the only southerners to vote for it were Jefferson

12. A graph of prices from 1795 is in Ulrich B. Phillips, *American Negro Slavery; A Survey of the Supply, Employment and Control of Negro Labor as Determined by the Plantation Régime* (N. Y. and London, 1918), opposite p. 370. For the southward trade, Bancroft, *Slave-Trading*, 11-24; *Minutes Abolition Convention* (1801), 20, 31, (1804), 7-8; John Parrish, *Remarks on the Slavery of the Black People; Addressed to the Citizens of the United States . . .* (Phila., 1806), 20; Thomas Jefferson to Thomas Mann Randolph, Washington, June 8, 1803, Edwin M. Betts, ed., *Thomas Jefferson's Farm Book, with Commentary and Relevant Extracts from Other Writings* (Princeton, 1953), 19; [John Edwards Caldwell], *A Tour through Part of Virginia, in the Summer of 1808*, ed. William M. E. Rachal (Richmond, 1951), 9-10. In the Constitutional Convention C. C. Pinckney had pointed out that if South Carolina and Georgia were prohibited slave imports, Virginia's slaves would rise in value. Farrand, ed., *Records Federal Convention*, II, 371, also III, 325.

13. John Richard Alden, *The First South* (Baton Rouge, La., 1961), 35-49.

and Hugh Williamson of North Carolina. Next year a similar provision met the same fate: the northern states voted unanimously for, Maryland two to one for, Virginia two to one against, the remaining southern states against. On the third try, in 1787, proponents of exclusion were successful; evidently some political bargain was involved, since only a lone New York delegate voted against prohibiting slavery in the Territory after 1800.[14]

That same year when the Constitutional Convention met in Philadelphia, delegates found that forging a new national government necessitated dealing with the far from malleable facts of slavery. One major issue concerned slave representation and taxation: the several states' disparate proportions of Negroes raised the question, which no one much wanted to discuss, whether slaves were persons or property. If slaves were to be included when apportioning representation, northerners asked, why not cattle as well? Despite the broad ramifications of this question, the dispute involved political definition and practice, not ethical evaluation of Negroes. No one claimed that slaves were not human beings. In the end, of course, the Convention decided to count three-fifths of a state's slaves for apportionment of representation and taxes. This famous compromise, for which there were precedents in the Confederation period, was a practical resolution of political interests, but it embodied more logic than has commonly been supposed. For the slave was, by social definition, both property and man, simultaneously partaking of the qualities of both; the three-fifths rule treated him accordingly, adding only a ludicrous fractional exactitude.

It was with a novel starkness that the founding fathers' legal ambidextrousness exposed the ambivalent judgment on the Negro's nature imposed by the institution of chattel slavery. The Negro was of course a man, but *insofar as he was property* he ranked with the beast of burden. This logic inhering in the three-fifths compromise was explicitly elaborated by James Madison in *The Federalist* No. 54. "One of our southern brethren might observe," Madison argued

14. Worthington C. Ford *et al.*, eds., *Journals of the Continental Congress, 1774–1789*, 34 vols. (Washington, 1904–37), XXVI, 247, 277, XXVIII, 164–65, XXXI, 669–73, XXXII, 334n, 343; Boyd, ed., *Papers of Jefferson*, VI, 603–8, 611–12, VII, 118–21. For the political bargain, Nathan Dane to Rufus King, N. Y., July 16, 1787, Edmund C. Burnett, ed., *Letters of Members of the Continental Congress (1774–1789)*, 8 vols. (Washington, 1921–36), VIII, 622; William Grayson to James Monroe, N. Y., Aug. 8, 1787, *ibid.*, VIII, 632. See also Joseph L. Arbena, "Politics or Principle? Rufus King and the Opposition to Slavery, 1785–1825," Essex Institute, *Historical Collections*, 101 (1965), 56–77. Sectional alignments in Congress owed something, perhaps, to the tradition of calling the roll in geographical order, from New Hampshire to Georgia.

with ingratiating indirection in a New York newspaper, that slaves were both persons and property,

that they partake of both these qualities; being considered by our laws, in some respects, as persons, and in other respects, as property. In being compelled to labor not for himself, but for a master; in being vendible by one master to another master; and in being subject at all times to be restrained in his liberty, and chastised in his body, by the capricious will of another, the slave may appear to be degraded from the human rank, and classed with those irrational animals, which fall under the legal denomination of property. In being protected on the other hand in his life and in his limbs, against the violence of all others, even the master of his labor and his liberty; and in being punishable himself for all violence committed against others; the slave is no less evidently regarded by the law as a member of the society; not as a part of the irrational creation; as a moral person, not as a mere article of property. The Federal Constitution therefore, decides with great propriety on the case of our slaves, when it views them in the mixt character of persons and of property. This is in fact their true character.

. . . Let the compromising expedient of the Constitution be mutually adopted, which regards them as inhabitants, but as debased by servitude below the equal level of free inhabitants, which regards the *slave* as divested of two fifths of the *man*.

Framing a national constitution forced men to say it outright: the Negro as a slave was but three-fifths a man. To many Americans, Madison included, this was precisely the wrong of slavery.[15]

But manifestly the Convention could not consider even the eventual termination of domestic slavery; propositions on this head would have sent half the delegates packing. The overseas slave

15. Jacob E. Cooke, ed., *The Federalist* (Middletown, Conn., 1961), 367–68, 369, opening clause's verb transposed. The wrong was built into the system. A lawyer pleading a freedom suit in Pennsylvania in 1790 claimed that no legislature could declare a person a slave when the Constitution proclaimed all men free: "It is no answer to this . . . that he is a Black. All are alike in the sight of God. . . . No legislature has such a power over white men; and none, therefore has such a power over black." The opposing lawyer replied, "On principles of nature, there can be no slavery. But we live under an express constitution; and on constitutional principles, there can be no slave, for the constitution declares all men born free; and the question is are these of human species? Another section protects property: this was a species of property; and the protection of the constitution is claimed for it. . . . These sections relate only to the parties to the contract. These negroes were not parties to it; they were none of the people. If it apply to all men, and a negroe be a man, there is an end of the question. If negroes be property, this can only be taken away by consent of the owner." Case of Aberilla Blackmore *v.* Pennsylvania (1790), Pennsylvania Abolition Society Papers, Legal Section, Acting Committee Cases, Habeas Corpus Cases, Hist. Soc. Pa. For later ramifications, see Albert F. Simpson, "The Political Significance of Slave Representation, 1787–1821," *Jour. Southern Hist.,* 7 (1941), 315–42.

trade, so widely reprobated, was another matter. An overwhelming majority of delegates wished to ban the traffic immediately or after a few years. But South Carolina and Georgia, probably with some support from North Carolina, were, as Madison put it, "inflexible on the point of the slaves." C. C. Pinckney of South Carolina warned that while he did not favor the traffic personally, the two southernmost states would most certainly reject the Constitution if denied slave imports. The founders wanted union more than an end to the slave trade; and with the aid of New England votes obtained by concessions on navigation laws, the twenty-year prohibition on federal action was inserted in the Constitution, a monument to pragmatic politics and to the ideal of national union.[16]

Ironically, implementation of that ideal helped expose the existence of sectional disunity. As the Convention painstakingly pieced together a plan of government in the simmering heat of the Pennsylvania State House, there was growing recognition of the pervasive and overriding influence of Negro slavery. Luther Martin of Maryland, less taken than most delegates by the need for unity, bluntly pointed out that "at the Eastward Slavery is not acknowledged, with us it exists in a certain qualified manner, at the Southward in its full extent." [17] James Madison, always very much taken with political realities, calmly commented: "It seemed now to be pretty well understood that the real difference of interests lay, not between the large and small but between the N. and Southn. States. The institution of slavery and its consequences formed the line of discrimination. There were 5 states on the South, 8 on the Northn. side of this line." [18] Acutely conscious of sectional interests, the Convention frankly and openly compromised. And the slavery com-

16. For Madison, Farrand, ed., *Records Federal Convention*, III, 135, 325; for Pinckney, II, 371. The intransigence of South Carolina and Georgia is broadcast through the records. North Carolina was occasionally included by those reporting the southern stand, but more often not. This confusion arose partly because North Carolina had not actually prohibited the slave trade but had recently enacted a prohibitive duty, a fact noted once during debate (*ibid.*, II, 373). Richard Dobbs Spaight, a North Carolina delegate, later told the North Carolina ratifying convention that the state's delegation had felt unable to vote for national prohibition because the state itself had not actually prohibited the trade. But James Iredell, not a delegate to the federal Convention, told the North Carolina convention that South Carolina and Georgia had blocked immediate banning of the slave trade and that all delegates had "reprobated this inhuman traffic." Elliot, ed., *Debates in State Conventions*, IV, 100–101, 178. On this matter as on so many others, North Carolina stood between the two Souths. For the bargain with New England, Farrand, ed., *Records Federal Convention*, II, 373, 415–16, III, 210–11, 367.

17. Farrand, ed., *Records Federal Convention*, IV, 25.

18. *Ibid.*, II, 9–10; also I, 476.

promises proved successful outside the Convention, at least for a time, perhaps owing partly to the frankness with which they were forwarded. In many ratifying conventions there was some grumbling, chiefly from delegates disaffected toward the Constitution for other reasons, but in no state did the slavery clauses in the Constitution become a major issue.[19]

3. A NATIONAL FORUM FOR DEBATE

Far from soothing sectional disagreements, inauguration of a new national government directly fostered sectional tension over Negro slavery. A powerful federal Congress looked like a magnificent fulcrum to antislavery organizations, and in 1790 petitions against the slave trade were presented to the House of Representatives by New York and Philadelphia Quakers and by the Pennsylvania Abolition Society. Several southern Representatives wanted the House to refuse consideration of the petitions, and an acrimonious debate ensued in which sectional interests were laid bare before the nation. (President Washington, alarmed by the dangers of disunion, privately declared the Quaker memorial to be "very mal-apropos.") [20] During the debate, Representative Thomas Scott of Pennsylvania set forth the antislavery case in language which would have been almost inconceivable a generation earlier: "I look upon the slave trade to be one of the most abominable things on earth; and if there was neither God nor devil, I should oppose it upon the principles of humanity, and the law of nature." [21] James Jackson of Georgia jumped to his feet to defend the interests of his state with a speech which moved eighty-four-year-old Benjamin Franklin to pen his last public paper, which was very

19. In addition to Elliot, ed., *Debates in State Conventions*, see DuBois, *Suppression of the Slave-Trade*, 62–69.

20. To David Stuart, N. Y., Mar. 28, 1790, Fitzpatrick, ed., *Writings of Washington*, XXXI, 30. For the debate, *Annals of Congress*, 1st Cong., 2d sess., 1182–91, 1197–1205, 1413–17, 1450–64, 1466–71, 1472–74; and Edgar S. Maclay, ed., *Journal of William Maclay, United States Senator from Pennsylvania, 1789–1791* (N. Y., 1890), 196–97, 221–23. See also Warner Mifflin, "Queries Addressed to a Committee of Congress," *American Museum*, 8 (1790), 61–65, 156–58. Vols. I and II of *Annals of Congress*, covering the 1st Congress, were published in two editions, not marked as such, both 1834 but with differing pagination and running heads. The edition used throughout is the second, which has running heads: "History of Congress/History of Congress." See Marion Tinling, "Thomas Lloyd's Reports of the First Federal Congress," *Wm. and Mary Qtly.*, 18 (1961), 520*n*.

21. *Annals of Congress*, 1st Cong., 2d sess., 1199.

Franklinish—a defense of slavery by an Algerian pirate.[22] An outraged reader of the *New York Daily Advertiser* assailed Jackson less
subtly: "An oration, delivered at this enlightened period, in favour
of domestic slavery, must be sufficient to crimson the face of a
Botany-Bay politician!"[23] Jackson's effort paled beside that of William Loughton Smith of South Carolina, whose bitter speech on the
same issue later in the session lasted two hours. Smith dwelt insis-
tently on the horrors of racial intermixture, to which every man in
the House, he hoped, had the utmost aversion. Like so many southerners after him, Smith lectured the nation on the peculiar sociol-
ogy of the South: "It is known, from experience, that the whites had
such an idea of their superiority over the blacks, that they never
even associated with them; even the warmest friends to the blacks
kept them at a distance, and rejected all intercourse with them."
"The truth was," Smith declared, "that the best informed part of
the citizens of the Northern States knew that slavery was so in-
grafted into the policy of the Southern States, that it could not be
eradicated without tearing up by the roots their happiness, tran-
quillity, and prosperity." Smith's diatribe revealed the near impossibility of defending slavery without derogating the Negro: "It was
well known that they were an indolent people, improvident, averse
to labor: when emancipated, they would either starve or plunder."
Representative Scott, appalled beyond eloquence by Smith's speech,
could only gulp out in reply that advocacy of slavery was *"a Phenomenon in Politics."*[24]

Smith went out of his way to throw barbs at the Quakers for
broaching the subject of the slave trade, which was, he said, protected by the Constitution. In that compact between North and
South "we took each other, with our mutual bad habits and respective evils, for better, for worse; the Northern states adopted us with
our slaves, and we adopted them with their Quakers." A fair exchange. When Delaware's John Vining announced his resentment
of Smith's "comparison" of Quakers with Negroes, Smith retorted
that Quakers should feel no resentment at being compared with
persons they claimed as equals, "though of a different colour, . . . as
good as themselves, in every respect."[25]

When it came to voting, defenders of slavery stood revealed as

22. *Ibid.*, 1st Cong., 2d sess., 1200; Smyth, ed., *Writings of Franklin*, X, 87–91.
23. Reprinted in *Maryland Journal and Baltimore Advertiser*, Apr. 2, 1790.
24. *Ibid.*, Apr. 6, 1790.
25. Ibid., Apr. 2, 8, 1790. Smith's speech is in *Annals of Congress*, 1st Cong.,
2d sess., 1455–64.

more vocal than numerous, for they mustered only fourteen votes. Not all names were recorded, but the sectional pattern was evident. Of those opposed to considering the petitions, only one was from the North; Maryland was three to one for consideration and Virginia eight to two; North Carolina was not yet present, and South Carolina and Georgia voted unanimously against. The correlation with the geographical pattern of Negro slavery could hardly have been more striking.[26]

Various aspects of the slavery issue continued to arouse debate in Congress during the 1790's, though members tried frequently to sweep the entire matter under the rug. Resentful Representatives replied to antislavery petitions by attacking the petitioners. With William Loughton Smith sitting in the House there was bound to be bitterness: in 1792 he labeled a petition by the prominent Quaker abolitionist, Warner Mifflin, "a mere rant and rhapsody of a meddling fanatic, interlarded with texts of Scripture, and concluded with no specific prayer." [27] Yet gradually the acrimony of sectional aspersion over slavery seemed to subside. Congress evenhandedly enacted a fugitive slave law in 1793 and next year a law barring United States citizens from participation in the international slave traffic. On the latter occasion, significantly, petitions from the abolition societies aroused favorable action but little debate.[28] Three years later in 1797 a Quaker petition concerning some Negroes re-enslaved in North Carolina kindled discussion of considerable warmth, but there were no diatribes against the North, no militant defenses of the southern institution. Nathaniel Macon of North Carolina, speaker of a later Congress, assured the House that "there was not a gentleman in North Carolina who did not wish there were no blacks in the country. It was a misfortune—he considered it as a curse; but there was no way of getting rid of them. Instead of peace-makers, he looked upon the Quakers as warmakers, as they were continually endeavoring in the Southern States to stir up insurrections amongst the negroes." [29] Despite these asperities, there was a tone of restraint in the 1797 debate which had been notably lacking in 1790.

26. *Annals of Congress,* 1st Cong., 2d sess., 1205.
27. *Ibid.,* 2d Cong., 2d sess., 730.
28. *Ibid.,* 3d Cong., 1st sess., 36, 38–39, 349, 448, 455, 469, 483; *Minutes Abolition Convention* (1794), 26–28; *The Public Statutes at Large of the United States of America, 1789–1873* . . . , 17 vols. (Boston, 1850–73), I, 302–5, 347–49.
29. *Annals of Congress,* 5th Cong., 2d sess., 661; the debate is on 656–70, 945–46, 1032–33.

Congressmen seemed increasingly to sense a delicate explosiveness in the slavery issue. When George Thatcher, from the Maine district of Massachusetts, moved to bar extension of slavery into the newly organized Mississippi Territory in 1798 he was treated by many Representatives much as if he had oafishly violated the rules of a game everyone was supposed to know how to play. Southerners claimed that westward expansion would thin the dangerous concentration of slaves on the seaboard and then castigated Thatcher for broaching the matter. Despite support from Albert Gallatin, Thatcher's proposition gained only twelve votes.[30]

There was again a spate of discussion generated by a petition in 1800, but it proved to be the last one for many years. Representative Robert Waln, a wealthy Philadelphia Quaker, introduced a petition signed and marked by Absalom Jones and other free Negroes of Philadelphia which asked for restriction of the slave trade and modification of the fugitive slave law; the petition also expressed hope for an eventual day of general emancipation. The explosion was instantaneous.[31] John Rutledge, Jr., of South Carolina vigorously berated white abolitionists, whom he detected as the real perpetrators of the petition. They had been heard from before, he said, and have "now put it into the hands of the black *gentlemen.*" Rutledge, a firm Federalist, saw the insidious import of such petitions: "Already had too much of this new-fangled French philosophy of liberty and equality found its way and was too apparent among these *gentlemen* in the Southern States, by which nothing would do but their liberty." Another stout Federalist, Harrison Gray Otis of Massachusetts, thought the danger was contagious: "To encourage a measure of the kind would have an irritating tendency, and must be mischievous to America very soon. It would teach them the art of assembling together, debating, and the like, and would soon, if encouraged, extend from one end of the Union to the other." Federalist John Brown of Rhode Island spoke with the vigor and aggressiveness which characterized his business dealings and came out with an astonishingly forthright defense of the slave trade.

30. *Ibid.*, 1306–12, 1313. Two years earlier a House committee had rejected a petition to allow slaves into the Northwest Territory, *ibid.*, 4th Cong., 1st sess., 1171, 1349.
31. The following account is drawn from *ibid.*, 6th Cong., 1st sess., 229–45, 686–90, 699–700. The quotations: Rutledge, 230; Otis, 231; Brown, 233, 686–87; Thacher, 232, 236–37 (the *DAB* gives "Thacher," or "Thatcher"); Jones, 235; Edmond, 237; the House resolution and first vote, 244–45; vote on the bill, 699–700. The act of 1800 is in *Statutes U. S.*, II, 70–71. See also DuBois, *Suppression of the Slave-Trade*, 81–84. Otis later strongly opposed extension of slavery during the Missouri Compromise debates.

Eleven years earlier he had belligerently defended the traffic in an unseemly battle in the public press with his brother Moses, fellow businessman but Quaker and abolitionist. Since then he had been widely suspected, correctly, of fitting out a slaver in violation of both Rhode Island and the federal law. Now on the floor of the House with the public-be-damned air of a nineteenth-century tycoon, Brown demanded repeal of the federal prohibition of 1794: "why should we see Great Britain getting all the slave trade to themselves; why may not our country be enriched by that lucrative traffic?" The act of 1794, he sneered, represented inexcusable capitulation to dunning by "the Abolition Society, otherwise the Society of Friends." It was "ill policy" to prohibit citizens from the trade, even "wrong" since Negroes benefited by removal to this country. John Brown was the entrepreneur rampant.[32]

Despite the partisan Federalism of Brown and Otis, individual and sectional feeling rather than party lines determined the division of opinion in the debate of 1800, just as in the debates of the previous ten years. Robert Waln, who set off the explosion, was also a Federalist. So too were those Representatives most vigorous in refuting aspersions on the Negro's character. When the Negro petition was attacked on grounds that some of its signers could not write their names, Federalist George Thatcher, already too familiar to the South, declared repeatedly, "A great reason why they could not write was their being brought up in early life in slavery." On the other side, James Jones, Republican of Georgia, thought the petition tended toward emancipation and even equality: "I would ask the gentlemen whether, with all their philanthropy, they would wish to see those people sitting by their sides deliberating in the councils of the nation?" He presumed not. These rather telling questions were parried by William Edmond, Federalist of Connecticut, who declared that "it mattered not whether the people were black or white; the petition only was to be regarded, and not the color of the persons."

When the acrimonious debate finally culminated in balloting, members of the House fell back on common ground, achieving a remarkable consensus which belied a nearly universal fear of the

---

32. *Providence Gazette,* Feb. 14–Apr. 11, 1789, for reference to which I am indebted to James Francis Reilly, Moses Brown and the Rhode Island Antislavery Movement (unpubl. M.A. thesis, Brown University, 1951). For evidence of Brown's trading after 1754, James B. Hedges, *The Browns of Providence Plantations: Colonial Years* (Cambridge, Mass., 1952), 82–84, notes p. 341. Brown could have abstained from trafficking without serious financial loss and perhaps with real saving.

divisive nature of the problem of slavery. The House voted eighty-five to one "that the parts of the said petition which invite Congress to legislate upon subjects from which the General Government is precluded by the Constitution, have a tendency to create disquiet and jealousy, and ought therefore to receive no encouragement or countenance from this House." Only independent George Thatcher voted against this refusal to consider the question of domestic slavery. At the same session, however, a bill which aimed at reinforcing the 1794 ban on American participation in the slave traffic passed the House sixty-seven to five. In opposition were John Brown, George Dent of Maryland, Joseph Dickson of North Carolina, and Benjamin Huger and John Rutledge, Jr., of South Carolina. Of these holdouts, only John Brown had explicitly endorsed the trade.

For several sessions after 1800 Congress was undisturbed by the slavery issue. Antislavery petitioners no longer importuned the House—a reflection of growing timidity and declining zeal in the antislavery movement. Relative quiet might have prevailed until termination of the slave trade's twenty-year immunity from congressional prohibition had not South Carolina reopened old wounds in 1803. Legal resumption of the traffic in South Carolina aroused proposals in Congress for a $10 duty on imported slaves, the maximum permitted by the Constitution. Debate was warm and vigorous but by no means unrestrained. Samuel Latham Mitchill of New York, though strongly antislavery, stressed joint sectional responsibility: "the citizens of the navigating States bring negroes from Africa, and sell them to the inhabitants of those States which are more distinguished for their plantations." [33] Such meticulously euphemistic phraseology was characteristic of the debate. More striking still was the pathetic need for reassurance that the slave trade received no public support: speaker after speaker arose to declare that he and everyone present reprobated the noxious traffic, and South Carolina's Representatives, while vigorously opposing the tax, were at pains to point out that they personally would have opposed their state's action. The tax was defeated, but the issue was blurred by suggestions that South Carolina would soon reverse her decision and would take offense at federal action and also by the reluctance of some northern Congressmen to "endorse" the traffic by taxing it. During the next few years the same subject came up repeatedly, and there was further aggravation over admitting slaves into the southern portion of the Louisiana Territory.

33. *Annals of Congress*, 8th Cong., 1st sess., 1001; for the whole debate, 820, 876, 992–1036; DuBois, *Suppression of the Slave-Trade*, 86–87.

All efforts against the trade, including proposals for constitutional amendment by North Carolina and other states, were unsuccessful.[34] The time of legal termination was too near. When that time finally came in the session of 1806–07, debates on the bill prohibiting the trade were hard-fought and bitter, but significantly they bore on enforcement and on disposal of contraband slaves, not on whether a bill should be passed. Ominously, however, Peter Early of Georgia announced that the nation must recognize that southerners generally did "not consider slavery as a crime" and that many did not regard it even as "a political evil." John Randolph of Virginia, never one to mince words, warned that "if ever the time of disunion between the States should arrive, the line of severance would be between the slaveholding and the non-slaveholding States." Yet there was no doubt about the legal termination of the trade; some law must and would be passed.[35]

And with enactment of the law which was to take effect January 1, 1808, slavery was no longer a critical divisive issue in the Union. The chief aggravation was relieved: the albatross of the slave trade no longer hung painfully on the national conscience, no matter how actively the traffic actually continued. The sense of victory and elation was heightened by Britain's prohibition of the trade that same year. Congress and the nation turned their energies to quarreling with Great Britain and when the second war for independence came in 1812, it brought, in striking contrast to the first, no benefit to the Negro. Not until westward expansion reanimated sectional bitterness in the Missouri Compromise debates of 1819–20 did Congress find itself wracked again by the problem of Negro slavery. Americans had learned to fear its divisive power, particularly after the first and bitterest clash in 1790. Jefferson's "firebell in the night" of 1820 was actually a second alarm. The first conflagration had been brought under control and even quenched, many thought, in 1807.

4. NATIONHOOD AND IDENTITY

For Americans of the post-Revolutionary generation, heightening national consciousness of differing sectional viewpoints was a comparatively external and less profound manifestation of the impact of nation-forming than was the compelling necessity for

34. DuBois, *Suppression of the Slave-Trade*, 87–93.
35. *Annals of Congress*, 9th Cong., 2d sess., 167–90, 200–203, 220–28, 231–44, 264–67, 270–74, 477–78, 483–85, 486–87, 527–28, 626–27, 636–38, 1266–70; the remarks of Early and Randolph being 238, 626. DuBois, *Suppression of the Slave-Trade*, 94–108.

finding the inner logic—the *raison d'être*—of the new republic. Part of this logic Americans found in the realm of governance. An important aspect of American nationalism was that the Revolution, the War for Independence, had been fought on a specific platform of political principles. At the time of the struggle over ratification of the Constitution many proponents argued, as one wrote, "The revolution cannot be said to be compleated till that [Constitution] or something equivalent is established." * Antifederalists of course disagreed, but they did *not* disagree with the assumption that the Revolution and its ideology entailed a system of government upon America. Almost everyone thought that there should be *some* sort of national union and that it as well as the state governments should be constructed along republican lines. This is to say that there was broad agreement that government in America would be non-monarchical, balanced and checked, and representative of the people in whom resided ultimate sovereignty. There was also considerable agreement as to the best institutional forms and practices of republican government—bicameral legislatures, an independent judiciary, and bills of rights.

These aspects of American nationalism are important particularly for two reasons relevant to changing attitudes toward Negroes. To many contemporaries the Revolution was not the end but the beginning of a glorious chapter in the history of man, the opening act of a glorious drama to be played out on the open stage of a virgin continent, with sympathetic vibrations confidently expected in the Old World. It was not the past which required elucidation so much as the present and future—including the future of America's Negroes. The Revolution may be considered to have been one of unfinished business.

Related to this anticipatory mood was the circumstance that Americans inherited from the Revolution a virtual textbook of instruction in only one area of this business—government. Thus the Revolution imparted a peculiarly *political* bias to American nationalism; it entailed instructions to establish governments suitable for the peculiar "republican genius" of the American people. But it failed to give guidance concerning the peculiar nature of the American people other than that they were "republican," which was principally a political concept. Important questions were left unanswered: Who were these people to be governed? What were they like? Why was there any reason to place them under one national government?

* David Ramsay to Benjamin Rush, Feb. 17, 1788, Robert L. Brunhouse, ed., "David Ramsay on the Ratification . . . ," *Jour. Southern Hist.*, 9 (1943), 553.

To some extent the assumption of republicanism did answer these questions. As it bore upon Negroes the republican self-image was logically negated or blurred by chattel slavery, and as the national destiny continued to unfold, the antislavery people seized upon what was in a very real sense a violation of self. As Theodore Dwight proclaimed in 1794,

And if any thing can sound like a solecism in the ears of mankind, it will be this story—That in the United States of America, societies are formed for the promotion of freedom. Will not the enquiry instantly be made—"Are the United States of America not free? Possessed of the best country, the wisest government, and the most virtuous inhabitants, on the face of the earth; are they still enslaved?" No—America is not enslaved; she is free. Her country is still excellent, her government wise, and her inhabitants virtuous. But this reply must be mixed with one base ingredient. The slavery of negroes is still suffered to exist.[36]

This slavery violated republicanism in another way by inviting an opulent, aristocratic way of life more suited for degenerate Europe than for virtuous America. An anonymous antislavery writer played lovingly upon this theme of yeoman virtue:

Many persons of opulence in Virginia, and the Carolinas, treat their unhappy slaves with . . . the most deliberate indifference. Surrounded with a numerous train of servants, to contribute to their personal ease, and wallowing in all the luxurious plenitude of riches, they neglect the wretched source, whence they draw this profusion. . . . While those miserable degraded persons, thus scantily subsist, all the produce of their unwearied toil, is taken away to satiate their rapacious master. He, devoted wretch! thoughtless of the sweat and toil with which his wearied, exhausted dependants procure what he extravagantly dissipates, not contented with the ordinary luxuries of life, is perhaps, planning, at the time, some improvement on the voluptuous art.—Thus he sets up two carriages instead of one; maintains twenty servants, when a fourth part of that number are more than sufficient to discharge the business of personal attendance.[37]

Was it right that any American republicans have "two carriages instead of one"?

While Americans knew themselves to be a republican, virtuous, and politically independent people, their character nonetheless remained unclear. Economically the nation was still tied to Britain's apron strings; despite widespread reluctance to acknowledge this unpleasant reality, many Americans, like Alexander Hamilton in his *Report on Manufactures,* faced it squarely and called upon the

36. Theodore Dwight, *An Oration, Spoken before "The Connecticut Society for the Promotion of Freedom and Relief of Persons Unlawfully Holden in Bondage." Convened in Hartford . . . 1794* (Hartford, 1794), 3.

37. "Essay on Negro-Slavery. By Another Hand," in James O'Kelly, *Essay on Negro-Slavery* (Phila., 1789), 46–47.

nation to strive for economic independence. As for other ties to England, so intangible yet so binding and pervasive, the problem of asserting independence was far more difficult. The struggle for cultural independence involved fighting on two fronts, proving both difference from the Old World and unity among Americans. With non-political institutions, perceptible progress was possible. Americans could point proudly to more than a dozen new colleges and scores of academies, more than a few medical schools and medical societies, Peale's literally wonderful Philadelphia Museum, Rittenhouse's unique observatory, the Massachusetts Historical Society, the South Carolina Society for Promoting and Improving Agriculture, and a one-man research organization at Monticello, to name but a few. There were hopes for a national university. The Anglican and Methodist churches were reconstituted on a national basis, and American Roman Catholics were given their first resident bishop.

Genuine cultural independence from England could not, however, be adequately assured by a proliferation of extra-political organizations. How could one be *sure* that Americans had acquired their own truly independent culture? An answer was urgently needed, and urgency made for a frantic quality in the quest. Joel Barlow's *Vision of Columbus,* lovingly inflated into the *Columbiad,* was expansively aggressive. Thomas Jefferson's *Notes on Virginia* strove to demolish European derogations of the American world. Noah Webster cried passionately for a truly American language. Equally hortatory were the attempts to create an American history; the nation already *had* a future, but where was its past? After the Revolution there were numerous attempts, all of which focused on the nature of the new society in the New World.[38]

On one very real level of historical reality this quest for national identity has been from the time of the Revolution the governing fact of American development. At first, inevitably, the search for identity assumed shape in assertions of and pleas for independence from England and the Old World. Independence itself was not sufficiently explanatory, however, for at best it described what America was not. Positive identification and delineation of American culture were needed, else the quest would go on perpetually, with Jeremiahs incessantly announcing, as Emerson did in the American

38. Demands for an American national literature, before 1815, are covered in Benjamin T. Spencer, *The Quest for Nationality: An American Literary Campaign* (Syracuse, 1957), chaps. 1–2.

Scholar address, that America had not yet achieved independence.

Emerson's famous plea was made possible by American political independence and union. Had there been no separate American nation, if the struggles for political independence and union had failed, Emerson could scarcely have summoned Americans to create an American culture. Perhaps this is to say merely that for any individual or society, assured self-identity is possible only if there exists a rudimentary self which both feels need for identity and provides some framework on which to build it. The *national* "self" came into being in the years just prior to and during and after the Revolution. The country emerged from the war politically independent but precariously unified, and the most crucial question of the postwar years was that of national union. For the nation's identity the year 1787 and those immediately following were absolutely critical. If the concept of national identity is at all meaningful, then it reveals an inner psychic meaning in the fathers' almost inexplicably poignant phrase—"a more perfect Union." If we may speak of the American nation as an individual—and we do more often than we realize—then the new government represented a partial integration of national self.

The search for national self-identity after the Revolution, and particularly the crisis of 1787–88, was intimately linked with white American attitudes toward Negroes. At least many of the historical "facts" in the remainder of this book point toward the existence of some connection between the incomplete success of Americans at becoming American and the changing pattern of American assessments of the Negro. Indeed it would be preposterous to suppose that efforts at cultural independence and national unity had no connection with American thoughts and feelings about a category of the populace which was so distinctly different and separate. For embedded in these efforts lay certain assumptions about the people to whom all this was happening, assumptions which helped guide the direction of the national quest.

5. NON-ENGLISH ENGLISHMEN

For a century and a half the people of the American continent had often thought of themselves primarily as colonial Englishmen. The Revolution undercut this self-conception with disconcerting suddenness, even though Americans had already become conscious of their divergence from the people of the mother country. Political independence discredited the old self-image by

strongly implying that Americans were not in fact Englishmen of
any sort. To proclaim convincingly non-Englishness as an accomplished fact was at once essential and impossible; the clash between
political independence and the inertia of cultural heredity made for
uncertainty and ambivalence. Americans still spoke English. Institutions such as family, churches, learned societies, and representative government had arisen on English models, no matter how
markedly transformed by New World conditions. Americans could
scarcely toss these aside as mere excess baggage. Even the repudiation of English imperial authority had been grounded on the rights
of Englishmen, half-transmuted into generalizations about the
rights of men. Somehow Americans had to find a way out, to deny
that they were English without denying their English heritage.

By far the easiest and most reassuring method was to concentrate
on the American environment. The assumption that colonial Englishmen had been happily remade by natural conditions in the New
World had pronounced advantages: it implied grateful acknowledgment of the English heritage while at the same time it stressed the
beneficent character of the American environment and hence the
likelihood of further improvement. Among the many reasons why
Americans assumed an environmentalist posture, the need both to
embrace and repudiate their own Englishness was one of the most
compelling.

For additional confirmation of their own distinctive character,
Americans might perhaps have seized upon the indisputable fact
that their continent had not been settled by Englishmen exclusively
but by peoples from all the western regions of the Old World. In
describing themselves, Americans might have pointed to a new
amalgam of nationalities as confirmation of American distinctiveness. Physically, by blood, the American could accurately have been
described as a new man.

On this matter it has lately become *de rigueur* to quote St. Jean
de Crèvecoeur's *Letters from an American Farmer* (1782) :

. . . whence came all these people? they are a mixture of English, Scotch,
Irish, French, Dutch, Germans, and Swedes. From this promiscuous breed,
that race now called Americans have arisen. . . . What then is the American, this new man? He is either an European, or the descendant of an
European, hence that strange mixture of blood, which you will find in no
other country. I could point out to you a family whose grandfather was an
Englishman, whose wife was Dutch, whose son married a French woman,
and whose present four sons have now four wives of different nations. . . .
Here individuals of all nations are melted into a new race of men, whose
labours and posterity will one day cause great changes in the world.[39]

39. [Crèvecoeur], *Letters from an American Farmer*, 48, 51–52.

These are striking words; few observations on the American people have been quoted more frequently, almost invariably with approval, as demonstrating both the fact of amalgamation and America's warm welcoming of the process. But in fact Crèvecoeur (a naturalized American who was born and died in France) was not expressing a common view, and historians have since placed heavy reliance on his words because at the time virtually no one else was saying the same thing. Certainly no one else put such heavy emphasis on the fusion of bloods, not even Thomas Paine (another temporary American) when he claimed in *Common Sense* that "Europe, and not England, is the parent country of America." In the late eighteenth century the idea that the "American" was a "new man" by reason of physical amalgamation was the exceptional opinion of a romantic French immigrant. Even those Americans who chose to acknowledge and emphasize the diversity of national backgrounds in America, such as David Ramsay in his *History of South-Carolina* (1809), presented a picture of the American people very different from Crèvecoeur's:

So many and so various have been the sources from which Carolina has derived her population, that a considerable period must elapse, before the people amalgamate into a mass possessing an uniform national character. This event daily draws nearer; for each successive generation drops a part of the peculiarities of its immediate predecessors. The influence of climate and government will have a similar effect. The different languages and dialects, introduced by the settlers from different countries, are gradually giving place to the english. So much similarity prevails among the descendants of the early emigrants from the old world, that strangers cannot ascertain the original country of the ancestors of the present race.

Ramsay's amalgamation was occurring as a natural cultural process, greatly hastened by the environmental factors of climate, form of government, and language.[40]

40. Foner, ed., *Writings of Paine*, I, 19–20; David Ramsay, *The History of South-Carolina, from Its First Settlement in 1670, to the Year 1808*, 2 vols. (Charleston, 1809), I, chap. 1, quotation pp. 22–23. In 1776 the Continental Congress appointed a committee, comprised of John Adams, Franklin, and Jefferson, to devise a seal for the new nation. They consulted P. E. Du Simitière, a Geneva-born artist who had been in America eleven years. The committee's report included six national symbols, for England, Scotland, Ireland, France, Germany, and Holland, which served as "pointing out the Countries from which these States have been peopled." Though approved by the three Americans, this celebration of the diversity of (European) national backgrounds in America was not their original intention. Franklin and Jefferson had suggested the theme of Israel's migration from Egypt and Adams the choice between virtue and vice. Here again, the theme of diversity was promulgated by a recent non-English immigrant. Ford, ed., *Journals of the Continental Congress*, V, 517, 689–91; Boyd, ed., *Papers of Jefferson*, I, 494–97; L. H. Butterfield, ed., *Adams Family Correspondence*, 2 vols. (Cambridge, Mass., 1963), II, 96–97, 108.

Of course physical amalgamation had in fact occurred. Non-English people had flocked to America in large numbers and in many cases had lost their genetic as well as cultural distinctiveness. An arresting picture of the amalgamative process was drawn by a Swedish Moravian minister visiting some settlements of his country-men (or so he had hoped) along the Delaware River in 1745. His description was like Crèvecoeur's, yet very different.

I found in this country scarcely one genuine Swede left, the most of them are either in part or in whole on one side or other descended from English or Dutch parents, some of them have had a Dutch, German or English father, others a Swedish mother, and others a Dutch or English mother and a Swedish father. Many of them can just recollect that their grand-fathers or mothers were Swedish. In general there is such confusion in their lineage, that they themselves can't tell, if they spring from English or Dutch, Swedish or German parents. The English are evidently swallowing up the people and the Swedish language is so corrupted, that if I did not know the English, it would be impossible to understand the language of my dear Sweden.[41]

Abraham Reincke's pathetic lament is highly revealing. By crying out that the "English are evidently swallowing up the people" and in instinctively pointing to language as evidence, he laid his finger upon the pulse of amalgamation. For in fact the English did "swallow up" other peoples. By the Revolutionary era, many of the non-English peoples in the American colonies had lost much of their cultural distinctiveness to the voracious dominance of English language, customs, and institutions, and their original genetic character to English numerical superiority. Absorption was most thorough in the settled regions along the coast, especially in urban centers where homogenization was bound to be most rapid. One only need call a roll of such names as Paul Revere, James Bowdoin, John Jay, Anthony Benezet, Henry Laurens, Stephen Van Rensselaer, Robert R. Livingston, and James Logan to realize how completely men of non-English background could be absorbed. In the latter part of the century much of the concern and resentment about Germans in Pennsylvania abated as they became less isolated.[42]

One of the most powerful forces making for cultural homogenization in the colonies was the overwhelming preponderance of the

41. John W. Jordan, ed., "Reincke's Journal of a Visit among the Swedes of West Jersey, 1745," *Pa. Mag. of Hist. and Biog.*, 33 (1909), 101.
42. See particularly Glenn Weaver, "Benjamin Franklin and the Pennsylvania Germans," *Wm. and Mary Qtly.*, 14 (1957), 536–59.

English language. Among some of the most numerous of the "non-English" settlers, the Scots, Irish, and Scotch-Irish, a large majority spoke English and had had some contact (not always pleasant) with English culture at home. Moreover, English cultural influence in America cannot be measured accurately by a simple process of weighing the proportion of English-derived people in the American population. The best available estimate is that in 1790 between 61 and 66 per cent of white Americans were of English origin and that between 80 and 84 per cent were of English-speaking origin.[43] One can scarcely assume on this basis that the American cultural background was 60 or 80 per cent English. Various other factors were of critical importance, such as primacy of arrival and language, economic and imperial ties, governmental institutions, and the localization of cultural deviance. England was actually *the* mother country.

This is to say that Americans had good reason for thinking of themselves as modified Englishmen rather than as products of a European amalgam. In perverse fashion, the break with England served to confirm this conviction. The paper war for liberty inevitably focused attention on ties with the British government: in a manuscript published in 1774 as *A Summary View of the Rights of British America,* Thomas Jefferson insisted that "our ancestors, before their emigration to America, were the free inhabitants of the British dominions in Europe." The military alliance with France was an affair of expediency, not cultural affinity. The postwar need for strong unified government tempted Americans to emphasize the nation's historic unity even to the point of utterly ignoring existing diversities. As John Jay wrote in the first Federalist paper, "Providence has been pleased to give this one connected country, to one united people, a people descended from the same ancestors, speaking the same language, professing the same religion, attached to the same principles of government, very similar in their manners and customs." [44] The struggle for economic and cultural independence following the military victory further deepened and exacerbated American awareness of pervasive English influence. Noah Webster's nationalistic project aimed not at forging a new language but at purifying English so that Americans would speak better English

43. American Council of Learned Societies, "Report of Committee on Linguistic and National Stocks in the Population of the United States," Amer. Hist. Assoc., *Annual Report* (1931), I, especially pp. 124–25, 310. This is the standard and infinitely the best study, yet one still sees in the 1960's assertions that the proportion of English was 75% or higher.

44. Boyd, ed., *Papers of Jefferson,* I, 121; Cooke, ed., *Federalist,* 9.

than contemporary Englishmen.[45] The same process of affirmation and rejection operated less obviously in the political battles of the 1790's. Federalists frequently discoursed on their nation's essential Englishness, but Republicans, significantly, did not think to reply by acclaiming French influence in America or by extolling the melting pot. That suggestive image attracted Americans only in a later day, when the impact of millions of immigrants from the European continent grew obvious and when the tension engendered by dependence on England had in some measure dissipated.

To assess the nature of the American people was to assess the Negro by implication, simply because Negroes lived in America. Inevitably the process of self-assessment patterned the way in which conclusions about the Negro would be reached. Americans' conclusions about themselves, no matter how vague or inconsistent, virtually precluded their arriving at certain conclusions about Negroes. Because they viewed the architecture of their culture as modified-English rather than fused-European, most Americans were not led to ponder the dynamics of cultural amalgamation in America, much less the pronounced African element involved. In fact there was little consideration given to the possibility that Negro language and manners had contributed to American uniqueness.[46] In his opening chapter on "Population" David Ramsay discoursed on the contributions to South Carolina made by the Scots, Swiss, Irish, Germans, New Englanders, and Dutch—all without once mentioning even the presence, much less the importance, of African Negroes in his state. And because Americans did not regard themselves as a new race blended from the bloods of many European nations, they had no special reason to be attracted by the notion that Negroes had contributed heavily to a new mixture. Indeed Americans had already conceived that miscegenation between whites and blacks was less than desirable, and this conclusion itself inhibited the flowering of the melting-pot idea. To endorse mixture of bloods as a general principle was to throw open the door to a repulsive prospect. Even St. Jean de Crèvecoeur could praise physical amalgamation in America only by ignoring utterly the single most important element in the process as it was actually occurring: "What then is the

45. Daniel J. Boorstin, *The Americans: The Colonial Experience* (N. Y., 1958), 280–82.

46. There were some complaints that southern children stood in such close contact with Negroes that they were in danger of imbibing Negro manners and particularly speech. Significantly, most of these assertions came from foreigners (or sometimes unsympathetic northerners) who disliked both slavery and Negroes; all were critical of the trend or possibility they described.

American, this new man? He is either an European, or the descendant of an European. . . ." Presumably the Negro was not an American.

And was this just the point? In itself, the quest for a national identity laid down no principles concerning Negroes, but by pressing the question of who Americans were, it raised the question whether Negroes were truly American. Definite questions tend to elicit definite answers, much more so than no questions at all. The search for American national selfhood thus rendered the old question of Negro participation in American society more urgent and more susceptible of definite answer. Was the Negro supposed to be accepted into the fold or rejected? Usually, assessments and answers concerning the Americanness of the Negro were veiled and less than completely conscious: they have to be looked for embedded in such diverse fields as the antislavery movement, the ideology of the late rebellion, and the achievements of American natural scientists. Occasionally, however, answers were required not by a half-recognized urge to attain integral national identity but in the most obvious manner by a specific question posed directly by creation of a genuine national government: the most clearcut instance was that the first federal naturalization law applied to "white" foreigners only.[47] Insofar as American nationalism involved consciousness of Englishness, it provided a negative answer—the Negro was *not* an American—basically because he could never even look like an English American. On the other hand, Americans had of necessity to reject Englishness. Hence no final answer was to be found in nationalism itself. Moreover, the prevailing view that Americans were Englishmen remodeled by New World conditions tended to throw the whole question of the Negro's Americanness into the lap of the American environment, where natural philosophers pondered it cautiously and arrived at strange conclusions. Then too, the basic principles upon which Americans thought their nation had been founded were relevant to the question which an uncertain nationalism posed. Taken at face value, these principles demanded that Negroes participate in freedom equally with other Americans; at the same time, with a critical double-edged implication, they strongly suggested that Negro slavery was thoroughly un-American. To trace the vicissitudes of antislavery after the Revolution is to see how Americans in all sections of the nation came to live with the un-Americanness of racial slavery.

47. *Statutes U. S.*, I, 103 (1790), also 414, II, 153, 292.

IX THE LIMITATIONS OF ANTISLAVERY

THE REVOLUTION ENDED WITH ALL THE STATES HAVING PRO-
hibited the slave trade but with only two having moved against
slavery itself. Yet it was perfectly clear that the principles for which
Americans had fought required the complete abolition of slavery;
the question was not *if*, but *when* and *how*. Although the majority
of Americans failed to face this question, thus effectively answering
the *when* with *later*, some men felt that abolition must come soon if
not at once. No one, of course, pondered the possibility of direct
revolutionary action—except, as will become evident in the next
chapter, by Negroes themselves. Much of the energy of antislavery
was discharged into newspapers, magazines, and pamphlets, leaving
its traces lying scattered confetti-like throughout this literature.

If the antislavery organizations are also taken into account, it is
possible to detect a significant chronological pattern which dovetails
with the timing of economic changes in the South and the development of American nationhood. Unquestionably there was an element of causality here, but it should not be overestimated. Certain
characteristics of antislavery thought may also be said to help account for the decline of antislavery after the early 1790's. These
characteristics pertained especially to the nature of Revolutionary
ideology, and accordingly it is scarcely surprising that the Quakers
stand out as exceptions; indeed certain incompatibilities emerged
between the religious and secular impulses in antislavery. The
over-all pattern was rendered still more interesting and complex by
development of two additional interrelated impulses, humanitarianism and sentimentality, which themselves were not altogether
compatible. All of which suggests that antislavery was not merely
destroyed from without but weakened from within.

1. THE PATTERN OF ANTISLAVERY

The first effective private societies for public secular reform in America had originated long before the Revolution as attempts to cope with increasingly pressing problems of urban life. The antislavery societies which sprouted up after the Revolution introduced an important new dimension, for while they were locally sponsored and aimed at local problems concerning Negroes, they shared similar problems and purposes which caused them to draw together into a national reform organization. It remained true, though, that most of the effective work was done at the local level, where benevolent individuals were able to derive satisfaction from tangible, if infrequent, local victories. Most antislavery societies were ostensibly state-wide, but in fact their memberships and activities centered in the larger cities, where organization was most feasible. In Pennsylvania, Delaware, Maryland, and Virginia, that is, in states facing great but not insuperable difficulties, there were also a few local societies, but south of Virginia there were no antislavery organizations (except Friends Meetings in North Carolina): the name "South Carolina Abolition Society" would have been a contradiction in terms.

The first secular antislavery organization was founded in 1775, The Society for the Relief of Free Negroes, Unlawfully Held in Bondage. Philadelphia was in several respects the most likely place for the antislavery movement to start. A variety of successful reformist organizations, most of them sparked by Benjamin Franklin, offered good example; there was an appreciable Negro population, both slave (a call to action) and free (a pattern to follow); and Quakers had always been in the vanguard of antislavery.[1] Not civic consciousness, however, but a freedom suit in the courts first suggested formation of a society. The case affords a certain prophetic irony: the slave in question was an Indian rather than a Negro, and the suit was lost.[2]

Inactive during the war, the Pennsylvania Society reorganized in 1784 and bent its efforts especially toward "the relief of free negroes unlawfully held in bondage."[3] Kidnapping of free Negroes cen-

1. Turner, *Negro in Pa.*, 209–15. For abolition societies more generally, Mary S. Locke, *Anti-Slavery in America from the Introduction of African Slaves to the Prohibition of the Slave Trade (1619–1808)* (Boston, 1901), 97–110.

2. Turner, *Negro in Pa.*, 209.

3. In the 1780's the official designation was "The Pennsylvania Society for Promoting the Abolition of Slavery, for the Relief of Free Negroes Unlawfully Held in Bondage, and for Improving the Condition of the African Race."

tered in Pennsylvania, though the problem existed in all the states. In New York, where slavery remained on secure legal footing, a Manumission Society was founded under the presidency of John Jay in 1785. Then, as the country pulled out of the economic depression of the mid-1780's and debated the question of a national government, there was a spasm of organizational effort. By 1792 state and local antislavery societies were scattered from Massachusetts to Virginia. While antislavery writing was dominated by obscure and often anonymous men, the societies enlisted the names though not always the efforts of eminent and respectable gentlemen such as Jay, Alexander Hamilton, Melancton Smith, George Clinton, Moses Brown, Samuel Hopkins, James Pemberton, Benjamin Franklin, Benjamin Waterhouse, and Benjamin Rush.[4]

The new concentration of political power in a federal government provided both an example and a point of attack for antislavery organizations, and early in 1794 some twenty-five delegates from nine societies gathered in Philadelphia and proceeded to memorialize everyone, including their own membership and the federal Congress. Thus refreshed, the Convention published its proceedings and resolved to meet on an annual basis. But this original energy dissipated rapidly. An apparently promising organizational movement came apart at the seams within a dozen years. In 1798 the somewhat bewildered Convention sadly recorded its pessimism: "In many of the United States a peculiar degree of caution in the management of this business becomes necessary." After that year New England sent no delegates, the Maryland and Virginia societies simply sank from view a few years later, and the Convention did not even meet in 1799 and 1802. A committee of the 1804 Convention proved unable to compose a plan of gradual emancipation for the United States, and two years later the Convention (by now a rump by default) tacitly confessed to its weakened condition by resolving on triennial meetings. From about 1806 until after the War of 1812, the national organ of antislavery was virtually moribund, and the most healthy of its component organizations, the New York and Pennsylvania societies, were less active than ever before.[5]

4. For important membership lists, Bartlett, ed., *Recs. Col. R. I.*, 382–85; *Public Laws of the State of Rhode-Island . . . 1798* (Providence, 1798), 607–11; Mitchell *et al.*, eds., *Statutes Pa.*, XIII, 424–32; Charles C. Andrews, *The History of the New-York African Free-Schools, from their Establishment in 1787 . . . Also a Brief Account of the Successful Labors, of the New-York Manumission Society* (N. Y., 1830), 10.

5. The changing condition of the abolition societies is best revealed in the minutes of the national convention, published in Philadelphia after each meet-

While many factors contributed to this process, organized anti-slavery contributed to its own decline by achieving one of its major goals. A measure of success had come rather rapidly. Vermont banned slavery in its 1777 constitution. Pennsylvania, appropriately, was first to pass an abolition law (1780), though the society was not active in sponsoring it. In the next few years judicial decisions in Massachusetts found slavery to be a violation of the state's new constitution. Elsewhere, emancipationists pushed through gradual abolition laws in Rhode Island (1784), Connecticut (1784), New York (1799), and New Jersey (1804). Northern slavery seemed almost to be withering gradually away. In New Hampshire no court or legislative action seems to have been taken, but in 1800 the state reported only eight slaves and in 1810 none.[6]

In all these states except Vermont and Massachusetts, cautious legislators were at pains to provide that emancipation not be abrupt. Generally, the acts declared that all Negroes born after the date of passage, or soon (often July 4) thereafter, were to be free; these young Negroes were to serve their mother's owner until some such age as twenty-one or twenty-eight. Freedom was thus conferred upon a future generation and the living were given merely the consolation of a free posterity. Yet this apparent reluctance should

---

ing, cited as *Minutes Abolition Convention*. The first was entitled *Minutes of the Proceedings of a Convention of Delegates from the Abolition Societies Established in Different Parts of the United States, Assembled at Philadelphia . . .* (Phila., 1794). The title later varied slightly, the only important changes being insertion of ordinal numbers before "Convention," as "Second" and "Third." From 1794 to 1812 there were 13 meetings: 1794–98, 1800, 1801, 1803–06, 1809, 1812. For a list of constituent societies and what they thought they were accomplishing, *Minutes Abolition Convention* (1797), 37–43. The quotation is from *ibid*. (1798), 11.

6. Francis N. Thorpe, ed., *The Federal and State Constitutions, Colonial Charters, and Other Organic Laws . . .* , 7 vols. (Washington, 1909), VI, 3739–40; Mitchell *et al.*, eds., *Statutes Pa.*, X, 67–73; Moore, *Notes on Slavery in Massachusetts*, 200–222; Bartlett, ed., *Recs. Col. R. I.*, X, 7; *Public Laws R.-I.* (1798), 607–11; Charles J. Hoadly *et al.*, eds., *The Public Records of the State of Connecticut . . .* (Hartford, 1894—), VIII, xvii–xviii; *Laws of the State of New York, 1777–1801*, 5 vols. (Albany, 1886–87), IV, 388–99; Henry S. Cooley, *A Study of Slavery in New Jersey* (Baltimore, 1896), 26; and for New Hampshire, Locke, *Anti-Slavery in America*, 117n. It is not entirely certain that Massachusetts courts actually declared slavery unconstitutional in the early 1780's: William O'Brien, "Did the Jennison Case Outlaw Slavery in Massachusetts?" *Wm. and Mary Qtly.*, 17 (1960), 219–41; John D. Cushing, "The Cushing Court and the Abolition of Slavery in Massachusetts: More Notes on the 'Quock Walker Case,'" *American Journal of Legal History*, 5 (1961), 118–44; but by 1787, perhaps earlier, contemporaries certainly thought they had. The story is told in Arthur Zilversmit, *The First Emancipation: Slavery and Its Abolition in the Northern States* (Chicago, 1967), 112–16.

not obscure the dimensions of the achievement: slavery had been put on the road to extinction in the eight states from Pennsylvania northwards. Public opinion in the North would no longer tolerate chattel slavery.

That this victory was not wholly responsible for the demise of antislavery is suggested by the situation in the southern states and Delaware. In Georgia and South Carolina, of course, the antislavery movement ended by never beginning, and the same was largely true of North Carolina except among the Quakers.[7] In Virginia, Maryland, and Delaware, however, criticism of slavery was, if hardly universal, at least acceptable and widespread. Antislavery societies represented a visible but very small portion of this sentiment, as was natural in an agricultural region where organization was difficult and slavery well entrenched. Particularly in Virginia, men of various backgrounds denounced slavery in private conversation and in print and in the legislature. The committee charged with drafting the revisal of Virginia's laws in 1777 laid plans for gradual abolition, but these grand hopes came to nothing, and a 1785 petition to the same purpose encountered resentful opposition.[8] Maryland's legislature debated emancipation bills in 1789 and the following year.[9] The College of William and Mary conferred an LL.D. on Granville Sharp in 1791, which was to bestow a benediction on antislavery itself.[10] But by 1796 when the Virginia Senate thanked a prominent Virginia jurist for submitting a plan of gradual emancipation, there was in the Senate's words, despite the pious references to natural rights, a tone of firm refusal.[11] After 1800 public denunciation of

7. Stephen B. Weeks, *Southern Quakers and Slavery; A Study in Institutional History* (Baltimore, 1896), 217–27.

8. Editorial discussion of the revisal in Boyd, ed., *Papers of Jefferson*, II, 472–73; *Journal of the House of Delegates of the Commonwealth of Virginia; Begun . . . The Seventeenth Day of October in the Year of our Lord One Thousand Seven Hundred and Eighty Five* (Richmond, 1828), 27, 30–31 (Journals of the Virginia General Assembly are available on microfilm, Early State Records Project, and are hereafter cited as *Virginia House Journal* and *Virginia Senate Journal* followed by dates of session.); Clark *et al.*, eds., *Journal of Francis Asbury*, I, 498; James Madison to Thomas Jefferson, Richmond, Jan. 22, 1786, Boyd, ed., *Papers of Jefferson*, IX, 199.

9. Brackett, *Negro in Md.*, 52–55.

10. William F. Poole, *Anti-Slavery Opinions before the Year 1800* (Cincinnati, 1873), 73.

11. "You certainly judge rightly in supposing that to an enlightened Legislature no object can be more grateful than to restore upon a plan not injurious to Society; the Freedom to a part of our Fellowman, which the God of Nature gave them. That the time may come when Liberty in our Country shall be inseparable from Life, is a wish in which you are sincerely joined by Your . . . Hble. Servant." Ludwell Lee (on behalf of the Virginia Senate) to St. George Tucker,

slavery became increasingly muted and occasional, and the antislavery societies simply collapsed. In the very early years of the new century the antislavery movement of the Upper South melted away like some wispy vision. In 1805 Thomas Jefferson confided gloomily, "I have long since given up the expectation of any early provision for the extinguishment of slavery among us." [12]

Yet southern antislavery was neither utopian nor a total failure. Its principal success lay in the passage of laws facilitating private manumission, laws which in the North had often preceded the laws providing for gradual abolition. In this way the states from Delaware to North Carolina conceded a certain legitimacy to individual antislavery sentiment while balking at the sweeping action which the state alone could effect. Frequently memorialized by the antislavery societies and by Friends' Meetings, the legislatures of the five states which constituted what may be called the antislavery South one by one opened the door to private action—first Virginia in 1782 (where as a result the free Negro population doubled in two years), then Delaware in 1787, and Maryland (after a struggle lasting many sessions) in 1790 and 1796. Kentucky and Tennessee followed suit in 1798 and 1801.[13] In North Carolina the issue appeared to hang in the balance for at least twenty years. Despite a 1777 law which tightened manumission procedures, masters were still permitted to free their slaves if granted permission by a county court. In 1785 the lower house passed a bill which would have allowed persons with conscientious scruples to manumit their slaves, but the measure failed in the upper chamber. The following year the legislature evinced sympathy with the principle of emancipation by ordering that slaves brought into North Carolina from states which had "passed laws for the liberation of slaves" be returned within three months. During the next few years a number of slaves were freed by private acts of assembly implementing the wishes of deceased owners. But the tide turned. A law of 1788 continued existing manumission procedures but pointed to the dangers arising from Negroes

Richmond, Dec. 5, 1796, in Mary Haldane Coleman (Mrs. George P.), comp., *Virginia Silhouettes: Contemporary Letters Concerning Negro Slavery in the State of Virginia; To Which Is Appended a Dissertation on Slavery with a Proposal for the Gradual Abolition of It in the State of Virginia* (Richmond, 1934), 5.

12. To William A. Burwell, Washington, Jan. 28, 1805, Paul L. Ford, ed., *The Works of Thomas Jefferson*, 12 vols. (N. Y., 1904–05), X, 126–27.

13. Hening, ed., *Statutes Va.*, XI, 39–40; *Laws Del.*, II, 884–88, 1321–24; Virgil Maxcy, ed., *The Laws of Maryland . . .* , 4 vols. (Baltimore, 1811), II, 354–55, 359–61; Brackett, *Negro in Md.*, 150–54; Locke, *Anti-Slavery in America*, 121. For the flood of manumissions, Russell, *Free Negro in Va.*, 61.

freed by masters with religious scruples (a swipe at the Quakers) ; ominously, the act oiled the court machinery for prosecuting illegal manumissions. In 1796 the assembly reaffirmed the absolute neces- sity of court approval for manumission and in 1801, citing the likelihood of indigence and consequent financial burden on the public, required owners to post a £100 bond for each slave freed.[14] In summary, after the Revolution, North Carolina took a few faltering steps on the road toward emancipation but then about 1787 began retreating to more familiar ground. South Carolina and Georgia, where neither the law nor public opinion ever took a happy view of private manumission, rendered the procedure more difficult at the turn of the century, Georgia allowing it only upon appeal to the legislature.[15]

Restriction of private manumission in the three southernmost states was paralleled by a similar trend in the Upper South, the more striking because a growing tendency to encourage freedom was directly reversed, far more noticeably than in North Carolina and at a somewhat later date. In 1791 the Maryland House of Delegates roundly censured the Maryland Abolition Society for its memorial concerning two Negro criminals and came within three votes of resolving that the Society was utterly inimical to the inter- ests of the state. In 1795 Virginia reinforced the master's position in freedom suits and in 1798 barred members of emancipation societies from sitting on juries considering such cases. Finally, an increas- ingly vigorous campaign to stem the flood of private manumissions succeeded in the Virginia General Assembly in 1806; by law, slaves freed thereafter were required to leave the commonwealth within twelve months. This was, of course, a key decision in a key state. Virginia's neighboring states to the north and west, faced with an influx of freshly manumitted slaves, hastily prohibited immigration of free Negroes. By 1807, abolition of slavery in the Upper South appeared a much dimmer prospect than it had in 1790. A noble vision had proved a mirage.[16]

14. Clark, ed., State Recs. N. C., XX, 30, XXIV, 14–15, 794, 850, 859, 929–30, 963, 964, XXV, 37; James Iredell and François-Xavier Martin, comps., The Public Acts of the General Assembly of North-Carolina, 2 vols. in 1 (Newbern, 1804), II, 88, 179. Also Weeks, Southern Quakers and Slavery, 222.

15. Cooper and McCord, eds., Statutes S. C., VII, 442–43; A Compilation of the Laws of the State of Georgia, Passed by the Legislature Since the Political Year 1800, to the Year 1810, Inclusive . . . (Augusta, 1813), 27.

16. Annapolis Md. Gaz., Dec. 29, 1791; Brackett, Negro in Md., 54–55; Samuel Shepard, ed., The Statutes at Large of Virginia, from October Session 1792, to December Session 1806, Inclusive, New Ser., continuation of Hening, 3 vols. (Richmond, 1835–36), I, 363–65, II, 77, III, 252; Russell, Free Negro in Va., 66–72; Brackett, Negro in Md., 176.

Even a brief review of efforts at abolition in the American states makes possible detection of certain important patterns of development. Divided according to final results, the states fell into the two groups made so very familiar by events later in the nineteenth century. Divided according to their willingness to entertain the hope of abolition rather than by hindsight, however, four distinct groups of states emerge. Between 1777 and 1804, all states from Pennsylvania northwards provided effectively for eventual abolition of slavery; in fact all but two, New York and New Jersey, had done so by 1784. In the same period, in the antislavery South the tide of public sentiment and action moved tentatively in the direction of abolition until the 1790's, but then in that decade turned and, after 1800, flowed so swiftly that by 1807 it was clear that the region was committed to slavery for many years to come. North Carolina showed a roughly similar pattern, but since the steps taken were far more hesitant and the turning point came earlier (well before Tennessee became a separate state), North Carolina's experience was unique. Finally, South Carolina and Georgia took no steps toward abolition and even tightened up long-standing restrictions on manumission after 1800.

In themselves these patterns do little to explain the fact that antislavery, as a national mood and program, lost its vigor after the 1790's. Initially, abolitionists had hoped for eventual total victory. The first Philadelphia Convention had proudly said of its own member societies in 1794, they "hope, their labours will never cease, while there exists a single slave in the United States." [17] Yet ten years later the national organ of antislavery had gone a fair way toward disintegration, while there were more slaves in the United States than ever before. Plainly something had gone wrong. In fact there were many factors which sapped the energy of the antislavery movement and foreclosed the possibility of general abolition in the foreseeable future.

2. THE FAILINGS OF REVOLUTIONARY IDEOLOGY

Much of this energy had derived from the Revolutionary struggle against Great Britain. The triumphant achievement of independence at Yorktown and Paris gave added stature to the ideology of the Revolution, of which antislavery was a part, by sealing it with success. Indeed the ideology of the Revolution proved sufficiently dynamic that Americans wondered if it was not dangerously contagious—but this is a theme of separate importance.

17. *Minutes Abolition Convention* (1794), 25.

In the postwar years the natural rights philosophy, no longer needed as a handbook for action, easily became a diploma of political achievement, suitable for framing as a certificate of republican virtue. During the postwar years of governmental drift and economic depression, moreover, the rhetoric of natural rights became increasingly irrelevant to the nation's problems. Americans found that the philosophy of rights, bedrock of the Revolution, could not be made to serve as the cornerstone of effective government. It was thoroughly characteristic of the situation that the Bill of Rights was tacked on after the new edifice had been erected.

Diminished relevance in the natural rights philosophy profoundly endangered the vitality of antislavery, the more so because men were not entirely aware of what was happening. Achievement of independence undercut the striking analogy of enslavement— Americans by Britons and Negroes by Americans. A more insidious tendency was that men found it easy to speak the language of natural rights when defending the Negro without at all recognizing a certain hollowness in their words. Something was wrong when at about the turn of the century the only documents which could be invoked were already a generation old. Obeisance to national doctrine could so easily become mechanical: in attacking slavery in the 1790's the Quaker Thomas Mifflin cited congressional documents written twenty years earlier, including the Declaration of Independence, which most Quakers had opposed.[18] The waning influence of the natural rights doctrine was also revealed more directly. As time went on, antislavery writers appealed to its principles less directly and less often.

Even in full force the Revolutionary philosophy was of limited benefit to the American Negro. For one thing, the ideas of freedom and equal rights were intimately linked with the concept of private material property. As Locke had said, men possessed a "property" in both themselves and their possessions; they had a natural right to their life, liberty, and "estates." American revolutionaries saw no reason to readjust this view of private property as a basic natural right; more important, they rarely thought of the right of private property as distinct from, much less antagonistic to, other natural liberties. Arbitrarily deprive a man of his possessions, and you have a slave. It was no indication of hypocrisy that Americans had cried

18. Warner Mifflin, *A Serious Expostulation with the Members of the House of Representatives of the United States* (Phila., 1793). Also, *To the Senate and House of Representatives of the United States, In Congress Assembled, the Memorial and Address of the People Called Quakers, from Their Yearly Meeting Held in Philadelphia . . .* ([Phila., 1797]).

"liberty" when Parliament proposed novel measures of taxation. The issue of private property was central to the Revolutionary agitation, and for the colonists this issue was not financial or economic. It was in keeping with the character of the Revolution that some of its earliest martyrs were delinquent taxpayers. It was equally characteristic that one of the most common antislavery arguments was that enslaved Negroes were being wrongfully deprived of the fruits of their labor.

The absence of any clear disjunction between what are now called "human" and "property" rights formed a massive roadblock across the route to abolition of slavery. It was obvious that compulsory manumission would violate the right of masters to their own property. Insofar as slaves were property, their masters possessed an inherent right to dispose of them as they wished. A revolution carried forward in the name of this right was in this sense a serious and enduring impediment to compulsory abolition. In Massachusetts the preamble to the state's constitution had been taken literally by the courts, and some men evidently felt that such interpretation violated an even more basic principle. As Judge James Winthrop complained, "By a misconstruction of our State Constitution, which declares all men by nature free and equal, a number of citizens have been deprived of property formerly acquired under the protection of law." [19] Almost a century afterwards Abraham Lincoln seriously considered the possibility of paying slaveowners for their human property.

Despite this limitation, the concept of natural rights was ideal as a weapon against personal or national slavery. Yet it was permeated by a strong tone of negativity. The only duty it enjoined on government and men was negative—that they *not* violate the rights of other men. Thus the extent of social duty was defined by the scope of personal rights! (For some heirs of this ideology it requires an effort of the imagination to realize that social duty can be defined in other ways.) It afforded few hints about protecting life against the four horsemen, about preserving liberty in the face of more subtle threats than outright enslavement, or about providing necessary property to those who somehow had acquired none. John Locke had laid down a trinity of rights—life, liberty, and property—which Revolutionary Americans generally found sufficient and self-explanatory. There were virtually no elements in the character of

19. To Jeremy Belknap, Cambridge, Mar. 4, 1795, "Letters and Documents Relating to Slavery in Massachusetts," *Belknap Papers*, 2 vols. (Mass. Hist. Soc., *Collections*, 5th Ser., 3 [1877]) , 389–90. Also Trenton *N. J. Gaz.*, Apr. 11, 1781.

the Revolutionary struggle which might have served to broaden this definition: the traditional trinity encompassed America's grievances very nicely—redcoats, political dictation, and Parliamentary taxation. Accordingly Americans were led to seek an end to the Negro's slavery and to feel that they had fulfilled their obligation once they had ceased to violate his "rights." The natural rights philosophy was virtually silent on how the Negro was to be treated when he became "free."

That this was the tendency of the natural rights idea does not mean that it was inherently empty of other possibilities. For the definition of rights could logically be broadened to include other areas beyond the legal status of personal "freedom." If the mundane and explicit matters of education, housing, and livelihood could be included, then the claims of the Negro to what other men might not do to him would be broadened, and, in effect, the duties of the white community enlarged. This would involve a shift from the concept of society as a collection of individual units cemented by legal relations toward a less mechanistic view of social cohesion, but there has proved no reason why the philosophy of rights could not make the shift. Current American terminology points up the subtle change. We speak of the "right to vote" but of "fair housing." Similarly, everyone knows that "right to work laws" are not the same thing as "fair employment practices," and indeed that advocates of the one are not much given to advocating the other. An essential element in this change has been the very plasticity of the natural rights idea, its ability to absorb an expanding content like a balloon. Thus it was not so much the inherent logic of the philosophy of rights which failed to meet the Negro's needs in the late eighteenth century as the genesis of that philosophy and the political context in which it first achieved popular currency in America.

The fact was, however, that during the period of antislavery successes the problem of the Negro's future condition did not get much attention.[20] Northern abolition laws simply abolished slavery by degrees. Little was done to meet the most obvious needs of newly freed Negroes (except perhaps in Quaker Philadelphia) and, more

20. A straightforward news item in the Annapolis *Md. Gaz.*, Mar. 31, 1791, described the Spanish practice of freeing slaves gradually and giving them plots of ground to work on their own account. Significantly, most antislavery writers, despite their gradualism, failed to take up this possibility. For an example of thinking about improvement of free Negroes, "An Address to the Public, From the Pennsylvania Society for Promoting the Abolition of Slavery . . . ," *Amer. Museum*, 6 (1789), 383–85.

surprisingly, little was proposed.[21] On the few occasions when planters freed large numbers of their slaves, consideration of future
condition became an immediate necessity; George Washington, for
instance, provided for tenancy or apprenticeship.[22] It was characteristic of this prevailing failure that expressions of optimism concerning the future of America's black population were rare and un-
realistic. The anonymous author of "Thoughts on the Probable
Termination of Negro Slavery in the United States of America"
tried to erase the problem by saying that the condition of slavery
and the increase in private manumissions would result before long
in white men vastly outnumbering their slaves.[23] Apart from proposals for Negro colonization, only a handful of writers offered suggestions for handling emancipated Negroes or for preparing slaves
to meet the burdens of freedom. Significantly, one such brief proposal came from John Morgan Rhees, one of the few antislavery
pamphleteers from the Lower South. If Rhees's proposition sounds
a trifle quaint in light of later developments, at least he recognized
that real emancipation required more than paper and ink: "Let the
legislators of the different states, therefore enact, that every slaveholder shall instruct his negroes in the duties of citizenship, and
use them in every respect as citizens for the term of   at
which period they are to have full liberty to choose their own masters, or form a settlement together in such parts of the union as
shall be appointed for them." [24] Thomas Pownall, a sometime American viewing the problem from a rather lofty perch in England, suggested that slaves be freed gradually and be barred from owning
property so that freed Negroes would remain the staple of American labor.[25] Noah Webster perhaps made most sense of the situation. After recounting the noxious effects of slavery on both master
and slave, Webster considered two possibilities, immediate full-scale

21. For efforts by the Pennsylvania Abolition Society to help Negroes obtain
suitable employment, Turner, *Negro in Pa.*, 123–25, 210–11; *Minutes Abolition
Convention* (1797) , 31–34.

22. Fitzpatrick, ed., *Writings of Washington*, XXXVII, 276–77; Eugene E.
Prussing, *The Estate of George Washington, Deceased* (Boston, 1927) , chap. 13.

23. By "H. L.," *Monthly Magazine, and American Review*, 2 (1800) , 81–84.

24. [John Morgan Rhees], *Letters on Liberty and Slavery: In Answer to a
Pamphlet, Entitled, "Negro-Slavery Defended by the Word of God." By Philan-
thropos*, 2d ed. (N. Y., 1798), 20–21. These were addressed to Mr. John
Lawrence, South Quay, Va., from both Charleston and Savannah. The refuted
proslavery pamphlet has not been found.

25. T[homas] Pownall, *A Memorial Addressed to the Sovereigns of America*
(London, 1783) , 108–10.

emancipation and colonization. Both remedies, he concluded force-
fully, were attended by ruinous difficulties. The answer, then,
would be to make slaves into tenants. The trick was to begin with
a few especially virtuous slaves so that the others might then follow toward freedom with a good example set firmly before them.
Good husbandry, Webster felt, was example enough.[26]

While Webster's proposal of tenancy was unusual, his gradualism
was not. No emancipation act in the North provided for immediate
abolition. This gradualist approach derived partly from prevailing
assumptions about social change: men were confident of progress
but saw no reason to suppose that social evils were amenable to
radical acts of social engineering. Gradualism also represented realistic assessment of certain practical difficulties, not the least being
the necessity of winning support so that some action could be taken.
Certainly the abolition laws and tracts strongly suggest that the
principal reality being faced was the immediate welfare of masters
rather than the future benefit of manumitted slaves. Gradual emancipation not only recognized the claims of property but avoided
cataclysmic rearrangement of social relationships. Though gradual
emancipation may (or may not) have benefited Negroes, they were
not intended as the primary beneficiaries.[27]

The prevalent inability of Americans to think beyond emancipation is particularly striking because they seemed to have in their
hands a master key to problems of individual and social improvement. Americans were coming to think of education as a device of
great power and as one of the chief means of uplifting the republic.
Nonetheless, attempts at providing rudimentary education for
Negroes were scattered, ephemeral, and, on the whole, unsuccessful.
A few Negro schools were established, mostly in northern cities, but
keeping them going always proved an uphill struggle.[28] To some
extent practical difficulties stood in the way: money, buildings, and
suitable instructors were hard to obtain. Although some white

26. Noah Webster, Jr., *Effects of Slavery, on Morals and Industry* (Hartford,
1793).
27. Benjamin J. Klebaner, "American Manumission Laws and the Responsibility for Supporting Slaves," *Va. Mag. of Hist. and Biog.*, 63 (1955), 443–53; cf.
David Brion Davis, "The Emergence of Immediatism in British and American
Antislavery Thought," *Mississippi Valley Historical Review*, 49 (1962–63),
209–30.
28. For Negro education, in addition to sources cited in this chapter, see the
standard state histories on Negroes and Carter G. Woodson, *The Education of
the Negro Prior to 1861; A History of the Education of the Colored People of the
United States from the Beginning of Slavery to the Civil War* (N. Y. and
London, 1915), chaps. 3–5.

schools accepted Negroes, for the most part popular prejudice
barred them: the president of the New Jersey Abolition Society
once complained that "there occurs a serious difficulty in obtaining
their admission . . . into *white* schools," and suggested black
schools with black teachers.[29] Since Americans did not yet presuppose that education was primarily a state-supported enterprise,
widespread public schooling for Negroes was not to be expected,
though the most successful school for Negroes, a coeducational
operation with about one hundred students sponsored by the New
York Manumission Society, received some financial support from
the city as authorized by state law.[30] Only two states, New Jersey
and eventually New York, seized the obvious opportunity of requiring that young Negro slaves or apprentices be taught to read.[31]
More surprising still was the rareness of pleas and plans for Negro
education. It was of the utmost significance that such men as Thomas Jefferson, vastly interested in the promotion of American education, were to an equal extent uninterested in educating Negroes
so as to improve their chances of participating in the body politic.
On the other hand, a few men, possessing a different temperament
and a better situation from which to view the problem, saw education as the only solution to slavery. The most eloquent and prophetic plea for Negro education came from James Sullivan of
Boston, a wealthy, prominent lawyer and Democratic politician and
founding member of the American Academy of Arts and Sciences.
Sullivan had been brought to consider the difficulties inhering in
racial slavery by an inquiry originating from Virginia:

But there is, in my mind, this resource; and I am obliged to think that it
is the only one in the case, and that a very slow one. As there is no way to
eradicate the prejudice which education has fixed in the minds of the
white against the black people, otherwise than by raising the blacks, by
means of mental improvements, nearly to the same grade with the whites,

29. William Griffith, *Address of the President of the New-Jersey Society, for
Promoting the Abolition of Slavery* . . . (Trenton, 1804), 8–10.

30. Papers of the New York Society for Promoting the Abolition of Slaves, New
York City, IX, 55, 65, N.-Y. Hist. Soc.

31. In 1785 an unsuccessful emancipation bill in New York required that slaves
be taught to read and, if possible, to write. Finally, by an 1810 law, young
Negroes were to be taught to read. *Journal of the Assembly of the State of
New-York . . . 1785* (N. Y., 1785), 56–57; *Laws of the State of New-York,* VI
(Albany, 1812), 33. *Acts of the Thirteenth General Assembly of the State of
New-Jersey . . . First Sitting* (Trenton, 1788), 488; William Paterson, ed., *Laws
of the State of New Jersey* (New Brunswick, 1800), 310. A sweeping emancipa-
tion bill passed by the Connecticut House but rejected by the Council in 1794
included provision for education of Negroes; Hoadly *et al.,* eds., *Recs. State
Conn.,* VIII, xix.

the emancipation of the slaves in United America must be slow in its progress, and ages must be employed in the business. The time necessary to effect this purpose must be as extensive, at least, as that in which slavery has been endured here. The children of the slaves must, at the public expence, be educated in the same manner as the children of their masters; being at the same schools, etc., with the rising generation, that prejudice, which has been so long and inveterate against them on account of their situation and colour, will be lessened within thirty or forty years.[32]

For the most part, however, Americans failed to plump for the idea that education would render Negroes more useful. By 1805 the situation in Virginia was such that overseers of the poor, when binding out a Negro orphan, were prohibited from making any requirement that the master teach the child "reading, writing or arithmetic." [33]

Omission of Negroes from the American educational program rested on a mountain of practical difficulties, on fear of literacy among slaves, on the exclusion of Negroes from occupations requiring much use of the head, on the general tendency to set Negroes apart, and on widespread reluctance to think out the problem of future status. In the North, certainly, this reluctance was a critical factor. For if men should admit even for a moment that there *was* a problem beyond emancipation, then they would be led inexorably to consider the possibility of Negro education. Taken another way, if men should for some reason focus on the presence of enslaved Negroes as a moral problem, rather than on the status of slavery, then education would assume equal importance with abolition and both would appear as major components in a single ameliorative program. If there were any Americans inclined to view society as cemented more by moral relationships than by legal relations, then some attention would be accorded the Negro's condition as well as his status.

3. THE QUAKER VIEW BEYOND EMANCIPATION

There were, of course, such men, pre-eminently in the Society of Friends and less notably in some other Christian denominations. Quakers were especially concerned with the Negro's plight because they felt that enslavement was morally wrong, not merely a denial of rights. It was characteristic of this feeling that many

32. To Jeremy Belknap, Boston, July 30, 1795, "Letters Relating to Slavery in Mass.," *Belknap Papers*, 414.
33. Shepard, ed., *Statutes Va.*, III, 124.

Quakers, once they discovered a concern to free their slaves, actually compensated them for back wages. Indeed, Quaker attitudes toward Negroes seemed to operate in an atmosphere of moral bookkeeping. Quaker religious principles made the Negro their brother, and Quakers owed their brother special attention because they had wronged him. They had no great affinity for the natural rights philosophy which had called on God to verify men's contractual equality on earth. More than for other Americans, slavery for them was a particularly crying defect in moral social relations.

In fact, Quakers far more than other Americans interested themselves in the Negro's condition *after* emancipation. They concentrated especially on education of Negroes, though Quakers had never been noted for zealous educational activities.[34] Anthony Benezet, a virtual one-man abolition society, established a Negro school in 1759 and exercised his concern for Negro education until his death in 1784.[35] Robert Pleasants, a Virginia Friend, circulated his "Proposals for Establishing a free school for the Instruction of the Children of Blacks and people of Color" about 1782; his prospectus was revelatory of the Quaker approach as he "earnestly recommended to the humane and the benevolent of all denominations, chearfully to contribute to an Institute calculated to promote the spiritual and temporal interest of that unfortunate part of our fellow creatures, in forming their minds in the principles of virtue and religion, and in common or useful literature; Writing, Cyphering and Mechanic arts, as the most likely means to render so numerous a people fit for freedom and to become useful citizens." [36] Education for Negroes would as naturally include moral and religious instruction as more worldly means of rendering them "useful citizens."

After the war, many other Friends took a hand in the work. In 1789 one group organized the Philadelphia Society (or Association) for Free Instruction of Colored People, which corresponded with Quakers of similar mind in Baltimore, Providence, Newport, and

34. James, *A People Among Peoples, passim.*
35. Brookes, *Friend Anthony Benezet,* 45–52.
36. Quoted in Weeks, *Southern Quakers and Slavery,* 215. Pleasants established a school on his own land, "Gravelly Hills," which was still operating as late as 1824; he also experimented with slave tenancy and gradual emancipation: William C. Dunlap, *Quaker Education in Baltimore and Virginia Yearly Meetings with an Account of Certain Meetings of Delaware and the Eastern Shore Affiliated with Philadelphia . . .* (Phila., 1936), 173–77, 458–59. See this source, chap. 14, for Quaker interest in Negro education in the antislavery South and for the poor record of accomplishment.

Burlington, New Jersey, all of whom hoped for good progress.[37] Benjamin Hadwen of Newport wrote eagerly to the Philadelphia Association: "We feel great Satisfaction in thus far endeavouring to promote Usefull Learning Amongst them, And desire that they universally may be enabled to make a right Improvement." [38] Significantly, these efforts were expected to yield a double return: beyond instruction of the blacks, the Burlington School-Society saw benefit for the instructors: "Amongst other good effects, attendant on this our Undertaking, we have found it insensibly to unite us, more nearly, not only to the Blacks immediately under our Care, but to that People in general, and to enlarge in us, that disposition, which, dispelling the mists of prejudice, embraces all mankind as Brethren." [39] In a still larger view, education of Negroes would unveil the degradation which they had suffered and reveal the true cause of their apparent backwardness. The Newport group, for instance, hoped its work would help demonstrate to the world that Negroes "are of the Same species as Ourselves; possessing the same Capacities, and that Education only, forms the Apparent Contrast between us." [40] As the Philadelphia Association obliquely expressed this point, educating blacks would "do Something towards restoring them to that Rank in the Community which is the Right of every rational Being." [41] In this view, then, instruction of Negroes would be instructive to white men.

Negro schooling afforded other benefits which the teachers were less anxious to advertise, if, indeed, they were conscious of them. Some idea of the content of instruction may be gathered from "Essay 91" written by a Negro pupil, probably an adult living in Philadelphia, which took the form of a letter addressed to "Masters bartone": "dear masters i am verry thinkful to you For the lerning that i resieved from you to think not most a fected people a mung

37. *History of the Associations of Friends for the Free Instruction of Adult Colored Persons in Philadelphia* (Phila., 1890) ; Turner, *Negro in Pa.*, 129; Correspondence of the Philadelphia Society [or Association] for Free Instruction of Colored People, Department of Records, Philadelphia Yearly Meeting, 302 Arch St., Philadelphia. For all quotations from this correspondence I am indebted to Professor Sydney V. James.

38. Benjamin Hadwen to the Philadelphia Society for the free Instruction of the Blacks, Newport, Apr. 25, 1791, Correspondence of the Phila. Soc. for Free Instruction of Colored People, Dept. of Recs., Phila. Yearly Meeting.

39. Burlington School-Society to the Philadelphia School Society for the instruction of the Blacks, Burlington, Feb. 2, 1793, *ibid.*

40. Benjamin Hadwen to the Philadelphia Assoc. for free Instruction of Colored People, Newport, Apr. 16, 1794, *ibid.*

41. Association for Free Instruction of Colored People to Obadiah Brown, Phila., Jan. 11, 1794, *ibid.*

our Cullur but o my dear masters if you did not tiched aus to know you is Good to aus how Shoud i pursome to Set it down i render you thenthousand think for the pains that you has taken with me o my dear masters i nose not how to render you thinks e nuff but i hope god all Mighty will bless all of you for your trouble." [42] Evidently Negroes might fail to recognize how good their masters were to them unless they were "tiched" the idea. Negro education could be useful in a variety of ways.

Fully as important and revealing as these Quaker attempts at Negro education was the pervasive Quaker influence in the abolition societies and in the national Convention begun in 1794. Though the societies carried famous names on their membership rolls, there is considerable evidence to suggest that except in Connecticut much of the real work was done by Quakers, supported in Philadelphia by such benevolent physicians as Benjamin Rush and Caspar Wistar.[43] Quakers were conspicuously active in the two most active societies, New York's and Pennsylvania's. Without question the pronouncements of the national Convention were pronouncedly Quakerish in tone and approach. A declaration by the 1797 Convention might almost have been a paraphrase of Robert Pleasants's plea: in view of "the extensive influence of education on society," the Convention asked that attention be given not merely to "what is

42. Frances B. Richardson to "Masters bartone," n.p., Feb. 24, 1790, *ibid.*
43. Wistar came from a Quaker family. A thorough study of the abolition societies and the national convention is badly needed; until detailed investigation of memberships is made, this conclusion on Quaker influence must remain open to question. For evidence pointing in this direction, Turner, *Negro in Pa.*, 210; Drake, *Quakers and Slavery*, 90, 94, 98n; Alfred F. Young, *The Democratic Republicans of New York: The Origins, 1763-1797* (Chapel Hill, 1967), 252; John Cox, Jr., *Quakerism in the City of New York, 1657-1930* (N. Y., 1930), 62. Locke's *Anti-Slavery in America* discusses the societies but fails to consider religious affiliations. Zilversmit, *Abolition in the North*, 166, calls the societies often front organizations for Quakers. My own reading of the Papers of the New York Society for Promoting the Abolition of Slaves, New York City, N.-Y. Hist. Soc., makes me somewhat less confident of Quaker predominance in New York than these secondary authorities. Elsewhere, Moses Brown, Warner Mifflin, and Robert Pleasants, all Quakers, were especially prominent in the formation of the Providence, Delaware, and Virginia (Richmond) societies. Antislavery flourished wherever Quakers were numerous; the New Jersey Society reported in 1798, "No orations on the subject of slavery have been attempted in this state, being thought unpopular in East Jersey, and unnecessary in West Jersey," *Minutes Abolition Convention* (1798), 9; also (1801), 8ff. For an antislavery organization clearly without Quakers, see Whitefield J. Bell, Jr., "Washington County, Pennsylvania, in the Eighteenth Century Antislavery Movement," *Western Pennsylvania Historical Magazine*, 25 (1942), 135-42. For Connecticut, where there were few Quakers, Morgan, *Ezra Stiles*, 452. The *Minutes* of the national Convention shed considerable light on activities of member societies.

called school learning" but also to "sound principles of morality and religion as well as habits of temperance and industry." This would be "the greatest and perhaps the only important service we can render to them and to our country, to disseminate learning and morality among them, thus raising them gradually and safely to that level, to which they must, in the course of time, inevitably attain." [44]

Extension of this logic would imply a large measure of civil equality for Negroes, and indeed this was precisely what the Convention had in mind. The first meeting called upon the constituent societies "to use their utmost endeavours to have the children of the free and other Africans, instructed in common literature—in the principles of virtue and religion, and afterwards in useful mechanical arts; thereby to prepare them for becoming good citizens of the United States." This citizenship was "a privilege and elevation to which we look forward with pleasure, and which we believe can be best merited by habits of industry and virtue." Of what use to the Negro, they asked, was simple manumission? He must have "civil privileges" when he was fully prepared to exercise them. [45] Like various Quaker groups and individual Friends, the Convention reached this position without much explicit discussion of natural rights. Equally significant, non-Quaker antislavery writers outside the Convention often rang the changes on Revolutionary doctrine—and failed to reach this position. [46]

In this typically but by no means exclusively Quaker view, the Negro's status as a slave did not constitute the entire problem nor abolition the complete answer. Because the institution of slavery did not loom before them as a massive fortress of evil, as it was later to do, many reformers were able to see that other aspects of the Negro's degradation required ameliorative action. Slavery had no active defenders, nor could it yet be exclusively the fault of southerners—accordingly there was no temptation to fly to philippics against the institution and its sinful supporters. The reality that slavery was but one form of degradation for the Negro could be faced squarely and the immensity of the entire task be seen with considerable clarity. In 1795, the Convention in Philadelphia was

44. *Minutes Abolition Convention* (1797), 23.
45. *Ibid.* (1794), 8, 15–17, 20–21.
46. Unusual personal inclinations and political circumstances led, of course, to exceptions. Young DeWitt Clinton, an Antifederalist with a reforming bent, assailed a Federalist-sponsored emancipation bill (1790) in New York because it contained no provisions for support of freed children or "protection of their rights." Young, *Democratic Republicans of New York*, 253–54.

vigorously explicit in outlining the broader duties of the Negro's friends: "even should that great end [entire abolition] be happily attained," the Convention wrote, ". . . when we have broken his chains, and restored the African to the enjoyment of his rights, the great work of justice and benevolence is not accomplished." Instruction of Negroes would serve three good purposes: it would render the Negro "capable and desirous of fulfilling the various duties he owes to himself and to his country"; it would "do away the reproach and calumny so unjustly lavished upon us"; and it would demonstrate that Negro slaves were "in no wise inferior to the more fortunate inhabitants of Europe and America." [47] Only three years later when the Convention was already gloomy about prospects for abolishing slavery, it took the position that Negro education ought to be "the primary object of all the Abolition Societies." [48] Evidently education was going to have to run interference for "Abolition." By this time members of the Convention were thoroughly alive to the immensity of their task. They counted on education of Negroes to make a convincing display of the essential equality of Negroes with white men; just as significantly, they regarded popular acceptance of this equality as a precondition for attainment of the "great end" of "entire abolition." It was on the same assumption that the Convention issued hortatory addresses to free Negroes, urging the necessity of their behaving with such propitiatory propriety as to convince the world that emancipation was indeed a blessing.[49]

4. RELIGIOUS EQUALITARIANISM

The pervasive Quaker influence in organized antislavery points up the continuing vitality of religious equalitarianism. It seems certain that it was the specifically religious impulse in anti-

47. *Minutes Abolition Convention* (1795), 29–30. There was no retreat from this position, despite growing discouragement: "Although liberty be a blessing, when we obtain the freedom of the slave our work is not completed. It then becomes our peculiar charge to endeavour to teach the enfranchised man how to value, and how to employ the privileges which have fallen to his lot." *Ibid.* (1809), 28.

48. *Ibid.* (1798), 17–18.

49. For example, *ibid.* (1796), 12–15; (1797), 16–18; (1805), 38; *To the Free Africans and Other People of Color in the United States. The Convention of Deputies from the Abolition Societies in the United States, Assembled at Philadelphia, Have Undertaken To Address You upon Subjects Highly Interesting to Your Prosperity . . .* (Phila., 1796).

slavery, in contrast to the natural rights philosophy, which provided the energy and vision necessary to think and act beyond abolition of slavery, notably in the direction of "improvement" by education. In one sense, education of Negroes was taken up as the half-loaf imposed by the seeming impossibility of complete abolition, but this very refusal to demand all-or-nothing, as the philosophy of rights did, contained the critical affirmation that outward legal status was not all that mattered. It is clear, at any rate, that the ameliorative approach appealed to religious groups more than to those who drew faith primarily from the breast of Locke and the Revolution.

In practice many religious groups did very little to help Negroes obtain educational opportunities. Indeed, it almost appears that very little was ever done without Quakers having a hand in the work, though as with the successful school operated by the New York Manumission Society, their predilection for self-effacement always makes it hard to be sure. In Boston, Negro schooling was initiated by Negroes themselves.[50] Perhaps a good deal was accomplished in an offhand fashion by the many masters who, when freeing their slaves, required that they be taught to read and write.[51] Yet surely it is significant that many religious sects pronounced themselves in favor of Negro education, while the author of the Declaration of Independence remained silent. The Presbyterian Synod of New York and Philadelphia recommended in 1787 that masters give their slaves "such good education as to prepare them for a better enjoyment of freedom," and a Methodist conference took the same stand in 1790.[52] The Reverend Samuel Miller told the New York Manumission Society in 1797 that gradual emancipation must be accompanied by moral and intellectual cultivation.[53]

Indeed religious conviction was capable of generating sufficient power to eradicate mere practical obstacles. The Reverend Alexander McLeod, after demanding an end to slavery, unintentionally proclaimed both the inexorable force and the self-defeating rigor inherent in this conviction: "Every plan is accompanied with diffi-

50. Woodson, *Education of the Negro*, 95–96.
51. Wright, *Free Negro in Md.*, 138, also 200–201, found that in the period 1803–05 Maryland indentures began to omit expressly the obligation to teach Negro apprentices to read and write, except in the Baltimore area and the counties bordering Pennsylvania.
52. Woodson, *Education of the Negro*, 74.
53. Samuel Miller, *A Discourse, Delivered April 12, 1797, at the Request of and Before the New-York Society for Promoting the Manumission of Slaves, and Protecting Such of Them as Have Been or May Be Liberated* (N. Y., 1797), 30–32, 34–35.

culties. To export them to Africa would be cruel. To establish them in a separate colony would be dangerous. To give them their liberty, and incorporate them with the whites, would be more so. The sins of the fathers, it is to be feared, will be visited on their children. But it is more safe to adopt any one of those plans than continue the evil." [54] God would take care of the future, McLeod felt, if only men would act now. Paradoxically, this blind faith prevented formulation of specific plans of action while at the same time rigidly insisting that some action be taken.

The religious approach to the problem of racial debasement contained an older and larger ambivalence. Sermons addressed to Negro slaves were invariably freighted with assertions of inherent equality before God and the rightness of inequality on earth. When the Reverend Cary Allen urged upon a group of Virginia Negroes the central fact that Christ had died for them as well as for whites he was no more a "Christian" than the Reverend Jedidiah Morse (who hated slavery) when he cautioned Negroes, "Many eyes are upon you. Some doubtless are watching for your halting. Be contented in the humble station in which providence has placed you." [55] The tenor of these apparently divergent admonitions was, of course, new neither to America nor to Christianity. From St. Paul through Martin Luther to Cotton Mather and Bishop Asbury, Christianity had to grapple with the profoundly revolutionary implications of its own doctrine. Social stability always depended upon maintenance of rigid distinction between two spheres, a distinction which rationalized the equality of souls with the inequality of persons. For some men, the mode of thought and beliefs which informed the American Revolution had considerably blurred the traditional distinction; indeed some became caught up in a round of thought which imbued mankind with the spark of divinity by a circular process of naturalizing God, deifying Nature, and naturalizing man, a process which brought heavenly equality to earth, literally. For many others, however, the distinction remained as real as ever—or rather they thought it did—and they simply incorporated, rather than fused, the ideal of earthly equality into their way of

54. Alexander McLeod, *Negro Slavery Unjustifiable. A Discourse,* 11th ed. (N. Y., 1863), 42–43. The original edition was N. Y., 1802.

55. Allen quoted in William H. Foote, *Sketches of Virginia, Historical and Biographical, Second Series,* 2d ed. (Phila., 1856), 232–33; Jedidiah Morse, *A Discourse, Delivered at the African Meeting-House, in Boston, July 14, 1808, in Grateful Celebration of the Abolition of the African Slave-Trade, by the Governments of the United States, Great Britain and Denmark* (Boston, 1808), 18.

looking at the world without extensively remodeling their traditionally dualistic view of man.

The evident compatibility and mutual reinforcement of the natural rights doctrine and Christian equalitarianism during the Revolutionary period does not mean that they entirely coalesced. Many individuals, probably most, subscribed in a general way to both clusters of belief; certainly every American operated in a cultural context pervaded by some or other combination of the two ideologies. But as ideologies, whatever their interrelations, they contained certain incompatible elements, or at least incompatible emphases, with the result that men with special reason to identify with one or the other (most notably statesmen on the one hand and clerics and lay-clerics on the other) were likely to approach the problem of inequality in earthly status in different ways.

Certainly, if considered as distinct approaches to the Negro's condition, these two ideologies seem to have made rather different demands. While the natural rights philosophy directly undermined the logic of slavery, religious equalitarianism could, and in fact did, both attack and support the institution. This is to say not only that Christianity could be urged as a means of slave control, which the philosophy of rights never could, but that Christian equalitarianism retained its old ambivalence; it asked both less and more than freedom from slavery. In and of itself, it did not of necessity demand abolition, though it could be made to do so, as the Quakers had shown. On the other hand, because Christianity's focus was not exclusively upon external condition it allowed men to envision other possibilities than the wonder-stroke of abolition. It compelled concern both with the moral state of the slave and with his condition when freed. While the natural rights philosophy assayed the Negro as a slave, Christianity looked through external status to the man himself and his inner justification for existence, his soul. From this vantage point, abolition of slavery was not the cup of victory but a stride toward a better inherent condition. To the extent that religious and moral betterment required a better environment on this earth—and this extent was growing rapidly—religion demanded this better environment: hence the interest of religious men in Negro education and a mild regimen for slaves. The indefatigable Bishop Asbury outlined these claims of Christianity with such clarity as to lay bare at once their strength and their failing.

We are defrauded of great numbers [of converts] by the pains that are taken to keep the blacks from us; their masters are afraid of the influence of our principles. Would not an *amelioration* in the condition and treatment of slaves have produced more practical good to the poor Africans, than any attempt at their *emancipation?* The state of society, unhappily, does not admit of this: besides, the blacks are deprived of the means of instruction; who will take the pains to lead them into the way of salvation, and watch over them that they may not stray, but the Methodists? Well; now their masters will not let them come to hear us. What is the personal liberty of the African which he may abuse, to the salvation of his soul; how may it be compared? [56]

How indeed? It was as if the natural rights philosophy were seen in a mirror, with every element reversed yet the basic image unchanged.

5. HUMANITARIANISM AND SENTIMENTALITY

The religious demand for *"amelioration,"* which was almost as old as Negro slavery, found a new ally during and after the Revolutionary era. The growth of humanitarianism, one of the most profound and least explicable developments of the eighteenth century, resulted in increasingly humane treatment for slaves. More than that, humanitarian feeling was quietly but effectively equalitarian. Insofar as humanitarianism limited brutality it tended to undercut the notion that the Negro was a brute. It tended to legitimize the Negro's claim to humanness and to compel explicit recognition that Negroes, in such matters as family affection and physical pain, were similar to other men. Empathy was of course a strong element in humanitarianism, and empathy implied equality, if only in a very limited sense.

A number of circumstances combined to nurture an especially strong humanitarian movement in America. Perhaps most important was the pervasiveness of environmentalist thought: human misery had come to seem less inherent in the human condition and more a function of the surroundings in which man was placed. Ironically, the presence of two more primitive races tended to stimulate humanitarianism, especially after the flowering of the natural rights philosophy made it more necessary than ever to assert their essential equality with European settlers. Slightly more effective medical treatment, a slightly declining death rate, and a slightly rising standard of living all made for a new sense (which was *not* slight) that human misery was not inevitable. Urbanization probably increased human suffering, made it more apparent, and engendered the condition of some the concern of all. The decay

56. Clark *et al.*, eds., *Journals of Francis Asbury*, II, 591 (Feb. 1, 1809).

of articulate social hierarchy helped level the mental wall which separated the wealthy and powerful from the suffering of the less fortunate. And while some religious sects contributed conspicuously to the humanitarian movement, so did the decline of religiosity. It had become less possible to shrug off suffering as inherent in the God-ordained social order. As God became less the omnipotent arbiter, suffering became less virtuous. Growing rationalism meant witches hustled off to hospitals and debtors sprung from jails. The process of revising legal codes during and after the Revolution provided good occasion for making criminal punishments more rational and more humane. And driving all these and other factors was a snowball dynamic: the less suffering there was, the less reason why there should be any.

If ever there was a deserving claimant to humanitarian ministration, it was American slavery and the slave trade. Abuse of Negroes was a compelling invitation to reform, and widespread awareness of this abuse vigorously stimulated the humanitarian impulse. The humanitarian mood was always deeply earnest and serious minded, and the hideousness of slavery at its worst reinforced this bent. Humor is never possible when hyperbole fails to dwarf reality, as one writer unwittingly demonstrated by suggesting that Negroes be used as currency, with fractional currency to be obtained by chopping them up and salting the extremities.[57] Slaves were still branded ("I HILL" on the forehead and breast, read one advertisement) though not nearly so commonly as in the early years of the century.[58] Whipping was frequently so severe as to scar for life.[59] The less lovely aspects of slavery kept popping into the open in an embarrassing way, as in Charleston where in 1805 there was much

57. "Letter from an Enemy to the Society for the Abolition of Slavery, Phila., 29 May 1787," *Amer. Museum*, 4 (1788), 52.

58. *Raleigh Register*, Aug. 12, 1805; for other instances, Charleston *State Gazette of S. C.*, Aug. 12, 1793; Richmond *Examiner*, Sept. 2, 1800.

59. The files of almost any southern newspaper afford evidence. Some advertisements were unapologetic: "he is a noted rogue and runaway, as his back will shew, and went off with an iron collar on his neck." Annapolis *Md. Gaz.*, Nov. 15, 1792; others in *ibid.*, Nov. 26, 1795; Norfolk *Va. Chronicle*, Oct. 15, 1792, Nov. 24, 1794; Charleston *Carolina Gazette*, Jan. 16, 1800. Especially in the antislavery South, however, many advertisers were reluctant to admit whipping their slaves or were almost pathetically anxious to assert they never did so. In Maryland one owner claimed his slave's marks were acquired before his purchase (a common claim) another that the scars on the back and shoulders of a Negro woman had come from a scalding accident, and another described a "smooth face as well as back, he never had a stripe thereon by me who raised him." Annapolis *Md. Gaz.*, May 30, 1793, June 5, July 10, 1794. A foreigner's report on slave-whipping in New York and Virginia is in Roberts, trans. and eds., *Moreau de St. Méry's Journey*, 54, 59, 156.

indignation about "dead bodies" thrown from slave ships into the harbor. It was a dreadful affair: one traveler reported that "nobody would eat any fish." Juries brought in verdicts that the deaths had come "by the visitation of God," but a city ordinance declared the situation "extremely disgraceful" and provided that any future offender be fined and his name published in the gazettes for "public detestation." [60] Insofar as slavery stimulated cruelty, the institution itself became an object of humanitarian attack. Antislavery writers seized the opportunity of enlisting humanitarian sentiment in their cause, many of them pointing out that slavery gave play to the "most boisterous passions" of the masters. [61] (In some cases certainly they were right, as the occasional sadistic atrocities testified. Anger at Negroes was perhaps less likely to be securely hedged in than anger at persons who were not owned.) [62] In actuality, of course, antislavery and humanitarianism interlocked with each other; antislavery writing became more markedly humanitarian in tone toward the end of the century. [63] Every lash of the whip drove home the antislavery case.

Slavery did in fact become less cruel. It is impossible to ascertain just how much amelioration there was, since reports of mild treatment and public excoriations of brutality were perhaps as much reflections of hope as of actuality. Yet the new laws which prohibited gross maltreatment of slaves and made murder of a slave an offense equal to murder of a white man, no matter how well or badly observed in practice, were expressions of an important change in standards. [64] There is scattered evidence, moreover, that slave

60. John Lambert, *Travels Through Canada, and the United States . . .* , 2d ed., 2 vols. (London, 1814) , II, 166–67; Donnan, ed., *Documents Slave Trade*, IV, 526–27; *Digest of the Ordinances of the City Council of Charleston . . . 1783–1818* (Charleston, 1818) , 145.

61. Quotation is Jefferson, *Notes on the State of Virginia*, ed. Peden, 162.

62. How one interprets the following outburst by a little girl in Virginia depends upon one's view of children: a Negro enraged by a cat which scratched him had killed the animal, concerning which she demurely commented to her diary, "A vile wretch of new negrows, if he was mine I would cut him to pieces, a son of a gun, a nice negrow, he should be kild himself by rites." Sally Cary Fairfax, "Diary of a Little Colonial Girl," *Va. Mag. of Hist. and Biog.*, 11 (1904) , 213.

63. St. Jean de Crèvecoeur's description of a Negro punished by starvation in a cage was widely reprinted; an incomplete list is in Julia Post Mitchell, *St. Jean de Crèvecoeur* (N. Y., 1916) , 346–49. For the original, [Crèvecoeur], *Letters from an American Farmer*, 232–35.

64. *Acts of the Tenth General Assembly of the State of New-Jersey . . . Second Sitting* (Trenton, 1786) , 242; Hening, ed., *Statutes Va.*, XII, 681; Thorpe, ed., *Constitutions*, II, 801 (Georgia) ; *Laws State Ga. Since 1800*, 289; cf. Henry, *Police Control of the Slave*, 67–68. The natural rights philosophy sometimes came into play, reinforcing humanitarianism. North Carolina declared (1791) ,

punishments were indeed becoming less harsh and familial relations less subject to arbitrary disruption. In Virginia, at least, many planters insisted upon decent food and quarters, upon sparing use of the whip, and that slave families never be sold apart. More generally, it is difficult to imagine that slaves failed to benefit from the decline of overt brutality in American life which was so evident in punishments for crime. In terms of one kind of human happiness, this may have been one of the most successful revolutions in history.

The supreme irony in this happy development was that with slavery humanitarian victories over brutality left the real enemy more firmly entrenched than ever. As slavery became less brutal there was less reason why it should be abolished. Humanitarianism was less a program of reform than a quality of human need; as such it was satisfied by piecemeal accomplishments. The dangers inherent in such an approach to human slavery have perhaps never been more obvious. By concentrating on elimination of inhumane treatment, the humanitarian impulse helped make slavery more benevolent and paternal and hence more tolerable for the slaveowner and even for the abolitionist. In revealing contrast to this situation in the American South, slavery in the British West Indies helped doom itself by its notorious cruelty. To the extent that cruelty was inherent in slavery, humanitarian amelioration helped perpetuate cruelty. As for the future, the humanitarian outlook was in its own way as limited as the natural rights philosophy: it looked no further than stopping the flow of tears and blood.

Closely intertwining with the growth of humanitarianism in late eighteenth-century America was a growing mood of sentimentality. As a cast of mind, a mode of approach, sentimentality overlapped and interlocked with humanitarian feeling, bringing to good-hearted benevolence a half-intended emotionalism, a partially deliberate titillation of human sympathies. No matter how fluttery, sentimentality heightened empathy; as a mode of approach to Negro slavery, it implied that Negroes had feelings as deep and

---

"whereas by . . . act of Assembly passed in . . . 1774, the killing a slave, however wanton, cruel and deliberate, is only punishable in the first instance by imprisonment and paying the value thereof to the owner; which distinction of criminality between the murder of a white person and one who is equally an human creature, but merely of a different complexion, is disgraceful to humanity and degrading in the highest degree to the laws and principles of a free, christian and enlightened country"; willful killing of a slave was made murder, as of a white man, except if the slave resisted or died under moderate correction. Iredell and Martin, comps., *Acts N.-C.*, II, 8–9, also 179.

legitimate as white men. This implication was stated self-consciously in a letter from a young Virginian to his father.

I enclose a short note from Bob to his mother. Poor little fellow! I was
much affected at an incident last night. I was waked from a very sound
sleep by a most piteous lamentation. I found it was Bob. I called several
times before he waked. "What is the matter Bob?," "I was dreaming about
my mammy Sir"!!! cried he in a melancholy and still distressed tone:
"Gracious God"! thought I, "how ought not I to feel, who regarded this
child as insensible when compared to those of our complexion." In truth
our thoughts had been straying the same way. How finely woven, How
delicately sensible must be those bonds of natural affection which equally
adorn the civilized and savage. The American and African—nay the
man and the brute! I declare I know not a situation in which I have been
lately placed that touched me so nearly as that incident I have just
related.[65]

Sentimentality was equalitarian in that it assumed and played upon a sense of human sameness in feeling.

With its penchant for pretty feeling, sentimentality found its natural outlet in literature; indeed it has sometimes been regarded as a literary movement. While humanitarianism played somber fugues on the theme of human suffering, sentimentality pulled all the stops: "Methinks, I now see them dragged, with the most vigorous reluctance and resistance on their part, from their beloved habitations, on which they cannot forbear to look back; and, while they look back, tears flow in copious streams down their furrowed cheeks; and their heaving breasts sufficiently indicate the inexpressible anguish which they feel within." [66] It is difficult to tell whether

65. Henry St. George Tucker to his father, St. George Tucker, Winchester, Feb. 17, 1804, Coleman, comp., *Va. Silhouettes*, 9–10.
66. Thomas Branagan, *A Preliminary Essay, on the Oppression of the Exiled Sons of Africa* . . . (Phila., 1804), 32–33. Branagan's writings offered a tear-on-every-page; *The Penitential Tyrant; A Juvenile Poem* . . . (Phila., 1805) and *Avenia, or a Tragical Poem, on the Oppression of the Human Species; and Infringement on the Rights of Man* . . . , 2d ed. (Phila., 1810). He claimed to have been at one time a slave trader and plantation owner on Antigua. For biographical data, Lewis Leary, "Thomas Branagan: Republican Rhetoric and Romanticism in America," *Pa. Mag. of Hist. and Biog.*, 77 (1953), 332–52. Many American magazines carried sentimental tales about Negroes: "Observations upon the Genius, the Manners, and the Institutions of the People of India [From Robertson's *Ancient India*]," *New York Magazine, or Literary Repository*, 2 (1791), 338–39; "The Negro Trade. A Fragment," *American Moral and Sentimental Magazine*, [no vol.] (Sept. 11, 1797), 181–82; "Extracts from a Speech on the Slave Trade Spoken Before the Council of the Leeward Islands, March, 1798," *Literary Magazine and American Register*, 2 (1804), 45–47; "Horrors of West India Slavery," *ibid.*, 5 (1806), 7–13; [Benjamin Rush], "The Paradise of Negro-Slaves—a Dream," *Columbian Magazine*, 1 (1787), 235–38; L.B., "Slavery," *New York Weekly Magazine*, 2 (May 22, 1797), 303; "Petition of an African Slave, to the Legislature of Massachusetts," *Amer. Museum*, 1 (1787), 538–40; "Address

sentiment had become a vehicle for antislavery or vice versa; at any rate, sentimental antislavery verses achieved wide popularity. Best known, and reprinted in several American songsters, was the tale of an African prince in England who was asked what he had given for his watch: "What I will never give again:—I gave a fine Boy for it."

> His Father's hope, his Mother's pride,
>   Tho' black, yet comely to their view,
> I tore him helpless from their side,
>   And gave him to a ruffian crew;
>   To fiends that Afric's coast annoy,
>   I sold the blooming Negro Boy.

> From country, friends and parents torn,
>   His tender limbs in chains confin'd,
> I saw him o'er the billows borne,
>   And mark'd his agony of mind.
>   But still, to gain this simple toy,
>   I gave away the Negro Boy.[67]

And so on, for seven stanzas. The extent to which sentimentality encouraged empathy with the Negro's plight was evident in the novel vogue for what might be called the African Lament. Antislavery writers increasingly put themselves in the Negro's place by employing a simple literary device: "We were dancing on the green in the evening, and we dreaded not the hour of danger. But the tall ship anchored in the stream, and treachery lurked for our captivity. In vain we wept." [68] Africa was thus transformed into the despoiled sylvan idyl of aggrieved and tear-stained humanity.

In becoming more sentimental and more a specifically literary genre, antislavery writing seemed merely to reflect a change in American mood and taste. At a deeper level of development, however, this shift toward a romantic sentimentalism was a symptom of, and perhaps a subtle yet readily intelligible social signal for, a

to the Heart, on the Subject of American Slavery," *ibid.*, 540–44; "The African Boy," *ibid.*, 6 (1789), 328–29; Annapolis *Md. Gaz.*, Mar. 19, 1795. For other examples, *Reflections on Slavery; With Recent Evidence of its Inhumanity. Occasioned by the Melancholy Death of Romain, a French Negro. By Humanitas* (Phila., 1803); [William Roscoe], *The Wrongs of Africa, a Poem* (Phila., 1788).

67. *Providence Gazette*, Aug. 18, 1792; S. Foster Damon, "The Negro in Early American Songsters," Bibliographical Society of America, *Papers*, 28 (1934), 140–41, an article which makes evident the growth of sentimentality in stage plays and songs.

68. "The Negro," *Weekly Magazine*, 1 (Feb. 3, 1798), 11–12.

retreat from rational engagement with the ethical problem posed by
Negro slavery. Even if the more extravagantly sentimental antislavery tales are disregarded, it remains true that the rhetoric of antislavery as a whole was changing in the direction of *extravagance,* a
term whose derivation suggests very neatly what was happening.
Consider closely the following: "Slavery cannot be vindicated upon
any principles, but what comes directly or indirectly from the
infernal regions. Slavery like a poisoned river, has its source in his
Plutonic majesty's dominions, from whence its various meanderings
through this beautiful creation has transmitted its noxious quality
to every department of the inhabited globe." [69] To take a rather
different and infinitely more egregious example:

> Why shrinks yon slave, with horror from his meat?
> Heavens! 'tis his flesh, the wretch is whipp'd to eat.
> Why streams the life-blood from that female's throat?
> She sprinkled gravy on a guest's new coat! [70]

The hyperbole inherent in the new approach represented, on the
surface, a willingness to face the grim realities of slavery; but
excessive exaggeration, as it so often does, exposed an inner inability to face reality, an *un*willingness to admit the true dimensions of
the problem. In an important sense, atrocity-mongering attested less
to a decline in rationalism than to a failure of nerve. In the long
run, too, this shift toward extravagant sentimentality tended to
vitiate antislavery as a program of action. Removal from the political arena and failure to attend to practical goals made for a weaker
grasp on future problems and for blindness to the economic and
social mechanics of slavery. As for the Negro's future, the contribution of sentimental antislavery literature was to cloud it with tears.
At the same time, however, sentimentality helped turn America's
attention toward the slave trade, and action on this front was
prerequisite to progress at home.

It was therefore no happenstance that hands were wrung over the
African slave trade much more than over domestic slavery. Sentimentality found in the anguished partings and infamous cruelty of
the slave trade a perfect medium for literary exploitation. Not only

69. *Reflections on the Inconsistency of Man, Particularly Exemplified in the
Practice of Slavery in the United States* (N. Y., 1796), 17–18.

70. Timothy Dwight, *Greenfield Hill: A Poem, in Seven Parts* (N. Y., 1794), 40.
The pervasiveness of this change is suggested by the fact that a Congregational
minister could write a somewhat sentimental tract without mentioning Revolutionary doctrine; William Patten, *On the Inhumanity of the Slave-Trade . . .*
(Providence, 1793).

was the slave trade far more brutal than domestic slavery but it was further from home and therefore more susceptible to hyperbole and dramatization. What satisfying quivers might be obtained by reading of two lovers parted by abduction of the lady and her father, of the faithful suitor swimming out from shore to join them on the slave ship, of both men dying gallantly in a desperate brawl with the traders who sought to part them from the lady in the islands! Nor was the moral of this drama left hidden from the gentle reader:

> Hark! from yon ship the scream of woe I hear,
> Another quick succeeding fills my ear;
> What mean those screams? Ah! shudder to behold,
> These *Britons* barter *human blood* for *gold!* [71]

One of the earliest antislavery prints in America, borrowed from the British campaign against the trade, showed a plan of the lower decks of a slaving ship with Negroes lying packed like so many sardines.[72]

6. THE SUCCESS AND FAILURE OF ANTISLAVERY

Other factors contributed to this shift of attention toward the slave trade and thus in turn may have nurtured the growth of sentimentality. For one thing, since the trade was notoriously the most brutal facet of the Negro labor system, it became a principal target for humanitarian indignation. For another, blame for its brutalities might readily be foisted onto others, principally the British, even though everyone knew that some New England traders were (illegally) very active, Rhode Island being "the most exuberant in iniquity." [73] Most important, the slave trade invited

71. [Thomas George Street], *Aura: Or, the Slave, A Poem* . . . (Phila., 1788); quotation p. 8.

72. William Elford, *Plan of an African Ship's Lower Deck* (Phila., [1789]). This and similar pictures were used in antislavery pamphlets.

73. *Reflections on Slavery*, 11. For example, *Annals of Congress*, 8th Cong., 1st sess., 992, 997, 1000, 9th Cong., 1st sess., 373; Donnan, ed., *Documents Slave Trade*, IV, 517–19; Richmond *Virginia Argus*, Oct. 3, 1800; La Rochefoucauld-Liancourt, *Travels through the United States*, 505–6; Annapolis *Md. Gaz.*, June 5, 1794; Jonathan Edwards, *The Injustice and Impolicy of the Slave-Trade, and of the Slavery of the Africans: Illustrated in a Sermon Preached before the Connecticut Society for the Promotion of Freedom* . . . (Providence, 1792), 28–29; Elizabeth Donnan, "The New England Slave Trade after the Revolution," *New England Quarterly*, 3 (1930), 251–78; this charge runs through the *Minutes Abolition Convention* especially after 1800. For a typical defense of the trade, *Letter to Philo Africanus, upon Slavery* . . . (London, reprinted Newport, [1788]).

attack after the war because it was on its last economic legs. Slave importation was stopped as much by lack of demand for slaves as by antislavery attack. Between 1774 and 1794 every state acted to ban importation.[74] The first prohibition in South Carolina in 1787 was for only a few years, but the legislature extended it periodically until mounting demand for slaves led to reopening of the trade in 1803, an action which brought an outcry of protest from the rest of the nation.[75] Many states prohibited residents from participating in the trade, and the federal government reinforced these laws by barring all United States citizens from participation in 1794.[76] On no matter of policy concerning the Negro was there anything like such national consensus. It was only the adamantine resistance of South Carolina and Georgia which prevented the Constitutional Convention from prohibiting the trade outright. By the 1790's an overwhelming majority of Americans assumed that the constitutional prohibition of congressional action for twenty years meant in fact that the trade would be banned in 1808. From Virginia northwards the execrable traffic was almost universally condemned.

In moving against the slave traffic, Americans attacked the most vulnerable aspect of the Negro problem. The political, religious, humanitarian, and sentimental approaches toward Negro slavery —it sometimes seems useful to separate the inseparable—all converged upon this one point. The result was fairly effective suppression of the slave trade, yet success on this front proved damaging to the campaigns on others. A series of local triumphs against the trade and the long-awaited national victory of January 1, 1808, caused men to forget that much remained undone; it was partly for this reason that the antislavery drive began to sputter after about 1790 and finally stalled around 1810. The successful movement against the slave trade engrossed much reformist energy and, more important, salved the nation's conscience that *something* was being done about slavery. While the program against the trade rested upon the equalitarian assumption of human sameness, it said nothing definite about Negroes already in America and afforded a comfortable alternative to thinking about that problem. On the other hand it

74. DuBois, *Suppression of the Slave-Trade*, 222–36.

75. Cooper and McCord, eds., *Statutes S. C.*, VII, 449; Branagan, *Serious Remonstrances*, 27; Richmond *Enquirer*, Feb. 3, 1807, from a Baltimore newspaper which called the South Carolina Senate's rejection of the House's bill to end slave importation a "deep wound on the national character." See also George Washington to Gov. Charles Pinckney, Phila., Mar. 17, 1792, Fitzpatrick, ed., *Writings of Washington*, XXXII, 6; *Minutes Abolition Convention* (1804), 47, (1806), 18–19; *Annals of Congress*, 8th Cong., 1st sess., 820, 992–1036.

76. DuBois, *Suppression of the Slave-Trade*, 80–81, 229, 231–35, 239.

furnished Americans with the realization that progress could actually be made, that they were dealing with a problem which, if intractable, might someday yield to action.

In retrospect, the pity of antislavery's failure was that in the decade after the Revolution, success against slavery itself seemed almost within reach. If the Negro had been freed in the late eighteenth century rather than in 1863, if only in Virginia, he would have suffered far less degradation. The implications of the natural rights philosophy and religious equalitarianism would have operated directly upon his nature unimpeded by the glaring fact of his inferior status as a slave, and he would then have been in a far stronger position to meet the challenge of Darwinism. He would have undergone a shorter period of association with a radically debased status. The protracted battle for abolition in the nineteenth century generated by reaction defenses of slavery which deliberately subverted his equality; just as important, that battle forced reformist energies to concentrate more exclusively upon the single goal of abolition. After the Revolution the Negro would have been freed more for his fundamental equality and less because slavery nagged the nation's conscience as an anomaly in the civilized world. A general emancipation after the Revolution would have been more than an improvised weapon in a fratricidal war. It would have come as a glorious triumph, the capstone of the Revolution; guilt could easily have been foisted onto the British and the whole nation stirred with pride.

These possibilities were denied, of course, in part because antislavery was characterized by certain weaknesses and limitations. An expanding economy and the forging of a truly national union also worked to preclude them. And they were driven even further out of question by certain reverberations of the Revolution. White Americans discovered after 1790 that their own struggle for liberty was perhaps coming back to plague them. The threat of Negro rebellion was a major factor in the decline of antislavery, as the timing involved will suggest. Yet the importance of the threat went beyond the fact that it did a great deal to topple an antislavery movement which with all its limitations had considerable strength. As things turned out, some Negroes forced white Americans to see that their own dearest principles might serve as a lever for prying Negroes out from what they had always been sufficiently under—control. That, at very least, made for a highly charged social atmosphere.

X THE CANCER OF
REVOLUTION

ALTHOUGH THE REVOLUTION FAILED TO PROVIDE SUFFI-
cient impetus for abolition of slavery in the eighteenth century, it is
well known that the Revolution helped spark successful attempts at
freedom elsewhere. Ironically, the first triumphant imitators were
Negro slaves.

The reaction of Americans to the shocks of revolution which
swept through France and the West Indies was mixed. They hoped
for the triumph of liberty in the world but not for a complete one.
They delighted to talk of freedom but wished their slaves would not.
They assumed that their slaves yearned for liberty but were determined not to let them have it. To trace the spread of Negro
rebellion in the New World and to examine American responses to
what they saw as a mounting tide of danger is to watch the drastic
erosion of the ideology of the American Revolution. It is also to
glimpse a chronological pattern which virtually matched the
courses of nation building, agricultural change, and the fortunes of
antislavery. That there were numerous causal links among these
patterns is obvious, yet the precisioned parade of coincidences
points in a number of instances to chance. It was not unprecedented
in human affairs that causal and chance relationships worked together to weave one fabric of social change.

1. ST. DOMINGO

On New Year's Day 1804 the Republic of Haiti became
the second independent nation in the hemisphere, ruled by triumphant revolutionaries who were, of all things, black. France had lost
the pearl of her empire, hundreds of thousands of people on the
island had lost their lives, and millions of white men in other lands

wondered what had happened. Standing before a crowd of shouting blacks, Jean-Jacques Dessalines, the new Negro ruler, seized the tricolor in furious hatred and tore from it the band of white.

The new republic was born in bloody turmoil. By comparison the American Revolution was a quiet, polite affair, appropriately begun with a tea party. The revolution in St. Domingo (as most Americans then called the western French portion of the island of Hispaniola) actually began in Paris and was for at least a decade a distorted extension of the French Revolution. The calling of the Estates General in 1788 excited the white planters, some of whom, disregarding warnings from the more conservative, hustled off a delegation to Paris in hopes of undermining the arbitrary powers of the resident governor-general and intendant. Before the enthusiastic colonial deputies had a chance to do more than air their grievances, events in Paris took an ominous turn. The Bastille fell July 14, 1789, and six weeks later the National Assembly grandly issued its Declaration of the Rights of Man and Citizen, in language strongly reminiscent of the American declaration. Strange talk about equality gave the planter delegates reason for pause, the more so because an obvious corollary was being noisily expounded by *Les Amis des Noirs,* an abolitionist group with connections in Britain and the United States.

In addition to dividing the forty thousand whites of the colony, revolutionary principles infected the free colored caste, numbering some twenty-eight thousand, most of whom were mulattoes and all of whom suffered galling civil, political, and social disabilities. The National Assembly in Paris, entangled with domestic difficulties, played shuttlecock with the island time bomb by promulgating a vacillating series of decrees which several times granted and withdrew full political equality for mulattoes. The first mulatto revolt was viciously suppressed in 1791. But the example was not lost on the Negroes, and that summer many of the half million slaves seized firebrand and machete and devastated northern parts of the colony. The following years were characterized by bumbling confusion and barbarous atrocities on all sides. Negroes, whites, and mulattoes slaughtered each other by turns and the kaleidoscope of alignments whirred ever more rapidly as French troops, Jacobin commissioners, and English and Spanish armies poured in. In 1793 the leading port of Cap Français was the scene of a battle which ranged mulatto soldiery led by Jacobin commissioners against a French governor-general backed by white residents and sailors from the French fleet. Near defeat, the desperate commissioners summoned masses of blacks from the surrounding plain with promises of liberty and opportunity to pillage. The result was complete destruction of the town. A French fleet crowded with thousands of terrorized and destitute refugees set sail on June 23, 1793, for the United States.[1]

Eventually a semblance of order was impressed upon the troubled colony. Toussaint L'Ouverture, a full-blooded Negro, was an exslave who climbed to power on the ladder that chaos always seems to thrust before the able and ambitious. By 1801 he controlled the entire island. Toussaint's styling himself "first of the blacks" contained a suggestive parallel entirely unwelcome to the French emperor, who thought to make good use of a brief truce with England by dispatching troops to recover St. Domingo in 1802. The story of initial French successes, treacherous seizure of Toussaint, and eventual defeat at the hands of yellow fever and a British blockade is familiar, since these events opened the way for the sale of French Louisiana. The United States was not then nor afterward overwhelmed with gratitude for Haitian assistance, for by 1804 Americans could see in the new Republic of Haiti little else than a sample of Negro rule. Dessalines made the country truly black by massacring the remaining whites.

From the very first the momentous proceedings in St. Domingo aroused mixed reactions in the United States. St. Domingo had long been a focal point for American trading ventures. Shipmasters continued to return with information concerning the revolts, for chaos in the island stimulated demand for provisions and arms, and American merchants were eager to satisfy. Trading was hazardous in the troubled 1790's, for the United States became involved in undeclared war first with Britain and then France, and American relations with St. Domingo were inevitably entangled in larger diplomatic considerations. Accordingly, the American government did not take a forthright stand on Negro revolt in a foreign colony. During the naval war against France in 1799, the United States joined Great Britain in concluding a trade agreement with Toussaint but withheld diplomatic recognition. That year American and British naval squadrons contributed to his final victory by blockading harbors and even by bombarding forts controlled by his opponent, a French-supported mulatto. Under pressure from Napoleon the American Congress finally assented to a ban on American trade

1. The best detailed acount is T. Lothrop Stoddard, *The French Revolution in San Domingo* (Boston and N. Y., 1914). An excellent compendium by Earl Leslie Griggs is in Griggs and Clifford H. Prator, eds., *Henry Christophe and Thomas Clarkson: A Correspondence* (Berkeley and Los Angeles, 1952), 3–37 (p. 34 for Dessalines's gesture).

with the island in 1806, at a time of mounting tension with Great Britain; passage of the ban represented principally a victory for Jeffersonian Republicans unsympathetic to maritime interests.[2]

These vagaries of diplomacy were not accurately reflective of American opinion about the revolt. Americans had recently been rebels, were noted in the world as such, and knew it. Only a handful were willing to spell out completely the obvious implications, as one member of the Pennsylvania legislature did during a debate in 1791 on sending aid to St. Domingo planters: "it would be inconsistent on the part of a free nation to take measures against a people who had availed themselves of the only means they had to throw off the yoke of the most atrocious slavery; if one treats the insurrection of the negroes as rebellion, what name can be given to that insurrection of Americans which secured their independence?"[3] What name indeed? Most Americans, however, were reluctant to admit the exactness of the parallel.

Although far from being typical, a few participants in the flourishing antislavery movement actually welcomed the prospect of Negroes winning their own freedom. The monthly *American Museum*, which frequently carried antislavery pieces, printed in November 1792 a brief note by J. P. Martin entitled "Rights of Black Men" which directly praised the fighting efforts of St. Domingo slaves. Later that year the magazine published a poem which characterized the revolt as just retribution for the slave trade. Elsewhere, Theodore Dwight and the Reverend David Rice of Kentucky both cited it as proof of the evil nature of slavery. One anonymous author accused the creole planters of bringing on the current barbarities by their lust and cruelties and by enslaving the Negroes in the first place. The mulattoes, he explained, had become hostile because they had been treated as belonging to a lower rank than white men. In 1794 even the cautious Abolition Convention in Philadelphia cited St. Domingo as evidence telling against slavery. In general, though, abolitionists handled the revolt with extreme

2. Rayford W. Logan, *The Diplomatic Relations of the United States with Haiti, 1776–1891* (Chapel Hill, 1941), 1–183; Ludwell L. Montague, *Haiti and the United States, 1714–1938* (Durham, N. C., 1940), 29–46; Mary Treudley, "The United States and Santo Domingo, 1789–1866," *Journal of Race Development*, 7 (1916), 83–145, 220–74. Diplomatic recognition was withheld from Haiti until 1862 (when southerners could no longer block it), the only prolonged American refusal to follow the *de facto* principle until President Wilson found a Mexican dictator morally objectionable.

3. Reported by Jean de Ternant to Comte de Montmorin, Phila., Sept. 30, 1791, Frederick J. Turner, ed., *Correspondence of the French Ministers to the United States, 1791–1797* (Amer. Hist. Assoc., *Annal Report* [1903], II), 53, translated.

wariness, well aware of its explosive character. The Convention especially, conscious that its pronouncements might be regarded as the authoritative voice of antislavery, scrupulously avoided endorsing the revolt. Its members, with interests vested in southern emancipation, knew that a few indiscreet words would blast their hopes.[4]

Significantly, only a handful of antislavery advocates seized upon the Negro revolt to make an obvious and normally congenial point about Negroes. Two months before the outbreak in St. Domingo the *American Museum* published an "Account of a Plot by the Negroes of Goree, to Destroy All the White People on the Island." The anonymous writer explained that he wished to prove the error of those assertions "that the negroes are a distinct race of men, every way inferior to the whites; that their mental powers are weak, and unfit for great enterprises; and that they are destitute of genius and courage." In two other antislavery pieces, final establishment of Negro rule in St. Domingo was utilized to demonstrate the Negro's equal capacities, especially his courage and military aptitude. Most abolitionists, however, realized that to adopt this line of reasoning was to contract with a highly dangerous ally.[5]

Virtually the last note of positive approbation for Negro revolt was sounded in 1796 from a safe corner in the *Rural Magazine: or, Vermont Repository.*

> Whips, chains, swords, so long in tyrants' hands,
> Are now destroying—Is this more than just?
> If blacks are cruel, vengeful, and unfeeling,
> And deal to Christians terrors, sword, and fire,
> As they now strive to break their galling yokes—
> Do they not act from Christian precedent—
> Wrote, round the globe ten thousand times, in blood?[6]

This was all very well in Vermont, but elsewhere in the United States the appalling atrocities helped turn virtually everyone

4. J. P. Martin, "Rights of Black Men," *Amer. Museum*, 12 (1792), 299–300; "Lines on the Devastation of St. Domingo," *ibid.*, 12 (Appendix I, 1792), 13–14; Dwight, *An Oration before "The Connecticut Society,"* 18–19; Rice, *Slavery Inconsistent with Justice*, 9; *An Inquiry into the Causes of the Insurrection of the Negroes in the Island of St. Domingo* . . . (London, reprinted Phila., 1792), *passim; Minutes Abolition Convention* (1794), 23.

5. *Amer. Museum*, 11 (1792), 304–7, Goree being just off Senegal, West Africa; McLeod, *Negro Slavery Unjustifiable*, 22; "On the Consequences of Abolishing the Slave Trade to the West Indian Colonies," *Literary Magazine and American Register*, 4 (1805), 379.

6. "Reflections on the Slavery of the Negroes, Addressed to the Conscience of Every American Citizen," *Rural Magazine: or, Vermont Repository*, 2 (1796), 360, by "L.B.C." of Arlington, Bennington Co.

against the rebellion. The Quakers predominating in the antislavery movement were of course unable to applaud the scenes of violence on the island. Indeed, in the late 1790's the entire antislavery movement was clearly being debilitated by the news from St. Domingo.

As much as they were repelled by events in the island, Americans remained fascinated. The popular press regaled its readers with tales of horrible atrocities ("Who can read this and not drop a tear?") .[7] St. Domingo assumed the character of a terrifying volcano of violence, liable to new eruption at any moment. A single Negro rebellion was bad enough, but this was never-ending, a nightmare dragging on for years. Worst of all, the blacks were successful, and for the first time Americans could see what a community really looked like upside down.

The awful consequences of social inversion were dramatized in 1793 when refugees from Cap Français came streaming into American ports. In a fashion since become traditional, Americans turned out to aid the impoverished victims of revolutionary terror. Public subscriptions were raised, with Norfolk, Baltimore, Philadelphia, and New York leading the parade of philanthropy. Newark offered shoes. Relief was voted by the legislatures of Massachusetts, Pennsylvania, Maryland, Virginia, North and South Carolina, and by the federal Congress. This generosity was not entirely a matter of succoring fellow white men; refugees were in distress, and it was widely recognized that the disaster at Cap Français had resulted from conflicts more complex than simple slave rebellion. A report in the *State Gazette of South-Carolina* on the crowds of French at Norfolk gravely described the tragic plight of refugees driven from their homes "by the violence of political feuds." [8]

2. NON-IMPORTATION OF REBELLION

Hand in hand with these generosities, the year 1793 saw growth of a peculiar uneasiness, especially in Virginia where many refugees had congregated. In Richmond one Virginian deposed that he had overheard two Negroes discussing a plot against the whites

---

7. Annapolis *Md. Gaz.*, Apr. 19, 1792.

8. July 29, 1793; Aug. 12, 1793 (shoes) ; Annapolis *Md. Gaz.*, July 11, Aug. 22, 29, Nov. 28, 1793; Roberts, trans. and eds., *Moreau de St. Méry's Journey*, 50; *Annals of Congress*, 3d Cong., 1st sess., 153, 169–73, 349–52, 1417–19; Treudley, "U. S. and Santo Domingo," *Jour. Race Development*, 7 (1916) , 103–15; Frances S. Childs, *French Refugee Life in the United States, 1790–1800; An American Chapter of the French Revolution* (Baltimore, 1940) .

and referring to what the slaves had accomplished in the "French Island." That same year another citizen wrote the governor that "since the melancholy affair at Hispaniola" the inhabitants of the lower counties "have been repeatedly alarmed by some of their Slaves having attempted to raise an Insurrection, which was timely suppressed in this county by executing one of the principal advisors of the Insurrection." Similar alarms were raised in Charleston, where there were also many refugees. The meddlesome minister of the Jacobin government, Edmond Genêt, reported home in October that American slaveowners were terrified by the Negro insurrection in St. Domingo.[9] Two years later in Savannah there was a mass meeting of citizens aroused by reports of vessels arriving with "seasoned negroes" from the West Indies.[10]

Americans were the more alarmed when they discovered, as they thought, the vectors of the insurrectionary plague. Refugees from St. Domingo were bringing in their slaves. In October 1793 the *New-York Journal, and Patriotic Register* reported, "They write from Charleston (S. C.) that the NEGROES have become very insolent, in so much that the citizens are alarmed, and the militia keep a constant guard. It is said that the St. Domingo negroes have sown those seeds of revolt, and that a magazine has been attempted to be broken open." Two months later Secretary of State Thomas Jefferson wrote to warn the governor of South Carolina of two mulattoes coming from St. Domingo to incite insurrection. Jefferson never lost his conviction that St. Domingo might easily fall as a spark in the tinder box of the South. When Congress passed a bill opening trade with Toussaint in 1799 he commented to Madison, "We may expect therefore black crews, and supercargoes and missionaries thence into the southern states. . . . If this combustion can be introduced among us under any veil whatever, we have to fear it." [11] Similarly, John Cowper of Norfolk knew a dangerous black when he saw one; he wrote Governor Monroe in 1802 to express his own and his neighbors' consternation at the presence of French Negroes "whose dispositions, I apprehend, will be influenced by the accounts which are daily arriving and published concerning the

9. Palmer, ed., *Cal. Va. State Papers*, VI, 452–53, 651; Aptheker, *Revolts*, 96–97; Phillips, "South Carolina Federalists," *Amer. Hist. Rev.*, 14 (1908–09) , 734–35; Genêt to Minister of Foreign Affairs, N. Y., Oct. 7, 1793, Turner, ed., *Correspondence of French Ministers*, 245–46.

10. Charleston *City Gazette & Daily Advertiser*, July 9, 1795.

11. *New York Journal, & Patriotic Register*, Oct. 16, 1793; Phila., Dec. 23, 1793, Andrew A. Lipscomb and Albert E. Bergh, eds., *The Writings of Thomas Jefferson*, 20 vols. (Washington, 1903) , IX, 275–76; [Phila.], Feb. 12, 1799, Ford, ed., *Works of Jefferson*, IX, 39.

horrid scenes of St. Domingo." Cowper knew that "your Excellency" would understand his concern; Norfolk, he added meaningfully, was liable to fire. Three years later some citizens of that city apprehensively reported to the Assembly that "the black population of the burrough hath received a very formidable accession from the Island of St. Domingo." [12]

Uneasiness concerning French Negroes seems to have overtaken Virginia especially; but for some reason, Virginia was the only southern state not to adopt preventive measures. By comparison Maryland, which in 1792 had allowed refugees to bring in their slaves, took action in 1797 against what by then seemed a menace. Many French slaves in Baltimore, a new law declared emphatically, were disorderly and dangerous; those seized on suspicion by Baltimore authorities, if not removed from Maryland by their owners, were to be sold to the West Indies. Other states in the South were inhospitable from the first, perhaps conscious of greater vulnerability. In 1794 South Carolina barred entry of free Negroes from the West Indies or any part of the Americas except the United States. Georgia banned entrance of any Negroes from the West Indies and the Floridas in 1793; three years later the militia was authorized to seize any who had entered illegally. Moreau de St. Méry, onetime resident of St. Domingo, remarked in 1798 on Georgians' special fear of Negroes from Port-au-Prince. Apparently the entire Caribbean area was thought to be contaminated, a not inaccurate assessment perhaps, since Negroes had rebelled against outnumbered Europeans in several island colonies. In 1795 North Carolina barred entry of slaves from the West Indies over fifteen years old, traditionally the age at which white boys were considered fit for military duty. When South Carolina resumed slave importation in 1803 the legislature was at great pains to see that no cargo contained the seeds of rebellion. No colored person from the West Indies or South America was to be imported; and no colored person who had ever lived in a French West Indian island might enter South Carolina. No male slave over fifteen might be brought in from another state without a certificate attesting to good character and that he had never "been concerned in any insurrection or rebellion." [13] Such thoroughness bespoke genuine apprehension.

12. Palmer, ed., *Cal. Va. State Papers*, IX, 287; Johnston, Race Relations in Virginia, 96, citing Virginia Archives, Legislative Petitions, no. 4907, Norfolk, Dec. 8, 1805, Va. State Lib., Richmond. See also Palmer, ed., *Cal. Va. State Papers*, VI, 490.

13. Maxcy, ed., *Laws Md.*, II, 395–96; Cooper and McCord, eds., *Statutes S. C.*, VII, 433; *A Digest of the Laws of the State of Georgia, From* [*1755*] . . . *to the Year 1798, Inclusive, and the Principal Acts of 1799* . . . (Phila., 1800), 530,

That same year, 1803, the menace received national attention. The House of Representatives was memorialized by some inhabitants of Wilmington, North Carolina, concerning the arrival of Negroes and mulattoes from the French island of Guadaloupe, which had recently been shaken by a slave rebellion. The anxious petitioners claimed "that, in the opinion of the memorialists, much danger to the peace and safety of the people of the Southern States of the Union in particular, is justly to be apprehended from the admission of persons of that description into the United States, from the West India Islands"; and they prayed such action as Congress might deem fit. Immediately a committee of five Representatives was appointed, one member from each coastal southern state—a highly unusual procedure. The committee's report, to which the House assented without division, somberly stated "That the system of policy stated in the said memorial to exist, and to be now pursued in the French colonial governments of the West Indies, is fraught with danger to the peace and safety of the United States." In short order a bill was introduced which would have barred "any negro, mulatto, or other person of color" from the ports of states which legally prohibited their entrance. Not surprisingly, there was objection to such a sweeping measure. John Bacon of Massachusetts said the bill abridged the rights of free Negroes; New Jersey's James Mott and others thought it unconstitutional. Accordingly the bill was altered, over the protests of some southern members, to include only "any negro, mulatto, or other person of color, not being a native, a citizen, or registered seaman of the United States, or seamen, natives of countries beyond the Cape of Good Hope." All speakers agreed that the incipient menace must be countered in some fashion. The Senate similarly recognized where interests lay, for named to its three-man committee for consideration of the bill were senators from North and South Carolina and Georgia. The bill passed the Senate without division. Fear could scarcely be allayed by act of Congress, however, and several years later southern congressmen were still crying up the same danger.[14] In

---

601; Roberts, trans. and eds., *Moreau de St. Méry's Journey*, 308; Iredell and Martin, comps., *Acts N.-C.*, II, 79; Cooper and McCord, eds., *Statutes S. C.*, VII, 449–51. See also R. H. Taylor, "Slave Conspiracies in North Carolina," *N. C. Hist. Rev.*, 5 (1928), 25–26. After the Revolution, the age for militia service in North Carolina was raised from 16 to 18. Clark, ed., *State Recs. N. C.*, XXIV, 358, 710, XXV, 334; Iredell and Martin, comps., *Acts N.-C.*, II, 159. The lower age was evidently thought safer with slaves.

14. *Annals of Congress*, 7th Cong., 2d sess., 100, 101, 207, 385–86, 423–24, 459, 460–61, 467–73, 525, 534, 1564–65, 9th Cong., 1st sess., 30–31, 360. Southerners were still referring to the horrors of St. Domingo in the 1850's.

1805 Senator James Jackson of Georgia declared heatedly that "the honorable gentleman from Connecticut had been pleased to term his fears bugbears, [and it] might be no bugbear to him, safe and remote from the scene of action, near New Haven; but that it was a serious bugbear to him, and would be to the whole southern country, where the horrid scenes of that island would be reacted, their property destroyed, and their families massacred." [15]

Had Americans successfully shut out every dangerous West Indian Negro, they would still have felt themselves in jeopardy. Complete quarantine was impossible, for while news traveled slowly in the eighteenth century, some governments were unwilling and none were efficient enough to erect an effective iron curtain. Most Negroes were screened off to some degree by illiteracy, but many slaves lived so close to whites that they could hardly miss picking up topics of general conversation. Some Negroes, moreover, could read; it was advantageous if one's trusted slave could do so—if one could trust him. And it certainly was no comfort that literacy among free Negroes was more common than among slaves.

It was therefore an important result of the reverberating disaster of St. Domingo that many Americans came increasingly to feel that slavery was a closed subject, entirely unsuitable for frank discussion. Southern delegates in Congress began to claim that public airing of matters bearing on slavery was downright dangerous. In the midst of heated debate on the free Negro petition of 1800 an angry John Rutledge threw off the cloak of caution to bare the alarming facts: "There have been emissaries amongst us in the Southern States"; Rutledge cried, "they have begun their war upon us; an actual organization has commenced; we have had them meeting in their club rooms, and debating on that subject, and determinations have been made. It might be wrong in me to mention these things, because many of those people can read and write, and will be informed of what I am now saying, which they think I did not know, but knowing, I am determined to make use of." In a similar vein, the Richmond *Recorder* announced that American editors had been fomenting restlessness among Virginia's slaves by reprinting the St. Domingo constitution.[16] The ostentatiousness of all this caution is suggestive: beyond a reasoned fear of domestic insurrection seems to have lain a desire to banish the reality of St. Domingo.

But of course no one could forget. The height of feeling came

15. *Ibid.*, 9th Cong., 1st sess., 37.
16. *Ibid.*, 6th Cong., 1st sess., 242; Richmond *Recorder*, Nov. 10, 1802.

with complete Negro independence in the island, for now the worst
had happened; even the finest Napoleonic armies had proved incapable of preventing it. St. Domingo suggested an awful progression
in racial slavery: white rule, insurrection, black usurpation. Southerners were unwilling to concede inevitability to the process, for
obvious reasons, but the possibility of such progression could
scarcely be denied. Forthright description of the possibility was left
to antislavery northerners, like David Bard of Pennsylvania, arguing in 1804 for the tax on imported slaves.

> And what is to be expected from the people of this description, but that
> they will some day, and especially if their importation continues, produce a
> disturbance that may not be easily quieted, or kindle a flame that may not
> be readily extinguished. . . . If they are ignorant, they are, however,
> susceptible of instruction, and capable of becoming proficients in the art of
> war. To be convinced of this we have only to look at St. Domingo.
> There the negroes felt their wrongs, and have avenged them; they
> learned the rights of man, and asserted them; they have wrested the power
> from their oppressors, and have become masters of the island. If they are
> unarmed, they may be armed; European Powers have armed the Indians
> against us, and why may they not arm the negroes? [17]

Negro independence was so patently dangerous that there was no
necessity of thinking through exactly how it might possibly be
transmitted to American soil. No one seems to have pointed out, for
instance, that in St. Domingo the blacks outnumbered whites and
mulattoes combined by seven to one. Most northerners somehow
felt that they too had a stake in quarantining Haiti. In Congress in
1805, Senator George Logan of Pennsylvania asked, "is it sound
policy to cherish the black population of St. Domingo whilst we
have a similar population in our Southern States, in which should
an insurrection take place, the Government of the United States is
bound to render effectual aid to our fellow citizens in that part of
the Union?" Cherish? The new republic, exclaimed Pennsylvania's
Joseph Clay, was "black despotism and usurpation." For the South,
John W. Eppes of Virginia rattled the windows with a fanfare of
indignation: "Some gentlemen would declare St. Domingo free; if
any gentleman harbors such sentiments let him come forward
boldly and declare it. In such case, he would cover himself with
detestation. A system that would bring immediate and horrible
destruction on the fairest portion of America." [18] Eppes's concluding
phrase revealed how rapidly Negro slavery was pushing southerners

17. *Annals of Congress*, 8th Cong., 1st sess., 996.
18. *Annals of Congress*, 9th Cong., 1st sess., 29, 512, 515. See also Richmond
Enquirer, Jan. 15, 1805.

into a stance so familiar in the nineteenth century and, indeed, in the twentieth.

3. THE CONTAGION OF LIBERTY

Especially striking in all this bluster was the total lack of surprise that rebellion had occurred. For one thing, many Americans living in 1800 were old rebels; if rebellion had taken place in America, why not France and St. Domingo? Americans were disposed to regard their revolutionary doctrine of natural rights as highly contagious. Shortly after the Revolution was sealed at the peace table in 1783, the Reverend Ezra Stiles confidently predicted the spread of freedom to Europe: "Great and extensive will be the happy effects of this warfare, in which we have been called in providence to fight out, not the liberties of america only, but the liberties of the world itself. The spirited and successful stand which we have made against tyranny, will prove the salvation of *england* and *ireland:* and by teaching all sovereigns the danger of irritating and trifling with the affections and loyalty of their subjects, introduce clemency, moderation, and justice into public government at large through europe." As Jefferson had announced grandly to the citizens of Alexandria upon his return from Paris to the United States in 1790, "It is indeed an animating thought that, while we are securing the rights of ourselves and our posterity, we are pointing out the way to struggling nations who wish, like us, to emerge from their tyrannies also." And at about the same time, before the outbreak of rebellion in St. Domingo, Stiles blithely welcomed "the Inoculation of Germany, the Baltic Kingdoms, and all Europe with the epidemical contagion of Liberty the Rights of Man!"

Several years later, of course, Americans had grown rather less enthusiastic about the course that revolution seemed to be taking. Yet they remained deeply convinced that rebellion was infectious and now had reason to see that they might themselves be attacked in their peculiar vulnerability. By 1797 a deeply disturbed Jefferson fretted that "if something is not done, and soon done, we shall be the murderers of our own children . . . ; the revolutionary storm, now sweeping the globe, will be upon us, and happy if we make timely provision to give it an easy passage over our land. From the present state of things in Europe and America, the day which begins our combustion must be near at hand; and only a single spark is wanting to make that day to-morrow." From the very first, St. Domingo seemed a threat to American security. In 1791 when that colony's legislature requested armed assistance of South Carolina's Governor Charles Pinckney, he forwarded the plea to President Washington with the comment that if the situation in that island were not checked it would become "a flame which will extend to all the neighbouring islands, and may eventually prove not a very pleasing or agreeable example to the Southern States." [19]

Americans were fully aware where the "epidemical contagion" of "the rights of man" had originated. By definition these rights belonged to all men, despite the lurking temptation to regard them as essentially Anglo-American in origin and character. For Americans particularly, denial of the universal applicability of natural rights would have deprived their Revolution of its broader meaning and of its claim upon the attention of the world. Denial would have shrunk the new nation from a grand experiment to an episodic instance of political degeneration. If men throughout the globe possessed a right to liberty, there was no good reason why they should not fight for it. Americans had shown the way. The validity of the revolutionary logic had been tellingly confirmed by the manner in which rebellion in the island colony had actually begun. Who was to say where all this would stop?

Not that Americans were eager to spell out the dynamics of rebelliousness. Though consciously the heirs of revolution, as custodians of a new government they were perforce no longer revolutionary, at least not at home. Daniel Shays and the Pennsylvania Whiskey Boys had shown once again that every revolution must suppress its successors. There is no need to label the new mood a reaction; a doctrine of revolution simply no longer served American interests and was, indeed, inimical to them. Americans had not abandoned their allegiance to colonial wars of independence, but the menace of St. Domingo helped produce a novel hesitancy about revolutions in general that was strengthened in some quarters by the French Revolution in particular.

Given provocation some Americans were willing publicly to diagnose the pattern of contagion in order to attack it. The bitter election campaign of 1800 provided ample stimulus. Federalists, motivated by partisanship, linked slave rebellion with Jacobinism, which was to claim that Jeffersonian Republicans fomented slave

19. Ezra Stiles, *The United States Elevated to Glory and Honor* . . . (New Haven, 1783) , 48; Boyd, ed., *Papers of Jefferson*, XVI, 225; Morgan, *Ezra Stiles*, 455–56; Jefferson to St. George Tucker, Monticello, Aug. 28, 1797, Ford, ed., *Works of Jefferson*, VIII, 335; Pinckney quoted in Rogers, *William Loughton Smith*, 249.

revolt. Robert Goodloe Harper wrote to his constituents in South
Carolina that the French were planning to organize a black inva-
sion from St. Domingo against the southern states. The Federalist
Boston Gazette derisively labeled a conspiracy in Virginia "only a
branch of the French system of fraternity." Warming to its work the
paper continued, "If any thing will correct and bring to repentance
old hardened sinners in Jacobinism, it must be an *insurrection of
their slaves.*" A later issue carried a little item entitled "Natural
Cause of the Insurrection of the Negroes" in which the author
gleefully described a house slave overhearing conversation on natural rights (Jacobinism) at a southern dinner table and carrying it
to his fellows. A similar view of the "natural cause" of revolution
was advanced by Federalist John Rutledge during debate on the
Quaker petition of 1797: "considering the present extraordinary
state of the West India Islands and of Europe, he should insist that
'sufficient for the day is the evil thereof,' and that they ought to shut
their door against any thing which had a tendency to produce the
like confusion in this country." [20] From another quarter, Pennsylvania's David Bard, leading the fight to tax slave imports in 1804,
paraded the popular dinner-table theory of transmission.

> Gentlemen tell us, though I can hardly think them serious, that the
> people of this description can never systematize a rebellion. I will not
> mention facts, it is sufficient to say that experience speaks a different
> language—the rigor of the laws, and the impatience of the slaves will
> mutually increase each other, until the artifices of the one are exhausted,
> and until, on the other hand, human nature sinks under its wrongs, or
> obtains the restoration of its rights. The negroes are in every family; they
> are waiting on every table; they are present on numerous occasions when
> the conversation turns on political subjects, and cannot fail to catch ideas
> that will excite discontentment with their condition.[21]

Few Americans could disagree.

The Negro as potential rebel was of course presumed to crave
liberty. Indeed if there was one thing about which Americans of the
eighteenth century were certain (in fact there were a great many) it
was that men everywhere yearned for freedom. Nothing would have
surprised them more than to learn that later generations spoke
knowingly of the contented slave and, in the twentieth century, of
man's urge to escape from freedom. Surely God would not have

20. Phila., Mar. 20, 1799, Elizabeth Donnan, ed., *Papers of James A. Bayard,
1796–1815* (Amer. Hist. Assoc., *Annual Report* [1913], II), 90; *Boston Gazette*,
Oct. 9, 16, also 23, 1800; *Annals of Congress*, 5th Cong., 2d sess., 667.
21. *Annals of Congress*, 8th Cong., 1st sess., 995–96. Bard's claim that the
slaves' ability to organize had been questioned may have been rhetorical; the
records of debate show no such doubt.

conferred the natural right of liberty on all men and then failed to provide them with the desire to realize it! Not that Americans were blind to tyranny: having brandished pens and swords in the cause of freedom, they were hypersensitive to its enemies. They disagreed among themselves as to the most likely quarter from which the threat of tyranny might be expected, but the flintiest of aristocrats were among the first to acknowledge that the lower orders had an appetite for freedom. Indeed, from their standpoint this appetite was all too saliently characteristic of the lowly. From everyone's standpoint, too, this appetite was inherent in slaves, nonetheless real for being unwelcome.

The firmness of this assumption was demonstrated when in 1804 Congress debated the proper form of government for newly acquired Louisiana. The bill under consideration provided for a governor and council both appointed by the president. In the House there was strenuous objection that the territory ought to be permitted a legislature, and debate turned on the question whether the inhabitants were ready for some measure of democracy and self-government. Members who opposed a legislature had much to say on habit-forming French and Spanish tyranny and the consequent incapability of this foreign population to rule themselves. Tennessee's George Washington Campbell challenged this argument in the following terms.

One gentleman observes, that we ought to regard the people of Louisiana as totally distinct from, and as not possessed of any similar habits with ourselves. I trust, however, we shall consider them as a part of the human species. I believe the gentleman will find the human character the same in different parts of the globe. If this principle had been pursued, liberty had never flourished; if the people had never enjoyed liberty till they were ripe for it, how many ages of darkness would have passed away! But the fact is, the people suffer oppression to an astonishing degree—despotism grinds them down till human nature can endure no more, and then they break their chains in a revolt. I therefore can see no force in the argument of waiting till they are ripe for liberty. . . . I trust, therefore, we shall extend to them the same rights as are enjoyed by the other Territories.

Federalist Benjamin Huger of South Carolina, far from happy over this chitchat about self-government, grumbled that the people of the territory "ought to be looked upon as a certain portion of people among us and treated as such." Upon challenge from a young Virginia Republican, John G. Jackson, Huger withdrew his unfortunate analogy, but Jackson would not let the matter rest. "Admitting they are not to be compared to the slaves of the Southern States, or to those human beings who are made the subject of traffic, gentlemen allege that a system of free government will be inconvenient to them. I believe they are wrong in this position, and that man is the same, whether born in the United States or on the banks of the Ganges, under an African sun or on the banks of the Mississippi, and that a love of liberty is implanted in his nature." Jackson pressed on by drawing a striking parallel to the people of the territory.

Allow, for the sake of argument, that the people are slaves. This does not prove that they are not fit objects of a free Government. Look at the ensanguined plains of St. Domingo; the oppressed have there broken their chains, and resumed their long lost rights. The example proves more than a volume. There, notwithstanding the great debasement of the human character, the sacred fire of liberty is not extinguished. Wherever it exists, sooner or later, it bursts forth into an irresistible flame, and consumes everything opposed to it. And are the subjects of a monarchy, the inhabitants of Louisiana, more deficient in manly sentiment than the people of St. Domingo?

Other speakers joined in to disagree with Jackson, saying that man everywhere was not necessarily capable of free self-government. Significantly, however, no one denied that men everywhere *desired* to govern themselves; such desire was axiomatic.[22]

This American axiom, long since less patently valid though no less holy than it was in 1800, was at that time firmly rooted in widely held convictions about the nature of man. The eighteenth-century cast of mind leaned toward universalizing mankind, toward Newtonizing, as it were, men into man. In small part, at least, this inclination represented a posture of intellectual defense against the shock of discovering that the world was filled with peoples who seemed not at all like one another. Americans were less ready than Europeans to adopt this stance, however, since they had much more immediate experience, pleasant and otherwise, with ethnic diversity; a thoughtful journey from, say, tidewater Virginia to the Kentucky frontier and thence through Pennsylvania to New York was well calculated to clear the head of wispy notions concerning man-in-general. On the other hand, Americans had undertaken a revolution in a day when divorce from one's rightful rulers demanded better grounds than simple cruelty. Reluctant to generalize and still attached to the glorious rights of Englishmen, they nonetheless had placed their independence on the platform of man's right to freedom. And what could be more obvious than that a natural right was bound to be naturally and rightly sought after?

22. *Ibid.*, 8th Cong., 1st sess., 1054–79, 1129–30 (Huger quoted by Jackson). Campbell's proposal for a legislature lost 37–43. That session Jackson (then just 26) also spoke for a tax on slave imports: 1031–32.

By the 1790's Europe had offered ample confirmation. The American Revolution was vindicated as something more than a family squabble or the effect of fortunate environment, though Americans were thoroughly conscious that it was both of these. In the convulsions of Europe and St. Domingo lay proof of their generalizations. And, paradoxically, the ethnic diversity of their own country, which lessened the itch to generalize about man, afforded further evidence that all men in fact craved liberty. The Indian's grave refusal to submit found echo in the frontiersman's truculent demand for elbowroom. When the Negro grasped desperately at freedom too, he confirmed America's great expectations as well as one of America's greatest fears.

4. SLAVE DISOBEDIENCE IN AMERICA

Nor were Americans' fearful expectations unfounded, though the usual difficulties prevail in any attempt to ascertain how much Negro rebellion there actually was in the new United States. Negro witnesses had obvious reason to distort the facts, the direction varying with whether the witness was himself implicated, and talk by white men about conspiracies was sometimes nothing but wildest rumor. On the other hand, news of actual conspiracies was frequently suppressed lest publication stimulate further unrest.[23] It is incontrovertibly evident, nonetheless, that a period of pronounced unrest among American slaves began not long after word arrived of racial turmoil in St. Domingo.

There were no revolts involving large numbers of Negroes for many years after the shudders which swept through the colonies just before mid-century. During the Revolution, British armies provided opportunities for escape to freedom but, almost surprisingly, no important slave uprisings took place. A period of continued quiet after the war abruptly terminated in the spring and summer of 1792. Virginia was most seriously affected. The governor received numerous requests for arms, and white men reported hearing muffled Negro conversations about the "French Island."[24] This was the first summer following news of the slave uprising in St. Domingo. The source of the effect seems clear, but it is utterly impossi-

---

23. Aptheker, *Revolts,* 155–58; and below, note 34.

24. Palmer, ed., *Cal. Va. State Papers,* V, 534–35, VI, 470, 488–90, 547; Aptheker, *Revolts,* 209–19. Perhaps the most serious incident during these 50 years occurred in Georgia (1774): four whites killed and three wounded, two slaves burned, other punishments unrecorded. Savannah *Ga. Gaz.,* Dec. 7, 1774. The Charleston *State Gazette of S.-C.,* July 22, 1793, reported a bloody, unsuccessful revolt aboard a Rhode Island slaver.

ble to tell whether white men or black men, or both, had been affected! Very occasionally, to be sure, reasonably decisive evidence
does come to light: Smith Snead wrote the governor on July 9 that
three slaves had been executed for their part in an attack on a member of a slave patrol.[25] But the vast bulk of information concerning
slave rebelliousness completely eludes certainty of interpretation.

It seems safe to say, however, that the typical pattern in the 1790's
was some fire and much smoke. Slave resistance rarely involved
large numbers, though this fact can scarcely be taken as indicating
that slaves were docile and contented. Indeed, slaves struck frequently at the oppressive white world around them, but in most
instances violence involved spontaneous outbursts on the part of
individuals or small groups. Even that common bane of the plantation owner, slave absenteeism, was usually a small-scale enterprise;
slaves ran away alone or in threes and fours, very rarely in groups as
large as a dozen. The newspapers which carried the ubiquitous
runaway advertisements not infrequently carried reports of more
alarming manifestations of slave discontent. The *Maryland Gazette*
in 1795, for example, took note of a "Horrid Murder" perpetrated
by a slave upon his master. Two years later the same paper reported
that Negroes had killed two white men on a Georgia plantation and
that a Negro woman in Maryland, upon hearing that her master's
will provided for her freedom should he leave no heirs, had enter-
prisingly poisoned his three children. In 1806 two Negroes killed an
overseer in Georgia; one was hanged and the other burned, tied to a
tree. Next year the Richmond *Enquirer* announced the trial of a
Negro girl for poisoning her master and mistress. Slaves sometimes
turned to arson: the great fire of 1793 in Albany was set by Negroes
who for some reason held a grudge against their owner; three were
executed.[26]

The present need, of course, is for quantitative studies of these
occurrences; we simply do not know how much this sort of thing
went on, though even the most cursory reading in the newspapers
suggests persuasively that there was enough of it to give contemporaries genuine cause for alarm. Some very rough statistics are available for Virginia, though there is little reason to think Virginia
typical. From 1783 to 1814 the state recompensed owners of 434
executed slaves, an average of fourteen per year. Thirty-one slaves

25. Palmer, ed., *Cal. Va. State Papers*, V, 625, also 555.
26. Annapolis *Md. Gaz.*, Mar. 5, 1795, Mar. 23, Apr. 27, 1797; John Melish,
Travels through the United States of America, . . . 1806 . . . 1811 . . ., [2d ed.]
(London, 1818), 39; Richmond *Enquirer*, Jan. 24, 1807; Edgar J. McManus, *A
History of Negro Slavery in New York* (Syracuse, 1966), 85; also Aptheker,
Revolts, 215.

were executed for murder of masters or overseers in the period 1786–1810, twenty for poisoning (1772–1810), seven for arson (1789–1810). These figures underrepresent actual occurrences, since they do not include slaves transported (fifty-seven, 1801–06), pardoned, taking their own lives, killed by masters or overseers or patrols, owned by non-citizens of the state, or not caught.[27] Though in most cases the violence perpetrated by slaves could not have been rationally regarded, by either the slaves or their masters, as attempts at freedom, one suspects these incidents must often have involved very little in the way of rationality on either side. Because Negroes were slaves, Negro violence was for both blacks and whites an attack on slavery.

Certainly Americans knew from grim experience that slaves could be dangerous as individuals, and in the South, at least, Americans were understandably apprehensive of slaves in combination. Toward the end of a hot summer in 1800 the long-dreaded disaster finally struck: Virginia was confronted with genuine rebellion. Led by a tall slave named "General" Gabriel, Negroes in the Richmond neighborhood collected what arms they could lay hands on and gathered themselves for a march on the capital. There is a compelling irony in the fact that some of the slaves seem to have been influenced by Christian training. The most talkative witness in the affair was "Ben alias Ben Woolfolk," who disclosed that at a meeting of the conspirators "I told them that I had heard in the days of old, when the Israelites were in service to King Pharaoh they were taken from him by the power of God, and were carried away by Moses." Apparently they hoped that capture of key points in the city would trigger a general revolt throughout the state and beyond. Their plans were frustrated by two Negroes who warned the appropriate authorities and by a torrential downpour which rendered a vital bridge impassable. The time was long past when such heavenly intervention was clearly purposeful, and Virginians knew themselves lucky to have escaped so easily. No whites or Negroes had been killed, but future safety demanded some salutary executions. Within six weeks the affair was officially closed by thirty to forty hangings, Gabriel, "the main spring and chief mover," on October 7.[28]

Virginians could not possibly permit themselves to doubt their ability to suppress any Negro revolt, but they were thoroughly

27. Johnston, Race Relations in Virginia, 250–52.
28. Woolfolk's disclosure is in Palmer, ed., *Cal. Va. State Papers*, IX, 151. Two accounts are Joseph C. Carroll, *Slave Insurrections in the United States, 1800–1865* (Boston, 1938), 47–57; and Aptheker, *Revolts*, 219–26. Some important

shaken by the magnitude of the Gabriel plot. While it confirmed their fears about the Negro, it jarred their picture of slavery and themselves. For they had rightly taken pride in the gradual amelioration of slavery. The revolt, some Virginians felt, should logically have come much earlier and, indeed, elsewhere than Virginia. Young Governor James Monroe thought it somewhat "strange" that "this novel and unexampled enterprise" had occurred in an enlightened day when slaves were better treated and there were relatively fewer of them. Sustaining these thoughts was a feeling of unrequited rectitude, and one can detect here the seeds of an important change in attitude toward slave revolt. Yet Monroe went on to say, in words which were not yet a sterile formula, "Unhappily while this class of people exists among us we can never count with certainty on its tranquil submission." [29]

It is instructive to compare Monroe's remarks with those of Virginians a generation later. During the famous debate on slavery in 1832, which was partly a post-mortem on the last major slave rebellion in the United States, antislavery members of the legislature still sometimes referred to the "continual and abiding danger of insubordination from the natural love of liberty, which the great Author of our being has imparted to all his creatures." Yet this same speaker, George W. Summers, could also say, "I know that many of them, perhaps the larger portion of them, are content with their destiny." Proslavery members were far more confident of slave contentedness—or rather they claimed to be. They described the Negro in language which would have seemed nonsensical in 1800. James H. Gholson claimed that "Our slave population is not only a happy one, but it is a contented, peaceful and harmless one." [30] This

---

accessible sources are Stanislaus M. Hamilton, ed., *The Writings of James Monroe*, 7 vols. (N. Y., 1898–1903), III, 201–18, 234–43, 246–48, 261, 266, 292–95; Palmer, ed., *Cal. Va. State Papers*, IX, 128, 134, 138–39, 140–74; *Virginia Senate Journal* (1800); James T. Callender to Thomas Jefferson, Richmond Jail, Sept. 13, 1800, Worthington C. Ford, ed., *Thomas Jefferson and James Thomson Callender, 1798–1802* (Brooklyn, 1897), 25–27. The slave Ben Woolfolk gave interesting testimony on slave aims: "As far as I understood all the whites were to be massacred, except the Quakers, the Methodists, and the Frenchmen, and they were to be spared on account as they conceived of their being friendly to liberty, and also they had understood that the French were at war with this country. . . . They intended also to spare all the poor white women who had no slaves." Palmer, ed., *Cal. Va. State Papers*, IX, 152. Ben Woolfolk was the principal Negro witness willing to discourse endlessly and perhaps not always accurately about plot and plotters.

29. *Virginia Senate Journal* (1800), 11–13.

30. Joseph C. Robert, *The Road from Monticello; A Study of the Virginia Slavery Debate of 1832* (Durham, N. C., 1941), 67, 85, 87.

after the most serious slave insurrection in American history! In 1832 Virginians were strongly tempted to blame slave discontent on abolitionists, since it could no longer be regarded as coming from slaves themselves.

For most Americans the lesson to be drawn from the Gabriel plot was that "we can never count with certainty" on the Negro's "tranquil submission." As an anonymous Virginian declared firmly several years after the plot, slaves "entertain a rooted aversion to their masters." [31] When news of American slave unrest reached Ambassador William Vans Murray in The Hague he unburdened his fears to his friend John Quincy Adams. "A young South Carlinian who was with me when I had the papers observed, that he had long expected this misfortune, and had often wondered that they had not risen before. Certainly there are motives sufficiently obvious," Murray continued, "independent of the contagion of Jacobinism, to account for an insurrection of slaves; but I doubt not that the eternal clamour about liberty in V[irginia] and S[outh] C[arolina] both, has matured the event which has happened." [32] Whether the contagion was Jacobin was open to argument, but fear of it was certainly real enough. Upon hearing of the Virginia conspiracy, Mississippi Territory Governor Winthrop Sargent discreetly penned a private letter describing the plot and urging precautions, and then had printed copies sent round to a hundred leading planters. Sargent stressed "the impolicy of unnecessarily alarming *them,* by informations upon a *subject* which mild and wise Treatment may happily long keep from their Views and wishes." [33] Most striking of all reactions to the Gabriel plot was the virtually complete silence in the Charleston press, a silence not attributable to lack of interest.[34]

American reaction to the revolt was distorted because the

31. Richmond *Va. Argus,* Jan. 7, 1806.

32. Dec. 9, 1800, Worthington C. Ford, ed., "Letters of William Vans Murray to John Quincy Adams, 1797–1803," Amer. Hist. Assoc., *Annual Report* (1912), 663. Murray referred to disturbances in South Carolina as well as Virginia, though his news concerning South Carolina was grossly exaggerated. See Carroll, *Insurrections,* 66–67; Aptheker, *Revolts,* 151.

33. Grove Plantation, Mississippi Territory, Nov. 16, 1800, Dunbar Rowland, ed., *The Mississippi Territorial Archives, 1789–1803* (Nashville, 1905), 311–12. Sargent saw the hand of foreign influence and the shadow of St. Domingo. To my knowledge this was the most optimistic contemporary statement on the chances of avoiding slave revolt, but perhaps not, since "happily" had not then lost connection with the idea of chance ("haply").

34. Aptheker, *Revolts,* 158, found only one notice of the revolt, 75 words long, which reported executions of rebels in Virginia without mentioning they were Negroes. Equally distant Boston felt no such hesitation: for example *Boston Gaz.,* Oct. 13, 20, 1800.

Negroes' challenge came during the bitter contest for the presidency. Federalists were sure that this timing was far from coincidental, and they seized upon the insurrection (*"organized on the true French plan"*) as a cudgel for belaboring Jeffersonians. A contributor to the Fredericksburg *Herald* declared that "this dreadful conspiracy originates with some vile French Jacobins, aided and abetted by some of our own profligate and abandoned democrats. Liberty and equality have brought the evil upon us. A doctrine which, however intelligible, and admissible, in a land of freemen, is not only unintelligible and inadmissible, but dangerous and extremely wicked in this country, where every white man is a master, and every black man is a slave." The motivation was partisan, but one could hardly deny the force of the logic as the anonymous writer continued: "This doctrine, in this country, and in every country like this (as the horrors of St. Domingo have already proved) cannot fail of producing either a general insurrection, or a general emancipation. It has been most imprudently propagated at many of our tables, while our servants have been standing behind our chairs, for several years past. It has been, and is still preached by the Methodists, Baptists and others, from the pulpit, without any sort of reserve. What else then could we expect than what has happened?" [35] Republicans responded by accusing the Adams administration, not incorrectly, of supporting Toussaint.[36]

It was not long before Virginians realized that they were far from rid of danger. In 1802 several genuine conspiracies were unearthed; hangings that year ran to thirty-two—three times the annual norm.[37] Even in far-off Lexington, Kentucky, some anxious petitioners declared that the Negroes of the South "are strongly bent on insurrection" and asked strict enforcement of the town's laws.[38] Relative quiet in South Carolina and Georgia suggests that the more lenient slavery of the Upper South may have facilitated slave conspiracy; at any rate violence seems to have concentrated in

35. Phila. *Gazette of the United States*, Sept. 23, also Sept. 18, 1800; Fredericksburg *Virginia Herald*, Sept 23, 1800.

36. Partisan asperities may be traced in Richmond *Va. Argus*, Oct. 3, 1800; Charleston *Carolina Gazette*, Oct. 30, 1800; [Henry W. De Saussure], *Address to the Citizens of South-Carolina, on the Approaching Election of President and Vice-President of the United States. By a Federal Republican* (Charleston, 1800), 16–17; Aptheker, *Revolts*, 150–53.

37. Aptheker, *Revolts*, 228–30; Carroll, *Insurrections*, 58–64; Hamilton, ed., *Writings of Monroe*, III, 328–39, 344–49; *Virginia Senate Journal* (1801), 57–60; Palmer, ed., *Cal. Va. State Papers*, IX, 293–94, 296–311, 320.

38. Richard C. Wade, *The Urban Frontier: The Rise of Western Cities, 1790–1830* (Cambridge, Mass., 1959), 127.

Virginia and North Carolina. Citizens of the latter state had been apprehensive of slave unrest for a decade, and Gabriel's plot had strung their nerves to the highest pitch. When alarms rang in 1802, they jumped reactively. In heavily Negro Halifax County there was almost comical panic and recovery. A petition was forwarded to the governor requesting pardon for a Negro recently convicted of conspiracy; the petitioners now found the conspiracy to have been nonexistent in Halifax, though no doubt, they said, it was real enough in other parts of the state. In an impressive if undignified display of justice the petition had been eagerly signed by many citizens of Halifax, the entire court and two-thirds of the jury, and the state attorney who had prosecuted the Negro. The governor, showing rare judgment, granted the pardon.[39]

That same summer the *Raleigh Register* published an unusually levelheaded account of a conspiracy in Martin County which revealed that rumors could be handled more rationally. "J.R." undertook to set forth the true facts because, he said, some people had credited the wildest reports and others had believed none of the most sober. Some planters, he hinted, were financially interested in not having their slaves implicated. The plot had been laid for June 10. On the eighth, information from a neighboring county set off a flurry of rumors; the militia was called up and Negro males placed under guard. Then a special Committee of Enquiry took over. Allowing no communication among prisoners, the Committee first queried the youngest and told him that he had been implicated. A confession was obtained without lashes. This procedure was continued until twenty-five or thirty had been examined. Then the older leaders were brought before the Committee, most of whom had to be whipped into confession. Two were hanged after legal trial. Finally, every Negro was "chastised, more or less, according to his previous bad or good conduct, and ordered home." [40] Very tidy indeed, if it is correct to assume, as seems probable, that there was a real plot and that the Committee was not merely reviewing a parade of frightened Negroes telling white men what they needed to hear.

Violence and rumors of violence subsided somewhat after 1802, but not so far as to ease the public mind entirely. Violence was built

39. *Raleigh Register*, Aug. 24, 1802. For other North Carolina plots that year, *ibid.*, June 1, 22, 29, Aug. 10, 1802; Palmer, ed., *Cal. Va. State Papers*, IX, 307–8; Aptheker, *Revolts*, 231–32; Carroll, *Insurrections*, 67–70. For apprehensiveness in the 1790's, Iredell and Martin, comps., *Acts N.-C.*, II, 54, 80, 117; Taylor, "Slave Conspiracies in North Carolina," *N. C. Hist. Rev.*, 5 (1928), 23–24.

40. *Raleigh Register*, July 27, 1802.

into the system of racial slavery which rested, in the final analysis, on coercion. Violence perpetuated itself, permitting brutalities which contrasted anomalously with humanitarian amelioration. In 1805, for instance, North Carolina's Wayne County uncovered a Negro plot to poison whites and enslave the survivors. The authorities acted with exemplary justice. One woman was burned alive for poisoning her master, mistress, and two other white persons; three slaves were hanged, one transported, one "pilloried, whipped, nailed, and his ears cut off"; others were whipped or discharged. Fear seems to have been so great that there was no public protest.[41]

If white men rightly feared for their lives, they also feared for their women, but whether rightly is open to question. During the Virginia disturbances in 1802 one slave was reported as testifying that two Negroes intended to kill certain white men and take their wives. On the other hand another Negro's note of warning said all whites were to be killed, including "wemin and children," and a white man wrote that all white men between eight and eighty were supposed to die "and not a white woman on earth to live." The straightforward "J.R." of Martin County, however, reported the conspiratorial Negroes as saying they aimed at killing all white males over six or seven together with white and Negro women over a "certain age" but that "the young and handsome of the white women" they would "keep for themselves" and the young Negro women to be spared as "waiters."[42] Perhaps such reports were well founded. Hatred of the white man might easily have generated an urge to take his woman, to take the one liberty most emphatically denied. Perhaps the bewildered Negro conspirator under examination got the idea from his anxious questioner. Perhaps white reporters invented these assertions to satisfy their itch to discover Negroes libidinously yearning for white women. In fact, during this entire period of slave unrest there is no evidence of Negroes sexually assaulting white women. Though this lack is hardly final proof of anything, at very least it suggests that the danger of sexual violence by Negroes was exaggerated by white men. Certainly white

41. *Ibid.*, July 22, Aug. 12, 1805. Aptheker, *Revolts*, 241–42, cites other sources which give similar accounts. "Nailed" meant ears to the pillory before cropping.

42. Palmer, ed., *Cal. Va. State Papers*, IX, 294; Johnston, Race Relations in Virginia, 28, 52; *Raleigh Register*, July 27, 1802; also Richmond *Va. Argus*, Oct. 14, 1800. The 1831 Nat Turner insurrection killed more than 50 whites, but evidently there were no sexual attacks by slaves, despite opportunity. Aptheker, *Revolts*, 224n, found "that so far as the evidence shows there is no case of rape or attempted rape in the history of American Negro slave revolts."

men had compelling reasons to exaggerate. They had been doing so for a long time.

5. THE IMPACT OF NEGRO REVOLT

Certainly, too, there can be no doubt concerning the momentousness of the plots in their effect on white Americans. Gabriel, the terrible figure with the devastatingly ironic name, was set against a backdrop of Negro rebellion which included not only the "scenes of St. Domingo" but flashes of individual violence and revelations of conspiracies at home. The outburst of violence at the opening of the century had the immediate effect of hardening the determination of white Americans that slaves should have no opportunity for success. Virginia's slave code, which had been consolidated in 1792, received some reinforcement, but much of Virginia's response lay along other lines. In 1802 North Carolina passed a restrictive law hopefully preventive of conspiracies and insurrections. It was South Carolina, significantly, which responded to the heightened threat most vigorously, thereby demonstrating a willingness to meet the dangers of slavery head on. South Carolinians were committed to slavery and knew it. In December 1800 the Assembly enacted a stringent law which bore on all Negroes, free and slave. Negro gatherings for "mental instruction or religious worship" before dawn and after dark were prohibited outright, even if whites were present. Patrol regulations and the old requirement of an overseer for ten or more slaves were tightened up. A slave might be manumitted only with approval from a magistrate and five freeholders. The Assembly also clamped down on entry of slaves from other states and barred free Negroes entirely. The Assembly clearly went too far in its enthusiasm, for two years later it reacted favorably to petitions from "certain religious societies" by modifying the 1800 law so as to prohibit anyone from breaking up a meeting without a warrant before nine o'clock if a majority present were white. Just two years afterward in 1805, however, the legislature found occasion to denounce inflammatory writings and to declare that any person guilty of aiding slave insurrection should die for treason. Unlike the law of 1800, this latter act was probably a response to local disturbances. Georgia also passed a similar act the year before and strengthened patrol regulations the year after.[43]

43. Shepard, ed., *Statutes Va.*, I, 122–30 (1792), II, 279–80, 300 (1801); Carroll, *Insurrections*, 57 (Va.); Iredell and Martin, comps., *Acts N.-C.*, II, 200–201; Cooper and McCord, eds., *Statutes S. C.*, V, 503, VII, 436–49; *Laws State Ga. Since*

While South Carolina legislators gritted their teeth, elsewhere there was less assured determination. When South Carolina re-opened the slave trade the rest of the nation reacted as if orders had been placed for shiploads of rattlesnakes. Indeed, after the summer of 1800 the slave trade could be opposed solely on grounds of domestic danger, though there was no rush to deny its immorality. Thus the revolt heightened the already growing distinction being made between slavery and the slave trade and enabled men to reprobate the "inhuman traffic" without getting tangled up in dangerous principles about human rights. Slave insurrection joined in an unlikely partnership with humanitarianism to ensure legal termination of the trade which was now confirmed to be "impoli-tic" as well as "cruel."

A necessary concomitant was the weakening of abolition senti-ment. Virginia's Negro conspirators had not managed to kill a single white man but they did a remarkably effective job on Virgin-ian antislavery. Less than a month after disclosure of the Gabriel plot an anxious Elisha C. Dick wrote to Governor Monroe from Alexandria, home of an abolition society, that many free Negroes had come in from Maryland, that abolition societies were educating Negroes and filling them with ideas of equality, and that this was a patently dangerous combination.[44] Perhaps Dick did more than write letters; the Alexandria Society confessed some months later that the recent insurrection had forced abandonment of its Sunday School. The Virginia Abolition Society reported pessimistically that the plot had rendered its work much more difficult, an understate-ment at best. In 1805 a member of the defunct Alexandria Society specified the revolt as one cause of the Society's collapse, explaining gloomily, "We are in fact dead; and I may say, I have no hope of reanimation." [45]

While stressing the walloping impact of Negro insurrection on the antislavery movement, the inherent weaknesses and limitations of antislavery must be borne in mind; as the member of the Alexan-dria Society suggested, Negro revolt was (only) one cause of the Society's demise. The Gabriel plot was a blow to a movement which was already faltering badly. Yet even in the North the blow was

---

1800, 178, 333–34. For slave disturbances in South Carolina and Georgia, 1804–06, Jameson, ed., "Diary of Hooker," Amer. Hist. Assoc., *Annual Report* (1896), I, 881–82; "Chronicle of Memorable Occurrences, 1806–7," *American Register*, 1 (1806–07), separately paginated section, 10; Carroll, *Insurrections*, 70.

44. Sept. 26, 1800, Palmer, ed., *Cal. Va. State Papers*, IX, 178.

45. *Minutes Abolition Convention* (1801), 22, 32; (1805), 23.

almost audible. The Abolition Convention in Philadelphia, at its first meeting following the Virginia disaster, felt compelled to justify its cause. Pitching its address to the people of the South, the Convention fended off charges of subverting the laws and deprecated the recent insurrection while trying gingerly to transform it into an argument for gradual emancipation, amelioration, and education. From about 1803 there was a pronounced lull in Quaker antislavery activity; by then, it seemed plain that hapless Negroes rather than abolitionists were going to be martyred. Of the dwindling production of antislavery tracts after 1800, only one (anonymously) dared try bend the Gabriel plot to the antislavery bow.[46]

Of all reactions to slave insurrection by far the most complex and subtle occurred in Virginia. South Carolina, by comparison, reacted directly and with confident dispatch. Virginia displayed a hesitancy which betrayed inner conflict. Since the roots of Virginia's distress lay tangled in a multitude of factors other than revolt, including such diverse developments as the spread of Christianity among slaves, the beginnings of novel kinds of social separation, and the speculations of Thomas Jefferson and other natural philosophers in Europe and America, further discussion needs to be held in abeyance, except for the bald suggestion that Virginia reacted to a revolt of slaves by turning on freemen. That the freemen were Negroes affords striking demonstration that American slavery lay deeply enmeshed in problems of race which immeasurably complicated the dynamics of exploitation. No free Negroes were implicated in the Gabriel plot. During this period of slave agitation beginning in 1792 there seems to be no clear record of free Negroes actually involved in conspiracy of any kind.[47]

This was not, for Virginians or for Americans generally, the point. In the quarter century after the Revolution they had, many of them, contemplated the prospect of Negro freedom with diminishing equanimity as Negroes began to take a hand in the work.

46. *Ibid.* (1801) , 37–41, 45; [Humanitas], *Reflections on Slavery*, 7–8.
47. The most definite scrap of evidence which I have seen for free Negro involvement is thoroughly inconclusive: James Monroe wrote William Prentis (Richmond, Oct. 11, 1800) that "a man named Samuel Bird, a free mulatto of Hanover town, was arrested on suspicion of being concerned in the conspiracy of the negroes; he was sent here, commited to Jail, and finally discharged for want of evidence, it being decided that people of his own colour [i. e., Negroes], in slavery, could not give testimony against him. His son, a slave, was condemned, and executed yesterday." Hamilton, ed., *Writings of Monroe*, III, 215. This incident may have animated the Virginia Assembly when it passed laws restricting free Negroes in Jan. 1801, for included was a provision that slaves could now act as witnesses against free Negroes. Shepard, ed., *Statutes Va.*, II, 300.

The Revolution had entailed upon the institution of slavery a gigantic question mark and upon Americans the necessity of facing up to the prospect of what it would be like actually to have Negroes free. As they were forced to face this prospect they backed off from its inherent implications. In this period of economic and political crystallization, of successful and unsuccessful antislavery, and of reverberating revolts, whites and Negroes in America became separated from each other in ways which fit the pace and direction of the conglomerate pattern of social change of the post-Revolutionary era.

XI THE RESULTING PATTERN

OF SEPARATION

SHORTLY AFTER THE REVOLUTION, AMERICANS BEGAN haphazardly but with detectable acceleration to legislate Negroes into an ever-shrinking corner of the American community. Indications that Negroes were becoming more than ever walled off from white men fell into a pattern which coincided, roughly, with patterns of change in the economics of southern agriculture, national and sectional feeling, antislavery, and fear of slave revolt. For ten years after the war there were some signs of relaxation, but then came a trend which included tighter restrictions upon slaves and especially free Negroes, separation of the races at places of social gathering, and the founding of all-Negro churches. The American interracial mold was hardening into its familiar ante-bellum shape.

1. THE HARDENING OF SLAVERY

There was a period of uncertain eddying before the tide clearly turned. Before the mid-1790's many states extended to Negro slaves the right of trial by jury in capital cases.[1] In harmony with the spread of humanitarian feeling, some states made their slave codes more humane and occasionally less restrictive.[2] To prevent circumvention of their gradual emancipation laws, many northern states prohibited selling slaves out of state, thereby demonstrating

1. In the North, often in the gradual emancipation acts. *Laws State N. Y.*, II, 122; Hening, ed., *Statutes Va.*, XII, 345; Iredell and Martin, comps., *Acts N.-C.*, II, 38, 56; Georgia provided that no slave could be compelled to a second trial for the same offense: *Laws State Ga. Since 1800*, 133.

2. Hoadly *et al.*, eds., *Recs. State Conn.*, IX, 91–92; *Laws State N. Y.*, II, 675–79; Hening, ed., *Statutes Va.*, XII, 182–83; R. H. Taylor, "Humanizing the Slave Code of North Carolina," *N. C. Hist. Rev.*, 2 (1925), 323–25; but a 1798 act for proper maintainance of aged and crippled slaves (Iredell and Martin, comps., *Acts N.-C.*, II, 120–21) aimed more at their wandering about and becoming nuisances than at humanitarian treatment.

that they valued liberation of Negroes over riddance of them. Delaware drew an interesting distinction by requiring special license for sale of slaves to the Carolinas, Georgia, and the West Indies; two years later Maryland and Virginia were included.[3] Northern states and Maryland, Virginia, and North Carolina, as late as 1800, attached severe penalties to kidnapping of free Negroes, a not uncommon crime few people were willing to condone. Feeling on this matter was strong and lawmakers meant business: Delaware, thirty-nine lashes, both ears to the pillory for one hour and then cut off; Virginia, mandatory death without benefit of clergy. A North Carolina man was executed for this offense in 1806.[4]

After 1800, however, slave codes in the South were tightened up as occasion dictated, though the brutal punishments of an earlier day remained discarded, at least from the statute books. The principal occasion, of course, was Gabriel's plot, but while this was an important turning point, the pattern of restrictions on Negroes makes clear that Gabriel was not "the mainspring and chief mover" behind the new mood among white men. Two years earlier, for example, Virginia clamped down hard on harboring of fugitive slaves. As late as 1804 Virginia restricted nighttime religious meetings of slaves but the next year revised the law to permit whites to take their slaves with them to public worship. A special act in February 1808 provided strong penalties for burning stables, barns, stacks, ricks, and houses.[5] Hiring out had always been regarded with suspicion; a new Maryland act of 1787 curbing the practice was revealingly entitled "An ACT to prevent the inconveniencies arising from slaves being permitted to act as free." Virginia tightened regulations on slave hiring in 1792 but eased them slightly in 1808, perhaps because the practice was compellingly convenient in a region where many planters owned too many slaves. In 1794 North Carolina banned hiring out completely. Georgia forbade slaves working or transacting business for themselves in 1803.[6]

3. For example, Hoadly et al., eds., Recs. State Conn., VII, 379; Laws State N. Y., II, 676; Acts Assembly N. J. (1788), 487–88 (except to "neighbouring States") ; Laws Del., II, 884–85, 943.

4. Laws Del., II, 885, 1093–95; Maxcy, ed., Laws Md., II, 355–56; Hening, ed., Statutes Va., XII, 531; Shepard, ed., Statutes Va., I, 126, II, 147–48; Clark, ed., State Recs. N. C., XXIV, 220; Iredell and Martin, comps., Acts N.-C., II, 156–57; Franklin, Free Negro in N. C., 56. Though there were strong protests in Pennsylvania, nothing was done to strengthen the law until 1820; Turner, Negro in Pa., 115–18.

5. Shepard, ed., Statutes Va., II, 77–78, III, 108, 124, 377–78.

6. Maxcy, ed., Laws Md., II, 26–27; Shepard, ed., Statutes Va., I, 126, III, 372; Iredell and Martin, comps., Acts N.-C., II, 54; Laws State Ga. Since 1800, 133,

In somewhat random fashion, then, the structure of slavery was hardened and polished. Between 1796 and 1806, mounting irritation with antislavery agitation and free Negroes resulted in more stringent requirements for private manumission. Particularly where slavery was economically most viable it began to assume the qualities of the familier ante-bellum institution; it was becoming a "way of life" marked by apparently complex but functionally simple and unquestioned mores, a palladium deserving and demanding unreserved commitment and loyalty. For planters and probably for slaves themselves there was a deepening social gulf between house servants and field hands.[7] One senses, especially in South Carolina, not only the effects of time and handsome profits but a settling-in which could have come only from a feeling of permanence or at least a feeling that it was going to be a long siege. It was scarcely possible to doubt the perpetual existence of the social system when so much was at stake. Who could see the absurdities involved? Probably only a foreign critic could have dissected Charleston with one brief slice of description, as a British traveler, John Lambert, did so neatly about 1807.

I expected to find the Charleston stage well supplied with *sooty negroes,* who would have performed the *African* and *Savage* characters, in the dramatic pieces, to the life; instead of which the delusion was even worse than on our own stage; for so far from employing *real negroes,* the performers would not even condescend to *blacken* their faces, or dress in any manner resembling an African. This I afterwards learnt was occasioned by motives of *policy,* lest the negroes in Charleston should conceive, from being represented on the stage, and having their colour, dress, manners, and customs imitated by the white people, that they were very important personages; and might take improper liberties in consequence of it. For this reason, also, Othello and other plays where a black man is the hero of the piece are not allowed to be performed; nor are any of the negroes or people of colour permitted to visit the theatre.[8]

What had been drama two hundred years before was now life.

It is difficult not to see more "delusion" than "policy" in this. Not

---

457–58; also *Ordinances of Charleston,* 185–88. Ernest James Clark, Jr., "Aspects of the North Carolina Slave Code, 1715–1860," *N. C. Hist. Rev.,* 39 (1962), 148–64, shows that the courts liberalized their interpretations and accorded increasing protection to slaves in the period 1780–1830 but thereafter the trend was reversed.

7. My strong impression particularly from newspaper advertisements. Some distinction had always been drawn, but household status among slaves was almost certainly becoming more rigidly hereditary.

8. Lambert, *Travels through Canada, and the U. S.,* II, 138. Neutral on slavery, this is an informative source.

that the influence of hard realities was entirely negligible. A slave society depended on servility in the proper quarters. Charleston tradesmen fretted over competition from slaves in crafts and shop-keeping. Charleston cordwainers and master tailors were sufficiently aroused in 1793 to publish the relevant city ordinances at their own expense, and some years later the city authorities spelled out limitations on the number of slave apprentices a tradesmen might employ. Wherever there were complaints about slaves taking the jobs of white men (and there were few outside Charleston), they concerned skilled or at least nonagricultural activities. Virginia, for example, limited the proportion of slaves in crews of river and bay craft to one-third. Moreau de St. Méry commented in Philadelphia, "Workmen do not want to accept them, or to let them be apprentices." [9] That there were no complaints of slave competition in agriculture is scarcely surprising: Negroes had to do something, for idleness in slaves was inappropriate, expensive, and dangerous.

2. RESTRAINT OF FREE NEGROES

After 1790 it became increasingly apparent that southerners were less worried and irritated by Negro slaves than by Negroes who were not slaves. Mounting hostility to free Negroes was chiefly responsible for the portentous restraints on private manumissions, for in the Upper South, at least, men did not mind freeing Negroes but merely having them around once freed. There seemed to be more of them every day. From 1790 to 1810 the proportion of free Negroes in the total Negro population in the United States shot from almost 8 per cent to more than 13 per cent; the latter figure remained roughly stationary until it declined after 1840. During the last decade of the century the increase of free Negroes, for which manumissions rather than fecundity were largely responsible, was 82 per cent, while corresponding figures for slaves and whites were 28 per cent and 36 per cent. The increase was greatest in the Upper South. Almost one quarter of Maryland's Negroes were free by 1810. Virginia's proportion of Negroes who were free jumped well past North Carolina's in the period 1790 to 1810. The very small proportions in South Carolina and Georgia rose only slightly. Slavery in Delaware, by contrast, was completely under-

9. Charleston *State Gazette of S. C.*, Nov. 9ff., Dec. 5ff., 1793; *Ordinances of Charleston*, 182; Hening, ed., *Statutes Va.*, XI, 404; Roberts, trans. and eds., *Moreau de St. Méry's Journey*, 303.

mined, for by 1810 free Negroes outnumbered slaves three to one.[10]

Attempts to deal with the problem of free Negroes during the thirty years after the Revolution afford the clearest single index to the important modifications in the attitudes toward the Negro in that period. Most traditional restrictions on the freedom of free Negroes were recapitulated, extended, or strengthened. After 1790 the only slave state to relax any restriction on free Negroes was, predictably, Delaware.[11] In 1785 and 1792 when Virginia undertook to codify her slave "code," which was actually a jumble of accumulated statutes, most of the old caste regulations were retained—this shortly after the important act facilitating private manumissions. Free Negroes might lawfully possess only one gun; they were not to testify against white men in a court of law; no free Negro, on pain of thirty lashes, was to "at any time lift his or her hand in opposition to any person not being a negro or mulatto" unless in self-defense against wanton assault; and, by a separate act which placed a seal on existing racial arrangements, "No negro, mulatto, or Indian, shall at any time purchase any servant, other than of their own complexion."[12]

In addition to this clarifying of a third legal status of persons in the South, many laws aimed at specific abuses and dangers arising from the presence of free Negroes. Maryland particularly, with the largest free Negro population, claimed to be plagued by free Negroes operating as receivers for goods stolen by slaves; in 1796 free Negroes without visible means of support or found wandering about were ordered either to post bond, leave the state, or be

10. Figures compiled from U. S. Bureau of Census, *Century of Population Growth, 1790–1900*, 80; U. S. Bureau of Census, *Negro Population, 1790–1915* (Washington, 1918), 57.

Proportion of Negroes Free, Coastal Slave States, 1790 and 1810.

	1790	1810
Del.	30.5%	75.9%
Md.	7.2%	23.3%
Va.	4.2%	7.2%
N. C.	4.8%	5.7%
S. C.	1.7%	2.3%
Ga.	1.3%	1.7%

11. A minor change concerning free Negro legal testimony: *Laws Del.*, III, 80–81 (1799).

12. Hening, ed., *Statutes Va.*, XII, 182–83; Shepard, ed., *Statutes Va.*, I, 123–25, 181.

sentenced to six months' servitude. Everywhere they were regarded as thievish: the Duc de La Rochefoucauld-Liancourt explained that in Maryland "the judges attribute the multiplicity of robberies to the free negroes" and that he had "heard the same accusation preferred against them in all the states where slavery is permitted." Worse still, free Negroes seemed a threat to effective police control of slaves, more than ever now that slaves seemed to have been inoculated with the doctrine of liberty. Ten years of pertinent legislation in North Carolina is revelatory of the trend toward greater restrictiveness. In 1785 the legislature required free Negroes in certain towns to wear on the left shoulder a cloth badge bearing the letters "FREE"; plainly the requirement was intended for the wearer's protection. Two years later the Assembly cracked down, giving thefts as reason: free Negroes were restricted in their freedom to go aboard sailing vessels and to "entertain" slaves. Further, they were forbidden to marry or cohabit with slaves without first obtaining consent from the master and two justices of the peace. In 1795, finally, the Assembly ordered grand juries in the state to present free Negroes known to be dangerous and required that free Negroes entering the state and slaves freed thenceforth were to post a £200 bond which must ordinarily have been prohibitive and intended as such.[13]

Everywhere in the South the free Negro was pelted with restrictions, miscellaneous in character, growing in severity, and similar in underlying intent. In 1798 Virginia prescribed thirty-nine lashes (New England had long since mercifully abandoned the Scriptural number) for free Negroes convicted of harboring slaves and took further precautionary measures against free Negroes after the Gabriel plot. Virginia and Maryland both required licensing of free Negro guns in 1806, and Maryland offered salutary punishments for free Negroes found at tumultuous meetings of slaves. In 1808 Maryland made the radical departure of permitting slaves to testify in court against free Negroes on any matter. In the years 1806–08 Georgia went to more drastic lengths: the Assembly ordered that free Negroes were to be tried for felonies in the same manner as slaves; that in major towns they were subject to slave laws; and that "WHEREAS the permitting of free Negroes and persons of color to rove about the country in idleness and dissipation, has a dangerous tendency," free Negro boys over eight without guardians were to be

13. Maxcy, ed., *Laws Md.*, II. 358; also III, 55, 248–49; La Rochefoucauld-Liancourt, *Travels through the United States*, II, 281; Clark, ed., *State Recs. N. C.*, XXIV, 727–28, 890–91; Iredell and Martin, comps., *Acts N.-C.*, II, 79–80.

bound out until age twenty-one.[14] It could have been an Elizabethan statute except for the crucial difference "of color."

Both states of the Lower South enacted discriminatory taxes on free Negroes shortly after the Revolution, an oppression which in South Carolina elicited respectful petitions for relief. In Charleston free Negroes also petitioned the Senate in 1791 for repeal of the law forbidding Negro testimony against whites, but they were careful to add reverently that "Your Memorialists do not presume to hope that they shall be put on an equal footing with the Free white citizens of the State in general." [15] The presumption was the only safe one to make. Yet South Carolina distinguished itself in this period by *not* cracking down hard on free Negroes, in part because requisite legislation was on the books but in part also, perhaps, because white men remained confident of their ability to handle any challenge raised by a few free Negroes. In Charleston, where many of them were concentrated, the authorities showed no signs of great concern; the prescribed punishment for assaulting the City Guard, for example, remained the same for free Negroes as for white men.[16] It was not until 1822, after the Missouri Compromise, that South Carolina began tossing free Negro seamen into prison. Here, where the white community was in comparatively easy control of slavery both in actuality and in the mind, free Negroes seemed more a nuisance than a threat. In the Upper South they loomed much more as a threat precisely because the institution which their presence challenged was *not* under control, either in the mind or (as Gabriel had demonstrated) in actuality.

How much all this legislative tinkering represented a response to actual thievery, harboring of fugitives, and so forth must remain open to question, though surely free Negroes were not paragons of planter morality. Whatever their behavior, though, free Negroes

14. Shepard, ed., *Statutes Va.*, II, 77, 300–301, III, 274–75; Maxcy, ed., *Laws Md.*, III, 298, 398. Free Negroes could keep only one dog, with a license; *ibid.*, 297; *Laws State Ga. Since 1800*, 334–35, 369, 462–63. In 1798 Rhode Island re-enacted a 1770 law against free Negroes keeping disorderly houses; *Public Laws R.-I., 1798*, 611–12.

15. Candler, comp., *Col. Recs. Ga.*, XIX, Pt. ii, 403; Herbert Aptheker, "South Carolina Poll Tax, 1737–1895," *Jour. Negro Hist.*, 31 (1946), 131–39; Aptheker, ed., *Documentary History of the Negro*, 27, 29–31.

16. *Ordinances of Charleston*, 116 (1805), see also 38, 40–41, 47–48, 50–56, 62, 113, 138, 148, 150–56, 158–62, 165, 179, 231, 233. By 1813 there was evidence of a new feeling: a free Negro might not own any dog except one secured within a yard and having a collar bearing the name of some "creditable white person" who was to be considered the dog's owner. The city marshall and his deputies were authorized to enter Negro lots and enclosures to enforce this regulation, *ibid.*, 74–76.

constituted a threat to white society which was not owing so much as generally supposed to the fact that Negro freedom threatened to undermine the structure of slavery, for in many quarters men hoped genuinely for the institution's eventual extinction. It arose within the white man as a less than conscious feeling that a people who had always been absolutely subjected were now in many instances outside the range of the white man's unfettered power. The dislike, apprehension, and fear of free Negroes, which clearly had swelled out of proportion to any possible overt threat they might have posed, was thus in part an almost predictable response to loss of a once firm sense of control. Long accustomed to absolute dominion, white men could not readily or calmly surrender it, yet they could find compensation in despising what could no longer be absolutely controlled. To despise slaves as Negroes was redundant, but when Negroes were no longer slaves they became despicable only as Negroes. It was a tragic paradox that the spate of manumissions after the Revolution tended to heighten the white man's distaste for Negroes as such.

In considerable measure, too, that distaste merely represented continuation of long-standing feelings about the Negro. The growth of the free Negro population was bound to exacerbate these feelings. Certainly no one seemed to want them around. All southern and two northern states passed laws either restricting immigration of free Negroes, banning it altogether, or requiring emigration of emancipated Negroes. Delaware vacillated at first but after 1811 permitted no immigration.[17] On March 26, 1788, the Massachusetts General Court, having the previous day banned citizens of the state from engaging in the slave traffic and having tendered relief to families of kidnapped Negroes, passed an "act for suppressing and punishing of Rogues, Vagabonds, common Beggars, and other idle, disorderly, and lewd Persons" which provided that no "African or Negroe, other than a subject of the Emperor of *Morocco,* or a citizen of some one of the United States; to be evidenced by a certificate from the Secretary of the State of which he shall be a citizen shall tarry within this Commonwealth, for a longer time

17. Restriction of immigration: *Laws Ga., 1755–1799,* 530 (1793); Iredell and Martin, comps., *Acts N.-C.,* II, 79–80 (1796); Litwack, *North of Slavery,* 70n, 72 (Ohio, 1804 and 1807). Banned immigration: *Acts Assembly N.-J.* (1786), 242; Shepard, ed., *Statutes Va.,* I, 239 (1793); Cooper and McCord, eds., *Statutes S. C.,* VII, 433, 436–40, also 444–45 (1794 and 1800); Maxcy, ed., *Laws Md.,* III, 293 (1806); Hurd, *Law of Freedom and Bondage,* II, 15–16 (Ky., 1799 and 1808). Required emigration: Shepard, ed., *Statutes Va.,* III, 252 (1806); *Laws Del.,* IV, 108–10, 221, 400–404. Tennessee passed no ban until 1831; Hurd, *Law of Freedom and Bondage,* II, 92.

than two months." Violators were to be jailed, whipped ten stripes, and ordered to depart within ten days on pain of repeated penalties. Just how Negroes were to obtain certificates of citizenship, or even whether Massachusetts-born Negroes were citizens, was left unclear. Equally mystifying was the design of the law, though at very least it reflected some dislike of Negroes in a state where all Negroes had recently been freed.[18] The over-all pattern spoke for itself.

Given this trend toward exclusion, it is scarcely surprising that free Negroes were often barred from the presumed bulwark of American defense, the militia. It seemed unwise, to say the least, to offer military training to potential leaders of slave insurrection, especially in the South where one of the militia's main functions was guarding against such disaster. Yet the geographical pattern of exclusion suggests that actual danger was not the only consideration involved. Northern states, except New York for a few years and perhaps Rhode Island, excluded Negroes from the militia. In the South sectional differences in practice, so far as they can be determined from loosely written militia laws, point to where self-confidence lay. Maryland and Virginia excluded Negroes in definite terms. Maryland had drafted free Negroes during the Revolution but reversed itself when manpower was no longer needed after the war. North Carolina, by contrast, included free Negroes in the militia as late as 1812; thereafter they served as "musicians" only. The situation in South Carolina is unclear, though free Negroes may well have served in some capacities. Georgia did not exclude them, at least by law.[19] It is hard to tell exactly what this different practice in the Lower South reflected: the small number of free

18. *Acts and Laws Mass., 1786–87,* 626. The law remained a dead letter, though there were attempts to revive it in Boston in September 1800. Boston *Massachusetts Mercury,* Sept. 16, 1800; Phila. *Gaz. of U. S.,* Sept. 23, 1800; Boston *Independent Chronicle,* Sept. 25, 1800. Moore, *Notes on Slavery in Massachusetts,* 225–38, gives a full account. Dwight L. Dumond, *Antislavery: The Crusade for Freedom in America* (Ann Arbor, 1961), 121, suggests incorrectly that the act was meant to conform to the fugitive slave clause of the Constitution.

19. *Acts and Laws Mass., 1780–81,* 37, *1792–93,* 381; *Public Laws R.-I., 1798,* 422–42; Greene, *Negro in New England,* 127 (Conn.); Hoadly *et al.,* eds., *Recs. State Conn.,* VII, 376–88; *The Public Statute Laws of the State of Connecticut* (Hartford, 1808), 499; *Laws State N. Y.,* II, 220–29, III, 440–50, V, 452–66; Paterson, ed., *Laws N. J.,* 436; Turner, *Negro in Pa.,* 182n; *Laws Del.,* II, 1134, III, 82, IV, 123; Brackett, *Negro in Md.,* 196–97; Maxcy, ed., *Laws Md.,* III, 339–56; Shepard, ed., *Statutes Va.,* I, 345, III, 6; Iredell and Martin, comps., *Acts N.-C.,* II, 159–66, 285–92; Franklin, *Free Negro in N. C.,* 102–3, 193; Cooper and McCord, eds., *Statutes S. C.,* VIII, 485–517, IX, 679–80; Lambert, *Travels through Canada and U. S.,* II, 190; Candler, comp., *Col. Recs. Ga.,* XIX, Pt. ii, 348, 556; *Digest Laws Ga., 1755–1799,* 460; *Laws State Ga. Since 1800,* 408–22.

Negroes, exclusion in actual practice (neither explanation will do for North Carolina), or greater confidence in the white man's control of the Negro population. Militia service is not the only evidence suggesting presence of the latter feeling.

When the federal government passed a model militia law in 1792 only "white" men were included. Some states thereafter redrafted their militia laws to conform to this provision, but in others Negroes had already been barred. On all questions of color, national lawmakers inclined to the safer course of excluding black men. Whenever Congress laid down suffrage requirements, for instance, Negroes usually were excluded—in the District of Columbia in 1802 and the Mississippi and Indiana territories in 1808, though not in the Illinois territory in 1809.[20] Nationalization of political power tended toward nationalization of restrictions on the Negro.

As it was, the federal government did not set suffrage requirements throughout the nation, and various state regulations differed in a way which clearly foreshadowed the nineteenth-century sectional split. Throughout the free states free Negroes were legally entitled to vote, even before slavery was abolished. In practice they were often kept (or themselves stayed) away from the polls in accordance with local custom. Moreau de St. Méry declared that because of a "universal prejudice all over the United States" Negroes "are excluded from all elections." Certainly Moreau made the point too broadly, for at least a few Negroes seem to have voted. It was in the nineteenth century that they were pointedly excluded, mainly outside New England; Ohio in 1802 and New Jersey in 1807 were the first free states to disfranchise them by law. In the slave states the usual practice was to bar Negroes, except in North Carolina and Tennessee where Negroes voted until well into the antebellum period. In their constitutions of the Revolutionary era, Virginia, South Carolina, and Georgia excluded Negroes from the franchise. In the 1780's both Delaware and Maryland passed laws which excluded only Negroes freed after passage of the acts, but this reluctance to strip voting rights from Negroes already free was overcome in 1792 and 1802 when all free Negroes were disfranchised. Kentucky's first constitution of 1792 contained no ban but the second one of 1799 did.[21]

20. John K. Mahon, *The American Militia: Decade of Decision, 1789–1800* (Gainesville, Fla., 1960), 21–22; *Statutes U. S.*, I, 103, 271, 414, II, 196, 216, 455, 469, 514–16.

21. Roberts, trans. and eds., *Moreau de St. Méry's Journey*, 304; Thorpe, ed., *Constitutions*, VI, 3742, 3757–58, 3768 (Vt.), IV, 2459, 2461, 2463, 2477 (N. H.), III, 1898 (Mass.); Aptheker, ed., *Documentary History of the Negro*, 14–15; Moore,

Even in the more permissive North there seems to have been considerable resentment against Negro voting. The suffrage provision in the proposed Pennsylvania constitution of 1790 contained the word "white" until Geneva-born Albert Gallatin, objecting he said as a man of dark complexion, moved to strike it out.[22] In 1785 the New York Assembly passed a gradual emancipation bill which prohibited Negroes from voting or holding public office, but the bill was blocked by the Council of Revision. The Council objected that the prohibition "lays the foundation of an aristocracy of the most dangerous and malignant kind, rendering power permanent and hereditary in the hands of those persons who deduce their origin through white ancestors only." It then proceeded to the calculus of intermixture and concluded "that if only one thousandth part of the black inhabitants now in this State, should intermarry with the white, their posterity will amount to so many millions, that it will be difficult to suppose a fiftieth part of the people born within this State two hundred years hence, who may be entitled to share in the benefits which our excellent constitution intended to secure to every free inhabitant of the State." The divided and confused Assembly failed to pass a revised bill, so emancipation was defeated for the time being. Ironically, in the early part of the next century Negro voters, who were firm Federalists, wielded the balance of power in several elections. Finally in 1821 Republicans managed to subject them to a special property requirement which effectively disfran-

---

Notes on Slavery in Mass., 187–200; Thorpe, ed., *Constitutions,* VI, 3211–22 (R. I.); *Public Laws R.-I., 1798,* 114–26; Thorpe, ed., *Constitutions,* I, 544 (Conn., white only, 1818), see text for New York; Marion T. Wright, "Negro Suffrage in New Jersey, 1776–1875," *Jour. Negro Hist.,* 33 (1948), 171–77; Thorpe, ed., *Constitutions,* V, 3084, 3096, 3108 (Pa.), V, 2907 (Ohio); *Laws Del.,* II, 887, IV, 429; Thorpe, ed., *Constitutions,* I, 574 (Del.), III, 1691, 1698, 1705 (Md.); Olbrich, *Negro Suffrage,* 21 (Md.); Annapolis *Md. Gaz.,* Feb. 16, Mar. 22, 1792; Maxcy, ed., *Laws Md.,* II, 352; Thorpe, ed., *Constitutions,* VII, 3816, 3825 (Va.); Olbrich, *Negro Suffrage,* 9 (Va.); Thorpe, ed., *Constitutions,* III, 1269, 1278 (Ky.), VI, 3418, 3433–34 (Tenn.; with exceptions), V, 2790, 2796 (N. C.); Franklin, *Free Negro in N. C.,* 105–6; Weeks, "Negro Suffrage in the South," *Pol. Sci. Qtly.,* 9 (1894), 674–77 (N. C.); Thorpe, ed., *Constitutions,* VI, 3245, 3251–52, 3258–59, 3267 (S. C.); Georgia excluded Negroes in 1777 but did not do so expressly in the constitutions of 1792 and 1798 (*ibid.,* II, 779, 789, 800), almost certainly because it was assumed Negroes would not vote: there seems to be no record of Negroes voting in Georgia, but there is in North Carolina where the law clearly allowed them to. Chilton Williamson, *American Suffrage: From Property to Democracy, 1760–1860* (Princeton, 1960), contains little on Negro suffrage.

22. Olbrich, *Negro Suffrage,* 17–19. During debates on the gradual emancipation act of 1780 some legislators had objected that emancipation would give Negroes the vote; Turner, *Negro in Pa.,* 183.

chised many of them. It was, Republicans felt, about time.[23] Nor were New York Republicans alone. Between 1814 and 1838 Connecticut, New York, Rhode Island, Tennessee, North Carolina, and Pennsylvania prohibited or drastically restricted voting by Negroes; by 1840 less than 7 per cent of northern free Negroes lived in the several New England states which still admitted Negroes to the polls.[24]

The over-all pattern of Negro suffrage in this period is suggestive not only of the general trend toward more rigid exclusion of Negroes from the larger community but of the staying power of the ideology which had first powerfully implied the necessity of Negro freedom. The sectional pattern of liberality on Negro voting coincided, with the exception of Virginia, not with the prevailing degree of confidence in slave control but with willingness and ability to accept the implications of republican doctrine. Eventually the Negro lost the semblance of rights which the suffrage represented, but it is suggestive that political privilege lay open to the Negro longer than any other. The American Revolution seems to have given political ideas and institutions a strength which did not rapidly give way under mounting pressures to exclude the Negro from the white community.

3. NEW WALLS OF SEPARATION

Separation of Negroes from white persons—"segregation" now—assumed a new rigidity and meaning wherever slavery was abolished, though the pace of this change was impeded by the gradualness of abolition. Slavery was a genuine, if crude and perverse variety of common bond, which abolition snapped. Manumission of slaves resulted in fewer Negroes actually living in white families, a long step toward residential separation made firmer by

23. *Journal of the Senate of the State of New-York . . . 1785* (N. Y., 1785), 55–56; *Journal Assembly N.-Y.* (1785), 77, 86, 119–20; Alfred B. Street, *The Council of Revision of the State of New York; Its History, a History of the Courts with Which Its Members Were Connected; Biographical Sketches of Its Members; and Its Vetoes* (Albany, 1859), 268–69; *Laws State N. Y.*, II, 371–84; Thorpe, ed., *Constitutions*, V, 2630–31, 2642–43; Charles Thomson to his wife Harriet, Mar. 22, 1785, Charles Thomson Papers, Misc., Lib. Cong.; Edgar J. McManus, "Antislavery Legislation in New York," *Jour. Negro Hist.*, 46 (1961), 208–10. For later Negro voting, Dixon R. Fox, "The Negro Vote in Old New York," *Pol. Sci. Qtly.*, 32 (1917), 252–75. Republicans became much irritated by Negro voting (largely because it cost them elections) and tauntingly sang a campaign song in 1809 which began "Federalists with blacks unite."

24. Litwack, *North of Slavery*, 74–93; James Truslow Adams, "Disfranchisement of Negroes in New England," *Amer. Hist. Rev.*, 30 (1924–25), 543–47.

Negro poverty. Slavery had formalized and ritualized relations between Negroes and whites and accordingly had served to clarify the status of both. After abolition, only by separating the Negro, by law or by some less formal means, could clarity be retrieved. Clarity as to status was essential, since uncertainty about the Negro's position was proportionately as unwelcome as the Negro himself. There was nothing inevitable about the process, though, for knowledge and hence security concerning one's own position vis-à-vis the Negro might flow from either a personal sense of aristocracy or from firm equalitarianism—or, it should be emphasized, from both. Later, while the sense of aristocracy was decomposing in the ante-bellum North, equalitarianism received a strong boost after 1830 from a revived abolition movement; thus the degradation and separation of the northern Negro in the nineteenth century turned out to be a gradual process, not without striking reversals. Reinforcing the tendency toward exclusion, however, was a rapid trend toward urbanization. Free Negroes tended to congregate in cities; and slaves living in cities tended to act like free men. And it was only in an urban context that segregation made sense. In any age, formalized separation of distinct social groups becomes meaningful only when personal acquaintance is gone and strangers are thrown together in a fashion which can be taken to imply equality. Such separation made "sense" on mid-nineteenth-century Philadelphia streetcars but not in the farming counties of Maryland. Perhaps the most arresting aspect of this pattern of change is that it was recapitulated in the South after Emancipation, though with a new anthropology.[25]

In the period before about 1810, one can just begin to detect the ontogeny of segregation. The old tendency toward separation in places which might imply equality had not been noticably weakened by the Revolution. Some of the pride-stirring new institutions of humanitarian mercy, hospitals and penitentiaries, seem to have separated blacks from whites. Virginia's "Penitentiary House" seems to have been closed to Negroes.[26] Moreau de St. Méry, incurably interested in America's handling of her Negro population, was informative and probably not inaccurate. He mentioned a New York hospital which had separate wards for Negroes and reported that in Philadelphia prisons Negroes and whites ate separately and that

25. Richard C. Wade, *Slavery in the Cities: The South 1820–1860* (N. Y., 1964) ; Litwack, *North of Slavery*, and Woodward, *Strange Career of Jim Crow*.
26. Francis Baylor to Gov. James Monroe, Caroline, Aug. 31, 1800, Palmer, ed., *Cal. Va. State Papers*, IX, 135.

"a white servant, no matter who, would consider it a dishonor to eat with colored people." When it snowed in Philadelphia, Moreau claimed broadly, "any colored man who passes is sure to be showered with snowballs by white children"—a comment which comported with the childhood recollection of a man raised in Haddonfield, New Jersey, that one of his playmates had "in a disdainful manner, cursed a black boy, and called him *the seed of Cain*." Moreau's boundless curiosity was equaled only by his lack of humor: "Americans," he wrote as if commenting upon affairs of state, "ordinarily will not rent houses to colored prostitutes. In Philadelphia they are lodged for the most part on the outskirts of town or in alleys or small side streets." Just where else he had expected to find prostitutes, of any color, Moreau did not say; indeed his straight-faced comment serves as a warning against interpreting every instance of Negro separation and degradation as evidence of racism and a prototype of twentieth-century segregation.[27]

The hazards of interpretation on this matter are nowhere more apparent than with a funeral which attracted considerable attention in Philadelphia in 1792. Mrs. William Gray, "a black woman" married to one of the leading Negroes in Philadelphia, was laid to rest at a well-attended ceremony which one newspaper described as a "pleasing instance of total indifference to complexion." Scores of Negroes were joined on the "melancholy occasion" by about fifty "white persons," including Bishop William White and another Episcopal clergyman. Dr. Benjamin Rush, an eternally optimistic supporter of Negro equality, also attended. Rush found the presence of white people, "chiefly the neighbours of the deceased," most particularly animating: "The sight was a new one in Philadelphia, for hitherto (a few cases excepted) the negroes alone attended each other's funerals. By this event it is to be hoped the partition wall which divided the Blacks from the Whites will be still further broken down and a way prepared for their union as brethren and members of one great family."[28]

Though this incident may be made to serve a variety of interpre-

27. Roberts, trans. and eds., *Moreau de St. Méry's Journey,* 152, 302, 303, 311; for Haddonfield, [Charles Jones], *A Candid Examination, into the Origin of the Difference of Colour, in the Human Family* . . . (Phila., 1812), 3. Also La Rochefoucauld-Liancourt, *Travels through the United States,* II, 285.
28. Phila. *Independent Gazetteer,* June 23, 1792; Corner, ed., *Autobiography of Rush,* 221. Rush may have been wrong as to novelty, for an English woman living in Philadelphia reported in 1786 that white Quakers had attended the fine funeral of a Negro "who is reputed to have conducted himself with great reputation and was a man of some consequence." Sarah Cadbury, ed., "Extracts from the Diary of Mrs. Ann Warder," *Pa. Mag. of Hist. and Biog.,* 17 (1893), 460–61.

tations, it is clear that Rush's hopes never came to much. Certainly there are enough unmistakable straws in the period after the Revolution to indicate that the winds of change were against him. While there were schools attended by both Negroes and whites—one on Long Island, for instance, and another near Springfield, Massachusetts—and while John Chavis, a free Negro from North Carolina, attended (probably) college at Princeton, Boston Negroes were petitioning the General Court to remedy the "great grievance" they suffered because their children received no benefit from the free school system of the city.[29] John Chavis returned to North Carolina after being licensed to preach by the Lexington, Virginia, Presbytery "notwithstanding his colour"; he began teaching school but finally in 1808 was forced to advertise in the *Raleigh Register* that he was opening an evening school for colored children "as he intends, for the accomodation of some of his employers, to exclude all Children of Colour from his Day School." [30] Authorities in Richmond seem to have taken offense at Christopher McPherson, a prosperous free Negro who maintained a carriage and horses, for in 1810 they passed an ordinance which permitted Negroes to ride in carriages only as maids and coachmen.[31] Several years earlier when the "Richmond New Theatre" opened in that city, the managers inaugurated an apparently novel policy of restricting Negroes to the gallery: "No persons of colour admitted to the pit or boxes." Similarly, Negroes found themselves unwelcome as members of the Masonic Order. During the British occupation of Boston, more than a dozen free Negroes had joined a British army lodge and then after the war had obtained a charter from England for a separate African lodge. By 1797 there were African lodges in Philadelphia and Providence, but Philadelphia Negroes had been forced to appeal for association with the Boston group because, as one complained, "The white Masons have refused to grant us a Dispensation, fearing that black men living in Virginia would get to be Masons, too." [32]

Far more than these separate, middle-class Negro organizations,

29. *Minutes Abolition Convention* (1798), 8; Henry Wansey, *The Journal of an Excursion to the United States of North America in the Summer of 1794* (Salisbury, Eng., 1796), 56; Edgar W. Knight, "Notes on John Chavis," *N. C. Hist. Rev.,* 7 (1930), 326–45; Aptheker, ed., *Documentary History of the Negro,* 19.

30. Quoted in Knight, "John Chavis," *N. C. Hist. Rev.,* 7 (1930), 339.

31. Johnston, Race Relations in Virginia, 42–44, 49.

32. Richmond *Virginia Gazette, and General Advertiser,* Dec. 24, 1803, Feb. 5, 1806; Peter Mantone to Prince Hall, Phila., Mar. 2, 1797, Harry E. Davis, ed., "Documents Relating to Negro Masonry in America," *Jour. Negro Hist.,* 21 (1936), 425.

the long-established institutions of communal participation, the
churches, revealed the direction and potentialities of social change.
The long-standing arrangement of separate benches for Negroes
continued in many places; one Episcopal church in Virginia
avoided any possibility of confusion by painting certain benches
black.[33] The members of the Congregational church in North Bridgewater, Massachusetts, decided "to see what measure the Parish
will take to prevent the *blacks* from occupying the seats appro-
priated to the use of the white people, so as to prevent any disturbances in time of Public worshipe" and "voted that the side galleries
and the seats in the body [should be for the use] of the white
people, and the seats in the porch above to the use of the blacks."
The decision had an ominous ring: what other group of obstreperous worshipers could be so handily categorized and swept as a group
up into the "porch"? Separate seating in churches, as it turned out,
elicited what may have been the first protest against the kind of
racial stigmatizing which may properly be termed "segregation" in
the modern sense: Charles Crawford's pamphlet in 1790 urged that
Negroes "should be encouraged to sit in religious meetings, not on a
bench with Negroes only, but indiscriminately with white
people." [34]

Only in the Lower South, perhaps only in Charleston, was separate seating the standard practice among the churches. In the
Upper South, the burgeoning Methodist and Baptist churches were
more firmly established and were generally disposed to welcome the
Negro on terms which rendered his separation irrelevant and even
wrong. These sects had eschewed formalism and had thrown new
emphasis on individual salvation. Many of their members in the
Upper South entertained antislavery views, at least until 1800. Frequently they welcomed the lowly Negro into their churches if he
were one of God's own—an admission requirement which for once
the Negro could satisfy. By 1790 in Virginia one-fifth of the membership of the Methodist church was Negro, and the Baptists must

33. Roberts, trans. and eds., *Moreau de St. Méry's Journey*, 64, who also
reported (p. 302) that in Philadelphia there was an all-Negro cemetery, that the
Irish Catholic church on South Sixth St. did not permit burial of Negroes in its
cemetery, and that in the churches generally Negroes were "separated" from
whites. For further evidence of separate seating, Park, *Memoir of Samuel
Hopkins*, 166; and in Charleston, Clark *et al.*, eds., *Journal of Francis Asbury*, I,
535n; Lambert, *Travels through Canada and the U. S.*, II, 175–76; Jameson, ed.,
"Diary of Hooker," *Amer. Hist. Assoc., Annual Report* (1896), I, 853.

34. Bradford Kingman, *History of North Bridgewater, Plymouth County,
Massachusetts* . . . (Boston, 1866), 95; Charles Crawford, *Observations upon
Negro-Slavery*, 2d ed. (Phila., 1790), 118.

have had a higher proportion.[35] Together these two sects absorbed the great majority of Negroes flocking into the churches. The second Great Awakening at the turn of the century proved far less important for the Negro than the first, partly because the doorways to Christ had already been thrown open, partly because there had been many local awakenings ever since 1740, and partly because the revivals of 1800 were most fervent on the western frontier. As a form of worship, though, the camp meeting was well calculated to appeal to Negroes, who were starved for emotional outlets when serving as pieces of property and still hungry when free. Mrs. Mathew Carey, the genteel wife of the well-known publisher of the *American Museum*, was horrified by the wild emotionalism of Negroes at a meeting in western Pennsylvania.[36] Elsewhere, "goodly seasons" were held out of doors without formal seating. Even in church buildings, Negro men of God occasionally preached to blacks and whites together and even to white congregations.[37] Bishop Francis Asbury, who rode up and down the country exhorting Methodists and anyone else who would listen, wrote in his diary in 1781 that "Harry, a black man" spoke when Asbury had finished at a meeting in Virginia; "This circumstance was new and the white people looked on with attention."[38] After September 1800, however, public attention fastened on less amiable Negro activities, and such open-minded acceptance of Negro preachers became rare.

Of all American churches, the Society of Friends might have been expected to cast about most eagerly for converts to the faith. As it was, Quakers proved zealous in guiding Negroes into the confines of Christian morality, but they proved almost as eager to see converted Negroes enter some other church than their own.[39] While Friends labored to free the enslaved and to protect the free, while they tutored white and colored children together in the same little struggling schools, while particularly in North Carolina and the

35. *Minutes of the Annual Conferences of the Methodist Episcopal Church, for the Years 1773–1828* (N. Y., 1840) , 38–39.

36. Mrs. Mathew Carey to her husband, Octoraro, Lancaster County, Pa., Aug. 5, 1806, Mathew Carey Papers, Carey Section [Typescript] Selections from the Letters of Mrs. Mathew Carey, 1796–1815, 38, Hist. Soc. Pa.

37. Woodson, *History of the Negro Church*, 53–57; Richard Allen, *The Life Experience and Gospel Labors of the Rt. Rev. Richard Allen . . .* (N. Y. and Nashville, 1960) , 20–21, 23–24. In Pennsylvania a white Presbyterian church elected as minister a Negro "from Guinea"; Otto Chomet, trans., "Citizen Marsillac on Philadelphia," *Pa. Mag. of Hist. and Biog.*, 70 (1946) , 114.

38. Clark *et al.*, eds., *Journal of Francis Asbury*, I, 403. Asbury frequently preached to mixed congregations.

39. James, *A People Among Peoples*, 278–79, 291–96.

Upper South they faithfully brought Negroes to their meetings,[40] they made no efforts to bring Negroes into full membership in their religious society. Indeed, some Friends tried to exclude them.

Very possibly a few Negroes joined meetings earlier in the century, but in the 1780's an incident in Pennsylvania demonstrated dramatically that some Friends regarded color as grounds for refusing membership. Abigail Franks could scarcely have looked very black (she was half white, three-eighths Indian, and one-eighth Negro), but her application for membership in the Birmingham Meeting resulted in a query to the Concord Monthly Meeting, which in turn gingerly passed the question to the Chester Quarterly Meeting asking "whether person making application to be joined in membership with us as a religious Society and Friends being satisfied with respect to the sincerity of the one so applying, should be rejected on account of the color?" The subject "brought a weighty exercise" upon the Chester Meeting, and "diverse just observations were made thereon." Members of the committee appointed to investigate the matter were "desired to meet together and consider of this subject, and also to inquire more minutely into the disposition, color and circumstances" of the applicant. Friends who thereupon visited with Abigail Franks seemed fully as interested in her complexion as her religiosity, for they reported that "her disposition they apprehended to be worthy of Friends notice; and her color appeared to them not darker than some who are esteemed white," and then went on to pinpoint her racial ancestry with Quakerly precision. The matter was finally brought to the attention of Philadelphia Yearly Meeting which decided favorably that "Concord Monthly Meeting may safely consider the application of the person on the same ground in common with other applications for admission into membership." In 1784 Abigail Franks was admitted to the Birmingham Meeting, three years after she first applied.[41]

Perhaps owing to the lightness of her "color," her membership was not utilized by the Yearly Meeting as grounds for a rule of discipline. Indeed, James Pemberton noted that a year later the subject still "excited much attention." Finally in 1796 the Philadelphia Yearly Meeting, prodded by a mulatto woman's request for membership in Rahway, New Jersey, concluded that Friends had

40. See particularly "Joshua Evans's Journal," *Friends' Miscellany*, 10 (1837), 1–212, especially 139–43, 147, 167–71, 176, 195, 207.
41. Gilbert Cope, "History of Concord Monthly Meeting," in *Two-Hundred and Twenty-Fifth Anniversary of Concord Monthly Meeting of Friends* (Phila., [1911]), 33–35.

always lain under obligation to consider applications without regard to color and next year added this new rule to the book of
discipline. North Carolina Friends made the same decision in
1800.[42]

In the long run no other decision was possible. As so often
happened with the Quakers, in the midst of their laborious moral
calculations they were hosed down with their own principles by an
uncompromising member of the Society. Joseph Drinker reminded
Philadelphia Friends in 1795 that Christ "did not say there should
be one fold for Black sheep and other fold of white Sheep, as some
of our friends would have it, who say they should fold by themselves, and have Meetings by themselves, So that if Christ should
bring them to the fold, some of our foremost friends would try to
keep them out." Drinker made the point in more familiar language: "There is no People in the world that I ever heard of, who
hold forth such Liberal Universal Principles as the People called
Quakers, and yet to my astonishment they are the only People I
know who make any objections to the Blacks or People of Color
joining them in Church Fellowship." [43]

In large part the exclusionary tendency among Friends resulted
from their long-standing reliance on sectarian exclusiveness which
had been intensified by bitter experiences in attempting to govern
Pennsylvania during the French and Indian War and by sufferings
at the hands of their fellow countrymen during the Revolution.
The effect of their failure to encourage Negroes to become Friends
was to smudge their reputation as friends of the Negro and to lay
them open to the disingenuous arguments of hostile southerners. In
Congress, for instance, James Jackson of Georgia caustically suggested in 1790 that Quakers migrate to Africa, marry the inhabitants, and produce a "motley race of their own." [44] William Loughton Smith was reported as saying that "the Quakers asserted that
nature had made all men equal, and that the difference of color
should not place negroes on a worse footing in society than the
whites; but had any of them ever married a negro, or would any of
them suffer their children to mix their blood with that of a black?
They would view with abhorrence such an alliance." [45] Smith was
correct as to fact but doubly unfair, since the Society stood opposed

42. Cadbury, "Negro Membership in the Society of Friends," *Jour. Negro Hist.*,
21 (1936), 172–77.
43. Thomas E. Drake, ed., "Joseph Drinker's Plea for the Admission of Colored
People to the Society of Friends, 1795," *Jour. Negro Hist.*, 32 (1947), 110–12.
44. Baltimore *Md. Jour.*, Mar. 30, 1790.
45. *Annals of Congress*, 1st Cong., 2d sess., 1455.

to Friends marrying *anyone* outside the Society, to say nothing of Negroes. The ironic fact remained, however, that the most actively equalitarian of American religious sects was among the least interested in attracting their colored "brethren" into their "Church Fellowship." In 1805 the Philadelphia Monthly Meeting decided to hold no more meetings for Negroes, "as Friends upon weighty deliberation, were united in the belief that the service of them was over, and they have now several places for worship of their own." [46]

4. NEGRO CHURCHES

That Negroes were generally not welcomed as equal participants among American churches helps account for the development in the years after the Revolution of a dramatic and novel variety of separation of Negroes from the white community. Throughout the nation but most obviously in Philadelphia and other northern cities, the "Black sheep" of Christ's flock began to "fold by themselves." At least two independent Negro congregations had been founded in the South before the end of the war, but the rush of Negroes into "African" churches began in the same year and in the same city as the Constitutional Convention.

The critical break was led by two prominent Philadelphia Negroes, Richard Allen and Absalom Jones, but they received ample inducement from influential white men. Jones and Allen were leaders of a group of Negroes who worshipped at St. George's Methodist Church. There in 1787 they were told to take seats around the wall and then, one day, in the gallery. Though they complied, one of the church's "trustees" attempted to haul Absalom Jones to his feet during prayer. The indignant Negroes, who had recently subscribed to refurbishment of the church, walked out "in a body" when the prayer was over. Apparently on their own initiative, but with assistance from some Quakers, they formed a Free African Society which for a time showed promise of becoming a very Quaker-like organization. Philadelphia Friends seem to have been happy over the possibility that Negroes would develop true religion in an independent but decidedly Friendly way. Although the Free African Society lasted for more than a decade, it was rendered a rump in 1791 by the exodus of Jones and Allen, both of whom had been pupils at Anthony Benezet's school, and a number

46. Quoted in Cadbury, "Negro Membership in the Society of Friends," *Jour. Negro Hist.*, 21 (1936), 153.

of their followers.[47] Out of their efforts soon grew the first Negro Episcopal church in America, led by Jones, and the African Methodist Episcopal Church, of which Allen became the first bishop. For some Quakers this exodus seems to have been interpreted as a defection, for while they were usually happy to see Negroes embracing other faiths, the Negroes who hoped to establish an Episcopal church told Benjamin Rush that "Quakers were much displeased with them." This opposition by Quakers, Rush noted in his commonplace book, merely confirmed his own high estimate of the worth of the project.[48]

The erection of the "African Episcopal Church of St. Thomas" in 1793 occasioned a moving display of interracial harmony. The comptroller-general of Pennsylvania, John Nicholson, had loaned the Negroes £100 out of his own pocket, and at least one other prominent Philadelphian gave financial support. After the roof-raising, on Fifth Street below Walnut one block from the city jail, there was a festive dinner under some spreading trees at the edge of town where about one hundred white persons, many of them carpenters, were waited upon by the Negroes. Afterwards about fifty "black people sat down at the same table" and were waited upon by "Six of the most respectable of the white company." Nicholson and Benjamin Rush and two others "were requested to set down with them," which they did, "much to the satisfaction of the poor blacks."

A repast like this was just the fuel to warm the heart of the generous doctor, especially because his energies were "much fatigued" from tending the victims of the mounting yellow fever epidemic. Rush had happily devoted himself to the cause of this church and to the welfare of Negroes generally, whom he once described as "the scattered appendages of most of the Churches in the City." He was invariably enraptured by public manifestations of interracial brotherhood and noted with satisfaction the progress of Negroes in letters to his wife and in his commonplace book; he hoped that similar churches would be established in other states, "and who knows," he asked, "but that it may be the means of sending the gospel to Africa, as the American Revolution sent

47. Allen, *Life Experience*, especially 25–26; William Douglass, *Annals of the First African Church, in the United States of America, Now Styled the African Episcopal Church of St. Thomas, Philadelphia* . . . (Phila., 1862); Charles H. Wesley, *Richard Allen: Apostle of Freedom* (Washington, 1935); Charles H. Wesley s. v. "Jones, Absalom," *Encyclopaedia of the Social Sciences;* Cadbury, "Negro Membership in Society of Friends," *Jour. Negro Hist.,* 21 (1936), 153–56.
48. Corner, ed., *Autobiography of Rush,* 202–3.

liberty to Europe?" For Rush the separate African churches had the inestimable virtue of making the black people "happy," but he was too much the public-spirited physician not to regard them also as instruments for social hygiene. "It will be much cheaper to build churches for them than jails," he wrote toward the close of his life. "Without the former, the latter will be indispensably necessary for them." [49]

Similarly revealing feelings seem to have animated others among the white supporters of the new Negro Episcopal church in Philadelphia. The building was finally readied for public worship in July 1794. On a slab of marble on the outside wall of the church was inscribed, with the best intention, an appalling irony: "The People That Walked in Darkness Have Seen a Great Light." The Reverend Samuel Magaw, delivering the opening discourse in the church, dwelt tediously—and with no greater perceptiveness than the piece of marble—upon the "darkness" from which Negroes were so fortunately emerging. Turning from freemen to slaves, Magaw rang the changes on an age-old theme. "Your present situation," he counseled them, "gives you some advantages above what others have: yes, and very possibly, above what your Masters have,—in that your humbleness of mind, your patience, faithfulness, and trust only in God, will add to the greatness of your future happiness." He went on to remind the free Negroes of the debt of gratitude they owed their earthly benefactors, especially to Lay, Woolman, Benezet, Franklin, the Pennsylvania Abolition Society and, not least, the citizens of Philadelphia. He cautioned them to guard against pride, which was said to be increasing among them, and explained with perfect accuracy that "less allowance will be made for your failings, than for those of other people." Among the virtues they should cultivate, he suggested, was "an obliging, friendly, meek conversation." Magaw concluded his address by praising the generous character of Philadelphians.[50]

Plainly Negroes were not alone in deriving warm satisfaction from the establishment of separate Negro churches. In the ensuing years, the generally amicable pattern of separation in Philadelphia

49. The description of the dinner is also Rush's, *ibid.*, 202–3, 228–29; L. H. Butterfield, ed., *Letters of Benjamin Rush,* 2 vols. (Princeton, 1951), I, 624, II, 636–37, 639–40, 1071; Benjamin Rush, *Extract of a Letter from Dr. Benjamin Rush, of Philadelphia, to Granville Sharp* (London, 1792), especially 3–4. See Douglass, *Annals of First African Church.*

50. Samuel Magaw, *A Discourse Delivered July 17, 1794 in the African Church of the City of Philadelphia, on the Occasion of Opening the Said Church, and Holding Public Worship in It the First Time* (Phila., [1794]).

was repeated, with variations, in New York, Boston, and other northern cities. The circumstances of origination varied, and some of the new churches had white ministers at first, but the trend toward racially separate churches was well under way in the 1790's. The same process operated in the slave states as well. Not that the now-familiar arrangement of mutual exclusion had yet been approximated: in many churches, in one in Wilkes County, Georgia, in 1805, for example, Negroes and whites attended together. But unquestionably there were an increasing number of racially exclusive congregations: in Wilmington, Delaware, Negroes erected a church with aid from white persons; in North Carolina some free Negroes established a church that whites attended and that eventually became all white; in the same state a mixed congregation split apart when the whites erected a separate church for the Negro members.[51]

Few developments could have been so symptomatic of the changes which white attitudes underwent after the Revolution. The splintering of the churches along racial lines was not simply a matter of Negroes recognizing that they would be more welcome elsewhere. It symbolized an increasingly clear-cut and pervasive separation. It meant that the one institution which was at all prepared to accept the Negro as an equal was shattered—completely, as it turned out. The new Negro churches were equal but separate, prototypes of "separate but equal." When Christian equalitarianism ran head on into American racial mores the result was, institutionally and in the public mind, gradual fission along racial lines. Separation was facilitated by the fissiparous character of Protestantism, but it also exposed the waning social strength of religious principles and the power of deep-set social attitudes. Many Americans seemed unable to tolerate equality without separation. This inability proved critical in the years after the Revolution, for it raised the question of what would happen to the commitment to equality if separation seemed impossible. If Negroes were going to remain in America and in increasing numbers become free, white men would have every reason to ask more intensely than before the Revolution what manner of men these Negroes were. Thus while social relationships between whites and Negroes were undergoing change and examination, the very nature of the Negro was coming under closer scrutiny.

51. Woodson, *History of the Negro Church*, chap. 4; Jones, *Religious Instruction of Negroes*, 50–53, 56–58; Ralph B. Flanders, *Plantation Slavery in Georgia* (Chapel Hill, 1933), 174; *Minutes Abolition Convention* (1806), 17; Bassett, *Slavery in N. C.*, 57–58, 60–61.

Certain aspects of this intense process of assessment become clearest of all in the highly charged writings of one man who as much as any single person framed the terms of American assessment of the Negro's physical being and especially of his inherent qualifications for participation in the white man's community. His answer was physical separation.

Part Five

THOUGHT AND SOCIETY
1783—1812

XII THOMAS JEFFERSON

Self and Society

AGAINST THE BACKDROP OF CHANGING ATTITUDES AND
actions concerning Negroes and Negro slavery, the writings of one
man become a fixed and central point of reference and influence. In
the years after the Revolution the speculations of Thomas Jefferson
were of great importance because so many people read and reacted
to them. His remarks about Negroes in the only book he ever wrote
were more widely read, in all probability, than any others until the
mid-nineteenth century. In addition to his demonstrable impact
upon other men, Jefferson is important—or perhaps more accurately, valuable to historical analysis—because he permits (without
intending to) a depth and range of insight into the workings of
ideas about Negroes within one man as he stood in relationship to
his culture. Jefferson's energetic facility with the pen makes it
possible, uniquely so in this period of history, to glimpse some of
the inward springs of feeling which supported certain attitudes
towards Negroes. It then becomes possible to see the intricate interlacing of one man's personality with his social surroundings, the
values of his culture, and the ideas with which he had contact.
Thomas Jefferson was not a typical nor an ordinary man, but his
enormous breadth of interest and his lack of originality make him
an effective sounding board for his culture. On some important
matters, therefore, he may be taken as accurately reflecting common
presuppositions and sensitivities even though many Americans disagreed with some of his conclusions.

To contemplate any man-in-culture is to savor complexity. It will
be easiest to start with Jefferson's central dilemma: he hated slavery
but thought Negroes inferior to white men. His remarks on the
Negro's mental inferiority helped kindle a revealing public controversy on the subject which deserves examination. But it will also be

necessary to return again to Thomas Jefferson, to his inward world where Negro inferiority was rooted. There it is possible to discern the interrelationship between his feelings about the races and his feeling about the sexes and thence to move once again to the problem of interracial sex in American culture. Finally, by tacking back to Jefferson and to the way he patterned his perceptions of his surroundings, it becomes easy to see how he assimilated the Indian to his anthropology and to America. His solution with the Negro was very different.

1. JEFFERSON: THE TYRANNY OF SLAVERY

Jefferson was personally involved in Negro slavery. On his own plantations he stood confronted by the practical necessity of making slave labor pay and by the usual frustrating combination of slave recalcitrance and inefficiency. Keeping the Negro men and especially the women and children clad, bedded, and fed was expensive, and keeping them busy was a task in itself.[1] Nor was his load lightened by daily supervision of a system which he genuinely hated, nor by realization that his livelihood depended on its continuation. This dependence almost inevitably meant that, for Jefferson the planter, Negroes sometimes became mere objects of financial calculation. "I have observed," he once wrote, "that our families of negroes double in about 25 years, which is an increase of the capital, invested in them, of 4. per cent over and above keeping up the original number." Successful maintenance of several plantations made for a measure of moral callousness: "The first step towards the recovery of our lands," he advised John Taylor, "is to find substitutes for corn and bacon. I count on potatoes, clover, and sheep. The two former to feed every animal on the farm except my negroes, and the latter to feed them, diversified with rations of salted fish and molasses, both of them wholesome, agreeable, and cheap articles of food." [2] For a man of Jefferson's convictions, entanglement in Negro slavery was genuinely tragic. Guiltily he referred

1. Since Jefferson's writings are at present available in different editions of varying scope and editorial standards, the following have been used in order of preference: Boyd, ed., *Papers of Jefferson*; Lester J. Cappon, ed., *The Adams-Jefferson Letters: The Complete Correspondence between Thomas Jefferson and Abigail and John Adams*, 2 vols. (Chapel Hill, 1959) ; Ford, ed., *Works of Jefferson*; Lipscomb and Bergh, eds., *The Writings of Jefferson*. Material relevant to Jefferson's management of his slaves has been collected in Betts, ed., *Jefferson's Farm Book*, especially pp. 5–47 of the Commentary.

2. Notes on Arthur Young's Letter [June 18, 1792], Ford, ed., *Works of Jefferson*, VII, 120; to John Taylor, Monticello, Dec. 29, 1794, Lipscomb and Bergh, eds., *Writings of Jefferson*, XVIII, 197.

to his Negroes as "servants," thus presaging the euphemism of the nineteenth century. His hopes for transforming his slaves into tenants evidenced a desire to seek a way out, but financial considerations perpetually precluded action. In the end he freed a few of them, but more than a hundred remained in slavery.[3] He never doubted that his monetary debts constituted a more immediate obligation than manumission. Most Americans would have agreed.

Jefferson's heartfelt hatred of slavery did not derive so much from this harassing personal entanglement in the practicalities of slavery as from the system of politics in which he was enmeshed mentally. "Enmeshed" seems the appropriate term because the natural rights philosophy was the governing aspect of his theology and his science; it formed a part of his being, and his most original contribution was the graceful lucidity with which he continually restated the doctrine. Yet in Jefferson's hands natural rights took on a peculiar cast, for he thought of rights as being natural in a very literal sense. Rights belonged to men as biological beings, inhering in them, as he said in his draft of the Declaration of Independence, because "all men are created equal and independant" and because "from that equal creation they derive rights inherent and inalienable." [4] The central fact was creation: the Creator, whose primary attribute was tidiness, would scarcely have been so careless as to create a single species equipped with more than one set of rights. If Jefferson's own passion for order was reflected in these phrases, so was his agrarian penchant for solitude. What was reflected most clearly of all, though, was the extent to which the natural world dominated Jefferson's thinking. Creation was the central "fact" because it explained nature. And Jefferson was awed by nature, if "awe" may be used in connection with a man so immensely capable of placid receptivity. While apparently working from a "Supreme Being" to an orderly nature, in fact Jefferson derived his Creator from what He had created—a nature which was by axiom orderly. In the same way, he derived God-given rights from the existence of the class of natural beings known as men. To know whether certain men possessed natural rights one had only to inquire whether they were human beings.[5]

3. See especially Boyd, ed., *Papers of Jefferson*, XI, 653, XIII, 607–8, XIV, 492–93. Jefferson was wildly welcomed by his slaves upon his return from Europe: see the editorial note in *ibid.*, XVI, 167–68. Many school books still say that Jefferson freed his slaves.

4. Boyd, ed., *Papers of Jefferson*, I, 423.

5. I am much indebted to certain ideas in the analysis of Jefferson's ideology offered by Daniel J. Boorstin, *The Lost World of Thomas Jefferson* (N. Y., 1948). Jefferson pushed the concept of "natural right" into fields where many of his contemporaries were unwilling to follow in 1790: he described majority rule

Without question Negroes were members of that class. Hence Jefferson never for a moment considered the possibility that they might rightfully be enslaved. He felt the personal guilt of slaveholding deeply, for he was daily depriving other men of their rightful liberty. With "my debts once cleared off," he wrote with a highly revealing slip of the pen, "I shall try some plan of making their situation happier, determined to content myself with a small portion of their ~~liberty~~ labour." [6] His vigorous antislavery pronouncements, however, were always redolent more of the library than the field. Slavery was an injustice not so much for the specific Negroes held in bondage as for any member of the human species. It was not simply that Jefferson was a benevolent master and had little contact with the cruelty of slavery, but that his approach to human society was always phylogenic. His most heartfelt denunciation of the notorious horrors of the slave trade, for example, consisted of a reference to "the unhappy human beings . . . forcibly brought away from their native country." [7] Wherever he encountered human cruelty, as he assuredly did in France, he saw not cruelty but injustice; as in so many other matters he was inclined to universalize particulars. Yet he was always the observer of particulars and too much interested in the welfare of Virginia to let his vision of slavery remain entirely academic. Slavery was an evil as well as an injustice, and from this standpoint Jefferson wrote one of the classic denunciations of the institution. In his *Notes on the State of Virginia,* written in 1781–82 in reply to queries from the secretary of the French legation in Philadelphia, François Barbé-Marbois, Jefferson answered a question on the "particular customs and manners that may happen to be received in that state" by discussing one matter only—the deleterious effects of slavery.

There must doubtless be an unhappy influence on the manners of our people produced by the existence of slavery among us. The whole commerce between master and slave is a perpetual exercise of the most boisterous passions, the most unremitting despotism on the one part, and degrading submissions on the other. Our children see this, and learn to imitate it; for man is an imitative animal. . . . The parent storms, the child

as "the Natural law of every society" and claimed that "the right to have commerce and intercourse with our neighbors is a natural right." Boyd, ed., *Papers of Jefferson,* XVI, 179, 450. His original draft of the Declaration is in *ibid.,* I, 423–27.

6. To Francis Eppes, Paris, July 30, 1787, Boyd, ed., *Papers of Jefferson,* XI, 653; also to Nicholas Lewis, Paris, Dec. 19, 1786, *ibid.,* X, 615.

7. To Christopher Ellery, Washington, May 19, 1803, Ford, ed., *Works of Jefferson,* IX, 466.

looks on, catches the lineaments of wrath, puts on the same airs in the circle of smaller slaves, gives a loose to his worst of passions, and thus nursed, educated, and daily exercised in tyranny, cannot but be stamped by it with odious peculiarities. The man must be a prodigy who can retain his manners and morals undepraved by such circumstances. And with what execration should the statesman be loaded, who permitting one half the citizens thus to trample on the rights of the other, transforms those into despots, and these into enemies, destroys the morals of the one part, and the amor patriæ of the other. For if a slave can have a country in this world, it must be any other in preference to that in which he is born to live and labour for another: in which he must lock up the faculties of his nature, contribute as far as depends on his individual endeavours to the evanishment of the human race, or entail his own miserable condition on the endless generations proceeding from him. With the morals of the people, their industry also is destroyed. For in a warm climate, no man will labour for himself who can make another labour for him. This is so true, that of the proprietors of slaves a very small proportion indeed are ever seen to labour. And can the liberties of a nation be thought secure when we have removed their only firm basis, a conviction in the minds of the people that these liberties are of the gift of God? That they are not to be violated but with his wrath? [8]

While he recognized the condition of slaves as "miserable," the weight of Jefferson's concern was reserved for the malevolent effects of slavery upon masters. These effects had always concerned anti-slavery men of every stripe, but with most of them one is not left wondering what would have remained of their antislavery views had they found slavery beneficial to white society. Fortunately Jefferson went to his grave convinced that slavery was a blight on the white community. With slavery's effect on black men he simply was not overly concerned. [9]

Indicative of Jefferson's approach toward the institution was his horror of slave rebellion. His apprehension was of course shared by most Americans, but he gave it expression at an unusually early date, some years before the disaster in St. Domingo. When denouncing slavery in the *Notes on Virginia* he gave vent to forebodings of a possible upheaval in America in a passage clouded with dark indirection. "Indeed I tremble for my country," he wrote passionately, "when I reflect that God is just: that his justice cannot sleep for ever: that considering numbers, nature and natural means only, a

8. Jefferson, *Notes on Virginia*, ed. Peden, 162–63.
9. When confronted with the immediate practicalities of slave ownership Jefferson could more readily imagine its effect upon slaves; he ordered that his nailers not be whipped except in extreme cases, since whipping tended "to degrade them in their own eyes," Jefferson to Thomas Mann Randolph, Washington, Jan. 23, 1801, Lipscomb and Bergh, eds., *Writings of Jefferson*, XVIII, 232.

revolution of the wheel of fortune, an exchange of situation, is among possible events: that it may become probable by supernatural interference! The Almighty has no attribute which can take side with us in such a contest." The depth of his feeling was apparent, for he rarely resorted to exclamation marks and still less often to miracles without skepticism. Later, Negro rebellion in St. Domingo confirmed his fears, the more so because he was utterly unable to condemn it. Always blandly receptive to revolution as a mechanism of change, he foresaw a strange future for the Caribbean islands. "I become daily more and more convinced," he wrote in 1793, "that all the West India Islands will remain in the hands of the people of colour, and a total expulsion of the whites sooner or later take place." From the islands he gloomily turned to his own country. "It is high time we should forsee the bloody scenes which our children certainly, and possibly ourselves (south of the Potommac,) have to wade through, and try to avert them." St. Domingo, he became convinced, was merely "the first chapter"; and his mind dwelt on the possible second chapter almost morbidly: "if something is not done," he wrote melodramatically in 1797, "and done soon, we shall be the murderers of our own children." Then in the summer of 1800 the second chapter appeared to open, and Jefferson wrote self-consolingly from Monticello: "We are truly to be pitied." Twenty years later at the time of the Missouri Compromise he was still murmuring of his fears. Still adamant that Negroes must be free, he characteristically fused obligation with future fact: "Nothing is more certainly written in the book of fate than that these people are to be free." Only the means were at question: white men must liberate Negroes in justice, or Negroes would liberate themselves in blood.[10]

While Jefferson thus hitched fear of rebellion to the antislavery cause, he refused to allow strong feelings on both matters to override his judgment as to the appropriate course of practical action. As a youth, in the first blush of Revolutionary enthusiasm, he had urged upon his native Virginia a program of gradual emancipation. "But it was found," he wrote years later in 1821, "that the public mind would not yet bear the proposition, nor will it bear it even at

10. Jefferson, *Notes on Virginia*, ed. Peden, 163; to James Monroe, Phila., July 14, 1793, Ford, ed., *Works of Jefferson*, VII, 449–50; to St. George Tucker, Monticello, Aug. 28, 1797, *ibid.*, VIII, 335; to Benjamin Rush, Monticello, Sept. 23, 1800, *ibid.*, IX, 149; Autobiography (1821), *ibid.*, I, 77. For further evidence of his fears and of his certainty of eventual emancipation see his letter to William A. Burwell, Washington, Jan. 28, 1805, *ibid.*, X, 126–27; to Edward Coles, Monticello, Aug. 25, 1814, *ibid.*, XI, 416–20; to John Adams, Monticello, Jan. 22, 1821, Cappon, ed., *Adams-Jefferson Letters*, II, 569–70.

this day." [11] As early as the 1780's Jefferson fully recognized the difficulties involved in any practical program for freedom and shrank from publishing his *Notes on Virginia* because it contained strong antislavery expressions. His friend Charles Thomson agreed that there were just grounds for fearing southern reaction while agreeing too that if the "cancer" was not wiped out "by religion, reason and philosophy" it would be someday "by blood." James Monroe, on the other hand, thought the antislavery sentiments could well be published. They finally did appear, of course, but Jefferson remained pessimistic. [12] He wrote in 1786 concerning possible legislative action in Virginia that "an unsuccessful effort, as too often happens, would only rivet still closer the chains of bondage, and retard the moment of delivery to this oppressed description of men." Later he steadfastly refused to condemn slavery publicly, refused to join antislavery organizations, refused to endorse the publications of abolitionists, in each case because he thought that premature endorsement by a figure of his prominence might easily damage the antislavery cause. [13] It was neither timidity nor concern for reputation which restrained him; in fact he had good reason to think that antislavery pronouncements might solidify the institution. Francis Kinloch wrote him from South Carolina of "the general alarm" which a certain "passage in your Notes occasioned amongst us. It is not easy to get rid of old prejudices, and the word 'emancipation' operates like an apparition upon a South Carolina planter." [14] From wide experience Jefferson had acquired a strong sense of "how difficult it is to move or inflect the great machine of society, how impossible to advance the notions of a whole people suddenly to ideal right." He was acutely conscious of "the passions, the prejudices, and the real difficulties" compounded in American Negro slavery. [15]

2. JEFFERSON: THE ASSERTION OF NEGRO INFERIORITY

His sensitive reaction to social "passions" and "prejudices" was heightened by dim recognition that they operated power-

11. Autobiography (1821), Ford, ed., *Works of Jefferson*, I, 76–77.

12. Thomson to Jefferson, N. Y., Nov. 2, 1785, Boyd, ed., *Papers of Jefferson*, IX, 9; Monroe to Jefferson, N. Y., Jan. 19, 1786, *ibid.*, 190.

13. *Ibid.*, VIII, 184, 227, 245, 356–57, X, 63, XII, 577–78; to Dr. George Logan, Washington, May 11, 1805, Ford, ed., *Works of Jefferson*, X, 141–42.

14. Apr. 26, 1789, Boyd, ed., *Papers of Jefferson*, XV, 72.

15. To Walter Jones, Washington, Mar. 31, 1801, Lipscomb and Bergh, eds., *Writings of Jefferson*, X, 256; to St. George Tucker, Monticello, Aug. 28, 1797, Ford, ed., *Works of Jefferson*, VIII, 335; See also Jefferson, *Notes on Virginia*, ed. Peden, 159.

fully within himself, though of course he never realized how deep-seated his anti-Negro feelings were. On the surface of these thoughts lay genuine doubts concerning the Negro's inherent fitness for freedom and recognition of the tensions inherent in racial slavery. He was firmly convinced, as he demonstrated in the *Notes on Virginia,* that Negroes could never be incorporated into white society on equal terms.

Deep rooted prejudices entertained by the whites; ten thousand recollec-tions, by the blacks, of the injuries they have sustained; new provocations; the real distinction which nature has made; and many other circumstances, will divide us into parties, and produce convulsions which will probably never end but in the extermination of the one or the other race.—To these objections, which are political, may be added others, which are physical and moral.

The "real distinction which nature has made" was for Jefferson not only physical but temperamental and mental. Negroes seemed to "require less sleep," for "after hard labour through the day," they were "induced by the slightest amusements to sit up till midnight, or later" though aware that they must rise at "first dawn." They were "at least as brave" as whites, and "more adventuresome." "But," he wrote, withdrawing even this mild encomium, "this may perhaps proceed from a want of forethought, which prevents their seeing a danger till it be present. When present, they do not go through it with more coolness or steadiness than the whites." Negroes were "more ardent," their griefs "transient." "In general," he concluded, "their existence appears to participate more of sensa-tion than reflection. To this must be ascribed their disposition to sleep when abstracted from their diversions, and unemployed in labour. An animal whose body is at rest, and who does not reflect, must be disposed to sleep of course." Within the confines of this logic there was no room for even a hint that daily toil for another's benefit might have disposed slaves to frolic and to sleep.[16]

Of far more serious import for the Negro's future were Jefferson's remarks on mental capacity. More than any other single person he framed the terms of the debate still carried on today.

Comparing them by their faculties of memory, reason, and imagination, it appears to me, that in memory they are equal to the whites; in reason much inferior, as I think one could scarcely be found capable of tracing and comprehending the investigations of Euclid; and that in imagination they are dull, tasteless, and anomalous. It would be unfair to follow them to Africa for this investigation. We will consider them here, on the same

16. Jefferson, *Notes on Virginia,* ed. Peden, 138, 139.

stage with the whites, and where the facts are not apocryphal on which a judgment is to be formed. It will be right to make great allowances for the difference of condition, of education, of conversation, of the sphere in which they move. Many millions of them have been brought to, and born in America. Most of them indeed have been confined to tillage, to their own homes, and their own society: yet many have been so situated, they might have availed themselves of the conversation of their masters; many have been brought up to the handicraft arts, and from that circumstance have always been associated with the whites. Some have been liberally educated, and all have lived in countries where the arts and sciences are cultivated to a considerable degree, and have had before their eyes samples of the best works from abroad. . . . But never yet could I find that a black had uttered a thought above the level of plain narration; never see even an elementary trait of painting or sculpture.[17]

Despite his stress on the necessity for "great allowances," Jefferson seemed unable to push the logic of environmentalism very far; in fact he stopped at just the point where that logic made a case for Negro inferiority. He seemed incapable of complimenting Negroes without immediately adding qualifications. "In music," he continued, picking up a widespread popular belief, "they are more generally gifted than the whites with accurate ears for tune and time, and they have been found capable of imagining a small catch." Further ability was "yet to be proved."[18]

Not content with a general assessment, Jefferson went on to disparage the widely known Negroes who had been puffed by the antislavery people as examples of the Negro's equal capacities. Those known to him were poets, and by speculating on the theoretical effects of slavery upon poetry he twisted the environmentalist logic into anti-Negro shape. "Misery is often the parent of the most affecting touches in poetry.—Among the blacks is misery enough, God knows, but no poetry. Love is the peculiar oestrum of the poet. Their love is ardent, but it kindles the sense only, not the imagination." He dismissed Phyllis Wheatley with the airy remark that she was "not . . . a poet. The compositions published under her name are below the dignity of criticism." Ignatius Sancho he treated with

17. *Ibid.*, 139–40.
18. *Ibid.*, 140. On music compare Crawford, *Observations upon Negro-Slavery* (1790), 31; George Buchanan, *An Oration upon the Moral and Political Evil of Slavery. Delivered at a Public Meeting of the Maryland Society for Promoting the Abolition of Slavery, and the Relief of Free Negroes, and Others Unlawfully Held in Bondage* . . . (Baltimore, 1793), 10. Compare with the concluding sentence from a 20th-century work of scientific racism: "The Negro has the lower mental faculties (smell, sight, handicraftmanship, body-sense, melody) well developed, the Caucasian the higher (self-control, will power, ethical and aesthetic senses and reason)." Robert Bennett Bean, "Some Racial Peculiarities of the Negro Brain," *American Journal of Anatomy*, V (1906), 412.

more respect but decided that Sancho's works did "more honour to the heart than the head" and substituted "sentiment for demonstration." Sancho was the best of his race, but among literary figures in England "we are compelled to enroll him at the bottom of the column," if, Jefferson added pointedly, he was in fact the real author of the material "published under his name." This higher criticism was surprising in a man who wrote twenty years later that "of all men living I am the last who should undertake to decide as to the merits of poetry. In earlier life I was fond of it, and easily pleased." [19]

Jefferson was thoroughly aware that the environmentalist argument could serve (and actually had) to make a case for Negro equality, and hence he went to great lengths to prove that the Negroes' lack of talent did not stem from their condition. He turned to the slavery of classical times and wandered happily and discursively among the Romans and the Greeks, arguing that ancient slavery was more harsh than America's yet produced slaves of talent and demonstrable achievement. Unaware that he might be inverting cause and effect he noted that some ancient slaves excelled "in science, insomuch as to be usually employed as tutors to their master's children." There had been slaves, then, who had demonstrated significant attainments; and those who had "were of the race of whites." As for Negroes, he concluded, "It is not their condition then, but nature, which has produced the distinction." [20]

Having baldly stated his belief in innate inferiority, Jefferson immediately introduced his next subject by reopening the question he had just closed: "Whether further observation will or will not verify the conjecture, that nature has been less bountiful to them in the endowments of the head. . . ." What he now asked was suspension of decision, for he became increasingly aware of how far he had allowed himself to go. Genuine alarm underlay his admonition, toward the *end* of his passage on Negroes, that caution must be exercised "where our conclusion would degrade a whole race of men from the rank in the scale of beings which their Creator may perhaps have given them." But he extricated himself in highly satisfying fashion by dumping the whole problem in the broad lap of American science, thus permitting qualification of his previously stated position to the point of inconsistency. "The opinion, that they are inferior in the faculties of reason and imagination, must be hazarded with great diffidence. To justify a general conclusion,

19. Jefferson, *Notes on Virginia*, ed. Peden, 140–41; to John D. Burke, Washington, June 21, 1801, Ford, ed., *Works of Jefferson*, IX, 267.
20. Jefferson, *Notes on Virginia*, ed. Peden, 141–42.

requires many observations, even where the subject may be submitted to the Anatomical knife, to Optical glasses, to analysis by fire, or by solvents. How much more then where it is a faculty, not a substance, we are examining; where it eludes the research of all the senses; where the conditions of its existence are various and variously combined; where the effects of those which are present or absent bid defiance to calculation."

Growing happier with his solution he thus labored the obvious fact that assessing mental ability was an immensely difficult task. With nearly audible relief he remodeled an anti-Negro diatribe into a scientific hypothesis, thus effectively depersonalizing a matter which was for him obviously of some personal importance. "To our reproach it must be said, that though for a century and a half we have had under our eyes the races of black and of red men, they have never yet been viewed by us as subjects of natural history. I advance it therefore as a suspicion only, that the blacks, whether originally a distinct race, or made distinct by time and circumstances, are inferior to the whites in the endowments both of body and mind. It is not against experience to suppose, that . . . [they] may possess different qualifications." A "suspicion only" of "different qualifications" represented a rather different proposition from "It is not their condition then, but nature, which has produced the distinction." [21]

In assessing one important quality in Negroes, however, Jefferson always remained firmly consistent. The "moral sense" was as fully developed in Negroes as in whites. On this subject Jefferson suddenly pressed environmentalist logic as far as it would go. "That disposition to theft with which they have been branded," he declared categorically, "must be ascribed to their situation." With dry detachment he explained the justice of Negro thievery: "The man, in whose favour no laws of property exist, probably feels himself less bound to respect those made in favour of others." Might not the slave "justifiably take a little from one, who has taken all from him?" [22]

Jefferson's strikingly divergent conclusions on the Negro's moral sense and on his intellect were reached without a particle of inconsistency, for the two qualities were, as far as he and many of his post-Revolutionary contemporaries were concerned, thoroughly discrete. The "moral sense, or conscience," as Jefferson explained, was "as much a part of man as his leg or arm" and was "made a part of

21. *Ibid.*, 142–43.
22. *Ibid.*

his physical constitution, as necessary for a social being." [23] To say that the Negro possessed it was the Jeffersonian analogue of the Christian axiom that the Negro possessed a soul. Just as the traditional Christian God had provided the soul, the Jeffersonian Creator had endowed men with the properties necessary for their existence, and no kinds of men could be assumed to lack what they could not live together without. Had the Creator not provided men with a moral sense He would have been "a pitiful bungler." [24] The moral sense might be temporarily impaired by slavery, but Negroes must be said to possess it, else Negroes could never be free. Indeed they could not even be men without it. No such requirement, on the other hand, pertained to the Negro's intellectual endowment.

3. THE ISSUE OF INTELLECT

This striking dichotomy between morals and intellect gave evidence of both the staying power of traditional Christian dualism and the alterations which had been produced in it by the growth of mechanistic naturalism. John Locke's epistomology, which emphasized the blank mind's reception of "sensations" from the external world, had paved the way for re-elaboration of the old concept of "faculties" of the mind. The faculties were now conceived as mechanisms for manipulating sensations, and it was owing chiefly to Locke that the most popular term for describing mental

23. To Peter Carr, Paris, Aug. 10, 1787, Boyd, ed., *Papers of Jefferson*, XII, 14–15; to John Adams, Monticello, May 5, 1817, Cappon, ed., *Adams-Jefferson Letters*, II, 512.

24. Letter to Carr, previous note. On an earlier occasion he wrote that "Nature has written her moral laws" in "the head and heart of every rational and honest man . . . where every man may read them for himself." Opinion on French Treaties, Apr. 28, 1793, Ford, ed., *Works of Jefferson*, VII, 286. See also Jefferson to Maria Cosway, Paris, Oct. 12, 1786, Boyd, ed., *Papers of Jefferson*, X, 450; to Thomas Law, Poplar Forest, June 13, 1814, Bergh and Lipscomb, eds., *Writings of Jefferson*, XIV, 138–44, where Jefferson compared lack of moral sense in some individuals to physical birth defects. The same reasoning applied to liberty also, which was "given" to man "by the author of nature, because necessary for his own sustenance." Howell *v.* Netherland, Ford, ed., *Works of Jefferson*, I, 474. See also Adrienne Koch, *The Philosophy of Thomas Jefferson* (N. Y., 1943), chap. 3; Gladys Bryson, *Man and Society: The Scottish Inquiry of the Eighteenth Century* (Princeton, 1945). Benjamin Rush once admitted that some savage men, for instance certain African and Russian tribes, lacked the intellectual and the moral faculties. Rush carefully explained, however, that this lack did not mean such savages had never possessed them; the moral faculty might be asleep and could be wakened. Rush was arguing particularly that the moral faculty was as much influenced by external factors as were the other faculties, "Inquiry . . . Moral Faculty," *Medical Inquiries and Observations*, 2d ed., 4 vols. (Phila., 1805), II, 16–18.

talents had become "capacities." Dr. Benjamin Rush, who was as much of a psychologist as anyone in America, cataloged the faculties (under the heading "Physiology") as instinct, memory, imagination, understanding, will, passions and emotions, faith, and the "Moral faculties in which are included what is called the moral sense,—Conscience, and the sense of Deity." [25] An important result of this psychological taxonomy was an unprecedentedly clear-cut separation of what we would call intelligence from the capacity for religious experience, a separation of considerable relevance to changing assessments of Negroes in the second half of the eighteenth century. In one area of experience, this separation smoothed the path for converting Negroes to the religion of their masters by allowing conversion to proceed without implying anything very drastically positive about over-all equality. In another, it meant that the Negro could be judged inferior in certain respects without any implication that he was less than human, as Jefferson amply demonstrated. It helped also to bring the debate on the Negro's nature down to earth, away from heaven which offered better protection, to the realm of his future status in American society. By rendering the concept of mental ability less amorphous than previously, it helped channel much of the debate on the Negro toward the gratifyingly specific question of whether or not he was the mental equal of the white man.

In the years before the Revolution antislavery men had increasingly recognized the importance, even the necessity, of asserting Negro mental equality, but Jefferson's suspicions as advanced in the *Notes on Virginia* greatly heightened the urgency of the question and stimulated much more widespread debate. Publication of the *Notes*—1785 in Paris, 1787 in London (more widely circulated) and 1788 (a pirated edition) in Philadelphia—was followed almost immediately by public criticism of Jefferson's views as well as by a marked increase in the frequency of speculation on the matter in general terms. In 1792 Gilbert Imlay, a man of strange fortunes who had lived for a time in Kentucky, set out to refute Jefferson at some length, saying flatly that "it is certain" that Negroes and whites "are

25. Benjamin Rush, *Sixteen Introductory Lectures, to Courses of Lectures upon the Institutes and Practice of Medicine . . .* (Phila., 1811), 18–19. Rush's psychology may be illustrated by his assertion that we are able "to reject the doctrine of innate ideas, and to ascribe all our knowledge of sensible objects to impressions acting upon an *innate* capacity to receive ideas." Rush, *Medical Inquiries and Observations*, II, 451. The concept of "moral sense" was widely disseminated in American colleges after the Scottish Common Sense philosophy was introduced at the College of New Jersey by John Witherspoon in the early 1770's.

essentially the same in shape and intellect." Jefferson's whole case
for mental inferiority, Imlay declared, was absurd because it rested
on comparison between slaves and free men.[26] Equally specific attacks on Jefferson became more frequent after his involvement in
national politics, and there were audible crescendos in the election
years of 1796, 1800, and 1804. Often these volleys gave evidence of
sincere disagreement with his views on the Negro, despite the fact
that primary interest lay in defaming Jefferson the politician.
Clement Clarke Moore, for example, a New York scholar of Hebrew
with Federalist sympathies, controverted the *Notes on Virginia* in
considerable detail in 1804. On the subject of Negro poetry Moore
wrote indignantly that "one would have thought that modern philosophy herself could not have the face to declare that the wretch
who is driven out to labour at the dawn of day, and who toils until
evening with the whip flourishing over his head, ought to be a poet."
He went on to ask: "And does justice bid us examine their mental
powers, while in a state of servitude, rendered sullen by ignominy,
and broken down by labour? And although in large and civilized
communities there never appear more than a few scattered genuises
who deserve attention, does impartiality command us to criticise the
talents and literary productions of a few negroes who have escaped
the unhappy lot of their brethren; and because they fall far short of
European excellence, to degrade their whole race below the rest of
mankind?" Negroes could not meaningfully be compared to Roman
slaves, Moore concluded in a flourish which bared the logical weaknesses of the extreme environmentalist case, because Negroes were
"uncivilized." [27]

Jefferson's remarks were also attacked by a man who, as will
become clear in the next chapter, was an important defender of the

26. G[ilbert] Imlay, *A Topographical Description of the Western Territory of
North America* . . . (London, 1792), 194–97. The best biographical information
is in Ralph L. Rusk, "The Adventures of Gilbert Imlay," *Indiana University
Studies,* 10, no. 57 (1923), 1–26.

27. [Clement Clarke Moore], *Observations upon Certain Passages in Mr. Jefferson's Notes on Virginia, Which Appear to Have a Tendency to Subvert Religion,
and Establish a False Philosophy* (N. Y., 1804), 24–25; also published under the
same title in the *Port Folio,* IV (1804), 244–45, 250–52, 268–69. See also the
speech of William Loughton Smith, *Annals of Congress,* 1st Cong., 2d sess.,
1455–56; William Loughton Smith to Ralph Izard, Phila., Nov. 8, 1796, Ulrich B.
Phillips, ed., "South Carolina Federalist Correspondence, 1789–1797," *Amer. Hist.
Rev.,* 14 (1908–09), 785; Branagan, *Preliminary Essay on Oppression,* 234. Typical
political vindications of Jefferson which cited his antislavery but not his anti-
Negro views are [John Beckley], *Address to the People of the United States: With
an Epitome and Vindication of the Public Life and Character of Thomas
Jefferson,* 2d ed. (Phila., reprinted Newport, 1800), 8–9; Richmond *Va. Argus,*
Oct. 3, 1800.

underlying sameness of mankind. The Reverend Samuel Stanhope
Smith presented a brief and thoroughly inconclusive discussion of
the possibility that environmental influences might have altered the
Negro's skull and hence his thought; then he turned to the effects of
slavery upon the intellect and effectively utilized Jefferson's own
case against slavery, turning it on its head by presuming Negroes to
be the principal victims.

> I am inclined, however, to ascribe the apparent dullness of the negro
> principally to the wretched state of his existence first in his original
> country, where he is at once a poor and abject savage, and subjected to an
> atrocious despotism; and afterwards in those regions to which he is trans-
> ported to finish his days in slavery, and toil. Genius, in order to its
> cultivation, and the advantageous display of its powers, requires freedom:
> it requires reward, the reward at least of praise, to call it forth; competi-
> tion to awaken its ardor; and examples both to direct its operations, and to
> prompt its emulation. The abject servitude of the negro in America,
> condemned to the drudgery of perpetual labor, cut off from every mean of
> improvement, conscious of his degraded state in the midst of freemen who
> regard him with contempt, and in every word and look make him feel his
> inferiority; and hopeless of ever enjoying any great amelioration of his
> condition, must condemn him, while these circumstances remain, to per-
> petual sterility of genius.[28]

Smith went on to demolish the logic which Jefferson had employed
in unfavorably comparing Negroes with Indians. Negroes, he
pointed out, were cut "off from employments which, along with
conscious freedom and independence, often awaken the untutored
savage to the boldest enterprizes"; Negroes were placed "in the
midst of a civilized people with whom they cannot amalgamate, and
who only humble them by the continual view of their own inferiority." To place the Indian in that condition would be to "annihilate

28. Samuel Stanhope Smith, *An Essay on the Causes of the Variety of
Complexion and Figure in the Human Species. To Which Are Added, Animad-
versions on Certain Remarks Made on the First Edition of This Essay* . . . , ed.
Jordan, 1810 ed. (Cambridge, Mass., 1965), 161–64; and similar attacks in *New
York Magazine, or Literary Repository*, 2 (1791), 338–39; Edward Rushton,
*Expostulatory Letter to George Washington . . . on His Continuing to Be a
Proprietor of Slaves* (Liverpool, 1797), 10–11. A few travelers quoted Jefferson's
remarks on the Negro: William Priest, *Travels in the United States of America;
. . . 1793 . . . 1797 . . .* (London, 1802), 185–95; but more frequently foreign
travelers and abolitionists simply quoted Jefferson's antislavery remarks while
ignoring his views on Negroes as such: [Rhees], *Letters on Liberty and Slavery*,
title page and p. 9; G. W., "Slavery," *New York Weekly Magazine*, 3 (Mar. 23,
1798), 324–25; W. Winterbotham, *An Historical, Geographical, Commercial, and
Philosophical View of the American United States, and of the European Settlements in America and the West-Indies*, 4 vols. (London, 1795), III, 110; Melish,
Travels through the United States, 173–75; Charles W. Janson, *The Stranger in
America, 1793–1806*, ed. Carl S. Driver (N. Y., 1935), 388–89.

among them all the noble qualities which you had admired in their savage state." Smith turned finally to Jefferson's argument from classical slavery. "But has this philosopher sufficiently adverted to the infinite difference that must subsist between enslaved savages, destitute of the first elements of liberal knowledge, and held in contempt by their oppressors, and an ingenious and enlightened people, cultivated in the schools of philosophy, and practised in all the liberal arts, reduced to slavery by force of arms; and, even in slavery, respected by their masters?" [29] Heavy-handedly, Smith had groped his way toward realization that not only slavery but the "contempt" of whites might affect the Negro's intellect; but he did not see, or dared not say, that explicit assertions of inferiority (like those by Jefferson) might breed inferiority in actuality.

Heightened interest in the relative mental capacities of the various races derived not only from Jefferson's remarks on the subject and a changed conception of intelligence, but also from a growing tendency to regard man in general as a highly suitable object for scientific investigation. Anything proper to man lay within the scope of science, a presumption which shone brightly in the self-conscious optative pronouncements of American philosophers on the subject of their own endeavors. A signal occasion occurred in 1780 at the opening meeting of the American Academy of Arts and Sciences (Boston's answer to Philadelphia's American Philosophical Society), when founder and president James Bowdoin called the long roll of the Academy's legitimate interests. His multifarious topics necessarily included "Natural History," under which he discussed man, and he apparently thought it appropriate to dilate upon the problem of racial equality. As for mental abilities, he proclaimed, man's "beneficient CREATOR, the first and the supremely great Naturalist" (it could have been Jefferson speaking) had endowed him with "sufficient faculties" to gain knowledge of nature. But man's "natural faculties" varied, collectively, as "between *Europe* and *Africa*" and elsewhere. From an original equality, human faculties had come to vary because human beings had

---

29. Smith, *Essay on Variety* (1810), ed. Jordan, 164, 167. Despite the pronounced trend toward separation of inherent capacity from environmental influences, some writers remained mired in the old confusion. One wrote, "In their mental faculties, I believe . . . this race are inferior to whites. The native African is also inferior to the mulatto." But he went on, "Who knows but did they possess the same civil priviledges and literary advantages that whites do, philosophers, poets and orators might arise among them equal to this or any other country, to those either of ancient or modern times." George Fowler, *The Wandering Philanthropist* . . . (Phila., 1810), 289.

dispersed into varying climates. Too much heat and too much cold adversely affected the mind: "Hence, in both cases, an inferiority of intellects." A moderate climate was best suited to the "exertions both of mind and body." Even in the same climate, however, "the exertions of different nations" might vary, depending on such factors as "education, religion, government, and other circumstances, or the appearance of some happy genius to instruct and direct them." If there were differences of intellect between nations inhabiting similar climates, Bowdoin concluded tentatively, they "must be casual, arising from some certain adventitious circumstances." [30] Though hardly Jeffersonian in felicity of style, Bowdoin shared with Jefferson the assumption that questions about the human mind must be appealed to science and the conviction that for the moment such questions could only be answered tentatively. Bowdoin's environmentalism was characteristic of the mood of American scientists generally and his position on mental equality demonstrative of the fact that the injunctions of natural philosophy implied nothing definite about Negro inferiority. Clearly, a "scientific" affirmation of Negro inferiority would have to derive at least in some measure from imperatives extraneous to science itself.

Some Americans, however, had every reason not to hesitate in providing final answers. Clutching the lamp of environmentalism the antislavery people set out to discover an equality of mental capacity in the Negro, a discovery requisite both to the logic of their cause and to vindication of the Negro's ability to lead life in freedom. For the most part they were successful, and their near unanimity causes Jefferson's tentatively contrary views to stand out in sharp relief.

4. THE ACCLAIM OF TALENTED NEGROES

What is especially striking is that most antislavery writers became interested in vindicating the Negro's intellectual capacity only after the antislavery movement had been under way for some years, specifically, after 1787. The date suggests stimulation by Jefferson's *Notes on Virginia,* yet most antislavery writers did not mention the *Notes;* and indeed there are good reasons for supposing that Jefferson's remarks were not the only stimuli which generated

30. James Bowdoin, "A Philosophical Discourse, Publickly Addressed to the American Academy of Arts and Sciences, in Boston . . . [1780]," American Academy of Arts and Sciences, *Memoirs,* 1 (1785), 8–11; also published separately in 1780.

the remarkably sudden surge of interest in the question of the Negro's mental abilities. For one thing, adoption of a new Constitution may well have stimulated consideration of the nature of the men who were (for the most part) excluded from participation in the new nation. Certainly the widely discussed Constitution raised specific questions about Negro slavery and the slave trade. By the early 1790's, too, disturbing news began to arrive from St. Domingo. And there was perhaps a self-reinforcing mechanism in operation: once the matter had been thoroughly broached it was difficult to avoid discussing it. As it turned out, the argument for mental equality became a standard theme in the antislavery repertoire.

Whatever the cause, widespread concern with mental equality appeared with remarkable suddenness. Charles Crawford, a recent arrival in America and an active member of the Pennsylvania Abolition Society, barely touched upon the subject in his *Observations upon Slavery* in the first edition of 1784. Six years later in 1790, however, he brought out a much enlarged second edition which included an entire chapter of thirteen pages devoted to defense of the Negro's mental capacities. He pointed out that James Beattie (the Scottish professor of moral philosophy) had refuted David Hume's well-known diatribe against the Negro; he cited the success of Anthony Benezet's school for Negroes; and he went on to parade before his readers a succession of Negroes who had demonstrated to all the world the fact and hence the possibility of Negro intellectual achievement, including Ignatius Sancho and Phyllis Wheatley. While Charles Crawford was unusually radical in his desire to extend to Negroes "all the rights of men," including suffrage and freedom to marry whites, his new emphasis on mental equality was typical of the outpouring of antislavery literature from 1788 through the mid-1790's.[31] Hannah More wove the antislavery case into rhyme in 1788.

31. Crawford, *Observations upon Negro-Slavery* (1784) ; Crawford, *Observations upon Negro-Slavery* (1790) , 20–32, 117–18; J. P. Brissot de Warville, *New Travels in the United States of America, 1788*, trans. Mara Soceanu Vamos and Durand Echeverria, ed. Echeverria (Cambridge, Mass., 1964) , 217, 232–37; J. P. Brissot de Warville, *A Critical Examination of the Marquis de Chatellux's Travels, in North America, in a Letter Addressed to the Marquis; Principally Intended as a Refutation of His Opinions Concerning the Quakers, the Negroes, the People, and Mankind. Translated from the French* (Phila., 1788) , 51–63; "Education of Negro Children," *Amer. Museum*, 6 (1789) , 383; O'Kelly, *Essay on Negro-Slavery*, 45; [William Belsham], *An Essay on the African Slave Trade* (Phila., 1790) , 5; Charles Crawford, "Observations upon Negro-Slavery," *Universal Asylum, and Columbian Magazine*, 5 (1790) , 333–34; Annapolis *Md. Gaz.*, Jan. 20, Feb. 3, 1791; Buchanan, *Oration upon Slavery*, 10–11 (a work dedicated to Jefferson) ; Miller, *Discourse, Delivered April 12, 1797*, 13–15; "On the Consequences of Abolishing the Slave

> Perish th' illiberal thought which wou'd debase
> The native genius of the sable race!
> Perish the proud philosophy, which sought
> To Rob them of the pow'rs of equal thought!
> Does then th' immortal principle within
> Change with the casual colour of a skin?
> Does matter govern spirit? Or is mind
> Degraded by the form to which 'tis join'd? [32]

In 1791 Moses Brown, the prominent Quaker merchant of Providence, happily seized upon the success of a free school for Negroes in his city which, he declared, "may be reckon'd, among the numerous Evidences of their being Men capable of Every Improvement with ourselves where they [are] under the Same Advantages." An "Address to the Public" by the Pennsylvania Abolition Society, signed by its president, Benjamin Franklin, in 1789, declared that the chains which bound the slave's body "do also fetter his intellectual faculties; and impair the social affections of his heart." In 1789 the antislavery *American Museum* reprinted a defense of innate equality written (ostensibly) by a free Negro in England and in 1791 a translation of a French work entitled "The Negro Equalled by Few Europeans." William Pinkney of Maryland, later to attain fame as an orator, raised his huge bulk in the state legislature to attack slavery on two occasions in 1789. Negroes and whites, Pinkney rumbled, were "endued with equal faculties of mind and body"; Negroes were "in all respects our equals by nature; and he who thinks otherwise has never reflected, that talents, however great, may perish unnoticed and unknown, unless auspicious circumstances conspire to draw them forth, and animate their exertions in the round of knowledge." Warming to his work, Pinkney summed up the antislavery case in twenty-two words: "Thus the

---

Trade to the West Indian Colonies," *Literary Magazine and American Register*, 4 (1805) , 378–80; John Burk, *The History of Virginia, from Its First Settlement to the Present Day*, 4 vols. (Petersburg, Va., 1804–16) , I, 212; Branagan, *Preliminary Essay on Oppression*, 102–8; Parrish, *Remarks on the Slavery of the Black People*, 24; A[bsalom] J[ones] and R[ichard] A[llen], *A Narrative of the Proceedings of the Black People . . . in Philadelphia, in the Year 1793 . . .* (Phila., 1794) , 24. The contemporary attack on the slave trade in Great Britain may have had some influence on Americans; see the forceful statement of equality, ostensibly by a Negro but probably ghosted, Ottabah Cugoano, *Thoughts and Sentiments on the Evil and Wicked Traffic of the Slavery and Commerce of the Human Species, Humbly Submitted to the Inhabitants of Great Britain* (London, 1787). For biographical information see Lewis Leary, "Charles Crawford: A Forgotten Poet of Early Philadelphia," *Pa. Mag. of Hist. and Biog.*, 83 (1959) , 293–306.
32. Hannah More, *Slavery. A Poem* (N. Y., 1788) , 6.

ignorance and the vices of these wretches are solely the result of situation, and therefore no evidence of their inferiority." Benjamin Rush, too, announced as a general principle—Rush was much given to enunciating general principles—that "Slaves are stupid, because they have no wills of their own." [33]

Though antislavery writers continued in many cases to reiterate what had by this time become standard antislavery doctrine, the urgent need for restatement seems to have subsided somewhat after about 1793. With no very convincing method available of proving Negro equality it was not possible to develop further a case already made. As the antislavery movement began to lose energy the question of the Negro's intellectual endowment was left to drift, awaiting the definitive verdict of science which has since proved such a mirage. Occasionally, cracks showed in the solid antislavery structure, indicating that Jefferson was not entirely alone. The Maryland Abolition Society declared in 1789, "The human race, however varied in color or intellects, are all justly entitled to liberty"; and the Reverend Alexander McLeod told the New York Manumission Society in 1802 that the inferiority of blacks to whites had been "greatly exaggerated" and that while there was "no reason to suppose the blacks destitute of mental powers" possible superiority would give whites no right of dominion.[34] The assertion of mental equality was a plausible weapon for antislavery, but not, as Jefferson had shown, absolutely requisite to the cause.

One reason for the sudden outburst of interest in mental equality around 1790 was the sudden, and far from fortuitous, appearance of several Negroes to whose fresh example men might readily appeal. Benjamin Rush, first engaged in antislavery controversy in 1773,

33. Brown quoted in Michael Kraus, "Slavery Reform in the Eighteenth Century: An Aspect of Transatlantic Intellectual Cooperation," Pa. Mag. of Hist. and Biog., 60 (1936), 62; Smyth, ed., Writings of Franklin, X, 67; "Letter on Slavery. By a Negro," Amer. Museum, 6 (1789), 77–80; ibid., 9, 10 (1791), passim; William Pinkney, "Speech of William Pinkney, Esq. in the House of Delegates of Maryland, on the Discussion of a Report from a Committee, Recommending the Adoption of Certain Measures for Ameliorating the Condition of the African Race; and for Repealing a Law Which Prohibited the Manumission of Slaves; Delivered at Their Session in November, 1789," The American Museum: or, Annual Register of Fugitive Pieces, Ancient and Modern. For the Year 1798 (Phila., 1799), 86. Pinkney seems to have spoken twice, for see Amer. Museum, 6 (1789), 74–77; Rush, Sixteen Introductory Lectures, 108; also Corner, ed., Autobiography of Rush, 304–5.
34. From the constitution of the Maryland society, reprinted in Poole, Anti-Slavery Opinions Before 1800, 50n; McLeod, Negro Slavery Unjustifiable, 22, but see p. 16.

contributed again in 1788 by publishing a brief account of a Negro physician from New Orleans, James Derham. Dr. Rush was happy to call Dr. Derham a brother in science and commended him to the Pennsylvania Abolition Society as evidence of Negro achievement.[35] Rush was also responsible for bringing to light the strange case of Thomas Fuller, a Maryland Negro who received more widespread attention than Derham because he was nearer to home and because he perfectly embodied the hopeful proposition that a slave might demonstrate great natural talent despite his slavery. "Negro Tom," as his death notice in the Boston *Columbian Centinel* described him in 1790, was a *"self-taught Arithmetician"* born in Africa and brought to America at age fourteen. This "famous African Calculator" humbly commenced his mathematical career by counting hairs on the tails of cows and horses he had been set to tend, and though illiterate, became able to perform complicated arithmetical calculations in his head. When called upon to calculate the number of seconds a man has lived when age 70 years, 17 days, and 12 hours, he popped out the answer after only a few minutes' thought and, upon being charged with error, correctly suggested to his examiners that they had failed to account for leap years. What better possible evidence of native ability than this? Overnight he became an anti-slavery hero, often referred to simply as "the Negro mathematician." The *Columbian Centinel* was unrestrained, to put it mildly, in praise of "this *untutored Scholar!*—Had his opportunities of improvement been equal to those of thousands of his fellow-men, neither the Royal Society of London, the Academy of sciences at Paris, nor even a Newton himself, need have been ashamed to acknowledge him a Brother in Science." [36]

The most widely known exemplar of the interracial brotherhood of science was Benjamin Banneker, also something of a mathematician. Born free in Maryland, he interested himself in mathematical

35. "Certificate to the Pennsylvania Society for Promoting the Abolition of Slavery," *Amer. Museum*, 5 (1789) , 61–62; "From the Pennsylvania Society for Promoting the Abolition of Slavery, and the Relief of Free Negroes," *Columbian Magazine*, 2 (1788) , 742–43; Crawford, *Observations upon Negro-Slavery* (1790) , 28–29; Butterfield, ed., *Letters of Rush*, I, 498 (editor's note) . References and descriptions of talented Negroes became very numerous especially in the five years after 1788.

36. "Account of a Wonderful Talent for Arithmetical Calculation, in an African Slave, Living in Virginia," in *Amer. Museum*, 5 (1789) , 62–63, and in *Columbian Mag.*, 2 (1788) , 743–44; Rush, *Sixteen Introductory Lectures*, 450; Crawford, *Observations upon Negro-Slavery* (1790) , 29–30; Boston *Columbian Centinel*, Dec. 29, 1790 (italics reversed) .

puzzles, supposedly constructed a clock, and when loaned some books by a kindly neighboring Quaker manufacturer, Andrew Ellicott, became fascinated by astronomy. He was appointed member of the commission to survey the new national district; the Georgetown *Weekly Ledger* reported in March 1791 the arrival of Major Pierre Charles L'Enfant, a second member, and "Benjamin Banneker, an Ethiopian whose abilities as surveyor and astronomer already prove that Mr. Jefferson's concluding that that race of men were void of mental endowment was without foundation." Ironically, Banneker's nomination had come from the Secretary of State, Thomas Jefferson.[37] Banneker's fame rested particularly, however, on his almanacs, published from 1791 through at least 1796 alternatively in Baltimore, Philadelphia, Petersburg, and Richmond.[38] The first contained an introduction by James McHenry of Baltimore, once a medical student under Benjamin Rush and by this time a prominent soldier and statesman, who provided biographical facts and his personal assurance that Banneker had performed the calculations in the almanac without assistance. McHenry had been careful to investigate these particulars, he said, "as they form an interesting fact in the History of Man." "I consider this Negro," he went on, "as a fresh proof that the powers of the mind are disconnected with the colour of the skin, or, in other words, a striking contradiction to Mr. *Hume*'s doctrine, that 'the Negroes are naturally inferior to the whites, and unsusceptible of attainments in arts and sciences.' " In every civilized country, he added, there are many whites inferior to Banneker "in those intellectual acquirements and capacities that form the most characteristic feature in the human race." The "system" which attempted to assign Negroes a different origin would fall "as similar instances multiply," which must frequently happen, McHenry predicted, as slavery gradually disappeared. The Balti-

37. Henry E. Baker, "Benjamin Banneker, the Negro Mathematician and Astronomer," *Jour. Negro Hist.*, 3 (1918), 99–118, the Georgetown *Weekly Ledger* quoted p. 112. Banneker was probably the first Negro to serve the United States government in a civilian capacity.

38. The first was *Benjamin Banneker's Pennsylvania, Delaware, Maryland and Virginia Almanack, and Ephemeris, for the Year of Our Lord, 1792 . . .* (Baltimore, [1791]). Titles varied. The best collection, some eight items, is in the American Antiquarian Society, Worcester, Mass. One for the year 1795 (Phila., [1794]) has a picture showing him as a full-blooded Negro, which casts doubt on recent claims that he had white ancestors. Jefferson, it should be noted, thought he was the "son of a black man born in Africa, and of a black woman born in the United States." To Condorcet, Phila., Aug. 30, 1791, Ford, ed., *Works of Jefferson*, VI, 311.

more printers of that first issue left no doubt as to the purposes for which the *Almanac* was to be used. It "must be considered an extraordinary Effort of Genius" by a Negro "who, by this Specimen of Ingenuity, evinces, to Demonstration, that mental Powers and Endowments are not the exclusive Excellence of white People, but that the Rays of Science may alike illumine the Minds of Men of every Clime . . . particularly those whom Tyrant-Custom hath too long taught us to depreciate as a Race inferior in intellectual Capacity." The *Almanac* had been approved, they added significantly, by David Rittenhouse. Since Rittenhouse was far and away America's greatest luminary in the field of astronomy, this was benediction indeed. Rittenhouse had in fact written privately that Banneker's calculations represented "a very extraordinary performance, considering the color of the author." "Every instance of genius among the negroes is worthy of attention, because their oppressors seem to lay great stress on their supposed inferior mental abilities." [39]

Since Banneker's *Almanac* was a scientific feat, it might appropriately be forwarded to one of the nation's most prominent scientists; as an antislavery tract it might logically go to an eminent man of antislavery views; and as a defense of the Negro's abilities it might well be offered to a man who had traduced them. When Banneker sent a manuscript copy of his almanac to the Secretary of State on August 19, 1791, he gave no hint that he knew of the Secretary's views on the Negro's nature but confined his long letter to a brief suggestion that the almanac was evidence of Negro ability and to lengthy remarks on the injustice of slavery. Jefferson replied to the old Negro briefly and courteously. Both letters were almost immediately published as a pamphlet.

No body [Jefferson wrote] wishes more than I do to see such proofs as you exhibit, that nature has given to our black brethren, talents equal to those of the other colors of men, and that the appearance of a want of them is owing merely to the degraded condition of their existence, both in Africa and America. I can add with truth, that no body wishes more ardently to see a good system commenced for raising the condition both of their body

---

39. McHenry's and the printers' remarks are in the first almanac, 2–4. McHenry's letter was widely reprinted: *Amer. Museum,* 12 (1792), 185–87; *Universal Asylum and Columbian Magazine,* 2[7] (1791), 300–301; *New York Magazine or Literary Repository,* 2 (1791), 557–58; *The Bee, or Literary Weekly Intelligencer* (Edinburgh), 13 (1793), 291–93. Rittenhouse to Mr. Pemberton, n.p., Aug. 6, 1791, on the back of *Copy of a Letter from Benjamin Banneker, to the Secretary of State, with His Answer* (Phila., 1792) in the John Carter Brown Library, Brown University.

and mind to what it ought to be, as fast as the imbecility of their present existence, and other circumstances which cannot be neglected, will admit.[40]

It was a careful, courteous, and resoundingly ambiguous letter; the condition of the mind and body of the Negro was to be raised "to what it ought to be." Jefferson was still unconvinced, still awaiting the dictates of science. Political partisans detected an inconsistency of tone between his letter and the *Notes;* William Loughton Smith refused to let him get away with even a few words of courtesy about the Negro. "What shall we think of a *secretary of state* thus fraternizing with negroes, writing them complimentary epistles, stiling them *his black brethren,* congratulating them on the evidences of their *genius,* and assuring them of his good wishes for their speedy emancipation?" [41]

Jefferson, an avid collector of both books and miscellaneous scraps of scientific information, promptly shipped off the manuscript almanac to the Marquis de Condorcet. He was "happy," he wrote Condorcet, to proffer this evidence that a Negro had become "a very respectable mathematician." "I have seen," Jefferson continued, "very elegant solutions of Geometrical problems by him. Add to this that he is a very worthy and respectable member of society. He is a free man. I shall be delighted to see these instances of moral eminence so multiplied as to prove that the want of talents observed in them is merely the effect of their degraded condition, and not proceeding from any difference in the structure of the parts on which intellect depends."[42] As these remarks so clearly indicate, Jefferson had been thrown into confusion by his unsettling confrontation with Banneker. Having attempted to transform Banneker's achievement into an instance of "moral eminence," thereby dodging the problem of intellectual ability, he forced himself back to the issue at hand and suggested that "moral eminence" might offer proof that Negroes were not deficient "in the structure of the parts on which intellect depends." In light of his firm conviction that the "moral sense" and the faculties of intellect constituted completely separate entities, this simply made no sense.

40. *Letter from Banneker to Secretary of State;* Jefferson to Banneker, Phila., Aug. 30, 1791, Ford, ed., *Works of Jefferson,* VI, 309–10; the exchange between Jefferson and Banneker was also published in *Universal Asylum and Columbian Magazine,* 2[9] (1792), 222–24. Jefferson's letter was used by at least one southern Federalist as evidence of Jefferson's wicked scheme of emancipation; [De Saussure], *Address to the Citizens of South-Carolina,* 16.

41. [William Loughton Smith], *The Pretensions of Thomas Jefferson to the Presidency Examined . . .* ([Phila.], 1796), 7–14.

42. Phila., Aug. 30, 1791, Ford, ed., *Works of Jefferson,* VI, 311.

Jefferson's confusion at times became monumental. On the one hand he had intellectually derived his belief in human equality from the existence of an orderly creation which had shaped every natural species each to its own mold; and on the other he possessed a larger unquestioning faith, strengthened by his political experience, which predisposed him toward equality. The problem of the Negro's intellect stripped these approaches of their apparent congruity. For he could not rid himself of the suspicion that the Negro was naturally inferior. If this were in fact the case, then it was axiomatic that the Creator had so created the Negro and no amount of education or freedom or any other tinkering could undo the facts of nature. Thus Jefferson suspected that the Creator might have in fact created men unequal; and he could not say this without giving his assertion exactly the same logical force as his famous statement to the contrary. His science-theology rammed squarely into his larger faith, and the result was intellectual wreckage. In the *Notes*, for example, he explained the Indian's apparent deficiencies as resulting wholly from environmental influences. Yet in 1785 he wrote to the Marquis de Chastellux, "I believe the Indian then to be in body and mind equal to the whiteman. I have supposed the blackman, in his present state, might not be so. But it would be hazardous to affirm that, equally cultivated for a few generations, he would not become so." [43] This was all very well as a declaration of faith, but intellectually it made no sense at all. Logically the Indian could retrieve an original equality. But if the Negro was not originally equal he could never "become" so, not if equality really stemmed from "that equal creation" from which Jefferson had derived it in the Declaration.[44]

As he grew older Jefferson grew increasingly irritated on the subject, dimly aware of the trap in which he was placed. When in 1809 the Abbé Henri Gregoire sent him a book puffing the extraordinary achievements of various Negroes, he replied to Gregoire with his usual protestations of inconclusiveness. "Be assured that no person living wishes more sincerely than I do, to see a complete refutation of the doubts I have myself entertained and expressed on the grade

43. Boyd, ed., *Papers of Jefferson*, VIII, 186.

44. Jefferson felt that the alterations made in his draft of the Declaration, which included substitution of "that all men are created equal, that they are endowed by their Creator with certain unalienable Rights" for his "that all men are created equal and independant, that from that equal creation they derive rights inherent and inalienable," had weakened the force of the document. Boyd, ed., *Papers of Jefferson*, I, 423, 429; Dumas Malone, *Jefferson and His Time* (Boston, 1948—), I, 230–31.

of understanding allotted to them by nature, and to find that in this respect they are on a par with ourselves. My doubts were the result of personal observation on the limited sphere of my own State, where the opportunities for the development of their genius were not favorable, and those of exercising it still less so. I expressed them therefore with great hesitation." But then his nervousness came spilling forth, revealing the gap between his science and his equalitarian faith: "but whatever be their degree of talent it is no measure of their rights. Because Sir Isaac Newton was superior to others in understanding, he was not therefore lord of the person or property of others." The reference to Newton was a dangerous red herring and the separation of the rights of a group from their talent, while vindicating freedom for the Negro, came perilously close to impugning the tidiness of the Author of Nature from whom freedom was derived. Jefferson exploded to his friend Joel Barlow that the book in question was a fantastic collection of unauthenticated tales, though he had given Gregoire "a very soft answer." "The whole do not amount, in point of evidence, to what we know ourselves of Banneker." As for that case, Jefferson declared, "We know he had spherical trigonometry enough to make almanacs, but not without the suspicion of aid from Ellicot, who was his neighbor and friend, and never missed an opportunity of puffing him. I have a long letter from Banneker, which shows him to have had a mind of very common stature indeed." [45] Jefferson had become irritated, one might well conclude, by contact with an issue he could not successfully handle.

And on this issue one looks in vain for indications of a happily receptive scientific mind patiently awaiting appropriate evidence. Had he been so inclined Jefferson could easily have welcomed Banneker as a fragment of proof; many other men had done so, including southerners like James McHenry. Banneker's achievements, moreover, were of just the sort to appeal to Jefferson, for scientific endeavor, however modest, was always of interest to him.

45. To Henri Gregoire, Washington, Feb. 25, 1809, Ford, ed., *Works of Jefferson*, XI, 99–100; to Joel Barlow, Monticello, Oct. 8, 1809, *ibid.*, 120–21. When supporting the antislavery cause Jefferson tended to take a more environmentalist position: "From those [statesmen] of the former generation who were in the fulness of age when I came into public life, which was while our controversy with England was on paper only, I soon saw that nothing was to be hoped. Nursed and educated in the daily habit of seeing the degraded condition, both bodily and mental, of those unfortunate beings, not reflecting that that degradation was very much the work of themselves and their fathers, few minds have yet doubted but that they were as legitimate subjects of property as their horses and cattle." To Edward Coles, Monticello, Aug. 25, 1814, *ibid.*, 416.

He had lionized David Rittenhouse whose principal achievement was a mechanical model of the universe, the famous orrery. "Consider," he wrote its constructor urging continued endeavor, "that the world has but one Ryttenhouse." [46] Banneker's almanac was indeed modest by comparison, but Banneker possessed that virtue which most attracted republican scientists to Rittenhouse—he was "self-taught." [47]

Indeed it was the scientific aspect of Banneker's achievement which confirmed his celebrity, and that also of Derham and Fuller. If evidence of intellect was sought, what more likely field than science? Banneker was better proof even than Phyllis Wheatley. Nothing could point more clearly to the late eighteenth-century separation of intellect from morals than the arresting fact that no abolitionist seized upon Negroes like Richard Allen, Absalom Jones, and Prince Hall as exemplars of Negro capacity. Allen and Jones, both well-known ministers in Philadelphia, and Hall, leader of the active Negro community in Boston, were in all probability more able men than Banneker. Benjamin Rush was well acquainted with Allen and Jones, yet he never attempted to parade them as examples of Negro equality, nor did any other antislavery writer. No Negro minister, such as John Chavis, who attended Princeton, was so used. Nor did the fame of individual Negroes depend upon getting their writings into print, for Fuller and Derham did not publish anything, while Allen and Jones did. White Americans simply assumed that Negroes possessed religious and even quasi-political abilities; doubts on this point would have been doubts about the Negro's status as a human being. The Negro was to be judged on a thoroughly distinct matter—his intellectual capacity.[48]

Until well into the nineteenth century Jefferson's judgment on that matter, with all its confused tentativeness, stood as the strongest suggestion of inferiority expressed by any native American. To some extent sectional differences help account for his opinion, for Jefferson was the only person in Virginia or southward to tackle the problem, and his opponents were chiefly northerners. He wrote at length on a matter upon which Virginians generally were silent, but he may well have been speaking for many of them. His acquaint-

46. Monticello, July 19, 1778, Boyd, ed., *Papers of Jefferson*, II, 202–3.
47. Joseph Perkins, *An Oration upon Genius . . .* (Boston, 1797), 19.
48. The only exception I have seen was a casual reference to Negro achievements of the "desk, and the pulpit" in E[lihu] H[ubbard] Smith, *A Discourse, Delivered April 11, 1798, at the Request of and Before the New-York Society for Promoting the Manumission of Slaves, and Protecting Such of Them as Have Been or May Be Liberated* (N. Y., 1798), 28.

ance St. George Tucker, a Virginia lawyer, referred casually in 1795 (after, it should be noted, he had read the *Notes on Virginia*) to "the general opinion [in Virginia] of their mental inferiority," but this statement appears to be the only contemporary testimony concerning what Virginian opinion actually was.[49] It is striking that even when defending slavery Virginians seem to have felt no need to advance suggestions of Negro inferiority. No such suggestions were made, for example, in several emphatic petitions to the legislature which defended slavery in advocating repeal of the 1782 act facilitating manumission. Similarly, Governor John Drayton of South Carolina, one of a handful of men in that state to aspire successfully to authorship (in conscious imitation of Jefferson's *Notes*), defended slavery at some length in 1802 chiefly on grounds of necessity and without once mentioning the possibility of Negro inferiority. The only southerner to object directly to Jefferson about the remarks in the *Notes* was David Ramsay. Both a physician and a historian, Ramsay had been born in Pennsylvania and had migrated to Charleston at age twenty-three, where he became a moderately successful politician; though he owned slaves he was regarded by many persons in the state as distinctly unsound on the subject of slavery. It is therefore perhaps not surprising that after reading Jefferson's *Notes* in manuscript he wrote to congratulate the author and commented unfavorably on only one passage: "I admire your generous indignation at slavery; but think you have depressed the negroes too low." [50]

Opinion in the North, on the other hand, was distinctly different though far from unanimous. When St. George Tucker addressed queries concerning Negroes in Massachusetts to Jeremy Belknap in 1795, he asked specifically for information concerning mental capacity, and Belknap in turn made enquiries among his prominent friends in Boston. Judge James Winthrop replied magisterially, "There are a few instances of their appearing as authors, and some of their productions are not contemptible. I have not heard of their dipping into the more abstruse parts of science, and in general they are not estimated for speculative abilities." James Sullivan, less pompous but more verbose, explained that Negroes were not now

49. Tucker to Jeremy Belknap, Williamsburg, June 29, 1795, "Letters Relating to Slavery in Mass.," *Belknap Papers*, 407.

50. Legislative Petitions, Brunswick Co., Nov. 10, 1785; Pittsylvania Co., Nov. 10, 1785, Va. State Lib., Richmond; John Drayton, *A View of South-Carolina, As Respects Her Natural and Civil Concerns* (Charleston, 1802), 144–49, and 222 for explicit endorsement of the unity of the human species; Ramsay to Jefferson, N. Y., May 3, 1786, Boyd, ed., *Papers of Jefferson*, IX, 441.

the equal of whites but that if they were given the same "prospects," "motives," and "advantages" for three or four generations "they may exceed the white people." Belknap summarized his little survey by reporting that gentlemen in Massachusetts who had studied the matter "do not scruple to say, that there is no more difference between them and those whites who had have had the same education, and have lived in the same habits, than there is among different persons of that class of whites. In this opinion I am inclined to acquiesce. It is neither birth nor colour, but education and habit, which form the human character." [51]

Though it is difficult to judge exactly what most Virginians or other southerners would have thought of this statement, it is clear that only one man in the South felt compelled to take the opposite position publicly. Jefferson alone spoke forth, and this fact in itself suggests, at very least, strong feeling on his part, an uncommon need to discourse upon the subject. It was not that he alone felt need for scientific experiment. George Wythe, Jefferson's much-admired mentor, undertook to give both his own nephew and his mulatto servant boy classical educations as a comparative test of the Negro's ability. [52] On the other hand, Jefferson, who delighted in compiling the facts of the natural world, never attempted any such experiment despite ample opportunity. And the structure of his relevant passage in the *Notes*, where his appeal to science followed lengthy and very definite pronouncements on Negro inferiority, indicated clearly that his appeal to that highest court was not the starting point for his thoughts about Negroes but a safe refuge from them.

5. JEFFERSON: PASSIONATE REALITIES

Jefferson started, in fact, with a brief assertion of the necessity for colonizing Negroes elsewhere once they had been freed. [53] "Why not retain and incorporate the blacks into the state?"

51. "Queries Respecting the Slavery and Emancipation of Negroes in Massachusetts, Proposed by the Hon. Judge Tucker of Virginia, and Answered by the Rev. Dr. Belknap," Mass. Hist. Soc., *Collections*, 1st Ser., 4 (1795) , 209; "Letters Relating to Slavery in Mass.," *Belknap Papers*, 390, 415.

52. John P. Kennedy, *Memoirs of the Life of William Wirt, Attorney-General of the United States*, rev. ed., 2 vols. (Phila., 1854) , I, 141–42; Nathaniel Dwight, *The Lives of the Signers of the Declaration of Independence* (N. Y., 1860) , 269–70. For these references I am indebted to Dr. W. Edwin Hemphill of the South Carolina Archives Department. See also his "Examinations of George Wythe Swinney for Forgery and Murder: A Documentary Essay," *Wm. and Mary Qtly.*, 12 (1955) , 547; and [B. W. Leigh], *The Letter of Appomattox to the People of Virginia . . .* (Richmond, 1832) , 43.

53. The entire passage is in Jefferson, *Notes on Virginia*, ed. Peden, 137–43.

Only later did his answer find wide acceptance in Virginia, especially after September 1800. "Deep rooted prejudices entertained by the whites; ten thousand recollections, by the blacks, of the injuries they have sustained; new provocations; the real distinctions which nature has made; and many other circumstances, will . . . produce convulsions which will probably never end but in the extermination of the one or the other race." His ensuing remarks made evident which factor carried greatest weight with him, for he immediately entered into a long discussion of other "objections" which were "physical and moral." "The first difference which strikes us" he wrote in accurate summary of his countrymen's perceptions, "is that of colour." Accepting the chromatically inaccurate but universally accepted metaphor of the Negro's "black" color, he continued, "Whether the black of the negro resides in the reticular membrane between the skin and scarf-skin, or in the scarf-skin itself; whether it proceeds from the colour of the blood, the colour of the bile, or from that of some other secretion, the difference is fixed in nature, and is as real as if its seat and cause were better known to us." For Jefferson, the overwhelming aspect of the Negro's color was its *reality;* he simply shelved the important scientific question of its cause. Even when he considered the question in a more neutral context, in his discussion of albino Negroes in the section on "Productions Mineral, Vegetable and Animal," he refused (or perhaps was unable) to offer a word of speculation about a matter on which other scientists speculated freely. Instead he rushed on, spilling forth words which revealed what the "reality" of the "difference" was for Thomas Jefferson. The passionate underpinnings of his feelings were laid bare.

And is this difference of no importance? Is it not the foundation of a greater or less share of beauty in the two races? Are not the fine mixtures of red and white, the expressions of every passion by greater or less suffusions of colour in the one, preferable to that eternal monotony, which reigns in the countenances, that immoveable veil of black which covers all the emotions of the other race? Add to these, flowing hair, a more elegant symmetry of form, and their own judgment in favour of the whites, declared by their preference of them, as uniformly as is the preference of the Oran-ootan for the black women over those of his own species. The circumstance of superior beauty, is thought worthy attention in the propagation of our horses, dogs, and other domestic animals; why not in that of man?

With this geyser of libidinal energy Jefferson recapitulated major tenets of the American racial complex. Merely on a factual level he passed along several notions which had long been floating about, some since the first years of confrontation in Africa. Red and white were the ingredients of beauty, and Negroes were pronouncedly less beautiful than whites; Negroes desired sexual relations especially with whites; black women had relations with orang-outangs. On a deeper level the pattern of his remarks was more revealing of Jefferson himself. Embedded in his thoughts on beauty was the feeling that whites were subtler and more delicate in their passions and that Negroes, conversely, were more crude. He felt Negroes to be sexually more animal—hence the gratuitous intrusion of the man-like ape. His libidinal desires, unacceptable and inadmissible to his society and to his higher self, were effectively transferred to others and thereby drained of their intolerable immediacy. Having allowed these dynamic emotions perilously close to the surface in the form of the orang-outang, he had immediately shifted to the safe neutral ground of horse-breeding, thus denying his exposure by caricaturing it. Without fully recognizing the adversary within, he continued to flee, taking refuge on higher and higher ground. "They have less hair on the face and body." Not quite safe enough, but he was reaching the safe temple of science. "They secrete less by the kidnies, and more by the glands of the skin," he wrote, carefully placing the rationale before the important fact, "which gives them a very strong and disagreeable odour." Having taken as given the facts of Negro secretion, about which many contemporaries were uncertain, he applied them as proof to a less emotion-laden folk belief. "This greater degree of transpiration renders them more tolerant of heat, and less so of cold, than the whites." He came to rest finally in convoluted speculation. "Perhaps too a difference of structure in the pulmonary apparatus, which a late ingenious experimentalist [Adair Crawford, *Experiments . . . on Animal Heat*] has discovered to be the principal regulator of animal heat, may have disabled them from extricating, in the act of inspiration, so much of that fluid from the outer air, or obliged them in expiration, to part with more of it."

Yet Jefferson was never completely at rest. His picture of Negroes as crudely sensual beings, which was at once an offprint of popular belief and a functional displacement of his own emotional drives, kept popping up whenever Negroes came to mind. That it did not appear on other, irrelevant occasions indicated that there were limits to its personal importance, yet most of Jefferson's widely-read remarks on the Negro were tinged by it. When discussing the Negro's over-all temperament he wrote, "They are more ardent after their female: but love seems with them to be more an eager

desire, than a tender delicate mixture of sentiment and sensation."
In the original manuscript he had stated this even more baldly. Elsewhere in the *Notes* he commented in defense of the masculinity of
Indian men despite the sparsity of their hair: "Negroes have notoriously less hair than the whites; yet they are more ardent." [54]

Jefferson had framed old beliefs about the Negro's sexuality in
newly deprecatory terms, and defenders of the Negro rose in his
behalf. Gilbert Imlay laid his finger on the core of Jefferson's
argument with acute intuition but faltering analysis:

> Were a man, who, with all the ardour of a youthful passion, had just been
> gazing upon the fair bosom of a loved and beautiful mistress, and after-
> wards marked the contrast of that paradise of sublunary bliss, to the
> African or Indian hue, to exclaim in the terms which Mr. Jefferson has
> used, he might be judged excusable on account of the intoxication of his
> heated senses—But when a grave philosopher, who has passed the meridian
> of life, sits down to meliorate, by his writings and opinions, the condition
> of the slaves of his country, whose fetters have fixed an obliquity upon the
> virtue and humanity of the southern Americans, I confess it appears to me
> not a little jejune and inconsistent.

The Reverend Samuel Stanhope Smith of Princeton, however, was
affronted by Jefferson's assertions of ardency which kindled "the
senses only, not the imagination," and seized the opportunity of
reading an environmentalist lecture in morals to slaveowners.
"With what fine tints can imagination invest the rags, the dirt, or
the nakedness so often seen in a quarter of negro labourers? Besides,
to awaken the exquisite sentiments of a delicate love, and to sur-
round it with all the enchantment of the imagination, this passion
requires to be placed under certain moral restraints which are
seldom formed in the coarse familiarity, and promiscuous intercourse permitted, and too often encouraged among the American
slaves." Smith was careful to discharge the other barrel by declaring
that he had seen many instances of the highest sentiments of love
among Negroes.[55] Jefferson never replied to these attacks.

While the depth of emotional intensity underlying his thinking
about the Negro seems sufficiently evident, the sources of his feeling

54. *Ibid.*, 138–39, 70–71, 61, and 288n: "but love is with them only an eager
desire, not a tender delicate excitement, not a delicious foment of the soul."

55. Imlay, *Topographical Description*, 192; Smith, *Essay on Variety* (1810), ed.
Jordan, 277n. Imlay attempted to refute Jefferson's arguments point by point
(pp. 192–200), asserting, for example, that whites like Negroes secreted more in
hot climates, that Negroes' odor was owing partly to a different manner of living,
and that Phyllis Wheatley was indeed a respectable poetess. In the latter years of
the 18th century there seems to have been no subsidence of comment on the
Negro's smell.

remain obscured by his unsurprising failure to articulate emotional patterns and processes of which he was unaware. As has often been remarked about him, few men have written so much yet revealed so little of themselves. This fact is in itself enormously suggestive, though it has been a disappointment to historians that he did not include in his papers some remarks on parents and childhood, some few letters to his beloved wife. Yet if one draws back the velvet curtain of his graceful style to regard the *pattern* of his life and thought, it is possible to detect certain of the currents running beneath the structure of his intellect.

6. JEFFERSON: WHITE WOMEN AND BLACK

Two interrelated currents seem especially relevant to his thoughts on the Negro, the more deep-seated one having to do with his relationships with members of the opposite sex. Jefferson grew up in a world of women. His father, a man of more imposing physique even than Jefferson, died when his son was fourteen. At that critical age he was left with a mother about whom we know almost nothing, four sisters, and one brother. He was never really congenial with his brother, and their infrequent correspondence in later life merely exposed the enormous gulf between them in interests and talents.[56] He never said much concerning his mother and sisters. As a young man, leading a life thoroughly lacking in direction, he filled his letters with talk about girls, but his gay chitchat ended abruptly after a keenly disappointing one-sided romance with Rebecca Burwell, an attractive sixteen-year-old orphan. Consoling himself with outbursts of misogyny, Jefferson turned to the companionship of men. Nearly ten years later he made a level-headed match with Martha Skelton Wayles, a twenty-three-year-old widow whose young son died shortly before the wedding. On the marriage bond he at first inserted the word "spinster" but then corrected himself with "widow."[57] The marriage lasted from 1772 until her death in 1782, but again Jefferson left no picture of the woman sharing his life. She bore him six children: three girls died in infancy, as did their only son (whom Jefferson referred to as such before the birth!),[58] and two daughters survived. His wife's failing health

56. Collected in Bernard Mayo, ed., *Thomas Jefferson and His Unknown Brother Randolph* . . . (Charlottesville, Va., 1942) .

57. Albert Jay Nock, *Jefferson*, intro. Merrill D. Peterson (N. Y., 1960) , 18. The most authoritative biographical information may be found in Malone, *Jefferson and His Time*.

58. Malone, *Jefferson and His Time*, I, 434.

worried him terribly—it was in this period that he wrote the
Notes—and her death left him shattered with grief, not untinged, as
so often happens, with self-pity.[59]

Throughout his life after the Burwell affair, Jefferson seemed
capable of attachment only to married women. Several years before
his marriage he had made, on his own much later admission,
improper advances to the wife of a neighboring friend.[60] In Paris, as
a widower, he carried on a superficially frantic flirtation with Mrs.
Maria Cosway, a "love affair" in which the "love" was partly play
and the "affair" non-existent. The only woman outside his family
for whom he formed some attachment was John Adams's remarkable
wife, Abigail; with good reason he admired her intellect. With
women in general he was uneasy and unsure; he held them at arm's
length, wary, especially after his wife's death, of the dangers of
over-commitment. Intimate emotional engagement with women
seemed to represent for him a gateway into a dangerous, potentially
explosive world which threatened revolution against the discipline
of his higher self. His famous "Dialogue of the Head and the
Heart," written to Maria Cosway, revealed his dim awareness of the
struggle within, for beneath its stiltedness one senses a man not
naturally cool but thoroughly air-conditioned. Of necessity, the
Head emerged victorious in the dialogue, just as it did in real life,
declaring pontifically to the Heart, "This is not a world to live at
random in as you do." [61] The sentence might have served as a motto
for his life.

As Jefferson matured, he seems to have mitigated this inner
tension by imputing potential explosiveness to the opposite sex and
by assuming that female passion must and could only be controlled
by marriage. Not long after the Burwell affair, he wrote or copied a
solemn passage which characterized marriage as best founded on a
wife's self-restraint and constant attentiveness to the wishes of her
husband: "marriage, be a husband what he may, reverses the prerogative of sex." Certainly Jefferson lived in a culture which assumed dutiful wifely submission, but there was a particular urgency
in his stress upon the necessity of female decorum. In any age, his
strictures on toilet and dress to his unmarried daughter would seem

59. See the revealing description by his daughter in Sarah N. Randolph, *The
Domestic Life of Thomas Jefferson . . .* , intro. Dumas Malone (N. Y., 1958) , 63.
60. Malone, *Jefferson and His Time*, I, 153–55, 447–51, is a definitive account.
61. Jefferson to Maria Cosway, Paris, Oct. 12, 1786, Boyd, ed., *Papers of
Jefferson*, X, 443–53.

egregiously detailed. "Nothing is so disgusting to our sex," he warned her, "as a want of cleanliness and delicacy in yours." [62] It is scarcely surprising, therefore, that when living in Paris, Jefferson dashed off frequent warnings of the sexual corruptions awaiting American youths in Europe: "in lieu of this ["conjugal love"] are substituted pursuits which nourish and invigorate all our bad passions, and which offer only moments of extasy amidst days and months of restlessness and torment." And, he added, characteristically seizing an opportunity to salute republican virtue, "Much, very much inferior this to the tranquil permanent felicity with which domestic society in America blesses most of it's inhabitants." [63] If unrestrained sex seemed a dangerous trap to Jefferson, he was deeply certain which sex had set it. On one occasion, in his rough "Notes on a Tour of English Gardens," he jotted down an arresting mental picture, in an otherwise matter-of-fact account, of "a small, dark, deep hollow, with recesses of stone in the banks on every side. In one of these is a Venus pudique, turned half round as if inviting you with her into the recess." It was a revealing description, as much of Jefferson as of the statue. Most revealing of all was a letter to James Madison in 1786. The recent revisal of Virginia laws had included mitigation of criminal punishments, but the *lex talionis* had been preserved in two cases, death for treason or murder and castration for rape and buggery, etc. Jefferson wrote from Paris an interesting commentary. "The principle of retaliation is much criticised here, particularly in the case of Rape. They think the punishment indecent and unjustifiable. I should be for altering it, but for a different reason: that is on account of the temptation women would be under to make it the instrument of vengeance against an inconstant lover, and of disappointment to a

---

62. Marie Kimball, *Jefferson: The Road to Glory, 1743 to 1776* (N. Y., 1943), 166–68; to Martha Jefferson, Annapolis, Dec. 22, 1783, Boyd, ed., *Papers of Jefferson*, VI, 416–17; to Martha Jefferson Randolph, N. Y., Apr. 4, 1790, *ibid.*, XVI, 300. The 1783 letter contained the admonition: "A lady who has been seen as a sloven or slut in the morning, will never efface the impression she then made with all the dress and pageantry she can afterwards involve herself in. Nothing is so disgusting to our sex as a want of cleanliness and delicacy in yours. I hope therefore the moment you rise from bed, your first work will be to dress yourself in such a stile as that you may be seen by any gentleman without his being able to discover a pin amiss, or any other circumstance of neatness wanting."

63. To Charles Bellini, Paris, Sept. 30, 1785, Boyd, ed., *Papers of Jefferson*, VIII, 568–69, also 636–37; Jefferson's theme of sexual promiscuity as the ultimate corruption is noted in a perceptive portrayal by Bernard Bailyn, "Boyd's Jefferson: Notes for a Sketch," *New Eng. Qtly.*, 33 (1960), 386–87.

rival." [64] Evidently women loomed as threats to masculinity, as dangerously powerful sexual aggressors.

Jefferson's transferal of sexual aggressiveness to women helps explain certain otherwise puzzling aspects of his expressions on the Negro. He was greatly concerned with the Negro's lack of beauty —in his culture a highly feminine attribute—and it was with some justification that a political opponent charged that "The desire of preserving the beauty of the human race predominates . . . in the mind of our philosopher." [65] Moreover, Jefferson failed to offer even a hint concerning the Negro male's supposedly large organ, and though this failure may have stemmed from an understandable reluctance to broach the matter publicly, he gave no suggestion even indirectly of the sexual aggressiveness of Negro men; nor did he ever do so privately. In fact—and it is an arresting one upon re-reading the passage—his previously quoted remarks concerning beauty and breeding had reference not to Negro men, nor to Negroes in general, but, in implicit yet highly specific fashion, to Negro women!

It is in the light of this emotional pattern that Jefferson's widely discussed relationship with the Hemings family should be considered. The subject is an unpalatable one for many Americans: the assertion that a great national figure was involved in miscegenation—this is the central supposed "fact" of the Hemings matter—is one that Americans find difficult to treat as anything but a malicious accusation. Malice *was,* indeed, the animating force behind the original claim, but we need to brace ourselves into an intellectual posture from which we can see that the importance of the stories about black Sally Hemings and Thomas Jefferson lies in the fact that they seemed—and to some people still seem—of any importance. The facts of the matter require attention not because Jefferson's behavior needs to be questioned but because they are of some (but not very much) help in understanding Jefferson's views about miscegenation and, far more, because they shed light on the cultural context in which he moved and of which we are heirs. Viewed in the context of his feelings about white women, the problem of Jefferson's actual overt behavior becomes essentially irrelevant to the subject of this book; it is to the inner world of his

---

64. Boyd, ed., *Papers of Jefferson,* IX, 372, X, 604. This comment accurately but fortuitously forecasts later incidents in the 19th and 20th centuries where the charge of rape was used by white women against Negro men.
65. [Smith], *Pretensions of Jefferson,* 6.

thought and feeling that we must look for significant behavior and, even more, to his culture for the larger significance of the matter.

In 1802 James T. Callender charged in the Richmond *Recorder* that it was "well known" that Jefferson kept Sally, one of his slaves, as concubine and had fathered children by her. The features of "Tom," the eldest offspring, were "said to bear a striking although sable resemblance to those of the president himself." [66] Callender was a notorious professional scandalmonger who had turned upon Jefferson when the President had disappointed his hope for federal office. Despite the utter disreputability of the source, the charge has been dragged after Jefferson like a dead cat through the pages of formal and informal history, tied to him by its attractiveness to a wide variety of interested persons and by the apparent impossibility of utterly refuting it.[67] Ever since Callender's day it has served the varied purposes of those seeking to degrade Jefferson for political or ideological reasons, of abolitionists, defamers of Virginia, the South, and even America in general, and both defenders and opponents of racial segregation. Jefferson's conduct has been attacked from several angles, for in fact the charge of concubinage with Sally Hemings constitutes not one accusation but three, simultaneously accusing Jefferson of fathering bastards, of miscegenation, and of crassly taking advantage of a helpless young slave (for Sally was probably twenty-two when she first conceived). The last of these, insofar as it implies forced attentions on an unwilling girl, may be summarily dismissed. For one thing, indirect evidence indicates that Sally was happy throughout her long period of motherhood, and, more important, Jefferson was simply not capable of violating every rule of honor and kindness, to say nothing of his convictions concerning the master-slave relationship.

As for bastardy and miscegenation, the known circumstances of the situation at Monticello which might support the charges were, very briefly, as follows. The entire Hemings family seems to have received favored treatment. Sally's mother was mulatto and had come to Jefferson with her still lighter children from the estate of

66. Sept. 1, 1802.
67. By far the best account is Merrill D. Peterson, *The Jefferson Image in the American Mind* (N. Y., 1960), 181–87, though a complete history would require a volume. For more recent rehabilitations of the charge see the pseudo-scholarly article, Pearl N. Graham, "Thomas Jefferson and Sally Hemings," *Jour. Negro Hist.*, 44 (1961), 89–103, and the even less excusable tale in Raymond L. Bruckberger, *Image of America*, trans. C. G. Paulding and Virgilia Peterson (N. Y., 1959), 76–77.

his father-in-law, John Wayles, in 1774. Most of Sally's siblings were
personal servants; one brother became a skilled carpenter and two
of Sally's children were eventually charged to him for training. Sally
herself and her mother were house servants, and Sally (described as
very fair) was sent as maid with Jefferson's daughter to Paris. All
the slaves freed by Jefferson were Hemingses, and none of Sally's
children were retained in slavery as adults. She bore five, from 1795
to 1808; and though he was away from Monticello a total of roughly
two-thirds of this period, Jefferson was at home nine months prior
to each birth. Her first child was conceived following Jefferson's
retirement as Secretary of State with nerves raw from political
battling with Hamilton. Three others were conceived during Jefferson's summer vacations and the remaining child was born nine
months after his very brief return to Monticello for the funeral of
his daughter. In short, Jefferson's paternity can be neither refuted
nor proved from the known circumstances or from the extant testimony of his overseer, his white descendants, or the descendants of
Sally, each of them having fallible memories and personal interests
at stake.[68]

If we turn to Jefferson's character we are confronted by evidence
which for many people today (and then) furnished an immediate
and satisfactory refutation. Yet the assumption that this high-
minded man *could not* have carried on such an affair is at variance
with what is known today concerning the relationship between
human personality and behavior. If the previous suggestions concerning his personality have any validity, Jefferson's relations with
women were ambivalent, and in the Hemings situation either tendency could have prevailed.

Assuming this ambivalence in Jefferson, one can construct two
reasonable (though not equally probable) and absolutely irrecon-

68. This is a highly telescoped account; a full and *unexcited* discussion of the
matter is needed. A possible earlier daughter supposedly born in France can be
quite safely ruled out. For the timing of the births and certain blood relationships, see Betts, ed., *Jefferson's Farm Book, passim,* points which the fine brief
discussion by Peterson does not consider. See also Rayford W. Logan, ed.,
*Memoirs of a Monticello Slave, As Dictated to Charles Campbell in the 1840's by
Isaac, One of Thomas Jefferson's Slaves* (Charlottesville, Va., 1951), *passim;*
Waverly, Ohio, *Pike County Republican,* Mar. 13, 1873; Hamilton W. Pierson,
Jefferson at Monticello: The Private Life of Thomas Jefferson . . . (N. Y., 1862),
110–11; Henry S. Randall to James Parton, Courtland Village, N. Y., June 1,
1868, in Milton E. Flower, *James Parton: The Father of Modern Biography*
(Durham, N. C., 1951), 236–39; codicil to Jefferson's will, Mar. 17, 1826, Lipscomb
and Bergh, eds., *Writings of Jefferson,* XVII, 469–70.

cilable cases. It is possible to argue on the one hand, briefly, that Jefferson was a truly admirable man if there ever was one and that by the time he had married and matured politically, in the 1770's, his "head" was permanently in control of his "heart." Hence a liaison with a slave girl would have been a lapse from character unique in his mature life. It would have represented, on a deeper level, abandonment of the only grounds on which he was able to maintain satisfactory relations with women, their safe incarceration in the married state. It would have meant complete reversal of his feelings of repulsion toward Negroes and a towering sense of guilt for having connected with such sensual creatures and having given free reign to his own libidinous desires, guilt for which there is no evidence. On the other hand, however, it is possible to argue that attachment with Sally represented a final happy resolution of his inner conflict. This would account for the absence after his return from Paris in 1789 of evidence pointing to continuing high tension concerning women and Negroes, an absence hardly to be explained by senility. Sally Hemings would have become Becky Burwell and the bitter outcome of his marriage erased. Unsurprisingly, his repulsion toward Negroes would have been, all along, merely the obverse of powerful attraction, and external pressures in the 1790's would easily have provided adequate energy for turning the coin of psychic choice from one side to the other. One is left fully persuaded only of the known fact that any given pattern of basic personality can result in widely differing patterns of external behavior.

The question of Jefferson's miscegenation, it should be stressed again, is of limited interest and usefulness even if it could be satisfactorily answered. The *Notes* had been written years before, and Jefferson never deviated from his "aversion," as he wrote just before he died, "to the mixture of colour" in America.[69] One aspect of the history of the Hemings family, however, offers possible clarification on several points. It appears quite probable that Sally and some of her siblings were the children of his father-in-law, John Wayles.[70] It must have been a burden indeed for Jefferson, who probably knew this, to have the Hemingses in the same house with their half-sister and aunt, his beloved wife, who almost certainly was ignorant of the situation. This burden might well have embittered

69. Jefferson to William Short, Monticello, Jan. 18, 1826, Ford, ed., *Works of Jefferson*, XII, 434.
70. Logan, ed., *Memoirs of a Monticello Slave*, 13; Waverly *Pike County Republican*, Mar. 13, 1873; Peterson, *Jefferson Image*, 184.

his thoughts on miscegenation in general and have helped convince him to his dying day that it was a social evil.[71] It would also have heightened his conviction that slavery was degrading to white men. And while it does not settle anything concerning his relations with Sally, it would explain the favored treatment the Hemings family received at Monticello.

For many people it seems to require an effort of will to remember that the larger significance of the Hemings matter lay not in Jefferson's conduct but in the charges themselves. Callender's words went echoing through the anti-Jefferson press (with help from Callender) because they played effectively upon public sentiment. The motivation underlying the charges was undoubtedly political; some of his opponents were willing to seize any weapon, no matter how crude, for berating Jefferson, but that a white man's sleeping with a Negro woman should be a weapon at all seems the more significant fact. It is significant, too, that the charge of bastardy was virtually lost in the clamor about miscegenation. Hamilton's admission of sexual transgressions with a white woman had done little to damage *his* reputation. Jefferson's offense was held to be mixture of the races, and Callender and his fellow scandalmongers strummed the theme until it was dead tired.

> In glaring red, and chalky white,
>   Let others beauty see;
> Me no such tawdry tints delight—
>   No! *black's* the hue for me!
>
> Thick pouting lips! how sweet their grace!
>   When passion fires to kiss them!
> Wide spreading over half the face,
>   Impossible to miss them.
>
> Oh! Sally! hearken to my vows!
>   Yield up thy sooty charms—
> My best belov'd! my more than spouse,
>   Oh! take me to thy arms! [72]

71. The bizarre development in his household may have accounted for both an absence of strong feeling in his description of miscegenation, in a lawyer's brief *before* his marriage, as "that confusion of species, which the legislature seems to have considered as an evil," and the alteration, for which he may have been responsible, of the legal definition of a mulatto from one-eighth to one-fourth Negro in the Virginia revisal, five years *after* his marriage. Ford, ed., *Works of Jefferson*, I, 471; Boyd, ed., *Papers of Jefferson*, II, 476; Hening, ed., *Statutes Va.*, XII, 184.

72. Reprinted from *Boston Gazette* in Richmond *Recorder*, Dec. 1, 1802.

The same theme could easily be transformed into ridicule of Jefferson's equalitarianism.

> For make all like, let blackee nab
>   De white womans. . . . dat be de track!
> Den Quashee de white wife will hab,
>   And massa *Jefferson shall hav de black.*
> Why should a judge, (him alway white,)
>   'Pon pickaninny put him paw,
> Cause he steal little! dat no rite!
> No! Quashee say he'll hab no law.[73]

Jefferson's personal transgression could be handsomely enlarged to represent a threat to society, according to what might be called the law of gross expansion. "Put the case that every white man in Virginia had done as much as Thomas Jefferson has done towards the utter destruction of its happiness, that eighty thousand white men had; each of them, been the father of five mulatto children. Thus you have FOUR HUNDRED THOUSAND MULATTOES in addition to the present swarm. The country would be no longer habitable, till after a civil war, and a series of massacres. We all know with absolute certainty that the contest would end in the utter extirpation both of blacks and mulattoes. We know that the continent has as many white people, as could eat the whole race at a breakfast." [74]

7. INTERRACIAL SEX: THE INDIVIDUAL AND HIS SOCIETY

Callender's grossness should not be allowed to obscure the fact that he was playing upon very real sensitivities. American tenderness on mixture of the races had been unrelieved by the Revolutionary upheaval of thought concerning the Negro. Indeed certain shifts in thought in the latter part of the eighteenth century may have served to deepen objection to intermixture. While conceiving of man's social and political activities as taking place within the ordered realm of nature (most obviously in the natural rights philosophy), Americans also brought biological preconceptions to the consideration of human beings. In nature, likes begat likes in ordered succession. Could Americans be entirely happy, then, with even the superficial confusion of appearances brought about by miscegenation? The "mulatto breed" was an affront to anyone with

73. *Ibid.*, Sept. 1, 1802.
74. *Ibid.*, Sept. 22, 1802.

a sense of tidiness. In the 1790's, too, the Negro rebellions added urgency to all consideration of interracial relationships, and the growing sense of the separateness of Negroes meant more frequent expressions of alarm concerning mongrelization. Given a new nation, with slavery now recognized as a national concern, the omnipresent fact of miscegenation was perforce seen in a somewhat different light than in earlier years. Cases of intermixture once of only local pertinence had now become ingredients in the larger problem of the integrity of the blood of the national community. Hence national councils became forums for denunciation of intermixture. Pennsylvania's James Wilson announced during discussion of the three-fifths clause in the Constitutional Convention that he "had some apprehensions also from the tendency of the blending of the blacks with the whites, to give disgust to the people of Pena." William Loughton Smith, defending slavery in the congressional debate of 1790, declared that any "mixture of the races would degenerate the whites" and that as far as the future of America was concerned if Negroes intermarried "with the whites, then the white race would be extinct, and the American people would be all of the mulatto breed." And a nationalistic President Jefferson remarked concerning the Negro's future that "it is impossible not to look forward to distant times, when our rapid multiplication will expand itself beyond those [present] limits, and cover the whole northern, if not the southern continent, with a people speaking the same language, governed in similar forms, and by similar laws; nor can we contemplate with satisfaction either blot or mixture on that surface." [75]

This theme was to emerge as a dominant one especially in his own state during his presidency; by that time many other important individuals throughout the nation were speculating upon matters concerning the Negro. Important intellectual changes took place during the thirty years after he wrote the *Notes*, but Jefferson grew increasingly silent and depressed about the future of Africans in America. For the moment these individuals and changes may be held aside so as to permit concentration upon the problem of the relationship of one individual's attitudes to those of his society.

Beneath all pronouncements on the undesirability of racial mixture lay a substructure of feeling about interracial sex. Jefferson's feelings were of course partially molded by specific beliefs about

75. Farrand, ed., *Records Federal Convention*, I, 587; *Annals of Congress*, 1st Cong., 2d sess., 1455, 1458 (Smith had just finished reading aloud the relevant excerpts from the *Notes on Virginia*); Jefferson to Gov. James Monroe, Washington, Nov. 24, 1801, Ford, ed., *Works of Jefferson*, IX, 317.

Negroes which constituted readily visible manifestations of feelings prevailing in his culture not merely about Negroes but about life in general. It seems legitimate and profitable to speak of an entire culture as having feelings, partly because every society demands—and gets—a large measure of the behavior it "wants" (i.e., needs) from individuals and partly because in a literate culture expressions of individual feeling accrete through time, thus forming a common pool of expressed feelings. Usually, but by no means always, these expressions are highly intellectualized, that is, detached from direct functional connection with powerful emotional drives. Sometimes they are not, as they sometimes were not when Thomas Jefferson wrote about Negroes. It seems evident that his feelings, his affective life, his emotions—whatever term one prefers—were being expressed in some of his beliefs or opinions about the Negro. His opinions were thus sometimes quite directly the product of his repressions. And it seems axiomatic, given the assumptions about the nature of culture prevailing in the twentieth century, that variants of his repressions operated in so many individuals that one can speak of deep-seated feelings about the Negro as being social in character, that is, as characterizing an entire society. It seems important to remember that the explicit *content* of social attitudes stemmed not directly from the emotions being repressed but from the mechanisms of repression. The resultant attitudes, moreover, through constant communication within society, acquired autonomous energy and a viability independent of emotional underpinnings. Hence many individuals subscribed to beliefs about Negroes which performed no very vital function in their personality, and these beliefs may be considered as being part of the cultural environment.

It is with this final consideration in mind that such manifestations of attitudes as laws on interracial sexual relations must be considered; it saves us from despair at being unable to obtain much personal information on individual legislators. Again, it constitutes a useful way of looking at sectional differences in attitudes. Differences between North and South concerning interracial sex were not in kind but in vehemence, if vehemence is defined as the product of the degree of individual involvement and proportion of people involved. In New York in 1785, for example, the assembly passed a gradual emancipation bill which would have barred Negroes from the polls and from marrying whites. The senate objected to the intermarriage clause because "in so important a connection they thought the free subjects of this State ought to be left to their free choice." The assembly again voted narrowly to retain the clause and then, after conference with the senate, finally receded on it by a narrow margin, though later for other reasons the entire bill was lost.[76] In Massachusetts, however, an act of 1786 on the "Solemnization of Marriage" voided marriages between whites and Negroes. Rhode Island passed a similar law in 1798. The Pennsylvania emancipation bill also contained a similar provision which was dropped before final passage.[77] On the whole, this random pattern in the North suggests both the existence of sentiment against intermixture and a lack of great vehemence underlying it.

In the South, on the other hand, where there were more Negroes (wearing fewer clothes) [78] there is evidence suggesting greater tension. For the most part laws prohibiting racial mixture were already on the books and nobody wanted them off.[79] The Virginia legislature's refusal to accept Jefferson's provision in the revisal for banishment of white women bearing mulattoes stemmed more from objection to the harsh penalty than from willingness to countenance interracial matches. One foreign traveler observed that the unusually large number of mulattoes in the state was occasioned only by greater length of settlement and that public opinion was firmly set against interracial unions. Liaisons were carried on in secrecy, he explained, for "no white man is known to live regularly with a black woman." [80] The converse relationship was of course

76. Quote is from Charles Thomson to his wife, Harriet, Mar. 22, 1785, Charles Thomson Papers, Misc., Lib. Cong.; *Journal Assembly N.-Y.* (1785), 77, 86; also McManus, "Antislavery Legislation in New York," *Jour. Negro Hist.*, 46 (1961), 208–10.

77. *Acts and Laws Mass., 1786–87*, 10; *Public Laws R.-I., 1798*, 483; Phila. *Pa. Packet*, Mar. 4, 1779; Mitchell *et al.*, eds., *Statutes Pa.*, X, 67–73. In the year 1800 Rhode Island cleared up ambiguity in an earlier law by declaring that no paternity suits could be brought by Negro women against white men, *Public Laws of the State of Rhode-Island and Providence Plantations, Passed Since . . . 1798* (Newport, [1813?]), 41.

78. Rodman, ed., *Journal of a Tour by William Attmore*, 25, 44; Annapolis *Md. Gaz.*, Sept. 16, 1790; Davis, *Travels in the United States*, ed. Morrison, 97, 422; Robert Sutcliff, *Travels in Some Parts of North America, . . . 1804 . . . 1806 . . .* (Phila., 1812), 51–52, 97; Louis B. Wright and Marion Tinling, eds., *Quebec to Carolina in 1785–1786: Being the Travel Diary and Observations of Robert Hunter, Jr., a Young Merchant of London* (San Marino, Calif., 1943), 267; Janson, *Stranger in America*, ed. Driver, 381–82; O'Kelly, *Essay on Negro Slavery*, 26; "Extract from a Diary Kept by the Hon. Jonathan Mason of a Journey from Boston to Savannah in the Years 1804–1805," Mass. Hist. Soc., *Proceedings*, 2d Ser., 2 (1885–86), 22.

79. Delaware banned intermarriage in 1807 and repealed the ban in 1808, owing to confusion over other matters in the law, *Laws Del.*, IV, 112, 221.

80. *Report of the Committee of Revisors* in Boyd, ed., *Papers of Jefferson*, II, 471; La Rochefoucauld-Liancourt, *Travels through the United States*, II, 82. Other foreign travelers reported specific (though anonymous) instances of masters or their sons sleeping with their slaves; Davis, *Travels in the United States*, 56, 414; Sutcliff, *Travels in North America*, 53. Cases of sexual relations

another matter; though white women still occasionally slept with Negro men,[81] southern society was as determined as ever to punish rigorously any Negro sexual attacks on white women. In 1769, Virginia had excluded castration from the penal code except as punishment for that offense. The brutality of castration had become offensive to humanitarian sentiment, however, and the legislature refused to enact Jefferson's revisal bill based on the *lex talionis*. Yet as late as 1792 emasculation was specifically declared by the legislature to be permissible punishment for any slave "convicted of an attempt to ravish a white woman." In practice the courts seem usually to have hanged such offenders but there was at least one case of sentence to castration, in 1797. The penalty was finally abolished in a general amendment to the penal code in 1805. Despite tension on the matter, some Virginians refused to be blinded by their feelings. In the 1800's several petitions to the governor asked clemency for Negroes condemned for rape on grounds that the white woman involved was of low character.[82] Elsewhere in the South, however, there was evidence of smoldering emotion. In North Carolina a tradition was inaugurated at the turn of the century when lynching parties burned a Negro for rape and castrated a slave for remarking that he was going to have some white women. Georgia in 1806 enacted a mandatory death penalty for any Negro raping or attempting to rape a white woman. As late as 1827 a Georgia court sentenced a Negro to castration and deportation for attempted rape, and the *Macon Telegraph* castigated the court for its leniency.[83]

---

came to light in curiously different ways. Rev. James Fowles of Virginia admitted fathering mulattoes; a Virginia man appealed to the legislature for permission to free his mulatto child; a North Carolina law confirmed a planter's leaving property to his bastard children by "his negro slave Hester" and freed her and the children (1789—ten years later legislators probably would have been less lenient); and in Wilmington, N. C., a Dr. Nesbitt killed a Negro whose mulatto wife the doctor had previously been keeping. Johnston, Race Relations in Virginia, 178, 175; Clark, ed., *State Recs. N. C.*, XXV, 36–37; *Raleigh Register*, Aug. 10, 1802.

81. Ten petitions (1798–1808) for divorce by white men on grounds of the wife's adultery with a Negro are cited in Johnston, Race Relations in Virginia, 199–202, 206–7, 211, 221. Other instances of the same combination are in Annapolis *Md. Gaz.*, July 31, 1794; Edgar J. McManus, Negro Slavery in New York (unpubl. Ph.D. diss., Columbia University, 1959), 262; Melish, *Travels through the United States*, 49; Franklin, *Free Negro in N. C.*, 37–39.

82. Hening, ed., *Statutes Va.*, VIII, 358; Shepard, ed., *Statutes Va.*, I, 125, III, 119; Troy, N. Y., *Farmer's Oracle*, Oct. 3, 1797 (for reference to which I am indebted to McManus, *Negro Slavery in New York*, 97); the petitions in Johnston, Race Relations in Virginia, 206–7.

83. Janson, *Stranger in America*, ed. Driver, 386–87; *Laws State Ga. Since 1800*, 334–35; Flanders, *Plantation Slavery in Georgia*, 267.

The dynamics of the interracial sexual situation did not, of course, invariably tend toward emotional abandon. For one thing, in regions where slavery was firmly rooted in a high proportion of Negroes, the traditional European double standard for the sexes was subject to caricatural polarization. More sexual freedom for white men meant less for white women. Throughout the eighteenth century South Carolina had shown the effects of this tendency, though far less than the British West Indian societies. Despite difficulties created by the biases of travelers, it seems clear that the same tendency still operated in the deep South in the early years of the nineteenth century. One American traveler, the prominent ornithologist of Philadelphia, Alexander Wilson, described his unfavorable impressions by first lamenting that the "superabundance of Negroes" had "destroyed the activity of the whites," who "stand with their hands in their pockets, overlooking their negroes." In his letter to William Bartram in 1809 (here given as published much later in the century), Wilson went on to say,

These, however, are not one-tenth of the curses slavery has brought on the Southern States. Nothing has surprised me more than the cold, melancholy reserve of the females, of the best families, in South Carolina and Georgia. Old and young, single and married, all have that dull frigid insipidity, and reserve, which is attributed to solitary old maids. Even in their own houses they scarce utter anything to a stranger but yes or no, and one is perpetually puzzled to know whether it proceeds from awkwardness or dislike. Those who have been at some of their Balls [in Charleston] say that the ladies hardly even speak or smile, but dance with as much gravity, as if they were performing some ceremony of devotion. On the contrary, the negro wenches are all sprightliness and gayety; and if report be not a defamer— (here there is a hiatus in the manuscript) which render the men callous to all the finer sensations of love, and female excellence.[84]

While one suspects that the "hiatus" may not have been the author's, the description clearly points to deep alienation on the part of white women. Their rightful consorts were often otherwise engaged, and their resulting shell of "dull frigid insipidity" was hard-

84. Wilson to Bartram, Savannah, Mar. 8, 1809. Alexander B. Grosart, ed., *The Poems and Literary Prose of Alexander Wilson, the American Ornithologist*, 2 vols. (Paisley, Scotland, 1876), I, 167–68. A foreign traveler remarked on a concomitant phenomenon in 1819: "The ladies of Carolina, it is said, prefer a fair effeminate kind of man to one of a robust habit, and swarthy dark complexion. This preference of delicate complexions originates in their antipathy to any colour approaching to that of the negro or mulatto, or yellow man, whom it is sometimes difficult to distinguish from a white or brown person." William Faux, *Memorable Days in America, Being a Journal of a Tour to the United States [1818–1820]* . . . (London, 1823), in Reuben G. Thwaites, ed., *Early Western Travels, 1748–1846* . . . , 32 vols. (Cleveland, 1904–07), XI, 100.

ened by the utter necessity of avoiding any resemblance to women of the other race. Perhaps they sensed, too, that the protection they received against Negro men constituted a very perverse variety of affection. Their proper function, moreover, was to preserve the forms and symbols of civilization—they were, after all, bearers of white civilization in a literal sense—and to serve as priestesses in the temples, performing, in Wilson's perceptive phrase, a "ceremony of devotion."

The relationship between miscegenation and society was intricately reciprocal. While miscegenation altered the tone of society, the social institution of slavery helped reshape the definition of miscegenation from fusion of that which was different to fusion of higher and lower; hence slavery was of course responsible for much of the normative judgment implied in the concept of miscegenation. Yet both slavery and miscegenation rested, in the final analysis, upon a *perception of difference* between the races, a perception founded on physiognomic fact. When Jefferson, for example, set out to prove that emancipated Negroes must be removed from white society he predicated "the real distinctions nature has made," moved immediately into a discussion of appearance, and only then went on to less tangible differences in temperament and intellect. Underlying his discussion of the Negro, and everyone else's, was an axiomatic separation of Negroes from white men based on appearance.

8. JEFFERSON: A DICHOTOMOUS VIEW OF TRIRACIAL AMERICA

Yet two puzzles present themselves, the one concerning an individual's unusually extreme views and the other a more general problem of illogical perception. As for the first, Jefferson laid uncommonly great stress on the physical distinction between Negroes and whites. This emphasis derived partly from his emotional responses to women but also from a pervasive temperamental characteristic, a habit of mind not unconnected with his views of the opposite sex. He always regarded the world of men as utterly distinct from the strange world of women in which he could never feel at ease; his division was even sharper than that of the culture in which he lived, which was sharp enough, to be sure. (The English word *sex* itself derived from terms indicating cutting, separation, division.) On a different level, in terms of his "thought," Jefferson gave every evidence of a predilection for bifurcating men and issues and even his perceptual environment, for thinking of the world in terms of—it is significant that we cannot avoid a play on words here—black or white. His approach to the external world became most obvious perhaps during his involvement in the stormy partisan politics which elicited in so many Americans a tendency to regard the political world as composed of two conflicting opposites, Republican and Federalist, France and England, honest men and knaves. Jefferson pressed this tendency as far as anyone, and he may be said to bear some responsibility for the cleancut division of domestic politics in the 1790's, however much he deplored it. He always insisted that hard-core Federalists were "monocrats," i.e., utterly antirepublican, and that, on the other hand, the great body of Federalists were really Republicans at heart. This inability to admit a possible middle ground assumed only slightly different shape in his famous optative statement in the First Inaugural—"We are all republicans: we are all federalists"; here he resolved wide differences by a doubly incorrect denial of their existence.[85] This was partly a matter of shorthand phrasing, but no terminology is innocent of meaning; earlier Jefferson had frequently described European social and political conflicts with such pairs as "hammer and anvil" and "sheep and wolves." He never shared in the contemporary enthusiasm for a balance of powers in government; indeed his picture of society as composed of the people and their enemies precluded any necessity for balancing various interests. It is virtually impossible, for example, to imagine Jefferson as author of the Federalist No. 10; Madison's stress on a multiplicity of factions was

---

85. First Inaugural Address, Ford, ed., *Works of Jefferson*, IX, 195. Some idea of this tendency may be gained from Jefferson's summary of the political situation in 1795, a time of great frustration for him. "Two parties then do exist within the U. S. they embrace respectively the following descriptions of persons.

The Anti-republicans consist of

1. The old refugees and tories.

2. British merchants residing among us, and composing the main body of our merchants.

3. American merchants trading on British capital. Another great portion.

4. Speculators and Holders in the banks and public funds.

5. Officers of the federal government with some exceptions.

6. Office-hunters, willing to give up principles for places. A numerous and noisy tribe.

7. Nervous persons, whose languid fibres have more analogy with a passive than active state of things.

The Republican part of our Union comprehends

1. The entire body of landholders throughout the United States.

2. The body of labourers, not being landholders, whether in husbanding or the arts."

Notes on Prof. Ebeling's letter of July 30, 1795 (undated, probably late 1795), *ibid.*, VIII, 209–10.

entirely foreign to him. Jefferson was at his best on occasions calling for the vigor of simple dichotomy, as in 1776 when he contrasted the virtues of a free people to the crimes of a tyrannical King.

A similar penchant for orderly division became apparent in his relations with individual persons.[86] With a mind too intelligent to classify all men as good or bad, Jefferson nonetheless was temperamentally incapable of subtle analysis of other men's character, incapable of restraining himself from an all-inclusive value judgment. Gouverneur Morris sensed this quality when he wrote in his diary after a call upon Jefferson in Paris, "I think he does not form very just estimates of character, but rather assigns too many to the humble rank of fools, whereas in life the gradations are infinite and each individual has his peculiarities of fort and feeble." [87] For his most famous love letter Jefferson seized upon the one literary form which could most adequately convey his conception of his own personality, a "dialogue" between "the head and the heart."

Jefferson's pervasive temperamental bent for order, symmetry, and normative dichotomy was nowhere more obvious than in his anthropology. Entirely aside from helping to clear the way for his seemingly paradoxical denunciation of both slavery and Negroes, it resulted in what was for Jefferson a highly satisfying resolution of the problem posed by the American Indian. Here his individual temperament came into contact with his society's perception of Indians as being utterly distinct from Negroes. Indians did not in fact look like white persons, yet Americans evinced either indifference or downright unwillingness to admit the fact. With Jefferson the unwillingness was monumental. Confronted by three races in America he determinedly turned three into two by transforming the Indian into a degraded yet basically noble brand of white man. Some of the most heartfelt passages in the *Notes on Virginia* were devoted to a defense of the Indian against the famous French naturalist, Buffon, whose aspersions Jefferson declared to be "just as true as the fable of Æsop." Indians, he asserted, were actually brave and manly and by no means deficient in attachment to family and friends. They were notably eloquent, Jefferson claimed in an extravagant panegyric climaxed by the announcement that the speech of Chief Logan was not in the least inferior to the "whole orations

86. His rigid ordering extended to his architecture, though here there are other obvious influences. See the drawings in S. Fiske Kimball, *Thomas Jefferson: Architect* (Boston, 1916) ; see also his rigidly rectilinear division of the western territory into states in the maps in Boyd, ed., *Papers of Jefferson*, VI, 591, 593, opposite 605.

87. Quoted in Nock, *Jefferson*, 79.

of Demosthenes and Cicero." In contrast with Negroes "they aston-
ish you with strokes of the most sublime oratory; such as prove their
reason and sentiment strong, their imagination glowing and elevated." Unlike the Negroes, he explained, "They will crayon out an
animal, a plant, or a country, so as to prove the existence of a germ
in their minds which only wants cultivation." Physically, too, Jefferson argued, the Indian was by no means inferior to the white man.
Buffon had claimed that "The savage is feeble, and has small organs
of generation; he has neither hair nor beard, and no ardor whatever
for his female." Stung, like other Americans, by this slander on the
natives of his own environment, Jefferson responded with the sharp
rejoinder that the Indian "is neither more defective in ardor, nor
more impotent with his female, than the white reduced to the same
diet and exercise." Their natural supply of hair was the same "as
with the whites" but they "pluck the hair as fast as it appears,"
considering it "disgraceful to be hairy on the body." Indian women,
Jefferson continued, did indeed "raise fewer children than we do,"
but the causes lay "not in a difference of nature, but of circumstance." When married to white traders and leading a suitably
regular life, Indian women "produce and raise as many children as
the white women." [88]

Jefferson thus rescued the Indian from his detractors by appealing to the "circumstances" of their life and, wherever possible, by
outright denial of difference from the white man. In appropriately
altered circumstances Indians would become white men, a happy
transformation indeed. It was precisely this transformation which
Jefferson thought the Negro could never accomplish. By constantly
referring to environment for one group and to nature for the other
he effectively widened the gap which Americans had always placed
between the two. While stressing the "reality" of the Negro's blackness he denied the Indian's tawny color by not mentioning it, not
even venturing the usual suggestion that the Indian's tawniness

88. Jefferson, *Notes on Virginia*, ed. Peden, 58–64, 140. See also Charles
Thomson's commentaries on Jefferson's remarks, *ibid.*, 199–202; Jefferson to
Morgan Brown, Phila., Jan. 16, 1800, Lipscomb and Bergh, eds., *Writings of
Jefferson*, X, 138; Benjamin Rush, *Medical Inquiries and Observations, upon the
Diseases of the Mind* (Phila., 1812), 355; Abraham Bradley, *A New Theory of
the Earth; Or, the Present World Created on the Ruins of an Old World . . .*
(Wilkesbarre, Pa., 1801), 55; Samuel Williams, *The Natural and Civil History of
Vermont* (Walpole, N. H., 1794), 156–58, 183–84, 190; Richard McCausland,
"Particulars Relative to the Nature and Customs of the Indians of North-
America," *Amer. Museum*, 5 (1789), 17–19. There is a long discussion of the
Jefferson-Buffon argument and of the original peopling of America in Charleston
State Gazette of S.-C., July 29ff., 1793.

came not from nature but from bear grease.[89] With both Indians and Negroes Jefferson appealed decisions on mental powers to the court of facts, but he clearly expected radically differing verdicts. In contrast to his "suspicion" concerning Negroes, he announced that with the Indians "we shall probably find that they are formed in mind as well as in body, on the same module with the 'Homo sapiens Europaeus.' " Nothing could demonstrate more clearly Jefferson's prejudgment of the verdict than the different slants with which he made his appeal to environmental influences. While comparing Negroes unfavorably with Roman slaves, he declared that a comparison of Indians "in their present state with the Europeans North of the Alps" during the Roman Empire "would be unequal" because of the greater density of European population.[90] The only "respectable evidence" which might be said to militate against Indian equality, Jefferson wrote in 1785, was that of Don Antonio de Ulloa. Jefferson's method of refuting this evidence was, in light of his passage on the Negro, little short of extraordinary.

But he [Don Ulloa] saw the Indian of South America only, and that after he had passed through ten generations of slavery. It is very unfair, from this sample, to judge of the natural genius of this race of men: and after supposing that Don Ulloa had not sufficiently calculated the allowance which should be made for this circumstance, we do him no injury in considering the picture he draws of the present Indians of S. America as no picture of what their ancestors were 300 years ago. It is in N. America we are to seek their original character: and I am safe in affirming that the proofs of genius given by the Indians of N. America, place them on a level with Whites in the same uncultivated state.[91]

Consistency of argument was no barrier when the final judgment had already been made.

In defending the Indian Jefferson was vindicating the American environment, for his remarks on the Indian in the *Notes* formed only part of his refutation of Buffon's claim that animals in the New World were smaller and weaker than in the Old and of Abbé Raynal's extension of that claim to white Americans. These charges stung Jefferson not only as nationalist but also as scientist, since they imputed inferiority to his natural laboratory equipment. In employing an environmentalist defense of the Indian he had to work carefully, however, since the Indian was both a portion of the

89. Weld, *Travels through North America*, 375–76; Burk, *History of Virginia*, III, 46.

90. Jefferson, *Notes on Virginia*, ed. Peden, 62, 63.

91. To Marquis de Chastellux, Paris, June 7, 1785, Boyd, ed., *Papers of Jefferson*, VIII, 185.

American environment and the product of it. In order not to disparage his own natural environment he was careful to avoid any suggestion that the backwardness of the Indians was the effect of their surroundings and to attribute it (where he could not deny it) to the "circumstances of their situation," that is, to the way they lived. Unfortunately, this attribution left him completely unable to explain why Indians lived that way. At any rate, he was not prepared to let the Indians be subjected to the indignity of being called recent immigrants to America. Appealing the question of Indian origins to the evidence of language, he called for compilation of Indian vocabularies, collected many himself, and concluded categorically as early as 1781 that the wide disparity of Indian tongues "proves them of greater antiquity than those of Asia." [92] Neither Jefferson nor anyone else tried to gain knowledge of Negro languages.

Nowhere was Jefferson's effort to Americanize the Indian more apparent than in his reiterated hope for cultural and physical amalgamation of Indians with white Americans. Together they formed one nation: "We, like you," he once addressed an Indian chief, "are Americans, born in the same land, and having the same interests." His purchase of Louisiana raised the possibility of encouraging the Indians to remove beyond the Mississippi, but he preferred that they be encouraged to give up hunting for farming and cede the resultant surplus of land to the United States. "In truth," he wrote, "the ultimate point of rest and happiness for them is to let our settlements and theirs meet and blend together, to intermix, and become one people." This would "best promote the interests of the Indians and ourselves, and finally consolidate our whole country to one nation only." Ten years later in 1813 he wrote regretfully that war had now intervened: "They would have mixed their blood with ours, and been amalgamated and identified with us within no distant period of time." [93]

Amalgamation and identification, welcomed with the Indian, were precisely what Jefferson most abhorred with the Negro. The

---

92. Jefferson, *Notes on Virginia*, ed. Peden, 100–102. See Chinard, "Eighteenth Century Theories on America," Amer. Phil. Soc., *Proceedings*, 91 (1947), 27–57; Gerbi, *Disputa del Nuovo Mondo*.

93. Speech to Jean Baptiste Ducoigne, Charlottesville, June 1781, Boyd, ed., *Papers of Jefferson*, VI, 60; Jefferson to Benjamin Hawkins, Washington, Feb. 1803, Ford, ed., *Works of Jefferson*, IX, 447–48; to William H. Harrison, Washington, Feb. 27, 1803, Lipscomb and Bergh, eds., *Writings of Jefferson*, X, 368–73; to Horatio Gates, Washington, July 11, 1803, Ford, ed., *Works of Jefferson*, X, 13; to Baron von Humboldt, n. p., Dec. 6, 1813, *ibid.*, XI, 353–54.

Indian was a brother, the Negro a leper. While Americans had always regarded the two peoples as very different, Jefferson under-lined the dichotomy with a determined emphasis not matched by other men. His derogation of the Negro revealed the latent possibil-ities inherent in an accumulated popular tradition of Negro inferi-ority; it constituted, for all its qualifications, the most intense, extensive, and extreme formulation of anti-Negro "thought" offered by any American in the thirty years after the Revolution. Yet Thomas Jefferson left to Americans something else which may in the long run have been of greater importance—his prejudice for freedom and his larger equalitarian faith. It was this faith which must have caused him to fall gradually more silent on a subject which many of his fellow intellectuals were taking up with interest. For Jefferson more than for any of his known contemporaries, the subject was not an easy or a happy one.

XIII THE NEGRO BOUND BY THE

CHAIN OF BEING

NATURAL PHILOSOPHERS IN THE YOUNG REPUBLIC WERE LESS
willing than previously to act as humble collectors for the learned
naturalists of Europe, less willing, that is, to accept colonial status
in the empire of science. Newly won political independence did
nothing to undermine the old tradition of trans-Atlantic scientific
cooperation, but cooperation, Americans had come to feel, implied
equality among participants. In the face of this change, however,
the structure of their conceptual world remained fundamentally the
same. The fusion of traditional Christianity and Newtonian mechanics had helped generate a world view which was remarkable for
its cohesiveness, energy, and passion for system, qualities not unconnected with such well-known facets of the Enlightenment as the
deliberate reconstruction of governments and the maturation of a
money economy. If anything, the old structure seemed firmer than
ever, though in retrospect we can detect some of the cracks which
belied a growing fossilization. Indeed the eighteenth-century penchant for order actually grew stronger in many quarters after the
Revolution.

One notable apparent discordancy in nature concerned man himself and therefore elicited especially strenuous efforts at resolution.
Mankind existed in an untidy variety of shapes and colors, and it
was essential that this natural disarray should submit to some
universal, ordering principle of nature. Americans, especially, had
reason to sense a discordant note when they contemplated the status
of Africans in their new empire of liberty. Here lay the makings of
an interesting dilemma: what would happen if the passion for
system in nature should conflict with the yearning for a harmoni-
ously ordered society?

That any scientific answer concerning the variability of man would have ramifications for a vital social issue did not alter the necessity of finding some explanation. Most philosophers hoped that their findings would comport with the dictates of benevolence, but the misery of the slave could never be allowed to dictate to God's creation. It would be pleasant if the world were both happy and tidy, but there was no question as to which was the preferable condition if the two should happen to conflict. Fortunately for their peace of mind, many men who were engaged in the fight against the slave trade and slavery were convinced that no conflict was possible; men like Benjamin Rush were deeply convinced that slavery violated the prescriptions of Nature. Probably many antislavery advocates were impelled unknowingly toward a vision of order in creation by their empathy with their fellow creatures, but these men thought they reasoned in the opposite direction, from order to benevolence.

1. LINNAEAN CATEGORIES AND THE CHAIN OF BEING

All these themes—the self-searching and assertiveness of a new nation, the desire for order, and the continued presence of slavery in post-Revolutionary America—ran contrapuntally through the attempts of Americans to assess the nature of the Negro and his rightful place in a natural order which derived from divine decree. These attempts were framed, necessarily, in old terms, ones which had become international coin during the first, less revolutionary half of the century.

By the final quarter of the eighteenth century the concept of the Great Chain of Being had become highly popular and widely popularized. It still found expression at various levels of mental construction; traces of the concept cropped up in formulations ranging from Charles Bonnet's elaboration of the Chain (handsomely adorned with pictorial representation), through the singsong popularization of Alexander Pope, to innumerable offhand references to the "scale of beings" or "rank in Creation." For Americans the most widely known statement was Pope's; his *Essay on Man* became a runaway best seller and was printed in America no fewer than sixty-eight times between 1747 and 1809.[1] Aspiring American poets were not to be outdone in admiration for the Creator's plan.

1. Agnes Marie Sibley, *Alexander Pope's Prestige in America, 1725–1835* (N. Y., 1949), 23.

From animalcula, progress to man,
Explore each link of nature's wond'rous chain:
Say, can'st thou mark a nothing throughout space,
Or one minutia miss'd from race to race?
Then, if thou can'st not, study not in vain,
To alter nature, or unlink the chain.[2]

The popularity and pervasiveness of the Great Chain was by no means prescriptive, for the Linnaean tradition of classification remained a separate, viable means of imposing order on the Creation. The eminent naturalist's terminology and reputation still dominated the study of natural categories in America.

As for his teminology, in that era it was eminently suitable that similarities and likenesses in nature should be discussed within the confines of a limited and accurately pitched vocabulary. Despite occasional doubts it had been clear for a century that *species* described those categories originally created by God and that *varieties* pointed only to those differences *within* a species which had come about, as it was characteristically phrased, "accidentally." The discrete existence of each species seemed to be maintained by the providential inability of any species to procreate with another beyond the first generation, though on this point doubt had been cast, doubt which was to prove of considerable importance. As for his reputation, Linnaeus was revered as the father of classification; certainly there was no reason to assume that he was a proponent of the Great Chain. In 1789, for example, when the popular *Columbian Magazine* of Philadelphia published in translation a passage by the great naturalist, Americans were treated to a homily of praise for the wondrous variety of God's handiwork without the slightest suggestion of hierarchical arrangement.[3] The Chain of Being remained merely a readily available, even tempting way of ordering Nature's differences, not an intellectual imperative.

While the supply of systematizing concepts thus remained much the same as earlier in the century, political and social developments after the Revolution worked to heighten the temptation to draw upon them. When Edward Long and the author of *Personal Slavery Established* utilized the Great Chain to lower the status of the

2. *The Age of Error; or, A Poetical Essay on the Course of Human Action* (Phila., 1797), 12, quoted in Sibley, *Alexander Pope's Prestige*, 32.
3. "REFLECTIONS *on the Study of* Nature: *translated from the Latin of the celebrated* Linnaeus," *Columbian Magazine*, 3 (1789), 3–6, 82–87, 153–56. The weight of Linnaeus's prestige in America is made evident in Miller, *Brief Retrospect*, I, 112–45, 496.

Negro in 1773–74, they demonstrated that an antislavery campaign was bound to run into opponents equipped with dangerous scientific concepts. The thrust of antislavery was apt to generate a counterthrust of biological inequality. Yet these two works remained the most extreme expositions of their kind, partly because derogatory assessments of the Negro's nature were always more than a matter of involuntary responses to the threat of abolition. Several other major factors affected these assessments during the forty years after 1773. As will become evident, a more eager and more knowledgeable interest in human and comparative anatomy was bound to reshape discussion about Negroes. Less obviously but no less powerfully, the great upheaval of the French Revolution affected the discussion by stimulating the appetite of European and American opponents of that Revolution for a measure of order in the face of its chaotic excesses. In the realm of politics in America, principles of natural philosophy were called to serve novel purposes, as, for example, when a Federalist partisan chanted the following imprecation upon Jeffersonian leveling.

> Next, every man throughout the nation
> Must be contented with his station,
> Nor think to cut a figure greater
> Than was design'd for him by Nature.[4]

For purposes of politically partisan rhetoric, the Great Chain had a bleak future, but it served in this instance to soothe an itch which was becoming general in certain quarters in the 1790's and after. As will become evident, too, the principle of order was enormously attractive to anyone who for whatever reason felt that his social community was going to pot—it was perhaps no accident that the two men in America who had most to say about the nature of the Negro were a Virginia governor and a college president.

Most subtly but perhaps most powerfully of all, the process of nation-forming established a context within which a great deal of the discussion of the Negro's nature took place. Indeed there is an aroma of causality emanating from the coincidence of an outburst of discussion about Negroes in 1787–90 and the formation of the federal union. Partly, it was that a people's and a nation's identity were undergoing assessment. And although a vast majority of Americans felt that their society was by no means in total disarray, many were agreed on the need for a better-ordered and better-ordering

4. Quoted in Merle Curti, *The Growth of American Thought* (N. Y. and London, 1943), 193.

political mechanism. As the Virginia Plan which was presented at the opening of the Constitutional Convention expressed the necessity: "Resolved . . . that the national legislature ought to be empowered . . . to legislate in all cases to which the separate states are incompetent, or in which the harmony of the United States may be interrupted by the exercise of individual legislation." [5]

This outburst of discussion about the Negro coincided also with the first rumblings of an Anglo-American surge of antislavery protest and the accompanying discovery of remarkable Negroes like Benjamin Banneker. Undoubtedly mutual stimulation was involved. More immediately, discussion broke out in 1787–88 because Jefferson's *Notes on Virginia* specifically broached the question of the Negro's rank in creation. And, in 1787, independently, an aspiring college president undertook the first major American study of the races of mankind.

2. TWO MODES OF EQUALITY

Samuel Stanhope Smith was the son of a Presbyterian minister; he graduated from that nursery of Presbyterian ministers, the College of New Jersey, in 1769, and obtained license to preach from a synod. After a term of active ministry in piedmont Virginia he accepted the professorship of moral philosophy back at Princeton, married President John Witherspoon's daughter, and succeeded to his father-in-law's post in 1795. He stood in the front rank of American academicians and received honorary degrees from Yale in 1783 and Harvard in 1810, accolades which he valued no higher than his election as an honorary member of the American Philosophical Society in 1785. In grateful response to that honor Smith prepared a scientific paper for delivery before the Society; it was his maiden excursion into natural philosophy and though he elaborated his thesis some years later it proved to be the only one of his life. Smith's piece was published in 1787 with the promising title, *An Essay on the Causes of the Variety of Complexion and Figure in the Human Species. To Which Are Added Strictures on Lord Kaims's Discourse, on the Original Diversity of Mankind.*

Smith's point of departure in the *Essay* revealed his basic purpose. On the first page he took notice of the theories which held mankind to be of different stocks and summarily dismissed them: "we are not at liberty to make this supposition." The impossibility

5. Quoted in Irving Brant, *James Madison*, 6 vols. (Indianapolis and N. Y., 1941–61), III, 24.

of determining the exact number and types of originally separate human species, Smith argued, was clear indication that they had never existed. "This supposition" of separate creations, he wrote (shifting into Jeffersonian terminology), "unavoidably confounds the whole philosophy of human nature." Having thus cleared the stage in a few short pages Smith turned to constructive work, and it took him the rest of the book to demonstrate his basic proposition —that mankind constituted a single species and that human varieties had come to differ in appearance through the operation of natural causes, which were, as he described them, "climate," "state of society," and "habits of living." The energy of his argument plainly derived from Smith's abhorrence of the contrary possibility that men varied in appearance because they had originally been cast in different molds.

No one felt the need for system more irresistibly than Samuel Stanhope Smith, and his answer to the problem of human diversity was the one which, for a time, predominated in American and European thinking. His resolution of varieties into a single entity provided relief from the tension of disorder; his *Essay* was a prolonged Handelian ending. Smith was thoroughly conscious of the far-reaching importance of his system, and in 1787 he called upon the world to admit the disastrous consequences of its denial.

The writers who, through ignorance of nature, or through prejudice against religion, attempt to deny the unity of the human species do not advert to the confusion which such principles tend to introduce. The science of morals would be absurd; the law of nature and nations would be annihilated; no general principles of human conduct, of religion, or of policy could be framed; for, human nature, originally, infinitely various, and, by the changes of the world, infinitely mixed, could not be comprehended in any system. The rules which would result from the study of our own nature, would not apply to the natives of other countries who would be of different species; perhaps, not to two families in our own country, who might be sprung from a dissimilar composition of species. Such principles tend to confound all science, as well as piety; and leave us in the world uncertain whom to trust, or what opinions to frame of others.[6]

Smith concluded in obvious relief with a résumé of the advantages to be derived from his system. "The doctrine of one race, removes this uncertainty, renders human nature susceptible of system, illustrates the powers of physical causes, and opens a rich and extensive field for moral science." If illustrating "the powers of physical

---

6. Samuel Stanhope Smith, *An Essay on the Causes of the Variety of Complexion and Figure in the Human Species. To Which Are Added Strictures on Lord Kaims's Discourse, on the Original Diversity of Mankind* (Phila., 1787), 109–10.

causes" had its particular attractions for Americans dwelling close to untamed nature, Europeans could join wholeheartedly with Smith in contemplating with satisfaction the fundamental unity of the human species.

In effect, Samuel Stanhope Smith had marshaled Linnaean classification and the power of environmental influences in support of the Book of Genesis. Yet his book was not the work of a reactionary minister; rather it represented an age of special faith that inquiry into the natural world could do nothing but support the tenets of revealed religion because true inquiry could only reveal the handiwork of God. It was in this sense that the Reverend Mr. Smith shared the same cosmology with the other principal author on race in 1787, Thomas Jefferson.

Smith's *Essay* and Jefferson's *Notes on Virginia* did not, however, offer similar conclusions concerning the Negro, though as should become clear in the next chapter Smith's explanation of the Negro's color suggests that he shared some of Jefferson's predilections. It was not that the two men began with radically different views about man, but rather that they elaborated their assumptions with different basal modes of logic. Both started with human equality. After grounding equality in the *brotherhood* of man as embedded in the story of Genesis, Smith could scarcely permit merely physical distinctions among men to override the fundamental kinship of all human beings within one family. But Jefferson, by grounding human equality in men's common taxonomic participation in a natural species, was forced to suppose that physical distinctions among men were of the utmost importance. Perhaps this is to say that the two men's assumptions were very different, that one was a secularized version of the other. Perhaps, though, it would be more to the point to say that Jefferson's inability to think in terms of essentially familial relationships doomed his equalitarian faith to self-negation. He could never have brought himself to say with his friend Benjamin Rush that Negroes "are our brethren not only by creation but by redemption."[7]

Not merely the dangerous flaw in Jefferson's biologic conception of equality but also the ambiguousness of the *Notes on Virginia* and

7. Rush to Jeremy Belknap, Phila., Aug. 19, 1788, Butterfield, ed., *Letters of Rush*, I, 482–83. Much of Rush's differing emphasis as to the roots of equality may be summarized by his statement: "A Christian cannot fail of being a republican. The history of the creation of man, and of the relation of our species to each other by birth, which is recorded in the Old Testament, is . . . the strongest argument that can be used in favor of the original and natural equality of all mankind." Rush, *Essays, Literary, Moral and Philosophical* (Phila., 1798), 8–9.

the profundity of his disparagement of the Negro stand out all the more sharply when viewed in the light of Linnaean terminology and the Great Chain of Being. His remarks in the *Notes* bore all the earmarks of deliberate ambiguity, of an attempt to dodge the implications arising from his deep-seated sentiments. At a conscious level Jefferson's evasiveness involved gingerly referring to Negroes as a "race," a term then characterized by total absence of any precise meaning. At best the term *race* was used, as one writer, John Augustine Smith, explained, "merely to express the fact, that differences do exist." [8] Thus Jefferson hedged himself doubly when he hesitated to declare the Negro inferior in mental capacities because such a conclusion "would degrade a whole race of men from the rank in the scale of beings which their Creator may perhaps have given them." [9] Jefferson's determination (and inability) to commit himself was further demonstrated by his reference to "the blacks, whether originally a distinct race, or made distinct by time and circumstances," an almost frank evasion which was reiterated in his ensuing remark that "different species of the same genus or varieties of the same species, may possess different qualifications." This was as close as he came to broaching the key question—whether Negroes were of the same species with whites. Even to suggest the possibility that they were a different species of the same genus was, considering the precision of this terminology, a radical step which implied a degree of difference far greater than most men were willing to allow.

In brushing aside (ostensibly by postponing) a decision as to the proper category for the Negro, Jefferson left the door open to a sensible conceptualism which he did not develop fully for another thirty years.[10] In the *Notes on Virginia* he shunned the customary terminology even when expounding the most rigid of all corollaries of the Great Chain. "Such is the economy of nature," he commented on his search for the living mammoth, "that no instance can be produced of her having permitted any one race of her animals to become extinct; of her having formed any link in her great work so

8. J[ohn] Augustine Smith, "A Lecture Introductory to the Second Course of Anatomical Instruction in the College of Physicians and Surgeons for the State of New-York . . . ," *New-York Medical and Philosophical Journal and Review*, 1 (1809) , 33.

9. This and the following quotations from Jefferson are from his *Notes on Virginia*, ed. Peden, 53–54, 138–43. There is little evidence to support the suggestion that Americans were more inclined than Europeans to use "Chain of Beings" in preference to the more metaphysical "Chain of Being."

10. His most comprehensive statement was to Dr. John Manners, Monticello, Feb. 22, 1814, Lipscomb and Bergh, eds., *Writings of Jefferson*, XIV, 97–103.

weak as to be broken." Here the term *race* became a synonym for *species*. Despite his eventual realization that the categories of nature were imposed by man, he never expressed doubt as to the objectively hierarchical character of natural variation. As the years went by the concept of the Chain became less appealing to him and to his contemporaries, but in the *Notes* he accepted the concept axiomatically, utilizing it to express his deep-felt sense that the Negro was not the equal of the white man.

Jefferson's repugnance for sexual "mixture" of Negroes with whites was also expressible with special force in terms of the Linnaean terminology and the Great Chain. Once again Jefferson deliberately beclouded his words when he asked whether lovers of natural history would not, in viewing "the gradations in all the races of animals with the eye of philosophy, excuse an effort to keep those in the department of man as distinct as nature has formed them?" *Races* and *departments* were thoroughly *un*philosophical categories. Jefferson was attempting to emphasize distinctiveness in Negroes without denying their humanity. Similarly, he was able to convey an analogously veiled judgment by utilizing the standing facts of the Chain of Nature. At a general level of analysis it was obvious that sexual union between creatures of differing ranks in Creation constituted a violation of Nature's ordered plan. Jefferson was certain that mixture between Negroes and whites involved the inferior with the superior. "The improvement of the blacks in body and mind," he wrote in the *Notes,* "in the first instance of their mixture with the whites, has been observed by every one, and proves that their inferiority is not the effect merely of their condition of life."

More specifically and more powerfully, the Great Chain afforded a circuit pattern for the flow of the charged sexuality with which Jefferson vested relations between the two races. Here he was able to draw upon a centuries-old tradition, probably without even knowing it. He revealed to his readers the existence of an ordered hierarchy of sexual aggressiveness by referring to the Negroes' "own judgment in favour of the whites, declared by their preference of them, as uniformly as is the preference of the Oran-ootan for the black women over those of his own species." Here at last, proclaimed in language at once passionate and clinical, was the Negro's true rank in nature's scale—exactly midway between ("as uniformly as") the white man and the most man-like ape. This connection with the ape was forged by Jefferson in his passage on the superior beauty of white women.

3. THE HIERARCHIES OF MEN

This persistent confluence of sexual myth and supremely intellectual construct was one of the most bizarre in Western history; it may serve as a striking reminder that the "mind" of any age arises from widely disparate levels of psychic activity and that "ideas" persist according to the measure of their deep-rootedness in psycho-social necessities. Ever since the days of confrontation in Africa the sexual connection between Negro and ape had served to express the deep-seated feeling that the Negro was more animal —and accordingly more sexual—than the white man; or put another way, the Negro-ape connection served as a sufficiently indirect means by which the white man could express his dim awareness of the sexual animal within himself—an awareness that has become less pervasively dim in the twentieth century and which reveals civilized man as actually *more* "sexual" than primitive peoples. At the time, attachment of this pattern of feeling to a highly rationalized schema, the Great Chain of Being, had several profoundly satisfying results. It embedded the pattern in the cosmos, vindicating sexual feelings by adorning them with intellectual respectability and the endorsement of the Creator. (If this was blasphemy it was not the first of its kind.) It opened the way for elaboration of the fortuitous physiognomic similarities between ape and Negro. And, given the circumstance of Negro slavery, it gave vent to the deep social sense that society was, like nature, properly and naturally a harmonious hierarchical structure with each element set fixedly in its appointed place.

The union of sexuality and the Chain was most glaringly apparent in the acidulent remarks of the Jamaican historian Edward Long. In the opening months of 1788 the *Columbian Magazine,* then edited by a strong supporter of the new Constitution, Francis Hopkinson, dredged up Long's *History of Jamaica* (1774) and reprinted certain passages under the title "Observations on the Gradation in the Scale of Being between the Human and Brute Creation. Including Some Curious Particulars Respecting Negroes." [11] It was these passages, now frankly advertised as dealing

11. The title of the book was indicated, but not the author's name, *Columbian Mag.,* 2 (1788), 14–22, 70–75; [Long], *Jamaica,* the selected passage being II, 352–77, but see 320–83, 484–85. Bryan Edwards objected to many of these contentions in his MS. notes on Long's *History of Jamaica,* John Carter Brown Library, Brown Univ., Providence.

with the Chain, which had been stimulated by the burgeoning antislavery movement on both sides of the Atlantic. Long's "particulars" were indeed "curious," for his description of Negroes proved to be a romp through the garden of infantile sexuality. With the greatest sobriety he enumerated the Negro's "covering of wool, like the bestial fleece," round eyes, thick lips, large nipples on the females (to fit the lips, Long suggested), black lice, and "bestial or fætid smell." Long's formulations on the Negro's less tangible qualities were not much further removed from the lost pleasures of the nursery: Negroes were "void of genius" and had "no moral sensations; no taste but for women; gormandizing, and drinking to excess; no wish but to be idle."

Having concluded to his own very evident satisfaction that Negroes possessed no laudable qualities whatsoever, Long proceeded to divulge the Negro's position on the scale of nature. Must not Negroes, he asked, constitute "a different species of the same GENUS?" And "why shall we insist, that man alone, of all other animals, is undiversified in the same manner, when we find so many irresistable proofs, which denote his conformity to the general system of the world? In this system we perceive a regular order and gradation from inanimate to animated matter; and certain links, which connect the several genera one with another." Long was all but carried away with the magnificence of this vision in which the infinite gradations combined "all together in a wonderful and beautiful harmony, the result of infinite wisdom and contrivance."

Having made clear that his contentions had been underwritten by the Deity, Long turned to reinforcement of what he rightly sensed might be considered the weakest portion of his Chain. He hammered away industriously at proving that the "oran-outang" (the chimpanzee) possessed quasi-human characteristics: Apes ate at dinner tables; the mechanic arts of the Negroes were no more than an orang might be brought to do; orang-outangs might be taught to speak. Orangs did not "seem at all inferior in the intellectual faculties to many of the negroe race; with some of whom it is credible that they have the most intimate connexion and consanguinuity. The amorous intercourse between them may be frequent; the Negroes themselves bear testimony, that such intercourses actually happen; and it is certain, that both races agree perfectly well in lasciviousness of disposition." Long found this sexual theme irresistible, and he was eminently successful at weaving it into the Great Chain. "Ludicrous as the opinion may seem, I do not think that an oran-outang husband would be any dishonour to an Hottentot female." Orangs, he declared, "conceive a passion for the Negroe women, and hence must be supposed to covet their embraces from a natural impulse of desire, such as inclines one animal towards another of the same species, or which has a conformity in the organs of generation." This latter suggestion of corporal resemblance was not one which Long thought necessary to elaborate, though in more general form it was shortly to prove of vital importance. He contented himself with the announcement that the orang-outang "has in form a much nearer resemblance to the Negroe race, than the latter bear to White men."

The conclusion to which Long's argument was pointing represented calculation from nature to society, a procedure for which especially in that century there was more than ample precedent. After knowingly alluding to the orang's dominion over "his *slaves, the inferior animals,*" Long concluded with the only slightly veiled suggestion that the institution of Negro slavery was modeled upon the unalterable structure of divinely-ordained Nature: "The Negroe race (consisting of varieties) will then appear rising progressively in the scale of intellect, the further they mount above the Oran-outang and brute creation. The system of man [i.e., slavery] will seem more consistent, and the measure of it more complete, and analagous to the harmony and order that are visible in every other line of the world's stupendous fabric."

In transforming the most man-like ape nearly into a man and by emphasizing his affinity to the Negro, Long did *not* imply that the Negro was actually a beast, even though he was tempted, he said, to think that Negroes and whites were not of the same species and did not have common parents. It is of the utmost significance that the most virulent traducers of the Negro were forced to wildly strenuous and preposterous attempts at proving that the orang-outang was nearly human. Essentially what Long's attempt involved was eradication of the clear distinction between men and beasts, and such an attempt (even with powerful assistance from the concept of the Chain) was clearly going to have considerable difficulty wiping out a basic presupposition thousands of years old. The Judaic-Christian tradition was inflexible on the discrete conditions of man created "in his own image" as contrasted to "the fish of the sea," "the fowl of the air," "the cattle," and "every creeping thing that creepeth upon the earth," and the tradition remained very much alive in the latter part of the eighteenth century. Even Darwinism utterly failed to eradicate this distinction. The same verse of Genesis, whether interpreted literally or as a primal myth, helps illuminate the reasons for the alarm raised by attempts such as Long's; for God had given man "dominion" over living creatures, and if the Negro were an inferior sort of man perhaps his superior's dominion was implied. In a sense this brings matters back full circle to the fact that it sometimes was difficult for the white man to see the Negro as created in God's own image.

If some of these implications escaped the editor of the *Columbian Magazine*, he seemed determined to give the question of the Negro's rank a complete airing, for in the issue following the final selection from Long's *History of Jamaica* readers were offered a passage on the Negro drawn from Jefferson's *Notes on Virginia*.[12] Though the famous Virginian's classic denunciation of slavery was omitted, the magazine evidently had no intention of defending slavery or degrading the Negro, since the next month it published an able refutation of the doctrines set forth by Long and less definitively by Jefferson. The little piece by "R." (probably an Englishman, perhaps the noted abolitionist James Ramsay) was headed "An Answer to a Circumstance on Which Some Writers, in Defence of the Slave-Trade, Have Founded Much of It's Legality"; it also appeared that month in the *American Magazine* with the running title, "The Owran-Outang a Distinct Species."[13]

Taken together the two titles are suggestive, since one seized upon the social implications of the Chain of Being and the other on the mediating term between the Chain and sexuality. "R." maintained that the rationale of the slave trade now rested on *"that power delegated to man, of enslaving the animals lower in the scale than himself, and which those* [recent] *writers would extend to the natives of Africa, from an idea that he has a mixture of brute blood in his body."* This was not, of course, precisely the ground which Long had taken, but it afforded an excellent point of departure for effectively dismantling Long's whole argument by appeal to his basic premise. The axiomatic harmony of nature could as easily be utilized to separate the orang-outang from the Negro as to connect them:

If a creature had been produced by the connection of the African women with the Owran-Outang, and *vice versa*, capable of procreation, the har-

12. *Columbian Mag.*, 2 (1788), 141–44.
13. *Ibid.*, 2 (1788), 266–68; *American Magazine*, 1 (1788), 391–94. The original appeared as "An Argument Used by Some Writers in Defence of the Legality of the Slave Trade, viz., the Mixture of an Owran-Outang with a Female African, by Which They Think a Race of Animals May Be Produced, Partaking of the Nature of Each, Refuted," *European Magazine and London Review*, 13 (1788), 75–76. The text used here is from the *American Magazine*.

mony of the animal system must have been ruined. The new animal, neither brute nor human, might possibly again mix with an animal not of its own species; the consequence of which would be, the production of another new creature, partaking of the nature of both its parents, but differing essentially from one and the other; and so on *ad infinitum*. Thus might this promiscuous intercourse proceed, till the whole order of animals would be in the utmost confusion. But the all-wise Creator of the Universe foreseeing that such unnatural propensities would sometimes take place, has guarded against their effects by raising an insurmountable barrier, which is no other than rendering the offspring of such an intercourse STERILE. So that it is impossible a new race of animals should be produced by the mixture of a male and female of different species, as in the female African and Owran-Outang.

Clearly the principle of order in nature could as easily be used to defend the Negro's sameness with the white man as to deny it.

"R.'s" use of infertility of offspring as the criterion of species and as (thereby) the mark of the Negro's humanity, although coming under increasingly severe challenge, was by no means scientifically disreputable. Many scientists, Hugh Williamson for example, agreed with "R." that the strongest argument for regarding the Negro as "of the same stock with the European" was that the mixed offspring was "as fruitful as its parents." [14] On a level deeper than scientific doctrine, moreover, the firmly established fact that whites and Negroes were capable of interbreeding *ad infinitum* provided assurance of a fundamental affinity, a kind of shared experience against which no amount of speculation about Negroes and orangs could possibly compete. On this level, on the other hand, the orang-outang served as a symbol for the white man's sense that in interracial sexual union the Negro was not only the inferior partner but the more aggressive and more animal one. Even a fully committed equalitarian like Benjamin Rush subscribed to the still unchallenged assumption that it was African *women* who were "debauched" by orang-outangs.[15]

Thus in a very fundamental way the issue of the orang-outang was tied to the question of the Negro's nature, and it was with sure instinct that the anonymous "R." concentrated on the man-like ape. While he was able to cite Linnaeus, Buffon, and Camper in proof of the clear distinction between orang-outang and Negro, he could not entirely disentangle himself from the principle of continuity in the

14. Hugh Williamson, *Observations on the Climate in Different Parts of America* . . . (N. Y., 1811) , 35.

15. Benjamin Rush, "Observations Intended to Favour a Supposition That the Black Color (As It Is Called) of the Negroes Is Derived from the Leprosy," *Amer.* Phil. Soc., *Transactions,* 4 (1799) , 291.

Chain of Being. "Though the Owran-Outang is not in my opinion sufficiently allied to man to produce an intermediate species," he wrote, "yet I believe he may be the link which connects the rational creature to the brute." At last he fell back on the procrustean bed of the standard terminology. "From the united authority of able naturalists," he declared categorically, "there is not a doubt but man and the Owran-Outang are of distinct and widely-separated species." He did not, however, go on to claim that the Negro was the equal of the white man, perhaps feeling that to enroll the Negro in the human species was going far enough.

For the most part antislavery people were unwilling to take up battle along this line, since the concept of the Chain was exceedingly difficult to handle. On the one hand the existence of the Chain of Being was difficult to deny categorically without implying that Nature was not so highly ordered as it might be. Contrarily, to admit the possibility that Nature was hierarchically ordered was to open the door to inherent inferiority, no matter how strenuously the unity of the human species was objected. The difficulty may be illustrated by the position taken by William Dickson, an English antislavery advocate whose work was extracted in the *Columbian Magazine* in 1790. Without denying the existence of the Chain, Dickson denied its relevance to Negroes, declaring that there was "a chasm" between Negroes and brutes, which was to say that the Chain of Being was something nearly everyone had always said it never could be—broken.[16] In general, then, antislavery advocates simply ignored the concept; less often they blindly berated the "pseudo Philosophers" for classifying the Negro with the orangoutang.[17] Only one person, Gilbert Imlay in his indignant criticism of the *Notes on Virginia*, displayed even a partial consciousness of the importance of the orang as a mediating term between sexuality and cosmologic construct. After applauding Jefferson's antislavery views Imlay turned on him for having "attempted to make it appear that the African is a being between the human species and the oran-outang; and ridiculously [having] suffered his imagination to be carried away with the idle tales of that animal's embracing the negroe women, in preference to the females of its own species." This

16. "An Extract from [William] Dickson's Letters on Negro Slavery," *Columbian Mag.*, 4 (1790), 18–23, 73–80. The contention that there were "some chasms" between the three kingdoms of creation and "smaller intervals" between the various classes of animals was not the usual view of the "connecting chain." See C[harles] W[illson] Peale and A. M. F. J. Beauvois, *A Scientific and Descriptive Catalogue of Peale's Museum* (Phila., 1796), vi.
17. [Joseph Sansom], *A Poetical Epistle to the Enslaved Africans, in the Character of an Ancient Negro . . .* (Phila., 1790), 9n.

was, Imlay declared indignantly, "paltry sophistry and nonsense!" [18] At one level of psychic logic, of course, it was nothing of the sort.

The safest refuge for antislavery remained the position taken up by Samuel Stanhope Smith, but as it turned out even that fortress was not impregnable to incursions by the concept of the Great Chain. In 1789 "A.B." submitted to the *American Museum* some disparaging remarks on Smith's *Essay* by "the critical reviewers, of London" together with his own defense of Smith.[19] These reviewers had described the *Essay* as "extremely vague and inaccurate" and, with more justice, had charged Smith with "unreasonable diffuseness." The Mosaic account applied only to one race, they declared, and the white man's rank in creation was superior to that of other men. Interfertility would afford a strong argument for the unity of man, but recently unions of different species such as dogs and wolves had produced fertile offspring. Furthermore, they pointed out, Smith had fallen into factual error concerning the colors of many peoples around the globe.

In refutation "A.B." had little difficulty in exonerating Smith on this final point, but he was unable to offer contradictory evidence on the question of interfertility. More significant, he permitted his vigorous defense of Smith's *Essay* to collapse almost completely at the end by admitting the existence of ranks in creation: "We must not leave this enquiry, without remarking, that whatever conclusion we form of the distinct species, it ought not to affect the work of humanity in securing a better treatment to the Negroes. If they are found to be of a *different* species, they are still men; and if it appears that our own rank in the creation is the superior one, it should only suggest that mercy and compassion which we hope for from beings infinitely superior to ourselves. At any rate, a work of benevolence and importance ought not, in the slightest degree, to be influenced by a speculative question—by a question which it is possible will never be decided." In the face of man's age-old sense of dominion over beings inferior in nature, this was scarcely a convincing disclaimer.

4. ANATOMICAL INVESTIGATIONS

It was significant, too, that "A.B." should conclude that his opponent was "evidently an anatomist," for anatomical investigation proved to be the means by which the highly schematic Chain

18. Imlay, *Topographical Description*, 201.

19. A. B., "Reviewers' Opinion of Dr. Smith's Essay on Complexion and Figure; With Remarks on the Same," *Amer. Museum*, 6 (1789), 241–49.

of Being could be moored securely to the operative facts of nature. The study of human anatomy and physiology advanced rapidly during the final quarter of the century, much more so in Europe than America, of course, though intellectuals in the new republic followed developments with interest. It was burgeoning interest in the nature of the human body, indeed, which revealed how thoroughgoing a shift had taken place toward a primarily naturalistic view of man. The alteration was centuries in the making, to be sure, but the introduction of anatomical investigation into the long-standing problem of differences among human groups came with relative suddenness. When, after 1775, large numbers of human corpses were brought under the same scrutiny which Edward Tyson had applied to his "orang outang" in 1700, there were bound to be repercussions upon ideas about the Negro.

The trend first became evident in Peter Camper's work on the "facial angle," a method of measuring skulls which Camper himself, as indicated earlier, employed in the service of the concept of the Chain of Being. In Great Britain, Camper's suggestions were picked up by Dr. John Hunter, that country's most prominent surgeon in the late 1780's. An avid collector of natural specimens and a valued customer of the London body-snatchers, Hunter adorned the borders of a pool outside his private museum with animal and human skulls. No less impressed than Camper with the regular gradation in form from European to monkey, Hunter was acutely aware of the dangers involved in including the Negro in this series. "He understood," the English abolitionist James Ramsay reported after hearing Hunter lecture on "the gradation of skulls" at the Royal Academy, "that the very doubt whether they might not be an inferior race, operated against the humane treatment of them; and God forbid, said he, that any vague conjecture of mine should be used to confirm the prejudice." Ramsay was sufficiently set on edge by the implications which could be drawn from racial variations in skull structure that he went round to seek Hunter's assurances on the matter; he was immensely relieved to be able to report that Hunter "drew no conclusion from the difference in them respecting African inferiority." [20]

The appeal to the hard facts of anatomical structure was carried furthest by another English surgeon whose book was largely responsible for the subsequent reentry of Samuel Stanhope Smith into the

20. Ramsay, *Treatment and Conversion of African Slaves*, 219-30. In addition to the *DNB*, see John Kobler, *The Reluctant Surgeon: A Biography of John Hunter* (Garden City, N. Y., 1960).

field of controversy. Dr. Charles White was a member of the Royal Society and author of a treatise on midwifery that was well known in America. He became interested in the subject of comparative anatomy and hence the Negro, though equally with Dr. John Hunter, he was anxious that his scientific conclusions should not "be construed so as to give the smallest countenance to the pernicious practice of enslaving mankind." He wished merely "to investigate the truth." [21] As the title of his study suggested, however, *The Regular Gradation of Man, and in Different Animals and Vegetables* (1799) was something other than a straightforward investigation. "Every one who has made Natural History an object of study," White exclaimed enthusiastically, "must have been led occasionally to contemplate the beautiful gradation that subsists amongst created beings, from the highest to the lowest. From man down to the smallest reptile . . . Nature exhibits to our view an immense chain of beings, endued with various degrees of intelligence and active powers, suited to their stations in the general system." [22] At considerable length White set forth the orthodox doctrine of the Chain, but significantly he felt it necessary to make elaborations which would render the concept more consonant with stubborn natural facts. The gradation from man to animals, he explained, was "not by one way," for with each quality such as size, form, hearing, sight, and voice, the gradation might descend through different animals, as for example, "the person and actions descend to the orang-outang, but the voice to the birds." When deciding upon precisely which animals most nearly approached man in form, intelligence, and speech White resurrected Sir William Petty's old trinity of orangs, elephants, and parrots. Succumbing completely to the implications of the principle of continuity in the Chain of Being, White declared almost belligerently that infertility was no criterion of species, since, for example, Dr. John Hunter had proved that unions of wolves, jackals, and dogs could produce fertile offspring. Here was a suggestion which struck at the heart of the Linnaean (if not the mature Linnaeus's) system. Nonetheless, White was unable to rid himself completely of the ancient idea that likes begat likes, for he admitted that "these unnatural unions" were "seldom obtained without some stratagem." This brought him to the problem of the ape, one which he handled with uncharacter-

21. Charles White, *An Account of the Regular Gradation in Man, and in Different Animals and Vegetables; and from the Former to the Latter* (London, 1799), iii.
22. *Ibid.*, 1.

istic circumspection. Orang-outangs, he wrote, "have been known to carry off negro-boys, girls, and even women, with a view of making them subservient to their wants as slaves, or as objects of brutal passion: and it has been asserted by some, that women have had offspring from such connections. This last circumstance is not, however, certain. Supposing it to be true, it would be an object of enquiry, whether such offspring would propagate, or prove to be mules." That White felt it appropriate to call for inquiry into the matter spoke volumes in itself.[23]

Dr. Charles White had first been led to his subject, he confided, by conversation with Dr. John Hunter and by seeing all Hunter's skulls lined up in order of declining facial angles. The downward progression of European, Asiatic, American Indian, Negro, orang-outang, and monkey had impressed White enormously, and it occurred to him "that Nature would not employ gradation in one instance only, but would adopt it as a general principle."[24] Even the parrot and elephant possessed high facial angles! When White turned to apply his "general principle" to man, he discovered that of all the sorts of men, Europeans were highest and Negroes lowest on the scale. White saw nothing *a priori* about his procedure. "I did not carry my enquiries into provincial or national varieties or features," he explained, "but confined them chiefly to the extremes of the human race: to the European, on the one hand, and, on the other, to the African, who seems to approach nearer to the brute creation than any other of the human species. I was persuaded, that if I could prove a specific distinction betwixt these two, the intermediate gradations would be more easily allowed."[25] If this seemed to assume the existence of what was about to be proved, it should be remembered that for most Europeans and Americans Negroes and whites were indeed the "capital varieties" of mankind.

Much of Charles White's remaining argument was merely a lengthy catalog of the particular ways in which the Negro more closely resembled the ape than did the European.[26] He had carefully examined skeletons of Europeans, Negroes, Tyson's orang-outang, and a monkey, as well as the bodies of living whites and Negroes (from Liverpool). The Negro's skull, he found, was not only flatter but had a smaller capacity than the "European's." (White consist-

23. *Ibid.*, 11–40, especially 11–12, 19, 34, 39.
24. *Ibid.*, iii, 41.
25. *Ibid.*, 42.
26. *Ibid.*, 41–98.

ently used that term rather than the more American "white" man.)
The Negro possessed longer arms, thicker skin, less sweat but ranker
smell, shorter life span and earlier maturation, larger breasts and
nipples, greater ease of parturition, "gibbous" legs, and perhaps
greater susceptibility to certain diseases. Negroes excelled Europeans, on the other hand, in certain areas where apes excelled
man—seeing, hearing, smelling, memory, and mastication. For support of his contention that Negroes were inferior mentally, White
relied not only upon his evidence of lesser cranial capacity but on
the authority of an eminent American scientist, Thomas Jefferson,
whom he quoted at length.[27]

Dr. Charles White's book was of considerable importance not
only because it was read (not widely but in important quarters) in
America but because it established a striking precedent for grounding opinions about the Negro in the ostensibly ineluctable facts of
comparative anatomy. His case for Negro inferiority rested upon an
unprecedented if not always reliable array of physiological detail.
To discover whether the Negro was in fact a highly sensual creature, for example, one had only to turn to White's scientific evidence. "That the PENIS of an African is larger than that of an
European," he announced airily, "has, I believe, been shewn in
every anatomical school in London. Preparations of them are preserved in most anatomical museums; and I have one in mine." His
own investigations of living Negroes had confirmed this: *"Haller, in
his primae Liniae, speaking of the Africans, says, 'In hominibus
etiam penis est longior et multo laxior'; but I say Multo firmior et
durior."* [28] Furthermore, lest the facts of human anatomy be allowed
to repose slag-like in meaningless disorder, White had assembled
them in a fashion guaranteed to provide white men with gratifying
satisfaction.

Ascending the line of gradation, we come at last to the white European;
who being most removed from the brute creation, may, on that account, be
considered as the most beautiful of the human race. No one will doubt his
superiority in intellectual powers. . . . Where shall we find, unless in the
European, that nobly arched head, containing such a quantity of brain
. . . ? Where the perpendicular face, the prominent nose, and round pro-

27. *Ibid.*, 63–67.
28. *Ibid.*, 61. This was in direct contradiction to Soemmering's statement, "The
parts of generation, contrary to a vulgar notion, are of no uncommon size."
(*Ibid.*, clvii.) Otherwise, White placed great reliance on Soemmering's *Ueber die
Korperliche Verschiedenheit des Negers von Europaër* (Frankfurt and Mainz,
1785) , quoted at length in translation by White, cxxxix-clxvi.

jecting chin? Where that variety of features, and fulness of expression;
those long, flowing graceful ringlets; that majestic beard, those rosy cheeks
and coral lips? Where that erect posture of the body and noble gait? In
what other quarter of the globe shall we find the blush that overspreads the
soft features of the beautiful women of Europe, that emblem of modesty,
of delicate feelings, and of sense? Where that nice expression of the amiable and softer passions in the countenance; and that general elegance of
features and complexion? Where, except on the bosom of the European
woman, two such plump and snowy white hemispheres, tipt with vermil-
lion? [29]

Where indeed?

Certain other conclusions which the amiable Charles White derived from his study of gradation in man were less likely to appeal
to popular tastes in England and America. For he declared flatly
that mankind was divided into several species, that all men had not
derived from a single pair, that the Mosaic account suggested creation of other pairs beside Adam and Eve, and that, after all,
Revelation ought not be regarded as a handbook of natural history.
At the very end he nervously protested once again that his book had
no relevance to the execrable slave trade. The capacities of thousands of Europeans, he confided, were no better than those of
Negroes. After 140 pages of innate Negro inferiority these assurances must have seemed lame to antislavery advocates.

5. UNLINKING AND LINKING THE CHAIN

On a variety of counts, plainly, Charles White's anatomical investigations were bound to alarm many Americans, though
evidently no one thought of challenging his aesthetic judgment on
the European woman. In fact there were outcries in America
against degrading the Negro during the year following publication
of White's book, but these were owing not to White's book but to
Thomas Jefferson's candidacy for the presidency. Political pamphleteers bent on proving Jefferson's alleged atheism gleefully seized
upon various suggestions in the *Notes on Virginia*, including the
hint that Negroes were perhaps originally a distinct "race." In a
campaign of intense vituperation one Federalist almost shrieked at
Jefferson: "You have degraded the blacks from the rank which God
hath given them in the scale of being! You have advanced the
strongest argument for their state of slavery! You have insulted
human nature! You have contemned the word of truth and the

29. White, *Regular Gradation*, 134–35.

mean of salvation!" [30] Jefferson wisely maintained silence in the face of such attacks.

Predictably, Jefferson's re-election in 1804 was marked by similarly delicate aspersions, and one Federalist author produced a book (also published partially in the magazine *Port Folio*) devoted solely to the task of ferreting out infidelity from the *Notes on Virginia*.[31] Clement Clarke Moore, born in 1779 the son of a New York Episcopal clergyman, attained some fame as a Hebrew scholar and much more, much later, as the author of "The Night Before Christmas." Although religious and political considerations strongly tinged his argument when he earnestly assailed Jefferson in 1804, Moore rose above invective to make the most perceptive contemporary assessment of the intellectual assumptions underlying Jefferson's remarks on the Negro, particularly the concept of the Chain.

What troubled Moore was a somewhat vague realization that the principles of the Chain of Being tended to corrode the all-important distinction between human beings and the beasts that perish. It was not altogether easy for Moore to mount his objection effectively, for the concept of the Chain, when carefully formulated, had seemed to most men entirely compatible with man's exclusive participation in rationality and salvation. Only by proffering a conceptually extreme version of the Chain, therefore, was Moore able to demonstrate that the principle of continuity threatened the Christian presumption that man was a unique being. "It is a favourite object with modern philosophers," he began, "to persuade themselves and others, that man is of the same nature with the rest of the animal creation; that he is not rendered distinct from them by an immortal soul, but merely by the superiority of his faculties; that he is to all intents of the same *genus* with them, but only of a higher *species*." This was a distortion of the vocabulary and intentions of "modern philosophers," yet Moore's ensuing elaboration of the principle of continuity did effectively expose the implications of the naturalistic approach. "They have observed how wonderfully minute the gradations are from the inanimate spar, up to man, the lord of the creation; how the three kingdoms of nature encroach upon each other, rendering it impossible to define the limits of

30. [William Linn, assisted by John M. Mason], *Serious Considerations on the Election of a President: Addressed to the Citizens of the United States* (N. Y., 1800), 13; also [John M. Mason], *The Voice of Warning, to Christians, on the Ensuing Election of a President of the United States* (N. Y., 1800), 14–17; "People of Colour," *Port Folio*, 1st Ser., 1 (May 23, 1801), 163–64.

31. [Moore], *Observations upon Jefferson's Notes on Virginia*, 19–28; under the same title in the *Port Folio* [1st Ser.], 4 (1804), 244–45, 250–52, 268–69.

each." By abandoning demarcations and by concentrating on "corporeal properties," Moore implied strongly, this view of man threatened man's exclusive possession of an immortal soul.

When Moore turned to analysis of the Chain's application to Negroes he was on firmer ground, for his remarks accurately summarized not merely the implications of that concept but the way in which it had actually been worked out. He continued:

But the intellectual faculties of man were found to set him at such an immense distance from all other animals, that it was absolutely necessary to devise some scheme for filling up the chasm. The resemblance of the bodily structure of the orang-outang to that of the human species, and the consequent similarity in many of its actions to those of men, were not overlooked; but every art was employed to prove that it was endued with reason, and that it ought to be reckoned a lower order of man. But as there was still a long jump from an ape to a man, some happy geniuses bethought them of setting the Africans as a step which would make the transition perfectly easy. So that in the same proportion as the ape was raised above its proper sphere, the inoffensive negro was pulled down from his just rank in the creation. And thus was the golden chain of nature strained and new-linked, to serve the purposes of these gentlemen. The man with a high nose and fair skin was honoured with the first place among the beasts; the man with a flat nose and black skin with the second; Pongo, or the wild man of the woods, with the third; and then came the other animals in their proper order.

It required Moore little further effort to demonstrate that the *Notes on Virginia*, while not openly exalting "the orang-outang to the station of a rational being, . . . debases the negro to an order of creatures lower than those who have a fairer skin and thinner lips." Moore swooped down on Jefferson's seemingly casual reference to the sexual preferences of the orang-outang and, after quoting it, declared triumphantly, "Now, can any one who knows what candour is, deny that this sentence savours strongly of the aforementioned theory? The orang-outang prefers the female black, as being of an order superior to himself; and for the same reason, the negro shows a decided preference in favour of the whites. Where Mr. Jefferson learnt that the orang-outang has less affection for his own females than for black women, he does not inform us. No doubt," Moore said, unwilling to withhold a good Federalist jibe, "from some French traveller."

Moore's critique of the doctrines of "modern philosophers" was by far the most perceptive but by no means the only instance of objection to the "new-linking" of nature. For one thing, application of the principle of gradation to the Negro threatened the cause of antislavery as much as it threatened religious orthodoxy. That same year, 1804, an antislavery writer committed an entire chapter to the question, "Whether the African Negroes be a part of the Human Species, capable of intellectual, moral, and religious Improvement, no less than the other Nations of Mankind; or, an inferior Order of beings, occupying a middle Place between Men and Brutes?" And next year the Abolition Convention in Philadelphia took careful notice of the question for the first time: "Many remain under the erroneous notion," the Convention acknowledged unhappily, "that the blacks are a class of beings not merely inferior to, but absolutely a species different from the whites, and that they are intended, by nature, only for the degradations and suffering of slavery." [32]

Perhaps the convention overestimated the danger, for in those years only one American naturalist unequivocally expounded the Negro's inferior rank in the Great Chain of Being. Dr. John Augustine Smith was no kin to the Princeton Smith, though he, too, was the son of a minister and became a college president. Born in Virginia, he attended the College of William and Mary, studied in London, and in 1807 took a position in New York. Later he became president of William and Mary—where it was alleged that he was a deist—and eventually rebounded to the presidency of a New York medical institution. It was as a young man of twenty-six that Smith delivered a lecture in 1808 to a group of New York medical students; his remarks relied heavily on eminent authorities in Europe, whence he was freshly returned with his medical degree, and he was able to discourse learnedly on such abstruse technical matters as the facial angle and the *rete mucosum*.[33] At the outset the young doctor from Virginia announced his intention of proving that the "anatomical structure" of the "European" (significantly he borrowed Charles White's term) was "superior" to the Asiatic, Indian, and Negro, "or, at least, that it is farther removed from the brute creation." Europeans and Negroes had been "placed at the opposite extremes of the scale." Enthusiastically the youthful doctor appealed principally to a single index of gradation—the facial angle—and summoned as witnesses Camper, Cuvier, Hunter and White. In Nature the slope of the head flattened progressively from Europeans through Negroes to apes and monkeys and to still lesser creatures. The strikingly high facial angles of the Greeks and Romans as determined by statues (and, Smith might have added, by

32. Branagan, *Preliminary Essay on Oppression*, chap. 6; *Minutes Abolition Convention* (1805), 35.

33. J. A. Smith, "A Lecture," *New-York Medical and Philosophical Journal and Review*, 1 (1809), 32–48.

several plates in Charles White's book) probably attested to the historical degeneration which those unacquainted with facial angles had long suspected on other grounds. Perhaps, Smith added rapturously, the owl had been chosen as the symbol of wisdom because of its exceedingly high facial angle.

The by now rather breathless Dr. Smith was by no means intent on degrading the Negro—any further than warranted by anatomical facts. He summoned his students manfully to face them. The Negro's brain was firmer and smaller (by one-thirteenth) than the European's. Negroes had longer arms, often an extra bone in the back, and a peculiar articulation of the legs which made their gait more awkward. Too many known exceptions vitiated the pretended rule of Ray and Buffon that fertility of offspring indicated identity of species.

After dropping this broad hint, Smith the anatomist went on to castigate Smith the dabbler in science for throwing his weight around in the laboratory when he belonged in the pulpit. As his clinching demonstration that the Negro's color was not merely an accidental effect of climate or the state of society he asked President Smith to explain how these environmental factors could possibly account for the Negro's distinctive bones. Despite the effectiveness of this sally, in drawing his lecture to a close John Augustine Smith hastily modified his posture of confidence. He apologized that the causes of the differences he had enumerated were "unknown," while piously assuring his students that they were certainly "secondary," that is, in operation since the Creation. "But on this subject," he concluded carefully, "as on every other which may occur, I hold it my duty to lay before you all the facts which are relevant, all the opinions which are plausible, leaving you then to judge for yourselves. Different minds are satisfied with different degrees of evidence; and far be it from me to fix the bounds of your faith." In effect Smith kicked down the scientific enclosure around Revelation, refused (publicly, at least) to leave the ground himself, but then assured his students that they were welcome to do so.

6. FAITHFUL PHILOSOPHY IN DEFENSE OF HUMAN UNITY

In a sharply contrasting maneuver, President Samuel Stanhope Smith of Princeton, far from conceding that the barricades were down, emerged once again in 1810 to defend the "outworks" of true fidelity and to carry his attack "into the enemy's camp." As his combative language suggested, Smith sensed how much the situation had changed since his initial attempt in 1787 to explain the causes of human physical variations. During the quarter century between the two editions of his *Essay* transformations occurred in his immediate social world, in the American nation, in world politics, and in the international realm of ideas. At his college, Smith found himself under pressure from two directions. At all the American colleges, students at times went wildly out of control and rioted destructively. Their elders underwent considerable puzzlement and distress, for which they may perhaps be pardoned. Smith sniffed the air after a great fire at Nassau Hall in 1802 and detected the aroma of "irreligious and demoralizing principles which are tearing the bands of society asunder, and threatening in the end to overturn our country." Like many of the older generation, Smith liked to find order *wherever* he looked. It was not religious bigotry which animated him; indeed he was pressured from another direction, by a theologically and socially conservative clerical board of trustees, into resigning in 1812. It was partly that Smith found that his disorderly student body was mirrored in the nation as a whole and in the world at large. He served as an elector in 1800 in a futile attempt to keep Thomas Jefferson out of the presidency. He decried the influence of "jacobinic and anti-religious principles" in the colleges and thereby denounced the French Revolution. And in the realm of ideas he brought the second edition of his *Essay* to bear upon infidelity as it appeared in science.

Here, though, without fully realizing it, he confronted an insidious difficulty. For one of the handsomest ways of introducing order into nature, the Great Chain of Being, was one which he as a Christian minister could not possibly embrace. Indeed as a defender of Genesis he had logically to repudiate the concept of the Chain. But Smith only half sensed how damaging the incursions of that concept had become. Even though he had obtained a copy of the third edition of Blumenbach's *De Generis Humani Varietate Nativa* (1795) and made extensive use of it, he did not utilize Blumenbach's almost fearful denunciation of the principle of hierarchy in nature. But perhaps as a scholar in the cultural provinces Smith may be excused, since even Blumenbach had taken no notice of the Chain of Being in his 1775 and 1781 editions. More, possibly, than Charles White's explication of that concept in 1799, the world-famous German scholar's warning in 1795 of the dangers inherent in the Chain gave evidence of its erosion of the equalitarian view of the races of men.

Samuel Stanhope Smith was fully aware, however, that he had to combat specific suggestions that any group of men was inherently inferior to any other. With complete assurance that sound study of natural philosophy could only confirm the revealed Word, Smith manfully attempted to battle Charles White and John Augustine Smith on their own ground.[34] Indeed he could scarcely dodge a challenge which had arisen from the inductive principles of science, and he scurried about the kitchens of Princeton bravely brandishing a foot rule and thermometer. Smith concluded that his opponents had failed to take into account the changes which the American environment was producing especially in domestic slaves and free Negroes. Was the formation of the jaw, the teeth, or the nose of the Negro of inferior quality? This portrait was "sufficiently accurate" for the Negro in Africa but "in the United States, the physiognomy, and the whole figure and personal appearance of the African race is undergoing a favorable change." Were the legs of the Negro more gibbous? So they were in Africa and almost as much so among the neglected field slaves of America, but among the domestics of the South and even more among the free Negroes of Princeton are limbs "as handsomely formed as those of the inferior and laboring classes, either of Europeans, or Anglo-Americans." And the facial angle? Dr. J. A. Smith had confused his mathematics, misread his Blumenbach, and neglected to mention that the angle in American-born Negroes had become "considerably *less acute.*" Finally, Smith pleaded, let the opponents of fidelity come out into the open instead of skulking about in the alleys of natural science; let them cease "this species of wily ambuscade" and "appear in their true form"; let *us,* he cried in desperation, "see the enemy in the open day."

Though Samuel Stanhope Smith tried valiantly to stamp out infidelity as it had appeared in science, he failed to strike at the root of his opponents' argument. The concept of ordered hierarchy in Nature underlay all the myriad propositions concerning the Negro's inferiority, and if the axe was not laid to that concept these propositions would continue to blossom in one form or another. Yet Smith was no more capable than anyone else of denying absolutely the principle of hierarchy, and like a refutation of White by Dr. Hugh Williamson, Smith's *Essay* never negated the proposition of "gradation in man."[35] His utter failure to challenge the concept of the

---

34. Smith, *Essay on Variety* (1810), ed. Jordan, which see for information about Smith.

35. Williamson, *Observations on the Climate,* 47–49. Samuel Latham Mitchill thought Williamson's an able reply; see the review of *ibid.* in *Medical Repository,* 3d Hexade, 3 (1812), 171.

Chain masked an unwitting acceptance of several of its most critical principles. His answer to the Negro's lower facial angle was neither denial of the facts nor a declaration of their irrelevance but a claim that the head of the Negro was changing toward resemblance of the white man's higher form! In effect Smith was denying *inherent* inferiority yet conceding *present* inferiority. His whole book shouted that the Negro was going to be the *equal* of the white man only when the Negro came to look like one.

This half-articulated feeling lay at the very heart of the entire issue. So long as concentration fell on the Negro's appearance and physical characteristics it was impossible to say that he was the same as the white man. The burgeoning science of comparative anatomy, especially when hitched to the concept of the Chain, was bound to elaborate differences between the races (and, in the circumstances, exaggerate them), thus lending to racial differences an inherency and technicality which they had never had before. And again given the dovetailed circumstances of slavery, the Chain of Being, ethnocentrism, and accumulated tradition, racial *differences* were not going to be left lying around unassimilated to the prevailing system of social values. Differences in the Negro were, in short, going to be seen as indications of *inferiority*. Only by ignoring physical characteristics (as many antislavery people, especially the religious-minded, did), only by insisting on an essential brotherhood somehow independent of the body, only by acquiescence in the ancient mystical proposition that all nations were of one blood, would the proposition of the current and inherent equality of the Negro remain safely confirmed. Perhaps Samuel Stanhope Smith might have done better not to have rushed forth to defend his "outworks."

7. THE STUDY OF MAN IN THE REPUBLIC

Scientific inquiry was, of course, incapable of abandoning its concentration on physical (and by extension mental) characteristics. As the nineteenth century wore on, however, the pervasive concept of the Chain of Being lost much of its popularity and relevance. During the ante-bellum period a small but noisy "American school" of anthropologists stridently denied the original unity of man while their clerical opponents grew increasingly rigid and dogmatic in defense of Genesis. An overwhelming majority of southerners remained faithful to the Scriptural account at the cost of passing up an opportunity for vindicating slavery. Then just prior to the sectional war Darwin exploded not merely the Chain of Being but (some thought) the Mosaic account as well. Darwinism offered a pattern of order in the world which seemed to be based on something the eighteenth-century temperament found so difficult to accept—chaos. Eventually, the concept of natural selection gave startling confirmation to the environmentalist faith; Samuel Stanhope Smith's fortress was shattered and his outworks erected into an imposing edifice. Early in the twentieth century a prominent anthropologist confidently announced, without so much as a nod to the long-dead president of Princeton, that the head shapes of the children of recent immigrants were conforming to the native American pattern.[36] Much more important, by the twentieth century the way seemed clearer, to those so disposed, for discussion of racial differences as mere differences. Even in this radically changed atmosphere, however, remnants of the old concept of hierarchy were still lying about, for no exploded idea dissipates completely. The very phraseology of Darwinism—"higher" and "lower forms" and so forth—testified to the residual strength of the hierarchical principle, and there were many men, especially in the early years of the twentieth century, very much disposed to apply it to mankind. Of the more specific remnants of the Chain as it pertained to the Negro, perhaps the most important was the vague association of the Negro with the ape.[37]

Perhaps this legacy is in itself sufficient evidence of the importance of the concept of the Chain. It is instructive to remember that the concept could never have gained such widespread popularity during the eighteenth century without having roots thrust deep in men's conception of the world. Though it was an "idea" susceptible of analysis as a viable entity, it was never devoid of underpinnings at the deepest levels of mental formulation. To put the matter boldly and hence to overstate it, the Chain of Being was only one (unusually specific) projection of a profound sense of and yearning for hierarchical arrangement.

Some of the reasons for this yearning have become obvious. Natural philosophers were confronted by rapidly accumulating data; the muting of God's imminence and sovereignty threw into question man's place in the universe; and the structure of society was altering in such a way as to make the principle of hierarchy seem neither accurately descriptive nor normatively desirable. In-

---

36. [Franz Boas], *Changes in Bodily Form of Descendants of Immigrants*, in *Reports of the Immigration Commission*, vol. 38 (61st Cong., 2d sess., Senate Document no. 208, Washington, 1911), 1–7.

37. Flagrantly, for instance, in Charles Carroll, *"The Negro a Beast,"* or, *"In the Image of God"* . . . (St. Louis, 1900), particularly the illustrations.

deed by the beginning of the nineteenth century this sense of hierarchy showed signs of being battered and strained by fundamental changes in American thought and society, changes not altogether unconnected with the persistence of Negro slavery in a nation committed to the Revolutionary ideal of equality. In a process not yet fully understood—and by no means ever to be fully understood by tracing a single vector of social change—more and more individual Americans came to think of themselves as the social equals of any of their neighbors. A Chain of Being could never survive in such an atmosphere.

Yet racial slavery persisted in an increasingly frankly egalitarian society, in part of a huge young republic in which men were still struggling to discover the essential elements of their nationhood. Given a heightening awareness of man's physical attributes, given a plurality of races in America, given an intense interest in the special character of their continent, it is scarcely surprising that the ancient problem of the Negro's color assumed enlarged importance and became, indeed, a major challenge to the first generation of republican intellectuals. It is instructive to watch their efforts to wrestle the Negro's complexion into conformity with the symmetry of nature and with the social requirements of a white America.

XIV ERASING NATURE'S STAMP

OF COLOR

OF ALL THE NEGRO'S PHYSICAL ATTRIBUTES, THE ONE WHICH
had especially attracted the attention of Europeans was his color. As
a scientific puzzle, the cause of the Negro's complexion was almost
as poorly understood in 1800 as it had been two centuries earlier;
yet there were some signs of better understanding during the early
years of the nineteenth century. Blackness in men had always been
more than a problem in science, however, and as a social problem in
1800 it had been transformed from what it had been a generation
and even a dozen years earlier. Indeed during the last twenty years
of the eighteenth century there were signs that the Negro's complexion was becoming for many Americans a more urgent, pressing
difficulty. Their attempts to *explain* (in whatever manner) the
Negro's blackness are revelatory of the interaction between specific
ideas about Negroes and slavery, the assumptions of pre-genetic
science, and cultural pressures operating within the nation which
would have existed—perhaps less powerfully—if there had been no
Africans in America. Particularly, the facts that the campaign
against slavery ran into insurmountable obstacles and virtually
collapsed, that a new nation was struggling into workable existence
in a hostile international atmosphere, that religious and ethnic
distinctions had somehow to be overridden or overlooked, and that
Americans had so many good but weakening reasons to discover
positive beneficence in their continental environment—all these
acted to shape assessments of the Negro's color.

1. NATURE'S BLACKBALL

Of itself, the persistence of racial slavery in a land of
liberty drew closer to the surface the social meaning of blackness in

men. White Americans had been being brought (or driven) to realization that the relationship of master and slave was white to black. This realization was evident at different levels of self-awareness. One may be instanced by the indignant remark by a Virginia woman that "The People are all stird up over old John Bagwel whipping his black Wench nearly to death. Such a black hearted Rascal oughn't (be) allowed to have black People." Blackness was not meant to be governed by blackness. Another, more fully aware, level may be found in the schematic equation of two dichotomies. Just as slavery was the opposite of freedom: "In that conspicuous property of colour," one observer wrote, "we and our slaves are not different, but opposite; our badges of distinction are black and white." When an antislavery speaker pleaded that people were wrong in thinking that "nature has black-balled these wretches out of society," he merely pointed up precisely what Nature had done in America.[1]

The notion that Nature had permanently blackballed any set of men from participation in America was not one with which many Americans could feel comfortable. It was a notion that seemed to question the unity of man and that at the same time was too easily extended from one set of men to another. For some white Americans, though, complete exclusion of Negroes seemed the only way out of the morass of slavery. Among these was Thomas Jefferson, for whom the "reality" of difference in color was so overwhelming that he refused to speculate on its cause and insisted only that Negroes had to be removed, physically, from America. This insistence formed an important strain in American thinking, as should become clear in the next chapter. For the time being, another line of thinking needs examination, one which attempted to solve the problem of exclusion by painting all the balls white.

2. THE EFFECTS OF CLIMATE AND CIVILIZATION

To do so one had to get at the ancient problem of why men came in different colors. The most ambitious, persistent, and in some ways the most sensible attempts at explicating variations in man were by Samuel Stanhope Smith; certainly it would be unfair to characterize his *Essay* of 1787 and 1810 as merely a repaint job.

1. Polly Davis to Thomas Davis, Broadfield, Spotsylvania Co., Va., Nov. 6, 1792, "Two Old Letters," *Va. Mag. of Hist. and Biog.*, 12 (1904–05), 437; H. L., "Thoughts on the Termination of Slavery," *Monthly Magazine, and American Review*, 2 (1800), 82; "Speech of William Pinkney," *Amer. Museum, 1798*, 85.

The essentials of his argument were simple in 1787, and they remained so in the second edition. Mankind had originated somewhere in Asia, not barbarian but fully civilized. Man's gradual dispersion had been followed by degeneration into savagery in unfavorable locations and by gradual alterations in appearance. Here was the key to physical variations. Even superficial observation pointed to an approximately regular gradation of human complexions from the pole to the equator. What could be more obvious than that this was the effect of difference in heat? Admittedly this regularity was interrupted in many instances, but so was the gradation of heat by the elevation of land, proximity to the sea, the soil, state of cultivation, winds, and other factors. A gradation of color existed among Europeans, among Jews living in different climates, and even among Americans; in the lowlands of the Carolinas and Georgia men degenerated to a shade not much lighter than the Iroquois.[2] The effect of heat, Smith explained, was to thicken the skin and to free the bile which deposited a residue in the middle of the three layers of skin. It had been observed, he said (in what has since proved a highly accurate metaphor), "that colour may be justly considered as an universal freckle." [3]

These contentions were far from original. Rather, they represented a distillation of prevalent thinking on the subject and had, indeed, been set forth in explicit and comprehensive fashion in an Edinburgh medical dissertation by John Hunter (no relation to the famous anatomist) in 1775.[4] The second portion of Smith's argument, however, had never before received so much emphasis. The state of society and mode of living, he proclaimed, powerfully affected the human complexion. "The vapours of stagnant waters with which uncultivated regions abound; all great fatigues and hardships; poverty and nastiness, tend as well as heat, to augment the bile." Having taken this path Smith could not avoid linking savagery to dark complexion: "Hence, no less than from their nakedness, savages will always be discoloured, even in cold climates." [5] His examples—the Esquimaux, Indians, Negroes and so on—disclosed the near inevitability of the association; for in fact all the peoples which European expansion had uncovered were in a less advanced state of civilization.

2. Smith, *Essay on Variety* (1787), 19–24.

3. *Ibid.*, 10–15, a term not original with Smith; Ramsay, *Treatment and Conversion of African Slaves*, 215–16, declared that "a freckle may be defined a partial black skin; a black skin an universal freckle."

4. Bendyshe, trans. and ed., *Treatises of Blumenbach*, 359–88.

5. Smith, *Essay on Variety* (1787), 16.

It was perhaps not merely chance that it was an American rather than a European who first emphasized so strongly the importance of "the state of society" and "manner of living." Smith treated the complexion and physiognomy of the white man not merely as indication of superiority but as a hallmark of civilization. As Smith announced glowingly, "man, being designed for society and civilization, attains, in that state, the greatest perfection of his form, as well as of his whole nature." From this point it was no jump at all to saying that God had intended men to be white. In temperate latitudes, Smith exclaimed with evident satisfaction, the human constitution would be "seen most nearly in that perfection which was the original design and idea of the Creator." Lest American readers miss the point he added a congratulatory footnote: "It may perhaps gratify my countrymen to reflect that the United States occupy those latitudes that have ever been most favourable to the beauty of the human form. When time shall have accomodated the constitution to its new state, and cultivation shall have meliorated the climate, the beauties of Greece and Circassia may be renewed in America; as there are not a few already who rival those of any other quarter of the globe." Beauty, the perfection of human form, was here effectively harnessed in service of cultural nationalism.[6]

Just as Dr. Charles White was to do a dozen years later, Smith concentrated upon the "capital varieties" among men; indeed he sometimes wrote as if he felt the spectre of Negro inequality peering over his shoulder. He was oblivious to the iron ring of environment he had thrown around the Negro in Africa, in part because he saw savagery as degeneration and in part because dealing with Negroes in America was far more urgent. Partly, of course, he wished to assert the plasticity of the Negro's form so as to combat the irreligious principles which had been advanced by proponents of the Great Chain. There were other reasons for this insistence. In America, he declared, not only were Negroes in general becoming more ingenious and more capable of instruction, but the features and perhaps the color of domestic slaves had already changed more than those of field workers; even the latter were losing the strictly African countenance, though more slowly. The antislavery corollary followed easily: "The great difference between the domestic and field slaves, gives reason to believe that, if they were perfectly free, enjoyed property, and were admitted to a liberal participation of the society, rank and privileges of their masters, they would change

6. *Ibid.*, 49*n*, 43 and note.

their African peculiarities much faster." Smith had no liking for slavery, but he was glacially conservative concerning programs for abolition. He was always vastly more interested in the cause of human unity than in abolition of a merely temporal tyranny.

In discussing the impact of the American environment, Smith stressed that the most pronounced and rapid alterations were to be expected in the Negro's features, not in his complexion. Skin color, he thought, was less susceptible to change than any other bodily characteristic; he added also that while a light skin darkened easily, a dark skin lightened very slowly even under the most favorable circumstances. Here was a revealing emphasis, for it displayed once again the primacy of color in the white man's mind, the long-standing feeling that the most Negro thing about the Negro was his blackness. Though he stressed that "the negroe colour" could "be rendered almost perpetual," he never closed the door on the possibility that America was going to whiten black men.[7]

Smith's discovery of the revolutionary "fact" of physiological alteration in the Negro was the more striking because few other men could see much improvement. One who agreed with Smith was his brother-in-law, Dr. David Ramsay of Charleston, who chided his friend Thomas Jefferson for depressing Negroes "too low"; "I believe all mankind to be originally the same and only diversified by accidental circumstances. I flatter myself that in a few centuries the negroes will lose their black color. I think now they are less black in Jersey than Carolina, their [lips] less thick, their noses less flat. The state of society has an influence not less than climate. Our back country people are as much savage as the Cherokees." [8] But this was a minority view. It required strong conviction to see the lightening of Negroes in America as anything other than the result of sexual intermixture.

Yet the notion that environmental influences could cause Negroes gradually to become less Negroid was by no means ridiculous or scientifically disreputable. For Smith, defending the unity of man, it was eminently logical since deviations in the descendants of common parents necessarily would be rectified by the operation of forces opposite to those which had produced the deviations. Moreover, he was careful to emphasize that "habits both of mind and body" were "created, not by great and sudden impressions, but by continual and almost imperceptible touches" and that "national

7. *Ibid.*, 57–60.
8. N. Y., May 3, 1786, Boyd, ed., *Papers of Jefferson*, IX, 441. Brackets are the editor's. Ramsay may well have visited Smith at Princeton.

features, like national manners become fixed, only after a succession of ages." But they became "fixed at last," since the qualities acquired by parents were "transmitted to offspring." On this point Smith was as vigorous with man as Lamarck later was with the giraffe: the peoples living in cold climates, he suggested, had short necks because for ages they had hunched their shoulders against the cold. At the time this did not seem absurd; there was no reason to object when Smith declared, "Every remarkable change of feature that has grown into a habit of the body, is transmitted with other personal properties, to offspring." [9]

Smith's unbridled environmentalism and his stress on man's adaptability were bound to appeal to transplanted Europeans. So too was his unquestioning assumption that the natural, best, and original—for Smith the three were virtually indistinguishable—color in man was white. And many Americans were also attracted by the way in which his logic supported antislavery by vindicating human equality in general and by blanching the Negro in particular. Small wonder his book was widely known in America and even read in Europe.[10]

There were latent implications in Smith's arguments which told less favorably for the Negro's future. No one seized upon them explicitly, but the ancient connection between climate and color which he so meticulously expounded could easily be turned around. If the Negro had grown suited to the heat of Africa, was he not therefore a better candidate than the Englishman for toil in the hotter portions of America? If natural causes had fitted Negroes for life in Africa, moreover, did not the ones now living in America more naturally belong back at home? The only hope for Americans who balked at Negro slavery, at transportation to Africa, and of course at intermixture, lay in the proposition that Negroes in America were going to whiten up. Just how powerful that hope had become was evidenced by the extraordinary ingenuity with which some men tried to feed it.

3. THE DISEASE OF COLOR

Foremost among Americans who could tolerate neither the wrong of slavery nor the brutality of transportation was Dr. Benjamin Rush. Distinguished antislavery advocate, active leader in the conventions of abolition societies in the 1790's, and publici-

9. Smith, *Essay on Variety* (1787), 8, 39–40, 68.
10. Reprinted Edinburgh, 1788, and London, 1789.

zer of talented Negroes, Rush was also one of the nation's eminent physicians and humanitarians. A slavish worshiper at the temple of environment, Rush sometimes leaves the modern reader wondering if he realized that human beings had parents. When fused to his ardent patriotism and republicanism, Rush's environmentalism became an engine capable of grinding rocky facts into nonexistence. Some years after the Revolution he declared happily that "from a strict attention to the state of mind in this country, before the year 1774, and at the present time, I am satisfied, the ratio of intellect is as twenty are to one, in these states, compared with what they were before the American revolution." [11] All in all, it had been quite a revolution. Upon this as upon all subjects, Benjamin Rush advanced his opinions with an amiable dogmatism.

It was thoroughly in keeping with these qualities that Rush should have made his well-known, astonishing attempt to explain the Negro's color. In 1792 he presented his scientific hypothesis to the American Philosophical Society; it was published in 1799 in the sober pages of the Society's *Transactions* under the descriptive title, "Observations Intended to Favour a Supposition That the Black Color (As It Is Called) of the Negroes Is Derived from the Leprosy." [12] Why Africans particularly should have contracted leprosy was no mystery, Rush felt, since it was well known that an unwholesome diet conduced to the disease and that Africa was characterized by "greater heat, more savage manners, and bilious fevers." Leprosy sometimes resulted in a blackening of the skin and a "smell" which "continues with a small modification in the native African to this day." Leprosy produced also a morbid insensitivity to pain which, Rush affirmed, Negroes had exhibited on many occasions. Even the Negro's features were to be explained by the disease, for big lips and a flat nose were symptoms, and woolly hair the result of its spreading to the head.

All these contentions pertained with sufficient logic to individuals, but Rush's case required extension through generations. Leprosy, he explained patiently, was a most durable disease in descending to the posterity. Why, then, was there no infectious quality in the Negro's skin? In the first place, leprosy had lately become much less infectious; in the second, perhaps the Negro's skin was a trifle infectious after all, as instanced by two white women who had

---

11. Rush, *Medical Inquiries and Observations*, II, 42; Rush, *Sixteen Introductory Lectures*, 109–10, 256. In addition to the *DAB* see Nathan G. Goodman, *Benjamin Rush: Physician and Citizen, 1746–1813* (Phila., 1934); and the various *Minutes Abolition Convention* cited in chap. 9.

12. Amer. Phil. Soc., *Transactions*, 4 (1799), 289–97.

turned darker while living with Negro husbands. It was no objection that many Negroes lived on into old age, for a disease of local character would not impair longevity. Further evidence of a leprous quality in Negroes lay in their notorious sexuality: "Lepers are remarkable for having strong venereal desires. This is universal among the negroes, hence their uncommon fruitfulness when they are not depressed by slavery; but even slavery in its worst state does not always subdue the venereal appetite, for after whole days, spent in hard labor in a hot sun in the West Indies, the black men often walk five or six miles to comply with a venereal assignation."

Rush's central contention possessed no reputable contemporary scientific validity, nor, indeed, any basis in fact.[13] No matter. Benjamin Rush was not a man to permit such puny obstacles to impede the swath of his convictions. Nor was he willing to let the reader escape the "reflections" to be drawn from his "facts and principles."

1. That all the claims of superiority of the whites over the blacks, on account of their color, are founded alike in ignorance and inhumanity. If the color of the Negroes be the effect of a disease, instead of inviting us to tyrannize over them, it should entitle them to a double portion of our humanity, for disease all over the world has always been the signal for immediate and universal compassion.

Rush seemed totally unaware of the irony involved in transforming Negroes into lepers: of all diseases leprosy had for ages been treated with something less than "compassion" and "humanity."

Yet Rush knew the reputation of the disease and seized upon it for a second revealing "reflection."

2. The facts and principles which have been delivered, should teach white people the necessity of keeping up that prejudice against such connections with them, as would tend to infect posterity with any portion of their disorder. This may be done upon the ground I have mentioned without offering violence to humanity, or calling in question the sameness of descent, or natural equality of mankind.

13. As with so many 18th-century observations about the Negro, there seems to have been an ancient, vague tradition, in this instance extremely tenuous, from which Rush's very explicit contention may have flowed. Its point of origin probably rested in the fact that leprosy was most prevalent in warm climates; at any rate, in the 16th century Jean Bodin's wide reading of ancient and medieval authorities led him to associate black bile, leprosy, and "southerners." Certainly leprosy was rampant among the African slaves brought to the Americas, and the reputable Hans Sloane disclosed in 1707 that he had observed in the West Indies an instance of a disease, reported to be peculiar to the blacks, which, he speculated, "might come from some peculiar indisposition of their black skin." Bodin, *Method for Easy Comprehension of History*, trans. Reynolds, 106–7; Sloane, *Voyage to the Islands*, I, cvi.

With supreme ease Benjamin Rush had transformed what he called "the existing prejudices against matrimonial connections with them" into an obviously necessary measure of human hygiene.[14] Even though he dined with Negroes in Philadelphia, both privately and publicly, this good-hearted undeviating equalitarian drew the line at sleeping with them. This was a degree of social distance which virtually every American agreed must be maintained.

Rush reserved his most far-reaching "reflection" to the last, in what was surely one of the most optative pleas of Baconian science.

3. Is the color of the negroes a disease? Then let science and humanity combine their efforts, and endeavour to discover a remedy for it.

This was no utopian hope. "Nature has lately unfurled a banner upon this subject. She has begun spontaneous cures of this disease in several black people." But man was not required to wait helplessly for nature; he could make "artificial attempts to dislodge the color in negroes." When it came to practical measures, the good doctor's confidence seemed to flag slightly; indeed all he had to offer was a hopeful report that a Negro boy's chin and hand had been whitened by contact with the juice of unripe peaches. Still, the implications of his argument were too happy to permit discouragement.

To encourage attempts to cure this disease of the skin in negroes, let us recollect that by succeeding in them, we shall produce a large portion of happiness in the world. We shall in the first place destroy one of the arguments in favor of enslaving the negroes, for their color has been supposed by the ignorant to mark them as objects of divine judgments, and by the learned to qualify them for labor in hot, and unwholesome climates.

Secondly, We shall add greatly to *their* happiness, for however well they appear to be satisfied with their color, there are many proofs of their preferring that of the white people.

Thirdly, We shall render the belief of the whole human race being descended from one pair, easy, and universal, and thereby not only add weight to the Christian revelation, but remove a material obstacle to the exercise of that universal benevolence which is inculcated by it.

No matter how sandy the foundations, Rush's edifice had a certain magnificence. If only blackness were leprosy, slavery and intermixture stood condemned and Scripture and humanitarian benevolence confirmed. It was a big *if*, though, much too big for his countrymen, and even the antislavery people passed over his suggestion in wistful

14. In a letter to Jefferson, Phila., Feb. 4, 1797, Butterfield, ed., *Letters of Rush*, II, 785–86.

silence. More damning still, almost nobody bothered to refute it.[15]

In retrospect, it seems remarkable how absurd Rush could be, but it is also worth remarking that his central contention was, as far as white men were concerned, correct and impressively predictive: Negroes have been regarded in America as outcast and diseased. At an important level of human logic, Rush's diagnosis of blackness was entirely accurate.

4. WHITE NEGROES

Rush's clinching demonstration that this hope might materialize was Henry Moss, "a name which, for many years afterward," as his pupil Dr. Charles Caldwell put it with perhaps a little exaggeration, "was almost as familiar to readers of newspapers and other periodicals . . . as was that of John Adams, Thomas Jefferson, or James Madison." Moss turned up in Philadelphia from Virginia about 1795, suspecting quite rightly that his strangely altered appearance was not an unmitigated misfortune, and (Caldwell wrote) "procured a comfortable subsistence by exhibiting himself as a show." He was evidently a startling sight, with fully Negroid features, white hair, some of which was straight and smooth, and large white blotches all over his body which were still gradually spreading. The curiosity of the public was matched by that of the local scientific fraternity; Caldwell paid for Moss's lodging for several weeks in order to study him, and Benjamin Smith Barton summarized the curious facts of the case before the American Philosophical Society with speculations plagiarized (so Caldwell said) from Charles Caldwell. Interest in Moss was high and the facts well known, but scientists were baffled.

The difficulty of the problem presented by Henry Moss did not arise from lack of precedent. Several similar cases had come to light in preceding years, and, as it turned out, Moss was not the last. A blotchy Negro had been exhibited in Charles Willson Peale's museum in Philadelphia five years earlier in 1790 and Dr. John Morgan had presented two other living specimens before a meeting

15. For the only refutation, see Charles Caldwell's remarks below. I have seen only one other contemporary suggestion that the Negro's color might be "a leprous disease"; the author hoped that medical men would "exert their skill in pointing out a remedy," [Rhees], *Letters on Liberty and Slavery,* 9n. The hope that Negroes would lighten did not altogether fade in America; an assertion that they actually were getting lighter is in Ray Stannard Baker, "The Tragedy of the Mulatto," *American Mag.,* 65 (1908), 585.

of the Philosophical Society in 1784. Morgan, one of the new nation's most prominent physicians, was unable to explain the cause of the puzzling phenomenon any better than William Byrd had a century earlier.

Obviously the persistence of interest in white Negroes was more than a matter of scientific curiosity. It fed upon the same poignant hope which had animated Benjamin Rush, who was not the only republican physician who was susceptible to the pressures of living in America. In 1801 Dr. Samuel Latham Mitchill, a Republican politician and a talented, versatile scientist, described a man similar to Henry Moss and assured his readers that the alteration in color "militates powerfully" against the opinion of "some modern philosophers" that Negroes are a different species. Mitchill's hostility to slavery nudged him further: "Facts of this kind are of great value to the zoologist. How additionally singular would it be, if instances of the spontaneous disappearance of this sable mark of distinction between slaves and their masters were to become frequent! They would then be no less important to the moralist and political economist." Plainly Mitchill's opinions as scientist were affected by his sensitivities as American, for he entitled his report of a second case "Another Ethiopian Turning to a White Man." [16]

The existence of anomalous whiteness in black men seems to have remained a puzzle for Americans longer than for Europeans. A minor source of difficulty was the prevalent inability to sort out the two phenomena of mottled blanching and true albinism in Negroes: there was confusion as to whether spotted Negroes and albinos ended up with the same sort of skin. But the real difficulty lay elsewhere. Jefferson's interest in this "anomaly of nature" con-

16. Harriot W. Warner, ed., *Autobiography of Charles Caldwell, M. D.* (Phila., 1855), 163–64, 268–69; Benjamin Smith Barton, "Facts relative to Henry Moss, a white negroe, now in this city," *Early Proceedings of the American Philosophical Society . . . 1744–1838* (Phila., 1884), 241, 272, for Peale, 197; C. W. Peale, "Account of a Person Born a Negro, or a Very Dark Mulattoe, *Who afterwards Became* White," *Universal Asylum and Columbian Magazine,* 2[7] (1791), 409–10; Phila. *National Gazette,* Oct. 31, 1791; John Morgan, "Some Account of a Motley Coloured, or Pye Negro Girl and Mulatto Boy, Exhibited before the Society in the Month of May, 1784, for Their Examination, by Dr. John Morgan, from the History Given of Them by Their Owner Mons. Le Vallois, Dentist of the King of France at Guadaloupe in the West Indies," Amer. Phil. Soc., *Transactions,* 2 (1786), 392–95; *Early Procs. Amer. Phil. Soc.,* 142. One of the most detailed descriptions of Moss is La Rochefoucauld-Liancourt, *Travels through the United States,* II, 133–34; S[amuel] L[atham] M[itchill], "Another Instance of a Negro Turning White," *Medical Repository,* [1st Hexade], 4 (1801), 199–200; [Mitchill?], "Another Ethiopian Turning to a White Man," *ibid.,* [1st Hexade], 5 (1802), 83–84 (almost certainly by Mitchill). The first of these was copied verbatim in Edinburgh: *Scots Magazine,* 63 (1801), 470.

tinued after he wrote the *Notes*,[17] but despite the availability of suggestive evidence neither Jefferson nor for many years any other American seemed capable of realizing that albinism was common to all races of men and many animals and plants. In 1800 a writer in a Charleston newspaper, for example, described some pure white rats with weak red eyes without drawing any parallels with other species.[18] Although almost certainly there were albino persons in the American white population, there seem to have been no cases described by contemporary Americans. This omission was the more striking because the universal character of albinism was gaining wider recognition in Europe following Buffon's authoritative suggestions around 1770. The widely respected Dr. John Hunter noted in 1786 in his *Animal Economy* that various "lusus naturae, such as the white negro, the pure white child of fair parents, the white crow, the white blackbird, white mice, etc." had a similar coloring of the pigmentum of the eye. Hunter displayed a common sense on the matter which Americans never seemed able to muster. Dr. Charles White took much the same position in 1795, explaining that all albinos had poor vision in sunlight because their lack of "the black *mucus*" let in too much light. Not until 1814 was there a flicker of recognition in America: in that year Dr. Charles Caldwell cited a man in Philadelphia, descended from Europeans, who was afflicted with Henry Moss's "disease." [19]

Surely this was an arresting instance of deafness to European scientific knowledge. Jefferson was not alone in failing to admit the existence of this common bond—of color indeed—between whites and Negroes. The Reverend James Madison of the College of William and Mary passed on to Jefferson a curious communication from President Ezra Stiles of Yale concerning a Connecticut Indian whose body was gradually acquiring "a clear English White with *English Ruddiness*." Madison added a pessimistic codicil: "I know the Albinos are found among the Indians," he wrote, ". . . as well

17. *Amer. Museum*, 3 (1788), 37–39; 4 (1788), 501–2; 5 (1789), 234; also 6 (1789), 243; Jefferson, *Notes on Virginia*, ed. Peden, 70–71; Henry Skipwith to Jefferson, Hors du Monde, Jan. 20, 1784, Boyd, ed., *Papers of Jefferson*, VI, 423, 473–74; Charles Carter to Jefferson, Fredg., Feb. 9, 1784, *ibid.*, VI, 420, 534–35. The Annapolis *Md. Gaz.*, Aug. 23, 1792, offered an account of a white Negro baby.

18. Charleston *Carolina Gaz.*, Sept. 25, 1800.

19. Hunter, *Observations on Certain Parts of the Animal Œconomy*, ed. Owen, 289; White, *Regular Gradation*, 119–23, 145; [Charles] C[aldwell], review of Smith, *Essay* (1810), in *Port Folio*, 3d [i.e., 4th] Ser., 4 (1814), 264. The fullest early account of albinism in English was Thomas S. Trail, "On Albinoes," *Journal of Natural Philosophy, Chemistry, and the Arts* [ed. William Nicholson], 19 (1808), 81–86.

as I recollect Buffon, but I doubt whether this gradual Conversion, together with the Ruddiness acquired, be mentioned by any one. It differs remarkably in the last particular from what the poor Black experiences.—It seems as if Nature had absolutely denied to him the Possibility of ever acquiring the Complexion of the Whites." [20] It seemed almost as if Nature's paint was indelible.

Madison's remark probably epitomized the opinions of a sizable majority of Americans, certainly of those south of Mason's and Dixon's line. The contrast of the Negro's color to the "white" man's was so sharp that for most men albinism remained a point of interest rather than a point of similarity. The proper color of man was white: the Negro was simply not measuring up to a standard which was not, after all, excessively high, since white men universally had no difficulty reaching it.

In a sense, the most enlightening commentary on whitening black men was advanced in 1792 by Hugh Brackenridge in his satire on American society, *Modern Chivalry*.[21] Brackenridge managed to approach the problem with something no one else could seem to muster—levity. A gentleman in Maryland, so it seemed, had forwarded a stone found by one of his Negroes to the Philosophical Society, which duly adjudged it to be a petrified Indian mocassin. The grateful Society invited the gentleman to membership, but he deferred in honor of his slave, who in due course was elected and called upon to deliver the annual oration. Having no idea what he should say, the slave asked his master. "Colonel Gorum attending a good deal to literary matters, had heard of an oration delivered before the society, the object of which was to prove that the Africans had been once white, had sharp noses, and long hair; but that by living in sun-burnt climates, the skin had changed colour, the hair become frizzled, and in the course of generation, the imagination of the mother, presenting obtuse objects, had produced an offspring with flat noses." Cuff was thereupon advised to deliver an address which would honor his own people; he did so, announcing at the outset, "Now, shentima, I say, dat de first man was de black a man, and de first woman de black a woman."

Brackenridge was not content to rest with these gentle jibes at the philosopher of Princeton. As he went on to say in the next chapter, "There is no fact that has proved more stubborn than the diversity

20. Madison to Jefferson, Williamsburg, Dec. 28, 1786, Boyd, ed., *Papers of Jefferson*, X, 643.
21. Hugh Henry Brackenridge, *Modern Chivalry*, ed. Claude M. Newlin (N. Y., 1937), 114–18.

of the human species; especially that great extreme of diversity in the natives of Africa. How the descendants of Adam and Eve, both good looking people, should ever come to be a vile negro, or even a mulatto man or woman, is puzzling." But Brackenridge was on to an answer. He briskly demolished the customary explanations and continued quietly to resolve the entire question of the contrasting colors of Africans and Europeans. "I am of opinion that Adam was a tall, straight limbed, red haired man, with a fair complexion, blue eyes, and an aquiline nose; and that Eve was a negro woman." White man. Black woman. Q.E.D.[22]

5. THE LOGIC OF BLACKNESS AND INNER SIMILARITY

Yet the intermixture implied in Brackenridge's burlesque of Genesis was precisely what Americans could not accept. They were impelled to an environmentalist approach toward the Negro's appearance partly because they had to hold to the Mosaic account and had also to retain Adam in their own image. So the Negro had of necessity to be a man who had been turned black.[23] Embedded in any environmentalist explanation of this process was the teleological question: to what purpose was black skin? By the end of the eighteenth century a Biblical curse was no longer a widely satisfactory answer.

Most men were inclined to see the Negro's burnt color as purposively fitting him especially for life in hot climates. The opportunity for justifying slavery was obvious, but men actually seized upon it only when compelling need arose (as it had earlier in Georgia) to vindicate the institution. Charles Cotesworth Pinckney, for example, hinted in the South Carolina legislature during debate on a bill to prohibit slave importation in 1785 that Negroes could labor in climates forbidden by nature to white men; and three years later he defended the constitutional clause on the slave trade with the same argument. Other South Carolinians, including of course William Loughton Smith, took the same stand.[24] Elsewhere men were not

22. There is an interesting plate of a door panel (*ca.* 1710) of an apothecary shop in Calw, Germany, showing the Garden of Eden with Adam clearly a white man and Eve clearly a Negro woman; Curt Stern, "The Biology of the Negro," *Scientific American,* 191 (1954), 80.

23. Very few commentators took the position advanced earlier by John Mitchell and John Winthrop, IV, that man had originally been tawny or brown.

24. Though Edward Rutledge disagreed with this "general opinion"; Donnan, ed., *Documents Slave Trade,* IV, 482–83, 486; Elliot, ed., *Debates in State Conventions,* IV, 285, 309; *Annals of Congress,* 1st Cong., 2d sess., 1459–60.

normally defending slavery; occasionally the climatic logic was simply accepted without much thought or as an explanation for the geographical distribution of slaves in America.[25]

No one, least of all proponents of slavery, was able to support the climatic argument with a convincing explanation of exactly why the Negro was suited to heat. Samuel Stanhope Smith thought the Negro's greater tolerance of heat might stem from several characteristics, from thicker skin, from "the refrigerating nature" of the black mucous, and/or from more effusive sweating (a natural function which he referred to delicately as "the more copious transpiration of the hydrogene principle in which the bile is floated to the surface"). Elsewhere, James Bowdoin hazarded a tentative suggestion that a black skin might afford protection against the sun. Another New England scientist, Samuel Williams, put forward a rigidly Newtonist explanation which failed totally to account for the effect of the sun and hence was hardly an explanation at all. Dr. Hugh Williamson came up with much the same answer in more polished form. Knowledgeably he cited Franklin's experiment with two cloths on a snowbank to prove that white reflected heat and black absorbed it. The Negro, according to Williamson, possessed a thicker and harder middle layer of skin (the "reticular membrane") which provided better protection against heat. White skin, on the other hand, was a poor conductor and hence tended to confine heat within the body. Finally, in a dizzying reversal Williamson declared first that white clothes should be worn in the sun because they reflected its rays and then that white skin was a misfortune in the same circumstances because its reflective power created heat by "resistance." As the question stood in the opening years of the nineteenth century it was not the slightest advanced beyond the position taken by Benjamin Franklin fifty years earlier, when he had suggested to Dr. John Lining of Charleston that more rapid perspiring in Negroes made them better able to bear the sun's heat even though their dark skins absorbed it.[26] Underlying the

25. St. George Tucker, *A Dissertation on Slavery; With a Proposal for the Gradual Abolition of It, in the State of Virginia* (Phila., 1796), 13–16; Robert Boucher Nickolls, "Letter to the Treasurer of the Society Instituted for the Purpose of Effecting the Abolition of the Slave Trade," *Amer. Museum*, 3 (1788), 407; Edwards, *The Injustice of the Slave-Trade*, 22–23. The logic was widely accepted by foreign travelers.

26. Smith, *Essay on Variety* (1810), ed. Jordan, 38, 169–70; Bowdoin, "A Philosophical Discourse," Amer. Academy of Arts and Sciences, *Memoirs*, 1 (1785), 11; Samuel Williams, *The Natural and Civil History of Vermont*, 2d ed., 2 vols. (Burlington, Vt., 1809), I, 496; Williamson, *Observations on the Climate*, 28–29, 50–56; Franklin to Lining, London, June 17, 1758, Smyth, ed., *Writings of Franklin*, III, 449.

confusion was a lack of accurate information on a subject which still has not been satisfactorily studied.[27]

That fruitful scientific speculation could be based on evidence then in existence was convincingly demonstrated only a few years later by William Charles Wells. Born in 1757 in Charleston, he spent some of his early years there, including several as apprentice to the city's eminent scientist, Alexander Garden. After the Revolution he finally settled permanently in England. In 1813 he read before the Royal Society a paper (published in 1818 after his death) which has since become famous as a suggestive and not inaccurate pre-Darwinian statement of natural selection. Wells seized upon the concept of blackness as protection against heat and suggested that human types might have derived, in the case, say, of the Negro, from higher rates of survival among those persons in hot climates who happened to be born with a somewhat darker complexion than usual and who would in turn tend naturally to bear somewhat dark offspring. Wells was even able to extend this concept to some of the Negro's features, but his suggestions simply went unattended.[28] Men continued to fumble for years with the directly environmentalist connection between climate and appearance.

Given the state of scientific knowledge, Americans had to grope their way in the dark toward the *reason* for the Negro's different appearance. Given the prevailing assumption that acquired characters could be passed on to the progeny and an entire lack of acquaintance with the concept of natural selection and the mechanism of inheritance, even the most judicious natural philosophers were bound to flounder. It is instructive, though, that so many wished to thrash around with such an unmanageable problem as nature-versus-nurture then was. Plainly they were under greater compulsion to sort the two elements from one another than men had been a century earlier. One senses here the first twinge of the impulse to separate innate from acquired attributes which came to dominate discussion of human differences in the early twentieth century.

Before turning to the heightening pitch of debate on the issue as

27. See the brief remarks in Note on the Concept of Race, below.

28. William Charles Wells, *Two Essays: One upon Single Vision with Two Eyes; the Other on Dew. A Letter to the Right Hon. Lloyd, Lord Kenyon and an Account of a Female of the White Race of Mankind, Part of Whose Skin Resembles That of a Negro; With Some Observations on the Causes of the Differences in Colour and Form between the White and Negro Races of Men* (London, 1818), 423–39; Richard Harrison Shryock, "The Strange Case of Wells' Theory of Natural Selection (1813): Some Comments on the Dissemination of Scientific Ideas," in M. F. Ashley Montagu, ed., *Studies and Essays in the History of Science and Learning* (N. Y., [1946?]), 195–207.

it concerned the Negro's external color, there is profit in looking at the way it was conceived during a crisis concerning internal health and characteristics. As has already become clear, there was no pronounced tendency earlier in the eighteenth century to impute an essential *internal* distinctiveness to Negroes. Suddenly, in 1793, an epidemic of yellow fever swept through Philadelphia, and some interesting assertions about Negroes were advanced by, of all people, Benjamin Rush. Healthy men and women were desperately needed for nursing and burial duties, and Rush, eagerly seizing upon the old suggestion by Dr. John Lining, published an appeal to Negroes to aid the city which had first emancipated them. Negroes would not, he declared, contract the disease. Thus summoned and assured, considerable numbers of Negroes came forward to help. It soon became drastically apparent, however, that Negroes were far from immune and were taking the disease and dying of it like everyone else. More than three hundred were carried off before the end. Rush soon recognized his error, but not before an unpleasant controversy had broken out involving Mathew Carey, editor of the *American Museum,* and the two prominent Negro religious leaders Absalom Jones and Richard Allen.[29]

As the grim evidence of death accumulated, a degree of consensus emerged on the subject of Negro immunity. Carey, for one, noted that Lining's statements had now been proved erroneous but then went on to suggest that Negroes contracted the disease less often and more mildly than whites. Dr. William Currie suggested that Negroes native to America were susceptible to yellow fever, though not so readily as whites, and he called attention to a recent medical work by an English doctor, Robert Jackson, which indicated that Negroes from Africa and creoles who had lived constantly in the

---

29. John Lining, "A Description of the American Yellow Fever, in a Letter from Dr. John Lining Physician at Charles-Town in South Carolina, to Dr. Robert Whytt Professor of Medicine in the University of Edinburgh," *Essays and Observations, Physical and Literary* [Edinburgh], 2 (1756), 370–95; John Lining, *A Description of the American Yellow Fever, Which Prevailed at Charleston, in South Carolina, in the Year 1748* (Phila., 1799), 7; Benjamin Rush, *An Account of the Bilious Remitting Yellow Fever, As It Appeared in the City of Philadelphia, in the Year 1793* (Phila., 1794), 95–97; Mathew Carey, *A Short Account of the Malignant Fever, Lately Prevalent in Philadelphia . . .* (Phila., 1793), 76–78; J[ohn] H. Powell, *Bring Out Your Dead; The Great Plague of Yellow Fever in Philadelphia in 1793* (Phila., 1949), especially 94–101, 254, 293–94; J[ones] and A[llen], *Narrative of the Proceedings of the Black People.* See, too, Henry D. Biddle, ed., *Extracts from the Journal of Elizabeth Drinker, from 1759 to 1807, A.D.* (Phila., 1889), 194; College of Physicians of Philadelphia, *Facts and Observations Relative to the Nature and Origin of the Pestilential Fever, Which Prevailed in This City, in 1793, 1797, and 1798* (Phila., 1798), 19, 31.

islands were not subject to the disorder. The College of Physicians of Philadelphia was inclined to this view; when yellow fever struck again in 1797 the College recommended employment of Negroes native to Africa.[30] Though in 1793 reports had appeared as far away as Charleston that Negroes did not contract the fever,[31] that idea gradually faded before the onslaught of deadly facts. Apparently no special attempt was made to employ Negroes when the disease struck New York in 1805, and David Ramsay reported in 1809 that unseasoned Negroes in Charleston were less likely than whites to take the fever and that their illness was milder when they did. Ramsay added that both blacks and whites arriving from the West Indies enjoyed exemption from the horrible infection.[32]

American physicians had in fact groped their way toward a reasonably accurate conclusion on racial immunity. For yellow fever actually was endemic in West Africa and a large proportion of the population there contracted it during childhood; survivors acquired prolonged immunity or relatively high resistance which accounts not only for contemporary suggestions concerning Negroes in America but also for the reports of relative immunity among creoles, for the disease was nearly endemic in the West Indies.[33] A tentative suggestion (by an ardent equalitarian) that Negroes differed in their internal processes was refuted by the facts of death; plainly Americans in the new republic felt no compulsion to discover a radical internal difference in the Negro.

---

30. Carey, *Account of the Malignant Fever*, 77–78; William Currie, *A Treatise on the Synochus Icteroides, or Yellow Fever, As It Lately Appeared in the City of Philadelphia . . .* (Phila., 1794), 13–14; Robert Jackson, *A Treatise on the Fevers of Jamaica, with Some Observations on the Intermitting Fever of America . . .* (London, 1791), 162–63, reprinted Philadelphia, 1795; Richard Folwell, *Short History of the Yellow Fever That Broke Out in the City of Philadelphia, in July, 1797 . . .* , 2d ed. (Phila., 1798), 32; Thomas Condie and Richard Folwell, *History of the Pestilence, Commonly Called Yellow Fever, Which Almost Desolated Philadelphia, in the Months of August, September and October, 1798* (Phila., [1799]), 57.

31. Charleston *State Gaz. of S.-C.*, Oct. 31, 1793; Roberts, trans. and eds., *Moreau de St. Méry's Journey*, 57; Priest, *Travels in the United States*, 199; Thomas Jefferson to Thomas Mann Randolph, Germantown, Nov. 2, 1793, Ford, ed., *Works of Jefferson*, VIII, 57.

32. James Hardie, *An Account of the Malignant Fever, Which Prevailed in the City of New-York; During the Autumn of 1805* (N. Y., 1805), *passim*; Ramsay, *History of S.-C.*, II, 85; also James Hardie, *An Account of the Malignant Fever, Lately Prevalent in the City of New-York* (N. Y., 1799), 48.

33. Whether Negroes possess in addition a true racial resistance to yellow fever, as they definitely do to subtertian malaria, is uncertain. Henry R. Carter, *Yellow Fever: An Epidemiological and Historical Study of Its Place of Origin*, ed. Laura A. Carter and Wade H. Frost (Baltimore, 1931).

Indeed the concept of disease could be employed in the service of the environmentalist case for Negro equality. Benjamin Rush's predilections made it easy for him to construct a case which made slavery not merely immoral, inhumane, and impolitic, but also unhygienic. During the outbreak of discussion about Negroes in 1788 Rush offered readers of the *American Museum* "An account of the DISEASES peculiar to the negroes in the West-Indies, and which are produced by their slavery"—a title which effectively announced his purpose.[34] The "locked jaw" was caused by the heat and smoke of slave cabins; "hipocondriasis" by grief over enslavement; difficult parturition by heavy burdens and the kicks of masters; and numerous diseases by an all-vegetable diet. Finally, Rush argued, the singing and dancing of slaves evidenced misery rather than happiness; mirth, he explained for the laity, was frequently a symptom of melancholy. As he did with the Negro's color, Rush managed to make great sense by advancing absurdities which contained a large measure of truth, for as a description of slavery's impact upon Negroes this was not badly wide of the mark.

Benevolent, speculative physicians like Benjamin Rush came increasingly to realize that any pronouncements they made about Negroes were likely to be interpreted as reflecting on the questions of slavery and Negro equality. An arresting instance of this sensitivity appeared in the nation's first medical journal, *The Medical Repository*, in 1810. Dr. John Archer, an elderly Maryland physician, reported on two cases of Negro women whose labor had been hindered by nearly complete closure of the entrance of the vagina. Archer went out of his way to explain pointedly that Negro female children were more susceptible than whites to this condition "not because they are blacks, but from the occupation of the mothers, who have not time from their daily labour to attend their children and keep them clean by frequently washing." [35] Evidently he sensed that physiological investigations might lead to anti-equalitarian formulations.

6. THE WINDS OF CHANGE

Archer had reason to take care, for in 1810 the status of investigation into the physical peculiarities of the Negro was no

34. *Amer. Museum,* 4 (1788), 81–82. See also Ramsay, *History of S.-C.,* II, 92–94, 110.
35. John Archer, "Facts Illustrating a Disease Peculiar to the Female Children of Negro Slaves . . . ," *Medical Repository,* 3d Hexade, 1 (1810), 319–21.

longer where it had been left by the half-dozen years of discussion beginning in 1787. Quantitatively there was a measurable lull in writing about Negroes between 1793 and 1807. Antislavery was in retreat to the anodizing victory over the slave traffic. Samuel Stanhope Smith's environmentalist explanation fulfilled the modest intellectual needs of most antislavery supporters, as Charles Crawford acknowledged in his second edition (1790) by citing Smith in support of his contention that true philosophy "will tell us that the Negro is in every respect similar to us, only that his skin, or rather the skin of his ancestors, had been darkened by the sun." [36]

During this lull there were important pertinent developments across the Atlantic, such as Blumenbach's third edition and Charles White's litany to the Chain, and these were bound to reverberate eventually in America, especially as more young Americans returned from medical studies in Europe. In the same period, the spirit of disorder and what Smith called "infidelity" strutted brazenly into the open. In the very year Thomas Jefferson was first elected president an obscure Pennsylvanian named Abraham Bradley published a work ominously entitled *A New Theory of the Earth* in which he insisted that there had been two creations, one before the great deluge and one after. Worse than this, Bradley maintained that "not less than six or seven original pairs" of human beings had been created, each adapted to their several climates, that the "native Africans are considerably inferior in point of understanding to the Asiatics and very far below the Europeans," and that he was at a loss to see why Europeans "do virtually claim a blood relation to them." [37]

It is doubtful whether Samuel Stanhope Smith read Bradley's book, but he could scarcely ignore the rude shocks that were being administered to his environmentalist system. He had Blumenbach to support him, but opponents seemed to crop up at every hand. Dr. Charles White, the surgeon-anatomist, had gone out of his way to dissect the errors in Smith's 1787 *Essay;* White flatly denied that men changed color by removing to new climates.[38] Closer to home, John Drayton, statesman-author, drew upon a lifetime of experience in South Carolina to correct Smith on the same point: Negroes were not whitening up except by intermixture, Drayton declared,

36. Crawford, *Observations upon Negro-Slavery* (1790), 12–19.

37. Bradley, *New Theory of the Earth, passim,* quote p. 47. He was unrepentant in an ensuing work, *A Philosophical Retrospect on the General Out-Lines of Creation and Providence . . .* (Wilkesbarre, 1808).

38. White, *Regular Gradation,* 99–137.

though he went on to say disarmingly that he was in agreement with Smith on the unity of man.[39] Still less agreeable to Smith was the bumptiously personal onslaught of Dr. John Augustine Smith, anatomist-educator, who accused him of inadequate knowledge of the structure of the skin and of endeavoring "to prop Revelation" with his system.[40]

In the face of these attacks Smith grew adamant and combative. In explaining why he had devoted "so much time to studies which seem to be only remotely connected with the offices of piety peculiarly belonging to a Christian minister," he lapsed into the vocabulary of a conflict the existence of which he sought to deny: "From Natural Science, which has been cultivated with more than common ardour and success in the present age, she ['infidelity"] now forms her chief attacks against the doctrines, and the history of religion." By asserting that irreligion was mounting its attacks "from Natural Science," Smith showed himself less confident than he had been that (as he still insisted) "true religion, and true philosophy must ultimately arrive at the same principle." [41] It is easy to see here the clouds of a storm which was to break later in the century.

Yet it is important not to view Smith primarily as a harbinger of the conflict of science with organized religion in America. Rather, the importance of his book lies in its fulsome environmentalism, a special faith which by 1810 was beginning to sink in America like an island amid a rising tide of interest in the inherency of human (and social and political) characteristics.

In constructing his expanded case for the power of environment Smith retained his contention that human bones were more susceptible of change than man's external covering. His doing so was in keeping with the prevailing refusal to impute *inner* difference to the Negro. Indeed he attempted to wriggle out of the charge that he had said "that the black complexion of the American negroes is growing sensibly lighter." He claimed to have made "no such assertion" but to "have assigned reasons why no very sensible effect of this kind should yet be expected." Yet Smith had by no means brought himself to abandon his original hope. The critical term in his disclaimer was "yet," for he immediately went on to announce that he thought it "very probable" that "time will efface the black

39. Drayton, *View of South-Carolina*, 222–24.
40. Smith, "Lecture Introductory," *New-York Medical and Philosophical Journal and Review*, 1 (1809), 32–48.
41. Smith, *Essay on Variety* (1810), ed. Jordan, 4, 21.

complexion in them." [42] His presentation of the famous Henry Moss, moreover, could scarcely have been taken as pointing toward the ineradicability of the Negro's color. He had examined Moss in the company of two physicians and had found him to have no symptom of the "scrophulous or albino whiteness." Though he had not seen Moss since his return to Virginia he had been reliably informed "that the whitening process was soon afterwards completed, and that, in his appearance, he could not be distinguished from a native Anglo-American." To wed this astonishing claim to his theory of climatic alteration Smith announced triumphantly that his examination of Moss had revealed that the remaining black patches of Moss's skin lay directly beneath rents in his clothing! [43]

7. AN END TO ENVIRONMENTALISM

It was of course impossible to maintain an extremely environmentalist posture for very long, and Smith's claims concerning Henry Moss epitomized the virtual collapse of an intellectual stance in America. Environmentalism showed signs everywhere of giving way during the early years of the nineteenth century. Before asking why, it would be well to look at three instances which illustrate aspects of this change as it took place in assessments of the Negro's complexion.

One was a lengthy review of the second edition of Smith's *Essay* by Dr. Charles Caldwell, who was by this time estranged from his old medical instructor, Benjamin Rush. Caldwell's whole path through life was strewn with the litter of his vanity and dogmatism, and this review was no exception. He caustically twitted Smith for "dogmatical" assertions, "harshness of language," and for treating anyone who disagreed with him "as an infidel at heart, and hostile to the interest of holy religion." Yet Caldwell conceded that Smith's *Essay* was by no means absurd, for climate, state of society, and manner of living did, Caldwell thought, actually alter the appearance of men. But Smith had gone too far. White men, for example, might darken to some degree but they would never become Negroes. If house slaves were better looking than field Negroes, it was not that they had become so but that they had been selected for house service because of their better looks. Besides, compared with whites,

---

42. *Ibid.,* 155n.
43. *Ibid.,* 52n, 58–59. Similar conclusions were drawn even in Edinburgh, where the issue of Negro equality was isolated from the immediate social problem. "Negro Turning White," *Scots Mag.,* 63 (1801), 470.

they were still ugly. In actuality, he went on, house servants were
darker than their companions in the fields; blackness was natural to
them and, as with whites, natural color was brought to its height by
good health and cleanliness. Negroes were born relatively light-
skinned not because they had an inherent disposition to whiteness
but because sun and air were needed to bring out their *natural*
predisposition or constitution. This was as far as Caldwell could
seem to go, since he did not think that the races of man had been
separately created. He proved to have found nothing except holes
in another man's arguments and had to content himself with keeping the highway of scientific investigation clear for later traffic.
Smith, he declared, had forced investigators into a position where
"we must either abandon forever the study of nature, or our faith
must cherish as holy, what our reason would renounce as erroneous
and profane." [44]

In silencing Scripture Caldwell was in one sense performing a
valuable service, for Smith's mustering science into the service of
religion was hardly conducive to further investigation and was even
dangerous to religion. As Caldwell pointed out in a second review
three years later, the logical alternative to Smith's argument was
separate creations. With this suggestion Caldwell accurately forecast
the development of the ante-bellum American school of anthropologists. And in his corrections of Smith's claims concerning the Negro's complexion—in the unfamiliar terminology of "predisposition" and "constitution" and the outright *inversions* of Smith's
arguments—there is an audible murmur against the tyranny of
extreme environmentalism.[45]

A different instance suggests that even men committed to an
environmentalist approach found their thoughts slipping unaware
into an entirely opposite mode. Like many of his fellow natural
philosophers, Samuel Williams was the son of a minister and became a minister himself. After fifteen years in Bradford, Massachusetts, he accepted the Hollis Professorship of Mathematics and
Natural Philosophy at Harvard, but he became entangled in unfortunate financial difficulties and retired to Vermont in 1788. There
he devoted his abundant energies to the ministry, surveying, magazine editing, the new University of Vermont, and natural and civil

44. [Charles Caldwell], "An Essay on the Causes of the Variety of Complexion
and Figure in the Human Species . . . ," *American Review of History and
Politics*, 2 (1811) , 128–66.
45. C[aldwell], "An Essay on the Causes of the Variety of Complexion . . . ,"
Port Folio, 3d [i.e., 4th] Ser., 4 (1814) , 8–33, 148–63, 252–71, 362–82, 447–57.

history. The second edition (1809) of his *History of Vermont* (1794) included a long discussion of the color of man.[46]

In many ways Williams's speculations were characteristic of widely held views on the subject. His discussion of the processes of color-change was always in terms of the transformation of black into white. While "the negro color is the most deeply impressed of any," he announced in a revealing phrase, "white is more soon and easily sullied, and changed, than any of the other colors." Through inter-mixture, he argued, the Indian's color disappeared after three generations and the Negro's only after five. His explanation of the causes of variation in man was virtually the same as Samuel Stanhope Smith's: the list comprised "different climates . . . intermixtures of different nations, migration, differences in food, diseases, cleanliness, health and many other local circumstances and causes." Yet Williams wavered where Smith stood firm. Despite his respect for the power of environment, he proved to be less than certain that human differences could be laid entirely to climate and other "circumstances." Utterly unwilling to acknowledge this uncertainty, he became confused and collapsed completely into doubletalk. "Whatever those causes are which have served to form and fix the colors of men, they are causes which have been in operation, from the beginning of the creation of God. If there were any differences in the natural constitutions of men, so as to form what has been called different races, those differences must have been original; and therefore as ancient as those supposed races of men." If climate was the cause of color, he continued, it had been operating ever since men's residences had become fixed. "With regard then to all those nations which have long resided in the same part of the globe, their colors must be viewed as the effect of causes, which have been in operation either from the beginning of the creation, or from the time when they began to reside in their present situations, or countries." What this amounted to was certainty that color differences were ancient (but he does not say how ancient) and complete inability, despite his penchant for climatic causation, to rule out original "differences in the natural constitutions of men." Innateness had crept into the discussion without Williams's comprehending his own dissatisfaction with a rigidly environmentalist view.

Williams was banal and verbose, and perhaps his style reflected the fact that his thinking was rooted in an intellectual faith and

46. Williams, *History of Vermont* (1809), I, 493–503 (the 1794 edition was published at Walpole, N. H.). In addition to the *DAB*, Ralph N. Miller, "Samuel Williams' 'History of Vermont,'" *New Eng. Qtly.*, 22 (1949), 73–84.

style which was rapidly losing its predominance. While reveling in
the knowledge that "the general law of nature respecting color, is
marked with as much regularity, uniformity, design, and order, as
any other law of nature," he betrayed his awareness that the existence of this law did not foreclose the question of the Negro's color.
He insisted that the "systems" recently advanced to explain physical
differences by "different creations, and races of men" were not only
wrong but that they did not provide answers to important questions. "Still the inquiries would remain," he wrote plaintively,
"What is the seat of color in these different men? Why do the rays
of light appear of such different colors, upon the skin of the one,
and the other? Why does one color appear most common in a hot,
and another color prevail the most in a cold climate? And how is
the change of color produced by marriage and mixture?" How
indeed? Williams threw empiricism into the teeth of environmentalists and polygenesists alike. "Impatient of the fatigue of inquiry,
collecting and comparing phenomena, some philosophers, with
great precipitation, have pretended to decide it by system."

The collapse of the environmentalist temple was also heralded
by a scientist whose musings, together with those of Charles Wells,
most clearly pointed in the direction that future thinking was
actually to take. Over the course of ten years Dr. Samuel Latham
Mitchill worked himself into increasingly confident dissatisfaction
with the environmentalist case for the molding influence of climate. Reviewing a book by a Spanish sea captain and naturalist in
1806, Mitchill expressed great interest in the author's suggestion
that human form and color derived from a "generative agency," as
yet unknown, which might occasionally produce alterations in the
color of offspring and which would then carry the alteration
through the generations. This suggestion, Mitchill pointed out with
unusual open-mindedness, might be used to explain either the
derivation of white men from black or vice versa. Though unwilling to endorse the suggestion explicitly, Mitchill thought it "well
deserving of examination by all the speculative reasoners who call
in the aid of climate to explain almost every thing that they do not
understand." By 1812, in a lengthy review of the second edition of
Smith's *Essay*, Mitchill had become convinced that climate was
actually the *least* important of the agencies affecting man's appearance. Not that he was prepared to plump for separate creations, "a
supposition both gratuitous and unnecessary." For one thing, he
suggested, there probably had been an "Original Dissimilitude"

among the individuals of the original family of man. For another, "The Power of Imitation" was known to produce changes in appearance: among Quakers and tailors, individuals came to resemble one another, just as kennel-keepers, hostlers, and shepherds sometimes came to resemble the animals they tended. The most important agency, however, was the "Generative Influence": by some as yet unknown operation at conception or birth an animal might undergo an alteration in some feature. Mitchill's instinct on this matter remained entirely sound, for he decided in 1816 that the "generative influence" was "of the greatest moment" and that "the procreative power" could "shape the features, tinge the skin, and give other peculiarities." That anyone thought it necessary to call attention to the possibility of a "generative agency" affecting man's appearance testified eloquently as to the dimensions of eighteenth-century America's faith in environment.[47]

The dissipation of the older mode of thought—or mood of intellect—is not altogether easy to explain, especially because it had never been confined to the realm of natural philosophy, much less to discussion of the Negro's skin. Perhaps environmentalism collapsed partly of its own weight, or rather the weight which had been imposed upon it. In its extreme form it generated absurdities which put off sensible men. It was also bound to be undercut by empirical investigations into such matters as human anatomy; as interest in man's physical structure grew, faith in his plasticity diminished. Perhaps, also, the environmentalist temper which prevailed during the period of the Revolution and the first years of nation-building was undercut by the weakening of certain obvious supportive pressures—the necessities of asserting the legitimacy of restructuring the governments of the states and later the nation, of proving to European critics the beneficence of the American habitat, and of assuring the people (themselves) that they lived not merely in an age but an environment conducive to liberty. The mood of the Revolution itself, the prevailing sense of incompleteness and of embarking upon a new era in the course of human events, was itself bound to dissipate as Americans came quite rapidly in the early years of the nineteenth century to take the existence and the viability of an American nation more for what it had

47. Samuel L. Mitchill, unsigned review of Felix D'Azara, *Essais sur l'Histoire Naturelle des Quadrupedes . . .* , *Medical Repository,* 2d Hexade, 3 (1806) , 69–70; William Stanton, *The Leopard's Spots: Scientific Attitudes Toward Race in America, 1815–59* (Chicago, 1960) , 9.

never been before—granted. In these circumstances it is perhaps no wonder that views about the relationship of men to their surroundings should have changed.

8. PERSISTENT THEMES

Of course these views did not change overnight, and old ideas persisted amid the changing intellectual climate. In 1812 a book appeared in Philadelphia which inadvertently revealed how deeply the argument concerning human variations was mired in assumptions older, even, than the age of European exploration and discovery overseas. It was written by an obscure American named Charles Jones and intrepidly entitled *A Candid Examination, into the Origin of the Difference of Colour, in the Human Family. Shewing, the Reason Why, the Time When, the Place Where, and the Merciful Design of the Author, in Bringing About This Great Variety of National Distinctions*. Jones simply postulated mankind's origin from a single stock, but he held that the various colors of man had not, contrary to President Smith, resulted from climate. If whites lived in Africa for ten generations, for example, they would become tawny but not Negro, and if they then returned to Philadelphia they would bear truly white children in the first generation. How then had men come to vary? Jones's answer came easily. Before the Tower of Babel everyone was the same color—white. But when God introduced the confusion of tongues, He also mercifully changed manners, customs, habits, tempers, and colors so that men would have no recollection of their former united state and hence would be willing to separate. Jones acclaimed this benevolent dispensation (unaware that he was letting the climate theory in by the back door), because it had suited each nation to the region into which God was about to send it. It demonstrated "the wise economy of the Governor of the whole, in causing those to be directed to settle under the meridian of the sun, who had skins calculated to bear its glowing beams without being injured thereby." The facts he had set forth, Jones explained, were so obvious that the authors of the Old Testament had not bothered to include them.

The ancient association of color with climate simply would not down. Readers of Jones's book must have been mystified if they pondered the implications of his remarks for the Negro's future in America. For here were black men in a country calculated for white men—scarcely an instance of "wise economy"; but if color had been decreed suddenly and directly by God then it seemed unlikely that it could be changed by any agency less august than His direct intervention—an act which Jones did not appear to anticipate and which most men in the early nineteenth century had come to regard as excessively unlikely.

Jones's book caught up some of the important threads of assumption and thought which derived from Europe, from the centuries prior to settlement of the English colonies in the New World. Similar contentions had indeed been advanced forty years earlier by Lord Kames.[48] Yet much of the discussion of the Negro's color in America was shaped by peculiarly American concerns. Some of the most persistent of these concerns become clearest of all in a book published in 1811 by Dr. Hugh Williamson.[49]

His background and career were such as to bring him into contact with many of the cultural threads which were woven into the problem of complexion for Americans. Born in Pennsylvania in 1735, he had originally been destined for the Presbyterian ministry. Though never ordained, he obtained license and engaged in preaching but grew disgusted with doctrinal squabbles within the church. He turned to other interests, without ever abandoning his rather orthodox religious convictions. His versatile abilities carried him through mathematical, astronomical, electrical, and medical investigations, successful mercantile pursuits, sponsorship of colleges and learned societies, and writings in economics and history. He was active in the Revolutionary cause and served both in the North Carolina House of Commons and in the Continental Congress. He became North Carolina's most active delegate in the Constitutional Convention and an enthusiastic proponent of the new national instrument during the ratification campaign. Williamson's reputation rested on science as much as politics, however, and he received international honors for his work on the American climate. He brought to his work the assumptions of a Protestant Christian, a

48. Jones appeared to be totally unaware of the fact; his book seems very much *sui generis*.

49. Williamson, *Observations on the Climate, passim.* See Ralph N. Miller, "American Nationalism as a Theory of Nature," *Wm. and Mary Qtly.*, 3d Ser., 12 (1955), 74–95. An extended elaboration of the idea that the air affected men's form, complexion, temperament, and language is in John Arbuthnot, *An Essay Concerning the Effect of Air on Human Bodies* (London, 1733); for a recent discussion of this ancient concept, Johnson, "'Of Differing Ages and Climes,'" *Jour. Hist. Ideas*, 21 (1960), 465–80.

Pennsylvanian who lived in the South, a Jeffersonian intellectual, a gentlemanly go-getter, and an American nationalist. It would be difficult to find a more "representative" man.

Williamson regarded his book on "climate" as "introductory" to the "history of North Carolina." In the tradition of Montesquieu and indeed of the eighteenth century, he conceived of "climate" not simply as involving temperature and rainfall but as the critical aspect of the natural environment which constantly affected man's energy, intellect, health, morals, and appearance. The North American climate, Williamson proclaimed proudly, was becoming more moderate; it was surely going to lead to great achievements in arts, science, and liberty. The beneficial alteration was owing partly to natural change but partly also to the industry of American farmers; as others had claimed, the spread of agricultural cultivation tended to improve the atmosphere.

In discussing the pervasive influence of climate in general, Williamson the nationalist joined hands with Williamson the Christian. In his "Remarks on the Different Complexions of the Human Race," he proved eager to see his findings comport with Revelation, which they easily did since he was convinced that mankind had been varied by natural causes. The number of human races, he pointed out, could as well be considered fifty as five since the colors of man formed a spectrum without demarcations. Were cows of differing colors to be considered separate species? The features and color of all human beings could be altered by changes in "climate, food, and education or habits." And assuredly these alterations would be inherited: "I have seen a family of dogs, in Carolina, continue for three or four generations without tails, because one of their ancestors had lost her tail by some accident." Physical differences among types of men were largely superficial, Williamson contended, and Negroes and whites were internally much the same. It was no surprise, therefore, that the Negro's color and features were being altered in America, although it was far harder for black men to become white than vice versa. Climate, which like all things in the material world was governed by "the constant, universal agency of the God of nature, who is every where present always," invariably altered men so as to suit them to itself.

As late as 1811, then, Williamson was elaborating the case for the power of environment in general and the American environment in particular. Black Negroes were to be transformed by the American habitat. They were to be changed, though not in the twinkling of an eye. It would *not* be through *their* efforts: whiteness was to be *bestowed* upon them by America. The new land was not for black men; even the Indians, Williamson pointed out, had not been rendered black despite their savagery because the climate was not hot enough. Here, in the language of natural philosophy, was the absolutely literal claim: America was a white man's country. The urges behind this claim were not confined to a small group of speculators about the causes of the Negro's blackness.

XV   TOWARD A WHITE MAN'S

COUNTRY

IF THERE WAS ONE THREAD OF DEVELOPMENT WHICH
showed how deeply Americans felt about Negroes, it was a campaign which developed in the 1790's especially in Virginia for
ridding the state (and the entire nation) of black men. Perhaps
"campaign" is too strong a term for the wishful proposals which
were so obviously doomed to failure, but it was the enormity of the
obstacles rather than any weakness in the wish which kept the early
colonization movement from accomplishment. The proposals are
worth examining precisely because they could not have been implemented and because they therefore suggest the existence of extraordinary pressures making for pathetic hopes. The language and
underlying animation of the proposals for Negro removal are also
revealing of some of the important dynamics of attitudes toward
Negroes in America. Particularly they point to the pervasiveness
and profundity of thought and feeling about sexual intermixture.

1. EMANCIPATION AND INTERMIXTURE

One of the most interesting and revealing aspects of
American attitudes was the nearly universal belief that emancipation of Negroes from slavery would inevitably lead to increased
racial intermixture. What is arresting about this opinion is that no
one attempted to give reasons *why* such a development was inevitable and that there *were* in fact no good reasons. (So far, a century
and a half later, emancipation has actually lessened the rate of
intermixture.) The problem becomes, then, one of inquiring why
Americans adhered (and in many quarters still adhere) to this
belief.

Perhaps the real reasons for this expectation (those other kinds of human "reasons") lay in the hopes that white men had invested in America. A darkened nation would present incontrovertible evidence that sheer animal sex was governing the American destiny and that the great experiment in the wilderness had failed to maintain the social and personal restraints which were the hallmarks and the very stuff of civilization. A blackened posterity would mean that the basest of energies had guided the direction of the American experiment and that civilized man had turned beast in the forest. Retention of whiteness would be evidence of purity and of diligent nurture of the original body of the folk. Could a blackened people look back to Europe and say that they had faithfully performed their errand?

It was perhaps not merely chance that one of the clearest restatements of this incompatibility of racial mixture with the American mission came from the uncompromising heir of the man who had thought more deeply than any American on the nature of the American experiment. Jonathan Edwards the younger carried forward a modified version of his father's Calvinism into an era which found little interest in the intense religious scrupulosities of a New Divinity minister. But men could understand (especially in Connecticut) the fitness of the Reverend Edwards's setting the damnable sin of slavery in the larger context of the justification for possessing the new continent. What he relentlessly, mercilessly thrust before the assembled members of the Connecticut Abolition Society in 1792 was an appalling choice. The "facts" he had demonstrated, Edwards intoned, "plainly show, what the whites in the West-Indies and the southern states are to expect concerning their posterity, that it will infallibly be a mungrel breed, or else they must quit the country to the Negroes whom they have hitherto holden in bondage."

Thus it seems [Edwards continued], that they will be necessitated by Providence to make in one way or another compensation to the Negroes for the injury which they have done them. In the first case, by taking them into affinity with themselves, giving them their own sons and daughters in marriage, and making them and their posterity the heirs of all their property and all their honours, and by raising their colour to a partial whiteness, whereby a part at least of that mark which brings on them so much contempt will be wiped off. In the other case, by leaving to them all their real estates. . . . If therefore our southern brethren, and the inhabitants of the West Indies, would balance their accounts with their Negro slaves at the cheapest possible rate, they will doubtless judge it prudent to leave the country, with all their houses, lands and improvements, to their

quiet possession and dominion; as otherwise Providence will compel them
to much dearer settlement, and one attended with a circumstance inconceiv-
ably more mortifying than the loss of all their real estates, I mean the
mixture of their blood with that of the Negroes into one common posterity.[1]

Here was the brutally real dilemma: the sin of slavery required
wholesale abandonment of America or loss of original identity;
either way it was a failure of mission. Edwards's intense Puritan
conception of this mission led him to pose superficially ridiculous
alternatives which were actually in the very long run probably the
only ones possible.

Most Americans must have shared in some measure this half-
conscious concern for retention of physiognomic identity. As Patrick Henry put it, "Our country will be peopled. The question is,
shall it be with Europeans or with Africans?" Almost none of the
antislavery people advocated intermarriage as a long-range solution
to the problem of racial antipathy, and even the radical Charles
Crawford suggested merely that Negroes ought to be allowed to
marry white women without prosecution. The pre-eminent and
perhaps the only exception was, of all people, Samuel Stanhope
Smith, who told his students that emancipated Negroes might be
settled on western lands and white persons encouraged to go there
and intermarry. This would be "to bring the two races nearer
together, and, in a course of time, to obliterate those wide distinctions which are now created by diversity of complexion" and augmented "by prejudice." This proposal was all very well in a Princeton classroom, but it demonstrated how far Smith's zealous system
had transported him from the realities of America's racial situation.[2]

Defenders of slavery would have none of this nonsense; rather,
they could be expected to play gleefully upon concern over intermixture when attacking emancipation proposals. Solicitous concern
for the color of America's posterity reverberated in Congress in 1790
when William Loughton Smith of South Carolina proclaimed that
"a mixture of the races would degenerate the whites, without im-

1. Edwards, *Injustice of the Slave-Trade*, 36–37. The father's influence was
strong but partially indirect, for he died when the younger Edwards was six.

2. William Wirt Henry, *Patrick Henry: Life, Correspondence and Speeches*, 3
vols. (N. Y., 1891), I, 115–16; Charles Crawford, *Observations upon Negro-
Slavery* (1790), 118; Samuel Stanhope Smith, *The Lectures, Corrected and
Improved, Which Have Been Delivered for a Series of Years, in the College of
New-Jersey; On the Subjects of Moral and Political Philosophy*, 2 vols. in 1
(Trenton, 1812), II, 176–77.

proving the blacks." Smith sneered at the "fanciful schemes" for shipping emancipated Negroes out of the country, schemes which proved that "the advocates for Emancipation acknowledge that the blacks, when liberated, ought not to remain here to stain the blood of the whites by a mixtures of the races." The "friends to manumission," Smith claimed, had said that after emancipation "in process of time the very color would be extinct, and there would be none but whites." He was "at a loss to learn how that consequence would result. If the blacks did not intermarry with the whites, they would remain black to the end of time; for it was not contended that liberating them would whitewash them; if they would intermarry with the whites, then the white race would be extinct, and the American people would be all of the mulatto breed." [3] Smith was claiming that a black stain in white Americans was tantamount to *extinction*. Evidently the real American people would have disappeared.

Smith had not been altogether accurate in contending that no one thought emancipation would help whitewash the Negro, but for the most part he was right: the great majority of antislavery people were probably not expecting the mass of Negroes to follow the lead of Henry Moss. Accordingly they remained mired in the discomfiting position of advocating a program which most people agreed threatened the future purity of the American people. The painful character of their problem was clearly evident in their tortured efforts to resolve it.

In the fortunate North the alternatives for abolitionists were less distasteful than elsewhere. On the one hand, emancipation presented no towering problems of police control or economic dislocation, and on the other, intermixture did not loom as a threat of great proportions, despite its unattractiveness. As Jonathan Edwards said, "It is not to be doubted, but that the Negroes in these northern states also will, in time, mix with the common mass of the people. But we have this consolation, that as they are so small a proportion of the inhabitants, when mixed with the rest, they will not produce any very sensible diversity of colour." Edwards put the best face on a bad business, but he had a point. In a region where every twentieth rather than every third person was a Negro, it was easier for principles to override unpalatabilities.[4]

3. *Annals of Congress*, 1st Cong., 2d sess., 1505–8.
4. Edwards, *Injustice of the Slave-Trade*, 37; see also Sullivan to Jeremy Belknap, Boston, July 30, 1795, "Letters Relating to Slavery in Mass.," *Belknap Papers*, 414.

2. THE BEGINNING OF COLONIZATION

When considered from a southern vantage point, however, American slavery presented the fundamental difficulty in full
force, since wholesale emancipation looked as if it would result in
wholesale intermixture. The most common antislavery solution at
least had the virtue of simplicity: remove emancipated Negroes
from America. Other problems besides intermixture contributed to
the attractiveness of this solution, but objection to a mulatto posterity was rarely far from the heart of the numerous proposals for
Negro removal.

There had been a scattering of such proposals prior even to the
Notes on Virginia, but these seem to have been highly miscellaneous in inspiration and purpose. For example in a Philadelphia
newspaper in 1768, a contributor denounced Negro slavery and
went on to propose a "Negro colony" on some lands which His
Majesty might be petitioned to cede "to the southward." Evidently
there was room for Negroes in the Empire but not in the portion
already pre-empted by white men, but the author gave no reason
why.

Thomas Jefferson of course did. When freed, the Negro was "to
be removed beyond the reach of mixture" so that he would not
stain "the blood of his master." He disclosed in the *Notes* that the
Virginia revisal of 1777 (in which he had been very active) had
included an emancipation bill which provided that Negroes born
free after a certain date "should continue with their parents to a
certain age, then be brought up, at the public expence, to tillage,
arts or sciences, according to their geniusses," and then as young
adults "be colonized to such place as the circumstances of the time
should render most proper, sending them out with arms, imple-
ments of household and of the handicraft arts, seeds, pairs of the
useful domestic animals, etc. to declare them a free and independent people, and extend to them our alliance and protection, till
they shall have acquired strength; and to send vessels at the same
time to other parts of the world for an equal number of white
inhabitants." Throughout his life Jefferson never deviated from his
conviction that Negroes must be "removed" when freed, nor from
the ground for that necessity. Six months before he died in 1826 he
closed the matter with an octogenarian's finality: "The plan of
converting the blacks into Serfs would certainly be better than
keeping them in their present condition, but I consider that of

expatriation to the governments of the W. I. of their own colour as entirely practicable, and greatly preferable to the mixture of colour here. To this I have great aversion; but I repeat my abandonment of the subject." [5]

Jefferson's term for ridding America of Negroes was suggestive, for "expatriation" expressed precisely his desire to have Negroes out of his country. On this point his vision of an expanding empire for liberty in America was crystal clear: there was no social room for inclusion of Negroes. As newly elected president, prior to the Louisiana Purchase, he wrote glowingly of the future of his continent: "it is impossible to not look forward to distant times, when our rapid multiplication will expand itself . . . and cover the whole northern, if not the southern continent, with a people speaking the same language, governed in similar forms, and by similar laws; nor can we contemplate with satisfaction either blot or mixture on that surface." [6] Manifestly America's destiny was white.

Just as publication of the *Notes on Virginia* in 1787 helped generate a lively discussion of the Negro's nature, it seems to have catalyzed sentiment for colonization of Negroes. In 1788 "Othello," ostensibly a free Negro of Baltimore, pleaded for gradual emancipation or immediate freedom with colonization in the western territory.[7] Other men of equally indisputable antislavery conviction stepped forward to declare Negro removal indispensable to the accomplishment of emancipation. An anonymous New Hampshire author, whose title *Tyrannical Libertymen* (1795) epitomized his indictment of American slavery, declared that emancipated slaves must be put in "a state of dependence and discipline" because they were unused to freedom. Perhaps some should be returned to Africa, he suggested, but preferably they should be sent to lands in the west and supplied with provisions and magistrates. He conceded that "difficulties would attend the achievement" but pointed out

5. Jefferson, *Notes on Virginia*, ed. Peden, 143, 137–38; Jefferson to William Short, Monticello, Jan. 18, 1826, Ford, ed., *Works of Jefferson*, XII, 434, also Jefferson to Edward Coles, Monticello, Aug. 25, 1814, XI, 416–20, in which he wrote that Negro "amalgamation with the other color produces a degradation to which no lover of his country, no lover of excellence in the human character can innocently consent."

6. To Governor James Monroe, Washington, Nov. 24, 1801, Ford, ed., *Works of Jefferson*, IX, 317.

7. "Othello," "Essay on Negro Slavery," *Amer. Museum*, 4 (1788), 417; also published in O'Kelly, *Essay on Negro-Slavery*, 37–48. Earlier proposals are in Phila. *Pa. Chronicle*, Nov. 28, 1768; Benezet to John Fothergill, Philadelphia, Fourth Month, 28th, 1773, Brookes, *Friend Anthony Benezet*, 302–3. On another occasion Benezet rejected the idea of sending Negroes back to Africa; see his *Some Historical Account of Guinea*, 138–41.

"what a flattering project would it open to the wellwisher of mankind."

We might reasonably expect soon to see a large province of black freemen, industrious and well regulated, improving in arts and learning, happy at home and at peace with us, affording some revenue and adding some strength to the nation, an asylum for other unfortunate Africans, a nursery from which might in time proceed able missionaries and teachers to the land of negroes. Might not the establishment of such a colony be of extensive influence in bringing about the universal spread of light, liberty, and benevolence. Ye republican Pharaohs, how long will ye harden your hearts, and not let the people go!

The sons of Ham were to be repatriated to a new, separate land of Canaan.

The New Hampshire author was certain that "if the negroes should remain among us, though fully enfranchised, they will not be treated upon terms of equality; and perhaps never rise to that rank which they deserve. Let them go, therefore, be formed into a state, and, in due time, have a voice in Congress. They will never be men, till they are treated like men; they will never be citizens, till they feel themselves so." [8] What was striking in this proposal was that fervent equalitarianism led directly to Negro removal. Evidently the right to live in the white man's country was not one of "the rights belonging to human nature," since Negroes did not seem to share in it.

Certainly a majority of antislavery advocates in the North were not especially attracted by such proposals. Only once did the Convention of Abolition Societies in Philadelphia so much as briefly allude to the possibility of colonization. Its silence indicated hesitancy to endorse a program which might easily be cruel and would be treating Negroes as essentially unequal. Correspondingly, their silence suggests that they saw no great evil or danger in Negro removal, no great conspiracy to promote slavery by removing free Negroes. No one denounced colonization as a proslavery instrument, as the next generation was to do, for the good reason that the project was supported only by men of genuine antislavery feeling.

8. *Tyrannical Libertymen. A Discourse upon Negro-Slavery in the United States: Composed at ———, in Newhampshire; On the Late Federal Thanksgiving-Day* (Hanover, N. H., 1795), 9–11. Several years later Benjamin Dearborn of Boston forwarded to the American Philosophical Society a quaint scheme "for abolishing Negro Slavery, by purchasing the negroes and employing them to cut a Canal across the Isthmus of Darien and from Buzzard's Bay to Cape Cod," *Early Proceedings of the Amer. Phil. Soc.*, 338.

Indeed, by far the most heartfelt of the denunciations of colonization—and there seem to have been extremely few—came from the most vociferous proponent of slavery, William Loughton Smith. His sudden solicitude for the poor Negroes was transparently polemical and hypocritical.[9]

Colonization was an emancipationist scheme calculated primarily to benefit the emancipators. Essentially it was a means of profiting white Americans by getting rid of the twin tyrannies of Negroes and slavery. Thomas Branagan, for instance, though the most prolific of antislavery writers, was appalled at the thought of permitting revengeful, oversexed, emancipated Negroes to remain in the country. In 1805 he suggested establishment of a separate black state somewhere in the Louisiana Territory where, he noted with unconcealed satisfaction, Negroes might be as many as two thousand miles away. It would be a Negro country, although any white people "who wish to be manufactured to black" might migrate thither. Much more typical of the prevailing abolitionist spirit in the North was John Parrish, a Maryland Quaker, who offered a plan of removal without any clear explanation of why removal was necessary. Parrish first proposed gradual emancipation and praised the Spanish plan of allowing slaves to buy themselves with their own labor. As for the objection that manumission would encourage intermixture, Parrish declared, whites and Negroes possessed "a natural aversion and disgust" for each other which had been heightened by slavery. With the momentous problem thus easily swept aside, he went on to propose voluntary colonization of Negroes in the western territory.[10]

Probably a large measure of the support for Negro colonization stemmed from similarly vague feelings that Negroes and whites were incompatible peoples and belonged apart. This seems to have been the case with the rather frenetic activity of William Thornton, one of the handful of men who actually took steps toward accomplishing transportation of Negroes. In 1788 this naturalized Ameri-

9. *Minutes Abolition Convention* (1804), 21; *Annals of Congress*, 1st Cong., 2d sess., 1505; [Smith], *Pretensions of Jefferson*, 5–6.

10. Branagan, *Serious Remonstrances*, 22n, 36–37, and *passim*; Parrish, *Remarks on the Slavery of the Black People*, 41–44. Cf. the pamphlets by Lewis Dupré, an eccentric southern (probably North Carolinian) abolitionist, especially L. Dupré, *A Rational and Benevolent Plan for Averting Some of the Calamitous Consequences of Slavery, Being a Practicable, Seasonable and Profitable Institution for the Progressive Emancipation of Virginia and Carolina Slaves* (n.p., 1810).

can, originally from the Virgin Islands, was encouraging some free Negroes in Rhode Island and Boston in their efforts to emigrate to Africa. He also corresponded with several Englishmen interested in the establishment of Sierra Leone, where four hundred Negroes had actually been sent from Nova Scotia and England in 1787. Thornton seems to have felt that the animosities generated by slavery made colonization desirable. Like John Parrish, he depended upon mutual repugnance to prevent widespread intermixture, yet he was by no means prepared to abandon the customary double sexual-racial standard: "If the taste of a white man should be so depraved as to prefer a black to a white they ought to be joined" in marriage, he wrote, but "it would be injustice to permit such depravity to contaminate a white woman." After a time, Thornton seems to have lost interest in colonization, just as many other men were to do in the next half century.[11]

A more explicit impulse was at work in Reverend Samuel Hopkins of Newport. Immediately before the Revolution he had helped educate two free Negroes for missionary work in Africa. In America this hope for the Christianization of Africa was primarily a logical extension of converting American slaves. Yet while it found expression in many proposals for African colonization, it was not one of the important driving forces behind the movement, at least during the post-Revolutionary period. Hopkins, who was as much interested as anyone in Christianizing Africa, had discovered by 1793 that sending free Negroes to their old homeland offered advantages which had not occurred to him before the Revolution: he suggested publicly that it might be best to send emancipated Negroes back in order to make them "a free and happy people" since it was impossible that whites would treat them as equals. Thus they might be encouraged to return for their own good as well as for spreading the gospel, civilization, and science in Africa. Hopkins did not find prospects bright, however, for as he confided in 1794, "The Friends are always backward in promoting such settlement, and are the most active members [of the Providence Abolition Society], and nothing can be done without them." It was ironic, then, that the only man actually to transport Negroes to Africa until after the War of 1812 was a Negro Quaker. That achievement by Paul Cuffe

11. Quotation from W[illiam] T[hornton], *Political Economy: Founded in Justice and Humanity. In a Letter to a Friend* (Washington, 1804), 20–21. See Hopkins to Moses Brown, n.p., Mar. 7, 1787, Park, *Memoir of Samuel Hopkins,* 139; Gaillard Hunt, "William Thornton and Negro Colonization," Amer. Antiq. Soc., *Proceedings,* New Ser., 30 (1920), 32–61; Brissot de Warville, *New Travels in the United States,* trans. and ed. Vamos and Echeverria, 149, 250–52.

of Massachusetts, whose primary motive *was* conversion, stands out the more strikingly because it was a lonely one.[12]

Some of the heightened interest in returning Negroes to Africa was stimulated by the British experiment in Sierra Leone, which for years teetered between uncertain success and complete disaster. The project attracted considerable and for the most part sympathetic attention in the American press.[13] As colonizationist proposals multiplied after 1787, however, it became perfectly apparent that the basic urge was not to get Negroes over to Africa but to get them out of America. It became clear, too, that this urge was especially strong in one state; indeed, the colonization of Negroes in this period was the subject of widespread interest only in Virginia.

3. THE VIRGINIA PROGRAM

For only in Virginia did wholesale emancipation look at once extremely difficult yet seemingly within the realm of possibility. The statute of 1782, facilitating private manumissions, seemed a good beginning. Eventually, of course, statesmen like Jefferson came to realize that emancipation was not to be the work of their generation, but in fact there was some basis for the assumption by contemporaries that Virginia would be the first southern state to act against slavery. In the last quarter of the century Virginia's leaders, who had been foremost in expounding the doctrines of the Revolution, provided capable aristocratic leadership which aroused little antagonism. In many ways Virginia was an unusually homogeneous

12. Park, *Memoir of Samuel Hopkins*, 129–65, especially 149; Samuel Hopkins, *Discourse upon the Slave-Trade, and the Slavery of the Africans* . . . (Providence, 1793), 18–22 and appendix; Henry Noble Sherwood, "Paul Cuffe," *Jour. Negro Hist.*, 8 (1923), 153–229; and Sherwood, "Early Negro Deportation Projects," *Miss. Val. Hist. Rev.*, 2 (1915–16), 484–508, which contains useful information on most but not all such proposals. The earliest clear statement of the missionary idea was by Benjamin Lay, *All Slave-Keepers That Keep the Innocent in Bondage, Apostates Pretending to Lay Claim to the Pure and Holy Christian Religion* . . . (Phila., 1737), 54–55.

13. Granville Sharp, *"An Account of a FREE SETTLEMENT of NEGROES, now Forming at Sierra-Leona in Africa,"* *Columbian Mag.*, 3 (1789), 234–40; Thomas Clarkson, "Account of the New Colony at Sierra Leone," *Amer. Museum*, 11 (1792), 160–62, 229–31; Annapolis *Md. Gaz.*, Jan. 12, Feb. 16, Mar. 1, 8, Aug. 16, 1792; Charleston *State Gazette of S.-C.*, Nov. 26, 1793; *Substance of the Report Delivered by the Court of Directors of the Sierra Leone Company* . . . *March 27th, 1794* (Phila., 1795); *Substance of the Report of the Court of Directors of the Sierra Leone Company* . . . *26th of February, 1795* (Phila., 1795); "Account of the Sierra Leone Colony," *Literary Magazine and American Register*, 2 (1804), 538–41. One account of the project is by J. J. Crook, *A History of the Colony of Sierra Leone, Western Africa* (London, 1903).

state, in ethnic composition of the white population, in personal wealth, in its commitment to an agrarian economy, and most of all in social consensus. More important still, there was in Virginia little economic justification for continuing slavery and, by comparison with South Carolina at least, a manageable proportion of Negroes. A unique combination of favorable circumstances meant that of all the states where slavery's deep entrenchment precluded easy solution, Virginia was the one where the question of emancipation seemed furthest open. And in Virginia there lived 40 per cent of the nation's Negro population.

As the years went by and it became increasingly evident that emancipation was not going to materialize automatically out of Revolutionary principles Virginians turned to closer examination of the difficulties involved. The concomitant half-thinking disappointment was itself likely to generate unflattering assessments of the Negro, since it was easier and hence more "logical" to blame him than his master for the momentary failure to effect emancipation. Thus for white men the Negro's character became more than ever a likely dumping ground for the white man's burden. At first, though, this tendency was inhibited by the lingering conviction that remedial action was being undertaken and that emancipation might be accomplished in the foreseeable future. At the end of the eighteenth century, therefore, examination of difficulties principally involved realistic assessments of the barriers to emancipation rather than forthright attempts to deprecate the Negro.

After Jefferson opened the discussion in 1787 the possibility of Negro removal had to be considered by anyone interested in emancipating Virginia's Negroes. In 1788 James Madison took time from his political activities to correspond with William Thornton on the subject; he cautiously endorsed Thornton's plans for an African settlement as a means of encouraging manumission. As the situation now stood, Madison explained, general emancipation would benefit neither society nor freedmen. For the well-being of society "a compleat incorporation" of freedmen would be required, but this development was "rendered impossible by the prejudice of the whites, prejudices which proceeding principally from the difference in colour must be considered as permanent and insuperable." A settlement on the African coast was preferable to the American interior because Negroes in the West would be destroyed by the "Savages" if too distant and would soon be at war with the whites if too near.[14]

Several years later Madison was gingerly considering *required*

14. Hunt, "Thornton," *Amer. Antiq. Soc., Proceedings*, New Ser., 30 (1920), 51–52.

removal upon manumission, "there being arguments of great force for such a regulation, and some would concur in it who in general disapprove of the institution of slavery." This unpalatable question whether Negroes should be forced to leave was never even faced by many advocates of removal, but eventually it became apparent that forcible colonization was for the Negro little better than continued slavery and for the white man an impractical negation of the principles supporting emancipation. By 1820 Madison had decided against force, but he remained certain that removal was necessary: "The repugnance of the Whites to their continuance among them is founded on prejudices themselves founded on physical distinctions, which are not likely soon if ever to be eradicated." [15]

The idea of Negro removal spread rapidly in Virginia during the 1790's. In a modest contribution to the new *Collections* of the Massachusetts Historical Society, one Virginian declared that "whenever this [gradual emancipation] takes place, . . . they ought to be sent to colonize some new country; for there will be no happiness here, while they remain mixed with the whites." An important planter in heavily Negro Lunenberg County offered the General Assembly a plan for gradual emancipation and colonization in the Northwest Territory which included giving Negroes a suitable basic education and putting the colony on the same footing with the government as Indian tribes. In neighboring Maryland a newspaper contributor had "no doubt but a general manumission might take place—on exportation." [16] And an observant Frenchman touring the United States in the 1790's described the idea of removal almost as if it were the subject of daily conversation in Virginia: "They talk here of transporting all the negroes out of the country at once, either to Africa or to the southern parts of America, in order to found a colony." The Duc de La Rochefoucauld-Liancourt went on to complain that the measure was "so full of difficulties in its execution" and "attended with so many unpleasant consequences, that it cannot possibly be carried into effect." But he had no doubts why Virginians favored the measure: "The plan

15. To Robert Pleasants, Phila., Oct. 30, 1791, Hunt, ed., *Writings of Madison*, VI, 61, to Robert J. Evans, Montpellier, June 15, 1819, VIII, 437–39, and to Lafayette [1821], IX, 85n. His letters on the subject are conveniently assembled in "James Madison's Attitude toward the Negro," *Jour. Negro Hist.*, 6 (1921), 74–102.

16. John J. Spooner, "A Topographical Description of the County of Prince George in Virginia, 1793," Mass. Hist. Soc., *Collections*, 1st Ser., 3 (1794), 92; Sherwood, "Early Negro Deportation Projects," *Miss. Val. Hist. Rev.*, 2 (1915–16), 489–90; Archibald Alexander, *A History of Colonization on the Western Coast of Africa* (Phila., 1846), 61–62; Annapolis *Md. Gaz.*, Dec. 16, 1790; also Elliot, ed., *Debates in State Conventions*, IV, 101.

is supported by the fear which manifests itself in those who espouse it, that a mixture in the blood would take place if the Negroes were emancipated, or suffered to remain in the country: 'in future generations,' say they, 'there would not be a countenance to be seen without more or less of the black colour.' " [17]

It was all very well for a foreign visitor to call this problem an "inconvenience," but Virginians were facing their own future. Their fears cried out in every proposal for colonization. Ferdinando Fairfax, whose plan in 1790 was the first elaborated in detail, declared that it was "agreed" that manumitted Negroes could never be allowed "*all* the privileges of citizens." "There is something very repugnant to the general feelings," Fairfax continued, "even in the thought of their being allowed that free intercourse, and the privilege of intermarriage with the white inhabitants, which the other freemen of our country enjoy. . . . The remembrance of their former situation, and a variety of other considerations, forbid this privilege—and as a proof, where is the man of all those who have liberated their slaves, who would marry a son or a daughter to one of them? and if *he* would not, who would?" These "prejudices, sentiments, or whatever they may be called," Fairfax concluded, "would be found to operate so powerfully as to be insurmountable." The evident impossibility of finding anyone eager to tarnish his posterity led Fairfax to suggest the colonization of manumitted Negroes in "Africa, their native climate," where they would be at a suitable distance from America and would be neighbors of "the same kind of people." The officers of the colony would be appointed by Congress until it became self-governing, "suitable provision made for . . . support and defence," emigrants educated in useful arts and legislation, and "seminaries" established for spreading Christianity and civilization in Africa. Later when the American government was able, the project could be enlarged by encouraging manumission through compensation to slaveowners. Admittedly, in America Negroes would not labor without compulsion, Fairfax concluded reassuringly, but they might very well do so when placed in a situation offering sufficient incentives.[18]

---

17. La Rochefoucauld-Liancourt, *Travels through the United States*, II, asterisked p. 357. Other French travelers actually advocated intermarriage: the *Columbian Mag.*, 1 (1787), 479–80, carried Chastellux's suggestion that most Negro males be exported and the females taken as wives; see, too, Brissot de Warville, *Critical Examination of the Marquis de Chatellux's Travels*, 62.

18. Ferdinando Fairfax, "Plan for Liberating the Negroes within the United States," *Amer. Museum*, 8 (1790), 285–87. A protégé of George Washington, Fairfax was a wealthy planter.

Certain assumptions underlying Fairfax's proposal were important and revealing because almost certainly they were shared by a great many other Virginians. The desirability of emancipation, presumably a "radical" measure, was as much taken for granted as the "conservative" right of protection for private property. Still more obvious was Fairfax's presumption that the white man's claim to purity was of higher order than the Negro's claim on his future condition; after all, it was the white man's future which was at stake. Finally, prejudices ("or whatever they may be called") did not suggest alterability or remedial action; they were to be accepted for what they appeared—"insurmountable"—and action taken accordingly.

Similar assumptions supported another major proposal by St. George Tucker of Williamsburg. Born in Bermuda in 1752, Tucker came to Virginia as a youth and became ardently attached to his adopted homeland. After graduating from the College of William and Mary, he served as an officer in the war and subsequently became judge of the General Court, professor of law at William and Mary, judge of the Supreme Court of Appeals and finally of the federal circuit court of Virginia. By the 1790's he had developed a special interest in the problem of emancipation in Virginia, apparently through his studies in the law, and he took the lawyer-like step of inquiring into the situation in Massachusetts where emancipation had already been accomplished. The corresponding secretary of the new Massachusetts Historical Society, Jeremy Belknap, made extensive inquiries among his friends in Boston and even communicated with Prince Hall before replying to Tucker, who, grateful and stimulated, in turn replied at length to Belknap in June 1795, setting forth the difficulties which were preventing Virginia from following immediately in Massachusetts' steps.[19]

A major consideration, Tucker explained, was that the populous and heavily Negro eastern portion of the state would "bear an infinite disproportion" of the cost of "a general emancipation" and would almost exclusively bear "the dangers and inconveniences of any experiment to release the blacks from a state of bondage." Sectional disparity was by no means the core of the difficulty. "The calamities which have lately spread like a contagion through the

19. These and the following letters of Belknap, Tucker, and Sullivan are in "Letters Relating to Slavery in Mass.," *Belknap Papers*, 373–431, with the exception of Belknap's first report to Tucker which was published at the time: "Queries Respecting the Slavery and Emancipation of Negroes in Massachusetts . . . ," Mass. Hist. Soc., *Collections*, 1st Ser., 4 (1795) , 191–211.

West India Islands afford a solemn warning to us of the dangerous predicament in which we stand, whether we persist in the now perhaps unavoidable course entailed upon us by our ancestors, or, copying after the liberal sentiments of the national convention of France, endeavour to do justice to the rights of human nature, and to banish deep-rooted, nay, almost innate, prejudices." Gentlemen in Massachusetts had asserted that prejudices were "discernable" there; how much more they must be in Virginia. With considerable feeling Tucker sized up the intractable situation, borrowing heavily from a more famous Virginian's pronouncements on the subject.

Whatever disposition the first settlers in Virginia or their immediate descendants might have had to encourage slavery, the present generation are, I am persuaded, more liberal; and a large majority of slave-holders among us would cheerfully concur in any feasible plan for the abolition of it. The objections to the measure are drawn from the deep-rooted prejudices in the minds of the whites against the blacks, the general opinion of their mental inferiority, and an aversion to their corporeal distinctions from us, both which considerations militate against a general incorporation of them with us; the danger of granting them a practical admission to the rights of citizens; the possibility of their becoming idle, dissipated, and finally a numerous banditti, instead of turning their attention to industry and labour; the injury to agriculture in a large part of the State, where they are almost the only labourers, should they withdraw themselves from the culture of the earth; and the impracticability, and perhaps the dangerous policy, of an attempt to colonize them within the limits of the United States, or elsewhere.

Tucker went on to stress both the impracticality and inhumanity of Jefferson's proposal for Negro removal. Only "three courses" remained, one of which "must inevitably be pursued: either to *incorporate them with us*, to *grant them freedom without any participation of civil rights*, or to *retain them in slavery.*"

Tucker found none of these possibilities attractive. "If it be true that either nature or long habit have depraved their faculties so as to render them, in their present state, an inferior order of beings, may not an attempt to elevate them depress those who mingle and incorporate with them? May not such an attempt be frustrated by prejudices too deeply rooted to be eradicated?" Would not these prejudices lead to civil war between the races? As for the second possibility, to grant Negroes freedom without civil rights would tempt them to gain their rights by force. In the final analysis, Tucker leaned pessimistically toward the third course, deciding with the utmost caution that "the scene now passing in the West Indies prompts me to suspend my opinion, and to doubt whether it will not be wiser to set about *amending the condition of the slave* than to make him a miserable free man."

After reading Tucker's long and obviously pained letter, Jeremy Belknap turned it over to his friend James Sullivan, one of Boston's most prominent lawyers, whose long commentary on the subject was forwarded by Belknap to Tucker. Sullivan was in full sympathy with Tucker's efforts to unearth some fourth solution and was equally inclined to regard mass colonization as an impossibility. "We have in history but one picture of such an enterprize," Sullivan wrote, "and there we see it was necessary, not only to open the sea, by a miracle, for them to pass, but more necessary to close it again, in order to prevent their return." Apart from the miraculous, Sullivan knew of only one recourse, though entirely aside from its slow operation he was far from happy with it. There was "no way," he decided, "to eradicate the prejudice which education has fixed in the minds of the white against the black people, otherwise than by raising the blacks, by means of mental improvements, nearly to the same grade with the whites." To accomplish this feat would require time "as extensive, at least, as that in which slavery has been endured here."

The children of the slaves must, at the public expence, be educated in the same manner as the children of their masters; being at the same schools, etc., with the rising generation, that prejudice, which has been so long and inveterate against them on account of their situation and colour, will be lessened within thirty or forty years. There is an objection to this, which embraces all my feelings; that is, that it will tend to a mixture of blood, which I now abhor; but yet, as I feel, I fear that I am not a pure Republican, delighting in the equal rights of all the human race. This mode of education will fit the rising progeny of the black people either to participate with the whites in a free government, or to colonize, and have one of their own.

Such a program, Sullivan concluded, should be accompanied by the most gradual emancipation and by property qualifications for freedmen wishing to enjoy civil privileges.

Thus Massachusetts spoke to Virginia, sympathetically aware of the problem without feeling its full weight, hopeful that prejudices were not innate and might be overcome by education, hopeful, too, that the spectre of intermarriage would not prove an insuperable difficulty, and certain that true republicanism demanded full equality for all men. The fond wish that Negroes might simply go away was so compelling that it had cropped up once again at the end of Sullivan's letter despite his initial rejection.

His sober judgment impressed Tucker greatly, but where Sullivan hoped Tucker doubted. In another letter to Belknap he set forth not only his unresolved doubts but some proposals which formed the nucleus of a book he published the next year (1796) and which he later delivered as lectures to his law students. Tucker's *A Dissertation on Slavery: With a Proposal for the Gradual Abolition of It, in the State of Virginia* was addressed primarily to Virginians, but it effectively summarized the problems inherent in American Negro slavery wherever it existed. Three-quarters of the book was devoted to a history of the institution and its current legal status in Virginia, together with heartfelt denunciations of slavery on grounds of humanity and natural right; but it was the specific proposals for abolition which spoke so eloquently concerning the master's opinion of his slave.[20]

A general simultaneous emancipation was not to be countenanced. The habits of slavery had rendered Negroes unfit for freedom and white men incapable of treating freedmen as equals. Wholesale expulsion would be cruel and impractical, while permitting them to remain as freedmen would be throwing "so many of the human race upon the earth without the means of subsistence" where they would inevitably become "the caterpillars of the earth, and the tigers of the human race." General emancipation would invite "general famine" in some regions, and in every case men would deprive men unjustly of their legitimate property. To "incorporate the blacks" was impossible, as demonstrated by Jefferson. "Who is there," Tucker asked, "so free from prejudices among us, as candidly to declare that he has none against such a measure?" Secret supporters of domestic slavery had endeavored to show that abolition necessarily required extension of civil equality, yet was this actually a correct argument?

But have not men when they enter into a state of society, a right to admit, or exclude any description of persons, as they think proper? If it be true, as Mr. Jefferson seems to suppose, that the Africans are really an inferior race of mankind, will not sound policy advise their exclusion from a society in which they have not yet been admitted to participate in civil rights; and even to guard against such admission, at any future period, since it may eventually depreciate the whole national character? And if prejudices have taken such deep root in our minds, as to render it impossible to eradicate this opinion, ought not so general an error, if it be one, to be respected? Shall we not relieve the necessities of the naked diseased beggar, unless we

20. Published Philadelphia, 1796 and also in St. George Tucker, *Blackstone's Commentaries: With Notes of Reference, to the Constitution and Laws, of the Federal Government of the United States; and of the Commonwealth of Virginia,* 5 vols. in 4 (Phila., 1803), I, Pt. ii, 31–85; and reprinted New York, 1861. The portion discussed here is pp. 74–104 in the original edition.

will invite him to a seat at our table; not afford him shelter from the inclemencies of the night air, unless we admit him also to share our bed?

What was needed was "some middle course, between the tyrannical and iniquitous policy" of slavery ". . . and that which would turn loose a numerous, starving, and enraged banditti, upon the innocent descendants of their former oppressors."

Tucker's proposed "middle course" was bold, ingenious, complicated, and confusing. All female slaves born after adoption of the plan would be free and would transmit freedom to all their children. These persons would serve their mothers' masters until age twenty-eight, when they would receive twenty dollars and some clothing, and would be treated in the same manner as white servants. Tucker calculated at some length that this plan would bring an end to slavery in 105 years and that there would *always* be two-thirds to three-quarters of the Negro population serving until age twenty-eight. Whatever their status, Negroes were to be scrupulously disbarred from many civil privileges, from holding office, acquiring land other than by twenty-one-year lease, bearing arms except by special three-year authorization of the legislature, marrying whites, and serving as lawyers, jurors, witnesses against whites, executors, or trustees. Tucker conceded that these restrictions "may appear to savour strongly of prejudice," but he protested that he was merely trying to level as many obstacles to abolition of slavery as possible. He protested, too, that his proposal denied no one his lawful property since no man could rightly claim ownership of persons yet unborn.

Significantly Tucker was unable to thrust from his mind the hope that someday America would be rid of Negroes. "Though I am opposed to the banishment of the Negroes," he wrote pregnantly, "I wish not to encourage their future residence among us. By denying them the most valuable privileges which civil government affords, I wished to render it their inclination and their interest to seek those privileges in some other climate." The immense Spanish dominions of Louisiana and the Floridas might afford a place of settlement "more congenial to their natural constitutions."

Sustaining the ponderous weight of Tucker's proposals were assumptions which he saw no need to articulate, for he assumed his readers also accepted axiomatically that American Negroes could never be treated on an equal footing with other Americans. For Tucker, the route to abolition of slavery lay by way of accommodation to "deep-rooted, nay, almost innate, prejudices." His proposals made clear that entirely apart from property rights, economic dislocation, and depredations by ex-slaves, the termination of slavery could not be allowed to terminate white domination. His term "prejudices" succinctly subsumed the reticular complex of beliefs and attitudes which amounted in the last analysis to the proposition that Negroes as Negroes were inferior to white men or, at very least, that Negroes were so different that they could not be incorporated into white society on terms which ignored that difference which was, as Tucker put it, dictated by "Nature herself." The sanction of Nature was not in that age to be taken lightly. The firmly established opinions of men, moreover, seemed lacking in that plasticity which more recent generations have attributed to them. Even a rampant environmentalist like Benjamin Rush saw more hope in altering the Negro's color than in changing the white man's repulsion for it. St. George Tucker was less utopian, for he buttressed the ideal of abolition with realistic acknowledgment that abolition could not peacefully be accomplished without major concessions to the "prejudices" of white men. With the exception of his pitiful lingering hopes that Negroes would solve the fundamental problem by simply going away, Tucker's plan was startlingly portentous. A century later the Negro *was* free and in many areas of the South in a condition which, in an informal way, materially resembled the one he proposed.

4. INSURRECTION AND EXPATRIATION IN VIRGINIA

Tucker thought of his proposals as demanding serious consideration and forwarded copies of his *Plan* to both houses of the Virginia General Assembly when it convened that autumn of 1796. Reaction was mixed though scarcely heartening: the House of Delegates laid it on the table after several members had objected to even that measure of courtesy, while the Senate sent him a gracious letter thanking him for his effort. Tucker gloomily wrote Belknap that he had abandoned hope: "Actual suffering will one day, perhaps, open the oppressors' eyes. Till that happens, they will shut their ears against argument."

The first "suffering" descended upon Virginians all too soon, and their eyes and ears were indeed opened by the alarming events of the summer of 1800. Proposals for Negro removal suddenly assumed a somewhat changed character. Of course the danger of rebellion had been one of the arguments for removal from the beginning, and a very minor instance of Negro unrest in New Jersey had elicited a plea for removal as early as 1772,[21] but after 1800 the colonizationist movement became in much larger measure an effort to free America from the danger of slave insurrection.

That conviction settled especially on George Tucker, a young cousin of St. George, who was destined to become a literary figure. Shortly after the plot he published anonymously a pamphlet which announced dramatically that "the late extraordinary conspiracy has set the public mind in motion: it has waked those who were asleep, and wiped the film from the eyes of the blind." The situation in Virginia was "an eating sore" and was rapidly becoming worse: Negroes were increasing more rapidly than whites despite the heavy sale of slaves to the southern states; the "progress of humanity" precluded more rigorous discipline; and "the advancement of knowledge among the Negroes of this country" was turning them into just so many incendiaries. George Tucker knew the spirit of revolution when he saw it.

Every year adds to the number of those who can read and write. . . . This increase of knowledge is the principal agent in evolving the spirit we have to fear. The love of freedom, sir, is an inborn sentiment, which the God of nature has planted deep in the heart: long may it be kept under by the arbitrary institutions of society; but, at the first favourable moment, it springs forth, and flourishes with a vigour that defies all check. This celestial spark, which fires the breast of the savage, which glows in that of the philosopher, is not extinguished in the bosom of the slave. It may be buried in the embers; but it still lives; and the breath of knowledge kindles it into flame. Thus we find, sir, there never have been slaves in any country, who have not seized the first favorable opportunity to revolt.

Especially was this so in America: "The very nature of our government, which leads us to recur perpetually to the discussion of natural rights, favors speculation and enquiry."

In one sense, Tucker had offered rather prosaic reasons for suggesting that Negroes be removed from Virginia: with or without a sense of empathy, one throws a menacing tiger out of the house. Without perhaps fully realizing it, however, he had more effectively demonstrated the appalling fact that "the very nature of our government" was "the spirit we have to fear." Like virtually every commentator on the Gabriel plot, he detected the spark of liberty burning in the slave, a spark which made the spectre of Negro

21. Whitehead, *History of Perth Amboy*, 320. The earliest American suggestion of colonization included an observation that it was not "safe" to have Negroes free in America; Hepburn, *American Defence*, 33.

rebellion the more abhorrent because it confirmed that the rebellious Negro was merely responding to the claims of his nature and asking what was rightly his. Slave revolt was a deadly reminder that slaveholding violated the purpose for which the nation existed; it was a blow to self-respect especially sharp because it negated the presumption of inequality which served as the rationale for violating that purpose. It is of the utmost significance that when Tucker plumbed the reasons underlying the outbreak of Negro rebellion, he spoke of the Negro as indisputably capable of gaining knowledge, indeed as susceptible of republican enlightenment, in short, as culturally deprived but inherently equal.

Yet when Tucker turned to consider the sheer presence of Negroes in Virginia, his conclusions told in a very different direction. Emancipation as such, Tucker felt, was no remedy: Negroes "would never rest satisfied with any thing short of perfect equality"—and he was not prepared to extend this privilege. "The most zealous advocates for a general emancipation, seeing the impossibility of amalgamating such discordant materials, confess the necessity of qualifying the gift of freedom, by denying the negroes some of the most important privileges of a citizen." Having thus predicated that equality would result in amalgamation, Tucker proceeded to toss the Negroes out. Africa was too expensive and the West Indies too cruel, but western lands would be entirely suitable and might be obtained from the federal government. It would be an exclusively Negro community under United States protection.[22]

George Tucker's proposals found a far more receptive audience than his cousin's had five years earlier. Though he made no attempt to submit his plan to the General Assembly, that body was now very much in a mood for Negro removal. When it convened several months after the insurrection the Assembly's first thought was safety; behind "closed doors" and without recording the customary public minutes both houses passed a meticulously inexplicit resolution asking the Governor to correspond with the President of the United States concerning some area outside the state "whither persons obnoxious to the laws or dangerous to the peace of society

22. [George Tucker], *Letter to a Member of the General Assembly of Virginia, on the Subject of the Late Conspiracy of the Slaves; With a Proposal for Their Colonization* (Baltimore, 1801), also published in Richmond, 1801. Conclusive evidence for his authorship is in the letters of George Tucker to St. George Tucker, Richmond, Nov. 2, 1800; [Jan.] 18, 1800 [1801], Mar. 7, 1800 [1801], Tucker-Coleman Papers, Swem Library, College of William and Mary, Williamsburg, Va.

may be removed." [23] Governor James Monroe dutifully wrote his friend President Jefferson explaining that "motives of humanity" had moved the Assembly to seek some alternative to execution of rebels but that its resolution did not make clear whether the possibility of removal was intended exclusively for such offenders. Monroe himself was unwilling to rest on the threshold of opportunity without at least peering about.

As soon as the mind emerges, in contemplating the subject, beyond the contracted scale of providing a mode of punishment for offenders, vast and interesting objects present themselves to view. . . . We perceive an existing evil which commenced under our Colonial System, with which we are not properly chargeable, or if at all not in the present degree, and we acknowledge the extreme difficulty of remedying it. At this point the mind rests with suspense, and surveys with anxiety obstacles which become more serious as we approach them.

You will perceive that I invite your attention to a subject of great delicacy and importance, one which in a peculiar degree involves the future peace, tranquility and happiness of the good people of this Commonwealth.[24]

Next year, prodded by Monroe, the General Assembly cautiously clarified and expanded its intentions. With some effort the Assembly brought itself to speak the name of rebellion and stated its preference that convicted rebels should be sent to the "continent of Africa, or any of the Spanish or Portuguese settlements in South America." The Assembly resolved also that the President be asked to seek some location outside the United States to which free Negroes or those manumitted in the future "may be sent or choose to remove as a place of asylum." With the question of compulsion neatly side-stepped, the legislators washed their hands of Negroes by magnanimously renouncing any desire to acquire sovereignty over the projected colony.

Monroe and Jefferson continued to correspond on the matter and agreed that the most suitable location for Negroes would be where the climate was "congenial with their natural constitution," which

23. This and following quotations from the General Assembly's resolutions are in Alexander, *Colonization*, 62–72. See also George W. Munford to Gov. William B. Giles, Richmond, June 25, 1829, in Giles, *Political Miscellanies* ([Richmond, 1829]) , no. 57, pp. 26–27; *Virginia House Journal* (1804) , 84, 86, 98.

24. Monroe to Jefferson, Richmond, June 15, 1801, Hamilton, ed., *Writings of Monroe*, III, 292–95. Correspondence on this matter between Jefferson and the governors of Virginia is collected in *Annals of Congress*, 9th Cong., 2d sess., Appendix, 994–1000; also in Alexander, *Colonization*, 62–72.

meant the West Indies, Latin America, or Africa. Jefferson particularly, ever alive to new experiments, found Sierra Leone especially attractive.[25] Accordingly he wrote the United States minister to Great Britain, Rufus King, requesting him to inquire whether the Sierra Leone Company was receptive to the idea of including American Negroes in their coastal colony. Jefferson reviewed for King the events leading to his request. "The course of things in the neighbouring islands of the West Indies appears to have given a considerable impulse to the minds of the slaves in different parts of the U. S. A great disposition to insurgency has manifested itself among them, which, in one instance, in the state of Virginia, broke out into actual insurrection." The revolt had been "easily suppressed," Jefferson explained, and authorities in Virginia, casting about for a place to send the rebels, "have particularly looked to Africa as offering the most desirable receptacle." "It is material to observe," he continued, "that they are not felons, or common malefactors, but persons guilty of what the safety of society, under actual circumstances, obliges us to treat as a crime." Jefferson thought some sort of binding to labor in return for passage might be worked out—Negroes going to Africa would be treated like the servants who had come to America. In addition, he told King, larger aspects of the matter demanded cautious consideration. "The consequences of permitting emancipations to become extensive, unless a condition of emigration be annexed to them, furnish also matter of solicitude to the legislature of Virginia, as you will perceive by their resolution inclosed to you." Jefferson explained, in words of poignant irony, that "it is desirable that we should be free to expatriate this description of people." [26]

Interest in the freedom to expatriate continued in both Richmond and Washington, even after it became clear that the Sierra Leone Company was disinclined to invite convicted Negro conspirators to its colony.[27] Jefferson never ceased to eye St. Domingo as an eventual possibility, but in 1803 his attention was suddenly drawn to another area. He wrote Governor John Page of his hopes concerning the Louisiana Territory but explained that Virginia would

25. Jefferson to the Governor of Virginia, Washington, Nov. 24, 1801, June 2, 1802, in Ford, ed., *Works of Jefferson*, IX, 315–19, 373–75; Monroe to Jefferson, Richmond, Feb. 13, June 11, 1802, Hamilton, ed., *Writings of Monroe*, III, 336–38, 351–53.

26. Jefferson to the U. S. Minister to Great Britain, Washington, July 13, 1802, Ford, ed., *Works of Jefferson*, IX, 383–87.

27. C. Gore to Jefferson, London, Oct. 10, 1802, Palmer, ed., *Cal. Va. State Papers*, IX, 326–27.

have to wait to see how the national legislature disposed of it.[28] St. George Tucker also smelled fresh opportunity but was more doubtful than ever that action would be taken. He conceded unhappily in an anonymous pamphlet that colonizing Negroes there was a "Utopian idea, which I presume to suggest to the genuine friends of freedom, yet, I confess, without any sanguine hope, that it will receive countenance." Though wholesale emancipation seemed "a mere visionary project," Tucker pleaded that Louisiana offered an opportunity to "entice" free Negroes to leave. Manumission laws might then be somewhat relaxed and, come to think of it, Negro criminals might be sent to the colony.[29]

The Louisiana Purchase similarly aroused a spasm of interest within Virginia's General Assembly. Still cloaking discussion in secrecy, both houses adopted resolutions favoring Negro removal in 1804 and 1805; everyone agreed with Governor Page that it was a "delicate business." The resolution of 1805 instructed Virginia's congressmen to press for a portion of the Louisiana Territory for settlement of Negroes already free, freed in the future, and those who became dangerous to society. It was the last such resolution until 1816.

5. THE MEANING OF NEGRO REMOVAL

A variety of factors contributed to the sudden subsidence of the clamor for colonization after 1806. The nation was sucked into a whirlpool of international conflict, and removal of Negroes overseas seemed more out of the question than ever.[30] The ostensible abolition of the slave trade lessened the apparent need for immediate action, and at the same time the energy of the antislavery drive was flagging rapidly, thereby weakening a requisite impetus behind colonization proposals. Furthermore, the early movement for Negro removal was riddled with inconsistencies and confronted by nearly insurmountable obstacles. There was no general agreement on the key question whether Negroes were to be allowed, enticed, or forced to leave, and very little thoughtful consideration

28. Jefferson to Governor John Page, Washington, Dec. 23, 1803, Lipscomb and Bergh, eds., *Writings of Jefferson*, XIX, 138.

29. [St. George Tucker], *Reflections, on the Cession of Louisiana to the United States. By Sylvestris* (Washington, 1803), 25–26.

30. In 1816 the Virginia House of Delegates once again resolved (137 to 9) that the governor correspond with the U. S. president concerning a suitable territory; the House referred explicitly to the now-settled international situation. Giles, *Political Miscellanies*, no. 57, p. 27.

of the problem. There was no realistic or precise appraising of what a Negro colony would be like if one ever got started. In order even to approach success, a program for Negro removal would have to have been backed by massive popular support, by prodigious wealth, and by long-standing familiarity with both the necessity and the techniques of organized large-scale social engineering. None of these existed. The division of power in a federal system of government precluded concerted action; Jefferson was no mere stickler for strict construction in maintaining that the national government had no authority to finance a program of Negro removal and white immigration.[31] Virginia, on the other hand, had no authority to acquire an external site for a colony. So Virginia appealed (in vain) to the national government for assistance with her racial problems. Later developments were to put a stop to *that* spectacle.

The early movement for Negro removal needs to be recognized for what it was and not for what African colonization later became. The ten-year hiatus before the founding of the American Colonization Society in 1816–17 emphasized an alteration in purpose.[32] In that period, warhawk expansionism claimed the West for the American white man; thenceforward colonizationists thought in terms of Africa or sometimes the Caribbean. And by the 1820's and 1830's some, perhaps most, of the support for colonization came from men interested in perpetuating slavery; here was a complete reversal of intention. It is hard to imagine, for instance, any of the earlier colonizationists selling half their slaves to the deep South as the president of the Society did in 1821.[33] On the other hand, the same thread of abhorrence for the presence of emancipated Negroes was woven into the fabric of colonization in both periods. An underlying hostility to Negroes as equals in freedom was fundamental to any program of colonization, whether pro- or anti-slavery.

Whether the goal of colonizing Negroes was in any sense realistic is both a less easy and a more fruitful question. Viewed as a practical proposal, wholesale removal of Negroes was of course a

31. Jefferson to J. P. Reibelt, Washington, Dec. 21, 1805, Ford, ed., *Works of Jefferson*, X, 205.

32. The older authority, Early L. Fox, *The American Colonization Society, 1817–1840* (Baltimore, 1919) has been superseded in most respects by P. J. Staudenraus, *The African Colonization Movement, 1816–1865* (N. Y., 1961).

33. Bushrod Washington. Bancroft, *Slave-Trading*, 15–16; see also his "The Early Antislavery Movement and African Colonization," in Jacob E. Cooke, *Frederic Bancroft: Historian* (Norman, Okla., 1957). There was little continuity of personnel between the two periods, though Ferdinand(o) Fairfax attended the organizational meeting of the Society in Dec. 1816; Staudenraus, *Colonization*, 27.

"visionary project," and some men like St. George Tucker were willing to come out and say so even while they retained a tiny spark of hope. It was all too easy to accomplish things on paper: in 1806 a grandiose antislavery scheme in the *Virginia Argus* cleaned up the whole problem with a whiff of newsprint. If 12,520 Negroes of the right age and sex were sent to Africa each year, Virginia would be clear of Negroes in twenty years at an annual cost of only £103,620 which might be obtained by a tax on slave ownership; exportation of 30,000 annually would in twenty years empty the entire nation of Negroes, whose places could be filled by white Europeans.[34]

That the notion of colonizing America's Negro population in some remote region was so persistent while so preposterously utopian suggests that it was less a quirk of fancy than a compelling fantasy. That Virginians among the founding fathers, men noted by posterity as political realists above all, should have reiterated the utter necessity of accomplishing what was clearly an impossibility suggests that in this instance they were driven men. Caught, as they thought, between the undeniable necessity of liberating their Negroes and the inevitability of disaster if they did, they clutched desperately at the hope that the problem, Negroes, would simply go away. That they did not actually attempt a system of tenancy or half-freedom perhaps testifies more to the strength of their avarice than to the failings of their ideology, but their entertainment of the infinitely less hopeful solution of colonization suggests also that the fantasy of removing Negroes afforded them a measure of satisfaction of which they were unaware. It is possible that the idea functioned partly at a profound level as a symbolic gesture of their disgust with Negroes and the deep discomforts their importation had caused. If any white Americans conceived of their nation or community, at whatever level of conception, as a body of white men, as a white body, then the simultaneous expulsion of black men and noxious slavery could scarcely help but afford a measure of cathartic relief. This is to suggest that for some men the idea of Negro removal may have functioned, in part, as an expression of certain psychic impulses associated with the bodily function to which the idea corresponded with such arresting precision.[35]

While it is conceivable that Negro removal was thus a deeply meaningful gesture for the American or at least the Virginian community as a whole, the historical evidence points in a different

34. Richmond *Va. Argus,* Jan. 7, 1806.
35. "Cathartic" is intended here, of course, in its aesthetic (Aristotelian), not its psychoanalytic, meaning.

direction—to pronounced differences among individuals. Certainly a few colonizationists customarily spoke in precisely the figurative language one might imagine would arise from such a functionally meaningful commitment to Negro removal, while most did not upon any occasion employ this imagery. Indeed, most colonizationists did not employ an imaginative vocabulary of any kind but referred in flatly descriptive language to the necessity of "sending" or "removing" or "colonizing" Negroes so as to avoid racial strife and "mixture" or "amalgamation." By contrast, though he used these terms, William Loughton Smith several times spoke also of plans "to expel them" so that Negroes would not "stain the blood of the whites." Thomas Jefferson, after posing the question, "Why not retain and incorporate the blacks . . . ?" went on to explain that ineradicable antipathies would "produce convulsions" and that the Negro could not be freed "without staining the blood of his master." He was "to be removed." In contemplating the spread of Americans over the entire continent, Jefferson wrote, we cannot "contemplate with satisfaction either blot or mixture on that surface." Upon receiving several official communications from Governor Monroe concerning what Monroe repeatedly referred to as an "asylum" for Negroes, Jefferson wrote Rufus King that the Virginia Assembly "particularly looked to Africa as offering the most desirable receptacle." Perhaps it is unnecessary to point out that Smith and Jefferson, of all prominent men who spoke forth on colonization, felt the most vehemently about Negroes and slavery in America.[36]

Viewed in a different light, whatever the case with individuals, there was in the apparently preposterous proposition to colonize Negroes an important element of realism. During this period, in Virginia at least, some men were facing up to the necessity of doing something about slavery before it was too late, and at the same time they were also facing squarely the existence of "prejudices" and attempting to do the only thing they thought possible—to accommodate themselves to the reality that white men would not accept Negroes as equals. By acceding to this reality, of course, they hardened it and rendered it still more intractable. On the other hand, to think that "prejudices" would simply go away would have been

36. Smith in *Annals of Congress*, 1st Cong., 2d sess., 1505; Jefferson, *Notes on Virginia*, ed. Peden, 138, 143; Jefferson to Monroe, Washington, Nov. 24, 1801, Ford, ed., *Works of Jefferson*, IX, 317; Monroe to Jefferson, Richmond, Feb. 13, 1802, Hamilton, ed., *Works of Monroe*, III, 337, also 292–95, 321–22, 351–53, 378–79; Jefferson to [King], Washington, July 13, 1802, Ford, ed., *Works of Jefferson*, IX, 384.

even more utopian than hoping Negroes would. The measure of the tragedy was that Virginians were so paralyzed by the ineffaceable character of "prejudices" that they failed to nourish any hope that time and effort might change them. Nor was this pessimism merely a function of eighteenth-century assumptions about human psychology. Far from the scene in Massachusetts James Sullivan was able to suggest that time and education might alter the realities, but Virginians simply capitulated to them. As time went on in the nineteenth century, Virginians, realizing that colonization was utterly impractical and hating themselves as slaveowners, turned more and more to the self-solacing thought that the realities of "prejudice" were inevitable, innate, and right. Indeed they came to think that their opinions about Negroes were not prejudices at all but merely objective assessments of the realities of Negro inferiority. Eventually the defense of Negro slavery necessitated forthright vindication of the rationale upon which slavery rested, but as yet few people were pleased that white Americans regarded Negroes as inferior human beings.

EPILOGUE

XVI   EXODUS

I shall need, too, the favor of that Being in whose hands we are, who led our forefathers, as Israel of old, from their native land, and planted them in a country flowing with all the necessaries and comforts of life; who has covered our infancy with his providence, and our riper years with his wisdom and power; and to whose goodness I ask you to join with me in supplications, that he will so enlighten the minds of your servants, guide their councils, and prosper their measures, that whatsoever they do, shall result in your good, and shall secure to you the peace, friendship, and approbation of all nations.

These words concluded the second inaugural address of President Thomas Jefferson in 1805. Coming from him, from the Enlightenment, from rationalism and natural philosophy, from Virginia, they effuse a special illumination. It was exactly two and a half centuries since Englishmen had first confronted Negroes face to face. Richard Hakluyt was then in his cradle and the idea of America not yet fully alive in England. Now, what had once been the private plantations of the English nation was transformed into an independent state seeking not only the "peace" but the "approbation" of all the nations. The transformation had been accompanied by similarly impressive alterations in the character of society and thought. The people had become what so many sixteenth-century Englishmen feared they might become—the governors. As Jefferson said, magistrates were "servants" of the people. God no longer governed—much less judged—his people immediately; indeed "that Being" was now to be given "supplications" so that his "goodness" might endorse a people's continuance in peace and prosperity.

It would seriously mistake the meaning of Jefferson's words to see them as entirely a bland acclamation of the new society in America or as merely another stanza to God-on-our-side. They were these and more. His explicit identification of Americans with the covenanted people of Israel suggests that all Americans were very much in touch with what has been called too narrowly the old New England firm of Moses and Aaron. The American people had been led out "from their native land," though here there was a crucial difference, for Americans had once been truly "native" to England in a way that Israel had never been in Egypt. They had been planted in a land "flowing" with "comforts," a land of plenty, a land surely of milk and honey. In their earliest years, as the process of maturation was so persuasively described, they had "providence"; later they had "wisdom and power." As they grew they dispossessed the tribes of the land and allotted it in various portions to themselves. They killed and enslaved those people not of their own house, both the dispossessed tribes and the black sons of the cursed Canaanites whom their very ancient intellectual forefathers had driven out and killed when they achieved *their* deliverance from bondage.

All of which suggests that the most profound continuities ran through the centuries of change. Particularly, there were the tightly harnessed energies of a restless, trafficking, migrating people emerging from dearth and darkness into plenty and enlightenment. These were a people of the Word, adventuring into a New World; they sought to retain their integrity—their identity—as a peculiar people; they clamped hard prohibitions on themselves as they scented the dangers of freedom.

Which in turn rings of the twin themes which coursed through Elizabethan England—freedom and control. The same themes were changed upon in America; they may be summarized and at the same time most clearly illuminated by looking at a single, undramatic development in the heart of Jeffersonian America.

In 1806 Virginia restricted the right of masters to manumit their slaves.[1] On its face not a remarkable measure, in fact it was the key step in the key state and more than any event marked the reversal of the tide which had set in strongly at the Revolution. It was the step onto the slippery slope which led to Appomattox and beyond.

There had been some sentiment in Virginia favoring restriction of manumission ever since passage of the law permitting private manumissions by will or deed in 1782. However, the appearance of widespread and insistent demand for restriction may be dated precisely at September 1800. The next year in the Virginia Senate, an amendment was offered to a consolidated slave bill requiring anyone freeing a slave to post $1,000 bond as security that the freedman would leave the state within two months; the amendment failed, seven votes to eleven. Public pressure mounted inexorably during

---

1. Shepard, ed., *Statutes Va.*, III, 252. Jefferson's 2d Inaugural is in Ford, ed., *Works of Jefferson*, X, 136.

the next few years, especially as it became apparent that the Assembly's resolutions on colonization were not going to bring results. In 1805, the year of the last such resolution before 1816, a vigorous debate took place in the House of Delegates on a bill prohibiting private manumission; the bill was narrowly defeated, 81 to 72. At next year's session the House considered a similar bill which was finally defeated by only two votes. Undaunted, the proponents of restriction switched tactics by utilizing the popularity of Negro removal. Into a separate bill for the regulation of slaves the Senate quietly inserted an amendment providing that any Negro freed in Virginia had to depart the state within one year or face re-enslavement. The delegates, many of them now reconciled by the absence of direct restriction on the property rights of slaveowners, approved the provision 94 to 65.[2]

Although some newly manumitted Negroes actually did leave Virginia in the following years, this provision was in fact a drastic restriction on manumission and was intended as such by members of the General Assembly. At the time of passage, Ohio already prohibited the entry of Negroes, and within a year the other three key states, Kentucky, Maryland, and Delaware, predictably forbade Negroes from entering to take up permanent residence.[3] Furthermore, the Virginia act of 1806 effectively prevented benevolent masters from providing manumitted slaves with the one endowment they most needed—land. As it turned out, the act did help cut appreciably the rate of increase of the free Negro population, and the opponents of emancipation remained satisfied with the measure's effectiveness as long as slavery lasted.[4]

The pattern of voting in the House to some extent mirrored sectional differences, for of course the more heavily Negro tidewater and piedmont counties aligned generally in favor of restriction; but so many delegates voted against what might be presumed to be the interests of their locality that it is clear that differences in personal-

2. *Virginia Senate Journal* (1801–02), 67–68; *Virginia House Journal* (1804–05), 72, 73, 75, 76; *Virginia House Journal* (1805–06), 56, 59, 66, 68, 77, 87; *Virginia Senate Journal* (1805–06), 55, 56, 61, 67, 71–72. A slightly inaccurate account of the political movement for restriction is in Russell, *Free Negro in Va.,* 59–72. For an antislavery reaction, Barnaby Nixon, *A Serious Address, to the Rulers of America in General, and the State of Virginia in Particular* (Richmond, 1806).

3. Russell, *Free Negro in Va.,* 71–72. Members of the Assembly may not have realized that Ohio already forbade entry of Negroes, but everyone knew the obstacles to such migration were great.

4. This despite predictably lax enforcement in the early years after passage, *ibid.,* 156.

ity played fully as important a role in determining individual votes—as one would expect to begin with.[5]

No record of debate on the provision has survived, if in fact there was any. Fortunately, however, the spirited debates on the two directly restrictionist bills of 1805 and 1806 were partially reported in the Richmond newspapers.[6] Brief as they are, these reports reveal with unusual clarity the attitudes which led the Virginia legislature to repudiate Virginia's most tangible expression of dedication to the principle of liberty for all men.

Easily the most significant element in these debates was the deep substratum of agreement which underlay the opposing arguments. Every speaker echoed the general consciousness that restriction of private manumission would constitute a direct betrayal of the faith of the Revolution. On the one hand, John Minor, the most vigorous friend of manumission, passionately reminded the House that "In past days these walls have rung with eulogies on liberty. A comparison between those times and the present is degrading to us." Minor was able to shrink to absurd dimensions one of the most common arguments for restriction simply by setting it beside the altar of freedom: "Because a few men in detached neighborhoods complain of the loss of their sheep and hogs, shall you destroy a great principle?" Similarly utilizing the principle of liberty, John Love brought property rights to the defense of emancipation by reminding the House that to forbid private manumission was to deny masters the right to dispose of their property as they saw fit. On the other side, opponents of manumission frankly acknowledged that they were jettisoning the principles upon which the state and nation had been founded. Thomas B. Robertson argued that the bill proposed merely to renew an old prohibition, yet everyone knew that the long-standing prohibition of private manumission had given way, in 1782, to the impact of Revolutionary enthusiasm for liberty. No one knew this better than Robertson. All slaveholders, he declared, were offenders against principle: "The proposed meas-

5. From analysis of the 94 to 65 vote of 1806. See Earl G. Swem and John W. Williams, comps., *A Register of the General Assembly of Virginia, 1776–1918* . . . (Richmond, 1918); "The Census—A Tabular Statement of the Free White, Free Colored, Slave, and Total Population in Each County . . . 1790 . . . 1850," in *Documents Containing Statistics of Virginia* . . . (Richmond, 1851), no pagination; James Madison, *A Map of Virginia, Formed from Actual Surveys, and the Latest as Well as Most Accurate Observations* (Richmond, 1807).

6. Richmond *Enquirer*, Jan. 15, 1805; Richmond *Va. Argus*, Jan. 17, 1806. All the following quotations from the debates are drawn from these two reports.

ure is necessary. I advocate it from policy; and not because I am less friendly to the rights of men than those who oppose the bill." "Tell us not of principles," he cried; "Those principles have been annihilated by the existence of slavery among us."

Here in fact was precisely the agony in which Virginians writhed. The abandonment of the last vestige of emancipation was a stroke of realism, a confession of weakness, and a cruel confrontation with the damning fact that Virginia had failed to be true to herself. It was not, in 1806, an endorsement of slavery as a positive good. Restriction of manumission did not result, emphatically, from dedication to slavery or from special fondness for the institution and the style of life it sustained. *That* variety of attachment to slavery was to come later as the sharp spike of guilt sank deeper and deeper into Virginia's social consciousness. In 1806, Virginians stood upon the corner of that development; but they could only look back upon the generations of unheeding acceptance, upon their great awakening, and now upon the wreckage of their hopes for their society's regeneration.

The evident source of Virginia's mounting determination to bring a halt to individual acts of emancipation was fear of increase in the free Negro population. More correctly, it was fear of free Negroes *as such.* Long-standing hostility had been sharply aggravated by the sudden flood of manumissions after 1782. By the 1790's, free Negroes were being repetitiously characterized as lazy nuisances, harborers of runaways, and notorious thieves. They were further commonly depicted in the role of potential instigators of slave rebellion, as they had been occasionally for more than a century. After the Gabriel plot, of course, there was a barrage of such accusations: one petition to the General Assembly from a county well removed from the Richmond area complained that "it is notorious that the law for freeing Negroes hath tended to bring upon us our disturbed and distressed situation."[7] The arresting aspect of these accusations was, as always before, that they had little or no basis in fact. No free Negro had been implicated in the plot, despite the widespread disposition to suspect them on slightest provocation; yet Virginians for some reason seemed intent on regarding free Negroes as dangerous incendiaries.

Given these circumstances, one is virtually compelled to regard the reaction against free Negroes as functioning primarily on a

7. Johnston, *Race Relations in Virginia*, 35. See also Luther P. Jackson, "Manumission in Certain Virginia Cities," *Jour. Negro Hist.*, 15 (1930), 288–89.

symbolic level. Most directly, free Negroes stood as perpetual representatives of the freedom for which slaves had actually struggled
and were thought avidly to yearn. In this sense, especially in the
wake of a slave rebellion, the free Negro embodied all too effectively the failure of white Americans to remain true to Nature and
the corollary principles of liberty. From guilt concerning this failure to animosity toward the free Negro was an easy, perhaps a
necessary, step. Still more compellingly, the free Negro was feared as
an insurrectionary because his status was eminently suggestive of
the equality which white men half-consciously feared would result
from insurrection. Put another way, the free Negro and the slave
revolt both served as symbols of the loss of white dominion; as such
they were so inseparably linked to each other in the white man's
mind as to warp his perception of the external facts. Functionally,
free Negroes and insurrection were interchangeable manifestations
of, and hence synonymous expressions for, the loss of white control
over the Negro. In this sense, then, free Negroes *had* to be insurrectionaries.

It was in much the same sense, also, that the continued growth of
the free Negro population *had* to result in physical intermixture.
Proponents of the bills curtailing manumission were as fervently
insistent on the inevitability of this development as were Jefferson
and his fellow antislavery advocates for Negro colonization. Indeed
the opponents of emancipation were considerably more explicit on
the subject, not merely because a complete airing told to their
tactical advantage, but because intermixture stood in such intimate
relation with free Negroes and slave insurrection.

If these latter twin manifestations of Negro freedom implied the
loss of the white man's control, then physical amalgamation doubly
jeopardized his security by implying not only that Negroes were out
of control but that white men were too. Long accustomed to relying
upon slavery for the maintenance of social and personal controls,
white men tended to view its termination (pacific or violent, little
matter) as a cataclysmic, entire, and irrevocable disintegration of
indispensable restraints. Perhaps white men sensed how tightly the
institution had controlled the pattern of sexual relationships between the races, how handsomely it had afforded them a sexual
license and privilege which could be indulged without destroying
their most vital institution of cultural integrity, the family. The
controls of slavery were essential not only for curbing the licentious-
ness of Negroes but, as the "swarms" of mulattoes so eloquently
testified, for limiting the license of white men. For if the white
man's sexual license were not prudently defined and circumscribed,

might he not discover that it was he, as much or more than the Negro after all, who was licentious? Above all, the white man had to sustain his feeling of control; in restraining the Negro he was at the same time restraining and thereby reassuring himself.

The necessity of retaining control was the mediating and binding factor in the equation of free Negroes with intermixture and insurrection. And the character of the terms in the equation makes evident how desperately white men felt that necessity. For in advancing as the principal reasons for curbing the free Negro the dangers of intermixture and insurrection, white Americans were expressing—in the language in which such things are expressed —how greatly they feared the unrestrained exercise of their most basic impulses. Neither danger existed in anything like the proportions they saw; the proportions were much more theirs than the Negro's. In this sense, white men were attempting to destroy the living image of primitive aggressions which they said was the Negro but was really their own. Their very lives as social beings were at stake. Intermixture and insurrection, violent sex and sexual violence, creation and destruction, life and death—the stuff of animal existence was rumbling at the gates of rational and moral judgment. If the gates fell, so did humanness; they could not fall; indeed there could be no possibility of their falling, else man was not man and his civilization not civilized. We, therefore, we do not lust and destroy; it is someone else. We are not great black bucks of the fields. But a buck *is* loose, his great horns menacing to gore into us with life and destruction. Chain him, either chain him or expel his black shape from our midst, before we realize that he is ourselves.

To chain the free Negro, to re-enslave him, was an intolerable offense to conscience; the urge to do so was sufficiently assuaged by threatening newly freed Negroes with re-enslavement if they did not remove themselves. Preventing their increase was all that conscience would allow, since the intellectual and moral imperatives of Christianity, Revolutionary ideology, and "humanity"—taken collectively, the cultural conscience—placed effective, if somewhat indefinite, limits on what the white man could do to the free Negro. In other words, communal conscience prohibited extreme, overt manifestations of aggression against him. On the other hand, this same demand by the accretions of civilization that aggressions be restrained, also urged that the Negro be controlled because he was aggressive, that is, because he had been made to embody the white man's aggressions.

The supreme and tragic irony was that the white man's conflicting urges to liberate the Negro and to restrain him both derived from the same allegiance to his own higher self. Of the two inner necessities, the urge to curb projected aggressions was certainly the more complex and perhaps in the long run the more powerful; certainly in 1806 circumstances lent themselves to its expression. By then, the failure to implement the principles of the Revolution, the Gabriel insurrection and its reverberations, and the diffuse but very real sense of insecurity characteristic of a young nation had synergistically generated a heavy charge of anxiety concerning maintenance of American physical and cultural identity. Release was possible through the restriction of manumission—an admirable outlet indeed, for it conveyed precisely the pent-up impulses without producing excessive shock to self-respect. To restrict the free Negro and thereby intermixture and insurrection was to fight the good fight for civilization and its restraints, for whiteness and the inner purity it signified. Failure in this struggle would mean for the white man betrayal of the values of his culture and loss of those things most precious to him, self-esteem and his sense of who he was and where he was going.

All this was as clear in the debates on the bills restricting manumission as irrational phenomena are ever likely to be in the context of rational discussion. The white man's strong sense of racial identity and solidarity found reflection in the frequent assertions that all Negroes possessed this sense. Thomas B. Robertson made this presumed feeling of solidarity among Negroes an argument for controlling them all by slavery. "For if the blacks see all of their color slaves, it will seem to them a disposition of Providence, and they will be content." This was to say that white men would be content too. "But if they see others like themselves free," he continued, still talking as much about white men as black, "and enjoying rights, they are deprived of, they will repine. Those blacks who are free, obtain some education; they obtain a knowledge of facts, by passing from place to place in society; they can thus organize insurrection. They will, no doubt, unite with the slaves." Robertson was certain that "it is the free blacks who instil into the slaves ideas hostile to our peace." It would have been more consonant with the facts to say that it was the white man who instilled into others ideas hostile to his own peace of mind.

Another delegate, Alexander Smyth, was more troubled by the complementary term in the equation of Negro aggression. He opposed emancipation, he declared, because he assumed no one wanted "blacks indiscriminately blended with our descendants" nor America inhabited by "a blended and homogenous race." If Negroes were accorded equal political rights or even simple freedom, he argued, inevitably they would struggle for complete equality and then for mastery. Proof lay in St. Domingo. Smyth had no doubt what equality meant: "I presume . . . that no white man will look forward with any complacency to that condition of society, in which the two races will be blended together: when the distinctions of colour shall be obliterated: when, like the Egyptians, we shall exhibit a dull and uniform complexion. If this state of society, then, is so disagreeable to our feelings, surely we will not encourage the policy, which is fitted to introduce it." That Americans must not be allowed to become "Egyptians" was precisely the point; if Americans were not Americans as they conceived themselves to be they were lost. The people of a new nation had at all cost to prevent loss of nationality. Another delegate, thrusting home the case against emancipation, concluded with a poignantly explicit restatement of these most inner fears. "There are now 20,000 free blacks among us. When they shall become more numerous, they will furnish the officers and soldiers around whom the slaves will rally. We cannot now avoid the evil of slavery. Partial emancipation was not the proper remedy. If it proceeds, and they continue to mix with the whites as they have already done, as we daily see, I know not what kind of people the Virginians will be in one hundred years."

The dilemma was apparent. Virginia's distress was then America's writ large. The white American wanted, indeed *had,* to remain faithful to himself and to his great experiment. In doing so he was caught between the necessity, on the one hand, of maintaining his identity as the fruit of England's and Europe's loins and as the good seed of civilization planted in the wilderness, and on the other, the necessity of remaining faithful to his own image as the world's exemplar of liberty and equalitarianism, as the best hope of the civilization which he cherished. Whichever path he took he seemed to abandon part of himself, so that neither could be taken with assurance or good conscience. Individual Americans divided according to their private necessities, while at the same time the nation divided in response to pressures generated by economic, demographic, and cultural differences, but no American and no section of America could rest at ease with the decision. For Virginians especially, for many Americans, and for the nation as a whole it was impossible to make a clearcut choice.

Within every white American who stood confronted by the Negro, there had arisen a perpetual duel between his higher and lower natures. His cultural conscience—his Christianity, his humanitarianism, his ideology of liberty and equality—demanded that he regard and treat the Negro as his brother and his countryman, as his equal. At the same moment, however, many of his most profound urges, especially his yearning to maintain the identity of his folk, his passion for domination, his sheer avarice, and his sexual desire, impelled him toward conceiving and treating the Negro as inferior to himself, as an American leper. At closer view, though, the duel appears more complex than a conflict between the best and worst in the white man's nature, for in a variety of ways the white man translated his "worst" into his "best." Raw sexual aggression became retention of purity, and brutal domination became faithful maintenance of civilized restraints. These translations, so necessary to the white man's peace of mind, were achieved at devastating cost to another people set permanently apart because they looked different from the white man generation after generation. But the enormous toll of human wreckage was by no means paid exclusively by the Negro, for the subtle translations of basic urges in the white man necessitated his treating the Negro in a fashion which lacerated his own conscience, that very quality in his being which necessitated those translations. So the peace of mind the white man sought by denying his profound inexorable drives toward creation and destruction (a denial accomplished by correlated affirmations of virtue in himself and depravity in the Negro) was denied the white man; he sought his own peace at the cost of others and accordingly found none. In fearfully hoping to escape the animal within himself the white man debased the Negro, surely, but at the same time he debased himself.

Conceivably there was and is a way out from the vicious cycle of degradation, an opening of better hope demanding an unprecedented and perhaps impossible measure of courage, honesty, and sheer nerve. If the white man turned to stare at the animal within him, if he once admitted unashamedly that the beast was there, he might see that the old foe was a friend as well, that his best and his worst derived from the same deep well of energy. If he once fully acknowledged the powerful forces which drove his being, the necessity of imputing them to others would drastically diminish. If he came to recognize what had happened and was still happening with himself and the Negro in America, if he faced the unpalatable realities of the tragedy unflinchingly, if he were willing to call the beast no more the Negro's than his own, then conceivably he might set foot on a better road. Common charity and his special faith demanded that he make the attempt. But there was little in his historical experience to indicate that he would succeed.

NOTE ON THE CONCEPT OF

RACE

Since the presently difficult terms *race* and *racial* are used throughout this book, it seems desirable that their meaning be rendered clear. It is notorious that *race* has been defined in a great variety of (usually unfortunate) ways, but it is less widely known that in recent years race as a scientific concept has undergone a virtual revolution. Since about 1950 scientists have made notable advances in the study of human races and have dispelled much confusion on the subject. Though there remain broad areas of disagreement and many unanswered questions, most reputable investigators now share certain fundamental suppositions and modes of approach.

Increasingly the tendency has been to study human races within the context of human evolution and genetics. At first, some scientists directed their attention to physical features which seemed obviously susceptible to modification by natural selection. Attempts were made to link the more gross and obvious physiognomic characteristics with climatic factors: thus the typical Mongolian face and stature were declared admirably adapted to extreme cold. Partly because such characteristics are difficult to analyze genetically, other scientists set out to investigate certain characteristics, such as blood types, which are governed not by many genes but by one. Initially it was supposed that blood types of the major series A-B-O were selectively neutral (that is, that individuals were neither advantaged nor disadvantaged by having a given type of blood) ; but it now seems almost certain that some of these types are connected with susceptibility to certain diseases. More strikingly, it has been established that a gene responsible for sickle cell hemoglobin (which is especially common in Africa) often causes fatal anemia in homozygous individuals (both of whose parents contribute the gene) but affords protection against malaria to heterozygous individuals (those who inherit the sickle cell gene from one parent only and who do not develop the anemia) . In malarial areas the frequency of the gene remains roughly constant in the population as a whole: for while the sickling gene makes for a fatal disease in some persons, it saves others from death by malaria but itself does no harm, and it is thereby passed on to the next generation. In non-malarial areas, of course, the gene is entirely disadvantageous. Discovery of these facts has served to highlight man's plasticity under pressure of environmental change: elimination of mosquitoes may result eventually in elimination of a racial characteristic.

The sickling gene and indeed genes as such are not commonly thought of as racial characteristics. Obviously, however, human groups which differ markedly in appearance also differ genetically. One of the most important recent breakthroughs has been the conception of *race* as a group of individuals sharing a common gene pool. Such a definition emphasizes the fact that racial characteristics such as skin color are unlikely to remain stable over long periods of time. It underlines the fact that the continued existence of races is dependent upon geographical or social separation. It places in proper perspective the biological differences among human beings: all mankind shares a vast number of genes in common, yet at the same time various populations differ as to frequency of certain genes. With this in mind, racial characteristics may be defined as biological traits which various populations possess in varying frequencies. By this definition, arms and legs are not racial characteristics; on the other hand, blue eyes do constitute a racial characteristic, but blue-eyed people do not constitute a race. Finally, the genetic approach to race makes clear that permanent isolation of any group of individuals from the common gene pool of the species *Homo sapiens* would result eventually in development of a new species which would be incapable of genetic intermingling with its progenitor. In this sense, races are incipient species. Obviously, however, the biocultural attributes of *Homo sapiens* make the prospect of permanent reproductive isolation very unlikely.

There are several important, broad emphases implicit in this evolutionary view of race which run somewhat counter to widely held popular notions. It is now clear that mankind is a single biological species; that races are neither discrete nor stable units but rather that they are plastic, changing, integral parts of a whole which is itself changing. It is clear, furthermore, that races are best studied as products of a process; and, finally, that racial differences involve the relative frequency of genes and characteristics rather than absolute and mutually exclusive distinctions. It is also true, however, that the process of human raciation remains imperfectly understood. The evolutionary history of human races is still a subject of dispute, though at this writing a majority of investigators feel that present races derived from a single progenitor who had already developed into *Homo sapiens*.

Unfortunately, recent advances in the study of race have done little to settle certain important questions concerning racial differences in physiology and anatomy—let alone the slippery problem of mental abilities. It remains hazardous, for instance, to offer summary findings as to skeletal differences between whites and Negroes, except to say that such differences exist, have often been exaggerated, require discussion in terms of frequency, and need further investigation. It is perhaps more surprising that the facts concerning skin color remain in doubt. It is clear that the complex structure of the skin may be considered as consisting of three layers, that differences in skin color are quantitative in the sense that all peoples (except albinos) possess the granulated pigment melanin which is generated in the middle (Malpighian) layer, and that melanin is primarily responsible for dark skin color. Yet it is far from certain whether dark skin as such affords important protection against the sun. Some investigators have supposed that although melanin absorbs solar heat it protects the cells below (in the *cutis vera*) against ultra-violent radiation and hence against skin cancer. On the other hand, protection against skin cancer is probably of very minor evolutionary significance, since the disease is not highly lethal and does not usually develop until well after the sexually reproductive years. Other investigators have found that the outermost layer of the Negro's skin does often contain some melanin granules and that it is thicker than the white man's, but while the first of these facts seems sufficiently well established, the second does not. Certainly, the precise adaptive value of the Negro's skin is not as yet known. It is ironic that a scientific problem which has been acknowledged for several millenniums still remains unsolved, and, further, that scientists have not yet been able to fit one of the most socially explosive facts of human biology securely into the framework which now supports the study of human races.

ESSAY ON SOURCES

Properly, a study of attitudes toward Negroes in early America should be based upon examination of everything written in the period. Human beings are supposed, in theory, frequently to express social attitudes in the most tangential manner on the most unexpected occasions. In early America, in practice, they did. In doing so they produced a bewildering body of miscellany; only at the time of the Revolution did an appreciable number of white men in America begin to write directly about the Negro as such. Of course this partial transformation and proliferation of the historical sources was symptomatic of a major shift in attitudes, a shift which this study in some measure elucidates. Yet the development in the second half of the eighteenth century of a body of literature bearing directly and obviously upon the Negro does nothing (unfortunately) to diminish the obligation which pertains so clearly to the earlier period. Rather, the necessity of reading everything is heightened and the historian the more stupified. For plainly, if he attends only to the most readily obvious and available sources, he will see only the most salient expressions of attitudes and will be led not merely to generalize too freely as to their explicit content but also to overestimate the saliency and vehemence of attitudes prevailing in the culture at large. It seems probable that men who wrote about Negroes felt differently and more strongly about them than men who did not.

There persists in the sources for this study, then, an inherent bias which may be compensated but never wholly corrected. The distortive tendency may be countered in some measure by exercising due restraint, discretion, imagination, and, more particularly, by venturing beyond the most obviously pertinent writing about Negroes in search of more casual, tangential references. Only by undertaking this venture is it possible to say anything, however tentative, about the attitudes of Americans as a people. Yet it is important to remember that the prevailing bias will remain no matter how thorough the research. For if it were possible (fortunately it is not) to prowl through all the extant sources and thereby collar every fugitive allusion, the resultant evidence would still suggest the existence of more salient and more vehement attitudes than prevailed among the people as a whole.

Set over against this difficulty is the fact that, in literate societies, written and particularly printed ideas and fancies reverberate almost endlessly through space and time. Written records are not merely fossils of momentary opinion but links in a chain of cultural transmission. In varying measure, every written expression of attitude and opinion exerts influence on every reader. Insofar as they were widely disseminated, then, written expressions concerning the Negro (however indirectly) functioned as social memory traces, as fixed points of reference and departure. Written expressions of attitudes have, especially, a preservative, accretive effect. Some 2,500 years ago Aristotle made some offhand remarks about Africa whose reverberations may be tracked with considerable precision down to the present day. If we are interested in persistency and change in social attitudes, therefore, we may find both spread out for us in the public record of our culture. Indeed, attitudes prevailing today can scarcely be understood without attention to our literate historical experience.

Partly for these reasons, this study has drawn principally upon relatively public sources. The result has been to throw emphasis upon the communal aspects of social attitudes at the cost of de-emphasizing the functional importance of these attitudes as they operated within individuals. Here again, the nature of available sources has partially fixed the mode of approach, for with very few individuals do we have sufficient information to permit even the most tentative suggestions concerning the relationship between personality and specific attitude. Yet it would be difficult for the historian not to play his attention especially on the shared and interactive aspects of attitudes toward a social group since he must attend always to transmission through time.

In light of these considerations, one of the most valuable categories of evidence for this study has been the statutes passed by the colonial and state legislatures. The collections used are indicated in the notes, particularly to chapters 3, 4, and 11. Certain guides are especially useful: William S. Jenkins, comp., *A Guide to the Microfilm Collection of Early State Records* [ed. Lillian A. Hamrick] (Washington, 1950) and its *Supplement* (Washington, 1951) and Jack P. Greene, "The Publication of the Official Records of the Southern Colonies," *William and Mary Quarterly*, 3d Ser., 14 (1957), 268–80.

The danger of assuming that laws reflect actual practice is well known, but several observations need to be made about this rather shopworn problem. Reliance upon statutes almost always introduces a *systematic* distortion—which may therefore be partially compensated. Statutes provide a picture of race relations and slave control which is too clear cut, too highly rationalized, too formalized, and far too uniform. The slave codes do *not,* however, necessarily suggest more (or less) brutality in the system than there actually was. When the law required 39 lashes or prohibited gatherings of six or more slaves, who counted? When compared from one colony to the next, of course, the codes furnish a pattern of difference which probably underestimates actual differences in practice: in the eighteenth century Virginia's slave code was *slightly* less harsh than South Carolina's and treatment of slaves *far* less so.

For this book's purposes it is especially important that while statutes usually speak falsely as to actual behavior, they afford probably the best single means of ascertaining what a society thinks behavior ought to be; they sweep up the felt necessities of the day and indirectly expound the social norms of the legislators. This function marks an important distinction between the historical sources for English colonies and for Latin America, a distinction which comparisons between the two broad cultural areas have frequently ignored. Almost from the beginning the English colonies had representative assemblies and the French, Spanish, and Portuguese colonies did not. Laws promulgated in Madrid should be compared only with great caution to laws voted in Williamsburg; indeed a comparison between Madrid and London would seem more apt (and would yield a very different result). That Englishmen had representative assemblies in America makes it possible for the historian to ascertain communal attitudes with a thoroughness and precision which is impossible for the Latin colonies. That dozens of men voted on a piece of legislation confers a reliability—a representativeness—on statutes which the remarks of a single traveler can scarcely match. Colonial assemblies were of course not accurately representative of even the white population; like all such bodies they overweighted education, wealth, and ability; in addition they overrepresented slaveholders and the coastal areas where Negroes were concentrated—which means that statutes, like all other sources, reflected the views especially of men interested in "saying" something about Negroes.

Another important category of sources may also be said to contain a bias toward wealth, education, and even the seacoast. The reports of travelers are revealing not only of the traveler but of the society in which he moved, the difficulty being, of course, disentangling the one from the other. The difficulty is suggested implicitly in chapters 1 and 2 in discussion of English contact with West Africa and with various parts of the New World. Some men are inherently more credible as reporters of fact than others, as comparison between Richard Jobson, *The Golden Trade or the Discovery of the River Gambra, and the Golden Trade of the Aethiopians*

(*1623*), ed. Charles G. Kingsley (Teignmouth, 1904) and Francis Moore, *Travels into the Inland Parts of Africa: Containing a Description of the Several Nations for the Space of Six Hundred Miles up the River Gambia* . . . (London, 1738) —or reading a modern travelogue—will readily suggest.

In assessing attitudes toward Negroes, one is led especially to ask what pressures the reporter was under, what he wished to discover, into what presuppositions he had to assimilate his data. Reporters foreign to English culture were able to bring to bear a peculiarly external perspective which is frequently revealing. One of the earliest important visitors to America was a Swedish disciple of Linnaeus whose mid-eighteenth-century observations are set forth in Adolph B. Benson, trans. and ed., *Peter Kalm's Travels in North America. The English Version of 1770*, 2 vols. (N. Y., 1937). During and after the Revolution numerous Frenchmen recorded their impressions of the new society in America: the most useful, probably, is Duc de La Rochefoucauld-Liancourt, *Travels through the United States of North America* . . . *1795, 1796, and 1797* . . . , 2 vols. (London, 1799). Two others, who for different reasons were especially interested in the problem of American slavery, were the François, Marquis de Barbé-Marbois (Eugene P. Chase, trans. and ed., *Our Revolutionary Forefathers; The Letters of François, Marquis de Barbé-Marbois during His Residence in the United States as Secretary of the French Legation, 1779–1785* [N. Y., 1929]) and J. P. Brissot de Warville (*New Travels in the United States of America, 1788*, trans. Mara Soceanu Vamos and Durand Echeverria, ed. Echeverria [Cambridge, Mass., 1964]). The perceptive observations of a nobleman who traveled in the most influential circles in America have been beautifully edited in the Marquis de Chastellux, *Travels in North America in the Years 1780, 1781 and 1782*, trans. and ed. Howard C. Rice, Jr., 2 vols. (Chapel Hill, 1963). It might also be said that Englishmen visiting in the West Indies were equally foreigners in an alien culture; certainly some of the most interesting and informative books on their overseas dominions were written by such English observers. How early the divergence in culture began is evident in Richard Ligon, *A True and Exact History of the Island of Barbadoes* . . . (London, 1657); equally interesting is one by an important figure in the world of English science, Hans Sloane, *A Voyage to the Islands Madera, Barbados, Nieves, S. Christophers and Jamaica, with the Natural History* . . . , 2 vols. (London, 1707–25). The remarkable observations of a lady in the islands and in the continental colonies are recorded in [Janet Schaw], *Journal of a Lady of Quality; Being the Narrative of a Journey from Scotland to the West Indies, North Carolina, and Portugal, in the Years 1774 to 1776*, ed. Evangeline Walker Andrews and Charles McLean Andrews, 3d ed. (New Haven, 1939). One might argue even that the same sense of foreignness underlay the remarks of a young New Englander who journeyed to South Carolina: Mark Anthony De Wolfe Howe, ed., "Journal of Josiah Quincy, Junior, 1773," Massachusetts Historical Society, *Proceedings*, 49 (1915–16), 424–81. One English visitor to America bore the chip of his dislike for slavery on his shoulder and published the results as [Edward Kimber], ["Observations in Several Voyages and Travels in America"], *London Magazine*, [14] (1745), 395–96, 549–52, 602–4; [15] (1746), 125–28, 248, 321–30, 572–73, 620–24 (which make more sense if the 1746 pages are read before those of 1745). Of all the English travelers, Nicholas Cresswell was the most openminded and candid: Samuel Thornely, ed., *The Journal of Nicholas Cresswell, 1774–1777* (N. Y., 1924).

Observers who did not travel wrote "histories"; in the eighteenth century the discipline of history was less rigorous than today and its scope more broad. Virginia was lucky to have had two able accounts written early in the century: Robert Beverley, *The History and Present State of Virginia* [1705], ed. Louis B. Wright (Chapel Hill, 1947), and Hugh Jones, *The Present State of Virginia from Whence Is Inferred a Short View of Maryland and North Carolina* [1724], ed. Richard L. Morton (Chapel Hill, 1956). Two West Indian histories are works of central importance for a study of slavery and race relations in the English colonies. [Edward Long], *The History of Jamaica . . . , 3* vols. (London, 1774) was informative and brutally hostile to Negroes; Bryan Edwards, *The History, Civil and Commercial, of the British Colonies in the West Indies,* 3d ed., 3 vols. (London, 1801) was temperate, proslavery (like Long), but interested in amelioration of the Negro's condition. One should also consider the acerbic, persuasive writings of a leading opponent of the American Revolution though their purpose was frankly polemical; of all those dissaffected to the American cause, the Reverend Jonathan Boucher was most perceptive about the racial dilemma in his *A View of the Causes and Consequences of the American Revolution . . .* (London, 1797), much of which was composed as sermons during the years of impending crisis. Finally, of really important general works not focusing on some special subject pertaining to Negroes or Indians [St. Jean de Crèvecoeur], *Letters from an American Farmer . . .* (London, 1782) stands in a class by itself for reasons suggested in chapter 8.

It may be useful to those interested in pursuing investigations to list four valuable guides to travel accounts: James Masterson, *Records of Travel in North America: 1700–1776* (unpubl. Ph.D. diss., Harvard University, 1936 [available at the University Archives]); Ruth Henline, *Travel Literature of Colonists in America, 1754–1783: An Annotated Bibliography with an Introduction and an Author Index* (unpubl. Ph.D. diss., Northwestern University, 1948 [typed copy available on interlibrary loan]) ; Thomas D. Clark, ed., *Travels in the Old South; A Bibliography*, 3 vols. (Norman, Okla., 1956–59) ; and for broader scope, Edward Godfrey Cox, *A Reference Guide to the Literature of Travel . . .* , 3 vols. (Seattle, 1935–49).

Similar problems of interpretation are involved in use of personal diaries, though diaries of course tend to be less systematic and more tangential in their comments upon the diarist's social environment. As a species of source material diaries provide less information about attitudes toward Negroes in colonial America than travel accounts and histories, although they are often useful for miscellaneous snatches of information. A basic reason for their limited usefulness for this study is that the people who kept diaries did not keep many slaves. There seems to be only one revealing plantation diary in print, Jack P. Greene, ed., *The Diary of Colonel Landon Carter of Sabine Hall, 1752–1778* (Charlottesville, Va., 1965) ; there are only a very few others almost as revealing in manuscript collections, particularly in Virginia. William Matthews, comp., with the assistance of Roy Harvey Pearce, *American Diaries: An Annotated Bibliography of American Diaries Written Prior to the Year 1861* (Berkeley and Los Angeles, 1945) conveniently lists diaries fully and partially in print.

Private letters as such furnish a far better handle with which to grasp attitudes toward a specific group than do diaries, for letters more often focused upon a specific problem relevant to Negroes. The standard collections of the correspondence of Jefferson and Rush in themselves constitute indispensable sources; references to the correspondence of many other prominent men are scattered throughout the footnotes and may be obtained by reference to the index.

Some printed collections of journals and letters have special interest because the writer had reason for continually referring to Negroes and their condition in America. Particularly, men interested in converting heathen slaves were inclined to dwell at length upon the necessity and difficulty of doing so. An important example is Elmer T. Clark *et al.*, eds., *The Journal and Letters of Francis Asbury*, 3 vols. (London and Nashville, 1958), which, with an inadequate index, provides a revealing glimpse into the mind and experience of the itinerant Methodist bishop. Indeed what may be termed the literature of conversion constitutes a separable body of source material of the greatest importance. It is possible to trace an arresting lineage of exhortation from works which did not deal at all with Negroes, such as William Gouge, *Of Domesticall Duties: Eight Treatises* (London, 1622), through the earliest crises of Christian conscience concerning Negro slaves in the new plantations, such as G[eorge] F[ox], *Gospel Family-Order, Being a Short Dis-*

course *Concerning the Ordering of Families, Both of Whites, Blacks and Indians* ([London], 1676) and Richard Baxter, *A Christian Directory: Or, a Summ of Practical Theologie, and Cases of Conscience . . .* (London, 1673) and Morgan Godwyn, *The Negro's and Indians Advocate, Suing for Their Admission into the Church . . .* (London, 1680), to the efforts mounted in England as reflected by [Edmund Gibson], *A Letter of the Lord Bishop of London to the Masters and Mistresses of Families in the English Plantations Abroad; Exhorting Them To Encourage and Promote the Instruction of Their Negroes in the Christian Faith* (London, 1727), and [David] Humphreys, *An Account of the Endeavours Used by the Society for the Propagation of the Gospel in Foreign Parts, To Instruct the Negroe Slaves in New York . . .* (London, 1730). One of the very few intimate portrayals of the Negro's condition in South Carolina is reflected in the reports of an observant and good-hearted S.P.G. missionary: Frank J. Klingberg, ed., *The Carolina Chronicle of Dr. Francis Le Jau, 1706–1717* (Berkeley and Los Angeles, 1956). Native American efforts were by men in the Puritan tradition, such as Cotton Mather, among whose many writings touching upon Negroes was *The Negro Christianized. An Essay To Excite and Assist That Good Work, the Instruction of Negro-Servants in Christianity* (Boston, 1706), and Samuel Davies, *The Duty of Christians to Propagate Their Religion Among Heathens, Earnestly Recommended to the Masters of Negroe Slaves in Virginia . . .* (London, 1758). A sense of the importance of the Great Awakening in shaping attitudes toward Negroes may be gained also from *George Whitefield's Journals* (Guildford and London, 1960) and *Three Letters from the Reverend Mr. G. Whitefield . . . Letter III. To the Inhabitants of Maryland, Virginia, North and South-Carolina, Concerning Their Negroes* (Phila., 1740).

A closely related body of literature, more various and more subject to change through time, was accreted by the opponents of slavery. Anthony Benezet's many pamphlets made him the great publicist of the cause in America; his *Some Historical Account of Guinea, Its Situation, Produce and the General Disposition of Its Inhabitants. With an Inquiry into the Rise and Progress of the Slave-Trade, Its Nature and Lamentable Effects . . .* (Phila., 1771) is especially interesting for its attempt to reinterpret the nature of the Negro's homeland. The other great Quaker figure is of course John Woolman, whose special importance is suggested in chapter 7; Amelia Mott Gummere, ed., *The Journal and Essays of John Woolman . . .* (N. Y., 1922) is the best edition of his magnificent writings. Other important antislavery writers are discussed in chapters 7 and 9; of these, the names Cooper, Crawford, Hopkins, Rice, Rush, and Branagan are especially important. Chapter 15 utilizes Virginia antislavery works such as St. George Tucker, *A Disserta-*

tion on Slavery; With a Proposal for the Gradual Abolition of It, in the State of Virginia (Phila., 1796), which for persons who like comparisons between New England and the South may be read in conjunction with Jonathan Edwards, *The Injustice and Impolicy of the Slave-Trade, and of the Slavery of the Africans: Illustrated in a Sermon Preached before the Connecticut Society for the Promotion of Freedom* . . . (Providence, 1792). Two manuscript collections are helpful to an understanding of the organization of post-Revolutionary antislavery: Papers of Pennsylvania Society for Promoting the Abolition of Slavery, Historical Society of Pennsylvania, Philadelphia; and Papers of the New York Society for Promoting the Abolition of Slaves, New York City, New-York Historical Society, N. Y. C. The best bibliography is unannotated and incomplete: Dwight Lowell Dumond, *A Bibliography of Antislavery in America* (Ann Arbor, 1964).

Since the Negro was not merely a slave to white men, certain works which may be denominated scientific are crucial to an understanding of the development of attitudes in white America. Some of the most important seem at first sight of only tangential relevance but are nonetheless vital. It is necessary to go back to Aristotle's *Historia Animalium,* trans. D'Arcy W. Thompson (J. A. Smith and W. D. Ross, eds., *The Works of Aristotle,* IV [Oxford, 1910]), and such distillers of classical traditions as John Bodin, *Method for the Easy Comprehension of History,* trans. Beatrice Reynolds (N. Y., 1945). Ideas concerning the relationship between climate and man's nature are to be found specifically concerning Africa in Leo Africanus, *The History and Description of Africa and of the Notable Things Therein Contained* . . . , trans. John Pory, ed. Robert Brown, 3 vols. (London, 1896), and in Thomas Nugent, trans., with intro. by Franz Neumann, *The Spirit of the Laws by Baron de Montesquieu,* 2 vols. in 1 (N. Y., 1949). Far more even than the eighteenth- and nineteenth-century antislavery movement in the Atlantic world, science was international; for this reason the scientific literature utilized in this study is necessarily frequently European. The earlier important works did not focus upon Negroes but they are indispensable to an understanding of the more specific discussions which followed in the last quarter of the eighteenth century. The work of most central importance was Linnaeus's *Systema Naturae,* available as *A General System of Nature* . . . , trans. William Turton, 7 vols. (London, 1802–06). The other great natural history of the century is Buffon's *Histoire Naturelle, Générale et Particulière* . . . , 36 vols. [roughly, depending upon how one counts the supplements] (Paris, 1749–88), large portions of which are in Buffon, *Natural History, General and Particular* . . . , trans. [William Smellie], 9 vols. (London, 1781–85). Of works discussing Negroes specifically at some length, the remarks of Sir

Thomas Browne form an interesting bridge from essentially medieval to more modern notions concerning the Negro's color: Charles
Sayle, ed., *The Works of Sir Thomas Browne*, 3 vols. (London,
1904–07), II, 367–87. A post-Newtonian attempt at the same problem
in America is John Mitchell, "An Essay upon the Causes of the
Different Colours of People in Different Climates . . . ," Royal
Society, *Philosophical Transactions*, 43 (1744–45), 102–50. After
the pace of interest quickened in the 1770's the Negro's physical
nature came into discussion as an *issue* in such works as Samuel
Stanhope Smith, *An Essay on the Causes of the Variety of Complexion and Figure in the Human Species* (1810), ed. Jordan (Cambridge, Mass., 1965) and Charles White, *An Account of the Regular
Gradation in Man, and in Different Animals and Vegetables; and
from the Former to the Latter* (London, 1799). The most important work on what would now be called physical anthropology was
by Johann Friedrich Blumenbach; three swelling editions of his
great work may be followed in translation (complete for the 1775
and 1795 editions) in Thomas Bendyshe, trans. and ed., *The Anthropological Treatises of Johann Friedrich Blumenbach . . .*
(London, 1865), though the complexities of scientific Latin in the
eighteenth century make it necessary to check, for instance, Blumenbach's *De Generis Humani Varietate Nativa*, 3d ed. (Goettingen,
1795). Finally, it is important to gain acquaintance with the work
which more than any other shaped eighteenth-century thinking
about the nature of man: John Locke's *Essay Concerning Human
Understanding*. And Thomas Jefferson, whose *Notes on the State of
Virginia*, ed. William Peden (Chapel Hill, 1955), constitutes the
single most important American source for a study of attitudes ·
toward Negroes in early America, would not have thought it inappropriate to find his only book included with others bearing on
natural philosophy.

Hopefully, the first two chapters of this book make plain that
many sources for a history of attitudes toward the Negro in America
are to be found not merely in Europe but before English settlement
in the New World. The settlement of the English colonies represented merely one branch of European expansion overseas, and the
two great English sources for this enterprise are Richard Hakluyt,
*The Principal Navigations Voyages Traffiques and Discoveries of
the English Nation . . .*, 12 vols. (Glasgow, 1903–05) which reprints the original second edition of 1598–1600; and the 1625 work
by Samuel Purchas, *Hakluytus Posthumus or Purchas His Pilgrimes, Contayning a History of the World in Sea Voyages and
Lande Travells by Englishmen and Others*, 20 vols. (Glasgow,
1905–07), which never achieves the elevation of its predecessor. Just
as it is necessary to read Locke and Montesquieu for the eighteenth
century, acquaintance with works which did not pertain directly to

Negroes is essential for an understanding of how Negroes came to be the slaves of Englishmen. For these purposes Shakespeare's *Othello* is superbly revealing, as in a different way are such legal treatises as John Cowell, *The Interpreter: Or Booke Containing the Signification of Words* . . . (Cambridge, 1607) and Sir Edward Coke, *The First Part of the Institutes of the Laws of England: or, a Commentary upon Littleton* . . . , 12th ed. (London, 1738). Some of the "commonwealth" literature on the state of England in the sixteenth century does as much as anything to "explain" how it first was with Englishmen and Negroes: [William Harrison], *An Historicall Description of the Iland of Britaine* . . . [1577] in *Holinshed's Chronicles of England, Scotland, and Ireland*, 6 vols. (London, 1807–08), I, 1–42; and Sir Thomas Smith, *De Republica Anglorum: A Discourse on the Commonwealth of England* [1583], ed. L. Alston (Cambridge, Eng., 1906).

For an appreciation of how it was later, in America, there is no better way of finding one's way into the interstices of social thought in the colonies than through the newspapers, many of which are available on microfilm. Reading them strains the eyes and takes time from golf and the family, which may explain why they have not yet (certainly not in this study) been fully utilized by historians for understanding race relations in America. Unfortunately newspaper publication did not get fully under way in the colonies until the 1730's. The excellent standard guide is Clarence S. Brigham, *History and Bibliography of American Newspapers, 1690–1820,* 2 vols. (Hamden and London, 1962).

It may be useful particularly to readers not specializing in history and seventeenth- and eighteenth-century America to point up several of the large collections of documents relevant to this study. The *Calendar of State Papers, America and West Indies* . . . , presently 43 vols. (London, 1860—) affords valuable material and an entrée into imperial records of various kinds. There is a fine collection of material concerning the slave trade, Elizabeth Donnan, ed., *Documents Illustrative of the History of the Slave Trade to America,* 4 vols. (Washington, 1930–35), which despite its virtues should not be regarded as including all important material on the subject. It is characteristic of the political development of the colonies that the excellent collection by Helen T. Catterall, ed., *Judicial Cases Concerning American Slavery and the Negro,* 5 vols. (Washington, 1926–37), is of no great use until the early nineteenth century; in the nearly two hundred years previous, statute law was of enormously greater importance than the decisions of courts, especially, of course, for purposes of an inquiry into popular attitudes. Late in the eighteenth century circumstances combined to produce an interesting collection of opinion which may be found entitled "Queries Respecting the Slavery and Emancipation of Negroes in Massachusetts, Proposed by the Hon. Judge Tucker of Virginia, and Answered by the Rev. Dr. Belknap," Mass. Hist. Soc., *Collections,* 1st Ser., 4 (1795), 191–211. For religious affairs there is much valuable material in William Stevens Perry, ed., *Historical Collections Relating to the American Colonial Church,* 5 vols. in 4 (Hartford, 1870–78); the "church" is the Anglican, the one which circumstances brought into most direct contact with masses of Negroes. A major manuscript collection deserves attention in the same connection, the Society for the Propagation of the Gospel transcripts in the Library of Congress, Washington. Other valuable collections are at the Virginia State Library in Richmond, which houses all the county court records (in itself a major triumph of archival condensation) and the official Archives of Virginia, which contain materials indispensable for slave discontent after the Revolution, not all of which is contained in the useful *Calendar of Virginia State Papers* . . . , 11 vols. (Richmond, 1875–93). Of manuscript collections perhaps the most valuable, however, and certainly the most extraordinary, is the Parish Transcripts in the N.-Y. Hist. Soc. For some reason, in the late years of the nineteenth century Mr. Parish decided to assemble a collection of materials pertaining to slavery and Negroes. The result is a wildly disorganized assemblage of documents which range from verbatim typescript copies of relevant pages in books readily available in print to the immensely valuable transcribing done by W. F. Noble in the Public Record Office, London. Mr. Noble seems to have been paid to comb through the original records there and copy down any and every item which pertained to slavery and Negroes. Not only was he an accurate copyist but his handwriting was legible—which will recommend him for some historians and disbar him for others.

Finally, it should be heartening to non-specialists interested in pursuing any of the material cited in the footnotes of this study that a fairly large proportion of the books used are available at any major library in microform. Charles Evans's *American Bibliography* lists most books published in America through 1799, and these have been reproduced on microprint cards in the Early American Imprint series by the American Antiquarian Society. Many books listed in the following two guides are available on microfilm: A. W. Pollard and G. R. Redgrave, eds., *Short Title Catalog of Books Printed in England, Scotland and Ireland, and of English Books Printed Abroad, 1475–1640* (London, 1926); and D. G. Wing, ed., *Short-Title Catalogue . . . 1641–1700,* 3 vols. (N. Y., 1945–51). Good libraries have this "STC" film collection, though some of them seem bent on disguising the fact by improper cataloging—this jibe to balance the very genuine remarks of appreciation at the opening of this book.

In concluding this résumé of primary materials it should be made clear (as many readers will know anyway but which dawned on me only after long puzzlement over the meaning of other sources) that the Bible is the single most important historical source for an intellectual background of the development of attitudes toward Negroes in early America.

I have attempted in this study to let my conclusions arise as much as possible from reading in primary sources, but in numerous instances I have relied upon secondary accounts. I have used the accumulated efforts of scholars in three principal ways. Most important, many books and articles bearing on Negroes have afforded leads into primary materials which would otherwise have been missed. Frequently I have utilized in books on race and slavery specific references to a given primary source; I have acknowledged in the footnotes these various books but only in a few instances of specific citation to material which I would not possibly have seen have I indicated indebtedness for individual references. A different kind of utilization has been my reliance upon certain authoritative monographs for information about topics which are highly specialized or somewhat tangential to the main areas of investigation; these studies are referred to in the notes. Unless other references are given, biographical information may be taken as coming from the *Dictionary of National Biography* (the *DNB*) and the *Dictionary of American Biography* (the *DAB*); and of course the *Oxford English Dictionary* (the *OED*) is the great reference work on the history of the English language. Finally, I have benefited in varying measure from broader works bearing upon race relations and American culture. It is these studies which require comment in this essay; it seems useful to discuss only ones of considerable importance, some of which have not been alluded to in the footnotes.

There is no manageable body of literature which can be regarded as covering the "background" for the development of attitudes toward the Negro in America. There is, however, a recent study which enlarges our understanding of the meaning of slavery in America: David Brion Davis, *The Problem of Slavery in Western Culture* (Ithaca, 1966). Its earlier chapters on the moral problem of slavery in the ancient, medieval, and early modern periods do a great deal to illumine the cultural context into which American Negro slavery was born. The book was written as an introduction to the international abolition movement of the late eighteenth and nineteenth centuries, which he will cover in forthcoming volumes. It is an arresting instance of how fully an historian's perspective gives shape to the sources of history that Mr. Davis and I have had rather different things to say about the same historical materials.

A more traditional approach to slavery stands out for its thoroughness and special relevance to the problem of continuity from ancient to modern, racial slavery. Charles Verlinden, *L'Esclavage*

*dans L'Europe Médiévale. Tome Premier. Péninsule Ibérique;
France* (Brugge, 1955) massively documents the persistence of slavery from the Roman Empire through to the early modern period of Hispanic overseas expansion. There is no similar study of the disappearance of bondage in England, a development which of course did a great deal to shape initial English reaction to Negroes and Indians. Of the many works on English culture in the sixteenth and early seventeenth centuries, none is more revealing of the strains in and interrelationships between social arrangements and ideology than Christopher Hill, *Society and Puritanism in Pre-Revolutionary England* (N. Y., 1964). A study which contains implications beyond its apparently narrow topic is Edmund S. Morgan, *The Puritan Family: Religion and Domestic Relations in Seventeenth-Century New England,* rev. ed. (N. Y., 1966). There is an excellent, balanced survey by Roger Lockyer, *Tudor and Stuart Britain, 1471–1714* (N. Y., 1964) which is the place to strike up an acquaintance with the period.

There is no comparable volume, unfortunately, for early American history. There are available, however, several books which provide good introductions to significant portions of the field which have close bearing to the subject of this study. There are two excellent, though rather different, surveys of southern society: Wesley Frank Craven, *The Southern Colonies in the Seventeenth Century, 1607–1689* ([Baton Rouge], 1949), which is particularly good on relations between the English settlers and the Indians; and Carl Bridenbaugh, *Myths and Realities: Societies of the Colonial South* (Baton Rouge, 1952), a work which attended to the importance of the presence of Negroes before it became fashionable to do so. There is a durable study by Lewis Gray, assisted by Esther Katherine Thompson, *History of Agriculture in the Southern United States to 1860,* 2 vols. (Washington, 1933), which bears up very well after a generation of use. Two well-known books on the labor system of the colonies are useful. Abbot Emerson Smith, *Colonists in Bondage: White Servitude and Convict Labor in America, 1607–1776* (Chapel Hill, 1947), while covering with special thoroughness the recruitment of servants in England, fails to come to grips with the origin of the practice of indentured servitude. Richard B. Morris, *Government and Labor in Early America* (N. Y., 1946) is useful principally for its thousands of references to primary materials, though they are too frequently inaccurate. An interesting, pioneering article on the demography of the colonies must be treated with caution as to its conclusions: Herbert Moller, "Sex Composition and Correlated Culture Patterns of Colonial America," *Wm. and Mary Qtly.,* 3d Ser., 2 (1945), 113–53.

Population statistics used in this study were compiled from the following sources. U. S. Bureau of the Census, *A Century of Popula-*

tion Growth, from the First Census of the United States to the Twelfth, 1790–1900 (Washington, 1909); Evarts B. Greene and Virginia D. Harrington, *American Population before the Federal Census of 1790* (N. Y., 1932); Noel Sainsbury *et al.*, eds., *Calendar of State Papers, Colonial Series, America and West Indies*, 43 vols. (London, 1860—); Alan Burns, *History of the British West Indies* (London, 1954), 401, 454, 461, 465, 499, 500, 510, 511, 514, 515; Vincent T. Harlow, *A History of Barbados, 1625–1685* (Oxford, 1926), 338; C. S. S. Higham, *The Development of the Leeward Islands under the Restoration, 1660–1688: A Study of the Foundations of the Old Colonial System* (Cambridge, Eng., 1921), 145, 148; Frank W. Pitman, *The Development of the British West Indies, 1700–1763* (New Haven, 1917), 48, 370, 374, 378; Bryan Edwards, *The History, Civil and Commercial, of the British Colonies in the West Indies*, 3d ed., 3 vols. (London, 1801), II, 2. My figures are in substantial agreement with those which may be calculated from a table compiled by Stella H. Sutherland in U. S. Bureau of the Census, *Historical Statistics of the United States, Colonial Times to 1957* (Washington, 1960), 756, except in the case of North Carolina where her figures yield a proportion nearly 10 per cent too high. See William L. Saunders, ed., *The Colonial Records of North Carolina*, 10 vols. (Raleigh, 1886–90), *passim;* Walter Clark, ed., *The State Records of North Carolina*, 26 vols. (Goldsboro, 1886–1907), *passim.*

When one turns to histories bearing directly upon American Negro slavery it is arresting to find that none deal satisfactorily with the problem of how slavery and the degradation of the Negro got started. As I have tried to indicate in chapter 2, this problem is one of central importance and great difficulty. The two most direct assaults have been Oscar and Mary F. Handlin, "Origins of the Southern Labor System," *Wm. and Mary Qtly.*, 3d Ser., 7 (1950), 199–222, which is available without documentation in Oscar Handlin, *Race and Nationality in American Life* (N. Y., 1957); and Carl N. Degler, "Slavery and the Genesis of American Race Prejudice," *Comparative Studies in Society and History*, 2 (1959), 49–66, the main points of which are conveyed in his *Out of Our Past: The Forces That Shaped Modern America* (N. Y., 1959), a book which is especially interesting for its extensive treatment of Negroes and the problem of Negroes in American history. The Handlin and Degler articles take virtually opposite positions on the relationship between slavery and prejudice. I offered a still different view, as well as a discussion of the literature on the subject, in "Modern Tensions and the Origins of American Slavery," *Journal of Southern History*, 28 (1962), 18–30, which was written at a time when (as I now think) I was far from comprehending the origins of American slavery. More recently, Paul C. Palmer, "Servant into Slave: The

Evolution of the Legal Status of the Negro Laborer in Colonial Virginia," *South Atlantic Quarterly*, 65 (1966), 355–70, followed the same familiar trail of evidence and rested his case for evolution-from-servitude on the few bits of information in the 1620's which seem to me far too slight and ambiguous to support any certain conclusion.

Studies of slavery in operation are far more numerous and vary greatly in quality. It seems almost astonishing that we have no satisfactory histories of plantation slavery in the colonies. The best single work on eighteenth-century slavery remains an old one by Ulrich B. Phillips, *American Negro Slavery: A Survey of the Supply, Employment and Control of Negro Labor as Determined by the Plantation Régime* (N. Y. and London, 1918) which despite its outdated, gentlemanly racism has the virtues of thoroughness and a sense for change through time. A more modern and superior work by Kenneth M. Stampp, *The Peculiar Institution: Slavery in the Ante-Bellum South* (N. Y., 1956) describes slavery as it was in the nineteenth century, especially during the thirty years prior to the Civil War; its mastery of the sources and judicious handling of Negro life in slavery make it important for an appreciation of what slavery was like in the years when it was under effective challenge. One of the best discussions of the way in which his treatment of Negroes shaped the white man's treatment of his fellow (white) men is in William W. Freehling, *Prelude to Civil War: The Nullification Controversy in South Carolina, 1816–1836* (N. Y., 1966). An article by Charles G. Sellers, Jr., "The Travail of Southern Slavery," in Sellers, ed., *The Southerner as American* (Chapel Hill, 1960), chap. 3, stresses the burden of responsibility the Revolution entailed upon all Americans including southerners and the resultant guilt and its unhappy effects in the antebellum period; what is especially interesting in this is that there exists in this country reason to have to make this point. A very different study, Eugene D. Genovese, *The Political Economy of Slavery: Studies in the Economy and Society of the Slave South* (N. Y., 1965), makes evident that it is possible to say meaningful things about slavery as an institution without shedding much light on race relations—which the import of the present study would seem to suggest to be impossible. Leon F. Litwack, *North of Slavery: The Negro in the Free States, 1790–1860* (Chicago, 1961) makes abundantly clear that an end to slavery did not bring an end to the degradation of Negroes in the northern states.

Of historical accounts which deal with slavery and Negroes in early America, Melville J. Herskovits, *The Myth of the Negro Past* (N. Y. and London, 1941) affords the best introduction to the African cultural background but greatly overstresses how much of the Negro's culture survived the middle passage; his case stands up much better for the West Indies and Brazil than for the United States, for reasons which should be apparent to readers of this book. The best general history of Negroes in the United States is John Hope Franklin, *From Slavery to Freedom: A History of American Negroes*, 2d ed. (N. Y., 1956). Herbert Aptheker, *American Negro Slave Revolts* (N. Y., 1943) was a pioneering corrective work written from a Marxist viewpoint; as is now well known, it tends to inflate every scrap of evidence into an instance of servile conspiracy and rebellion and to identify rumors as revolts. A much older book, a byproduct of the nineteenth-century debate over slavery, constitutes a useful survey of and guide into the slave codes of all the colonies and states: John Codman Hurd, *The Law of Freedom and Bondage in the United States*, 2 vols. (Boston, 1858–62).

Much of the work on slavery in the colonial period has been written at the level of state history. Early in the twentieth century platoons of graduate students were set upon topics which conceived of slavery and free Negroes principally in institutional terms; the result is a large corpus of state histories which vary considerably. Two of the best and most useful were aimed at free Negroes but included much material on slavery as a system: John H. Russell, *The Free Negro in Virginia, 1619–1865* (Baltimore, 1913); and James M. Wright, *The Free Negro in Maryland, 1634–1860* (N. Y., 1921). A more thorough study was Edward R. Turner, *The Negro in Pennsylvania, Slavery—Servitude—Freedom, 1639–1861* (Washington, 1911). A more recent book is thorough but far from closing the subject and like all these studies does little to explain the genesis of the Negro's condition: Lorenzo Johnston Greene, *The Negro in Colonial New England, 1620–1776* (N. Y., 1942). Edgar J. McManus, *A History of Negro Slavery in New York* (Syracuse, 1966) surveys the situation in an important colony, but so many of its assertions are supported or rather unsupported by wildly inaccurate shotgun documentation that the book is unsafe for use.

An extremely helpful but non-interpretive work which contains fascinating material has not been published: James H. Johnston, Race Relations in Virginia and Miscegenation in the South (unpubl. Ph.D. diss., University of Chicago, 1937) —available on interlibrary loan. It is unfortunate that South Carolina has received perhaps the least attention of any important state, owing in part to relative paucity and inaccessability of the original sources. There is very interesting material, however, in Frank J. Klingberg, *An Appraisal of the Negro in Colonial South Carolina: A Study in Americanization* (Washington, 1941), which is based largely on S.P.G. materials. Another exception, written by someone with very close acquaintance with South Carolina sources, is the excellent article by M. Eugene Sirmans, "The Legal Status of the Slave in South Carolina, 1670–1740," *Jour. Southern Hist.*, 28 (1962), 462–73. Virginia has been more fortunate. Edmund S. Morgan, *Virginians at Home: Family Life in the Eighteenth Century* (Williamsburg, 1952) contains a good discussion of slave life. Extremely interesting results of a thorough combing of the sources are presented by Gerald Mullin, Slave Resistance in Eighteenth-Century Virginia (unpubl. Ph.D. diss., University of California, Berkeley, 1967). A more localized study seems to me to be the best single description of Negro life in the eighteenth century: Thad W. Tate, Jr., *The Negro in Eighteenth-Century Williamsburg* (Charlottesville, 1966) has a significance which extends far beyond the colonial capital. Finally, a book which bears directly upon an important period is Robert McColley, *Slavery and Jeffersonian Virginia* (Urbana, 1964); it reaches rather different conclusions than I have presented concerning the feelings of Virginians about slavery. McColley rightly stresses the importance of antislavery views among men animated by religious impulses. In calling them "the true emancipators" and in contrasting them to rationalist gentlemen planters who are presented as not really wanting to do anything about slavery, his study seems to me not to do justice to the facts. It rests heavily on the illogical presumption that because Virginia planters did not in fact succeed in abolishing slavery they did not wish to do so.

Historical writing on the opposition to slavery in America has been powerfully shaped, as have discussions of slavery, by the writers' own attitudes. There is no single work which covers adequately the development of antislavery in the eighteenth century, a fact which in itself reflects a prevalent partiality in approach. Thomas E. Drake, *Quakers and Slavery in America* (New Haven, 1950) covers his material meticulously and praises the Quaker record. It may be balanced by an excellent study which on occasion leans too far the other way: Sydney V. James, *A People Among Peoples: Quaker Benevolence in Eighteenth-Century America* (Cambridge, Mass., 1963). Dwight Lowell Dumond, *Antislavery: The Crusade for Freedom in America* (Ann Arbor, 1961) is a sweeping neo-abolitionist survey which permits moral righteousness to rewrite history in its own image. A good account of a related movement is Wylie Sypher, *Guinea's Captive Kings: British Anti-Slavery Literature of the XVIIIth Century* (Chapel Hill, 1942). Michael Kraus, "Slavery Reform in the Eighteenth Century: An Aspect of Transatlantic Intellectual Cooperation," *Pennsylvania Magazine of History and Biography*, 60 (1936), 53–66, makes a case for treating antislavery as an international development, as evidently David Brion Davis will in his forthcoming volumes. I think, however, that there still remains value in searching for indigenous, unique aspects of American antislavery. A useful survey is by Arthur Zilversmit, *The First Emancipation: The Abolition of Slavery in the North* (Chicago and London, 1967). Leon F. Litwack, "The Abolitionist Dilemma:

The Antislavery Movement and the Northern Negro," *New England Quarterly*, 34 (1961), 50–73, shows how in a later period white men could be badly trapped between their dislike of slavery and racial discrimination and their dislike of complete social equality for Negroes. There is a useful survey by William Sumner Jenkins, *Pro-Slavery Thought in the Old South* (Chapel Hill, 1935).

The Christianization of Africans in America has not been adequately covered in our historical literature. A good deal of piecemeal work has been done (and cited in the footnotes especially to chapter 5), but there is only one inadequate, though pioneering survey, Carter G. Woodson, *The History of the Negro Church*, 2d ed. (Washington, 1921). There are few fields in American history in such crying need of investigation.

As should be evident in the body of this book, it is impossible to discuss attitudes toward Negroes in early America without also dealing with attitudes toward Indians. The central work on the subject, Roy Harvey Pearce, *The Savages of America: A Study of the Indian and the Idea of Civilization*, rev. ed. (Baltimore, 1965), focuses upon the concept of civilization. This provides a very illuminating but occasionally distortive view, as is made plain in a review discussion by David Bidney, "The Idea of the Savage in North American Ethnohistory," *Journal of the History of Ideas*, 15 (1954), 322–27. That white Americans living on the frontier found the Indians rather less than totally admirable is made clear by Lewis O. Saum, "The Fur Trader and the Noble Savage," *American Quarterly*, 15 (1963), 554–71. It is symptomatic of the prevailing need for further work concerning attitudes toward Indians that the only general work on Indian slavery is a half-century old: Almon Wheeler Lauber, *Indian Slavery in Colonial Times within the Present Limits of the United States* (N. Y., 1913).

Attitudes toward other peoples are sometimes called anthropology. For purposes of this study several historical works on ideas about man's nature have proved useful for comprehending the broader intellectual contexts into which perceptions of Negroes were fitted by white men. Wilhelm E. Mühlmann gives a comprehensive survey in his *Geschichte der Anthropologie* (Bonn, 1948). Another history of ideas, John C. Greene, *The Death of Adam: Evolution and Its Impact on Western Thought* (Ames, Iowa, 1959), deals with many prominent intellectuals who grappled with the problem of human variation but fails to come fully to grips with the materials covered. The magnificent monograph by Arthur O. Lovejoy, *The Great Chain of Being: A Study of the History of an Idea . . .* (Cambridge, Mass., 1936) unfortunately weakens at the end in discussing eighteenth-century science; it takes an approach to "ideas" in history which is very different from the one in this book. Daniel J. Boorstin, *The Lost World of Thomas Jefferson* (N. Y., 1948) helped shape my thinking about Jeffersonian anthropology; it is a brilliant study which may perhaps be faulted on grounds that it homogenizes a rather disparate group of thinkers and does not deal with changes in Jefferson's thinking.

There are also a few studies bearing more directly upon the history of the idea of race and of race prejudice in America. Thomas F. Gossett, *Race: The History of an Idea in America* (Dallas, 1963), summarizes a good deal of interesting material, as does I. A. Newby, *Jim Crow's Defense: Anti-Negro Thought in America, 1900–1930* (Baton Rouge, 1965). John C. Greene, "The American Debate on the Negro's Place in Nature, 1780–1815," *Jour. of the Hist. of Ideas*, 15 (1954), 384–96 surveys some of the sources I have discussed in chapters 12, 13, and 14. A superior study is William Stanton, *The Leopard's Spots: Scientific Attitudes Toward Race in America, 1815–59* (Chicago, 1960).

So far as I am aware, the first attempt at learning the history of the ideology of race prejudice was made by one of the assistants in the project headed by Gunnar Myrdal; he was at first given six months to complete his report (!) but received several months' extension after making a case for the complexity of his assignment. Guion G. Johnson, *A History of Racial Ideologies in the United States, with Reference to the Negro* (1940), is in typescript in the Schomburg Collection, New York Public Library; a microfilmed copy is available for purchase. Another somewhat tentative probe into the problem was originally, I take it, an M.A. thesis, published as Naomi Friedman Goldstein, *The Roots of Prejudice against the Negro in the United States* (Boston, 1948).

More is to be learned than from these somewhat sketchy studies by reading in some of the books which deal with slavery and race relations in the Americas on an international scale. With few exceptions I have deliberately chosen not to draw comparisons between the English and the other European colonies in the New World for reasons stated in the introduction. In the years after World War II many such comparisons appeared; indeed there developed something of a controversy which generated a good deal of scholarly smoke which has inhibited understanding of the history of race relations in the United States as well as in Latin America. Perhaps the seminal study was a brief discussion by Frank Tannenbaum, *Slave and Citizen; The Negro in the Americas* (N. Y., 1947) which stressed that the slave was accorded a moral personality in Latin (particularly Portuguese) America and that in British America his status as a human being was denied. According to this view Latin American slavery was a less harsh and rigid system and could finally be abolished in the nineteenth century without the aid of a great armed conflict. The persistence of the Roman law of slavery in the Iberian countries and the great strength and leverage of the Roman Catholic church in the Latin colonies meant that the slave was accorded legitimacy as a person and was given opportunities to pass over into freedom which did not exist in North America. These points were linked to the proposition that there existed little racial prejudice in modern Latin America, again especially Brazil.

This last was a major thesis of a passionate, evocative re-creation of Brazilian life by Gilberto Freyre, *The Masters and the Slaves: A Study in the Development of Brazilian Civilization*, trans. Samuel Putnam, 2d Eng. ed. rev. (N. Y., 1956), one which was both widely accepted and severely challenged by historians and social scientists. There seems no point in reviewing this literature here except to say that it is now clear that Freyre greatly underrated the amount of race consciousness in Brazil. One foremost critic, C. R. Boxer (see his *Race Relations in the Portuguese Colonial Empire, 1415–1825* [Oxford, 1963] and *The Golden Age of Brazil: 1695–1750. Growing Pains of a Colonial Society* [Berkeley and Los Angeles, 1963]) virtually exploded Freyre's contention and with it the notion that Portuguese slavery was especially mild and benevolent, but in doing so he lapsed into the polemical tone which has marred so much discussion of the relative demerits of the various European slave systems.

Tannenbaum's suggestions were picked up by Stanley M. Elkins, *Slavery: A Problem in American Institutional and Intellectual Life* (Chicago, 1959), a work which did a great deal to fasten the attention of scholars on the impact of slavery upon the Negro's personality. The Elkins book derived the presumed greater harshness and rigidity of English slavery from "the dynamics of unopposed capitalism" and from the institutional weakness of the English church(es) in the colonies. There is great merit in these points, but Elkins's assumption that the Negro enslaved by Englishmen was infantilized by a closed system of slavery greatly distorts the facts, which he made little attempt to investigate. The impact of slavery upon Negroes is not the subject of this book, but I hope to write on this interesting matter shortly, focusing on the interaction between white attitudes toward Negroes and slavery and African acculturation during the century and a half prior to Emancipation.

In the hands of most scholars the comparative approach has proved to be extremely dangerous. Many absurd assertions have been made about both Latin and North American slavery and race relations by people who have undertaken to compare two things about one or both of which they were ignorant. To list the comparative studies which are in demonstrable error concerning the English colonies would be to list virtually all such studies. An exception

is David Brion Davis, *The Problem of Slavery in Western Culture,*
which manages to present a judicious picture of the similarities
between Latin and British slavery, though one can readily detect
the deleterious influence of an unjustified scholarly controversy in
the fact that he found it necessary so often to explain what conditions in the various colonies were *not.* His account may be assayed
against the evidence in Herbert S. Klein, *Slavery in the Americas:
A Contemporary Study of Virginia and Cuba* (Chicago, 1967).

Recently, two other brief books have offered valuable commentaries on European treatment of the overseas peoples. Marvin Harris, *Patterns of Race in the Americas* (N. Y., 1964) draws an
illuminating distinction between the patterns of race relations
which emerged in the highland areas of Latin America, where
Indians remained the largest group, and the lowland regions, where
large plantations and masses of Negroes predominated. As a way of
getting at current patterns of race relations in Latin America this
seems a very valuable distinction, but the concluding discussion on
the relationship between slavery and prejudice makes very little
sense concerning English America. A very different but equally
valuable and interesting little study is Henri Baudet, *Paradise on
Earth: Some Thoughts on European Images of Non-European Man,*
trans. Elizabeth Wentholt (New Haven and London, 1965), which
rightly seeks to understand these images as serving a functional
need built into European culture. The book shows that European
fashions in assessments of other peoples have fluctuated considerably from the middle ages on, though in the long run the American
Indian has been accorded the greatest admiration. His suggestions
concerning the myth of "le bon éthiopien" in the middle ages are
extremely interesting: "Ethiopia" was taken to be a Christian kingdom and therefore a strategically situated potential ally in the
struggle against Islam; "Ethiopians" filtered into European dreams
and iconography, most obviously in the case of the three Magi. I
think perhaps that the strength and the favorability of this assessment have been somewhat overestimated, though the essential point
stands. I have not discussed this tradition in the present study
because I found no evidence that it affected sixteenth-century Englishmen, who until the voyages were situated on the outskirts of
Europe. Henri Baudet himself refers to the connection of these
thoughts with "Latin Christianity," and it is suggestive that he
employed a French term to describe what later events made for
Englishmen in America "a good nigger."

When one turns to studies which deal with problems of prejudice
and the concept of race as they pertain to the Negro in America one
is confronted by a massive corpus of literature. By mentioning a few
such works it is scarcely possible to do more than draw upon one's
own personal preferences. A number of works by historians deal

with problems which from the perspective of this study seem very much like the end results of trends under way for centuries. I would single out as being especially useful several books which deal with the period after Reconstruction. C. Vann Woodward, *Origins of the New South, 1877–1913* ([Baton Rouge], 1951) is a work of major importance; his *The Strange Career of Jim Crow*, 2d rev. ed. (N. Y., 1966) deals directly with the controversial problem of the origin of racial segregation. Rayford W. Logan, *The Betrayal of the Negro from Rutherford B. Hayes to Woodrow Wilson*, new ed. (N. Y., 1965) surveys a dismal story. It is important that attitudes toward the Negro be kept in the largest context possible and to this end John Higham, *Strangers in the Land: Patterns of American Nativism, 1860–1925* (New Brunswick, 1955) is extremely helpful. W. J. Cash, *The Mind of the South* (Anchor Books, Garden City, 1954), is an impressively perceptive study which shows the importance of recognizing the influence of "frontier" elements upon the South's development. One of the best books on the current racial crisis is Charles E. Silberman, *Crisis in Black and White* (N. Y., 1964).

Social scientists have for a generation been crawling through every nook and cranny of the nation in search of answers to real and non-existent questions concerning Negro-white relations. It is impossible to discuss even a few of the results here, so I will merely mention one and refer readers to a good library and a daily newspaper. John Dollard, *Caste and Class in a Southern Town*, 3d ed. (Anchor Books, Garden City, n.d.) was a pioneering study in 1937, now dated but still valuable for its sensitive re-creation of life in a town in the deep South; its lack of rigid system will suit the biases of historians.

Of works dealing directly with the problem of race prejudice, Lillian Smith, *Killers of the Dream*, rev. ed. (Anchor Books, Garden City, 1961) seems to me one of the very best to grapple with the white southerner's attitude toward Negroes; the author brought to the problem the sympathies of a southern liberal and a superb amateur psychiatrist. A more sweeping survey was made by a Swedish scholar, Gunnar Myrdal, with the assistance of Richard Sterner and Arnold Rose, *An American Dilemma: The Negro Problem and Modern Democracy*, 2 vols. (N. Y., 1944), a work which the authors did not have the nerve to call "The White Problem," though its approach and conclusions concerning the tension between American ideals and practices would justify this now fashionable title. It has been criticized by Herbert Aptheker, *The Negro People in America: A Critique of Gunnar Myrdal's "An American Dilemma"* (N. Y., 1946); a recapitulation of the conflict between what have been called the idealist and the materialist schools is in Ernest Kaiser, "Racial Dialectics: The Aptheker-Myrdal School Controversy," *Phylon*, 9 (1948),

295–302. Aptheker has further elaborated his views in "The Central Theme of Southern History—A Re-examination," in his *Toward Negro Freedom* (N. Y., 1956), 182–91. To claim that "the central theme of Southern history, in my opinion, is the drive of the rulers to maintain themselves in power, and the struggle against this by the oppressed and the exploited" seems to me not so much wrong as insufficient. One does not have to accept Ulrich Phillips's view of Negroes to agree with his contention in "The Central Theme of Southern History," *American Historical Review*, 33 (1928), 30–43, that the white man's determination to maintain white supremacy has constituted the driving impulse in the history of southern society.

Of the more theoretically oriented discussions of racial prejudice, I have been especially impressed by the common sense and balance which pervade Gordon Allport, *The Nature of Prejudice* (abridged, without much loss) (Anchor Books, Garden City, 1958). A very large proportion of the studies by social psychologists and sociologists have been obtuse to the influence of historical experience, and this fact has been pointed out by non-historians such as Paul Kecskemeti, "The Psychological Theory of Prejudice: Does It Underrate the Role of Social History?" *Commentary*, 18 (1954), 359–66, and in an especially telling critique by Herbert G. Blumer, "Reflections on Theory of Race Relations," in Andrew W. Lind, ed., *Race Relations in World Perspective: Papers Read at the Conference on Race Relations in World Perspective, Honolulu, 1954* (Honolulu, 1955), 3–21. Of studies bearing upon the problem of European treatment of colored peoples in other areas of the globe I have found the following especially illuminating: I. D. MacCrone, *Race Attitudes in South Africa: Historical, Experimental and Psychological Studies* (London, 1937), and his "Race Attitudes: An Analysis and Interpretation," in Ellen Hellman, ed., assisted by Leah Abrahams, *Handbook on Race Relations in South Africa* (Cape Horn, 1949), chap. 33; [Dominique] O. Mannoni, *Prospero and Caliban: The Psychology of Colonization*, trans. Pamela Powesland (London, 1956); and Philip Mason, *Prospero's Magic: Some Thoughts on Class and Race* (London, 1962), an interesting and suggestive study by a sometime civil servant in India which is at once very perceptive and very British.

For a study of attitudes toward a racial group it seems to me indispensable to have clearly in mind precisely what *race* is and is not. Two older works on the Negro's physiology are still unsupplanted and moderately trustworthy: W. Montague Cobb, "Physical Anthropology of the American Negro," *American Journal of Physical Anthropology*, 29, (1942), 113–223, and Julian Herman Lewis, *The Biology of the Negro* (Chicago, 1942). In general, however, the best working rule is not to trust any work written before 1960 and exercise extreme caution with any after that. In revulsion against the racism which prevailed during the first third of this century, many scholars, such as Ruth Benedict and Gene Weltfish, *Race: Science and Politics. Including the Races of Mankind* (Compass Books, N. Y., 1959) and M. F. Ashley Montagu, *Man's Most Dangerous Myth: The Fallacy of Race*, 3d ed. (N. Y., 1952) threw out the baby of race with the bathwater of racism: the analogy is as unfortunate as the attempts in these books to wish human racial differences out of existence. A good idea of the controversy among scientists which swirled around the concept of race at mid-century may be gained by reading United Nations Educational, Scientific and Cultural Organization, *The Race Concept: Results of an Inquiry* (Paris, 1951 [1953]). That the issue of mental equality was (and is) very much alive is evident in William M. McCord and Nicholas J. Demerath III, "Negro versus White Intelligence: A Continuing Controversy," *Harvard Educational Review*, 28 (1958), 120–35. One of the best of the recent books to deal with the problem of race at a popular level is Philip Mason, *Common Sense About Race* (N. Y., 1961). The least unpersuasive case for Negro racial inferiority is by Carleton Putnam, *Race and Reason: A Yankee View* (Washington, 1961), whose principal qualification for writing on the subject seems to have been Yankee ancestry.

As suggested in the Note on the Concept of Race, there has been a revolution in scientific thinking about race in the last fifteen years. Of the many studies Stanley M. Garn, *Human Races,* rev. 2d printing (Springfield, Ill., 1962) is the best single book on race. Theodosius Dobzhansky, *Mankind Evolving: The Evolution of the Human Species* (New Haven and London, 1962) is an absorbing treatment; a different view is presented by Carleton S. Coon, *Living Races of Man* (N. Y., 1965).

Finally, I should like to enter a plea for the relevance of a great many books which have nothing to do, strictly speaking, with attitudes toward Negroes. My own thoughts on the subject have been affected by works of literature, psychological studies, and embracive interpretations of American culture in ways about which I am no doubt only partly conscious. Which leads to the core of the assumptions which have supported my reading of the historical sources in this book: that it is essential always to ask why did he write that?

SELECT LIST OF FULL TITLES

(This list is comprised only of works which are cited in more than one chapter and whose short titles are not easy guides into a library catalog.)

Allen, Don Cameron, *The Legend of Noah: Renaissance Rationalism in Art, Science, and Letters* (Urbana, Ill., 1949).

Ames, Susie M., *Studies of the Virginia Eastern Shore in the Seventeenth Century* (Richmond, 1940).

Anburey, Thomas, *Travels through the Interior Parts of America*, 2 vols. (Boston, 1923).

[Annals of Congress], *The Debates and Proceedings in the Congress of the United States, 1789–1824*, 42 vols. (Washington, 1834–56). See chap. 8, note 20.

Aptheker, Herbert, ed., *A Documentary History of the Negro People in the United States* (N.Y., 1951).

Bacon, Rev. Thomas, *Four Sermons, Upon the Great and Indispensible Duty of All Christian Masters and Mistresses . . .* (London, 1750).

[Bacon, Thomas], *Two Sermons, Preached to a Congregation of Black Slaves . . .* (London, 1749).

Bendyshe, T[homas], "The History of Anthropology," Anthropological Society of London, *Memoirs*, 1 (1863–64).

Benson, Adolph B., trans. and ed., *The America of 1750: Peter Kalm's Travels in North America. The English Version of 1770*, 2 vols. (N.Y., 1937).

Beverley, Robert, *The History and Present State of Virginia*, ed. Louis B. Wright (Chapel Hill, 1947).

Boucher, Jonathan, *A View of the Causes and Consequences of the American Revolution . . .* (London, 1797).

Brackett, Jeffrey R., *The Negro in Maryland* (Baltimore, 1889).

Bradley, Abraham, *A New Theory of the Earth . . .* (Wilkes-Barre, Pa., 1801).

Bricknell, John, *The Natural History of North-Carolina . . .* (Dublin, 1737).

Brookes, George S., *Friend Anthony Benezet* (Phila., 1937).

Bruce, Philip A., *Economic History of Virginia in the Seventeenth Century* . . . , 2 vols. (N.Y., 1896).

Buffon, [Georges Louis Leclerc], Comte de, *Histoire Naturelle, Générale et Particulière* . . . , 36 vols. (Paris, 1749–88).

Burnaby, Andrew, *Travels through the Middle Settlements in North-America* . . . (London, 1775).

Calhoun, Arthur, *A Social History of the American Family* . . . , 3 vols. (Cleveland, 1917–19).

Catterall, Helen T., ed., *Judicial Cases Concerning American Slavery and the Negro*, 5 vols. (Washington, 1926–37).

Cawley, Robert R., *The Voyagers and Elizabethan Drama* (Boston, 1938).

Chase, Eugene P., trans. and ed., *Our Revolutionary Forefathers; the Letters of François, Marquis de Barbé-Marbois during His Residence in the United States as Secretary of the French Legation, 1779–1785* (N.Y., 1929).

Chastellux, Marquis de, *Travels in North America in the Years 1780, 1781 and 1782*, trans. and ed. Howard C. Rice, Jr., 2 vols. (Chapel Hill, 1963).

Churchill, John and Awsham, comps., *A Collection of Voyages and Travels* . . . , 6 vols. (London, 1704–32).

Clark, Elmer E., J. Manning Potts, and Jacob S. Payton, eds., *The Journal and Letters of Francis Asbury*, 3 vols. (London and Nashville, 1958).

Cook[e], Eben[ezer], *The Sot-weed Factor: Or a Voyage to Maryland* . . . (London, 1708).

[Cooper, David], *A Serious Address to the Rulers of America, on the Inconsistency of Their Conduct Respecting Slavery* . . . (Trenton, 1783).

Crawford, Charles, *Observations upon Negro-Slavery*, new ed. (Phila., 1790).

[Crèvecoeur, St. Jean de], *Letters from an American Farmer* . . . (London, 1782).

Davies, Samuel, *The Duty of Christians to Propagate Their Religion Among Heathens* . . . (London, 1758).

De P[auw, Cornelis], *Recherches Philosophiques sur les Américains* . . . , 3 vols. (Berlin, 1770).

Dexter, Franklin B., ed., *The Literary Diary of Ezra Stiles, D.D., LL.D., President of Yale College*, 3 vols. (N.Y., 1901).

Donnan, Elizabeth, ed., *Documents Illustrative of the History of the Slave Trade to America*, 4 vols. (Washington, 1930–35).

Drake, Thomas E., *Quakers and Slavery in America* (New Haven, 1950).

Du Bois, William Edward Burghardt, *Suppression of the African Slave-Trade* . . . (N.Y., 1896).

Eben, Carl T., trans., *Gottlieb Mittelberger's Journey to Pennsylvania in the Year 1750 and Return to Germany in the Year 1754* . . . (Phila., 1898).

Edwards, Bryan, *The History, Civil and Commercial, of the British Colonies in the West Indies*, 3d ed., 3 vols. (London, 1801).

Edwards, Jonathan, *The Injustice and Impolicy of the Slave-trade and of the Slavery of the Africans* . . . (Providence, 1792).

[Fleetwood], William, *A Sermon Preached before the Society for the Propagation of the Gospel in Foreign Parts* . . . (London, 1711).

Fontaine, James, *Memoirs of a Huguenot Family* . . . , trans. and ed. Ann Maury (N.Y., 1872).

Force, Peter, ed., *Tracts and Other Papers* . . . , 4 vols. (N.Y., 1947).

Franklin, John Hope, *The Free Negro in North Carolina, 1790–1860* (Chapel Hill, 1943).

[Gibson, Edmund], *Two Letters of the Lord Bishop of London* . . . (London, 1727).

Godwyn, Morgan, *The Negro's and Indians Advocate* . . . (London, 1680).

Goldsmith, Oliver, *An History of the Earth, and Animated Nature*, 8 vols. (London, 1774).

Grant, Anne, *Memoirs of an American Lady* . . . , ed. James Grant Wilson, 2 vols. (N.Y., 1901).

Greene, Lorenzo J., *The Negro in Colonial New England, 1620–1776* (N.Y., 1942).

Hart, Levi, *Liberty Described and Recommended* . . . (Hartford, 1775).

Hepburn, John, *The American Defence of the Christian Golden Rule* . . . (n.p., 1715).

[Hewat, Alexander], *An Historical Account of the Rise and Progress of the Colonies of South Carolina and Georgia*, 2 vols. (London, 1779).

Hopkins, Samuel, *A Dialogue Concerning the Slavery of the Africans* . . . (Norwich, Conn., 1776).

[Horsmanden, Daniel], *A Journal of the Proceedings in the Detection of the Conspiracy* . . . (N.Y., 1744).

Hughes, Griffith, *The Natural History of Barbados* (London, 1750).

Humphreys, [David], *An Account of the Endeavours Used by the Society for the Propagation of the Gospel in Foreign Parts* . . . (London, 1730).

Hurd, John Codman, *The Law of Freedom and Bondage in the United States*, 2 vols. (Boston, 1858–62).

Jernegan, Marcus W., *Laboring and Dependent Classes in Colonial America, 1607–1783* . . . (Chicago, 1931).

Johnston, James H., Race Relations in Virginia and Miscegenation in the South, 1776–1860 (unpubl. Ph.D. diss., University of Chicago, 1937).

Jones, Charles C., *The Religious Instruction of Negroes in the United States* (Savannah, 1842).

Jones, Hugh, *The Present State of Virginia . . .*, ed. Richard L. Morton (Chapel Hill, 1956).

Kames, Henry Home, Lord, *Sketches on the History of Man*, 2d ed., 4 vols. (Edinburgh, 1778).

Klingberg, Frank J., *Anglican Humanitarianism in Colonial New York* (Phila., 1940).

———, *An Appraisal of the Negro in Colonial South Carolina . . .* (Washington, 1941).

———, ed., *The Carolina Chronicle of Dr. Francis Le Jau, 1706–1717* (Berkeley and Los Angeles, 1956).

Lawson, John, *A New Voyage to Carolina . . .* (London, 1709).

[Leslie, Charles], *A New History of Jamaica . . .*, [2d ed.] (London, 1740).

Lind, James, *An Essay on Diseases Incidental to Europeans in Hot Climates . . .*, 3d ed. (London, 1777).

[Long, Edward], *Candid Reflections upon the Judgment Lately Awarded by the Court of King's Bench . . .* (London, 1772).

[———], *The History of Jamaica . . .*, 3 vols. (London, 1774).

Luffman, John, *A Brief Account of the Island of Antigua . . .* (London, 1789).

Melish, John, *Travels through the United States of America . . . 1806 . . . 1811 . . .*, [2d ed.] (London, 1818).

Minutes of the Proceedings of a Convention of Delegates from the Abolition Societies . . . (Phila., 1794). See chap. 9, note 5.

Moore, George H., *Notes on the History of Slavery in Massachusetts* (N.Y., 1866).

Morris, Richard B., *Government and Labor in Early America* (N.Y., 1946).

Olbrich, Emil, *The Development of Sentiment on Negro Suffrage to 1860* (Madison, Wis., 1912).

Otis, James, *The Rights of the British Colonies Asserted and Proved* (Boston, 1764).

Park, Edwards A., *Memoir of the Life and Character of Samuel Hopkins, D.D.*, 2d ed. (Boston, 1854).

Perry, William Stevens, ed., *Historical Collections Relating to the American Colonial Church*, 5 vols. in 4 (Hartford, Conn., 1870–78).

Phillips, Ulrich B., *American Negro Slavery . . .* (N.Y. and London, 1918).

Ramsay, James, *An Essay on the Treatment and Conversion of African Slaves in the British Sugar Colonies* (London, 1784).

Rice, David, *Slavery Inconsistent with Justice and Good Policy* . . . (Phila., 1792, reprinted London, 1793).

Romans, Bernard, *Concise Natural History of East and West Florida* . . . (N.Y., 1775).

[Schaw, Janet], *Journal of a Lady of Quality* . . . , ed. Evangeline Walker Andrews and Charles M. Andrews, 3d ed. (New Haven, 1939).

Sewall, Samuel, *The Selling of Joseph* . . . (Boston, 1700).

Singleton, John, *A General Description of the West-Indian Islands* . . . (Barbados, 1767).

Sloane, Hans, *A Voyage to the Islands Madera, Barbados, Nieves, S. Christophers and Jamaica* . . . , 2 vols. (London, 1707–25).

Smith, William, *A Natural History of Nevis* . . . (Cambridge, Eng., 1745).

Smyth, J[ohn] F[erdinand] D., *A Tour in the United States of America* . . . , 2 vols. (London, 1784).

Stedman, J[ohn] G., *Narrative of a Five Years' Expedition, against the Revolted Negroes of Surinam and Guiana* . . . , 2 vols. (London, 1796).

Steiner, Bernard C., *History of Slavery in Connecticut* (Baltimore, 1893).

Stokes, Anthony, *A View of the Constitution of the British Colonies* . . . (London, 1783).

Thornely, Samuel, ed., *The Journal of Nicholas Cresswell, 1774–1777* (N.Y., 1924).

Thorpe, Francis N., ed., *The Federal and State Constitutions, Colonial Charters, and Other Organic Laws* . . . , 7 vols. (Washington, 1909).

Tryon, Thomas, *Friendly Advice to the Gentlemen-Planters of the East and West Indies* . . . ([London], 1684).

Turner, Edward R., *The Negro in Pennsylvania, Slavery—Servitude—Freedom, 1639–1861* (Washington, 1911).

Wallace, David D., *The History of South Carolina*, 4 vols. (N.Y., 1934).

Weeks, Stephen B., *Southern Quakers and Slavery* . . . (Baltimore, 1896).

Williams, John Rogers, ed., *Philip Vickers Fithian: Journal and Letters, 1767–1774*, 2 vols. (Princeton, 1900–34).

Williamson, Hugh, *Observations on the Climate in Different Parts of America* . . . (N.Y., 1811).

Woodson, Carter G., *The History of the Negro Church*, 2d ed. (Washington, 1921).

Wright, James M., *The Free Negro in Maryland, 1634–1860* (N.Y., 1921).

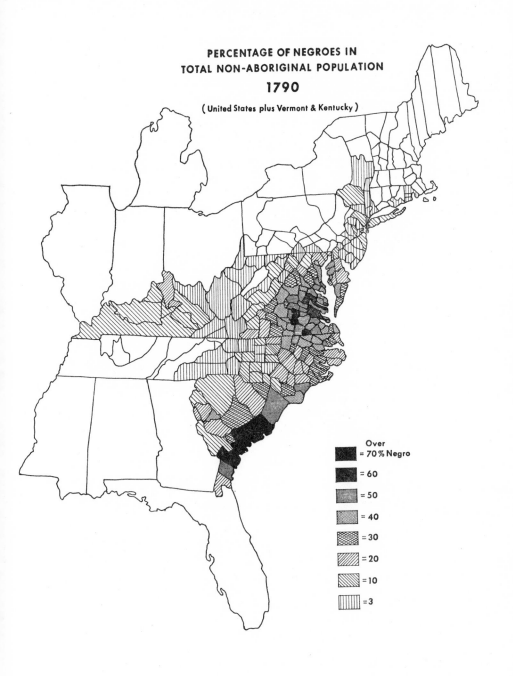

PERCENTAGE OF NEGROES IN
TOTAL NON-ABORIGINAL POPULATION
1790
(United States plus Vermont & Kentucky)

Over
= 70 % Negro
= 60
= 50
= 40
= 30
= 20
= 10
= 3

INDEX

A

Aaron, 574

Abolition. *See* Antislavery; Emancipation

Abolition societies. *See* Antislavery societies

Academy of Sciences (Paris), 449

Account of Two Voyages to New-England (John Josselyn), 245

Acculturation: of Indians, 94; Negroes learn English, 96n; of Germans, 102; use of hoe, 113; and sex among slaves, 160–61; effect of conversion, 183–84; pace of African, 184; and mental ability, 190. *See also* Churches; Conversion; Great Awakening; Negroes

Acquired characters, 244–45, 516–17, 527, 540. *See also* Color; Human reproduction

Adam, 23, 41, 242–43, 502, 525

Adam (slave of Saffin), 199

Adams, Abigail, 462

Adams, John, 264, 337n, 396, 462

Adams, John Quincy, 395

Ægopithecus, 30

Africa: European contact with, 3–4, 5–6, 12, 23; as land of new monsters, 30–31; associated with sexuality, 33; ancient reputation of, 39; social structure in, 58; slavery in, 58, 89; hoes used in, 113; cartography of, 158; inoculation in, 202–4; albinism in, 251–52; common diseases in, 260; in antislavery literature, 283, 370; in proslavery writings, 305–8; American hopes for Christianization of, 423–24; yellow fever in, 529. *See also* Apes; Beasts; Climate; Colonization; Color; Guinea; Heathenism; Orangoutangs; Savagery; Sexuality; Slave trade

African Episcopal Church of St. Thomas, 423–24

African Methodist Episcopal Church, 423

Africans: in England, 6, 34, 60, 224, 237; in Europe, 14–15; religious practices, 23; manner of living, 24–25, 28, 39–40; tribal distinctions among, 24–25, 90, 102, 111, 185; social order among, 26; helplessness against Europeans, 91; standard of dress, 161; native, in colonies, 184; in northern Africa, 254; paint devil white, 258. *See also* Hottentots; Moors; Slave trade; Slaves

Airey, Rev. (Anglican in Md.), 186

Akin, James, 121–22

Albany, N. Y., 105, 144, 392

Albinos, 585; discovered among Negroes, 243, 249–50; speculation concerning, 250–52; Negro called leprous, 258; discussed by Jefferson, 458; study of after Revolution, 521–25; S. S. Smith on, 533

Alexandria, Va., 320, 386, 400

Alison, Rev. Francis, 299

Allen, Rev. Cary, 363

Allen, John, 290

Allen, Rev. Richard, 422–23, 455, 528

Alsop, George, 193

Amalgamation. *See* Melting pot; Miscegenation

American Academy of Arts and Sciences, 355, 444

American Colonization Society, 566

American destiny: peopling of the continent, 69, 143, 269, 544, 547; as America itself, 115; compared to West Indian, 142–43; Paine on, 269; Stiles on, 269–70; and natural advantages of the continent, 288; meaning after Revolution, 332, 334–35; and miscegenation, 470, 580–81; Jefferson on,

480; aided by climate, 515, 540; and environmentalism, 537–38; belongs to whites, 541; exclusion of Negroes from, 547; violated by slaveholding, 562; and War of 1812, 566; as venture into a new world, 573–74. *See also* American Revolution; Miscegenation; National identity; Nationalism; Self-identity

American independence, 209, 333–36. *See also* American destiny; American Revolution; Declaration of Independence; National identity

American Magazine, 494

American Museum, 378–79, 419, 447, 497, 528

American Philosophical Society, 444, 486, 518, 521–22, 524

American Revolution: trends during and after, 264–65, 270–71; as turning point, 310–11; legacy, 332; and St. Domingo, 378; expected spreading of, 386–91; suggests all men crave liberty, 390–91; retreat from principles of, 401–2; and Negro voting, 414; betrayal of, 578–79; ideology of as cultural conscience, 579, 581. *See also* American independence; Declaration of Independence; Natural rights

Les Amis des Noirs, 376

Anality, 36, 39, 238, 256–57, 567–68

Anatomy, comparative, xiii, 222, 485; Tyson's early achievement, 32, 218–19; after Revolution, 497–502; J. A. Smith on, 505–6; effect of development of, 509; study of undermines environmentalism, 537; modern on races, 585. *See also* Color; Facial angle; Penis

Anglican Church, 206–7, 210, 211, 334, 418. *See also* Church of England

Anglicans, 199, 301. *See also* Ministers

Angola, 74

Animal Economy (John Hunter), 523

Animals, 16, 28, 218, 219. *See also* Beasts; individual animals

Anthropologists, 509, 534

Anthropomorpha, 221

Antifederalists, 325, 332, 360n

Antigonus, 12

Antigua, 154, 156n, 176n, 181. *See also* West Indies

Antislavery: Sewall on, 165, 195–96; slavery inconsistent with American liberty, 193–94, 279, 289–92, 333; among Quakers, 194–95, 196, 197,

256–57, 271–76; condemned by proponents of conversion, 197–98; abetted by religious revivals, 214; advocates on Negro's color, 255, 258, 545; advocated before Revolution, 278–80; and problem of savagery of Africans, 285–87; relationship to ideology of Revolution, 292–94; religious impulse in, 292–301; sinfulness of slavery, 297–301, 543–44; national action during Revolution, 298–300, 301–2; sectional pattern of, 301–2, 349; in Virginia, 303–4, 394–95; and concept of innateness, 305; petitions to Congress, 325, 326, 327, 328–30, 344, 388; decline of, 330, 346–47, 531, 565; writer denounces planter opulence, 333; after Revolution, 342, 486; and natural rights, 350–52; inattention to Negro's future condition, 352–54; gradualism of, 354; obstacles delineated, 362–63; becomes more humanitarian, 367; becomes sentimental, 368–72; weakened by ban on slave trade, 373; significance of failure of, 374; weakened by slave revolts, 374, 400–401; impact of St. Domingo on, 378–80; among Methodists and Baptists, 418–19; Jefferson's views, 430–35; and itch for order, 483; generates counter ideas of inequality, 485; and Chain of Being, 496, 504–5; advocates ignore Negro's physical characteristics, 509; S. S. Smith on, 515–16, 517; and albino Negroes, 519–20, 522; and miscegenation, 545; and colonization, 548–49. *See also* Colonization; Environmentalism; Humanitarianism; Mental ability; Prejudice; Quakers

Antislavery societies, 343–45, 346, 347; Pa., 290, 325, 343–44, 359, 424, 446, 447, 449; Alexandria, Va., 320, 386, 400; N. Y., 344, 355, 359, 362, 448; Md., 348, 448; Quaker dominance in, 359–60; Conn., 359, 543; France, 376; Va., 400; weakened by slave revolts, 400–401; Providence, 550. *See also* Convention of antislavery societies

Apes: associated with Negroes, 29–32, 65, 235–39, 490–97, 510; Linnaeus on, 222, 227; in Chain of Being, 222, 223, 225, 228, 229–32, 305; Blumenbach on, 223, 230; in Camper's gradation, 225–26; Buffon on, 225, 230; effect of geographical location, 229; facial angle of, 505. *See also* Orang-outangs

Apostles' Creed, 211
Appleton, Nathaniel, 286
Appomattox, Va., 574
Apprentices, 62, 80
Apprenticeship, 52, 60, 63, 406
Archdale, Gov. John, 92*n*
Archer, Dr. John, 530
Aristocracy, 115, 333, 415. *See also* Social hierarchy
Aristotle, 12, 31, 179, 309
Arms. *See* Militia; Slave codes
Army. *See* Continental Army; Militia
Asbury, Rev. Francis, 132*n*, 213*n*, 296, 363, 364–65, 419
Ascriptitius Glebae, 53
Asia Minor, 254
Asiatics, 217, 221, 240, 500, 505, 531. *See also* specific countries
Association, Continental, 302
Atkins, Dr. John, 17, 31–32
Atlantic Ocean, 45, 47
Attitudes, viii, 149–50, 470–71, 586–87. *See also* Prejudice
Attorney-General (of England), 128, 181

B

Babel, Tower of, 245, 538
Baboons, 29, 237, 238, 305
Bacon, Francis, 34, 224, 520
Bacon, John, 383
Bacon, Rev. Thomas, 182, 191–92
Bacon's Rebellion, 79
Bagwell, John, 513
Baker, Henry, 244–45
Baker, Robert, 4
Baltimore, 357–58, 380, 382
Banneker, Benjamin, 449–52, 454–55, 486
Baptism, 73, 93. *See also* Conversion
Baptists, 155, 199, 212, 213, 396, 418–19
Barbados: population, 63, 152*n*, 176; Irish and Scots in, 63, 87, 87*n*, 88; slavery develops in, 64–65; contact with New England, 67; influence on S. C., 84–85; prohibits kidnapping of white children, 86; insurrection and sex in, 152, 156; castration in, 156; compared to Jamaica, 176–77; issue of conversion in, 185, 188; Fox in, 194; Ligon describes Negroes in, 232; slaves likened to apes in, 238. *See also* Population; West Indies
Barbary, 33, 38
Barbé-Marbois, François, 283, 432
Bard, David, 385, 388

Bardon, Edward, 251
Barlow, Joel, 334, 454
Barton, Benjamin Smith, 521
Bartram, William, 474
Bastille, 376
Battell, Andrew, 33, 250
Baxter, Rev. Richard, 200, 214
Baynes, Rev. Paul, 61–62, 192
Beastly (term), 33
Beasts: Negroes seen as analogous to, 28, 33; in *Othello*, 38; slaves in same condition as, 50, 54, 56, 190; Negro conspirators likened to, 119; sense of man as one of, 138; slaves castrated like, 156*n*; affinity of men with in Chain of Being, 228–30; Negroes not thought literally to be, 230–34, 365, 493–94; scientific ideas of Negro's nature and, 234–36; question of taxing slaves like, 322–23; intermixture of with Negroes refuted, 494–95. *See also* Animals; Chain of Being; Sexuality; Species
Beattie, James, 446
Beauty: English ideal of, 8–11; in Negroes, 27–28; whites' held superior, 164–65; in Europeans, 248, 501–2; Jefferson on, 458–59, 464, 490; U. S. climate called favorable to, 515. *See also* Blackness; Whiteness
Behn, Aphra, 9, 27–28
Belknap, Rev. Jeremy, 456–57, 555–58, 560
Bell, Gov. Philip, 65
Benezet, Anthony, 338, 424; corresponds with S. P. G., 197; as publicist, 272; utilizes accounts of slave trade, 274; sees slavery producing contempt for Negroes, 275; on Negro's mental ability, 282–83; denies barbarism of Africa, 286; and natural rights, 289; on sin of slave trade, 300; quotes English antislavery writer, 308–9; school for Negroes, 357, 422, 446
Bering Straits, 240
Berkeley, Dean George, 191
Bermuda, 78*n*, 79, 87, 88–89
Bernier, François, 217–18
Best, George, 15, 17, 40–42, 43
Bestial (term), 33
Bestiaries. *See* Beasts
Bible, 6; on human unity, 12, 22, 27; quoted, 15, 34–35, 70*n*; story of Noah and Ham in, 17; relationship to natural history, 19, 488, 502, 506–8, 534, 540; creation of man in, 22; used to

explain African religion, 23; function for Puritans, 40, 199; on enslavement, 55n, 68, 199; as Hebraic law, 67–68, 69, 105, 294; works in Negro's favor in New England, 69–70; used by anti-slavery advocates, 195–96, 256, 273, 274, 294, 327; in proslavery argument, 201; Protestant emphasis on, 211; color imagery in, 215; cited on separate creations, 240, 502; Kames on Mosaic account in, 245; read by Phyllis Wheatley, 283–84; bogus proslavery passage, 307; less relevant to equality in Revolutionary era, 307–8; thirty-nine-lashes punishment in, 408; on relationship between man and beasts, 493–94; defense of in ante-bellum U. S., 509; defended by Rush, 520; satirized, 525; C. Jones on, 538. *See also* Ham; Jews

Bile, 13, 19n, 458, 514, 519n, 526

Bill of Rights, 350

Billey (slave of Madison), 303

Bird, Samuel, 401n

Birmingham Meeting (Pa.), 420

Bishop of London, 186, 188, 191, 207, 208

Black (term), 61, 95, 257

Blackbirds, 523

Blackmore, Sir Richard, 228–29

Blackness: early emphasis on Negro's, 4–6, 43; meaning for Englishmen, 7, 11; early reaction to Negro's, 9–11; as an infection, 15, 17, 518–21; as a curse, 19, 24; as God's providence, 19–20, 173; sets Negroes apart, 20, 21; linked with heathenism, 24, 27; inappropriate in the noble savage, 27–28; connection with apes, 30; and sexuality in *Othello*, 37–38; in Islam, 39n; meaning revealed in Bible, 41; serves badly to identify runaways, 108; and miscegenation, 146; of Negro's semen, 166; Mather on, 200–201; as protection against disease, 245n; as protection against heat, 245, 520, 526; as degeneration from original color, 248–49; of Negro's blood and brain, 249; as opposite color from Europeans', 252–53; serves unconscious needs, 255–57; meaning of in colonial America, 257–59; not extrapolated to Negro's internal organs, 259, 528; feared in American people, 270, 543, 544–45, 553–54; denied to be a justification for

slavery, 278–79; not permitted on stage in Charleston, 405; Negro Christians seen emerging from, 424; Jefferson on, 458; meaning of after Revolution, 512–13; thought to characterize Negroes, 516, 534; thought more permanent than whiteness, 516, 535, 540; purpose of, 525; and climatic theory, 525–27; as effect of sun, 531. *See also* Albinos; Antislavery; Color; Ham; Miscegenation; Prejudice; Whiteness

Blood: thought blackened by sun, 13; in New Testament, 22; as vehicle of human reproduction, 165–66; in Sewall's objection to miscegenation, 197; Negro's thought black, 249, 259; types, 583. *See also* Miscegenation

Blumenbach, Dr. Johann Friedrich: on Negro's penis, 158n; classifies mankind, 222–23; on Hottentots, 227; on apes and Negroes, 230; on albinism, 252; praises Phyllis Wheatley, 285; denounces Chain of Being, 507; influences S. S. Smith, 507–8, 531

Bob (slave missing mother), 369

Bodin, Jean, 31, 34, 35, 249, 519n

Body of Liberties (Mass.), 68

Bolton, Mr. (in Phila.), 133

Bomley, Francis, 76

Bond slavery. *See* Slavery

Bones, 506, 532

Bonnet, Charles, 223, 483

Booth, James, 122n

Boston, Mass., 118; and slave trade, 67, 299; population, 103, 119; regulates slaves, 104–5; sense of community in, 120; Negroes in, 126, 417, 455; Negro wedding in, 130; newspapers do not discuss miscegenation, 147; debate on slavery in, 199; inoculation in, 202–4, 260; Phyllis Wheatley in, 283; during Revolution, 303; Negro schooling in, 362, 417; Negro churches in, 424–25; opinion of Negro mental ability in, 456–57; colonization proposed in, 550; queries on condition of Negroes in, 555–56. *See also* Massachusetts

Boston Gazette, 388

Boston News-Letter, 121, 158

Boucher, Jonathan, 280

Bowdoin, James, 144, 338, 444, 526

Brabantio, 38

Brackenridge, Hugh, 524–25
Bracton, Henry de, 50–51
Bradford, William, 40
Bradford, Mass., 534
Bradley, Abraham, 531
Bradley, Richard, 218n, 241
Brain, 26n, 249, 259, 506. *See also* Skulls
Branagan, Thomas, 369, 549
Branding, 51, 60, 107, 112, 233, 366
Brazil, 57, 60
Briefe Treatise of Testaments and Last Willes (Henry Swinburne), 53
Briggins, Mr. (ship captain), 242
British officials: unconcerned with Negroes in the colonies, 84–85; early use "whites" and "blacks," 96n; and slaves as property, 104; ask free Negro suffrage, 127–28; denounce castration, 155–56; encourage intermarriage with Indians, 163n; ask law aiding conversion, 184; and Anglican Church, 207. *See also* Church of England
Brown, John (1736–1803), merchant and congressman, 328–29, 330
Brown, John (1800–59), abolitionist, 123
Brown, Moses, 329, 344, 359n, 447
Browne, Sir Thomas, 15–16, 19, 20
Bruno, Giordano, 12
Brunskill, Rev. John, 213
Buffon, Georges Louis Leclerc, Comte de, 163n; on animals nearest man, 225; on separation of apes and men, 230, 495; wavers on problem of species, 235; says orangs copulate with Negro women, 236; expects Negroes to lighten in cold climate, 243; on albinism, 251n, 252, 523–24; refuted by Jefferson, 477–80; on criterion of species, 506
Burdett, William, 76
Burial grounds, 132, 418n
Burlington, N. J., 276, 281, 357–58
Burlington School Society (N. J.), 358
Burnett, James. *See* Monboddo, James Burnett, Lord
Burnham, Rowland, 75
Burning alive, 106, 116, 118, 392, 398, 473
Burton, Daniel, 197–98
Burton, Mary, 117–18
Burwell, Rebecca, 461, 462, 467
Butler, Gov. Nathaniel, 64, 67

Bymba (Africa), 59
Byrd, William, 111, 143, 162n, 250, 316, 522

C

Caesar (slave of Bowdoin), 144
Cain, 242, 416
Cairo, 60
Caldwell, Dr. Charles, 521, 523, 533–34
Callendar, James T., 465, 468–69
Calmucks, 226
Calvinism, 23, 119, 205, 300, 543–44. *See also* Puritanism; Puritans
Campbell, George Washington, 389
Camper, Peter, 225–26, 230, 237, 495, 498, 505
Canaan (person), 17, 35, 36, 54. *See also* Ham
Canaan (land of), 43, 548
Canaanites, 36, 574
Canada, 269
Canary Islands, 59
Cancer, 585
A Candid Examination, into the Origin of the Differences of Colour, in the Human Family (Charles Jones), 538
Cap Français (St. Domingo), 376–77, 380
Cape of Good Hope, 225
Cape Verde, 4
Cape Verde Islands, 67
Capital, 47
Captivity, 60, 62; and concept of slavery, 54–56; and enslavement of Indians in Brazil, 57; of Africans, 58–59; of Irish, 63; of Scots, 63, 88; in New England, 67–70, 71; not used in Va., 72. *See also* Enslavement
Carey, Mathew, 528
Carey, Mrs. Mathew, 419
Carib Indians, 90
Caribbean. *See* West Indies
Caroline Co., Va., 113n
Cartagena, 61n
Carter, Landon, 214
Caspian Sea, 254
Caste, 93, 134
Castration: as legal punishment, 154–58; in N. C., 155, 473; in Va., 155, 157, 463, 473; in Ga., 473
Cataline, 111
Catechism, 133, 134
Catholicism. *See* Roman Catholicism

Caucasian (term), 222
Caucasians, 223
Caucasus, 30
Celebese, 226
Cemeteries. *See* Burial grounds
Central America, 63
Chain of Being, xii, 515, 531; eluci-
dated, 219–20; function of, 220, 510–
11; and Linnaean classification,
220–22, 484; not utilized by Blumenbach, 223; utilized for classifying
mankind, 223–25; and Camper's gradation of skulls, 225–26, 230; and
anatomical studies, 226, 497–502,
505–6, 509; Negroes ranked at bottom of, 226–28, 500–501; and social
hierarchy, 227–28; affinity of men
and beasts in, 228–30; place of apes
and Negroes in, 238, 495–96; and
valuation of color, 254; used by proslavery writers, 304–5, 308; Jefferson
on, 438, 489–90, 502–3; popularity in
America, 483–85; and sexuality, 490–
93, 494–95, 496–97, 500–502; Long on,
492–93; social implications of, 493,
494; and antislavery advocates, 496–
97, 504–5; White on, 499–502; Moore
on, 503–4; J. A. Smith on, 505–6; and
S. S. Smith, 507–9; remnants, 510.
See also Apes; Orang-outangs
Cham. *See* Ham
Chandler, Dr. (quoted by Dillwyn),
281–82
Charles II (King of England), 83
Charleston, S. C.: slave conspiracy in,
115; resentment of skilled Negroes
in, 129, 406; miscegenation in, 145–
47; white women's life in, 148–49;
smallpox in, 165; citizens irate at
Negro preacher, 209–10; antislavery
in, 283; exports rice, 317–18; slave
prices in, 321; dead slaves thrown
into harbor, 366–67; fear of conta-
gion from St. Domingo in, 381–82;
newspapers and Gabriel plot, 395;
blackness barred from stage in, 405;
regulates slave apprentices, 406; free
Negroes in, 409; church seating in,
418; yellow fever in, 529. *See also*
South Carolina
Charlton, Stephen, 75
Chastellux, Marquis de, 280, 453, 554n
Chauncy, Rev. Charles, 212
Chavis, John, 417, 455
Cherokees, 516
Chesapeake area, 72

Chester Co., Pa., 139
Chester Quarterly Meeting (Pa.), 420
Children: insubordination of in England, 42; abducted from England, 52;
subordination to parents, 54, 193;
Negro and white in early Va. and
Md., 82; Barbados prohibits kidnapping, 86; Negro and white thought
born fair, 248–49; race-awareness in,
257; effect of slavery on white, 273,
432–33; feared imbibing Negro's
speech, 340n; white girl rails at Negro man, 367n; Negro, 369, 530. *See
also* Education; Family; Schools
Chimpanzee. *See* Orang-outang
Chinese, 226, 241, 242n, 306n
Chisman, Capt. John, 75
Christian (term), 74, 93–97
Christianity: and curse on Ham, 18,
36; as mandate to proselytize, 21, 22;
makes Negroes seem similar and different, 22–23; as attribute of Englishness, 24, 93–94; in Tudor-Stuart England, 40; regarded as responsible for
end of villenage, 50, 56; struggle
against Islam, 55–56; universalism of,
180, 205–6; jeopardizes social hierarchies, 192; and Chain of Being,
220; and man as a unique being, 228,
503; conduces to amelioration of
slavery, 231–32, 364–65; as impulse
in antislavery, 292–94; and question
of equality, 363–64; influence on Gabriel plotters, 393; defended by S. S.
Smith, 487; Judaic-Christian tradition, 493–94; as cultural conscience,
579, 581. *See also* Bible; Churches;
Conversion; Equalitarianism; Human unity; Ministers; Protestantism;
Puritanism; specific denominations
Church of England, 133, 180–81, 205,
206–10, 297. *See also* Anglican
Church; Society for the Propagation
of the Gospel
Churches: pre-Reformation, 12; Negroes admitted to full membership,
93, 131, 205–6, 211–12; whites addressed by Negroes in, 130; separate
seating in, 132, 418; and Protestant
posture toward Negroes and slavery,
198–202, 205–10; in northern and
southern colonies compared, 206–7;
Negroes join especially after Great
Awakening, 213–15; congregational,
418; development of Negro, 422–25.
See also specific denominations

Churchills' *Voyages*, 16, 309
Chus, 20, 41, 60. *See also* Ham
Cicero, 478
Circassia, 515
Circassions, 254
Civil law, 53
Civil War (American), 131, 179
Civil War (English), 192, 194
Civilization: in apposition to savagery, 24; not to be brought to Africa by Englishmen, 27; as attribute of Englishmen, 46; desire to impose on Indians, 89, 91; West Indians grasp at, 142; associated with whiteness, 253, 305–6, 515; Africans admitted to be at different stage of, 286–87; declared lacking in Africa, 307; as man's original condition, 514; desire to maintain in America, 543; and white self-control, 579–82. *See also* Savagery
Clay, Joseph, 170–71, 385
Climate: effect on skin and hair, 12; of Africa, 13, 286–87; and logic of latitude, 13–14; in America, 14, 22; sexuality associated with hot, 151; claimed temperate in Va., 239–40; Negroes thought fitted for hot, 260–64, 459, 517, 525–27; Bowdoin on, 445; said to affect color and form, 487, 514–17, 538; and colonization, 517, 563–64; effect of minimized, 536; Williamson on, 539–41. *See also* Color
Clinton, DeWitt, 360n
Clinton, George, 344
Coddington secession, 70n
Coke, Sir Edward, Lord, 50–51, 54–55
College of New Jersey, 188, 441n, 455, 486, 507, 544; Negro at, 417
College of Physicians (Phila.), 529
College of William and Mary, 346, 505, 523, 555
Colleges, 507
Collyer, J., 209
Colman, Rev. Benjamin (1673–1747), 203
Colman, Deacon Benjamin (fl. 1775), 297, 298, 299, 300
Colonization, 517, 542, 544, 546–69, 575; denounced, 362–63, 545, 549
Color: as a marvel, 6–7; relativism concerning, 11; maternal impressions, 12; Indian's and Negro's distinguished, 14, 16–17; Negro's claimed to be permanent, 15–17; concept of

complexion, 19n; of Indians, 27, 98, 239–40, 241–42, 478–79; valuation of, 39, 170, 252–55; as basis of slavery, 94–98; of Europeans, 143, 253–55; decreed by God, 165, 538–39; as means of classifying mankind, 218, 226; of Chinese, 242n; physiology of, 245–47, 458, 514, 526; of original man thought to be white, 247, 251; of cuticles, 249; and Quaker membership, 420–22; fair preferred in S. C. men, 474n; whitening of American Negroes, 515–16, 532–33, 540–41; Negro's not expected to lighten in America, 545; modern knowledge of, 585

Problem of cause: ancient theories, 11; logic of latitude, 13–14, 20; effect of sun, 13, 16, 19–20, 24, 200, 531; whether Englishmen changed by climate, 13, 15–16, 20, 244, 538; question whether Negro's altered by cold, 14–15, 16, 243–44; quasi-genetic explanations of, 16, 20; Negro's as core of, 240–42; *Athenian Oracle* discusses theories on, 242–43; Mitchell on, 246–47, 536–37; early American scientists on, 247–49; ignored by Jefferson, 458; S. S. Smith on, 513–16, 517; satirized, 524–25; and natural selection, 527; discussed by Williams, 535–36; C. Jones on, 538–39. *See also* Albinos; Blackness; Ham; Human reproduction; Prejudice; Whiteness
Columbian Centinel (Boston), 449
Columbian Magazine, 484, 491, 494, 496
Columbus, Christopher, 14
Commandments. *See* Ten Commandments
Commercialization, 42–43, 104. *See also* Slave trade
Commissaries, 186, 207
Committee for Trade and Foreign Plantations, 86, 185
Common law, 49, 50
Common Sense (Thomas Paine), 337
Common sense philosophy, 441n
Community, sense of: among Puritans, 46; not strong in Va. and Md., 71; in Va. and New England, 98; and reaction to slave unrest, 101; in Boston, 104–5, 126; negated by Negro rule, 114–15, 120; lack in New York City, 119–20; in various cities, 120; ex-

cludes all Negroes, 123, 130–31, 134, 323n; enhanced by idea of racial superiority, 134; in continental colonies, 142; expressed by Sewall, 165; changing ideas concerning men's role in, 294–95; and Negro membership in body politic, 295–96; and St. Domingo as an inversion, 380; and miscegenation, 470. See also National identity; Self-identity; Tribalism

Comparative anatomy. See Anatomy

Conceptualism, 235–36, 489–90

Concord Monthly Meeting (Pa.), 420

Concubines, 145, 169, 174

Condorcet, Marquis de, 452

Congo, 6, 58

Congregationalists, 300, 418. See also Puritans

Congress (U. S.), 316, 421; antislavery petitions to, 325, 326, 327, 328–30, 344, 388; enacts fugitive slave law, 327; acts against slave trade, 327, 330, 331; and St. Domingo, 377–78, 381, 383–85; southern delegates object to discussion of slavery in, 384; debates taxing slave trade, 385, 388; debates form of government for La., 389–90; laws on suffrage, 412; emancipation denounced in, 544–45; and colonization, 548, 554. See also Continental Congress; Sectional divisions

Congress (Confederation), 321–22

Connecticut, 68, 69, 158; militia, 71, 411; prohibits sale of debtors to non-English, 86; population, 103, 615; castration in, 155n, 158; churches of, 207; Negroes and whites eat together in, 234; opposition to slavery in, 299; newspaper debate over slavery in, 307–8; abolishes slavery, 345; antislavery society in, 359; remote from slave revolts, 384; voting in, 414. See also Congress; Miscegenation; New England; Sectional divisions; Slave codes

Connecticut Abolition Society, 543

Connecticut Journal (New Haven), 307–8

Conspiracies. See Slave revolts

Constitution, 325, 326, 332, 446

Constitutional Convention, 322, 422, 470, 486, 539; and slave trade, 321n, 323, 324, 325, 373

Continental Army, 302

Continental Association, 302

Continental Congress, 298, 302, 321, 337n, 539

Control, social. See Social control

Convention of antislavery societies: history of, 344; states intentions, 349; Quaker dominance of, 359–60; on duties toward freed Negroes, 359–61; reaction to St. Domingo, 378–79; reaction to Gabriel plot, 401; protests claims of Negro inferiority, 505; Rush as leader in, 517; on colonization, 548. See also Antislavery societies

Conversion: of Negroes in Africa, 3–4, 21–22; implications re Negro's nature, 21, 180; of Indians, 21–22, 89, 94, 95, 211; of Negroes by Spanish and Portuguese, 22, 23; and skin color, 22, 258–59; progress among Indians, 92; and manumission, 92–93, 180–81; progress among Negroes, 93, 94, 181, 206n, 208, 211, 213, 214, 418–19; opposition to, 180–86, 192, 209; ambivalence toward, 186–87; in S. C., 186, 399; Mather on, 187, 189–90; and Negro's mental ability, 188n, 189; proponents recognize opposition to, 190–92; urged by Fox, 194; campaign compared to antislavery, 197–98; efforts by Church of England, 207–9; morphology of, 210–12; no longer chief aim of equalitarians, 296–97; worship by Negroes restricted, 399, 404; aided by changing psychological ideas, 441; and colonization, 550–51, 554. See also Baptism; Churches; Great Awakening

Convicts, 52, 67–68, 103

Cooper, David, 276, 290, 292

Cordwainers, 406

Cosway, Maria, 462

Cotton, Rev. John, 88

Cotton, 317–18, 319

Cotton gin, 316–17

Council for Foreign Plantations, 85

Council of Trade and Plantations, 128

Cowell, John, 50–51

Cowper, John, 381

Cows, 540

Cox, Rev. (Anglican in Md.), 186

Crawford, Adair, 459

Crawford, Charles, 418, 446, 531, 544

Cresswell, Nicholas, 277

Crèvecoeur, St. Jean de, 336–37, 340–41, 367n

Cromwell, Oliver, 40, 87, 88, 192

Crows, 523
Cuffe, Paul, 550–51
Currie, Dr. William, 528
Cuticles, 249
Cuvier, Georges, 505
Cynocephali, 29

D

Daemonology (James I), 30
Danbury, Conn., 299
Darien, Ga., 301
Darwin, Charles, 509
Darwinism, 374, 493, 509–10, 527
David (free Negro preacher), 209–10
Davies, Rev. Samuel, 183, 188
Davis, Hugh, 78
Davis, Susan, 76
De Generis Humani Varietate Nativa
  (J. F. Blumenbach), 222, 507
Dearborn, Benjamin, 548n
Death. *See* Mortality
Declaration of Independence, 271, 290,
  301, 350, 362; Jefferson's draft of,
  431, 453
Declaration of the Rights of Man and
  Citizen, 376
Degeneration (term), 248n
Delaware: militia in, 125–26, 411; for-
  bids Negroes punishing white crim-
  inals, 130–31; law on rape, 157n;
  population, 175, 339, 406–7, 615; ex-
  pected to abolish slavery, 315; anti-
  slavery societies in, 343, 359n; anti-
  slavery accepted in, 346; relaxes
  manumission laws in, 347; penalizes
  kidnapping and restricts sale of Negroes, 404; laws on free Negroes, 407,
  410, 575; Negro churches in, 425;
  bans intermarriage, 472n. *See also*
  Congress; Miscegenation; Sectional
  divisions; Slave codes
Delaware River, 338
Dell, Rev. (Anglican in Md.), 186
Demosthenes, 478
Dent, George, 330
De Pauw, Cornelis, 163n, 242, 252n
Derham, Dr. James, 449, 455
Desdemona, 37–38
Desire (vessel), 67, 68
Dessalines, Jean-Jacques, 376, 377
Devil: term links savagery and black-
  ness, 24; associated with apes, 30; as
  description of Desdemona, 37–38; as-
  sociated with color, 39n; connected
  with blackness and sexuality, 41; as-
  sociated with blackness, 256, 258; as-

sociated with whiteness by Negroes,
  258
Dialect. *See* Speech
*Dialogue Concerning the Slavery of the
  Africans* (Samuel Hopkins), 298
Dick, Elisha C., 400
Dickson, Joseph, 330
Dickson, William, 496
Dillwyn, William, 281–82
Dirt (term), 42
Dirt, 257
Dirty (term), 38
Discoveries: Portuguese, 2; and hea-
  thenism, 20; stimulate development
  of science, 25; and curse on Ham,
  36; and European thought, 216; con-
  duce to environmentalism, 288; im-
  pact on view of man, 390–91
Disease(s), 88; smallpox, 165, 259–60;
  and Linnaean classification, 218; Ne-
  gro's seen as similar to white's, 259–
  60; in debate on slavery in Ga., 263–
  64; White on Negro's, 501; blackness
  as, 518–21; in Africa, 583–84. *See also*
  Climate; Inoculation; Leprosy; Yel-
  low fever
Dissertation on Slavery (St. G. Tuck-
  er), 558
Diversity. *See* Ethnic diversity; Reli-
  gious diversity
Doctors. *See* Physicians
Dogs, 36, 540
Dominica, Isle of, 59
Dorchester, Mass., 93
Double standard. *See* Sexual mores
Douglass, Dr. William, 203–4, 247–48
Downing, Emanuel, 69
Drake, Sir Francis, 58
Drayton, Gov. John, 456, 531
Drinker, John, 421
Du Simitière, P. E., 337n
Duke's Laws, 84, 92n
Dulany, Daniel, 105
Dunbar, Eng., 88
Dunmore, John Murray, Lord, 303
Dutch, 23, 60; in Barbados, 65; as in-
  ternational slave traders, 65, 83; and
  Va., 72, 73; not making slaves of
  English, 73; as servants, 75; colonists
  in New Netherland, 83; cultural
  background, 84; in Md., 88; in melt-
  ing pot, 336, 338; considered one of
  six nations of immigrants to U. S.,
  337n; in S. C., 340

Duty of Christians (Samuel Davies),
183
Dwight, Theodore, 333, 378

E

Early, Peter, 331
East Indians, 17
East Indies, 60
Eaton, Theophilus, 68
Ebenezer, Ga., 263
Economic conditions, 83; in Elizabe-
than England, 42–43; on American
continent, 66; in New England, 66,
67, 71; in Lower South, 317–19; in
Upper South, 319–20. *See also* Com-
mercialization; Frontier
Eden, Richard, 14
Edinburgh, 309
Edmond, William, 329
Education: Gooch expects to change
Negroes, 127; little for Negroes, 133–
34; Protestant emphasis on in con-
version, 212; lack of interest in for
Negroes, 354–55, 356; of Negroes pro-
posed by Sullivan, 355–56, 557;
Quaker efforts, 357–61; of Negroes
and religious equalitarianism, 362–
63, 364–65; of Negroes restricted by
S. C., 399. *See also* Apprenticeship;
Schools
Edwards, Bryan, 175, 177, 237
Edwards, Rev. Jonathan (the young-
er), 543–44, 545
Egmont, Earl of, 129, 263
Egypt, 30, 574
Egyptians, 581
Election of 1796, 442
Election of 1800, 387–88, 396, 442, 502,
507, 531
Election of 1804, 442, 503
Elephants, 222, 225, 230, 499, 500
Eliot, Rev. Andrew, 279
Elizabeth I (Queen of England), 3, 8
Elizabethans, 135. *See also* England,
Englishmen
Ellicott, Andrew, 450, 454
Ellsworth, Oliver, 320
Emancipation, 326; laws, 70–71, 294,
302, 345–46; bills, 346, 360n, 413–14,
471–72, 546; effect on segregation,
414–15; feared as resulting in inter-
mixture, 542–69. *See also* Antislavery;
Free Negroes; Manumission
Emaniell (slave of Stone), 76
Emerson, Ralph Waldo, 334–35
England: Negroes in, 6, 34, 60, 209, 224,

237, 254–55; social conditions in, 39,
41–43, 49–52, 84–85; Scots not enslaved in, 88; absence of slave codes
in, 104; function of government in,
108; Baptists in, 155; castration in,
156n; no prejudice assumed in, 171;
Civil War, 192, 194; lower class
women in, described, 239n; Indians
in, 239–40; albinos in, 250, 252;
Americans still tied to after Revolution, 333–34; armies of in St. Domingo, 376–77; colonization of Negroes from, 550. *See also* British
officials; Church of England; Great
Britain; London
English (term), 93–97
English law. *See* Law
English officials. *See* British officials
Englishmen: as settlers in New World,
xiii–xiv, 18, 22, 36, 43, 45–46, 136,
239; as slave traders, 3–4; as traders
in Africa, 3–4, 6, 27, 56; as non-set-
tlers in Africa, 22; as Christians, 23;
as civilizers of New World, 27; as
adventurers overseas, 40–43; consider
selves free men, 46, 49–52, 54; learn
of enslavement of Negroes, 57–62; as
settlers in West Indies, 63; look down
on Irish and Scots, 86–88; mood on
eve of settlement, 135; encounter
Negroes in different contexts, 136;
misunderstand American slavery,
208–10; Americans need to differen-
tiate selves from, 335–36. *See also*
England
Englishness, sense of: in early years,
43, 46, 86–89; and early debasement
of Negroes, 93–94; expressed by
Franklin, 102; in West Indies and
continental colonies, 142; at question in S. C., 147; among Americans
undercut by Revolution, 335–41. *See
also* National identity; Nationalism;
Self-examination; Self-identity
Enquirer (Richmond), 392
Enslavement: of Ethiopians in ancient
times, 18; lack of evidence concerning, 44; in Va. and Md., 44, 71–83,
92, 94–95; of vagabonds in England,
51–52; of Englishmen by Turks and
Moors, 54, 55–56; self-sale, 55; by
Spanish and Portuguese, 56–57, 74;
English learn of Spanish and Portuguese, 57–61; by Dutch and Greeks,
60; and Irish and Scottish captives,
63; in Providence Island, 64; in Bar-

bados, 64–65; in West Indies, 65–66, 85–86; in New England, 66–71; in N. Y., 83–84; in continental colonies and West Indies, 83, 85–86; in S. C. and N. C., 84–85; none in England, 88; of Africans easier than of Indians, 89; of free Negroes, 327.

Of Indians, 22, 227; by Spanish and Portuguese, 57; in West Indies, 63, 64, 65; in New England, 66, 67, 68–69, 71; in English colonies, 85–86, 89–92. *See also* Captivity; Slavery

Environmentalism: early manifestation of, 26n; in explanation of slave diseases, 260; reliance on by antislavery advocates, 286–87, 307; development of in Revolutionary era, 287–89, 308–10; linked to naturalization of man, 294; found a barrier by proslavery writers, 305–8; connection with American sense of Englishness, 336; aids growth of humanitarianism, 365; in Jefferson's thought, 437–38, 439, 453, 454n, 478–80; in assertions of Negro equality, 445; especially attracts Americans, 487–88; questioned by J. A. Smith, 506; re Negro's color, 514–22, 525–27; Rush's, 518, 530, 560; decline of, 533–38; and America as a white country, 540–41. *See also* Climate; Color; Mental ability; Smith, Rev. Samuel Stanhope

Episcopal church. *See* Anglican Church

Episcopate, 209, 297

Eppes, John W., 385

Equalitarianism: among Quakers, 272; development of political, 295, 296–302; denounced by W. L. Smith, 326; secularization of, 363–64; and segregation, 415; Jefferson's, 453, 481; S. S. Smith's and Jefferson's compared, 488; erosion of, 507–9; Rush's, 519–20; leads to colonization proposal, 548; and self-identity, 581–82.

Religious, 295; supports early antislavery, 70, 194–96; compared to antislavery, 197–98; stressed by Puritans, 200–204; strength sapped by weakness of churches, 206–7; emphasized by Great Awakening, 214–15; in Revolutionary era, 279; channeled into political, 296–302; leads to thinking beyond emancipation, 361–63, 364–65; leads to separation of Negroes, 425. *See also* Antislavery; Christianity; Churches; Colonization; Human

unity; Mental ability; Natural rights; Sentimentality

Equality. *See* Slave revolts; Social leveling

Eskimos, 514

Essay on Man (Alexander Pope), 483

An Essay on the Causes of the Variety of Complexion and Figure in the Human Species (S. S. Smith), 486, 533

Estates General, 376

Ethiopia, 20, 30, 34

Ethiopians, 18

Ethnic diversity, 87–88, 90, 277–78, 390; characteristic of the colonies, 102; in N. Y. C., 119; greatest in Pa. and southern back country, 270. *See also* Melting pot

Ethnocentrism, 9–10, 25, 252

Europeans. *See* Beauty; Chain of Being; Races

Eve, 23, 502, 525

Evolution. *See* Natural selection

Ewes, 38

Explorations. *See* Discoveries

F

Facial angle, 225–26, 498, 500, 505–6, 508–9. *See also* Prognathism

Facial features. *See* Beauty

Fairfax, Ferdinando, 554–55, 566n

Fall of man, 54

Family: in Africa, 39–40; slaves in white, 105; slave, 160–61, 198, 368; equality of members asserted, 201–2; Puritan ideas about, 205; changes in, 295; and views of mankind, 488; miscegenation as violation of, 578. *See also* Children

Federalist Papers, 322, 339, 467

Federalists: on antislavery petitions, 328–30; stress Englishness of America, 340; on slave revolts, 387–88, 396; Negro, 413; Jefferson on, 476; decry social leveling, 485; attack Jefferson, 502–4. *See also* Congress (U. S.)

Fenner, George, 59

Fenning, Daniel, 209n

Field work. *See* Mulattoes; Women

Fingernails. *See* Cuticles

Fletcher, Rev. (Anglican in Md.), 186

Flood (Biblical), 17, 36, 41; Africans said to know of, 23; Raleigh on, 42n; property thought common before, 55; and problem of origins of Indians, 240

Florida, 262, 382, 559
Fowler, William, 59
Fowles, Rev. James, 473n
Fox, George, 194
France, 339, 377–78, 432, 588. *See also* French; Paris; St. Domingo
Franklin, Benjamin, 424; on Germans, 102, 143, 254, 270; on existence of superior beings, 143, 219–20; praises white peoples, 143, 254; on peopling of America, 143, 269; on prejudice, 276–77; on Negro's mental ability, 282; antislavery writings, 325–26, 447; helps design national seal, 337n; sparks reform organizations, 343; in Pa. Abolition Society, 344; on color and heat, 526
Franks, Abigail, 420
Free African Society (Phila.), 422
Free Negroes: in early Va., 74, 76–77, 81, 94; as leak in slave system, 108; and slave revolts, 122–23, 401; laws restricting, 122, 123, 124–28, 407–9, 410–11; thought to harbor slaves, 122n, 408, 409–10, 577; position in community, 123, 134; laws protecting, 124, 408; British authorities ask suffrage for, 127; attempt rape, 157; distinguished from free mulattoes in Antigua, 176n; in Revolution, 302; re-enslaved, 327; petition Congress, 328–30; kidnapping of, 343–44; number of in Va., 347, 348; immigration of prohibited by various states, 348, 382, 399, 575; literacy among, 384; fear of in Va., 400, 577–81; threat posed by, 406, 409–10; increase in number of, 406–7; thought thievish, 407–8, 409–10, 576, 577; barred from militia, 411–12; congregate in cities, 415. *See also* Colonization; Manumission; Negroes; Passing; Voting
Freedom. *See* Liberty
French: in Barbados, 65; in New Netherland, 83; in Md., 88; refugees in S. C., 173; influence in New Orleans, 174n; color of, 254, 255; as enemies of colonists, 269; in melting pot, 336; considered one of six nations of immigrants to U. S., 337n; influence in America not extolled, 340; lose St. Domingo, 375–77; Americans associate with tyranny, 389; to be spared by Gabriel plotters, 393n. *See also* France

French and Indian War, 269, 271–72, 300, 421
French Revolution, 328, 376, 387–88, 391, 485, 556. *See also* Jacobinism; Jacobins
Frobisher, Martin, 40
Frontier, 47, 48, 61, 103, 175, 419. *See also* Western territories
Fugitive slave law, 327, 328–30. *See also* Slave codes
Fugitive slaves. *See* Runaways
Fuller, Thomas, 449, 455
Fundamental Constitutions of Carolina, 85

G

Gabriel (slave leader), 393, 399, 404, 409
Gabriel plot, xi, 393–94; reaction to, 395–96; effect of, 399–401, 404; and colonization, 560–65; and fear of free Negroes, 577
Gallatin, Albert, 328, 413
Galley-slaves, 52, 55
Garden, Alexander, 527
Garrettson, Rev. Freeborn, 215
Genera (term), 235n
Genesis. *See* Bible
Genêt, Edmond, 381
Genetics, 583–84. *See also* Human reproduction; Natural selection
Geographia (Ptolemy), 13
Geographic conditions, 66, 71. *See also* Climate
Georgetown, D. C., 450
Georgia, 209; manumission laws, 124, 348; restricts free Negroes, 124, 408–9; voting in, 126–27, 169, 412–13; limits punishments, 155; encourages immigration of free mulattoes, 169–70; status of mulattoes in, 170–71; population, 175, 339, 406, 615; immigration to from West Indies, 182; Anglican church in, 206–8; Whitefield on Negroes in, 214; branding in, 233; trustees on smell of Negroes, 257; debate over necessity for Negroes in, 261–64; refuses to oppose slave trade, 301, 324, 373; refuses to enlist slaves in Revolution, 302; cotton in, 317; domestic slave trade in, 320; slave prices in, 321; attitude toward slavery in, 331, 346; fears Negroes from West Indies and Fla., 381–82; slave violence in, 392; absence of alarm over slave revolts,

396; tightens slave code, 399; militia in, 411; Negro churches in, 425; laws on rape, 473; white women in, 474–75; darkness of white men in, 514; debate on slavery in, 525. *See also* Congress (U. S.) ; Miscegenation; Sectional divisions; Slave codes

Georgians (Russia), 254

Germans: immigration of, 102, 270, 337n; Franklin on, 102, 143, 254, 270; in Pa., 143, 254, 338; ancient, 253; in Ga., 263; in melting pot, 336, 338; in S. C., 340

Gernsey Island, 86

Gesner, Konrad von, 29

Gholson, James H., 394

Gibson, Bishop Edmund, 191

Gibson, Edward, 174n

Gibson, Gideon, 172–73

Gibson family, 171–73, 174n

Glen, Gov. James, 121

Glorious Revolution, 289

Goats, 30

Godwyn, Rev. Morgan, 97, 229–30, 231

Goettingen, 285

The Golden Coast (anonymous), 35

Goldsmith, Oliver, 248, 254

Gooch, Gov. William, 122, 127

Goree Island, 379

Gorton, Samuel, 70n

Gouge, Rev. William, 56

Grant, Anne, 144

Graveyards. *See* Burial grounds

Gray, Mrs. William, 416

Great Awakening, 120, 212–14, 269–70, 296–97, 419

Great Britain, 116, 301, 331, 377–78. *See also* England

Greece, 219, 280

Greeks, 11–12, 60, 166, 253, 505, 515

Greene, Mrs. Nathaniel, 317

Greenland, 240

Gregoire, Abbé Henri, 453–54

Grenada, 233. *See also* West Indies

Groves, Thomas, 76

Guadaloupe, 383

Guinea, 58, 59, 60, 61n, 226, 282. *See also* Africa

Guinea Company, 28

H

Habersham, James, 188–89, 209–10

Hackensack, N. J., 117

Haddonfield, N. J., 416

Hadwen, Benjamin, 358

The Hague, 395

Hair, 8–9; cause of Negro's, 12, 518; Indian's and Negro's distinguished, 14; Negro's called innate, 16; and Chain of Being, 226; of Indians, 241; thought protection against sun, 245n; red used to ridicule slavery and prejudice, 277, 278–79

Haiti, Republic of. *See* St. Domingo

Hakluyt, Richard, 57, 573; fosters enthusiasm for colonization overseas, 3; discusses Negroes in England, 6; reprints Eden's account of Indians, 14; discusses purposes of English colonization, 46; accounts of Hawkins's voyages, 59; calls Negroes "slaves," 60

Halifax Co., N. C., 397

Hall, Prince, 455, 555

Haller, Albrecht von, 501

Ham (term), 18

Ham, curse on, 60, 62n, 84, 111; and Negro's color, 17–20; in Jewish and Christian thought, 17–18, 35–37; Jobson on, 35; exegesis by Best, 41–43; as cause of slavery, 54, 56; and Negro's penis, 158; discussed in colonies, 200–201; loses popularity, 243, 525; Josselyn on, 245–46; cited by proslavery writer, 308

Hamilton, Alexander, 282, 333–34, 344, 466, 468

Hamlet, 53

Hammond, John, 77

Hannibal (slave of MacSparran), 105n

Harper, Robert Goodloe, 388

Harrison, William, 49

Harry (Negro preacher), 419

Hart, Rev. Levi, 294, 297

Harvard College, 248, 308, 486, 534

Hathorne, John, 92

Haward, Bartholomew, 28

Hawkins, John, 3, 58–59, 60

Hawley, Gov. Henry, 64

Heat. *See* Climate

Heathenism, 20–25, 43, 91–96, 97, 119, 216. *See also* Conversion

Hebraic law, 67–68, 69, 105, 294

Hemings, Sally, 464–69

Hemings family, 464–69

Henderson, Rev. Jacob, 186

Henry I (King of England), 156n

Henry VIII (King of England), 40, 51

Henry (Prince), the Navigator, 3

Henry, Patrick, 163, 544

Herald (Fredericksburg, Va.), 396

Herbert, Sir Thomas, 231

Herder, Johann Gottfried von, 230
Heredity. *See* Human reproduction
Herodotus, 166
Hessians, 153
Hewat, Rev. Alexander, 261–62, 283, 293
Heylyn, Rev. Peter, 19–20, 53
Hierarchy. *See* Chain of Being; Social hierarchy
Hinrichs, Capt. Johann, 153
Hispanic languages, 95
Hispaniola, 59, 376. *See also* St. Domingo; West Indies
Histoire Naturelle (Buffon), 230
Historie of Foure-Footed Beastes (Edward Topsell), 29
History of Jamaica (Edward Long), 491, 494
History of South-Carolina (David Ramsay), 337
History of the Earth (Oliver Goldsmith), 254
History of Vermont (Samuel Williams), 535
Hoe, 113
Hollis Professorship, 248, 534
Home, Henry. *See* Kames, Henry Home, Lord
Hopkins, Rev. Samuel, 297, 300, 344; describes prejudice, 276; discusses impact of slavery on Negroes, 283; on slavery as sin, 298–99; proposes colonization, 550
Hopkinson, Francis, 491
Hoppius, Christianus Emmanuel, 221
Horses, 38, 190
Horsmanden, Daniel, 118–19
Hottentots: classified by Bernier, 217; Hoppius and Linnaeus on, 221; in Chain of Being, 223, 224, 229; Petty on, 225; in Camper's gradation, 226; thought most barbarous of men, 226–27; associated with Negroes, 227; Buffon on, 230; associated with orangs, 492
House of Representatives. *See* Congress (U. S.)
House slaves, 169, 174, 405, 508, 515–16, 533–34
Howe, Admiral Lord Richard, 291
Huger, Benjamin, 330, 389
Hughes, Rev. Griffith, 188
Human reproduction, 164–67, 244–45, 250–52, 536–37. *See also* Acquired characters; Natural selection
Human unity: enjoined by Christian tradition, xiii, 22–23; asserted by Bible, 12, 22; denied, 12, 17, 502; militated against by Christianity, 23; asserted in religious terms in 17th century, 179; individuals assert, 197, 247, 487, 516, 520, 531–32; reinforced by environmentalism, 288; concept of dependent on ignoring physical differences, 509; imperiled by color differences, 513. *See also* Antislavery; Chain of Being; Diseases; Equalitarianism; Natural rights; Prejudice; Races; Species
Humanitarianism, 232, 372; and Great Awakening, 214–15; and antislavery, 272, 292–93, 298, 367; flowering of, 365–68; effect on slave codes, 403; institutions of, 415; relation to science, 483; of Rush, 518, 519–20; as cultural conscience, 579, 581
Hume, David, 253, 254, 305, 307, 446, 450
Humors, 19n. *See also* Bile
Hunter, Dr. John (1728–93), anatomist, 498, 499, 505, 523
Hunter, Dr. John (d. 1809), theorist on skin color, 514
Huntingdon, Countess of, 209
Hurons, 223
Hybridization, 235–36, 497, 499. *See also* Interfertility

I

Iago, 37–38
Iboes, 237
Identity. *See* Self-identity
Idleness, 51
Idolatry. *See* Heathenism
Illinois Territory, 112
Imlay, Gilbert, 441–42, 460, 496–97
Immigrants, 510
Immigration: of foreign Protestants encouraged, 86; of non-English, 95, 102; discouraged by slavery, 129; efforts to encourage white, 147; after Great Awakening, 270; of free Negroes restricted or banned by many states, 410–11. *See also* Melting pot; Naturalization; Servants; Slave trade
Imperial officials. *See* British officials
Indentured servitude. *See* Servitude
Indentures, 52, 81
Independence. *See* American independence
India, 30, 242
Indian (term), 95

Indiana Territory, 412

Indians, xiv, 516; called part of Christ's flock, 12–13; color, 13–14, 27, 98, 241, 246, 535, 541; seed of white, 20; conversion of, 21–22, 89, 92, 94, 211; encountered in different context than Negroes, 22; seen as savages, 27, 95; attacks by, 45, 72; abuse by Spanish condemned, 57n; justice for in R. I., 70; in Mass., 71, 232; included in laws regulating Negroes, 82n; characteristics compared to Negro's, 89; as symbols of American experience, 90–91; subject to castration, 155; question of virility, 162–63, 460; seen different from Negroes, 162–63, 169, 239–40, 477–81; in Ga., 169; and miscegenation, 169, 480; remedy for snakebite, 203; and S. P. G., 208; impact of appearance of, 216; classifications of, 217, 220, 223; taken to England, 224, 239–40; in Chain of Being, 226, 500; problem of origins of, 240; Goldsmith on, 248; albino, 250, 523–24; as allies of French, 254, 271; prejudice against, 276–77; and ethnic diversity, 278; suit *re* slave, 343; assumed to crave liberty, 391; prohibited from having white servants, 407; Jefferson on, 439, 453, 460, 477–81; S. S. Smith on, 443–44, 514; anatomy of, 505. *See also* Enslavement

Indians (of India), 12

Indigo, 147, 317

Individualism, 212

Individuality, 90, 108

Inheritance. *See* Acquired characters; Human reproduction

Innateness, 199–200, 444, 527, 534; in Africans, 26; of mental ability, 189–90; concept of sharpens in Revolutionary era, 305, 308–10; in Williams's thought, 535. *See also* Color; Environmentalism

Inoculation, 259–60

Inquisition, 58

Institutes of the Laws of England (Edward Coke), 50

Insurrection. *See* Slave revolts

Intelligence. *See* Mental ability

Interfertility, 234–35, 495, 497, 499–500, 506

Intermarriage, 518–19; Dutch in Africa, 84; regional pattern, 138–39; prohibited in Montserrat, 140; with

Indians prohibited and advocated, 163; in S. C., 171–72; in New England, 175; Crawford defends right of, 446; banned by some northern states, 471–72; not advocated by antislavery supporters, 544. *See also* Miscegenation

Iredell, James, 324n

Ireland, 87, 170

Irish: as captive "slaves," 63; in Barbados, 65, 87; servants, 81, 91; as nonslaves, 86–88; in melting pot, 336; considered one of six nations of immigrants to U. S., 337n; language used by, 339; in S. C., 340

Iroquois, 514

Islam, 23, 39n, 55–56. *See also* Christianity; Muslims

Isle of Man, 86

Isle of Wight Co., Va., 157n

Israel, 25n; as migrating nation, 18, 36; law of, 67–68, 69, 105, 294; Puritans as new nation of, 199; identification with migration of, 337n; Negro rebels identify with, 393; exodus of likened to colonization, 557, 573–74. *See also* Canaan; Jews

Italians, 254

J

Jackson, James, 325–26, 384, 421

Jackson, John G., 389–90

Jackson, Dr. Robert, 528

Jacob (in Bible), 243

Jacob (Negro in Md.), 53

Jacobinism, 387–88, 395–96, 507. *See also* French Revolution

Jacobins, 376–77, 381

Jamaica: captured from Spanish, 63; discriminates against Irish, 86; Long on miscegenation in, 140; population, 141, 176, 177; comparison with S. C. and N. C., 145; slave revolt in, 152n; Edwards on mulattoes in, 175, 177; compared to Barbados, 176–77; educated Negro in, 253; and climatic argument, 264. *See also* West Indies

James I (King of England), 30

Jamestown, Va., 45, 71

Japheth, 17, 84

Jay, John, 338, 339, 344

Jefferson, Thomas: significance of, xii, 458–59; hatred of slavery, 273, 430–35; votes for exclusion of slavery from Northwest Territory, 321; pessimism on prospect of abolition, 331,

347, 551; refutes European derogations of America, 334; helps design
national seal, 337n; *Summary View*,
339; uninterested in educating Negroes, 355, 362; on spread of rebellion, 381, 386; influence, 429; personality, 429, 431–32, 461, 466–69,
475–77; as slaveholder, 430–31, 432;
ideas on human equality, 431–32;
compares Negroes to whites, 436–40,
475; asks scientific inquiry into racial
differences, 438–39; on Negro's place
in nature, 438, 489–90; on moral
sense, 439–40, 452; criticized by
equalitarians, 441–44, 450, 460, 496–
97, 516; political attacks on, 442,
452, 464, 468–69, 502–4; as secretary
of state, 450, 466; and Banneker,
450, 451–52, 454–55; on inferiority of
Negroes, 453–57, 481; on orang-
outang, 458–59; on Negro's sexuality,
458–60; on skin color, 458, 513; defends Indian's virility, 460; silent in
face of criticism, 460, 503; feelings
about women, 461–68, 475; relatives
of, 461–62, 466, 467–68; in Paris,
462, 463, 467, 477; and Hemingses,
464–69; views on miscegenation, 464,
467–68, 470, 472, 480, 490; and his
culture on interracial sex, 470–71;
on castration, 473; bifurcates world,
475–77; compares Indians and Negroes, 477–81; equalitarianism of,
481, 488; quoted by Hunter, 501;
election as president, 507, 531; on
albino Negroes, 522–23; on colonization, 546–47, 552, 558, 562–64, 566,
568, 578; criticized on colonization,
556; assumed to have called Negroes
inferior, 558; on American mission,
573–74. *See also* Declaration of Independence
Jenyns, Soame, 224
Jeremiad, 297–301
Jersey Island, 86
Jews, 18, 36–37, 65, 94, 493–94, 514.
    See also Bible; Hebraic law; Israel
Jobson, Richard, 22–23, 34–35, 61, 158
Johnson, Anthony, 74
Johnson, Gov. Robert, 172
Jones, Rev. Absalom, 328, 422–23, 455,
    528
Jones, Charles, 112–13, 538–39
Jones, Rev. Hugh, 191
Jones, James, 329
Josselyn, John, 245–46, 259

Jowan (Negro girl), 75
Judaic-Christian tradition, 493–94
Jury, 403
Just war. *See* Captivity
Justices of the peace, 51, 106, 108, 112

K

Kalm, Peter, 183, 243–44
Kames, Henry Home, Lord, 163n, 245,
    539
Kent, Eng., 55
Kentucky, 320, 347, 396, 412–13, 575,
    615. *See also* Congress (U. S.)
Keyser, Thomas, 70
Kidnapping, 81, 86, 343–44, 404, 410
Kimber, Edward, 261
King, Rufus, 564, 568
King, William, 59
Kinloch, Francis, 435
Kormantin (West Africa), 4

L

Laban, 243
Labor: free wage, 47; shortage in
America, 47, 72, 83, 91, 130; con-
sidered a positive good, 52; need for
conduces to non-freedom, 74; effect
of shortage, 107; skilled Negro, 128–
29, 172, 174, 406; whites dislike with
Negroes, 129; in antislavery argu-
ment, 351. *See also* Frontier
Lamarck, Jean Baptiste, 517
Lambert, John, 405
Language. *See* Acculturation; Speech
Lapland, 226
Lapps, 216
La Rochefoucald-Liancourt, François
Alexandre Frédéric, Duc de, 408,
    553–54
Latin America. *See* South America
Laurens, Henry, 173, 302, 338
Laurens, John, 302
Law, English: slavery in, 44; on eve of
settlement, 45; in favor of liberty,
61; on sexual offenses, 79; common
to all English colonies, 83; slaves as
property in, 104; castration alien to,
156.
    Other: statutory, 48, 49; common,
49, 50; Roman, 50; civil, 53; natural,
54, 144, 164; Hebraic, 67–68, 69, 105,
294; as historical source, 587
Lawrence, Richard, 79
Lawson, John, 162n
Lay, Benjamin, 424
Lee, Arthur, 309–10

Leeward Islands, 63, 86, 161n, 176, 233. *See also* Antigua; Montserrat; Nevis, St. Kitts; West Indies
Leisler's Rebellion, 119
Le Jau, Rev. Francis, 183
L'Enfant, Major Pierre Charles, 450
Leo Africanus, 33–34, 35, 60
Leprosy, 53, 258, 260, 518–21
Letters from an American Farmer (St. Jean de Crèvecoeur), 336
Lexington, Ky., 396
Lexington, Va., 417
Liberty: personal freedom, 48, 102; increasing in late medieval England, 50; Puritan concepts of, 69–70; slaves assumed to crave, 111, 115, 303–4, 394–97, 561–62, 578; negated by slave codes, 127, 147; slavery as negation of American, 134; grows with slavery, 135; acclaimed by Stiles, 269–70; all men assumed to crave, 388–91; reprobated by Federalists, 396; spread of American to Europe, 423–24; eulogies on, 576–77. *See also* Antislavery; Conversion; Natural rights
Libia, 20, 30, 33–34
Libians, 12
Lice, 249, 492
Ligon, Richard, 65, 232
Lincoln, Abraham, 351
Lining, Dr. John, 526, 528
Linnaean classification, xii, 304–5, 484, 488, 489–90
Linnaeus, Carolus, 238, 243, 305; inspires imitation, 216; classifies man with animals, 218–19; classifies mankind, 220–21; approach of and Chain of Being, 221–22, 223; on Hottentots, 227; on species, 234, 499; on hybridization and strange origin of Negroes, 236; cited as proving Negroes and orang-outangs distinct species, 495
Linné, Carl von. See Linnaeus, Carolus
Lions, 29n
Literacy, 384. *See also* Education; Schools
Littleton, Nathaniel, 74
Littleton, Sir Thomas, 50
Liverpool, 500
Livingston, Robert R., 338
Locke, John, 235–36, 287, 289, 350–51, 440–41
Logan, Chief, 477
Logan, George, 385
Logan, James, 338

London, 6, 29n, 64, 141, 224. *See also* Bishop of London
London Magazine, 153
Long, Edward: describes miscegenation, 140; on status of mulattoes in Jamaica, 177; on mulattoes and Chain of Being, 228; on white women wanting Negro men, 239n; claims Negro's lice black, 249; ridicules Negro poetry, 285; utilizes Chain of Being, 484–85; on Negro's place in nature, 491–93; refuted, 494–95
Long Island, N. Y., 84, 116
Longoe, Anthony, 74
Lord's Prayer, 211
Lot (in Bible), 242
Louisiana, 174n, 389, 559
Louisiana Purchase, 377, 480, 547, 564
Louisiana Territory, 330, 549, 564
L'Ouverture, Toussaint, 377, 381, 396
Love, John, 576
Lower South. *See* Antislavery; Georgia; Miscegenation; North Carolina; Sectional divisions; Slave codes; Slave trade; Slavery; South Carolina
Ludlow, Thomas, 76
Luffman, John, 174
Lunenberg Co., Va., 553
Luther, Martin, 39n, 192, 363
Lutherans, 19n
Lynching, 121, 473

M

McHenry, James, 450, 454
McLeod, Rev. Alexander, 362–63, 448
McPherson, Christopher, 417
MacSparran, Rev. James, 105n
Macon, Nathaniel, 327
Macon Telegraph, 473
Madison, Rev. James (1749–1812), college president, 523–24
Madison, James (1751–1836), statesman, 324, 381, 463; assumes his slave craves liberty, 303–4; on three-fifths rule, 322–23; describes sectional divisions, 324; compared to Jefferson, 476–77; favors colonization, 552–53
Magaw, Rev. Samuel, 424
Maine, 480
Malaria, 583–84
Malays, 216, 223
Malpighi, Marcello, 246
Malpighian layer, 585
Man, Isle of, 86
Man-stealing, 70, 294

Manadier, Rev. (Anglican in Md.), 186

Mandingoes, 34

Manigault, Peter, 173n

Mansa Musa, 158n

Manumission, Va.: law of 1782, xiii, 456, 551, 576; restrictions in southern states, 123–24, 399, 405, 574–81; regulated by northern colonies, 124; of mixed offspring, 169; and conversion, 92–93, 180–81; for service in Revolution, 302; changes in laws concerning, 347–48. See also Emancipation; Free Negroes

Marblehead, Mass., 303

Marmosets, 29n

Marriage. See Intermarriage; Family; Women

Martin, J. P., 378

Martin, Luther, 324

Martin Co., N. C., 397, 398

Martyr, Peter, 14

Maryland: slave codes in, 44; sense of Englishness in, 46; servitude in, 48; slavery develops in, 71–83; servants in, 80–81; discriminates against Irish, 86–87; naturalizes aliens, 87–88; laws re conversion and manumission, 92; calls Indians "pagans," 95; Negroes speak English in, 96n; population, 103, 175, 339, 406, 615; frees slave of cruel master, 109; slave conspiracies in, 121, 153–54; manumission in, 124, 347; militia in, 126, 411; voting in, 126, 412–13; laws on rape, 157n; progress of conversion in, 186–87; promotional tract, 193; Anglican churches in, 207–8; Woolman in, 272; might have abolished slavery, 315–16; domestic slave trade in, 320; antislavery in, 343, 344, 346; censures Abolition Society, 348; Quakers in, 357; aids St. Domingo refugees, 380; acts against slaves brought from St. Domingo, 382; slave violence in, 392; penalizes kidnapping of Negroes, 404; restricts free Negroes, 407–8, 575; colonization in, 549, 553. See also Congress (U. S.); Miscegenation; Sectional divisions; Slave codes

Maryland Abolition Society, 348, 448

Maryland Gazette (Annapolis), 392

Mason, George, 295–96, 301n, 320

Masons, 130, 417

Massachusetts, 298, 534, 545; sense of Englishness in, 46; in slave trade, 67;

first law on slavery, 67–68, 84; tries penal slavery, 68; punishes man-stealing, 70; militia in, 71, 126, 411; conversion of Indians in, 92; laws re manumission and conversion, 93; Spanish "slave" in, 96; lynching in, 121; bars Negroes from lottery, 130; punishment of rape in, 157n; degrades a "gentleman," 192–93; Negro church member in, 205–6; conversion in, 206n, 211; taxes Negroes with horses and hogs, 232; antislavery Negroes in, 291; voting in, 302; slavery found unconstitutional in, 345, 351; aids St. Domingo refugees, 380; orders out free Negroes not citizens, 410–11; Negro school in, 417; church seating in, 418; opinion of Negro's mental ability in, 456–57; bans intermarriage, 472; queries on condition of Negroes in, 555–56; and Va., 557; population, 615. See also Boston; Congress (U. S.); Miscegenation; New England; Sectional divisions; Slave codes

Massachusetts Historical Society, 334, 553, 555

Maternal impressions, 242–43

Mather, Cotton, 214, 363; stresses Englishness of New Englanders, 46; on mental ability and conversion, 187; urges instruction of Negroes, 189–90; asserts equality of Negroes, 200–201; in inoculation controversy, 202–4; argues blackness irrelevant to salvation, 258; contrasted to Woolman, 275

Maupertius, Pierre Louis Moreau de, 244, 250–51, 252

Maverick, Samuel, 71

Medical Repository, 530

Meeting for Sufferings (Phila.), 301

Meetings (Quaker), 271–72, 273, 300, 301, 420, 422

Melanin, 585

Melting pot, 336–41. See also Ethnic diversity

Mental ability, xii; of Africans, 26; and conversion, 187–90; Negro's belittled, 253, 285, 306–8, 531, 556; Negro's defended by antislavery advocates, 282–85; Jefferson on, 436–40, 479; conceived in terms of different "capacities," 440–41; debate on Negro's after Revolution, 441–57; White on, 501–2

Mestize (term), 175

Mestize, 150. *See also* Mustee

Metamorphosis Plantarum (René de Réaumur), 236

Metappin (Indian), 94

Methodists: benefit from Great Awakening, 212; Negroes join, 213; condemn slavery, 293; itinerant preachers, 296; church reorganized after Revolution, 334; advocate education of Negroes, 362; to be spared by Gabriel plotters, 393*n;* denounced for preaching liberty and equality, 396; equalitarian stance towards Negroes, 418–19; Negroes separate from in Philadelphia, 422. *See also* Churches

Mice, 523

Michaëlius, Rev. Jonas, 83

Microcosmus (Peter Heylyn), 19

Midrash, 18

Midrash Rabbah, 36

Mifflin, Thomas, 350

Mifflin, Warner, 327, 359*n*

Militia, 71, 109, 111, 125–26, 411–12

Miller, Rev. Samuel, 362

Mills, Alice, 156

Milton, John, 40

Mingo (Negro in Va.), 76

Mingrelians, 254

Minister(s): assert human unity, 12–13; on Negro's color, 19, 526, 534–36; explain origin of slavery, 54; protests degradation of Negro's nature, 54, 229–30; describe nature of slavery, 56, 61–62; arrives in New Amsterdam, 83; describes Scots in New England, 88; on complexion and slavery in 17th century, 97; punishes slave, 105*n;* required to read aloud slave codes, 108; describes Carolina back country, 110*n;* report opposition to mixed catechism, 133–34; and laws *re* manumission, 180–81; Anglicans, 186–87, 197–98, 206–9; on mental ability, 187–88, 283, 448; asserts equality of Negroes, 200, 201–2, 279, 293; claims Negro descended from cursed Ham, 201; in inoculation controversy, 202–4, 260; Negro, 209–13, 328, 419, 422–23, 455; preach to Negroes, 215; on religious diversity in Pa., 238; on blackness as mark of reprobation, 258; on necessity of having Negroes for hot labor, 261–62; on American destiny, 269–70, 543–44; describes prejudice, 276; describes color problem in America, 280; denounces slave trade, 294; preaches to whites and Negroes, 296; defend rights of colonies, 297; denounce slavery, 297–300, 371; wonders whether Negroes inferior, 309; petitions Congress, 328; Swedish Moravian, 338; urges Negro education, 362; delineates obstacles to abolition, 362–63; on spiritual equality and temporal inequality, 363–64; asks amelioration of slavery, 364–65; calls St. Domingo retribution against slave trade, 378; predicts spread of liberty to Europe, 386; on effect of slavery on Negroes, 442–44; fathers mulattoes, 473*n;* on albinos, 523–24; proposes colonization, 550. *See also* Anglicans; Churches; Conversion; Great Awakening; Mather; Smith, Rev. Samuel Stanhope; Society for the Propagation of the Gospel; Whitefield, George

Minor, John, 576

Miscegenation: in England, 15; in early Va. and Md., 78–80; in Bermuda, 79; in Md., 96, 164; in Va., 96, 125, 127–28; importance of, 136–37; rate of, 137, 542; based on perception of difference, 137–38, 144, 475; regional variations, 138–41, 148, 471–75; laws prohibiting, 139–40, 144; as failure of self-control, 143–44; in Albany and Boston, 144; in West Indies and Carolinas compared, 145; in S. C., 145–49, 164, 165, 166; generates "male" attitudes, 149–50; in West Indies, 152; restricted in Leeward Islands, 161*n;* and Indians, 163, 480; seen as an infection, 165; seen as mixture of bloods, 165–66, 168; Sewall on, 165, 197; Indian-Negro, 169; not punished as buggery, 232; Long on, 254–55; W. L. Smith on, 326; inhibits growth of melting pot idea, 340–41; calculation of future results, 413; utilized to twit Quakers, 421; question of Jefferson's supposed, 464–69; associated with slave revolts, 470; feelings on in N. C., 473*n;* effect of slavery on, 475; as assurance of human unity, 495; opposed by Rush, 519–20; and fear of emancipation, 542–69; relation to free Negroes and

slave revolts, 578–82. *See also* Inter-marriage; Mulattoes; Passing; Sexuality
Missionary efforts. *See* Conversion; Society for the Propagation of the Gospel
Mississippi Territory, 328, 395, 412
Missouri Compromise, 328n, 331, 409, 434
Mitchell, Dr. John, 246–47, 259, 260n
Mitchill, Dr. Samuel Latham, 330, 522, 536–37
Modern Chivalry (Hugh Brackenridge), 523
Moguller, 226
Monboddo, James Burnett, Lord, 236–37
Mongolians, 223, 583
Monkeys, 29, 228, 237, 305, 500, 505
Monroe, James, 381, 394, 400, 435, 563, 568
Montesquieu, Baron de, 261, 262, 278–79, 540
Monticello, 334, 465, 468
Montserrat, 140. *See also* West Indies
Moore, Clement Clarke, 442, 503–4
Moor(s), 6, 12, 254; considered black, 5; Othello as, 37–38; enslave English, 55; religious wars against, 56; on Hawkins's crest, 60; in Va. law, 94. *See also* Othello
Moral sense, 439–41, 452
Moravians, 338
More, Hannah, 446–47
Moreau de St. Méry, Médéric Louis Élie, 382, 406, 412, 415–16
Morgan, Dr. John, 521–22
Moriscos, 254
Morocco, Prince of, 13
Morris, Gouverneur, 477
Morse, Rev. Jedidiah, 363
Mortality, 63, 233, 262–63, 318n, 365
Moses, 23, 393, 574
Moss, Henry, 521–22, 523, 533
Mott, James, 383
Mount Vernon, 319
Mozambique, 60
Mulatto (term), 61, 167–68, 175
Mulattoes, 145; definition, status and treatment of, 163, 167–78; in Long's Chain of Being, 228; color of, 249; in St. Domingo, 376, 378, 385. *See also* Miscegenation
Mules, 234
Murray, William Vans, 395

Museums, 498, 521
Muslims, 23n, 94. *See also* Islam
Mustee (term), 168–69. *See also* Mestize

N

Nakedness, 161–62, 460, 472; in Africa, 4–5, 39–40; of slaves in Barbados, 65; of Negro boys, 159
Napoleon, 377–78
Narragansett Indians, 69
Narragansett region (R. I.), 66
Nassau Hall, 507
National Assembly (France), 376
National identity: Indians retain, 90; Negroes excluded, 208–10; association with whiteness, 259; and Negroes in American army, 302–4; problem of after Revolution, 316, 333–34; and formation of national union, 332, 335, 339, 485–86; question whether Negroes to be included in, 340–41; struggle for, 511; and the American errand, 581. *See also* American destiny; Christianity; Miscegenation; National union; Nationalism; Self-identity
Natural law, 54, 144, 164
Natural rights: ideology and environmentalism, 288–89; theory in antislavery, 289–91, 292–94; and social thought in Revolutionary era, 294–96; and slavery as sin, 298–99; not challenged by proslavery writers, 304; and antislavery after Revolution, 349–52; not embraced by Quakers, 357, 360; relationship to religious equalitarianism, 361–62, 364–65; and humanitarianism, 367, 368n; doctrine of regarded as contagious, 386–91; in Jefferson's thought, 431; and equality as Revolutionary ideal, 511. *See also* Liberty
National union, 315–16, 332, 335, 339, 446, 485–86. *See also* Nationalism
Nationalism, 24, 208–10, 331–34. *See also* American destiny; National identity; National union
Natural selection, 244, 257, 510, 527, 583–84. *See also* Acquired characters; Color; Human reproduction
Naturalization, 87–88, 341
Neau, Rev. Elias, 258
Negro (term), 61, 73–74, 95, 167

The Negro Christianized (Cotton Mather), 187, 258

Negro woman (term), 78n

Negroes (as active agents): slave owner, 74; as Masons, 130, 417; preachers, 209–10, 212–13, 419; poetess, 283–86; poet, 285n; petition against slavery, 291; in Revolution, 302–4, 321; ministers, 328, 422–23, 455; initiate schooling in Boston, 362; letter by, 358–59; in S. C. petition against restrictions, 409; vote Federalist in N. Y., 413; at funeral, 416; protest exclusion from schools, 417; teacher, 417; maintains carriage in Richmond, 417; becoming Methodists and Baptists, 418–19; applies for Quaker membership, 420; found own churches, 422–24; arithmetician, 449; physician, 449; mathematician, 449–52; famous albino, 521–22; in yellow fever epidemic, 528; attempts colonization, 550–51. *See also* Acculturation; Free Negroes; Gabriel plot; Intermarriage; St. Domingo; Slave revolts; Slave resistance, violence, and crime

Negro's and Indians Advocate (Morgan Godwyn), 97, 231

Nevis, 185. *See also* West Indies

New Amsterdam. *See* New York City

New Atlantis (Francis Bacon), 34

New Divinity, 276, 543

New England: sense of community, 46, 98; contrasted with Va. and Md., 46, 71–72; Scottish and Irish captives in, 63; slavery develops in, 66–71; population, 66, 103, 175, 339; in slave trade, 66–67, 68, 372; need for labor compared with Va., 72; Scottish prisoners well treated in, 88; less restriction on free Negroes and slaves, 125; intermarriage, 138, 175; permits Negroes relative sexual freedom, 141; sex ratio in, 175; churches in, 206–7; conversion in, 211–12; color of Negroes in, 243–44; protests against British tyranny in, 292; clergy defends right of colonists in, 297; antislavery Jeremiad in, 300–301; in 1787 slave trade compromise, 324; sends no delegates to convention of antislavery societies, 344; lessens punishments, 408. *See also* Miscegenation; Population; Sectional divisions; Slave codes

New Englanders, 340

New Hampshire, 291, 339, 345, 547, 615. *See also* Congress (U. S.); Miscegenation; New England; Sectional divisions; Slave codes

New Haven, Conn., 68, 69, 384

New Jersey, 276, 281, 416, 524; laws *re* conversion and manumission, 92; population, 103, 175, 339, 615; conspiracy in, 114; arson in, 117; Negro militia in, 125; lawyer in Charleston, 149; castration in, 154; law on rape, 157; Woolman in, 272; abolition of slavery, 345; requires Negroes be taught reading, 355; Quaker education of Negroes in, 357–58; sectional split in, 359n; helps St. Domingo refugees, 380; voting in, 412–13; and Quaker membership for Negroes, 420; S. S. Smith in, 508; slave violence, crime and resistance in, 560. *See also* Congress (U. S.); Miscegenation; Sectional divisions; Slave codes

New Jersey Abolition Society, 355, 359n

New Light ideas, 214. *See also* Great Awakening

New London, Conn., 158

New Model Army, 192

New Netherland. *See* New York

New Orleans, 174n

New Theory of the Earth (Abraham Bradley), 531

New York, 105; slavery develops in, 83–84; population, 84, 103, 175, 339, 615; Duke's Laws, 84, 92n; laws *re* conversion and manumission, 92; slave plots in, 115; slave violence in, 116; less rigorous regulation of free Negroes, 125; Negro militia in, 125, 411; miscegenation in, 144; mustees in, 169; conversion in, 189; color of Negroes in, 243–44; Negro albinos on show in, 251; Quakers of petition Congress, 325; abolishes slavery, 345; requires Negroes be taught reading, 355; abolition bill in, 360n, 413; arson in, 392; voting in, 413–14, 471–72; separation of races in, 415; Negro churches in, 424–25. *See also* Congress (U. S.); Miscegenation; Sectional divisions; Slave codes

New York City, 323, 505; population, 103, 119; slave conspiracies in, 116–18, 121, 122; sense of community in,

119–20; Negro Masons in, 130; slave plot and conversion in, 181; aids St. Domingo refugees, 380; yellow fever in, 529

New York Daily Advertiser, 326

New-York Journal, and Patriotic Register, 381

New York Manumission Society, 344, 355, 359, 362, 448

Newark, N. J., 380

Newburyport, Mass., 298

Newport, Christopher, 61*n*

Newport, R. I., 10, 120, 276; population, 103, 119; colonization in, 357–58, 550

Newton, Isaac: inspires imitation, 216; as pinnacle of mankind, 224, 449, 454; utilized in analysis of skin color, 246–47, 253; influence of, 390, 482, 526

Nichols, Rev. (Anglican in Md.), 186

Nicholson, Gov. Francis, 96*n*

Nicholson, John, 423

Nicholson, Thomas, 293

Nile River, 60

Nisbet, Richard, 306–7

Noah, 17–18, 23, 35, 36, 42*n*, 240. *See also* Ham

Noble savage, 9–10, 27

Noddles Island, 71

Nominalism. *See* Conceptualism

Norfolk, Va., 380, 381–82

Norfolk Co., Va., 79

North. *See* Miscegenation; Population; Sectional divisions; Slave codes; Slavery

North Bridgewater, Mass., 418

North Carolina: slavery develops in, 84–85; laws *re* conversion and manumission, 92; manumission laws in, 123–24, 347–48; regulations concerning free Negroes in, 124, 408; voting in, 126–27, 412–14; mixed schools refused in, 133; population, 145, 175, 316, 339, 406, 615; castration in, 154, 155, 157; law on rape, 157*n*; bans intermarriage with Indians, 163; defines *mulatto*, 168; mustees in, 169; Anglican churches in, 206–8; as borderland, 316; domestic slave trade in, 320; position on slave trade in Constitutional Convention, 324; presence of Negroes considered misfortune in, 327; planter opulence denounced, 333; Quakers in, 343, 346, 419, 421; acts against murder of

slaves, 367–68; aids St. Domingo refugees, 380; bars Negroes from the West Indies, 382, 383; slave revolts in after Gabriel plot, 396–98; tightens slave code, 399; penalizes kidnapping of Negroes, 404; Negro militia in, 411–12; free Negro teaches school in, 417; Negro churches in, 425; darkness of white men in, 514; Williamson in, 539. *See also* Congress (U. S.); Miscegenation; Sectional divisions; Slave codes

Northwest Passage, 40

Northwest Territory, 321–22, 328*n*, 553

Norwich, Conn., 299

Notes on the State of Virginia (Thomas Jefferson), 334, 546; first written, 432; Jefferson hesitates to publish, 435; stimulates discussion of Negroes, 441, 486, 547; assessed by Ramsay, 456; read by St. G. Tucker, 456; section on Negro in magazine, 494. *See also* Jefferson, Thomas

Nova Scotia, 550

Nova Zembla, 226, 229

Numidia, 20, 33

Nudity. *See* Nakedness

O

Observations upon Slavery (Charles Crawford), 446

Odor. *See* Smell

Ohio, 412–13, 575

Onesimus (slave of Mather), 202

Opticks (Isaac Newton), 246, 253

Orang-outangs: Tyson on, 218, 498; Camper on, 226, 230, 237; Monboddo on copulation of, 236–37; in Chain of Being, 305, 495–96, 499, 500; Jefferson on, 458–59, 490; relation to Negro women, 494–95, 499–500; Moore on place of in Chain of Being, 504. *See also* Apes

Order, xiii; new need for after Middle Ages, 25; social, 42–43, 134, 193, 485–86; different needs for among Americans and Europeans, 255–59; in Jefferson's thought, 431, 462, 475–77; S. S. Smith's desire for, 507

  In nature: search for necessitated by overseas discoveries, 216–17; imposed by Linnaean classification, 218–19; affirmed by Mitchell's theory of colors, 247; miscegenation as a violation of, 469–70; 18th century passion for, 482–83; S. S. Smith on,

487; destroyed by mixture of Negroes and orang-outangs, 494–95; offered by Darwinism, 510; Williams on, 536. *See also* Chain of Being
Ordination, 207
Orientals. *See* Asiatics
Oroonoko, 27–28
Oroonoko (Aphra Behn) , 9
Othello, 5, 34
Othello (William Shakespeare) , 37–38, 258, 405
"Othello" (pseudonym) , 547
Otis, Harrison Gray, 328–29
Otis, James, 278, 292
Overseers, 114, 256, 392, 393
Ovington, John, 227
Owl, 506
Oxen, 190
Oxford, Md., 186

P

Pagans (term) , 95
Page, Gov. John, 564–65
Paine, Thomas, 269, 294, 299–300, 302, 337
Panama, 250
Papists, 87, 88, 205. *See also* Popery; Roman Catholicism
Paris, 250, 376, 386, 462–63, 467, 477
Parliament, 302, 351, 352
Parrish, John, 549, 550
Parrots, 222, 225, 230, 253, 499, 500
Passing, 171–74
Peale, Charles Willson, 334, 521
Pemberton, James, 344, 420
Penis, 30, 34–35, 158–59, 163, 464, 501
Pennsylvania: population, 102, 103, 175, 339, 615; Germans in, 102, 143; militia in, 125–26, 411; attitude toward miscegenation, 139, 470; castration in, 154; law on rape, 157; First Pa. Regiment, 159; slave revolts feared in, 196; religious diversity in, 238; attitudes toward Germans in, 254, 270, 338; diversity greatest in, 270; Quaker position in, 271, 421; massacre of Indians in, 276–77; abolishes slavery, 302, 345; freedom suit in, 323n; State House, 324; antislavery societies in, 343; kidnapping of Negroes in, 343–44; debate on aid to St. Domingo in, 378; aids St. Domingo refugees, 380; fails to strengthen law on kidnapping, 404n; constitution of, 413; voting in, 413–14; camp meeting in, 419; Ne-

gro Quaker in, 420–22; bill banning intermarriage, 472. *See also* Congress (U. S.) ; Miscegenation; Philadelphia; Sectional divisions; Slave codes
Pennsylvania Abolition Society, 325, 359, 424, 446, 447, 449
Pennsylvania Packet (Phila.) , 307
Pequot War, 68, 72
Personal Slavery Established (anonymous) , 304, 305, 308, 484–85
Petty, Sir William, 224–25, 449
Phaëton, 11
Philadelphia: population, 103, 119; sense of community in, 120; mixed schools in, 133; Whitefield in, 213; antislavery in, 290; Paine in, 299; pamphlet debate over slavery in, 304–5, 307; Constitutional Convention in, 322; Quakers of petition Congress, 325; antislavery society in, 343; free Negroes in, 352; aids St. Domingo refugees, 380; attitudes of workmen in, 406; racial antipathy in, 415–16; interracial funeral in, 416; Negro Masons in, 417; burial grounds in, 418n; Negroes form churches in, 422–24; Negro ministers in, 455; Peale's museum in, 521; white Negroes in, 521–22; yellow fever in, 528–29; colonization proposed in, 546. *See also* Convention of antislavery societies
Philadelphia Monthly Meeting, 422
Philadelphia Museum, 334
Philadelphia Society for Free Instruction of Colored People, 357–59
Philadelphia Yearly Meeting, 271, 273, 420, 422
Phillips, Capt. Thomas, 11
Physicians, 17; and connection of ape with Negroes, 31; in inoculation controversy, 202–4; on Chain of Being, 228–29, 498–502, 505–6; on problem of color, 246–48, 516, 526, 539–41; not interested in degrading Negro, 259–60; in antislavery movement, 260, 359; on Negro's mental ability, 283, 456; investigate albinism, 521–23, 533; and yellow fever, 528–29; assert Negro equality, 530; criticize S. S. Smith, 531, 533–34. *See also* Rush, Benjamin
Pierce, Capt. William, 67
Pinckney, Gov. Charles, 387
Pinckney, Charles Cotesworth, 321n, 324, 525

Pinkney, William, 447–48
Pleasants, Robert, 357, 359
Pliny, 12, 249, 306
Plots. *See* Slave revolts
Pluralism. *See* Ethnic diversity; Religious diversity
Plutarch, 12
Plymouth colony, 45
Poisoning, 392, 393, 398
Polydactylism, 244
Pongos, 237
Poor laws, 42
Pope, Alexander, 219, 483
Popery, 23, 46, 118. *See also* Papists; Roman Catholicism
Population, 83; map indicating, 615; in West Indies and continent, 63; Providence Island, 64; New England, 66; Va., 73, 78*n*, 319; Bermuda, 78*n*; N. Y., 84; importance of ratios, 101, 106, 136–37; proportion of Germans in Pa., 102; proportion of Negroes in continental colonies, 102–3; in S. C., 106, 145, 147; northern cities, 119; Negro preponderance affects miscegenation, 141–42, 474; ratios in Barbados, 152*n*; sex ratios in various colonies, 175–76; as factor in sectional division, 315–16; proportion of English in white American, 339; St. Domingo, 385; increase, 406–7; effect of ratio in Va., 551; free Negro in Va., 575; historical sources on, 598–99. *See also* Mortality
Port-au-Prince, 382
Port Folio, 503
Portuguese: as explorers, 3, 56; in Africa, 3, 22, 59, 158; contact with Africa, 6; and conversion, 21–22, 23; enslave Africans in 15th and 16th centuries, 57; buy and sell Negroes with English, 59; character of slavery, 60; associated with slavery in minds of Englishmen, 60–61; captured and set free by English, 65; influence on American slavery, 72, 98; Africans captured from and brought to Va., 74; language, 95; definitions of mixed offspring by, 167; treatment of slaves compared with English, 198; more tawny than English, 242, 254–55; colonies proposed in dominions of, 563; absence of representative assemblies in colonies of, 588

Pott, Francis, 75
Pott, John, 75
Powell, George Gabriel, 173
Powhatan Indians, 94
Pownall, Thomas, 353
Predestination. *See* Calvinism
Prejudice (term), 276
Prejudice: question of early development, 80; problem of origin, 257–59; first recognition of, 273–78; and recognition of color problem, 278–81; denounced by antislavery advocates, 281–83; modern writers on, 317; Sullivan's plan to eradicate, 355–56; Quaker efforts to combat, 358; Jefferson on, 435–36, 458; against miscegenation supported by Rush, 519–20; S. S. Smith on, 544; Madison on, 552–53; Fairfax on, 554–55; G. Tucker on, 556; Sullivan on, 557; St. G. Tucker, 558–60; in Va., 568–69
Presbyterian Synod of New York and Philadelphia, 362
Presbyterians, 300, 301, 417. *See also* Churches; College of New Jersey
Presidential elections. *See* Election
Prices: of slaves, 65, 76–77, 89, 130, 174, 320–21; of servants, 76–77
Prince George Co., Md., 121
Prince George Co., Va., 320
Princeton, N. J., 508, 524. *See also* College of New Jersey
Princeton College. *See* College of New Jersey
Principal Navigations (Richard Hakluyt), 3
Prognathism, 225, 235, 237, 238. *See also* Facial angle
Projection. *See* Sexuality
Property: servants' labor as, 47–48; how thought to have arisen, 55; slaves as, 101, 104, 322–23; security of in America claimed, 269–70; ideas about in Revolution hurt antislavery, 350–51; right of recognized by antislavery gradualism, 354; ideas on a barrier to emancipation, 431–32; and colonization, 554, 558; in unborn persons, 559; rights in Va. debate, 576. *See also* Slaves
Proslavery: before Revolution, 199–200; arguments answered by Woolman, 274; writings in Revolutionary era, 304–8; in Congress, 325–30; views of James Jackson, 325–26, 384,

421; in Va., 394–95, 456, 577; Chain of Being in, 493; advocates on danger of miscegenation, 544–45; and inevitability of civil equality, 558; and colonization, 566; in 19th century, 569. *See also* Smith, W. L.
Protestant Reformation, 40
Protestantism, 24, 46, 205, 210–12. *See also* Churches; Conversion; Great Awakening; Puritanism
Protestants, 86
Providence, R. I., 70n, 357–58, 359n, 417, 447
Providence Abolition Society, 550
Providence Company, 64, 67
Providence Island, 63–64, 67, 68
Psychology, 287, 441. *See also* Innateness; Mental ability
Ptolemy, 12, 13, 34, 249
Puerto Rico, 61n
Punch, John, 75
Purchas, Rev. Samuel, 3, 12, 33, 57, 60
Puritanism, 293–94. *See also* Calvinism; Churches; Jeremiad; Protestantism
Puritans: in England, 40, 42, 51; and slavery, 54; in Providence Island, 63; accept slavery, 66–69; ideas on liberty, 69–70; compared with Virginians, 72; rule in Va., Md., Bermuda, 87; Americans as heirs of, 135; sense of community, 165; attitude toward Negroes and slavery, 199–205; sense of exclusiveness, 204–6; authoritative position in New England, 210; sense of mission, 544. *See also* Congregationalists; Mather; New Divinity; New England; Sewall
Pygmies, 25n
Pyle, Robert, 256–57

Q

Quadroon (term), 175
Quadroons, 150
Quakers: bury Negroes separately, 132–33; early antislavery among, 194–95, 196–97, 256, 257; as low church Protestants, 199; authoritative position of in Pa., 210; growth of antislavery among, 271–76; argue inconsistency of Negro slavery, 290; and natural rights ideology, 292, 293; on sin of slavery, 300, 301; petition Congress, 325, 326, 327, 328–30, 388; in vanguard of antislavery, 343, 359–60; in N. C., 343, 346, 348;

petition southern legislatures, 347; oppose Declaration of Independence, 350; concern with freed Negroes, 356–61; reaction of to St. Domingo, 380; to be spared by Gabriel plotters, 393n; lull in antislavery activities, 401; attend funeral of Negro, 416n; views on Negro membership, 419–22; tribalism, 421–22; assist founding of Negro churches, 422–23; and colonization, 549, 550–51
Quincy, Josiah, 145, 282

R

Race (term), 489–90
Races: early attempts to categorize, 217–18, 220–21, 241; classified by Blumenbach, 222–23; and Chain of Being, 225–26; Bible inspires division of mankind into three, 240; as separate creations, 240, 245, 493, 502, 531; albinos not thought of as, 251–52; superiority of whites asserted, 253–55; not separately created, 486–87, 534; Williams on, 535; problem of number of, 540; modern concept of, 583–84. *See also* Chain of Being; Human unity; Interfertility; Species
Rahway, N. J., 420
Raleigh, Sir Walter, 42n
Raleigh Register, 397, 417
Ram, 38
Ramsay, Dr. David, 337, 340, 456, 516, 529
Ramsay, Rev. James, 309, 494, 498
Randolph, John, 331
Rape, 155, 157, 398n, 463, 473
Rappahannock River, 75
Rats, 523
Ray, John, 506
Raynal, Abbé Guillaume Thomas François, 479
Reason, 277. *See also* Mental ability
Réaumur, René Antoine Ferchault de, 236
Recorder (Richmond), 384, 465
Redness, 8–9, 143, 277, 278–79, 458
Regular Gradation of Man (Charles White), 499
Regulators (in S. C.), 173
Reincke, Rev. Abraham, 338
Religious diversity, 70, 119, 238, 270
Religious revivals. *See* Revivals

Report on Manufactures (Alexander Hamilton), 333
Representation, 73, 103, 322–23, 588
Reproduction. *See* Human reproduction
Republicanism, 331–33
Republicans, 329, 340, 378, 396, 413–14, 476. *See also* Congress (U. S.)
Restoration (in England), 83
Rete mucosum, 505
Revelation. *See* Bible
Revere, Paul, 338
Revivals, 271. *See also* Great Awakening
Revolts. *See* Slave revolts
Revolution. *See* American Revolution; French Revolution; Glorious Revolution
Rhees, John Morgan, 353
Rhode Island, 10, 276; slavery in, 66; antislavery law of 1652, 70–71; population, 103, 615; slave punishment in, 105n; sense of community in, 120; law on rape, 157n; slave trade in, 291, 329, 372; raises battalion of Negroes, 302; abolishes slavery, 345; Negro education in, 357–58; militia in, 411; voting in, 414; bans intermarriage, 472; colonization proposed in, 550. *See also* Congress (U. S.); Miscegenation; New England; Newport; Providence; Slave codes
Rice, Rev. David, 378
Rice, 85, 103, 147, 233, 262–64, 317–18
Richmond, Va., 359n, 380, 393, 417, 564, 576
Richmond New Theater, 417
Rights of the British Colonies Asserted and Proved (James Otis), 292
Rittenhouse, David, 334, 451, 455
Robertson, Thomas B., 576, 580
Robertson, William, 163n
Rochefoucauld-Liancourt. *See* La Rochefoucauld-Liancourt
Rolfe, John, 73
Roman Catholic Church, 198, 334, 418n. *See also* Conversion
Roman Catholicism, 23, 119, 121n, 198, 210–11. *See also* Conversion; Papists; Popery
Roman law, 50
Romans, Bernard, 242n, 285, 305
Romans, 505
Rome, 280

Roxbury, Mass., 121
Royal Academy (England), 498
Royal African Company, 4, 185
Royal Society of London, 224, 244, 250–51, 449, 499, 527
Runaways, 109, 392; treatment in England, 51; in early Va. and Md., 75, 81; as major problem, 107–8; punished, 112–13; in swamps, 113; supposed harbored by free Negroes, 122, 124, 577; castrated in S. C., 154–55; maiming of, 155; with whites, 174n. *See also* Fugitive slave law; Slave codes
Rural Magazine: or, Vermont Repository, 379
Rush, Benjamin, 289, 450, 533; decries effect of slavery on slaves, 281; on mental ability, 283, 448–49, 455; twitted on issue of mental ability, 285; environmentalist argument regarding Negroes in Africa, 286–87; calls slavery a national crime, 300–301; environmentalist contentions of combatted, 305–6; in antislavery society, 344, 359; delights in interracial funeral, 416–17; welcomes Negro churches, 423–24; on moral sense, 440n; psychological taxonomy, 441; antislavery views, 483, 530; and Jefferson, 488; assumes Negro women debauched by orang-outangs, 495; on Negro's color, 517–21, 522, 560; on Negroes and yellow fever, 528
Russian aristocracy, 115
Russians, 254
Rutledge, John, 384, 388
Rutledge, John, Jr., 328, 330

S

Sabbath, 23, 70
Saffin, John, 199–200
Sahara Desert, 5–6
St. Augustine, 18
St. Augustine, Fla., 155
St. Christopher, 63
St. Domingo, xi, 390, 391, 446, 581; revolts in, 375–77; U. S. commerce with, 377; refugees from in U. S., 377, 380–81, 382; and U. S. diplomacy, 377–78; American reaction to revolts in, 378–85; slaves from in U. S., 381–86; population, 385; revolt feared spreading to U. S. from, 386–87; effect on slaves in U. S., 391–92; used by political partisans,

396; Jefferson on, 434; colonization proposed in, 564
St. George's Methodist Church, 422
St. Jerome, 18
St. Kitts, 63. *See also* West Indies
St. Paul, 363
Salem, Mass., 67, 118
Salzburgers, 263
Sambo (term), 150, 175
San Juan de Ulua, 58, 59
Sancho, Ignatius, 437-38, 446
Sandys, George, 60
Santee River, 172
Santo Domingo. *See* St. Domingo
Sargent, Gov. Winthrop, 395
Satyr, 29-30
Savagery, 216; of Africans, 24-28, 309-10; attractions of, 40; as basis for slavery, 97; associated with extreme temperatures, 226; exemplified by Hottentots, 226-27; antislavery advocates on, 285-87, 308; assumed an impermanent condition, 288; of Africans emphasized by proslavery writers, 305-8; linked to dark complexion, 514; as degeneration, 514, 515. *See also* Civilization
Savages (term), 95
Savannah, Ga., 170, 381-82
Saxons, 143, 254
Schools: Negro, 133, 354-55, 362, 400, 417, 447; Benezet's for Negroes, 283, 357; mixed, 354-55, 417; run by free Negroes, 417. *See also* Conversion; Education
Science, 12, 25, 255, 482-83. *See also* Anatomy; Bible; Chain of Being; Color; Jefferson; Linnaean classification; Order; Smith, Rev. Samuel Stanhope
Scorpion, 34
Scotch-Irish, 102, 339
Scots: as captive "slaves," 63; in Barbados, 65; in Mass. militia, 71; as servants, 75, 88; as non-slaves, 86-88; Cresswell on prejudice against, 277; in Ga., 301; in melting pot, 336; considered one of 6 nations of immigrants to U. S., 337n; language of, 339; in S. C., 340
Scott, Thomas, 325, 326
Scurvy, 88
Sectional divisions, 315-16, 349, 555, 575. *See also* Congress (U. S.); Free Negroes

Secularization, xiv, 573; and discoveries, 25; in rationale for slavery, 95-97; of ideas *re* human reproduction, 164-67; of equality, 192-93; fought by S. P. G., 208; of view of man, 216-17; of Chain of Being, 220, 510; of whiteness, 259; of concept of equality, 270-71, 363-64; and prejudice, 277; conduces to environmentalism, 287-88; in Revolutionary era, 294-95; and clergy in Revolution, 297-301; impact on humanitarianism, 365-66; and concept of moral sense, 439-41; and miscegenation, 469-70; and interest in anatomy, 498. *See also* Equalitarianism; Innateness
Seed. *See* Semen
Segregation, 128, 131-34, 414-22
Self-control, xiv, 135; in Englishmen, 40-43; exercised in slave codes, 109, 110; miscegenation a failure in, 143-44; and settlement of New World, 204-5; and Western civilization, 579-82. *See also* Castration; Civilization; Jefferson; Miscegenation; Sexuality; Social control
Self-examination: by Englishmen, 40, 42-43; characteristic of Puritans, 204-5; in Revolutionary era, 264-65, 269-71, 272, 310-11; among Quakers, 271-72; and habitat of America, 288. *See also* Prejudice; Woolman, John
Self-identity, xiv; among Christians, 21; of Englishmen, 24, 25; Americans' contrasted to West Indians', 142-43; affects status of mulattoes, 177-78; among Puritans and Protestants, 204-6; need for American in Revolutionary era, 288; and miscegenation, 544-45; and migration to New World, 574; and free Negroes, 579-82. *See also* Christianity; Community; Englishness; Miscegenation; Mulattoes; National identity
Semen, 20, 166, 249, 259
Senate. *See* Congress (U. S.)
Sentimentality, 368-72
Serfs. *See* Villenage
Serle, Ambrose, 291
Servant (term), 52-53, 55, 62
Servants: insubordination of in England, 42; early status in Va. and Md., 48, 73, 80-81; desired as protection against slave revolts, 63, 85; crowded out by slaves, 64; in Bar-

bados, 65; length of terms, 65, 70,
75, 76–77, 80–81, 88; in New England, 66; desire freedom, 69; prices,
76–77; exploited in early years, 86–
88; as labor source, 91; revolts of,
123; as mothers of free Negroes, 127;
desired in West Indies, 185; obedience urged on by Mather, 201; in
Ga. slavery debate, 263–64; Negroes
and Indians prohibited from having
white, 407; and colonization, 564.
See also Slave codes; Immigration
Service (term), 53
Servitude (term), 53
Servitude: essential character of, 47–
48; in Tudor-Stuart thought, 49;
concept of, 52–56; slavery seen as
different from, 53, 60; various kinds
distinguished, 61–62, 192; answers
needs of New England, 66; relation
to slavery in Va., 72. See also Servants
Severus, 258
Sewell, Samuel, 144, 307; on Spanish
"slave," 96; on miscegenation, 142,
163n, 165, 197; antislavery views,
195–97; replied to by Saffin, 199;
protests taxing Negroes with horses
and hogs, 232
Sex (term), 475
Sex ratio. See Population
Sexual mores, 136, 148, 474, 550. See
also Miscegenation
Sexual offences, 155. See also Rape
Sexuality: seen in Africans, 4–5, 32–35,
38–40, 43; associated with heat, 18,
151; and human physiognomy, 30;
of "apes," 30–32, 236–37; and curse
on Ham, 35–36; in Othello, 37–38;
seen in Negroes of Barbados, 65;
ideas about African, 136; overrides
differences between peoples, 138;
imputed to Negro women, 150–51;
imputed to Negro men, 151–54; pro-
miscuousness among Negroes, 159–
61; comparison between Negro's and
Indian's, 162–63; and Negro-ape association, 238–39, 490–93; fear of Negro in slave revolts, 398–99; Jefferson
and his critics on Negro's, 458–60;
in individuals and societies, 470–71;
and Chain of Being, 490–97, 500–
502; Moore attacks Jefferson re
orang-outang, 504; and Negro's
leprosy, 519; and American destiny,
543; of white men, 578–82. See also

Anality; Castration; Ham; Jefferson;
Miscegenation; Penis; Women
Shakespeare, William, 8, 37–39, 40
Sharp, Granville, 346
Shays, Daniel, 387
Sheep, 60
Shem, 17, 200
Shepard, Rev. Thomas, 211
Short, Elizabeth, 94
Sickle cell, 583–84
Sierra Leone, 59, 550, 551, 564
Sierra Leone Company, 564
Silk, 257
Simians, 221. See also Apes; Orang-
outangs
Sin, 54. See also Antislavery
Skin color. See Color
Skin-worms, 260
Skinner, Mary, 139
Skulls, 249, 500. See also Brain; Facial
angle; Prognathism
Slave (term), 52–53, 55, 62, 74–75, 80
Slave-breeding, 71, 160–61, 320
Slave codes, 147; in New England, 70,
71; in Va. and Md., 73, 81–82; in
Va., 78, 94–95, 127; S. C. borrows
from Barbados, 85; Bermuda, 96;
and pattern of representation, 103;
process of formation, 104; regional
variations, 104–5; in southern colonies, 106–7; as disciplining whites,
108–9, 112–13; serve to justify severity of slavery, 109–10; fundamental
purpose, 111; punishments in S. C.,
112–13; as reactions to slave plots,
116; free Negroes included in, 125;
lump mulattoes with Negroes, 168;
mustees included with Negroes in,
169; after Revolution, 399, 403–5.
See also Castration; Free Negroes;
Manumission
Slave hiring, 404
Slave resistance, violence, and crime,
112n; against weak master in N. Y.,
105; arson, 105n, 117, 393; variety
of, 113–14; wave of ca. 1740, 116,
120–22; sexual retribution, 151;
thought fostered by conversion, 182,
185–86; after Revolution, 392–93;
rape, 473. See also Runaways
Slave revolts: in Providence Island, 63;
not feared in New England, 66; fear
of, 110–15, 196, 328; in Va., 111–12,
113n, 122n, 394, 398n; number of,
113; in N. J., 114; Lord Dunmore's
call, 114, 303; make for sense of

sameness and difference, 115; and reaction in N. Y., 115–20; whites in, 117–18, 119, 123; in S. C., 120–22, 153, 399; in N. Y. C., 121, 122; in Md., 121, 153–54; and free Negroes, 122–23, 577–81; all whites assumed opposed to, 123; revealed by Negroes, 124; reaction to in Va., 127; associated with sexual fears, 152–54; no actual sexual assaults during, 152, 398–99; in Barbados, 156; thought fostered by conversion, 181–82, 185–86, 190–92; and Negro preacher in Charleston, 209–10; and attempts to curtail slave trade in Va., 301; during Revolution, 302–3, 391–93; Quakers charged with fomenting, 327; in Goree, 379; used to instance Negro's equality, 379; feared spreading from St. Domingo, 380–87; in Guadaloupe, 383; associated with French Revolution, 387–88; after St. Domingo, 391–93; after Gabriel plot, 396; politically partisan use of, 396; in Ga., 399; effect of, 399–401; feared by Jefferson, 433–35; associated with miscegenation, 470, 578–82. *See also* Gabriel plot; Liberty; St. Domingo

Slave trade, xi, 5–6; English participation in, 4, 22, 35, 58–59; development, 11; no justification required in 17th century, 27; makes Negroes seem like beasts, 28; early years, 56–60; opposition to in early 17th century, 61; begins in English West Indies, 63–65; Dutch in, 65, 83; New England participation in, 66–67, 68; first advocated in America, 69; to Va., 73, 74, 111, 143, 320; influx into Va. and Md., 82; Indian slaves in, 90; influx into continental colonies, 101–2; means many African-born Negroes in colonies, 184; new Negroes described, 233; accounts of utilized by Woolman, 274; Benezet on, 274, 300; called responsible for barbarism in Africa, 286; denunciation of, 293, 294, 371–72; cut off by Revolution, 296; different views on in Va. and Lower South, 301–2; prohibited by Continental Association, 302; federal prohibition of, 318–19, 331; to S. C., 318–19, 330; domestic, 320–21; origin of vessels in, 321; compromise on in Constitution, 323–24; petitions to Congress against, 325, 328–30; U. S. acts to restrict, 327, 330; defended by J. Brown, 328–29; in R. I., 329; Congress debates taxing, 330, 385, 388; banned by Great Britain, 331; banned by all states by end of Revolution, 342; dead bodies thrown overboard, 366–67; movement to end, 372–73; effect of ban on, 373–74, 531, 565; St. Domingo called retribution against, 378; opposed as dangerous, 400; from northern states banned, 403–4; Mass. bans citizens from, 410; Jefferson on, 432; defense of refuted, 494; deplored by White, 499, 502; defended with climatic theory, 525

Slavery (term), 291–92

Slavery, concept of: early development, 52–56; among Englishmen at end of 16th century, 60; affected by Spanish and Portuguese practice, 60–61; explained by Baynes, 61–62; essential ingredients described, 62–63; self-sale, 67; punishment for crime, 67–69; and religious disjunction, 68–69; not borrowed in Va. and Md., 72, 80; legal confusion concerning, 104.

Rationale of, 101, 115; and curse on Ham, 18–19; in tobacco colonies, 72; development of, 91–98; clearly rests on race, 134; undermined by miscegenation, 178; analyzed by Woolman, 272, 274–75; discovered in Revolutionary era, 279–80, 310–11; undermined by slave revolts, 562.

Social institution: problem of origins, x, 44–45; not deliberately established, 44; importance of early years of, 44, 98; essential character of, 47; emergence in America, 51, 57; in Iberian Peninsula, 56; in Africa, 58, 89; severities, 60, 109–10, 233; in West Indies, 63, 141; in Va., 73, 394–95, 563; characteristics of in 17th century Va. and Md., 82; in S. C., 85, 141; Indian not of importance, 89; in first half of 18th century, 101; classical, 111, 273, 432–33, 438, 444, 479; enhances social leveling, 134; unexamined before Revolution, 134–35; as un-American, 134, 341; as a condition of New World, 136; creates gulf between

Americans and English, 156; as agency of acculturation, 160; conflicts with ideal of human unity, 179; and conversion, 184; as deprivation of all rights, 198; and relationship between Negroes and whites, 227, 414–15; tends to make Negroes seem like beasts, 232–33; and Negro's place in ordered creation, 255; Woolman on effects of, 273–75; effect on Negroes explained by antislavery advocates, 275, 281–82, 283; changing economics of after Revolution, 316–25; question of in Northwest Territory, 321–22; attitude toward in Ga., 331; as viewed by Quakers, 356–57, 360; amelioration of and Christianity, 364–65; cruelty of stimulates humanitarianism, 367; amelioration of in late 18th century, 367–68; becoming a closed subject, 384; free Negroes as threat to, 410; affect of on miscegenation, 475; justified by climatic theory, 525–26. *See also* Antislavery; Climate; Emancipation; Enslavement; Manumission; Mental ability; Proslavery; Sectional divisions; Segregation; Villenage

Slaves: in North Africa, 60; attempts to regulate number of, 64; prices, 65, 76–77, 89, 130, 174, 320; in New England, 66, 125; held cheaper to maintain than servants, 69; as property, 101, 104, 322–23; taxation of, 104, 321–23, 330, 385, 388; assumed to crave liberty, 111, 115, 303–4, 388–91, 394–97, 561–62, 578; seen as contented, 115*n*; freed for extraordinary service, 124; skilled, 128–29, 172, 174, 406; criticized for fine dress, 130; more humane treatment of after Great Awakening, 214; debate over exclusion of in Ga., 262–64; surplus of in Va., 319–21; treatment of when freed, 352–54, 356–63; punishment of, 366–67; literacy among, 384; thought to learn of liberty from conversations of whites, 388; may actually have wanted white women, 398; protections for extended after Revolution, 403–4; in cities, 415. *See also* Acculturation; Conversion; Free Negroes; Galley-slaves; House servants; Runaways; Women

Sloane, Hans, 250, 519*n*
Sloth (animal), 218
Smallpox, 165, 259–60
Smell (of Negroes), 256–57, 459, 460*n*, 492, 501, 518
Smith, Adam, 309
Smith, Alexander, 580
Smith, Rev. Henry, 56
Smith, James, 70
Smith, Capt. John, 54
Smith, Dr. John Augustine, 489, 505–6, 508, 532
Smith, Melancton, 344
Smith, Rev. Samuel Stanhope, 498, 505, 510, 531, 535; criticizes Jefferson, 442–44; environmentalist argument *re* Negro sexuality, 460; on human variation, 486–88; faith in religion and science, 488, 532; and Chain of Being, 497; criticism of, 497, 506, 531–32, 533–34, 536, 538; combats infidelity, 506–9, 515, 532; on Negro's color, 513–16, 532–33; on acquired characters, 516–17; influence of, 517; satirized, 524; on Negro's tolerance for heat, 526; advocates intermarriage, 544
Smith, Sir Thomas, 50, 54
Smith, Rev. William, 185
Smith, William Loughton, 525; defends slavery, 326, 470; denounces Quaker petition, 327; assails Quakers, 421; attacks Jefferson, 452, 464; on danger of miscegenation, 470; connects emancipation and miscegenation, 544–45; on colonization, 549, 568
Snead, Smith, 392
Social control: need for felt in England, 41–43, 51; Africans as candidates for, 43; need for in early years, 45–47; slave codes as exercises in, 108–10; slavery as, 131, 134; slaves seem out of in Upper South, 409; fear of loss of, 578–82. *See also* Conversion; Free Negroes; Miscegenation
Social distance, 544; sense of in Englishmen, 86–88; slavery creates, 131; expressed by Negro-ape association, 239; need for from Negroes, 255–58; and Negro's appearance, 259; and miscegenation, 520. *See also* Attitudes; Prejudice; Social hierarchy
Social hierarchy, 164; in Tudor Eng-

land, 51; in churches, 132; and miscegenation, 137; in Latin colonies, 167; not based on color in English colonies, 168–74; changes in thought about, 192–94; decline of, 193–94, 510–11; in Puritan thought, 202; and Chain of Being, 228, 491; imagined based on complexion, 255. *See also* Chain of Being; Secularization

Social leveling, xiv, 511, 573; resented, 130; enhanced by slavery, 130, 134; progress in America, 192–93; unawareness of before Revolution, 193–94; impact on humanitarianism, 365–66; reprobated by Federalists, 396; decried, 485

Social thought. *See* Community; Secularization; Self-examination; Servitude; Slavery

Society for the Propagation of the Gospel: and laws *re* manumission, 180, 211–12; missionary efforts, 182–83, 189, 208; missionaries on mental ability, 188*n;* attitude toward slavery, 197–98; missionary on color, 258; squeezed out of colonies, 297

Society for the Relief of Free Negroes Unlawfully Held in Bondage (Pa.), 290, 343–44

Society of Friends. *See* Quakers

Sodom, 242

Soemmering, Samuel Thomas von, 501*n*

Solicitor-General (of England), 181

Songsters, 370

South. *See* Antislavery; Miscegenation; Sectional divisions; Slave codes; Slave trade; Slavery

South America, 563, 588, 604–6

South Carolina: slavery development in, 84–85; laws *re* conversion and manumission, 92; population, 103, 106, 141, 145, 147, 339, 406, 615; slave revolts in, 120–21, 152, 153; committed to slavery, 122, 147, 399–401, 405; restrictions on manumission, 123, 348; restricts free Negroes, 124, 409; voting in, 126–27, 412–13; views on mixed labor in, 129–30; openness of miscegenation in, 140, 145–48; social style in, 147–49, 474–75; Revolution in, 153, 302; castration in, 154–55, 156; mustees in, 169; passing in, 171–73; conversion in, 183, 186; opposition to conver-

sion in, 184, 185–86; commissaries in, 207; S. P. G. in, 208; heavy slave mortality in, 233; climatic theory in, 261–62, 525; opinion of Negro's mental ability in, 282; refuses to ban slave trade, 301, 324, 373; antislavery in, 302; Whitney in, 317; bans slave trade, 318, 373; opens slave trade, 318–19, 330, 373, 400; domestic slave trade in, 320; planter opulence denounced, 333; Ramsay on, 337, 340; absence of antislavery in, 346; reaction to slave plots in, 363, 395; aid to St. Domingo refugees, 380, 386–87; bars Negroes from West Indies, 382; tightens slave code, 399, 401; not alarmed by free Negroes, 409; Negro militia in, 411; reaction to *Notes on Virginia* in, 435; darkness of white men in, 514. *See also* Charleston; Congress (U. S.); Miscegenation; Sectional divisions; Slave codes

South-Carolina Gazette (Charleston), 150, 254; discusses miscegenation, 146–47; article on Creator's harmony of distinct colors, 165; article on mulatto's status, 170; letter from Antigua on revolt and conversion, 181; on conversion, 185–86; bogus runaway ad for baboon in, 238

South Carolina Society for Promoting and Improving Agriculture, 334

Spaight, Richard Dobbs, 324*n*

Spanish: in America, 3; contact with Africa, 6; convert Negroes, 22, 23; English struggle against, 24; enslave Africans in 15th and 16th centuries, 57; and Indians, 57*n*, 211; and John Hawkins, 58–59; character of slavery, 60; associated with slavery in minds of Englishmen, 60–61; lose Jamaica, 63; capture Providence Island, 64; in Barbados, 65; little influence on Va., 72; names given to first Va. Negroes, 73; language, 95; "slave" in Mass., 96; influence on American slavery, 98; feared in N. Y., 116, 118; in Fla., 120, 155; definitions of mixed offspring by, 167, 168; terms borrowed in West Indies, 174–75; influence in New Orleans, 174*n;* treatment of slaves compared with English, 198; climate, 239; Franklin on color of, 254; Ga. as bulwark against, 262; method of emancipation noted, 352*n;* 549;

armies in St. Domingo, 376–77; Americans associate with tyranny, 389; colonization proposed in dominions of, 559, 563; absence of representative assemblies in colonies of, 588. *See also* Conversion; Papists; Popery

Species: crosses between two regarded as infertile, 31–32; Linnaeus on, 222; planters accused of regarding Negroes as separate, 231–32; concept of, 234–36, 484; Negroes said to be a separate, 304–5, 308–9; Negroes denied to be a separate, 308, 505; Quakers hope to prove Negroes same as whites, 358; Jefferson on, 489–90; Negroes and orang-outangs called distinct, 495–96; question whether Negroes a separate, 497; whitening Negroes show Negroes same, 522; man as a single, 584. *See also* Chain of Being; Human unity; Interfertility; Races

Speech, 203–4, 340n

Sperm. *See* Semen

S. P. G. *See* Society for the Propagation of the Gospel

Spirit of the Laws (Montesquieu) , 278

Spock, Dr. Benjamin, 256n

Spooner, John J., 320

Spotswood, Gov. Alexander, 111

Springfield, Mass., 417

Staple crops, 66, 142, 261–62. *See also* Indigo; Rice; Sugar; Tobacco

State Gazette of South-Carolina (Charleston) , 380

Statute of Apprentices (English) , 42

Statutory law, 48, 49

Steendam, Jacob, 83–84

Stiles, Rev. Ezra, 132n, 248, 269–70, 299, 386, 523

Stone, James, 76

Stone, Roger, 76

Stono, S. C., 120, 153

Suffrage. *See* Voting

Sugar, 63, 84

Sullivan, James, 355–56, 456–57, 557–58, 569

Summary View of the Rights of British America (Thomas Jefferson) , 339

Summers, George W., 394

Sun. *See* Climate

Surgeons. *See* Physicians

Swan, John, 220n

Sweden, 243

Swedes, 88, 254, 336, 338

Sweet, Robert, 79

Swinburne, Henry, 53

Swiss, 88, 340

Syphilis, 260n

Systema Naturae (Linnaeus) , 218, 220

T

Tailors, 406

Talmud, 18

Tartars, 248, 253

Taxation, 104, 321–23, 330, 385, 388

Taylor, Rev. Jeremy, 54

Taylor, John, 430

Teat, Capt. (in Mass.) , 96

Temperature. *See* Climate

Ten Commandments, 211

Tennessee, 347, 412–14, 615. *See also* Congress (U. S.)

Thackstone, John, 76

Thatcher, George, 328, 329, 330

Theater, 405, 417. *See also* Othello

Thompson, Rev. (Anglican in Md.) , 186

Thomson, Charles, 435

Thornton, William, 549–50, 552

Three-fifths clause, 322, 470

To the Masters and Mistresses of Families (Edmund Gibson) , 191

Tobacco, 71, 319

Topsell, Edward, 29–30

Tories, 114

Toussaint L'Ouverture. *See* L'Ouverture

Tower menagerie (London) , 29n

Tower of Babel, 245, 538

Towrson, William, 6, 57

Tradesmen, 128–29, 172, 174, 406

Trial by jury, 403

Tribalism, 204–5, 212, 272, 421–22

Troglodytes, 221

Tucker, George, 561–62

Tucker, St. George, 456, 555–61, 565, 567

Turks, 54, 55, 94

Turner, Nat, 398n

Tyrannical Libertymen (anonymous) , 547

Tyson, Edward, 32, 218, 219, 225, 498, 500

U

Ulloa, Don Antonio de, 479

Ulster, Ireland, 102

Union. *See* National union

United Colonies (New England) , 69

United States Congress. *See* Congress (U. S.)

United States Constitution. *See* Constitution

University of Vermont, 534

Upper South. *See* Antislavery; Maryland; Miscegenation; North Carolina; Sectional divisions; Slave codes; Slave trade; Slavery; Virginia

Urbanization, 365, 415

Urbanna, Va., 246

Ury, John, 118

Utye, Nathaniel, 53

V

Vagrancy laws, 42

Van Rensselaer, Stephen, 338

Varieties, 235, 484. *See also* Species

Venice, 6

Venus, 34

Vermont, 345, 379, 534. *See also* Congress (U. S.)

Vestry. *See* Anglican Church

Villenage, 49–50, 53, 62, 67

Vining, John, 326

Virgin Islands, 550

Virginia, 45, 553; slave codes in, 44; first Negroes in, 44, 73, 93; sense of Englishness in, 46; servitude in, 48; Christopher Newport in, 61n; slavery develops in, 71–83; population, 73, 78n, 175, 319, 339, 406, 551, 575, 615; laws on aliens, 87; hangs Caribs, 90; laws re conversion and manumission, 92; bars free Negroes and Indians from owning whites, 94; inadequate transplantation of English institutions to, 98; fears revolt in early years, 110–12; occurrence of slave revolts in, 111, 113n; militia in, 111, 126, 411; free Negroes feared as insurrectionaries in, 122; slave plot in, 122n, 127; restrictions on free Negroes, 123; protects free Negroes, 124; regulates manumission, 124, 348, 574–81; free Negroes under slave codes in, 125; voting in, 126–27, 412–13; separate teaching in, 133; social structure, 147; castration in, 154, 157, 473; rape in, 157; nakedness in, 159; laws on intermarriage with Indians, 163; defines *mulatto*, 168; intermarriage in, 171; conversion in, 182; declares conversion impossible, 184; Anglican Church in, 206–8; progress of conversion in, 211, 213, 214; slave mortality

in comparison to West Indies, 233n; climate of, 239–40; Mitchell in, 246–47; Woolman in, 272, 274; Methodists in condemn slavery, 293; 1776 convention in, 295–96; antislavery in, 300; British thought responsible for slavery in, 301; anger at Lord Dunmore's call in, 303; antislavery during Revolution, 303–4; might have abolished slavery, 315–16; economic conditions in, 319–20; antislavery societies in, 320, 343, 344, 359n, 386, 400; domestic slave trade in, 320–21; planter opulence denounced, 333; antislavery accepted in, 346; revisal of the laws in, 346, 463, 472–73, 546; relaxes manumission laws, 347; restricts education of Negroes, 356; amelioration of slavery in, 368; fear of contagion from St. Domingo, 380–82; slave revolts during the 1790's, 391; statistics on slave violence in, 392–93; debate on slavery in, 394–95; slave revolts after Gabriel plot, 396–97, 398; tightens slave code, 399; demise of antislavery in, 400–401; penalizes kidnapping of Negroes, 404; limits number of slaves in boats, 406; restricts free Negroes, 407, 408; penitentiary house, 415; licensed Negro minister, 417; Methodists and Baptists in, 418–19; ideas on Negro mental ability in, 455–56, 457; feelings on miscegenation in, 472–73; colonization in, 542, 551–69. *See also* Congress (U. S.); Gabriel plot; Jefferson; Miscegenation; Population; Richmond; Sectional divisions; Slave codes

Virginia Abolition Society, 400

Virginia Argus (Richmond), 567

Virginia Company, 45

Virginia Gazette (Williamsburg), 255

Virginia Plan, 486

Vision of Columbus (Joel Barlow), 334

Voltaire, 251

Voting: laws on Negro, 126–27, 169, 412–14; in West Indies, 176; by Negroes debated in Mass., 302; by Negroes advocated, 446; N. Y. bill banning Negro, 471–72

Voyage to Suratt (John Ovington), 227

W

Wafer, Lionel, 250

Wainoake Indians, 94

Walloons, 83

Waln, Robert, 328, 329

War. *See* American Revolution; Captivity; Civil War; France; French and Indian War; Great Britain; Militia; Pequot War

War of 1812, 344, 550, 556

Warwick, R. I., 70n

Washington, Bushrod, 566

Washington, George, 292, 316, 319, 325, 353, 387

Washington, D. C., 412, 450, 564

Waterhouse, Dr. Benjamin, 344

Wayles, John, 466, 467

Wayles, Martha Skelton, 461, 467

Wayne Co., N. C., 398

Webster, Noah, 334, 339-40, 353-54

Weekly Ledger (Georgetown), 450

Weemes, Rev. John, 62n

Wells, William Charles, 527, 536

Welsh, 86-87, 88

Wesley, John, 214, 283

West Indies, xiv, 185, 306, 376; Portuguese and Spanish slave trade in, 57-58; Hawkins carries Negroes to, 59; Christopher Newport in, 61n; slavery develops in, 63-65; influence on New England, 66-69, 71; need for labor compared with Va., 72; and Indian slaves, 90, 92n; use of "whites" in, 96n; punishments severe in, 105, 233; fear of rebellion in, 110; slave revolts in, 113, 152, 181, 564; miscegenation in, 140, 152; population, 141, 175-76; social style compared to continental colonies, 141-42; comparison with S. C. and N. C., 145; influence on S. C., 147; white women in, 148, 474; books of, 150; castration in, 154, 156; influence on New Orleans, 174n; status of mulattoes in, 174-77; sex ratio in, 175-76; voting in, 176; migration from to Ga., 182; opposition to conversion in, 184; Quakers in, 194; Godwyn on degradation of Negroes in, 230n; slaves treated like beasts in, 233; claims in *re* Negro's blackness, 249, 259; antislavery in, 280; as source of anti-Negro writing, 304; cruelty of slavery in helps abolish slavery, 368; and fear of St. Domingo, 382-84; Jefferson predicts will become all black, 434; leprosy in, 519n; and yellow fever, 529; colonization proposed in, 547, 562, 564, 566;

St. G. Tucker on revolts in, 555-57. *See also* Antigua; Barbados; Hispaniola; Jamaica; Leeward Islands; Miscegenation; Montserrat; Nevis; Population; St. Domingo; St. Kitts; Slave codes

Western territories, 544, 547, 549, 552, 562

Wheat, 319

Wheatley, Phyllis, 283-86, 437, 446, 455, 460n

Whiskey Boys, 387

Whistler, Henry, 65

White, Dr. Charles, 507, 515; on Negro's place in Chain of Being, 499-502; influences J. A. Smith, 505-6; refuted by S. S. Smith and Williamson, 508; on albinos, 523; criticizes S. S. Smith, 531

White, Bishop William, 416

White (term), 95-96, 97

White Negroes. *See* Albinos

Whitefield, George, 181, 213, 214, 284

Whiteness, 39n; meaning for Englishmen, 7-9, 11; Negro's opinion of, 10, 11; in *Othello*, 38; as proper color for Americans, 143; and miscegenation, 146, 148; of souls of Negroes, 215; of a whale, 258; in Negroes as a disease, 251-52; associated with salvation, 258-59; associated with civilization, 305-6; praised by White, 502; valued by S. S. Smith, 515, 517; as original color of man, 523; and restriction of free Negroes, 580-81. *See also* Albinos; Antislavery; Beauty; Blackness; Color; Miscegenation

Whitney, Eli, 316-17, 321

Whittington, William, 75

Wilkes Co., Ga., 425

Willard, Rev. Samuel, 201-2

William and Mary, College of. *See* College of William and Mary

William the Conqueror, 55

Williams, Francis, 285n

Williams, Rev. Roger, 70n

Williams, Rev. Samuel, 526, 534-36

Williamsburg, Va., 129

Williamson, Rev. (Anglican in Md.), 187

Williamson, Dr. Hugh, 321-22, 495, 508, 526, 539-41

Willoughby, William, Lord, 87

Wilmington, Del., 425

Wilmington, N. C., 383

Wilson, Alexander, 474

Wilson, James, 470
Winchester, Rev. Elhanan, 297
Winthrop, James, 351, 456
Winthrop, John, 40, 67, 69
Winthrop, John, IV, 248
Wise, Rev. John, 293–94
Wistar, Dr. Caspar, 359
Witch hunts, 116, 117
Witchcraft, 38, 118
Witherspoon, Rev. John, 441n, 486
Women, Negro: valuable because of progeny, 7, 76; sexuality of, 35, 150–51; breasts, 39–40; ease of childbearing, 39–40, 151; and field work, 77, 130; as concubines, 140, 145, 169, 174; as wet nurses, 151; thought debauched by orang-outangs, 238, 495, 500; Jefferson on, 458–59, 490; and miscegenation in Lower South, 474; intermixture with orang-outangs denied, 494–95. *See also* Jefferson; Miscegenation
Women, white: not in field work, 130; marry Negroes, 138, 139–40, 171–72, 175, 518–19; sleep with Negroes, 139, 144, 148, 151; in West Indies, 140, 148, 176; in S. C., 148–49, 474–75; role in patterns of miscegenation differ from men, 149; thought desired by Negro men, 151, 152n, 398–99; thought to want Negro men, 151, 154, 159n, 239n; not assaulted during slave revolts, 393n, 398–99; in Ga., 474–75. *See also* Jefferson, Thomas
Woodmason, Rev. Charles, 110n, 238
Woolfolk, Ben, 393
Woolman, John, 272–75, 278, 279, 424
Worcester, Eng., 88
Work. *See* Labor
Wye, Rev. (Anglican in Md.), 186
Wythe, George, 457

Y

Yale College, 316, 486, 523
Yaws, 260
Yeardley, Argoll, 76
Yellow fever, 377, 423, 528–29
York Co., Va., 75
York River, Va., 303

Z

Zohar, 36